THE REFORMATION IN IRELAND
UNDER ELIZABETH

LONGMANS, GREEN AND CO. Ltd.
39 PATERNOSTER ROW, LONDON, E.C. 4
6 OLD COURT HOUSE STREET, CALCUTTA
53 NICOL ROAD, BOMBAY
MOUNT ROAD, MADRAS

LONGMANS, GREEN AND CO.
55 FIFTH AVENUE, NEW YORK
221 EAST 20TH STREET, CHICAGO
TREMONT TEMPLE, BOSTON
128-132 UNIVERSITY AVENUE, TORONTO

BY THE SAME AUTHOR

THE REFORMATION IN DUBLIN
1536-1558

FROM ORIGINAL SOURCES

8vo   20s. net

THE REFORMATION
IN IRELAND
UNDER ELIZABETH

1558-1580

(FROM ORIGINAL SOURCES)

BY

MYLES V. RONAN, C.C.

MEMBER OF THE ROYAL IRISH ACADEMY
FELLOW OF THE ROYAL SOCIETY OF ANTIQUARIES OF IRELAND
AUTHOR OF "THE REFORMATION IN DUBLIN, 1536-1558," ETC.

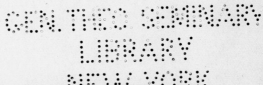
LONGMANS, GREEN AND CO.
LONDON • NEW YORK • TORONTO
1930

Nihil Obstat.

INNOCENTIUS APAP, O.P.,
Censor deputatus.

Imprimatur.

EDM. CAN. SURMONT,
Vic. Gen.

WESTMONASTERII,
die xiii Februarii, 1930.

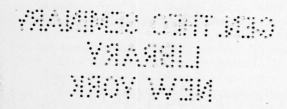
Made in Great Britain

FOREWORD.

My sincere thanks are due to those purchasers of my previous volume who thus enabled me to produce the present one, and likewise to the reviewers, Protestant and Catholic alike, who by their generous critiques encouraged me to continue my researches. Some of the reviewers pointed out a few blemishes in my work, which were minor ones, mainly concerned with annotations. Nevertheless, I am grateful for their kind help.

Protestant reviewers have acknowledged my honesty in endeavouring to come to impartial judgments, and a few considered that I did not completely succeed in my objective, mentioning one or two instances. One of these concerned George Browne, Protestant Archbishop of Dublin, on whom, I feel convinced, I was not unduly severe. Indeed, I have been asked by others where I got the whitewash for him.

On the other hand, some of my own co-religionists considered that I handled the Catholic Bishops too harshly. I should prefer to have erred on that side than to be charged with whitewashing them. In both cases I am satisfied that I was justified in my conclusions by the materials at hand. In the present volume I have endeavoured to pursue the same impartial policy, and I hope that I have succeeded to the satisfaction of both sides.

Unfortunately, I have to contend with historians who either for political or religious motives have distorted their accounts. On the Protestant side wrong conclusions of far-reaching importance have, in my opinion, been drawn, and I have considered it necessary to stress the Protestant position again and again, perhaps some will consider unduly.

On the Catholic side the Catholic reader is apt to accept unquestioningly a line of comment from a Catholic historian. I feel it my duty to call attention to the methods adopted by some of these writers both in the religious and the political domain.

In the religious domain I am sorry to have to admit that Dr. (Cardinal) Moran, over zealous to support his own side—a feature not unusual in polemists of both sides in the last century

v

—has allowed himself to suppress truth when it was inconvenient for his particular theory. Having done such useful research work it is a pity that he should have spoiled it by such a procedure, thus making the reader rather timid about accepting his authority.

In the political domain the case is equally deplorable. Catholic historians from partisan prejudices have coloured their pages. No doubt it will seem almost heresy to find fault with the *Four Masters*. Yet it has to be said that not only did they by their faithful transcription of the local chronicles thereby hand on the peculiar prejudices of those districts, but they were influenced by political considerations as well as by the glory of the House of Tirconaill in representing the adversaries of that House in a false light.

In general it may be said that the peculiar position of Catholics in the reigns immediately succeeding that of Elizabeth influenced Catholic historians to regard Catholic activities in the reign of Elizabeth solely from a political standpoint, thus ignoring the religious element, and showing little sympathy with those who suffered during that reign. Anxious to secure fair treatment for the Catholics of their own time they were unfair to those who preceded them. It is important in reading the works of the *Four Masters*, Campion, O'Sullivan Beare, Russell, O'Daly, etc., to bear this in mind.

Unfortunately these difficulties, as well as the labour, research, and reading necessary for the making of a volume of this kind, are not generally appreciated, otherwise more sympathy and support might be found for one who undertakes the onerous and indeed unprofitable (from the monetary standpoint) task.

I wish particularly to call attention to a series of articles appearing in the *Catholic Bulletin*, Dublin, entitled " Wine from the Royal Pope," to which I beg to acknowledge my great indebtedness. These brilliant and scholarly articles have simplified my task in the third and fourth parts of this book even though some of the *Roman State Papers* have been published since they began.

Finally, I wish to thank a few kind friends whose names I am not privileged to mention for valuable information and many useful suggestions.

MYLES V. RONAN.

Dun Laoghaire,
    6th January, 1930.

CONTENTS.

PART I.

"REFORM GOETH SLOWLY FORWARD."

Protestants Petition Elizabeth for Favours—Bishops of Tuam and Clonfert's Petition—Bishop of Leighlin takes the Oath—The English Service ordered for Irish Council—Martial Law and Mustering—Dublin Parliament of 1560; Bishops and the Supremacy—Alleged Acts of the Parliament—Common Prayer to be Translated into Latin—Commissions to Administer the Oath of Supremacy—Bishops Deprived of their Sees—The Pope Appoints an Archbishop and a Commissary—Elizabeth considers Secular Affairs more important than Religion—Shane O'Neill Fences with Elizabeth—Sussex's Expeditions to Armagh—Martial Law for the O'Tooles and O'Byrnes—Elizabeth's Bishops not Happy in their Sees—The Queen's Grievances against the Pope—A Protestant Archbishop for Armagh—Politics Enter into Religion —Shane at the Court of Elizabeth; Signs his Submission—Desmond Petitions Elizabeth for an Ecclesiastical Favour—The Bishop of Kildare Complains of Want of Preachers and of Poverty—Civil and Religious Law Set at Nought—Shane Frustrates Appointment of Loftus to Armagh— The Dean of Armagh and the Archdeacon of Meath; Commissioners for Ecclesiastical Causes—Irish Bishops at the Council of Trent—The Archbishop of Tuam and the Bishop of Clonfert—Sussex's plan for the Rule of Ireland—Desmond and O'Neill Defiant—Desmond Ratifies Treaty with Elizabeth—Another Expedition against Shane—Shane's Bond; Armagh Cathedral Restored for Divine Worship—O'Tooles and O'Byrnes Reported Obedient—Irish Ecclesiastics Forge Papal Letters—The Emperor Petitions Elizabeth for Toleration for Catholics—Both sides move in Religious Matters—Commissioners Report on State of Religion—Elizabeth Appoints Irish-Speaking Bishop to Kildare—The See of Meath a Sea of Troubles— Curwen Desires an English Bishopric—Curwen Disapproves of Suppression of St. Patrick's—Papal Letter to Shane O'Neill; Commends his Steadfastness in the Faith—Papal Commission for Creagh and Wolf—The Religious Duel Begins—Elizabeth's Orders to Proceed with the Reform—

vii

PART II.

" THE HOUR HAS NOW COME."

PART III.

"SPANISH ALE."

PART IV.

"WINE FROM THE ROYAL POPE."

APPENDICES.

MAP.

INTRODUCTION.

In the Introduction to our volume on *The Reformation in Dublin*, 1536-58, we surveyed the condition of the Irish Church which preceded that period. For the present volume another kind of survey is necessary, one that will elucidate the secular and political situation before the accession of Queen Elizabeth. It will be also necessary to obtain some idea of the Queen's early behaviour towards religion in England so that we may under-stand her efforts in that direction in Ireland. As to the first of these matters we cannot do better than give some extracts from the brilliant pages of Froude.[1]

Within two centuries from the date of the Anglo-Norman Conquest the descendants of the conquerors "could be dis-tinguished neither in soul nor body, neither in look, in dress, nor in disposition, from the Celts whom they had subdued. The Irish whom they had conquered in the field revenged their defeat on the minds and hearts of the conquerors ; and in yielding, yielded only to fling over their new masters the subtle spell of the Celtic disposition. In vain the government attempted to stem the evil. Statute was passed after statute forbidding the ' Englishry ' of Ireland to use the Irish language, or intermarry with Irish families, or copy Irish habits. Penalties were multiplied on penalties ; fines, forfeitures, and at last death itself, were threatened for such offences. But all in vain. The stealthy evil crept on irresistibly. Fresh colonists were sent over to restore the system, but only for themselves and their children to be swept into the stream ; and from the century which succeeded the Conquest till the reign of the eighth Henry."

Froude goes on to describe the system by which England usually governed Ireland : " At intervals, when the government was exasperated by unusual outrages, some prince of the blood was sent across as viceroy ; and half a century of acquiescence in disorder would be followed by a spasmodic severity, which

[1] *History of England*, c. viii.

xi

irritated without subduing, and forfeited affection while it failed
to terrify. At all other times, Ireland was governed by the Norman
Irish, and these, as years went on, were tempted by their convenience to strengthen themselves by Irish alliances, to identify
their interests with those of the native chiefs, in order to conciliate
their support; to prefer the position of wild and independent
sovereigns, resting on attachment of a people whose affections
they had gained by learning to resemble them, to that of military
lords over a hostile population, the representatives of a distant
authority, on which they could not rely."

But (he adds) there was another and a deeper cause at work :
" When a marked type of human character yields before another,
the change is owing to some element of power in that other, which
coming into contact with elements weaker than itself, subdues
and absorbs them. The Irish spirit, which exercised so fatal a
fascination, was enabled to triumph over the Norman in virtue
of representing certain perennial tendencies of humanity which
may at any moment develop. It was not a national spirit—
the clans were never united, except by some hatred ; and the
normal relation of the chiefs towards each other was a relation
of chronic war and hostility. It was rather an impatience of
control, a deliberate preference for disorder, a determination
in each individual man to go his own way, whether it was a
good way or a bad, and a reckless hatred of industry. The result
was the inevitable one—oppression, misery, and wrong. But, in
detail, faults and graces were so interwoven, that the offensive-
ness of the evil was disguised by the charm of the good ; and
even the Irish vices were the counterfeit of virtues, contrived
so cunningly that it was hard to distinguish their true texture.
The fidelity of the clansmen to their leaders was faultlessly
beautiful ; extravagance appeared like generosity, and improvi-
dence like unselfishness ; anarchy disguised itself under the name
of liberty ; and war and plunder were decorated by poetry as
the honourable occupation of heroic natures. Such were the
Irish with whom the Norman conquerors found themselves in
contact ; and over them all was thrown a peculiar imaginative
grace, a careless atmosphere of humour, sometimes gay, sometimes melancholy, always attractive, which at once disarmed
the hand which was raised to strike or punish them. These
spirits were dangerous neighbours. Men who first entered the
country at mature age might be fortified by experience against
their influence, but on the young they must have exerted a charm
of fatal potency. The foster-nurse first chanted the spell over

the cradle in wild passionate melodies. It was breathed in the ears of growing boy by the minstrels who haunted the halls, and the lawless attractions of disorder proved too strong for the manhood which was trained among so perilous associations. . . . At the opening of the sixteenth century, when the hitherto neglected barbarians were about to become a sword in the Pope's hands to fight the battle against the Reformation, the ' King's Irish enemies ' had recovered all but absolute possession of the island, and nothing remained of Strongbow's conquests save the shadow of a titular sovereignty and a country strengthened in hostility by the means which had been used to subdue it."

Outside the narrow strip of the Pale, some fifty miles long and twenty broad, " the common law of England was of no authority ; the King's writ was but a strip of parchment ; and the country was parcelled among a multitude of independent chiefs, who acknowledged no sovereignty but that of strength, who levied tribute on the inhabitants of the Pale as a reward for nominal protection of their rights, and as a compensation for abstaining from the plunder of their farms. Their swords were their sceptres ; their codes of right, the Brehon traditions. . . . These chiefs, with their dependent clans, were distributed over the four provinces in the following order : The Geraldines, the most powerful of the remaining Normans, were divided into two branches. The Geraldines of the South, under the Earls of Desmond, held Limerick, Cork, and Kerry ; the Geraldines of Leinster lay along the frontiers of the English Pale ; and the heads of the House, the Earls of Kildare, were the feudal superiors of the greater portion of the English counties. To the Butlers, Earls of Ormond and Ossory, belonged Kilkenny, Carlow, and Tipperary. The De Burghs, or Bourkes, as they called themselves, were scattered over Galway, Roscommon, and the south of Sligo, occupying the broad plains which lie between the Shannon and the mountains of Connemara and Mayo. . . . The Celtic chieftains had returned from the mountains, bringing back with them, more intensely than ever, the Irish habits and traditions. . . . The O'Neills and O'Donnells had spread down over Ulster to the frontiers of the Pale. The O'Connors and O'Carrolls had recrossed the Shannon, and pushed forward into Kildare ; the O'Connor Don was established in a castle near Portarlington, said to be one of the strongest in Ireland ; and the O'Carroll had seized on Leap, an ancient Danish fortress surrounded by bog and forest, a few miles from Parsonstown. O'Brien of Inchiquin, Prince—as he styled himself—of Thomond, no longer contented with his principality of Clare, had thrown a bridge across the Shannon five miles above Limerick, and was thus enabled to enter Munster at his pleasure, and spread his authority towards the South ; while the MacCarthys and O'Sullivans in Cork and Kerry, were only not dangerous to the Earls of Desmond, because the Desmonds were more Irish than themselves, and were accepted as their natural chiefs. In Tipperary and Kilkenny only the Celtic reaction was held in check. The Earls of Ormond, although they were obliged themselves to live as Irish chieftains, and to govern by the Irish law, yet partly from an inherent nobility of nature, partly through family alliances and a more sustained intercourse with their English kindred, partly, perhaps because of the inveterate feud of their House with both branches of the Geraldines, remained true to their allegiance and maintained the English authority so far as their power extended. That power, unfortunately, was incommensurate with their good will, and their situation prevented them from rendering the assistance to the Crown which they desired. Wexford, Wicklow, and the mountains of Dublin, were occupied by the highland tribes of O'Byrne and O'Toole, who, in their wild glens and dangerous gorges, defied attempts to conquer them, and who were able, at all times, issuing down out of the passes of the hills, to cut off communication with the Pale. Thus the Butlers had no means of reaching Dublin except through the County Kildare, the home of their hereditary rivals and foes."

In an important report drawn up in the year 1515, a document that exercised considerable influence in the shaping of the policy of Henry VIII, attention is devoted to the number of the Irish chiefs and to the relations, or want of relations, which existed between them : " There were in all Ireland some sixty regions inhabited by the King's enemies," some of which were as large as a county and some much smaller, each ruled by a chief captain, called a king, or a prince, or a duke, and the like, who " lives only by the sword and obeys to no other temporal person save only to himself that is strong . . . each makes war and peace for himself, and holds by the sword, and has imperial jurisdiction, and obeys no other person, English or Irish, except only to such persons as may subdue him by the sword . . . in every one of the said regions there be divers petty captains, and every one of them makes war and peace for himself, without licence of his chief captain . . . and there be no more than thirty of the English noble folk that follow this same Irish order, and keeps the same rule."

In such a state of things, according to Froude, it was no wonder

But if Henry allowed the Earl of Kildare to run the country in the old way, he took one step which in course of time was destined to have the most far-reaching results. The great difficulty had consisted in the unreliable nature of the information that had been reaching him from Ireland. He now had two men in the country who could be relied on to tell him what he wanted to know, and who were anything at all but disposed to send friendly reports about the Kildares. These were Wolsey's chaplain, Alen, whom he made Archbishop of Dublin, and Alen's first cousin, whom he appointed Master of the Rolls. " Henceforward," notes Froude, " there runs a clear stream of light through the fog and night of confusion." Their views were unmistakable—an English Deputy, condign punishment for the Geraldines, and a strong government, which in a few years would make the Irish " as civil, politic, and active as any other nation."

It was not long till this view began to appeal to Henry VIII, who, as a result of his matrimonial ventures, early in 1534, " learnt that excommunication was hanging over him, that a struggle for life or death had commenced, and that the Imperial armies were preparing to strike in the quarrel. . . . With a religious war apparently on the eve of explosion, he could ill tolerate a hotbed of sedition at his door; and Irish sedition was about to receive into itself a new element, which was to make it trebly dangerous.

In February of that year the Earl of Kildare was summoned to London, was at once arrested, and was made to see that Henry meant business this time. A month later the conditional excommunication of the King was published by the Pope. War with Spain was imminent, an agent of the Emperor's was known to have landed in Ireland and to have been in communication with the Munster Geraldines, and everything pointed to the probability of a Spanish invasion of Ireland. Immediately the Earl's son, known to History as Silken Thomas, threw off his allegiance.[1] No assistance came to him, the people gave an inadequate response to the young rebel's appeal, Dublin Castle was not taken, he was countered by the Earl of Ormond, and fresh appeals to Rome and Spain brought no result. In March of the following year the Fitzgerald stronghold of Maynooth, which they had deemed impregnable, fell under the strokes of a new weapon, which was to revolutionise warfare in Ireland, that of gunpowder and cannon. " The confederacy of the chiefs was broken up; first one fell away from it, and then another;

---

[1] Ronan, *Reformation in Dublin*, pp. xxiii-xxiv.

and before the summer had come, O'Brien of Inchiquin, O'Connor, who had married Fitzgerald's sister, and the few scattered banditti of the Wicklow mountains, were all who remained of the grand association which was to place the Island of Saints at the feet of the Father of Christendom. . . . So ended the rebellion in Ireland ; significant chiefly because it was the first in which an outbreak against England assumed the features of a war of religion, the first which the Pope was especially invited to bless, and the Catholic powers, as such, to assist." [1]

The subsequent history of the period is dealt with in our previous volume, which embraces the reigns of Henry VIII, Edward VI, and Mary. It now remains only to summarise Elizabeth's attitude towards religion in England in the first years of her reign.

Immediately after the death of Queen Mary, 17 November, 1558, Elizabeth, without opposition, was acknowledged, in accordance with the statute of 30 Henry VIII, as the rightful heir to the throne. She was then in the twenty-fifth year of her age, and the only surviving child of Henry. Though Mary and Elizabeth could not both be legitimate offspring of Henry, yet, strange to relate, both enjoyed successively the dominions of their father. And stranger still, the Catholics overlooked the fact that Elizabeth was the daughter of Anne Boleyn, and peaceably accepted her as Queen.[2] According to Catholic opinion, the rightful heir was Mary Stuart, grand-daughter of Henry's eldest sister, and wife of the French Dauphin. But neither Catholics nor Protestants would hear of her accession in view of the danger that England might come under Franco-Scottish influence. Moreover, although Elizabeth, who had been educated on strictly Protestant lines, had, after some slight opposition, professed to be a zealous Catholic during the whole of Mary's reign, and had gone so far as to gain an indulgence published by the Pope in September, 1555,[3] yet hardly anyone believed in the sincerity of her conversion. And the Venetian Ambassador, Michiel, bears witness, in his account of the year 1557, that people considered her to be a hypocrite who secretly cherished anti-Catholic opinions more strongly than ever.[4] So that, in the eyes of Catholics, Elizabeth held a very doubtful position so far as her religion was concerned. She inherited from her father not only a statesman-like and penetrating insight but an extraordinary gift

---

[1] *Catholic Bulletin*, August, 1925, p. 820 *seq.*
[2] Pastor, *Storia dei Papi*, vi. 576 *seq.*
[3] Machyn, *Diary (Camden Society, London*, 1848), p. 94.
[4] Michiel in *C.S.P.V.*, vi. 2, p. 1058 *seq.*

of deception and unfathomable subtlety.[1] She united to a passionate and ardent temperament the power of cool and systematic calculation and procrastination. Her behaviour, therefore, especially during the first months of her reign, was exceedingly guarded and careful in relation to the religious question.

She did not refer to religious matters in her proclamation from the throne, and, as she had done in Mary's reign, she continued to attend Mass and Vespers. The obsequies for Mary she had conducted according to the Catholic rites.[2] Thus, Catholic worship was allowed to remain unchanged so that the minds of zealous Catholics might be set at rest. Yet nothing could be further from the truth than to suppose that Elizabeth had not yet decided upon the course that she intended to adopt in religious matters. All the new members of the Privy Council, and those newly summoned to the court, were of the Protestant persuasion. She was thus cleverly making the ground firm under her feet, and at the same time, winning popularity with the people, before she launched her well-considered plan for the overthrow of the Catholic religion.

Scarcely two months had elapsed since her accession when she gave orders to the Bishop of Carlisle to omit the elevation of the Sacred Host at Mass. The Bishop refused, but, in order that she might not have to venerate the Sacred Host, she left the chapel before the offertory.[3] Two days later, a proclamation was issued which forbade preaching for the time being, and ordered the Epistle and Gospel at Mass to be said in English. This innovation was immediately carried into effect in the Royal chapel. Moreover, Elizabeth appointed married priests to serve there, who, in the prayers, omitted the names of the Mother of God, the Saints, and the Pope.[4] (She did not approve of the marriage of priests and snubbed an archbishop's wife. Priests who would marry were forbidden to do so until they had received her permission.)

These changes naturally caused much anxiety in the minds of the bishops in view of the approaching coronation of the Queen. Their refusal to attend that ceremony caused considerable perplexity to her and her chief adviser, Cecil, as they considered that it would upset the minds of the people. After long negotiation, the Bishop of Carlisle was induced to perform the ceremony;

[1] Meyer. I, ii.

[2] *C.S.P.V.*, vi. 3 *n.*, 1287. Hayward's *Annals (Camden Soc.*, 1840), p. 12.

[3] Report of Feria (*Kervyn de Lettenhove*, i. 365) ; Ambassador of Mantua (*C.S.P.V.*, vii. *n.* 2).

[4] *C.S.P.V.*, vii. *n.* 28 ; *Lettenhove*, i. 366.

this compliance he afterwards bitterly regretted.[1] Amid a display of great splendour, the coronation took place in Westminster Abbey, 15 January, 1559. Many changes were introduced into the Catholic Coronation Mass, the Elevation, in particular, being omitted.[2] By this action Elizabeth left no room for doubt that she intended to break the solemn coronation oath that she had just taken to protect the rights of the Church. Within a fortnight her intention became abundantly clear. On 25 January, at the opening of Parliament, the new Chancellor, Bacon, informed the members that they would be called upon—although the Queen could do it by her own power—to decide upon a comprehensive confession of faith, and a common form of divine service for the whole kingdom,[3] including, of course, Ireland.

Within another fortnight, Edward Carne, the English Ambassador to the Holy See, received orders to break off diplomatic relations with Pope Paul IV.[4] The Pope had no idea that the defection of Elizabeth from the Church was imminent. At this very moment the French Ambassador was endeavouring to induce him to make objections to a marriage between Elizabeth and Philip II of Spain. But Paul IV, who spoke in a perfectly friendly manner of the Queen, made it known that in the event of such a marriage he would not refuse the necessary dispensation. In the absence of any certain information as to the defection of the Queen, he openly expressed the hope that the opposition of the Catholics in Parliament would prevent a break with Rome.

The prospects of the avoidance of such a break did not appear quite hopeless. By means of extensive pressure on the members, the Queen had indeed succeeded in securing a safe majority for her plans in the House of Commons, but matters seemed less favourable in the Upper House. The Convocation of the bishops expressly declared its firm adherence to the Catholic doctrines of Transubstantiation, the Sacrifice of the Mass, and the Papal Supremacy, and declared that the decision concerning matters of Faith, the Sacraments, and religious discipline did not pertain

[1] Strype, *Annals*, i. no. 50.
[2] *Engl. Hist. Review*, xxii. 650 *seq.*; xxiii. 87 *seq.*; 533 *seq.*; xxiv. 322 *seq.*
[3] D'Ewes, *Journal of Both Houses*, 11 *seq.*
[4] *Acts of the Privy Council*, vii. 59; *State Papers, Foreign*, 1558-59, nos. 299, 474. For hundreds of years, owing to a calumny circulated by Sarpi, it was believed that Paul IV had hastened this turn of affairs by " his abrupt and discouraging answer," to the effect that Elizabeth, before everything else, should submit her claims to the throne to the decision of the Holy See. Maitland has conclusively shown that Sarpi's account was a spiteful fabrication. (See *Engl. Hist. Review*, xv. 324 *seq.*)

to any assembly of the laity, but only to the lawful pastors of the Church.[1]

The granting of tithes and first-fruits to the Crown was accomplished without any difficulty, but violent opposition was aroused by a draft of a Bill regarding the royal supremacy over the Church. The bishops did not fail to make strong remonstrances against it. Archbishop Heath, of York, in particular, set forth lucidly the reasons that made it impossible for Catholics to acknowledge the royal supremacy, and showed that, according to the clearly expressed text of the Holy Scriptures, a woman could not teach in the Church, or fulfil the duties of the supreme ecclesiastical office, and that, therefore, she could not be head of the Church.[2]

The force of such reasoning did not escape Elizabeth herself. She therefore had the title of " chief governor of all spiritual and ecclesiastical affairs " introduced into the Bill instead of " Head of the Church." In this form the Bill was passed, 22 March. Parliament was then prorogued until Easter, 1559. As to the Elizabethan primacy, it was limited in the *Thirty-Nine Articles* by the following clause : " We give not to our princes the ministering either of God's Word or of the Sacraments, the which thing the injunctions also lately set forth by Elizabeth our Queen do most plainly testify, but that only prerogative which we see to have been given always to all godly princes in Holy Scriptures by God Himself, that is that they should rule all estates and degrees committed to their charge by God, whether they be ecclesiastical or temporal, and restrain with the civil sword the stubborn and evil doers." This limitation made no change in the actual power of the Queen, for Parkhurst was able to write, 21 May, 1559, to Bullinger : " The Queen will not, it is true, be named the Head of the Church, although this title was offered to her ; she, however, willingly accepts the title of a Ruler of the Church, which comes to the same thing. The Pope is once more driven out of England, to the great sorrow of the bishops, and the whole gang of shaven priests." [3]

The bishops and the Abbot of Westminster, with Lord Montague and the Earl of Shrewsbury, remained firm in their opposition to the separation of the Church in England from Rome. The Spanish Ambassador, Feria, made an attempt, at the last moment, to restrain Elizabeth from confirming the fateful Act of Supremacy. But the Queen left no room for doubt as to her

---

[1] Cf. Birt, *The Elizabethan Religious Settlement*, London, 1907.
[2] Strype, i., App. VI.
[3] See Meyer, i. 19 *seq.* ; Lilly, *Dublin Review*, cix. 14 *seq.*

determination to proceed in a thoroughly autocratic manner in religious questions. Feria was of opinion that the Pope should now be informed of the state of affairs, and, in his over-estimation of the zeal of English Catholics,[1] believed that Elizabeth would not be able to hold out if Paul IV should now pronounce sentence of excommunication against her. But Paul IV did not proceed to this extreme penalty, acting probably on the advice of the Jesuit, Ribadeneira,[2] who was at that time in London, to deal cautiously with the Queen. At the beginning of May, 1559, he still hoped that the Spanish King would succeed in preserving England for the Church.

Philip II of Spain, in whom the English Catholics placed great hopes, preferred to have Elizabeth on the throne rather than Mary Queen of Scots, who was devoted to the interests of France. He also cherished the hope of obtaining the hand of Elizabeth either for himself or for a member of the House of Hapsburg. Thus, early in Elizabeth's reign, matters became complicated by the introduction of the political differences between France and Spain, which state of affairs had enormous influence on the trend of events in later years. In fact, those political differences destroyed all prospect of success on the part of the English as well as of the Irish Catholics in their opposition to Elizabeth's anti-Catholic rule. And without the help of either power, opposition, in view of the divided nature of the Catholic force, was doomed to failure. From the Catholic point of view, the mess that was made of the situation was pitiful in the extreme.

Elizabeth made use of the favourable situation thus created by quickly taking the second step for the establishment of the English State Church. She summoned a religious conference to be held in Westminster Abbey during Easter week. On account of the anti-Catholic legislation, the Catholics refused to continue in attendance. Elizabeth's answer to this was to throw the Bishops of Winchester and Lincoln into the Tower. In spite of this attempt to intimidate the opposition in Parliament, the Bill relating to the Mass and the introduction of the New Anglican liturgy aroused strong opposition. In the Upper House it only passed by a majority of three. On 24 June the new order of

---

[1] The statement of Feria that two-thirds of the English were Catholics has been questioned by Meyer (i. 7). However this may be, it is certain that the Catholics far outnumbered the Protestants, but the number of zealous or fighting Catholics was evidently small (cf. Michiel in *Brosch*, vi. 453, *n.* 1).

[2] Letter of Ribadeneira to Lainez, General of the Society of Jesus, 20 January, 1559 (Delplace, *Précis, dist.* 1900, 348). Paul IV was a close friend of Lainez.

things was to come into force, and the Sacrifice of the Mass to cease throughout the kingdom.

The new liturgy, with several alterations, closely followed the Second Book of Common Prayer of Edward VI, of the year 1552. The clergy who opposed it (i.e. who continued to use the Catholic liturgy) were at first to lose their income for one year, and to be imprisoned for six months ; for a repetition of their offence they were to be deposed and imprisoned for a year, and for the third offence they were threatened with imprisonment for life. In the case of the laity, fines were imposed to enforce attendance at the new services. Similar drastic punishments threatened those who refused to take the Oath of Supremacy, and who remained faithful to the Spiritual jurisdiction of the Pope. With regard to this offence the third act of resistance was to be punished by death.

Armed with these weapons, Elizabeth now proceeded to destroy the Catholic hierarchy in England, and to force the new State Church on her subjects. But it was too soon to give them a martyr. Elizabeth acted with great caution ; deposition, forfeiture of property, and imprisonment were sufficient for the present to punish the disobedient bishops. Only one bishop in the whole English hierarchy obeyed the royal summons of July, 1559. This was Antony Kitchin, Bishop of Llandaff, who had been a schismatic under Henry VIII, a Calvinist under Edward VI, and a Catholic under Mary.[1] When these blows were being dealt at the Catholic religion in England, Paul IV was a dying man.

The English Catholics did not give up their cause as lost. According to a memorial to Pius IV of the year 1559, the change of religion was built solely on the will of the Queen ; many lords and the mass of the people were still loyal to the ancient faith. Besides, Elizabeth had not executed the new law with the extreme penalty ; there was, therefore, still hope that with time, either spontaneously or constrained by circumstances, the Queen would seek union with Rome. Carney and Feria were also of this opinion, and so, too, was Bishop de la Quadra, Feria's successor in the Spanish embassy in London. To the Spaniards it seemed inconceivable that Elizabeth, by her religious laws, should alienate Spain, her only ally. But de la Quadra soon recognised that he was deceived concerning the young Queen, who, although given to vanity caprice, and erotism, yet was politically clear-headed, of extraordinary acumen and tenacity, and a master of intrigue and

---

[1] Bridgett-Knox, *Catholic Hierarchy Deposed by Elizabeth*. London, 1889. Bellesheim, *Historpolit. Bl.*, cxxxvi (1905), 991 *seq.*

finesse. Personally she was little affected by religious ideas; success was her god, and Machiavelli her gospel.[1]

For a right understanding of the period of this book it will be useful to have even a general outline of Catholic conditions in Ireland. This is especially so since the Catholic background is obscured by " reform " and wars, and we have very little documentation to show the ebb and flow of Catholic life. By means of the few references extant we are, however, enabled to throw some light on the prevailing conditions.

A few general principles must be noted. This was an age of insincerity, inconsistency, bluffing, and temporising on all sides. The bishops, in their dealings with the Sovereign, as a rule followed the lead of the local lord of the soil. This was apparent in the unseemly haste with which the bishops took the Oath of Supremacy under Henry VIII. Under Elizabeth, however, the lords as a rule remained firm, neither being asked, nor of themselves taking the Oath of Supremacy. Thus, the bishops, following their lords, were content with taking the oath of fealty and allegiance to the Queen and her Deputy when the occasion demanded it. It was only where English force prevailed that a few of the Marian bishops went over to the " Reform," some of them not for any love of the new religion, but just to keep their Sees. These conformers belonged to the Pale—Dublin, Ferns, and Leighlin—and to Waterford and Cork. Although the Earl of Clanricard in Connacht remained a " devout Catholic," not hesitating, however, to divorce a couple of wives and keep a few concubines, yet the pressure of English force was so great upon him, and he was so anxious to remain at peace with the English and in possession of his territories, that he elected to support two bishops who had taken the Oath of Supremacy.

The Church Temporalities provide another key to the situation. Wherever they could be gathered through the power of the ruling lord the bishop continued to remain in his See and fulfil his office. This is strangely exemplified in the case of the two Western Bishops already alluded to in Catholic Connacht. Another example of this method of holding office is provided in the case of Morgan MacBrien (son of Mac Ui Brien Arra who had accepted his lands from the hands of Elizabeth) who was appointed to Killaloe by the Queen because, as she said, " no person could enjoy the profits of the bishopric without the good-will of the

---

[1] See J. R. Green, *Short History of the English People*, pp. 386-9. John Knox, *History of the Reformation in Scotland*, ed. D. Laing, Edinburgh, 1846, ii. 174. Pollen, *The Month*, 1904, ii. 501.

said MacBrien Arra." Morgan was thus able to remain as Royal Bishop for forty-two years afterwards among the Catholic people of Killaloe, and receive the profits of the See.[1] On the other hand, where the Catholic lord and people, through personal dislike or otherwise, turned against the Catholic bishop, and refused to contribute to the temporalities the bishop thought it well either to resign or to get transferred to another See in order to preserve the temporalities for the Church. Thus it was that Bernard O'Higgins of Elphin resigned in 1561 and Redmund O'Gallagher of Killala in 1566 sought transference to Derry. The securing of the temporalities was then the first step towards gaining possession of the See. Where Elizabeth saw a chance of securing them she appointed her own nominee, in the hope, no doubt, that the control of the temporalities might ultimately lead those who had to supply them to recognise her bishop.

The temporalities were likewise the deciding factor in the ministration of the clergy, and it would seem that " no benefice no service " was but too common among them, otherwise it is impossible to understand the deplorable state of the people in religious matters in many places during the first twenty years at least of the reign of Elizabeth. Generally speaking, the Catholic Church in Ireland had not recovered completely from the confusion and disorganisation which pervaded it during the years of Henry and Edward, Mary's reign being all too short to pull it together again. The country had seen three changes of religion within the short term of twelve years, and ecclesiastics were appointed to benefices because of their recognition of or participation in these changes. The ministrations to the people suffered accordingly, and the people must in many places have been bewildered not only by new arrivals, but by old survivals in the persons of compliant " Vicars of Bray." No doubt the constant disturbances through wars had had a good deal to say to the confusion, but if the clergy had not been accustomed to rely on benefices as the charter of their ministrations they would have more readily given their services to the people who were

---

[1] Morgan MacBrien resigned his See in the year 1612, his conscience beginning to trouble him at the end of his days. Having made a general confession of all his sins to a Jesuit priest who was in the vicinity, having recited the profession of faith on his knees before the altar, having been absolved from his sins and from excommunication, and having heard Mass, he signed with his own hand in presence of witnesses his reconciliation with the Catholic Church. (*Litterae Annuae Missionis Hiberniae S.J.*, *anni* 1612, *Archiv. Gen. S.J.*, *Anglia* 41.) MacBrien died on 30 April in the following year.

left throughout the country without instruction and sacraments. They had not yet learned to depend on the charity of the people, and the apostolic spirit was little in evidence. No doubt there were many notable exceptions. In cities and walled towns priests and people seem to have banded themselves together for religious purposes, due largely to the Guild system of the Middle Ages, the religious and craft guilds which included the majority of the people of those cities and towns.

In general, also, it may be said that preaching was a thing of the past. On this point we have the lamentation of no less a person than James Fitzmaurice of Desmond when he endeavoured to introduce Franciscan preachers into the diocese of Cashel. Indeed the Franciscan friars alone seem to have had the courage necessary for this public preaching to the people. But even this was brief and insignificant. With the lack of teaching and preaching and the demoralisation of the clergy it was no wonder that the people grew up in ignorance not only of the sacraments but of the principles of religion and of the Creed itself. On this point we have the testimonies of Edmund Tanner, afterwards Bishop of Cork, and of Father Wolf, the Apostolic Commissary. Father Wolf saw it for himself, and Father Tanner learnt it in Louvain from the students who came from Ireland. One of the objects of Father Wolf's mission was to establish a university and schools. It seems not an unfair conclusion that he received little or no support from the Marian Bishops, who appear almost to have resented his presence among them.

Limerick seems to have been one of the few places where any attempt was made to carry on schools; there Bishop Leverous of Kildare, after his expulsion from his See, Creagh, Good and Daniel, two Jesuit students, taught for some years.

The morals of the people suffered in consequence, and there is no doubt that they became very lax. Divorces, too, were not uncommon. Two things helped to encourage them. On the one hand, in the towns and cities people kept very much to themselves, the merchant and craft classes having little in common with the country folk. As the roving bands of Irish and English soldiers went up and down the country the people found themselves much safer within the city or town walls. Considering the small population of these cities and towns at this time, intermarriage must have been considerable. Moreover, as the Irish apparently thought little of marrying within the strictly forbidden degrees of relationship, they thought little of repudiating the marriages when it suited them. On the other hand, throughout the country, the

ruling family system restricted the common people to a great
extent to intermarriage, with the same result of marrying within
forbidden degrees. Father Wolf says that when he landed at
Cork in 1561 thousands of people came to him even for many miles
to have their marriages legitimatised. After the Council of Trent
the faculty papers of the Irish bishops particularly called attention
to the fact that dispensations may be granted also in the fourth
degree, thus showing that up to that time it had been not unusual
to celebrate marriages of third cousins without dispensation.[1]
One redeeming feature, says Edmund Tanner, was that the people
were only too anxious to know what was right and to do it.

Father Wolf, 29 June, 1561, namely, shortly after his arrival
in Ireland, in a letter to the General of the Jesuits, gives a woeful
picture of the state of the clergy in general; matters, however,
seem to have mended somewhat during his six years among them.
But as the country grew more unsettled in succeeding years, through
the activities of Elizabeth's deputies and provincial presidencies,
the religious state of the clergy and people must have suffered
considerably in consequence. James Fitzmaurice's lamentation,
to which we have already alluded, seems to confirm the demoralisation that ensued, and, as Father Wolf stated, he left Ireland
not only on account of danger to his body but to his soul. When
such a noble soul as James feared for his salvation, it may well
be imagined in what state the ignorant people were. Although
Father Wolf succeeded in collecting good priests for some of the
western and southern Sees and had them consecrated, yet most
of these were unable to return to their dioceses on account of
Elizabeth's prohibition against Rome-runners, and were, therefore, quite useless for the organisation of their churches in clergy
and people. In addition to this a few bishops were expelled
from their dioceses by Elizabeth's agents and some others went
to the Continent as emissaries of James Fitzmaurice to seek men,
money, and munitions to withstand Elizabeth.

[1] Bodkin, schismatic Archbishop of Tuam, sanctioned marriages in Galway
within the forbidden degrees of the Church on the ground that there were no
marriage laws since Henry VIII. (Lynch, *De Presul. Hiber.*) Lynch also
narrates that a Provincial Council of Connacht, held in Galway in 1632, referred to a similar Council held in 1566 under Bishops O'Gallaghair, O'Crean,
and O'Hart in which it was enacted that all the decrees of the Council of Trent
should be observed in their entirety, and particularly to its decree of annulling
all clandestine marriages contracted without the presence of the parish priest.
These decrees were put into force in the dioceses of these three bishops, but not
in the dioceses of the schismatic bishops, Bodkin of Tuam and Kilmacduagh,
and Burke of Clonfert. It would seem, then, the abuse of clandestine marriages
had obtained in these several dioceses since the days of Henry VIII.

Such in general is the deplorable picture that presents itself during this period, relieved with high lights, no doubt, here and there throughout the country, especially in places like Meath and Co. Dublin,[1] where little zeal might be looked for on account of Protestant opposition. But though that is the condition of the Catholic religion, as may be impartially described, yet the attitude of the bishops, clergy, and people towards the " reform " is unmistakable in the main in its confirmed opposition. Nevertheless, it is true that the bishops of Ireland, unlike their fellow-bishops in England, took no united stand against the Acts of Supremacy and Uniformity.

---

[1] It is of interest to mention that the religious Guild of the Blessed Virgin Mary at Mulhuddard, Co. Dublin, founded in 1445, " so continued to the 15th Queen Elizabeth," namely, 1572. (Moran, *Archdall*, ii. 121.) What happened to it after that date, in its religious capacity, is a matter of doubt, but according to an inquisition, 5 November, 1613, " John Rise was chaplain to the chantry, but the jurors cannot find whether he celebrates divine service or not." The presumption is that the guild still continued its religious functions though unknown to the jurors. Again, almost within ear-shot of Dublin Castle, the nuns of Grace Dieu (3 miles north of Swords) were living as late as the year 1577 in a small house near the castle of Portrane, a part of their old property saved from the suppression in 1540. The prioress with her community and chaplain celebrated the Divine Offices in the parish church of Portrane.

BIBLIOGRAPHY.

GENERAL.

Annals, Camden (reign of Elizabeth, London, 1675).
Annals, Dowling (Irish Arch. Soc., Dublin, 1849).
Annals, Four Masters.
Annals, Hayward (Camden Society, 1840).
Annals, Loch Cé (W. M. Hennessey, London, 1871).
Annals, Loftus MS. (Marsh's Library, Dublin).

Bagwell, R., Ireland under the Tudors, ii., iii. (London, 1885, 1890).
British Museum, Cotton MSS.
British Museum, Egerton MSS., 1780.
Brosch, M., Geschichte Englands, vi. (Gotha, 1890).
Burke, J., Peerage (London, 1841).

Calendar, Ancient Records, Corporation of Dublin, i., ii.
Camden, Britannia (*trans.* Holland, 1610).
Campion, History (Ancient Irish Histories, Dublin, 1809).
Capgrave, J., De Illustribus Henricis (London, 1858).
Cox, R., Hibernia Anglicana (London, 1689).

Desiderata Curiosa Hibernica, i. (Dublin, 1772).
D'Ewes, Journal of all Parls. reign of Elizabeth (London, 1682).
Digges D., Compleat Ambassador (London, 1655).
Dublin Review, cix.

Froude, J. A., History of England, ix., x. (London, 1907).

Giraldus Cambrensis, Hist. and Works (Trans. Forrester, London, 1863).
Green, J. R., Short Hist. English People (London, 1878).

Hooker, J. (*alias* Vowell), Life and Times, Sir P. Carew (London, 1857).

Kervyn de Lettenhove, Relations Pol. des Pays-Bas et de l'Angleterre, i. (Bruxelles, 1882).
Kildare Archæol. Journal, i. (Dublin, 1891-95).

Leland, T., History of Ireland, ii. (Dublin, 1774).
Liber Munerum Publicorum Hiberniae, 1152-1827 (London, 1857).
Lingard, J., History of England, vi. (London, 1854).
Lodge, E., Peerage (London, 1846).

Machyn, Diary (Camden Society, London, 1848).

Rymer, Fœdera, i.-iv. (London, 1816-69).

State Papers, Foreign, Calendar, 1558-80.
State Papers, Ireland, Calendar, 1509-73, 1574-85.
State Papers, Ireland, Calendar, Carew, 1515-74, 1575-88.
State Papers, Ireland, Fiants, Elizabeth, Reports, D.K.R.I., 1879.
State Papers, Ireland, Patent Rolls, Calendar (1509-73, 1574-79).
State Papers, Ireland (Elizabeth), Public Record Office, London.
State Papers, Spanish, Calendar, 1558-67, 1568-79.
State Papers, Venetian, Calendar, vi., vii., 1558-80.
Stuart, Armagh (ed. Coleman, Dublin, 1890).

Tracts Relating to Ireland, ii. (Irish Arch. Soc. Dublin, 1841).
Trinity College, Dublin, MSS. E. 3, 18.

Ware, J., Antiquities (Dublin, 1745).
Webb, J. J., Guilds of Dublin (Dublin, 1929).

THE CHURCH ; THE IRISH BISHOPS.

Ancel, R., Nonciatures de France, i. (Paris, 1909).
Archivium Hibernicum, v., vii. (Maynooth, 1916, 1918-22).

Begley, J., Limerick in Sixteenth and Seventeenth Centuries (Dublin, 1927).
Bellesheim, A., Katholiscen Kirche in Irland, ii. (Mainz, 1890).
Birt, H. N., Elizabethan Religious Settlement (London, 1907).
Brady, W. M., Alleged Conversion of Irish Bishops, 5th ed. (London, 1866).
Brady, W. M., English State Church in Ireland (London, 1869).
Brady, W. M., Episcopal Succession, i., ii., iii. (Rome, 1877).
Brady, W. M., State Papers, Irish Church (London, 1868).
Bridgett-Knox, Catholic Hierarchy Deposed by Elizabeth (London, 1889).

Catholic Record Society, Miscellanea, ii., iii. (London, 1905-6).
Clifton Tracts : I. Reformation ; II. Historical Fallacies (London, 1854).
Costello-Coleman, De Annatis Hiberniae, i. (Dundalk, 1908).
Cotton, Fasti Eccl. Hiber. (Dublin, 1847).

English Historical Review, xv., xxii., xxiv., xxv. (London, 1907-10).

Franciscan MSS. Report (Historical MSS. Commission).
Frere, W. H., Engl. Church in Reigns of Eliz. and James I (London, 1904).

Haile, Martin, An Elizabethan Cardinal (London, 1914).
Harris, Ware's Bishops (Dublin, 1745).
Hergenrother, J., Staat und Kirche (Frieburg, 1872).
Hogan, E., Ibernia Ignatiana (Dublin, 1880).
Hore, A. H., Church of England (London, 1900).

Irish Ecclesiastical Record, i., ii., iii. (Dublin, 1865-67).

Kelly, M., Dissertations on Irish Church History (Dublin, 1864).
Kennedy, H. B., Christ Church Cathedral (Dublin, 1926).
Knox, John, History of Reformation in Scotland, ii. (Edin., 1846).
Knox, T., Records of English Catholics, ii. (London, 1822).
Kretzschmar, J., Die Invasions projeckte (Leipzig, 1892).

Lawlor, H. J., Reformation and Irish Episcopate (London, 1906).
Lynch, J., Cambrensis Eversus, iii. (*trans.* Kelly, Dublin, 1848-51).
Lynch, J., De Presulibus Hiberniae MS., T.C.D., K. 6, 15-16.

MacCaffrey, J., Catholic Church, Renaissance to French Revolution, ii. (Dublin, 1915).
Mant, R., History of the Church of Ireland, i. (London, 1840).
Mason, W. M., St. Patrick's Cathedral (Dublin, 1820).
Meyer, A. O., England und die katholische Kirche unter Elisabeth (Rom., 1911).
Moran, P. F. (Cardinal), Archbishops of Dublin (Dublin, 1864).
Moran, P. F. (Cardinal), Spicilegium Ossoriense, i. (Dublin, 1874-78).

Pastor, L. V., Storia dei Papi, vii., viii., ix. (Roma, 1923-25).
Pollen, J. H., English Catholics (London, 1920).
Pollen, J. H., The Month, 1902, 1904 (London).

Renehan, L. F., Collections on Irish Church History, i. (Dublin, 1861).
Ronan, M. V., Reformation in Dublin, 1536-58 (London, 1926).
Roth, D., Analecta (Colon, 1617).
Roth, D., De Processu Martyriali (Colon, 1619).

Shirley, E. P., Original Letters on Irish Church History (London, 1851).
Society of Jesus Archives (Rome).
Stephens, W. R., Helps to Study of Book of Common Prayer (Oxford, 1901).

Strype, J., Annals, Eliz., 1558-88 (London, 1725).
Strype, J., Life of Archbishop Parker (Oxford, 1821).

Theiner, A., Annales Ecclesiastici (Romae, 1856).
Theiner, A., Acta S. Concilii Tridentini, ii. (Zagabrii et Lipsiae, 1875).
Trinity College, Dublin, MS. F. 3, 17.

Vatican Archives, Urb. 1048, Misc. Armel.

Wood, A., Athenae Oxonienses (London, 1720).

FITZMAURICE EXPEDITION.

Boverius, Z., Annales Ord. Min. S. Francisci (London, 1632-39).

Carini, F. (Mgr. Ormaneto), Nuncio to Spain, 1572-77 (Roma, 1894).
Catholic Bulletin, " Wine from the Royal Pope " (Dublin, 1925-29).

Kilkenny Archæol. Assoc. ; Roy. Hist. and Archæol. Assoc. ;
    Roy. Soc. Antiquaries, Ireland, 1856-57, 1858-59, 1860-61,
    1870-71, 1879, 1890.

Maffei, G. P., Annali di Gregorio XIII (Roma, 1742).

O'Daly, Dom., Rise, Increase, and Exit of the Family of the
    Geraldines (trans. C. P. Meehan, Dublin, 1847).
O'Sullivan Beare, Catholic History of Ireland, 1821 (trans. M. J.
    Byrne, Dublin, 1903).

Sacchinius, F., Historia Societatis Jesu, iii. (Romae, 1649).
Simancas, Royal Archives.
State Papers, Rome, Calendar, 1558-71, 1572-85 (London, 1916,
    1926).

Vatican Archives, Sega, Relazione Compendiosa.

PART I.

"REFORM GOETH SLOWLY FORWARD."

Protestants Petition Elizabeth for Favours.

THREE days after Mary's death Elizabeth sent a letter, 20 November, 1558, to the Lord Deputy and Council of Ireland informing them of that event and commanding the proclamation of her own accession to be published in all convenient places.[1] The proclamation was accordingly made in Dublin, 12 December, and was attended by John Spensfeld, the Mayor, in state.[2] On the same day Sydney was elected by the Council as Lord Justice.[3] Two days afterwards he took the oath of office and received the sword of state, as was customary, before the high altar in Christ Church after the celebration of Mass. The next day Hugh Curwen, Archbishop of Dublin, was appointed keeper of the Great Seal,[4] although it was not until June of the following year that he was appointed Lord Chancellor.[5]

The proclamation of Anne Boleyn's daughter can hardly have caused much satisfaction in Ireland, but it was hailed with joy by some of Edward's Protestant officials whose prospects had been clouded during the late reign. Old Sir John Alen, who was Chancellor of Ireland under Edward, and who was allowed by Mary to live peacefully in England

---

[1] *C.S.P.I.*, Eliz., i. 3.

[2] Loftus, *Annals*. "The ceremony of Queen Mary's funeral was observed on the 12th of January [1559] and the 14th of the same month was celebrated the feast of Queen Elizabeth's coronation." These were performed according to the Catholic Ritual. Loftus states: "The service in English ceased to be read publicly from the death of Edward VI until the second coming over of the Earl of Sussex, but then, when he received the sword at Christ Church, Sir Nicholas Dardy sang the Litany in English."

[3] *C.P.C.R.I.*, *Eliz.*, i. 397.   [4] *Loc. cit.*   [5] *Ib.*, 418.

I

during her reign, was back in Dublin within a month after her death and restored to the Council. He lost no time in writing to Cecil (16 December), congratulating him on his recall to the office of Secretary, and reminding him of " the persecution he has suffered, having been chief in commission for the dissolution of the abbeys." [1] He enclosed a " token," the usual reminder that some favour would be appreciated.

Thomas Alen, who had profited, like his brother, by the dissolution of the Religious Houses, [2] also reminded the new Secretary of his great losses during Mary's reign, rejoiced that God had sent light after darkness, and that he and his friends were going to have their turn. [3]

Another Protestant who considered that he had a grievance was Edward Staples who had been appointed Bishop of Meath by the Pope, but who had been deprived of his See by Mary. He, too, lost no time in writing to Cecil (16 December) :—[4]

After most hearty recommendations, I cannot declare how much the people here doth rejoice of the coming of our most dear Masters to the governance of her noble realm, how cruelly I have been handled by the late Queen's days, it would be too long to set it forth in writing. After my service of thirty-five years I was driven almost to begging, thrust out of my house, cast from estimation, and made a jesting stock amongst monks and friars, nor any cause why was laid against me, but for that I did marry a wife, they did put an Irish monk [Wm. Walsh] in my place,

---

[1] *C.S.P.I., Eliz.*, i. 7.

[2] See Ronan, *Reformation in Dublin*, 1536-58, p. 509.

[3] Alen suggested that a sharp eye should be kept on Sir Oswald Messingberd, the prior of St. John's, Kilmainham, who was suspected of a design to pull down the priory lest its beauty and convenience should again attract the Lord Deputy. It should be noted that when the priory was dissolved by Henry VIII it became the residence of the Lord Deputy, but was afterwards restored by Mary to the Hospitallers, its former occupants.

Messingberd had probably sold the lead roofing, and the damage being aggravated by a great storm, the priory was not thought worth repairing. The Deputy's abode was accordingly transferred to Dublin Castle. Messingberd continued to hold his priory during the early portion of Elizabeth's reign. But Alen suggested that his revenue should be sternly restricted to 1000 marks, namely, about £10,000 in *1914 value*. This was about the revenue at the Dissolution. At the Dublin Parliament of 1560 a proclamation was made that Messingberd, " the pretensed Prior of St. John's of Jerusalem," should appear by a certain day otherwise to be adjudged and taken as a traitor. (Carew, 234.)

[4] *S.P.I., Eliz.*, i. 8, P.R.O., London. Shirley, 87.

whose chief matter in preaching hath been in rallying against our
old Master, wherewith I was more grieved than with my own
troubles. The Lord Cardinal [Pole] laid against me for a grievous
article that I presumed in my sermon to pray for his soul. Now, for
if it please you to be suitor to the Queen's Majesty for me, either
to have my living again, or else to obtain some state of living
to my vocation, you shall do no less than is my expectation at
your hands. I would have come myself to you, but surely such
is my poverty that I am not able to bear the charges of my journey,
and therefore I beseech you to pity my state, and accordingly
now show yourself my good master as I have always found you,
for I had never more need. The Lord Cardinal promised me that
I should have an honest stay of living out of the spiritualities
here that were granted to his disposition [disposal] by the act
of parliament, but nothing did he, but gave me leave almost to
beg my bread. If it please you to confer with my Lady Sydney
I trust she will further your suit for your poor friend. I trust in
the Lord by your means to find the Queen my gracious Lady,
her noble grandfather was my especial good Lord, and I think
I am the oldest chaplain that our old master [Henry VIII] hath
now living, and therefore trust that his noble daughter will not
see me lack living—And if this supplication herein enclosed [want-
ing] and directed to the Queen's Majesty seem unto you convenient, then I beseech you it may be delivered or else changed
as you think best, thus I take my leave of your good mastership,
beseeching the Lord to continue you long in much health with
increase of honour. Written at Dublin the XVIth day of December.

> Your poor bedesman and oratorman
> EDWARD STAPLE late Bishop of Meath.[1]

To the Right Honourable and my most especial good Master
Sir William Cecil, knight and secretary to the Queen's Majesty.

BISHOPS OF TUAM AND CLONFERT'S PETITION.

A petition of another kind, but of exceptional interest,
was presented to the Queen by Christopher Bodkin, Archbishop of Tuam, Rowland Burke, Bishop of Clonfert, and the

---

[1] Ware supposes Staples to have died about 1554, namely, before Elizabeth's
accession (*Bishops, Meath*). It is probable that he died soon after the sending
of this letter, as otherwise he would naturally have been restored to the See of
Meath.

Mayor and Commons of Galway in favour of the Earl of Clanricard, 15 February, 1559.[1] The signatories testify :—

Had it not been for the excellent order and government which the Earl maintained " we and all the rest of the confines had been cast away and not able to lie where we be . . . we have not had the like peer since his father departed this mortal life." We have no knowledge of the extent of his " living or lordship . . . but we do well know that his charge is great in maintaining of many men," which he must do to be ready to withstand such malefactors as been about his country. In our estimation the Earl is worthy to have a good living if it be your Grace's pleasure to grant him more than he hath. We recall the services performed by the Earl during the reigns of " your Grace's forefather, noble brother and sister, during their time we perceived no let in him." The Earl's exploit against the Scots on the 8 September was the best piece of service that was done in Connacht, the fifth portion of Ireland, when he and his men fought manfully against the Scots, they being the greater number than he was. " And as for us we have none other defender in spirituality or in temporality but only the said Earl under God and your Grace, for we are far distant from the Lord Deputy's power." In former times the Earls of Clanricard had the revenue of Your Grace's said town of Galway, Your Grace's only chamber [2] in Connacht, they being bound to defend the town and Commons, but since Henry VIII took the revenues of the late Earl " the said townsmen is not as bold upon [3] the said Earl as they were in times past, although there is nobody else who does any good for the town, and some of the Commons do not like to trouble the Earl to come and do justice to offenders, when they [the offenders] live at some distance away, and so would put the Earl to great expense, as he would have to come with great power," etc., to strike terror into the offenders and so they [Commons] remain outside his jurisdiction rather than put him to any trouble, but if her Grace would graciously restore the revenues it would once more entail upon the Earl the duty of defending the country.[4]

[1] *S.P.I., Eliz.*, i. 15, P.R.O., London.
[2] I.e. *camera*, court.
[3] Importunate with.
[4] In July, 1559, in answer to a suit made by Clanricard for a parcel of land within the English Pale, to the value of £10, granted to him by Henry VIII, Elizabeth was pleased to accede to it " in consideration of the good report of his service, and in expectation of its continuance." She likewise was pleased

From this letter it is clear that the two bishops, long suspected of anti-papal leanings, were not favourably regarded by the Catholic people of Connacht, and received the revenues of their spiritual offices as well as of their lands only by the aid of the strong arm of Clanricard. Their position in the Catholic hierarchy will be more fully treated later.[1]

Sir Ralph Bagenall, formerly lieutenant of Leix and Offaly, wrote to the Privy Council putting before them his particular grievance. During Mary's first Parliament in Dublin, he says, he denied the papal supremacy. For this he found himself so disliked that for safety he fled to France and lost thereby not only his office of lieutenant but his pension. In consequence of all this he incurred so much debt that he was forced to sell property of the yearly value of £500. Elizabeth had since granted him the non-residence fines of twelve bishoprics, but as there were legal obstacles

that her Deputy should grant him in fee-farm the nunnery of Kilcrenaught, in the Earl's county, at the rent of 22 marks sterling (1 mark = 13s. 4d.). (Carew, no. 219. *P.C.R.I.*, *Eliz.*, i. 448.)

In a memorial of answers given by the Queen to the Lord Deputy, 16 July, 1559, it is stated : " The Earl of Clanricard shall have the captainship of Connacht, as he has required, during her Majesty's pleasure, if the Deputy and Council shall think it meet. He has also required that his son by his first wife, who was divorced from him, might, notwithstanding the said divorce, be enabled to inherit him, and that his other sons by his present wife might be his heirs after his first son successively. The same shall be authorised by an act of Parliament, as it cannot be done otherwise." (Carew, *Cal.*, no. 219.) On 26 September, 1577, commissions were issued to William, Archbishop of Tuam, and others to make inquisition as to the legitimacy of Ulick Burke claiming to be the eldest son and heir of Richard, Earl of Clanricard, and his wife Margaret O'Brene, daughter of Maurice, late Earl of Thomond, on the complaint of Ulick against the Earl of Clanricard and John Bourke his son. (*Fiants*, no. 3117.)

[1] Before July, 1559, " the said Earl, the Archbishop of Tuam, and the Bishop of Clonfert, have written to Her Majesty in favour of the Dean of Tuam, William Lealy, for confirmation unto him of the deanery and the parsonages of Ballony, Aghasgaragh, Killosailaryn, and the prebend of Leekage, Her Majesty is pleased that the Deputy shall understand the nature of these things, and if he shall find no inconvenience to the service of Her Majesty, then, in her name and under Her Grace's seal, to make a confirmation thereof to the said Dean." (*P.C.R.I.*, *Eliz.*, i. 448.) In July, 1559, the Dean of Tuam and the Archdeacon of Enachdune (Sir John Bermingham) were appointed to the Privy Council. The Dean, in company with the Earl, the Bishop of Leighlin (who had already abjured the Pope's authority), Andrew Skiddye, a student in the Inner Temple, the Bishop of Clunye (Cloyne), and others, made several requests to Elizabeth. (*C.S.P.I.*, *Eliz.*, i. 155-7.)

he asked the Council to obtain for him a grant of lands in fee-farm or by lease worth fifty pounds a year.[1]

These petitions are a few samples showing, early in Elizabeth's reign, what those who had already accepted the Royal Supremacy expected from the new Queen whom they regarded as one who would reverse Mary's papal policy. As an indication of Elizabeth's mind on the religious question it may be well to mention here a letter that she wrote to Warham and Robert Sentleger commanding them to send over the books and writings of John Bale, late Bishop of Ossory during Edward's reign, which he left behind him " in the time of our late sister Queen Mary, when he was occasioned to depart out of Ireland." He had been deprived of his See by Mary. Elizabeth says he was " a man that hath been studious in the search for the history and anti-quities of this our realm " for the illustration and setting forth of its story.[2]

BISHOP OF LEIGHLIN TAKES THE OATH.

Although we have no document to show when Archbishop Curwen of Dublin (our cousin, as Elizabeth calls him) went over to Protestantism in this reign, it may be taken that, having been a compromiser in many reigns, he became obedient to the royal will immediately after the arrival of Sussex in August, 1559. But the recantation of Bishop Fihil of Leighlin is extant. Its date, 28 May, 1559, shows that he had not waited for the holding of the Dublin Parliament. As it was made at the Court then held at Greenwich, it may be that being in England at the time he was induced to make it. Its wording, however, shows the readiness with which he complied. The renunciation is as follows :—

I, Thomas ffyle, bishop of Laughlyn in the realm of Ireland, and contented to renounce and yield up to the Queen's Majesty all the temporal lands belonging to the said bishopric and lying

---

[1] *S.P.I.*, *Eliz.*, i. 11, P.R.O., London.

[2] *C.S.P.I.*, *Eliz.*, i. 85. Bale afterwards wrote a book on his tenure of the diocese, in somewhat scurrilous language, which was called " The Vocaycion of John Bale to the Diocese of Ossory " (see Ronan, *The Reformation in Dublin*, 1556-58, p. 413).

near to her Majesty's fort of Laughlyn [1] to be ordered as her Highness shall think fit in consideration of other spiritual possessions of like value to be annexed to the said bishopric which I promise to do by perfect order of the laws so soon as I shall by her Majesty's letters or by the Lord Deputy for the time being be commanded.

Item. I do profess that no foreign potentate [2] has or by the laws of God ought to have any temporal or spiritual power or jurisdiction within any of her Highness dominions but that the supreme governance thereof doth only appertain to her royal estate.

Item. I do renounce and refuse all Bulls or other sinister means whereby I did obtain the said bishopric,[3] and do humbly acknowledge and agree to receive the same of her Highness by her most gracious letters patents as the only way and means whereby I ought to enjoy the same. In witness whereof and for the better performance of the premises I have not only subscribed these articles with my own hand but also have taken a corporal oath upon the holy evangelist to keep, observe, and maintain the same to the uttermost of my power. Dated at the Court the XXVIII of May, 1559.[4]

Such an abject submission is inconsistent with the plea of pretence which has been made in Fihil's defence by some

---

[1] The episcopal lands near the fort were required for the use of the army of occupation, and it would seem that Fihil was summoned to England to come to an agreement with Elizabeth about the delivery of these lands, and then took the Oath.

[2] I.e. the Pope.

[3] I.e. his Papal appointment. In the memorial of the answers given by the Queen, 16 July, 1559, the eighth paragraph states : " Where Sir Thomas Fily, Bishop of Laughlyn, has acknowledged by his oath and writing his allegiance to her Highness, with a renunciation of all foreign authority and jurisdiction, making humble suit to have the said bishopric conferred on him ; the deputy shall make a grant to him of the same. Because certain of the temporalities of the bishopric so nearly adjoin the fort at Laughlyn, that they cannot be spared for the service of her Majesty, the Deputy is to deliver to the Bishop by way of exchange other spiritual possessions, and suffer him to enjoy the benefice of Dalighne [Delgany] in a *commendam* towards his better sustentation." (Carew, no. 219.)

In the Instructions given to Sussex, Lord Lieutenant of Ireland, 1560, by the Queen, is the following : " The Bishop of Laughlen is desirous to have the parsonage of Delgin [Delgany], in the diocese of Dublin, and the parsonages of Killessen and Killeban in the diocese of Laughlen, towards an increase of his living, which is very small. In consideration of his good conformity in matters of religion, the Lieutenant shall cause a grant of the said parsonages to be made to him by way of *commendam*." (Carew, no. 225.)

[4] *S.P.I., Eliz.*, i. 36, P.R.O., London.

Catholic historians ; and, as if this English document was not sufficient testimony to his abjuration of papal supremacy, he repeated the recantation in a Latin document in which his signature was witnessed by W. Howard, F. Knollys, and E. Rogers, members of the Privy Council. It has been likewise stated in his defence that, when he returned to his diocese, he gave no further proof of conversion. This, however, can no more be sustained than the former plea, for, as late as 6 October, 1564, he was appointed royal commissioner with Archbishop Loftus of Dublin, Bishop Brady of Meath, etc., to inquire into Catholic practices and "heretical opinions." [1] Moreover, Elizabeth appointed no one else to the See until after his death in 1567. Had he not continued to conform, it is scarcely credible that he would have been allowed to remain in such a stronghold of English power as Leighlin. His recantation was illegal as no Parliament in Dublin had as yet passed the Act of Supremacy. This makes Fihil's procedure all the more remarkable, and shows the anxiety of Elizabeth to secure the stronghold of Leighlin for a safe passage from the Pale to Munster, by coming to an early arrangement with him. No doubt the mere appointment on such a commission would not of itself be sufficient proof of conformity, but taking everything into account, the probability is that Fihil did conform. The same may be said of Alexander Devereux of Ferns.

Another example of the use of ecclesiastical authority by Elizabeth, before the holding of the Dublin Parliament, is found in the Queen's grant, 14 June, 1559, of protection for Matthew son of Cornelius MicBrien, and Maurice son of Matthew MicBrien, clerks, and confirmation in their benefices which they had previously obtained by papal provision, namely, Matthew in the archdeaconry of Emly, the prebend of Dunleisg, the vicarages of Karrygyninvis *alias* Templebrydan, Gryen, and Tuathclugin, and the chapel of Lyscormake ; and Maurice in the prebend of Lattyn, the vicarages of Dunmun and Lung, and of Ballunlocha, and in the chapel of Lathrechlay, in the diocese of Emly.[2]

---

[1] *P.C.R.I., Eliz.*, i. 489.   [2] *Fiants*, no. 84.

The English Service Ordered for Irish Council.

Thomas, Earl of Sussex, who had been Lord Deputy during the latter part of Mary's reign and a professing Catholic, and who continued in office for a short time under Elizabeth,[1] was reappointed on 3 July, 1559.[2] Though he struggled hard to avoid returning to the hated Irish service, pleading occupations public and private, yet the Queen would take no denial. After a fortnight she sent him the following instructions :—[3]

Her Majesty willeth and commandeth the said Deputy and all and every of her said Council that, in all their doings and governance, they set the service of Almighty God before their eyes and prefer the same in all cases. And that specially the said Deputy, and such others of that Council, which be native-born subjects of this our realm of England, do, as much as conveniently may with good order lie in them, use the rites and ceremonies of the service of God at the best in their houses, which is by law here approved and appointed, *for doing whereof, her Majesty's will is that none of them shall be impeached or molested.*[4]

In another draft of these instructions the following was originally added but was afterwards struck through with a pen, and these words added in Cecil's hand : " To be left out " :—

and that others native of that country be not otherwise moved to use the same otherwise than with their own contestations they shall be disposed, neither therein doth her Majesty mean to judge otherwise of them than well, and yet for the better example and edification of prayer in the Church, it shall be well done if the said councillors, being of that country born, shall

---

[1] In his expedition to the north, Sussex took with him the Mayor of Dublin, who was attended with a troop of horse and a foot company of the citizens, containing in number two hundred and twenty armed men, besides four-score archers with bows and arrows under the sheriff. An entry in the Assembly Roll of the Dublin Corporation of January, 1559, states : " that it is agreed that John Usher shall have allowaunce of XII. li. sterling, for iiii. mens wages towardes his greate chardges susteyned, being sheryffe appointed captain into the north, with a band of men to attend upon the lorde deputie into the Banne in the north. And also Patrick Buckeley, late sheriffe, that was petie captaine in the said journey, shall have allowaunce of iii. li. sterling, for one mans wages." (*Cal. Anc. Rec. Dub.*, i. 483.)

[2] *P.C.R.I., Eliz.,* i. 418.

[3] Shirley, 90. [4] Italics in Cecil's hand.

at times convenient cause either in their own houses or in the churches the Litany in the English tongue to be used, with the reading of the epistle and gospel in the same tongue and the ten commandments.

Elizabeth was extremely cautious in her first attempt at religious innovations. For the sake of example the English-born councillors in Ireland are ordered to use the Book of Common Prayer, but the Irish-born are merely advised to do so. Cecil thought it better to confine the Queen's instructions to the English-born and leave the Irish-born for the present in peace. He discreetly inserted the words that the English-born should in no way suffer for using the Protestant service. The Catholic ritual was thus left untouched for the present, as the Dublin Parliament had not yet passed the Act of Uniformity, but the Protestant wedge was being quietly driven in.

Meanwhile, however, indications were given that the religion of the State was to be Protestant in Ireland as well as in England. Two months before the above instructions of Elizabeth were issued, " orders had been sent to new paint the walls of Christ Church and St. Patrick's and instead of pictures and Popish fancies, to place passages or texts of Scripture on the walls ; and men had been employed for the execution of that work on the 25 May." [1] And so it happened that, during the painting-out of the " Romish fancies," and, for three months, the Latin Mass was being celebrated in the Dublin Cathedrals. It was one of those anomalies in religious matters to which the people had become accustomed since the death of Henry VIII. Within the short space of twelve years the people of Dublin had witnessed three changes in religion ; with the second coming of Sussex the third change was to take place. But a few years ago he had carried out Mary's orders for the restoration of the Catholic Liturgy, and now he returns with orders for the introduction of the English Liturgy in a modified form.

Sussex landed at Bullock Harbour, near Dalkey (27 August), and, on the following day, rode to Dublin, being

[1] Loftus, *Annals*.

received at St. Stephen's Green by the Mayor and Aldermen. Shaking hands with the Mayor, the Earl is reported to have said : " You be all happy, my masters, in a gracious queen." At his installation in Christ Church (30 August), Sir Nicholas Dardy sang the Litany in English,[1] and afterwards the Lord Deputy took his oath ; and then they began to sing " We praise Thee, O God " (*Te Deum* in English), at which the trumpets sounded. It is quite clear that the Service consisted of the Mass followed by the Litany and *Te Deum*.[2]

MARTIAL LAW AND MUSTERING.

Immediately after Sydney's appointment as Lord Justice hundreds of pardons [3] were issued to all classes of persons throughout the country who considered that they would be much safer with them under the new regime, and who accordingly asked for them. These included Curwen, Archbishop of Dublin, Eugene Maguiness, Bishop of Down and Connor, John Standish, Archdeacon of Glendaloch, Edward Barnewall, Treasurer of St. Patrick's Cathedral, Luke *alias* Fiegh O'Toole of Castlekevin, and the chief Anglo-Norman magnates of North Dublin and Meath, such as the Barnewalls, Nugents, Cusakes, etc. Grants of English liberty were issued to petitioners, including chaplains, chiefly in Cork, Waterford, Tipperary, and Limerick.

No time was to be lost in bringing the country into peaceful subjection to the new Queen. About twenty commissions [4] were issued early in the year 1559, to the prominent Anglo-Normans in the counties of Dublin, Leix, Offaly, Waterford, Louth, Westmeath, Kilkenny, Kildare, Carlow, Wexford, and Meath to execute martial law upon all such as have not an inheritance of 20s. The commissioners were to treat and make terms with the rebels and give them safe conduct in coming and returning. Patrick Barnewall of Kilmahioke was appointed for this purpose to the countries of O'Byrne and O'Toole and the marches or confines of Dublin. Among

---

[1] Loftus, *Annals. P.C.R.I.*, *Eliz.*, i. 418.

[2] The story circulated by the notorious forger Robert Ware as to the bleeding statue of Christ Church is not worthy of notice.

[3] *P.C.R.I.*, *Eliz.*, i. 397-408.   [4] *Ib.*, 408-12.

those appointed to Kildare was old John Alen of Alenscourt, near the New Bridge (at Celbridge), Co. Kildare.

Another series of commissions was issued for the assessment of taxes, to the Barons, Lords, and Gentlemen of various counties. In the commission for the County of Dublin the Archbishop of Dublin and Thomas Lockwood, Dean of Christ Church, were included. The commissioners were ordered " to muster the inhabitants of the county and the crosses [manor lands of the Archbishop], and the marches thereof ; to cause them to be assessed and arrayed, according to the quantity of their goods and chattels, to horses and arms of light cavalry, horsemen and footmen." [1] The account was to be sent to the Lord Justice.

In the commissions for Meath, Kildare, and Kilkenny, the bishops of these dioceses are included. But from all this it cannot be concluded that the commissioners, either bishops or laymen, even if they consented to act, thereby recognised Elizabeth as Head or Governor of the Church. Though the English Parliament had passed the Royal Supremacy, no Dublin Parliament had yet been held, and the religious question had so far not been forced on the country.

Shortly afterwards, however, indications were not wanting as to the impending changes. In remembrances from Draycott to Cecil (July) it is asked whether St. Patrick's Cathedral and the Priory of Kilmainham are to be suppressed, and it is suggested, that an account should be taken of Baron Bathe of the Irish Exchequer concerning " the spiritualities and such money as remaineth in his hand to be delivered to the Treasurer there for Her Majesty's use, and the arrearages of the Spiritualities to be called in. A new extent was to be made for the twentieth and First Fruits."

As to the Priory of Kilmainham, it was evident that unless the Government acted quickly, the Prior would have leased all the lands, vicarages, and parsonages in his possession. Evidently he, too, felt that his priory would be again suppressed, and he proceeded to lease the possessions he had recovered under Mary. In the cases of vicarages, he stipu-

---

[1] *P.C.R.I.*, *Eliz.*, pp. 410 ff.

lated that they should find an honest chaplain to serve in
each of the said churches where the Prior desired, to minister
God's service to the parishioners, and "to do that which a
curate ought to do " in every one of the churches. And a
curious feature about one of those leases, that to Sir Maurice
Fitzgerald and his wife, Dame Margaret Butler, of the
vicarages of Ardfinan, Rathronan, Mortelston, and the
parsonage of Kilmeloge, Co. Tipperary, parcel of the Commandery of Any,[1] is that it was signed by Thomas Sussex,
afterwards Lord Deputy, William FitzWilliams, Treasurer-
at-War, and Baron James Bathe. So that even these officials,
who presumably were aware of Elizabeth's new policy, were
not averse from helping the prior in his last hours of
possession to secure ready money. And the lease in this
case was for twenty-nine years, namely, eight years longer
than that allowed by the statute 32 Hen. VIII. The lease
of the possessions of the Commandery of Any, Co. Limerick,
shows that lands and tenements in the immediate neighbourhood of the Priory of Kilmainham, Dublin, were not the only
ones restored to the Hospitallers under Mary. The suppression of the priory, however, was not long forthcoming,
for in the following month (July) " the lands of the Hospital
of St. John are to be resumed to the Crown, and such persons
of that Order as shall seem like good, natural, quiet subjects
to deserve pension, to have the same assigned."

For the " increase of civil order " the Earl of Ormond
begged, through Sir Edward Bellingham, Lord Deputy,
that he be appointed Captain of Leinster, namely, of the
" Kavanaghs, Tooles, and Byrnes for the most part rebels."
He also desired that his house called Leighlin-Bridge in which
Bellingham had placed soldiers during his minority, should
be restored to him, and likewise he should be given charge of
a friary adjoining it which had been fortified at the expense
of his tenants. These shall always be at the service of the
Lord Deputy and will save the Queen a thousand pounds a
year. As a governor, then, of these parts for the Queen's
peace he desires to have victuals for the maintenance of his
men at the same prices as the Lord Deputy pays, and desires

[1] See Ronan, *The Reformation in Dublin*, p. 534.

the abolition of Coyne and Livery,[1] " the greatest mischief
to the public weal." He petitions likewise for the fee-farm
of O'Conaght (£6 13s. 4d. a year) as it stands " upon the
borders of the Irish country and very necessary for the
defence of the said Earl's liberty of Tipperary."[2] The
Earl who had been educated in England thus early ranged
himself on the side of the Queen, and became afterwards one
of her most powerful defenders, as his father had been an
ardent supporter of Edward VI and the Protestant Religion.

As it is important at this stage to have a general view of
the provinces and the ruling families, a few extracts from the
State Papers will show how matters stood.

The Geraldines are of Irish blood, not brought or reduced to
the English government. The Butlers, for the most part are
of English blood and name, or of the Irishry reduced already to
English government.

Of the Earl of Kildare, Sussex writes :—

If there be a full and speedy [temporal] reformation meant
of this realm, for that th' Earl of Kildare is not only the chief
head of this dangerous faction upon whom they wholly depend,
but also the direct seeker to overthrow all English government,

---

[1] For Irish customs, see Ware's *Antiquities*, c. xii.

[2] *S.P.I.*, *Eliz.*, i. 45, P.R.O., London. The abolition of Coyne and Livery
would mean that the Irish lords would themselves have to support their armed
followers instead of having them fed and housed by the tenantry. From the
Earl of Ormond's point of view the abolition of the custom would be desirable,
as the Irish lords would then find it difficult to maintain their fighting men.
In a State Paper of 23 August, 1559, this question is set forth thus by some
unnamed loyalist : " First there are two sets of laws and customs in Ireland,
(*a*) those obeyed and practised within the English Pale ; (*b*) those followed by
the Irishry who neither pay tribute or have never been conquered. It follows
that the lords of the Irish Pale, having no just laws, are compelled to maintain
large numbers of idle men simply to keep order in their own domains or to go
to war with their neighbours ; this entails a heavy charge upon the inhabitants
of the Irish Pale, and brings about decay of husbandry ; this oppression and
exaction is called ' Coyne and liverie,' and discourages the peasants from making
improvements and working hard, only to find their lord takes it from them to
feed and maintain his fighting men. The result is, the peasants being discouraged, become as bad as the men of war and go ' stealing by night and robbing
by day,' and fight one with another, but should they be attacked by the liege
people of the Queen, they promptly forget their own enmities and join together
to fight against the loyal subjects of the Queen. If this diversity of laws could
be abolished the land would soon be reduced to obedience." (*S.P.I.*, *Eliz.*, i.
72, P.R.O., London.)

and a manifest travailer to discredit and deface openly the Governor here, and living a discontented man, for that the government of this realm is not committed to him, as it hath been to others of his ancestors before, is the likeliest and most dangerous instrument to allure foreign aid for ambition, and to stir civil rebellion by such imps as depend upon him ; it shall be necessary for the surety of the Queen's Majesty and her crown of this realm, to withdraw wholely the said Earl of Kildare out of this realm, and to give him land in England of like value or better, so as there rest no further hope of his name here left by his long sufferance here. There may indeed ensue that which her Majesty of late had just cause to fear [rebellion, with foreign aid], and being now quelled by the good agreement made in Scotland, and the disability of the French, is not unlike, if time serve, hereafter to be revived. This danger is in my sight so fearful ; the matter, if it be attempted by foreign power and aided by civil faction, so easy to be compassed, and the resisting thereof so difficult, as I am forced by duty to give advice that it should in time be prevented not so much for the care I have of Ireland, which I have often wished to be sunk in the sea, as for that, if the French should set foot therein, they should not only have such an entry into Scotland as her Majesty could not resist, but also by the commodity of the havens here and Calais now in their possession, they should take utterly from England all kind of peaceable traffic by sea, whereby would ensue such a ruin to England as I am afeared to think on. This man taken away, some noblemen and gentlemen of England should be planted in places convenient, who upon all occasions might and would bring over force to defend their own.[1]

Ulster.—O'Neile is the chiefest of the Irishry, and heretofore ought for the most part to be king of Ireland, at some times, and others of the best of the Irishry as there turn went. The use of O'Neile is such that he never manures or tilleth any land for himself, but always had victuals sent him by his tenants and underlings (viz., certain cakes of oat bread and vessels of butter, being not good, but stinking and " heary ") from Tyrone, and from other lords hereunder written ; as also beeves and other lordships ; and he charges his tenants with bonnaught [coyne and livery], which is in keeping Scots and others in his country for his better defence and keeping. The people there are far more beastlike and barbarous than the people of the other countries —Lords under O'Neile ;—Maganyes (M'Guinness), Magwyre

---

[1] Carew, no. 227.

O'Cahan, M'Mahoun, O'Hanullan, Mack Cullivin, Mack Donell, consul [constable] of his Scots and galloglasses.

O'Donell is the second best lord in Ulster, and hath lords under him as the said O'Neile hath. He is the best lord of the fish in Ireland, and he exchangeth fish always with foreign merchants for wine, by which [he] is called in other countries, the king of the fish.—Lords under O'Donell ;—O'Dogherday, O'Boyle, O'Galluhur, three consulls, McSwynys, and divers others.

Connaught.—The Earl of Clanryckarde is the chiefest Irishman in Connaught, and in times past the kingdom of that province ought to be with O'Connor Roe. O'Connor Donn, O'Rorke, and O'Reyly are of the chiefest in Connaught ; the people there are good and civil, and full of cattle always. And the said lords in Connaught useth to have galloglasses in bonnaught upon their tenants. O'Rourke useth to have galloglasses and Scots upon bonnaught, and for forswearing his hand [1] they pay penalties according to the lord's calling.

As for curyn,[2] it is a thing which craftsmen useth to take up of tenants for duties, as smiths, sergeants of towns, and such like. They take certain cakes, flesh, and butter at two feasts, viz., Christmas and Easter.

Munster.—The Earl of Thomond his ancesters hath been the best in Munster, as O'Bryan [O'Brien] the said Earl now being in his place. Macara More [M'Carthy More] is the second best man in Munster, and the said Earl hath lords under him hereunder written. The people there are very civil and well fed, in manner the best in Ireland, and have the best havens.

Two McNeMarras, O'Loughlyn, O'Connour Corcam Roe, and divers others. The Lord of Cork Bask and Mackara Rivagh [M'carthy Reagh] is under Mackara More, and not under the Earl [of Thomond].

Instead of th' Earl of Desmond, there are Englishmen appointed from her Majesty, and the people in Desmond are very good and civil now, and [still] well fed with fish, beef, and wine.

Leinster.—Heretofore McMurghoe was the best Irishman there, and was King ; Mack Gilpatrick second, and O'Connor of Offaly third ; O'Byrne and O'Trahall [O'Toole] fourth and fifth. They were always strong, and would ever be at wars together. Now by means of English power they are become more civil,

---

[1] Note in margin : " For forswearing of O'Neile his hand, whatsoever he be that shall so do, shall forfeit as the bishops and the best learned in the country shall adjudge—sometime they forfeit three-score kine, and other times more."

[2] Probably *Soreyn* (Ware, *Antiqs.*, 74-5).

and also many Englishmen planted in their steads in the said province, by means whereof for the most part all their Irish customs and exactions be abolished as well there as in other places in the land.[1]

Of course, all this self-praise on the part of Sussex was mere whitewash, and had no justification in fact. As this history proceeds it will become abundantly clear with what difficulty and with what ill success the efforts of Sussex and other Lord Deputies were rewarded. At all events, Sussex wanted to show, however so much he hated the position, how businesslike were his methods.

Dublin Parliament of 1560; Bishops and the Supremacy.

So far the Catholic religion was the only one in Ireland recognised by law, but it would seem, although no documentary proof is extant, that Sussex was instructed to summon a Parliament in Ireland " to make such statutes as were lately made in England *mutatis mutandis.*" [2]

Parliament met in Christ Church, Dublin, on 11 January, 1560, but what happened there is wrapt in obscurity. Whether it lasted a day [3] or a month, according to the testimony of Loftus, it was dissolved the 1st of February " by reason of [its] aversion to the Protestant religion, and their ecclesiastical government." [4]

Another Protestant historian admits that " the perplexity of the case was perceived by the well-wishers of the Queen at the very beginning of the Parliament ; so that, after it had sat about a month, the Lord Deputy dissolved it and went over to England for the purpose of consulting Her Majesty about the affairs of the kingdom." [5]

No reliable account of the proceedings of this Parliament has yet been discovered, but there is a well-founded tradition that the acts ascribed to it reached the statute-book by fraud. Here is what seems to have happened. As so much

---

[1] Carew, no. 229.   [2] Cox, *Hib. Angl.*, 313.
[3] *Lib. Mun.*, ii. pt. 6, 10 ; i. 4, 113.   [4] Loftus, *Annals.*
[5] Mant, i. 264-5. Sussex ordered to repair to England, 18 January, 1560 ; sailed 13 February. (*C.P.R.I., Eliz.*, 428.)

opposition was made to the Act of Supremacy, Deputy Sussex prorogued the Parliament on 11 January, namely, the first day of its sitting, until 1 February, and set out for England on 13 February for further instructions from Elizabeth.

" The blame of these outrages on religion," writes the author of *Cambrensis Eversus*,[1] " must not be charged against all the members elected to serve in that Parliament. The deputy is recorded to have employed violence, and the speaker treachery. Finding that there was a very thin attendance of members on a certain day [2] and that the benches were almost untenanted, except by a few who were already resolved to abolish the old creed, he delivered an elaborate and specious harangue for the abrogation of the Catholic faith, and is said to have carried with him the votes of the House. I have been informed that it was previously announced in the House that Parliament would not sit on that very day ; but, in the meantime, a private summons was sent to those who were well known to be favourable to the new creed."

Another writer [3] adds further particulars : " In 1560, James Stanihurst, lord of Corduff, who was speaker of the lower house of Parliament, by sending private summons to some, without any intimation to the more respectable Irish, succeeded in carrying the penal law by surprise. . . . As soon as the matter was discovered, in the next full meeting of Parliament there was a general protest against the fraud, injustice, and deliberate treachery of the proceeding. But the lord deputy and others having solemnly sworn that the law would never be carried into execution the remonstrants were caught in the dexterous snare, and consented that the enactment should remain on the statute-book." [4]

[1] iii. 19.

[2] As 1 February was the Feast-day of St. Brigid, patroness of Ireland, it is easy to understand how the orthodox members might have absented themselves, and how it could have been hinted to them that no public business would be transacted on that day.

[3] Father George Dillon (*d.* 1650), *Rationes et Motiva*, 87 ; *Camb. Ever.*, iii. 21-3.

[4] Curry remarks that these penal acts " were well known to have been imposed upon the nation by force or fraud, though under the plausible appearance of parliamentary action." (*Historical Review*, II, c. iii.) Dr. Rothe, Bishop of Ossory, also attests these facts, and further states that the delegates of the

It was this depleted assembly then which gave Protestantism its first legal sanction in Ireland, and " the Speaker won for himself the name of being the chief author of the laws enacted against the Catholic religion." [1] Three days afterwards, 4 February, certificates of acceptance of the Supremacy were presented for signature to three of the bishops, only one of whom, as we shall see, complied with the request.

The composition of this Parliament is a matter of much importance as many rash conclusions have been drawn from it. A record [2] until recently preserved in the Rolls' Office, Dublin, gave " the following list of the Lords spiritual and temporal, knights, citizens and burgesses of the first Irish Parliament of Queen Elizabeth, held at Dublin, A.D. 1560." The list follows. It is to be noted that the record does not say that they were present at the Parliament, but that they were the lords, etc., of the Parliament. The list is merely a list of those who were summoned or were considered entitled to be present. Here it is :—

[Lords Spiritual] Hugh, Dublin ; Roland, Cashel ; Christopher, Tuam ; William, Meath ; Patrick, Waterford and Lismore ; Roger, Cork and Cloyne ; Alexander, Ferns ; Thomas, Kildare ; Thomas, Leighlin ; John, Ossory ; ——, Emly ; Hugh, Limerick ; Roland, Clonfert and Elphin ; Eugene, Down ; ——, Ross ; ——, Killaloe ; ——, Kilfenora ; ——, Killala ; ——, Ardfert ; ——, Ardagh.

[Lords Temporal] Thomas Butler, Ormond and Ossory ; Gerald, Kildare ; Gerald, Desmond ; Connacus, Thomond ;

Irish Parliament to King James in 1613, declared to the English monarch that the penal statutes of 1560 were passed in the fraudulent manner described above. (*Analecta*, 387.)

[1] *Camb. Ever.*, iii. 21. " It is strange," says the Editor, " that the proceedings of an assembly, which established by law a new state church in Ireland and proscribed the old faith, should be matter of conjecture. The crisis of a revolution so momentous ought, it would seem, to have been well known to all parties, especially as very minute details are preserved of the violent opposition given by the Irish parliament to less sweeping religious innovations in the reign of Henry VIII. It should be remembered, however, that the enactments of 2nd of Elizabeth could not be generally, nor vigorously enforced, and would not, therefore, provoke much inquiry regarding the manner in which they had been carried through parliament."

[2] *Tracts Relating to Ireland*, ii. 134-8.

2 *

Richard, Clanricard; James le Barry, Buttevant; Maurice Roche, Fermoy; —— Birmingham, Athenry; —— Cursy, Kinsale; Jenico Preston, Gormanston; Roland Eustace, Baltinglas; Richard Butler, Mountgaret; Richard Nugent, Delvin; James Fleming, Slane; Christopher St. Lawrence, Howth; Patrick Barnewall, Trimleston; Thomas FitzMorish, Lackenaway [Kerry]; Christopher Plunket, Dunsany; Edmund Butler, Dunboyne; Thomas Plunket, Louth; John Poer, Curraghmore; Bernard Fitzpatrick, Upper Ossory.

Seventy-six members are mentioned in the list as entitled to sit in the House of Commons. Ten counties returned each severally two knights, namely Dublin, Meath, West-meath, Louth, Kildare, Carlow, Kilkenny, Waterford, Wex-ford, and Tipperary. These were more or less " obedient " shires, and the others had no representation. The cities and boroughs honoured with representatives were those in which the royal authority was predominant. Seventeen were situated in Leinster, eight in Munster, two in Connacht (Athenry and Galway), and only one (Carrickfergus) in Ulster. These severally were entitled to two burgesses each. Curiously enough Kilmallock is omitted. As to the temporal peers, the twenty-three enumerated belonged to Anglo-Irish families, except O'Brien of Thomond and MacGillapatrick of Upper Ossory.

Our main concern is with the bishops, twenty in number, who are taken by some historians [1] as having been present at the Parliament, and who, with the exception of those of Meath and Kildare, are alleged to have " made no difficulty on the present occasion " in passing the anti-Catholic legislation.

Mant says: " Whilst many of the temporal lords re-tained their attachment to the religious principles in which they had been educated, and transmitted the same to their descendants, all, with two only exceptions, of the spiritual peers, who had been formerly friends of the Papacy, either saw cause to approve of the recent alterations, or, perceiving no disposition in the government to treat them with vigour, contentedly acquiesced in the existing order of things, whilst

---

[1] Bagwell, ii. 6. Mant, i. 278. Lawlor, 43 *seq.*

not a few of them took advantage of the uncontrolled power which they possessed over the property of their Sees, for enriching their kindred, and impoverishing the church and their successors." We shall see that it was chiefly Elizabeth's own bishops who were guilty of alienating Church property. Even if it be admitted for the sake of argument that the Acts were passed at a representative assembly of lords spiritual and temporal, and commons, there is no document to show that these twenty bishops were present. Again, if we take the list as a list of those who were present, how comes it, it may be asked, that seven of the Sees are given without the names of their occupants? Surely, if they were present their names would have been recorded as accurately as were those of the laity. As we have stated, the list simply enumerated those summoned or entitled to be present, and even in this respect it is faulty.[1]

At this time there were thirty-two dioceses, ten in the province of Armagh, five in that of Dublin, eight in that of Cashel, and nine in that of Connacht. Three were held by the Archbishop of Tuam, namely, Tuam, Anaghdune, and Kilmacduagh, and three by the Bishop of Clonfert, namely, Clonfert, Mayo, and Elphin.[2] The Archbishop of Armagh, Donat O'Taig, appointed 7 January, 1560, had not yet returned from Rome. There were thus only twenty-seven bishops available. Of these the list mentions the Sees of only twenty. The Christian names of thirteen of these are given with the names of the dioceses, in the other seven cases the names only of the dioceses are given. Of these thirteen, only two belonged to the province of Armagh, five to that of Dublin, four to that of Cashel, and two to that of Tuam.

[1] Errors are also found in the lists of the bishops who are supposed to have been present at the Parliaments of 1541 and 1585, which are given in the State Papers. And a list of the year 1574 gives the order in which all the lords spiritual and temporal sit in parliament (*S.P.I., Eliz.*, xlviii. 97, P.R.O., London), and this at a time when in most of the Sees there were no Elizabethan bishops.

[2] It would seem, however, that there were papal bishops in some of these Sees at this time, who were ousted or forced to resign by Bodkin, Archbishop of Tuam, and Burke, Bishop of Clonfert, through the power of Clanricard. Anaghdune was probably held by William Mor, Kilmacduagh, by Cornelius O'Dea, Mayo, by Eugene MacBrehon, and Elphin by Bernard O'Higgins (see List).

The seven dioceses mentioned without the names of their occupants are : Emly, Ross, Killaloe, Kilfenora, Killala, Ardfert, and Ardagh. The occupants at the time were Raymund de Burgh of Emly, Maurice O'Hea of Ross, Terence O'Brien of Killaloe, John O'Niallan of Kilfenora, Redmund O'Gallagher of Killala, James FitzMaurice of Ardfert, and Patrick MacMahon of Ardagh. For the reason already stated it may be presumed that none of these bishops was present at the Parliament. The list omits altogether to mention the dioceses of Clogher, Dromore, Derry, Kilmore, and Raphoe. These bishops were under the patronage of the great northern chieftains, and as Sir John Davis declared in 1613 " such archbishops and bishops as were resident in the more Irish counties, and did not acknowledge the King to be their patron, were never summoned to any Parliament." [1]

There is also no mention of Achonry or of Clonmacnoise. Thus, there are seven Sees not mentioned at all, six of which had occupants at the time, and seven others mentioned without the names of their occupants. Of the remaining thirteen bishops, two have gained notoriety by their categorical refusal to accept the Supremacy,—these were William Walsh of Meath, and Thomas Leverous of Kildare. And yet, according to the list, if it be accepted, as some Protestants contend, as a list of those who voted for the Supremacy, these two bishops are to be included in the number. It may be taken as absolutely certain that they neither voted for nor accepted the Supremacy. On the other hand, if the list is merely a list of those present, then it affords no clue as to the bishops who voted for the Supremacy. Having eliminated Walsh and Leverous, eleven bishops have to be accounted for. Curwen of Dublin, Alexander Devereux of Ferns (a married man, not deprived by Mary), Thomas O'Fihil of Leighlin, Patrick Walsh of Waterford and Lismore, Roger Skiddy of Cork and Cloyne, Christopher Bodkin of Tuam, and Roland Burke of Clonfert and Elphin, may be taken as having accepted in some form or other the Su-

---

[1] *Desid. Curiosa Hib.*, i. 186.

premacy—that is, seven in all.[1] Of only five of those seven can it be said with any degree of certainty that they accepted both Supremacy and Uniformity, and one of these, Skiddy of Cork, was most probably never consecrated. Although the two others, Bodkin of Tuam and Burke of Clonfert, accepted the Supremacy, there is no proof that they adopted Uniformity of Worship, the English Liturgy.[2] There remain then four of the eleven to be accounted for, namely, Lacy of

[1] Attention must be called to a piece of evidence which bears out the above conclusion. In a letter of 20 November, 1629, to Luke Wadding, Guardian of St. Isidore's, Rome, Thomas Strange, Guardian of the Franciscans in Dublin, states that Patrick Walsh, Bishop of Waterford, referred to above, was " a Catholic bishop by election and consecration, a man of learning and of great repute throughout the kingdom for his gifts of teaching and preaching, insomuch that in Parliament all the bishops of Ireland spoke *ad nutum ejus* (at his wish), and stood firm while he stood firm, and when he fell, all fell with him, save only the Bishop of Kildare. Not content with taking the Oath of Supremacy, he married. . . . Walshe died a confirmed heretic." (*Report on Franciscan MSS.*, *Hist. MSS. Commission*, p. 15.) Father Strange, a Waterford man, evidently relies here on tradition. He is quite right in his reference to the reputation for learning of Walsh, who having been *canonice institutus* was " A Catholic bishop by election." He was appointed by Edward VI in 1551, without any reference to Rome, but he was consecrated according to the Roman Ordinal as the Edwardine Ritual had not yet come into force. He was continued in office under Mary, because he repented and because he was not then a married man, although some of his children must have been born before this time. (We shall deal with this point later.) A very glaring mistake that Strange makes is in asserting that the Bishop of Kildare alone stood firm; his ignorance about Walsh of Meath and others is therefore apparent. This will be seen in the course of this history. That Walsh of Waterford died " a confirmed heretic " is most probably true in spite of the temporary conversion effected by Tanner, Bishop of Cork. He may have influenced the six bishops referred to above, but that he influenced others cannot be accepted for the reasons stated in our text. Strange seems to confuse the two Walshes, Waterford and Meath. All " stood firm while he stood firm " would refer to Walsh of Meath; " when he fell, all fell with him " would refer to Walsh of Waterford with the limitation just mentioned.

[2] As to Bodkin, Lynch in his MS. on the Bishops of Ireland states that he never omitted on a single day the celebration of Mass according to the Catholic rite although he was a schismatic. Bodkin was buried in the Catholic Cathedral of St. Nicholas in Galway, where a tomb was erected to him showing the effigy of the Archbishop with all the Catholic symbols. Lynch says that he himself saw the remains with a portion of the episcopal mitre made of silk and gold thread. As to Bishop Burke, Lynch says that he died a Catholic, and that a marble tomb was erected to him in the church of Tinach bearing his family and episcopal arms with Catholic episcopal symbols. He also states that the Bishop before he died in 1580 purchased a field at Tinach and gave it to the parish church, which he had embellished, for the support of four priests who would recite the Divine Office, and Lynch believed that this included Masses for his soul's pardon.

Limerick, Thonory of Ossory, Baron of Cashel, and Eugene Magennis of Down. Lacy, although he was threatened with deposition again and again, was not finally deposed until 1571, and, as we shall see, remained papal bishop all through. There is nothing to show that Thonory in any way conformed, and it is probable that he was deposed in 1561-62. His consecration is, however, doubtful, although Ware states that it took place at Inistiock about the close of the year 1553. The consecration of Baron is likewise doubtful, although Ware gives the date as December, 1553.[1] In this case also there is nothing to show any conformity. He died in 1561. Although Eugene Magennis of Down and Connor had assisted at Edwardine consecrations in Christ Church, yet he continued in his See under Mary, and may therefore be taken as having repented of his action. But there is no proof that he in any way accepted Supremacy under Elizabeth, although like many of the northern bishops he was quite ready to profess allegiance and fealty to Elizabeth whenever the occasion required.

To sum up then, the most that can be said about the Irish bishops is that out of twenty-seven (possibly thirty-one) who enjoyed their Sees at the time of the Parliament only seven can be regarded with any degree of certainty as having accepted the Supremacy, and only five of these accepted also Uniformity. As to the remaining twenty or twenty-four there is not a shadow of evidence to show that they in any way conformed either in the matter of Supremacy or Uniformity.

To conclude, therefore, that because they were not deposed they accepted the Supremacy is to ignore the utter powerlessness of Elizabeth's officials to depose them. It cannot be taken for granted that the Irish bishops as a whole were so enamoured of Elizabeth and her Supremacy that they would readily accept it after their determined opposition to her brother Edward and after the treatment that was meted out to those who had accepted Henry's supremacy. At all events, the onus lies on those who claim them as " Reform " bishops to bring forward the evidence against them. This

---

[1] See *Bishops at Dioceses.*

MARIAN BISHOPS.

Diocese.	Bishop.	Remarks.
Province of Armagh :		
1. Armagh	Vacant	Dowdall, *d.* 1558 (papal) [1]
2. Meath	William Walsh	deposed, 1560 (papal)
3. Clogher	Raymund M'Mahon	*d.* before 1560 (papal) [2]
4. Clonmacnoise	Peter Wall	*d.* 1568 (papal)
5. Kilmore	John M'Brady	*d.* before 1560 (papal) [3]
6. Ardagh	Patrick M'Mahon	*d.* before 1576 (papal)
7. Down and Connor	Eugene Magennis	*d.* before 1565 (papal)
8. Dromore	Arthur Magennis	*d.* before 1576 (papal)
9. Derry	Eugene O'Doherty	*d.* before 1569 (papal)
10. Raphoe	Art O'Gallaghair	*d.* 1561 (papal)
Province of Dublin :		
11. Dublin	Hugh Curwen	accep. Suprem. and Unifor.
12. Kildare	Thomas Leverous	deposed, 1560 (papal)
13. Ossory	John Thonory	deposed, 1561 (papal)
14. Ferns	Alexander Devereux	accep. Suprem. and Unifor.
15. Leighlin	Thomas O'Fihil	accep. Suprem. and Unifor.
Province of Cashel :		
16. Cashel	Roland Baron	*d.* 1561 (papal)
17. Waterford and Lismore	Patrick Walsh	accep. Suprem. and Unifor.
18. Cork and Cloyne	Roger Skiddy	accep. Suprem. and Unifor.
19. Limerick	Hugh Lacy	resig. or dep. 1571 (papal)
20. Emly	Raymund de Burgh	*d.* 1562-63 (papal)
21. Ardfert	James Fitzmaurice	*d.* 1583 (papal)
22. Ross	Maurice O'Fihil	*d.* 1558 (papal) [4]
23. Killaloe	Terence O'Brien	*d.* 1569 (papal)
Province of Tuam :		
24. Tuam	Christopher Bodkin	accepted Supremacy
25. Clonfert	Roland Burke	accepted Supremacy
26. Kilfenoragh	John O'Niallan	*d.* 1572 (papal)
27. Killala	Redmund O'Gallaghair	trans. (papal)
28. Kilmacduagh	Cornelius O'Dea	*d.* about 1576 (papal)
29. Anaghdune	William Mor (Murray ?)	*d.* after 1567 (papal)
30. Mayo	Eugene MacBrehon	*d.* before 1574 (papal)
31. Elphin	Bernard O'Higgins	resig. about 1562 (papal)
32. Achonry	Cormac O'Coyne	*d.* . . . (papal)

[1] Donat o' Taig appointed 7 January, 1560, by the Pope.
[2] Cornelius Macardel appointed 29 May, 1560, by the Pope.
[3] Hugh O'Sheridan appointed 7 January, 1560, by the Pope.
[4] Maurice O'Hea appointed 7 April, 1559, by the Pope. The word *papal* in the third column above denotes that the bishop was at the time of death, deposition, transference, or resignation, in union with the Holy See.

has never been done. Moreover, it is to be noted that it was only in the dioceses where there was any show of force to support the Parliament Act and carry it out that bishops accepted it, namely, in three within the Pale, Dublin, Leighlin, and Ferns, in Waterford and Cork, and in Tuam and Clonfert [1] under the strong hand of Clanricard. As English power extended throughout the country, Elizabeth appointed to the dioceses that came under her control, but in many cases these appointments were not made until late in her reign.[2]

ALLEGED ACTS OF THE PARLIAMENT.

The Acts that ultimately found their way to the Statute Book may be summarised :—

Firstly : An Act " restoring to the Crown the ancient jurisdiction (i.e. Henry VIII's) over the state, ecclesiastical and spiritual, and abrogating all foreign power repugnant to the same."

Acts of appeals and Faculties be revived : also as much of the Act of marriage as concerns consanguinity.

An Act of 3rd and 4th Philip and Mary reviving three statutes against heresy was repealed, except so much thereof as concerns *Premunire*. That the Queen and her successors may appoint commissioners to exercise ecclesiastical jurisdiction.

That all officers and ministers ecclesiastical or lay, all ecclesiastical persons, and everyone that has the Queen's wages, shall take the oath of Supremacy, on pain of losing

---

[1] A Vatican list of 1580 mentions Burke as having accepted the Supremacy but not Uniformity, and designates him a schismatic but not a heretic. The same may be said of Bodkin.

[2] See *Appendix II*. In this analysis we differ from Catholic and Protestant historians alike, such as MacCaffrey, Moran, Brady, Froude, Mant, etc. All the foregoing, two Protestants and two Catholics, except Mant, assert that " with the single exception of Curwen it cannot be proved with certain that any of the bishops proved disloyal to their trust." Froude, however, somewhat later admitted that O'Fihil of Leighlin might be admitted as having accepted the Supremacy. On the other side Mant and others who unquestioningly follow him, assert that as in about twenty dioceses no change of occupant occurred the bishops " contentedly acquiesced in the existing order of things " or saw cause to approve of the recent alterations. Our own view is based on facts of which these historians were not quite cognisant and which will appear during the course of this history.

his office. He that sues livery or takes Orders must take the oath. And a penitent, upon taking the oath, shall be restored to his office of inheritance.

He that shall extol, maintain or advance foreign juris-diction [1] shall for the first offence lose his goods : and if they be not worth twenty pounds, then a year's imprisonment without bail besides, and if it be an ecclesiastical person, shall likewise lose all his benefices, and the second offence to be *Premunire*,[2] and the third, high treason, provided the prosecution for words be within half a year after the speaking.

Nothing shall be judged heresy but what has been so by the Scripture, first four General Councils, or some other General Council, by express words of Scripture, or shall be by Act of Parliament ; the offence to be proved by two witnesses, before the party arraigned in person, face to face.

Secondly : An Act for " Uniformity of Common Prayer and service in the Church, and the administration of the Sacraments."

All ministers are commanded to use it ; and on such as should refuse to use it, or should use any other form, or should preach or speak in derogation of it, penalties are imposed ; first, the forfeiture of a year's profit of his benefice, and six months' imprisonment ; for the second offence, imprisonment for one year, and deprivation ; and for the third offence, deprivation and imprisonment for life. On all persons, also, who should despise or deprave the said book, or cause any other common and open prayer to be said or sung, or interrupt the minister in saying Common Prayer, or ministering the sacraments, fines and imprisonment, vary-ing according to the number of offences, be inflicted.

All persons not having reasonable excuse, are to resort to their parish churches on all Sundays and Holydays, and there to abide orderly during the service of God (i.e. of Common Prayer), on pain of the censures of the Church, and twelve-pence to be levied by the churchwardens for the use of the poor.

[1] This, of course, refers chiefly to papal jurisdiction in ecclesiastical as well as temporal matters. This portion of the statute is most important.

[2] I.e. the offence of introducing a foreign power within the realm in diminution of the authority of the Crown ; specifically, the offence of paying obedience to papal processes, or of maintaining the papal power in the realm.

All archbishops, bishops, and other ordinaries, are earnestly required and charged in God's name to put this Act in execution, and to punish offenders by the censures of the Church.

And the books, concerning the appointed services, are ordered to be procured in every parish and cathedral church before the next ensuing feast of St. John the Baptist (20 June), and the said service to be put in use within three weeks next after.

And all other laws and ordinances, for any other common prayer or administration of the sacraments, were to be utterly void and of none effect.

Thirdly : An Act for restitution of the first-fruits and twentieths of ecclesiastical benefices to the Crown.

Fourthly : An Act recited the delay, costs, and charges attending the election of archbishops and bishops by deans and chapters, and represented that such elections were indeed no elections, but only by a writ of *Congé d'élire* had pretence of elections, serving by no purpose, and seeming derogatory to the royal prerogative, to which only appertained the collation of all archbishoprics and bishoprics within the realm ; and thereupon enacted that no such election should be made, or *Congé d'élire* granted; but that the Queen and her successors by letters patent, or the governor of Ireland by warrant, should collate such persons as the Queen or her successors shall think meet. Persons so collated are required to be consecrated and invested, without any other election, and without suing to any foreign power. And the penalty of *Premunire* is enacted against these persons, who shall refuse to invest and consecrate within twenty days, or shall do anything to the contrary of this Act.

Fifthly : An Act of recognition of the Queen's title.

Sixthly : That it be *Premunire* to say that the Queen has no right to the Crown, and Treason to write it.

Seventhly : That the priory of St. John of Jerusalem (Kilmainham) be united to the Crown.

And forasmuch as in most places of this realm, there cannot be found English ministers to serve in the churches, or place appointed for common prayer, or to minister the sacraments to the people ; and that if some good men were provided, that they might use the prayer, service, and administration of sacraments set out and established by this act, in such language as they might best understand, the due honour of God should be thereby much advanced ; and for that also, that the same may not be in their native language, as well for difficulty to get it printed, as that few in the whole realm can read the Irish letters ; we do, therefore, most humbly beseech your majesty, with your highness's favour and royal assent it may be enacted, ordained, established, and provided, by the authority of this present parliament, that in every such church or place, where the common minister or priest hath not the use or knowledge of the English tongue, it shall be lawful for the same common minister or priest, to say and use the matins, even-song, celebration of the Lord's Supper, and administration of each of the sacraments, and all their common and open prayer in the Latin tongue, in such form and order as they be mentioned and set forth in the said book established by this act, and according to the tenor of this act, and none otherwise, nor in other manner ; anything before expressed and contained in this act to the contrary notwithstanding.

The form of this enactment differing so widely from that of the preceding ones affords reasonable ground for the opinion that it was " inserted by the parliament after the first transmiss of the bill, and possibly was procured by those who had opposed it." [1]

The Common Prayer to be Translated into Latin.

It does not appear that the framers of this enactment saw any inconsistency in their action. If they did, they preferred the way of compromise which was characteristic of the early policy of Elizabeth, and considered that by the use of Latin a similarity of the Common Prayer with the Mass might be sufficient to deceive Catholics and lead them to a gradual acceptance of the Protestant service. It is admitted that the translation of the Common Prayer into Latin was intended to allay the " prejudices of Catholics against the reformed worship by allowing it to be performed in the usual language of their devotions." [2] It does not appear from the enactment in what way the Latin version was to be provided, whether by public authority or by each individual minister, supposing he were competent to do so.

[1] Leland, ii. 225 *note*. Mant, i. 261.   [2] Leland, ii. 225 *note*.

Mant [1] doubts the benefit to be derived from a Latin version, for, he asks, would the people understand Latin more readily than their own Irish? He adds that the instruction of Edward VI was more practical, namely, that the liturgy in the Irish language should be used in places where it was needed. In the Regal Visitation of the year 1615 it is stated that in the diocese of Dublin the Common Prayer in Irish (*Liber Communis Hibernicus*) was used by the Protestant ministers, only in the deanery of Ballymore, in the Churches of Ballymore, Donard, Donaghmore in Ui Mail, Yago, and Rathmore, and the Latin version in only one parish, Tipper, in the same deanery.

It is stated that about the time of the holding of the Parliament, "a large Bible, the gift of the Archbishop of York to the two deans of Christ Church and St. Patrick's, was placed in the middle of the choir of each cathedral." It is also stated that there was a great trade done in small Bibles, as many as seven thousand copies being sold to booksellers in London for transportation to Ireland. [2]

Commissions to Administer the Oath of Supremacy.

Commissions were considered by Elizabeth and her officials in Ireland as the panaceas for all the ills of this country. They will appear in abundance. The Government did not trust itself to the goodwill of the people in either temporal or spiritual matters. As to the Supremacy of Elizabeth in ecclesiastical matters it saw from the start that if left to the people it was a dead letter. Something then had to be done to induce good obedience in them. A beginning should be made with bishops and officials whose salutary example it was presumed would be followed by the ordinary people. No sooner, therefore, were the Acts rushed

---

[1] i. 261.

[2] Loftus, *Annals, ad an.*, 1559. Mant, who quotes from Loftus, gives the reader to understand that the entire number were sold in Dublin (i. 265). Loftus's statement is not only vague, but appears exaggerated as the population of the City of Dublin at the period is given as about two thousand. It is not stated by whom the Bibles were bought. It is too much to presume that they were bought by the people of Dublin who were practically all Catholics. Probably they were bought by the Government for distribution among the Catholic citizens.

through Parliament than the Council proceeded to issue commissions to ecclesiastical and lay officials to minister the oath to one another, and to others specially mentioned. The cases of the Archbishop of Tuam and the Bishops of Meath and Kildare require first attention.

A commission was issued, 3 February, 1560, to Sir William FitzWilliams, knt., Vice-Treasurer; Sir George Stanley, knt., Marshal; John Plunkett, Chief Justice of the Common Bench; James Bathe, Chief Baron; John Parker, Master of the Rolls; James Wyngfelde, Master of the Ordnance; and Humfrey Waren, Privy Councillor; to administer the Oath of Supremacy under 2 Eliz., c. 1, to Christopher, Archbishop of Tuam, William, Bishop of Meath, and Thomas, Bishop of Kildare.

A certificate was issued the next day, 4 February, at 10 a.m. that the Oath of Supremacy was taken by the Archbishop of Tuam, and refused by the Bishop of Meath and the Bishop of Kildare, affirming their conscience to be their let.[1]

The question may be asked : why were these three bishops selected to sign a certificate of acceptance of the Oath of Supremacy, and why was a special commission issued for them alone ? Are we to conclude that they were the only bishops available at the time, and that the others, whoever they were, who were present at the first session of Parliament, 12 January, had gone home to their dioceses ? There is no mention of any commission to propose the oath to any of the other bishops, except Curwen, although many commissions were issued for other officials, clerical and lay.

In regard to Bodkin it will be convenient here to refer to a commission of the year 1564 which confirms in some way the position he had already taken up on the Supremacy question. It is dated 9 June, and was directed to him as well as others " to execute the Queen's ecclesiastical jurisdiction under Eliz. I in the territories of Connacht and Thomond." The terms of the commission also implied power to correct heresies and other offences subject to the ecclesiastical jurisdiction of the Queen, and to administer

[1] *Fiants*, nos. 198, 199.

to all persons in Connacht and Thomond, as may seem good to them, the Oath of Supremacy.[1] The other persons mentioned in the commission were Thomond, Clanricard, Roland Burke, Bishop of Clonfert, the Bishop of Killaloe, etc.

To return to the year 1560 : two weeks elapsed after the rebuff administered by Bishops Walsh and Leverous before any move was made in the issuing of further commissions for the taking of the oath. In compliance with the demand of a commission appointed 17 February, the following took it, 18th of that month : Hugh, Archbishop of Dublin ; Thomas Crief, Chantor of St. Patrick's ; Robert Nangill, Chancellor of the same ; Robert Wesseley, Archdeacon of Dublin ; and Christopher More, prebendary of Christ Church. The certificate also states that Christopher Rathe, Chantor of Christ Church, John Cardif, Treasurer ; Robert Lyde, prebendary ; and John Herman, Chancellor of the same, had refused the oath, affirming their conscience to be their let. Also that Edmund Barnewall, Treasurer of St. Patrick's, and the residue of the prebendaries, vicars, and priests of Christ Church, included in the commission had not yet been examined.[2]

It is clear that the commissioners were having a rough time of it in the way of refusals to take the oath. The statement that the other prebendaries, etc., of Christ Church had not yet been examined may very well mean that the commissioners had met with such opposition in that cathedral that they adjourned for more definite instructions from the Council. Very probably some of those prebendaries were afterwards deprived and others were induced to accept the oath. There is no reference to what happened. In the case of Sir Robert Luttrell, chaplain, and Archdeacon of Meath, who refused the oath when appealed to by a commission of 25 March, a certificate was issued, 20 April, to that effect. Afterwards he was deprived of his dignity which was given to John Garvey, 14 July.[3]

Commissions were also issued to deal with the judges of the civil courts, various officials, and justices of the peace. For the present these were confined to the counties of Dublin,

---

[1] *Fiants,* no. 668.   [2] *Ib.,* nos. 225, 226.   [3] *Ib.,* no. 262.

Meath, and Kildare. The issue of a commission to certain persons does not mean either that they carried it out or yet that they were in favour of it. It was generally taken for granted that the chief ecclesiastical and lay officials would carry out the Queen's wishes, although the presumption in many cases was unwarranted. It may be taken that the lawyers in general and the gentry of the Pale were opposed to the taking of the oath.

A commission was issued, 17 February, 1560, to Hugh, Archbishop of Dublin, Chancellor; John Plunket, Chief Justice; James Bathe, Chief Baron (who took the oath); and Sir Thomas Cusack, knt., to minister the Oath of Supremacy to Robert Dillon, Chief Justice of the Common Pleas, Luke Nettervyld, Second Justice of the Chief Place; Richard Talbot, Second Justice of the Common Pleas; Patrick White, Second Baron; James Barnewall, Attorney-General, and James Dowedall, Principal Solicitor.[1] There is no certificate to state that the persons to whom the oath was to be administered took it.

The same commissioners were deputed to minister the oath, same date, to Sir Henry Radclief, knt., lieutenant of Leix and Offaly; Sir John Stanley, knt., Marshal of the Army; John Parker, Master of the Rolls; Jaques Wyngfeld, Master of the Ordnance; Thomas Lockewood, Dean of Christ Church; Francis Agard, and Humfrey Warren, members of the Council; James Stanyhurst, Clerk of the Crown in Chancery; and Thomas Alen, Clerk of the Hanaper. All these took the oath. Sir Francis Harbert, knt., one of the Council, and Richard Fynglas, Serjeant at Law, also named in the commission, had not yet been examined, and of Bartholomew Russell, Clerk of the Crown of the Queen's Bench, also named in the commission, no return was made.[2]

A commission, same date, was issued to Gerald, Earl of Kildare; Roland, Viscount Baltinglass; Sir Henry Radclief, knt.; John Plunket, Chief Justice; Sir Thomas Cusack, knt.; Sir Francis Harbert, knt.; Francis Cosby, Sheriff of Kildare; Thomas Alen, Clerk of the Hanaper; and Giles Ovington; gent., to administer the Oath of Supremacy to all justices

[1] *Fiants*, no. 221. [2] *Ib.*, nos. 222, 227.

3

of the Peace, with the clerks and ministers thereof, and all town officers and other temporal ministers in the County of Kildare.

In pursuance of this, 20 February, John Alen, Chancellor of the Green Wax of the Exchequer, and Richard Fynglas, Serjeant at Law, took the oath ; so also did John Dunkerly, sovereign of Naas, Bartholomew Russell, Clerk of the Crown of the Chief Place, and Patrick Sarsfield, Justice of the Peace in the county (7 March), and likewise, Nicholas Wogan, of Rathcoffie, and John Sutton, of Tipper, County Kildare, Justices of the Peace in the county (8 March).[1]

A similar commission was issued, same date, to Sir George Stanley, John Plunket, John Parker, Sir Thomas Cusack, and Richard Fynglas, for County Meath, but no certificate to anyone as having taken the oath was returned.

It was not until four years afterwards (9 June, 1564) that a commission was issued to administer the oath in the counties of Carlow, Waterford, Kilkenny, Cork, Kerry, Limerick, and Tipperary.[2]

Bishops Deprived of their Sees.

Undue importance has been bestowed by certain historians on the enactments of the Dublin Parliament. They have taken it for granted that all that was required to turn Irish Catholics from their ancient faith was an Act of a Parliament in which they took little or no interest. Unmindful of the Catholic opposition to similar Acts in the reign of Edward VI, and unable to appreciate Catholic psychology, they con-cluded that practically the whole country was converted at once by a mere handful of men sitting in a chamber in a Dublin Cathedral and voting according to the wishes of a Protestant Queen. The Parliament might pass any laws it liked, but it had no machinery outside a limited area to enforce them. The tiny English garrison, many of them of the old faith, had little heart in the work of establishing the new. Consequently, the people went on as before, hearing Mass as their fathers had heard it, and snapping their fingers at laws passed by a mere fraction of the country. Indeed,

---

[1] *Fiants,* nos. 223, 224.   [2] *Ib.*, no. 666.

in view of the fact that the very cities and counties that had representatives in Parliament resisted stubbornly the introduction of the new religious service, and that most of the lay peers and gentry clung tenaciously to the Mass,[1] it is humanly improbable that they had anything to do with the passing of those Acts.

Sussex, as we have seen, returned from London some time in January, and presented the certificate of the Supremacy to Bishop Walsh of Meath and Bishop Leverous of Kildare for their signature on 4 February. Having met with a blunt refusal, he again left for England on 13 February, and was reappointed Lord Deputy or Lieutenant on 6 May. Meanwhile both bishops were deprived of their Sees. It was a safe procedure in view of the proximity of the Sees to Dublin, and it was to be a lesson to other non-conforming bishops.

Of Leverous it is recorded:[2] "The Lord Deputy required to know the cause of his refusal to take an oath already taken by many learned and illustrious men, to whom he made answer, that all ecclesiastical jurisdiction was derived from Christ, and since he thought not fit to confer ecclesiastical authority on the Blessed Virgin, His Mother, it could not be believed that supremacy, primacy of ecclesiastical power, was meant to be delegated by Christ to any other person of that sex; he added, likewise, that St. Paul commanded no woman should speak in the Church, much less should one preside and rule there; to confirm this opinion he adduced authorities from St. Chrysostom and Tertullian; the Deputy then represented to him, that if he should refuse to comply he must, of necessity, be deprived of all his revenues; he quoted, in answer, the text of Scripture, 'What shall it profit a man to gain the whole world and lose his own soul.'"

Having been deprived of his bishopric, Leverous quietly retired and was left at liberty.[3]

[1] The Earl of Kildare, a few months after the dissolution of Parliament, was charged with the crime of adhering to the Mass.

[2] *De Processu Martyriali* (Cologne, 1649), see Mason, pp. 163-4.

[3] For some time he enjoyed the hospitable protection of the Earl and Countess of Desmond, and then earned his livelihood by keeping a grammar school in the village of Adare, about ten miles from Limerick. A short time before his death he removed to that city where Richard Creagh, afterwards Archbishop of Armagh, had also taught school. He died in 1577, at the age

According to Loftus there was held in the year 1560 a " convocation of Bishops at the Queen's command for establishing the Protestant religion. Bishop Walsh would not conform thereunto, but for preaching against it was committed to custody, afterwards imprisoned and at length deprived of his living." [1] There is nothing to show who or how many were the bishops who attended. The synod evidently took place between February and July, namely, within a few months after the holding of Parliament, as the See of Meath was declared to be vacant on 14 July.[2] Presumably, the attendance was confined to the seven bishops, at most, who were partial to the Supremacy.

Shortly after his imprisonment in 1560 Walsh seems to have been released, and returned to his diocese to continue his opposition to the use of the Common Prayer. In 1565 he was summoned by the ecclesiastical commissioners, but " he openly protested before all the people the same day that he would never communicate or be present where the service should be ministered, for it was against his conscience and against God's word." He was a man, they say " of great

---

of 80 years and was interred in the church of St. David, Naas, in the burial-place of his family. (Mason, 164; Moran, *Spic. Ossor.* i. 83.)

[1] Loftus, *Annals.*

[2] *P.C.R.I., Eliz.*, i. 432. Walsh was a native of Meath, a member of the Cistercian Order, probably of the house of Bective, and chaplain to Cardinal Pole, in Rome. He was selected in Mary's reign to absolve the Irish bishops who had accepted Henry VIII's Supremacy, and was appointed then to the, See of Meath. (Ronan, *Reformation in Dublin*, 1536-58, pp. 412 *seq.*)

According to a Roman document, Walsh was in reality no longer Catholic Bishop of Meath. In the Acts of a Consistory held 6 September, 1564, it is stated that when Cardinal Pole was Legate, William Walsh obtained, as he asserted, sufficient authority to obtain the See and was provided to it with the obligation of obtaining within a year of the said provision further letters from the Pope in the form of a new and simple provision, otherwise the first provision would be null and void. William, it is alleged, on account of imprisonment and other impediments could not obtain the letters and yet had himself consecrated, took possession of his diocese, and received part of the revenues, and continued in the administration of the diocese, incurring thereby the pain of privation and other censures, for which reason that Church was considered still vacant; the Pope, however, provided William to that Church, thus or otherwise vacant, confirming the provision of the Legate, and absolving him from censures, etc., with retention of one priory of the Order of St. Augustine in the said diocese. (Costello-Coleman, *De Annatis Hiber.*, vol. i., Ulster.)

Walsh had allowed eleven years to elapse before he applied for the necessary letters of provision, his first appointment to the See having taken place in 1553.

credit among his countrymen, upon whom in causes of religion they wholly depend." [1] He was again thrown into
prison in 1565 where he lay until 1572 when he escaped to
France, and afterwards to Spain where he died in the
Cistercian monastery at Alcala in 1577.

Thonory of Ossory, who cannot be proved to have accepted the Supremacy, seems to have quietly left his diocese.
The See was mentioned in a State Paper as vacant about
1561-62.[2] It may safely be taken that it was intimated to
him to clear out of the diocese and that his successor was to
be appointed. With such an ardent reformer as the Earl
of Ormond and Ossory in the vicinity his safety there would
have been rather doubtful. The only other case in which
there was question of deprivation in the early years of
Elizabeth's reign, was that of Limerick. The State Papers,
3 July, 1562, state that "Limerick may be void by deprivation." But the threat was not carried out, and Hugh
Lacy continued in his See until 1572, when a former bishop,
William Casey, who had been deprived by Mary, was reappointed by Elizabeth.[3]

Elizabeth made no delay in filling the vacant See of Kildare,
and, almost within three months of the refusal of Leverous to
conform, appointed Alexander Craik. In her letter, 17 May,
to Sussex directing him to pass the patent for the bishopric
to Craik, she states : "We are pleased and contented that
the same, Alexander, for his better encouragement to take
this vocation upon him and to discharge the duty belonging
thereunto, shall have also, with the said bishopric, in manner
of augmentation and of a commendam, the deanery of St.
Patrick's, now being in our disposition, in like sort as the
late bishop of Kildare had." [4]

"Craik was consecrated in his own cathedral by Hugh

[1] Shirley, 220.

[2] *Ib.*, 101. This does not agree with the mention of Thonory's name
in the Commission of 1564. (*Fiants*, nos. 666-7.) Accuracy in issuing Commissions, however, cannot be relied on.

[3] Cotton, *Fasti*. Hugh Lacy continued as Papal Bishop until his death
in 1580.

[4] *P.C.R.I.*, *Eliz.*, i. 435. Mason, 164. Elizabeth was either unaware of,
or ignored the real constitution of this cathedral, in which neither the Archbishop
nor the Crown had the appointment of the dean.

Curwin, Archbishop of Dublin, and obtained orders for restitution of the temporalities, on the 22nd August." [1]   There
is no mention of any assistant bishops at the consecration,
according to the requirements of the Roman Ordinal.   In
the consecration of Elizabeth's bishops there is a want of
uniformity in the matter of the number of bishops who assisted
at these ceremonies, sometimes only one is mentioned, at
other times three.

To the other vacant Sees no appointments were made by
Elizabeth for some years ; Hugh Brady was not appointed
to Meath until 1563, and Christopher Gaffney to Ossory not
until 1565, namely, after the death of Thonory.   For the
first six years of her reign it may be said that Elizabeth did
little more than try to secure a few bishops for the dioceses
of the Pale where her government made some show of power,
and for a few other dioceses where it was important that she
should show that she possessed ecclesiastical authority.

The results of the Acts of Supremacy and Uniformity
so far are summed up by a Protestant historian [2] thus :—

" The partizans of Rome inveighed against the heretical
Queen and her impious ministers.   The clergy, who refused
to conform, abandoned their cures ; no reformed ministers
could be found to supply their places ; the churches fell to
ruins ; the people were left without any religious worship
or instruction.[3]   Even in places of most civility [i.e. of
obedience to English rule] the statutes lately made were
evaded or neglected with impunity.   The ignorant were
taught to abominate a government which they heard consigned to all the terrors of the divine vengeance ; were exhorted to stand prepared for a glorious opportunity of
asserting the cause of religion ; and assured of effectual
support, both from the Pope, whose authority had been
profaned, and from the King of Spain, now particularly
offended at Elizabeth." [4]

[1] Mason, 164.   [2] Leland, ii. 226.
[3] As far as Protestants were aware.
[4] This differs totally from the statement of Mant (i. 259) : " On the contrary,
the bishops complied with the alteration in the publick worship ; and the adherents of the Romish Church in Ireland resorted to the parish churches, where
the English service was used, during a great part, if not the whole, of Queen
Elizabeth's reign."   We shall see how far from the truth is this statement.

Substantially this description is accurate, but it is wrong to suppose that the people were left "without any religious worship or instruction." Even within the Pale the Catholics found places in which to worship according to their creed when they were deprived by the laws and forces of the Government of the use of the churches built by their Catholic ancestors. In the City of Dublin and in the principal towns of the Pale any commodious room, or outhouse—and they were many—was readily availed of for the offering of the Mass. In country places the residence of the Anglo-Norman Catholic nobility were at the disposal of priest and people. In the few dioceses in which the bishops conformed, the service of Common Prayer was carried out in the cathedrals. Without the Pale, the bishops who were beyond the Queen's power, and who therefore escaped deprivation, continued to enjoy their temporalities, and to celebrate the Mass, despite Parliamentary prohibitions. The clergy followed their prelates. When overawed by an English garrison, they refrained from public celebrations. When the soldiers retired, they offered the Mass in the churches as before. This, in general, is the state of religion at this early period of Elizabeth's rule ; particulars will be noted as they occur.

The Elizabethan "reform" did not begin happily, and it did not progress happily. Archbishop Curwen found Dublin more than he was able for, and he was anxious to return to an easier post in England. Accordingly Sussex wrote on his behalf to Cecil (2 November, 1560) :—[1]

Sir, my Lord Chancellor [Curwen] hath him heartily commended unto you, and beseecheth you to have his revocation into England to the bishopric of Harthford [2] in remembrance he is the man that of his coat hath surliest stood to the Crown either in England or Ireland, and therefore it shall be well her Majesty hath him in remembrance accordingly, to comfort him in his old years. I beseech you he may understand from you I have had him in remembrance.

Elizabeth did not accede to the request for some years. Her difficulty was to find bishops who would undertake the

[1] *S.P.I., Eliz.*, ii. 41, P.R.O., London. Shirley, 94.
[2] Elsewhere the name is given as Hochford, i.e. Oxford.

" reform," and she had no wish to be embarrassed by such
shirkers as Curwen.

The Pope Appoints an Archbishop and a Commissary

Primate Dowdall of Armagh died in London on 15 August,
1558. The guardianship of the spiritualities of the See
was then handed over to Terence Daniel or Donnelly, the
dean, who, 3 July, 1559, held a synod of the English clergy
of the diocese in St. Peter's, Drogheda.[1] The purpose of
the synod does not appear, but it may be that Terence wished
to test the attitude the clergy were likely to adopt in view
of Elizabeth's assumption of the headship of the Church
in England. Nor does it appear why the Pope left the See
vacant for eighteen months, until the year of the Dublin
Parliament. On 7 January, 1560, Donat O'Taig, a priest
of Limerick diocese, then present in Rome, was appointed
by Pius IV. It is probable that he was consecrated there
the same month as he received the pallium there on 27 March.
Evidently, on account of the proposed religious changes, he
lost little time in returning to his diocese, and on 22 November
he sent out a letter in Latin, given at Armagh, for his clergy
to appear before him.[2] During the early part of Elizabeth's
reign he continued to brave the dangers attached to his
occupancy of the archbishopric, to which was attached the
penalty of *Premunire*. But no attempt was made by Elizabeth
to appoint a Protestant primate for eighteen months.

The next move of Pius IV was the sending of a special
commissary to Ireland. Taught by his experience of England
he sent the Irish Commissary without any exterior pomp.
This important ecclesiastic was Fr. David Wolf, S.J., a
native of Limerick, and highly recommended to the Holy
See by Lainez, the General of the Society. He left Rome in
August, 1560, furnished with the papal commission (2 August)
appointing him visitor as well of regulars as of seculars in
Ireland with ample faculties for absolving all persons of
either sex in all cases, including even those reserved to the
Apostolic See and included in the Bull *Coena Domini*, and

---

[1] Coleman, *Stuart's Armagh*, 246.   [2] *Ib.*, 157.

whom by law and the grant of King Henry VIII the earldom of Tyrone belongs, may be restored to his lands and country, whereof Shane has dissiesed [dispossessed] him." In the West the Earls of Thomond and Clanricard were to be advised to combine against the O'Briens "who were lately come out of France," with promise of aid by sea from that country. Limerick, Waterford, and Cork should be guarded by soldiers. But the chief danger against the peace of the country was from the Earl of Kildare :

with the unseemly demeanour of the Earl in his open speeches against the English governance ; the mustering of his whole power ; his parliaments kept with the Irishry, his usage of open masses against the laws, his great rewards given to him for fostering of his son ; the earnest desires of the Irishry to retain his kinsmen with bands of men ; the declaration of Edmund Boy,[1] the said Earls nigh kinsman and trusty servant, of the determination of the Earls of Kildare and Desmond to join together to expel and betray the Deputy and the Englishmen, and to aid O'Bryne [O'Brien] at his return out of France ; the continual passing to and fro of the said Edmund Boye betwixt the said two Earls, and also Shane O'Neyle ; and beside this the general fear of the Englishman in Ireland of a rebellion of the Irishry this year ; with many other circumstances inducing doubtfulness of the said two Earls . . . her Majesty's Lieutenant of that realm should, at his coming thither, use his best discretion to procure the Earl of Kildare to come over into England. . . .

If he will not come over, the Lieutenant is to present to him the Queen's letter commanding him to do so. And if he will not come, he [Sussex] is to use the best means that may be to arrest the said Earl and commit him to safe custody, along with his chief adviser, and issue a proclamation showing the reasonable causes of his doings, tending only to the quietness of the realm.[2]

In her instructions Elizabeth continues :—

certain lords and captains of the Irishry, having lands of long continuance, desire to hold them of the crown. We authorize you to consider the matter, and upon surrender of their estates to make new grants from us under our Great Seal of Ireland tail male, using such means as you may therein to reserve either rents or corporal services, or both, to the augmentation of our crown. . . .

---

[1] I.e. *Buidhe* (yellow or fair).   [2] Carew MSS., i. nos. 223-5.

As our spiritualities remain at this day for the more part out of lease, in the demising thereof great regard shall be had for the augmentation of our revenue. We would that the tithes be letten, as in old times hath been, by couples of acres,[1] and thereupon, in some convenient places, that rent corn be reserved upon every couple for the furniture [furnishing, provisioning] of the households of you our said Lieutenant, our Chancellor, and other our principal officers of our Council that keep household, upon reasonable prices to be paid to us for the same. . . .

None of our freeholders shall be bought by any pretence or colour, directly or indirectly, to do any service to any manner of person, but at the appointment of you, our Lieutenant, except it be to our Chancellor or other principal officer there, being born in England. . . .

The Deputy is to see to the base money sent over to Ireland in Mary's reign and in the first year of our reign, which money is injurious to our subjects, and especially to our bands of men of war. . . .

It is enacted by Parliament there that upon the collation of any bishopric there by us, it should be lawful for us to make exchange for such temporal lands as should seem meet for our crown, delivering in lieu thereof as much in value of such spiritualities as remained within their dioceses. In such cases it shall be convenient for our service, upon the vacation of any bishopric, to make such exchange, You may proceed, following th' order, and yet foreseeing that such bishoprics as be very mean and of small dotation be not thereby decayed or diminished, but that favour therein be showed either utterly to be foreborne, or else to be put in needful cases dealt withal.

A P.S. at the end of the instructions states that as regards " An Act of Parliament, giving us authority to exchange certain temporalities with the bishoprics being void, We now understand that no such law is as yet enacted in Ireland, and therefore presently that article hath no force. Our pleasure nevertheless is that when hereafter any such Act shall be passed by Parliament that in such case our said Lieutenant shall proceed according to the words of the said article."   This shows the uncertainty as to what laws were passed by the Dublin Parliament.

In 1560, and for several years after, the state of secular

---

[1] Apparently according to the yield of acres in couples or bushels.

affairs in Ireland was so threatening that Elizabeth and her
advisers were more concerned with maintaining a foothold
in the country than with the abolition of the Mass. Her
indefatigable secretary, Cecil, made a note of this anxiety of
the Queen for further reference. The chief danger was evidently from the Earl of Kildare. This nobleman had refused
to abandon the Mass, and was in close correspondence both
with his kinsmen the Earl of Desmond, and with several of
the Irish chieftains. It was feared that a great Catholic
confederation might be formed against Elizabeth, and that
Scotland, France, Spain, and the Pope might be induced
to lend their aid. Sussex was instructed to persuade Kildare
if possible to go to England. If this failed, he and his most
prominent friends, including Desmond, were to be arrested
at the earliest opportunity. " And for satisfaction of the
subjects of the land, the Lord Lieutenant shall cause to
be published by proclamation or otherwise the reasonable
causes of his doings, leading only to the quiet of the realm." [1]
By detaining men like Kildare and Desmond in London,
and above all by getting possession of the children of the
Anglo-Irish nobles and educating them in England, it was
hoped that Ireland might be both anglicised and protestant-
ised. If there was peace between Desmond and Ormond
the Lord Lieutenant would have leisure to settle Shane
O'Neill's account, especially as all apprehension from France
was at an end through the death of the Regent and the
expulsion of the French from Scotland.

All pointed to the necessity of vigorous action ; but the
summer of 1560 passed, and nothing was done. Elizabeth
saw that nothing of importance could be done without
an effort, and being in one of her frugal moods, she was
disinclined to make that effort. She summoned Sussex
(3 January, 1561) to repair to England for a season for a personal conference, and reminded him that she had formerly
been charged with other items besides his salary, and suggested
that part of it should now be devoted to the payment of a
Lord Justice, " which, considering our other charges, we think
you cannot mislike." [2]

[1] Carew, *Cal.*, i. 292, 297, 301, 310. *C.S.P.I., Eliz.*, v. 42.
[2] *S.P.I., Eliz.*, ii. 50, P.R.O., London.

SHANE O'NEILL FENCES WITH ELIZABETH.

More trouble was anticipated in the North than elsewhere in Ireland. Its origin was due to the struggle for the earldom of Ulster. The two contestants were Shane, the eldest legitimate son of Con O'Neill, and Matthew Ferdorogh, his illegitimate son by a blacksmith's wife, named Alison Kelly of Dundalk. Notwithstanding Henry VIII's grant of the succession to Matthew, Shane asserted his own claim, robbed his father and mother of all they possessed, and drove them into the Pale where the unfortunate Con died early in 1559. And having, by assassination, secured himself against O'Donnell, his most dangerous rival, he claimed not only the earldom but the tribal sovereignty of the North. Elizabeth, seeing Shane in peaceful possession, did not trouble herself about her father's patent or Shane's legitimacy. In the absence of positive orders, Sydney had contented himself by summoning Shane to Dundalk, but the astute chief refused to go. Whilst he was loud in his profession of loyalty he feared possible loss of reputation among his own people if he obeyed the summons of an English governor. Sydney had perforce to visit Shane in his camp, listen to his claims and his irrefutable arguments, and be satisfied with his promise of keeping the peace, until the Queen should have pronounced on his claims. These were to the effect that : "Shane O'Neele claims to be O'Nele, remits to the Queen's judgment whether the superiorities of McMahon, Maginnis etc. ought to belong to her Majesty or to O'Neile ; and in the meantime the Queen to levy her duties, and he his claims upon them etc." [1]

As soon as the commission for Sir William FitzWilliams as Lord Justice arrived, Sussex took his passage from Howth to England on Wednesday, 29 January, 1561, and the Sunday following, 2 February, "the feast of the Purification of the Blessed Lady the Virgin," FitzWilliams was sworn Lord Justice of Ireland by the Archbishop of Dublin, in presence of the Peers and Council of the realm. [2]

Shane did not wish to let the Lord Lieutenant have the

---

[1] Carew, *Cal.*, no. 228.   Bagwell, ii. 2-4.
[2] *P.C.R.I.*, *Eliz.*, i. 452.

sole telling of his story. He was in communication with Philip of Spain who bade him not be discouraged, for that he should not want help. Letters to this effect were brought by the parish priests of Howth and Dundalk,[1] and O'Neill then wrote to the Queen in a very haughty strain. He asked leave to correspond freely with Cecil, and solicited the admission of his messenger to the Queen's presence. " There is nothing," he said, " I inwardly desire of God so much " as that " the Queen should know what a faithful subject I mean to be to her Grace." He stated his case against his rival Matthew Kelly (Ferdorach), his bastard-brother, and laid great stress on his own election by the tribe, adding that all the North for eighty miles had been waste, without people, cattle, or houses, " save a little that the spirituality of Armagh had," and now there was not one town uninhabited. If the Queen would give Ireland into his keeping, she would soon have a revenue where she had now only expense. Unable to trust Sussex, he had sent over the respectable Dean of Armagh, Terence Daniel, to bring a safe-conduct from the Queen herself, which would enable him to lay his case against Matthew Kelly before the English Council, and to return safely. For fear of mischances, Kildare and other men of rank should be directed to put him safely on board, and to deliver him at Holyhead into Sir Henry Sydney's charge. After his return Sussex should not be allowed to molest him for three months.

The fencing of these two great minds (Elizabeth and O'Neill) is one of the most interesting, if tiresome, episodes in the reign of the astute Queen. O'Neill bluffed her for many years, but Elizabeth had her satisfaction in the end. However, of this later. Meanwhile, Shane declared himself ready to make restoration wherever anything could be proved against him. His savagery, which he ingenuously confessed again and again, he thought could best be eradicated by an English wife, " some gentlewoman of some noble blood meet for my vocation, whereby I might have a friendship towards your Majesty." " By her good civility and bringing up, the country," he hoped, " would become civil, and my generation

---

[1] Bagwell, ii, 15 *seq.*

so mixed, I and my posterity should ever after know their duties." Some educated companion was necessary to him; for the men of the Pale would not even show him how to address his letters properly, and he feared to offend, whereas he desired nothing so much as Her Majesty's approbation and favour. As a matter of fact his letters, in Latin, were couched in the best court form, written by his secretary Fleming, or by the Dean of Armagh, Terence Daniel, who was also a better English scholar, judging by his autograph letters, than even the members of the Privy Council.

To enforce his demands, and to show how disagreeable he could be, Shane burned three villages on the border of the Pale which had been disloyal to him. He went so far as to threaten the disloyal town of Dundalk, and he demanded an authority for himself equal to that which Desmond had over the western seaports. His proposal to go to the Court was accepted in order to gain time. A safe-conduct was issued, and FitzWilliams was instructed to make his departure easy. While FitzWilliams was temporising with Shane in Ireland, Sussex was intriguing against him in Scotland with the Duke of Argyle whose sister was married to James MacDonnell. Large offers were made to MacDonnell and his brother Sorley Boy, and it was hoped that all the most powerful men in the North might be united against the redoubtable Shane.[1]

Warlike preparations were swiftly and silently made, and six hundred additional men were sent to Ireland, and a general hosting was ordered. Meanwhile, Shane had been acting, and, on the night of 14 May, he appeared at the gates of a Franciscan friary near Lough Veagh where Calvagh O'Donnell and his wife, the Countess of Argyle, and a few soldiers, women, and poets, lay defenceless. O'Donnell and his wife were carried off to Tyrone, the chief being confined to close quarters and the Countess becoming Shane's mistress. Through guilty admiration for Shane she had betrayed to him the defenceless position of her husband.

[1] *S.P.I., Eliz.*, iii. 14, 32, 51, 59.

Shane was proclaimed by the Government a rebel and a traitor.[1]

SUSSEX'S EXPEDITIONS TO ARMAGH.

Sussex landed at Dalkey on 2 June, 1561, and within three weeks advanced to Armagh. Shane would not parley with him as he had already received a gracious answer from the Queen, professed great readiness to go to London, and laid upon the Viceroy the whole responsibility of nullifying the Queen's good intentions. Sussex sent Ormond to Shane to have Calvagh O'Donnell set free. This Shane refused, and the attack began. Stuart describes the expedition as follows : [2] " But as time went on, Shane would not come to terms ; he was proclaimed a rebel in June, 1561, and, to overawe him, Sussex, the Lord Lieutenant, marched from Dublin to Armagh, at the head of five hundred men. This small army was reinforced by Bedlow and Gough, sheriffs of Dublin, with four-score men-at-arms and forty archers. Shane's adherents, having learnt that further reinforcements were to follow the deputy's corps, began to desert their standards and disperse. Sussex took up his position at Armagh, which had been previously fortified and provisioned for his troops. Shane, accompanied by O'Tighe [O'Taig] the primate, suddenly appeared with his army on a hill outside the walls of the town. Some friars, who were with them, celebrated Mass, and the primate walked three times up and down the lines, exhorting the Irish soldiers to go forward as God was on their side."

The whole expedition turned into a cattle raid, but the cattle were not brought to Armagh, and the moral effect of the check to Sussex was disastrous. It is interesting to have the account of the expedition from the Annals of the *Four Masters :*—

" The Lord Chief Justice of Ireland, Thomas Fitz-Walter [*recte*, Radcliffe, Earl of Sussex], proceeded into Tyrone, to

---

[1] *S.P.I., Eliz.,* iii. 84, P.R.O., London. See *Four Masters, ad an.* 1559. O'Sullivan Beare, *Catholic Hist. of Ireland,* i. 2, B. 4, c. 3. O'Sullivan who has a flair for the marvellous is not sufficiently impartial or reliable to quote from in his lurid account of this episode.

[2] *Armagh,* ed. Coleman, 160.

avenge the capture of Calvagh O'Donnell, and on account of his own enmity against that country. He pitched his camp of numerous hosts at Armagh ; and he erected strong raths and impregnable ramparts around the great Church of Armagh, in order that he might leave warders constantly guarding that place. When O'Neill (Shane) received intelligence of this, he sent some of his own faithful friends, and his servants of trust, to guard and keep Calvagh O'Donnell out of the way of the Lord Justice, from one island [1] and islet to another, in the wilds and recesses of Tyrone, until the Lord Justice should leave the country. The Lord Justice sent out from the camp at Armagh a company of captains, with one thousand men, both horse and foot, to take preys and spoils in Oriel." [O'Neill advanced into Oriel to meet them.]

" At this time O'Neill was harassing and plundering the territories of Bregia and Meath. Tirconnell was also subjugated and surrounded by him, after having already made a prisoner of Calvagh." " O'Neill (Shane) then assumed the sovereign command of all Ulster, from Drogheda to the Erne, so that at this time he might have been called with propriety the provincial King of Ulster, were it not for the opposition of the English to him."

The news of the disaster could not be kept from Elizabeth, and she ordered Wingfield to be dismissed from office. But on account of his services against the O'Byrnes, and other reasons, he remained Master of the Ordnance till his death in 1587.[2] After the failure of so many attempts to reduce O'Neill in the field, Sussex determined to try other methods. He hired one Neil Gray to murder O'Neill, and reported to Elizabeth that " if he will not do that he may in your service, there will be done to him what others may." [3] O'Neill, however, eluded the assassin.

Unhappy Sussex left 200 soldiers at Armagh, and, having spent all his victuals, returned to Newry to conduct " a new mass of victuals to Armagh " where he fortified the Cathedral.

---

[1] These were islands in fresh-water loughs, on which O'Neill had crannogs, or wooden houses. (See *Hist. and Arch. Assoc.*, 1870-71, p. 15.)
[2] *S.P.I.*, *Eliz.*, iv. 25, P.R.O., London. Carew, *Cal.*, no. 237.
[3] *C.S.P.I.*, *Eliz.*, iv. 42.

It was reported to the Queen that Maguire, Magennis, and others shrink from Shane, and that O'Reilly, O'Donnell, and Sorley Boy remain constant to the Queen.[1] But O'Neill cleverly vented his grievance against Sussex for the fortifying of the Cathedral of Armagh, the murder of those sent under protection to Sussex, and the assumption by Sussex of the name of the Earl of Ulster which Shane claimed.[2] Sussex was weary of the indifference, in fact opposition of the English Pale to himself and his army, and of the distracted state of the whole English race in Ireland.[3]

Of this muddled state of affairs Sir James Crofts narrates (12 February, 1561) : that the long continuance of disorders and disobedience in Ireland consisted in the lack of ministers of justice in all parts, and in the great invasion of the Scots in the North to spoil the counties but chiefly called in by the inhabitants to help to defend them and to revenge their wrongs. Some take lands by force, and others dispossessing the natives settle down in Connaught. He recommends that Grammar schools and other places for students be erected so that the people may be brought up to avail themselves of them. As a means of procuring obedience to her wishes the Queen ordered Sussex and the Council to commit such as do not come to church and to repair the gaols.[4]

Against the dismal outlook of the Government there was some consolation provided in the reports that Sir T. Cusack had gone to O'Reilly to take the oaths of O'Reilly, Maguire, Turlough, and Brian, that the Byrnes, Kavanaghs, and Tooles answer all men at the castle of Dublin " which was never heard of before " ; and that Ossory, O'Carroll O'Mulloy, McGeoghegan, McCoghlan, and all between Leix and Offaly and the Shannon answer the orders of Sir Henry Radcliffe. But the ominous note still pervades the reports, " if Shane be overthrown all is settled, if Shane settle [continue] all is overthrown." [5]

Sussex was not satisfied with the last expedition against Shane, and now strongly urged that a fresh campaign should

---

[1] *C.S.P.I., Eliz.*, iv. 11, 12, 22.
[2] *Loc. cit.*, 23. [3] *Loc. cit.*, 31, 66.
[4] *S.P.I., Eliz.*, iii. 17, 72, P.R.O., London.
[5] *C.S.P.I., Eliz.*, iv. 35, 37.

be prosecuted, or Shane should be left in full sway over Ulster, even over those who held their lands of the Queen. With a heavy heart he led an unusually large force to Armagh, with four of the five Irish Earls in his company. But Shane was nowhere to be seen. Again, the expedition developed into a cattle raid, and when Sussex withdrew southwards, Shane suddenly appeared on the borders of Meath, burning villages and taking cattle. Thus Sussex could neither conquer Ulster nor even defend the Pale.[1]

MARTIAL LAW FOR THE O'TOOLES AND O'BYRNES.

Troubles were meanwhile brewing for Elizabeth in other parts of the country, and commissions were issued to deal with them. On 27 January, 1561, Sir James Wingfield, Master of the Ordnance, received one[2] to execute martial law throughout the territory called the Byrnes' country and the O'Toole's country, the marches of Dublin, and the whole bounds and limits thereof, as well within the liberties as without, with power and authority

to investigate, by all ways and means, the disorders and offences committed within these territories by naughty and idle persons; and if, on trial, such persons should be found to be felons, rebels, enemies, or notorious evil-doers, that he should proceed, according to the course of martial law, to judgment and punishment of such persons, by death or otherwise, as the nature of their offences should require; Provided that this commission should not operate against any person having an estate of inheritance or freehold to the value of £10, or who was of good name or fame in the country;[3] with power to treat and parley with all enemies and rebels that should come within the limits to repair unto the commissioner for cause or occasion of treaty, and give them safe conduct in coming and returning, and to effect such good order and way with them as were expressed in the instructions sent by the lieutenant.

The following reasons are assigned for issuing this commission :—

[1] Bagwell, ii. 29-30.   [2] *P.C.R.I.*, *Eliz.*, i. 445.
[3] Elizabeth was not anxious to proceed to extreme measures against the powerful, for fear of reprisals, but only against the poorer sort.

For as much as the wicked, malicious, and disordered nature of sundry persons, being of vile and base condition, not having whereon to live, and, therefore, less careful of allegiance and obedience, requires that we should correct and repress the same by some more speedy and sharp means than by our common law, and considering our martial law to be necessary for the reformation of such naughty livers and idle vagabonds as do not cease to disquiet our liege people.

A similar commission (25 December, 1560) was issued to FitzWilliams for executing martial law within the Co. Westmeath and the county of Connaught. These commissions were followed up by an ecclesiastical one on 23 May, following, evidently with a view to making some show of opposition to the determined stand of the Bishop of Meath against the Supremacy Oath, and to reforming the diocese during his imprisonment. The commission was issued to John Parker, Master of the Rolls ; Sir John Garvy, Archdeacon of Meath ; James Nugent, Sheriff of Co. Westmeath ; and Sir Thomas Nugent, to execute ecclesiastical jurisdiction in Co. Westmeath ; to visit, reform, redress, and correct, all heresies, schisms, abuses, offences, and enormities whatsoever, which by ecclesiastical authority might be reformed, redressed or corrected, to the pleasure of Almighty God, the increase of virtue, and conservation of the peace and unity of the realm.[1]

Elizabeth's Bishops not Happy in their Sees.

The secular affairs of Ireland, since the holding of Parliament, had been sufficiently weighty to occupy most of the time of the Lord Deputy, and were not conducted with the success with which the Queen and himself expected them to be crowned. Until matters improved in this direction there was little use in endeavouring to push on the " reform." The soil was not yet ready for the seed. How could the Deputy be expected to support Protestant bishops in Sees where his authority was scouted and his force of no avail ? All he could do in the whole North was to carry off a few hundred cattle, and return to the Pale leaving matters

[1] *P.C.R.I., Eliz.*, i. 446-7.

much as they were. More than a year had now elapsed
since the passing of the Acts for the establishment of the
Queen's Supremacy and of Uniformity of Worship, and one
looks in vain to discover the Elizabethan Church that was
expected to spring up from them. Walsh, Bishop of Meath,
had been deprived in 1560, and no one had yet been appointed
to his See, indeed, not for two years more. Meath was
probably not yet considered a safe place on account of the
skirmishes of Shane in the locality. Elizabeth had appointed
Alexander Craik to Kildare, 22 August, 1560, on the deprivation of Leverous, but in a short time, he, like Curwen
of Dublin, was anxious to be relieved of the burden of a See
where he found himself unable to do what was expected of
him. Accordingly, he sent the following interesting letter to
his patron Lord Robert Dudley :—[1]

Right honourable and my Singular good Lord, my duty most
humbly remembered, whereas I have heretofore divers and sundry
times molested your honour with my writings, specify the heavy
burden of my conscience, with molestation of other injuries done
unto me ; and as yet never received comforts by word or writing,
wherefore I do most humbly beseech your honour that like as ye
were the instrument of this my continual and daily torment
(I mean of my preferment unto a bishopric in such place in Ireland
where neither I can preach unto the people nor the people understand me) [2] that ye will be the like instrument to the Queen's
Majesty that I may be exonerated and unburdened of the same,
for there is not a preacher to assist me in setting forth of God's
word saving one Mr. Lofthowse [Loftus] ; my own chaplain is
but lately come over to me. If this be a lamentable hearing or
not, I refer it to your honour's judgment and discretion, I do
most humbly beseech you, good my lord, to ponder this matter
well and deeply, for it is God's cause, wherein you shall do him
acceptable service and your duty. My first fruits [3] I trust your
honour will not forget, and the despatch of my servant which
hath so long attended upon your lordship. Dignity and promotion is good and acceptable for a worldly man, but quietness
of conscience and sincere serving of God is comfortable for a

---

[1] *S.P.I.*, *Eliz.*, iii. 62, P.R.O., London. Shirley, 95.

[2] The people of Kildare did not understand English.

[3] He wished Elizabeth to remit his payment to her of the first year's revenue
of the See.

man fearing God and acceptable unto him, which thing I do most
humbly crave of my Lord and God, for that I have not any other
help of man to aid and assist me herein, I trust the next messenger
that your honour shall receive from me, shall be myself, if I can
procure leave, and doth stand with the Queen's Majesty her
pleasure, and then I shall communicate my mind and affairs
unto your honour more largely. Thus leaving off the lamenting
of all my grief by pen, with distance and separation of our bodies
by the interval of seas which is not the least of my griefs. With
my most humble commendations unto my honourable and good
Lord, my Lord Ambrose, your Lord's brother, and unto my good
Ladies your sisters, I beseech the eternal God to preserve you all
in his faith, fear, and love, with much increase of honour, defacing
of your enemies, comforts, and consolation of your friends, and
to your hearts contentation. From my house at Saint Patrick's,
the last day of April by your honour his most humble and
addicted servant during life.

His patron, Dudley, having made no impression on Cecil,
Craik makes bold to write himself to Elizabeth's powerful
secretary, on 13 September following, asking to be relieved
of the bishopric of Kildare because, he says, he can neither
understand the people nor they him. He desires Cecil to
put before the Queen the necessity here of more preachers
of God's most Holy word, without whom " it is impossible
that this rude and barbarous people shall be obedient under
her Highness or obey her Grace's proceedings." " The
bishops here be so slow and negligent " that they do nothing
to aid the Queen in " the abolishing of idolatry and superstition." [1]

Neither letter brought any relief to Craik, so that he
repeated his request a year later (26 October, 1562) to be
released from his bishopric as, he says, " I cannot fructify
nor profit the people for as much as they understand not me
nor I them, which is a great grief to my conscience." [2]

Nothing better manifests the futility of Acts of Parliament
for the conversion of Ireland than the early letters of Curwen
and Craik in the very strongholds of English power. The
work was not the soft job Craik thought it, and his idea of
the ministry was something " comfortable " and " acceptable,"

---

[1] *S.P.I., Eliz.*, iv. 53, P.R.O., London.
[2] *S.P.I., Eliz.*, vii. 32, P.R.O., London.

" for a man fearing God," which he hoped to find on the other side of the Irish sea. As it was, he found for the present a more agreeable retreat in his deanery house of St. Patrick's, Dublin, than in his episcopal See, and a willing preacher during his non-residence in his diocese in Adam Loftus, the future Archbishop of Armagh, and afterwards of Dublin. As for Curwen he found the temper of the clergy and people none too pleasant and their opposition to his " reform" daily growing. Even the prebendaries of St. Patrick's were bold enough to scoff at his " reforming " methods. With very few helpers, he saw what " an unprofitable workman he was, and longed for the peace of Oxford. So far, then, these were the chief bishops of the " reform " passed by the Dublin Parliament, and the other few " reform " bishops, as Craik confesses, " be so slow and negligent " they are no use to the Queen for " the abolishing of idolatry and super- stition."

The Queen's Grievances against the Pope.

As has been already alluded to, Elizabeth opposed the coming of a papal nuncio to England. But from a letter,[1] 20 May, 1561, of John Francis Commendone, Nuncio in Lower Germany, to Hercules Gonzaga, Cardinal of Mantua, the mind of Elizabeth appears more clearly, and particularly in reference to the Irish Commissary. He says :—

As to the resolution of the Queen of England not to admit the nuncio Mgr. Martinengo, you will be more fully advised by other letters. After such a precedent I am more than ever in- clined to suspect that the King of Denmark will likewise refuse to admit me. The Queen, I understand, alleges three principal grounds for Martinengo's exclusion ; (1) that unlike other princes, she was not consulted as to the summoning of the Council [of Trent] ; [2] (2) that the Council is not free, pious and Christian, and that, had it been so, she would have sent to it men learned and pious in the name of the Anglican Church ; (3) that the Pope likewise seeks to stir up the Catholics in her kingdom and raise

---

[1] *C.S.P., Rome*, 1558-71, no. 81.

[2] The Council of Trent had been dispersed in 1552, and was not reopened until January, 1562. Provisions for its reopening, however, were made in the previous year.

sedition, and in that regard she complains that an Irishman [Wolf] was sent from Rome to Ireland for such a purpose. She adds that it is no new thing for the agents of the Pope to be refused admission to the kingdom and that her sister Queen Mary so treated the agent of Pope Paul IV, who brought the hat for father Peto.

She desired to give a written memorial of this resolution to the ambassador resident of the Catholic King [of Spain] through whom the safe-conduct was negociated, but he declined to receive it. Moreover, to make the affair yet more unfortunate, it fell out that, at the very time that the matter was being discussed, a poor priest was arrested in the neighbourhood of London for carrying a breviary, and for fear of torture informed against a number of Catholics, which discovery has greatly incensed the Queen.

A PROTESTANT ARCHBISHOP FOR ARMAGH.

Elizabeth had been feeling her way how to fill the See of Armagh with a Protestant prelate. The gesture was intended as a peaceful penetration of her " reform " in the turbulent North. With Shane's coming to terms with her, the acceptance of her bishop seemed to her an easy matter. For three years Sussex had been seeking for a fit man for the See, and at last found one in Adam Loftus or Lofthouse, then about twenty-six years of age, who had been the Queen's chaplain, his own chaplain, and a preacher with Craik of Kildare. On 30 October, 1561, Elizabeth wrote to Curwen to consecrate Loftus for Armagh and to restore to him the temporalities. An enclosure was addressed to the Dean and Chapter of Armagh granting them the *congé d'élire* (licence to elect) and commanding them to elect Loftus.

In the Acts of the Parliament of 1560 Elizabeth had abolished episcopal election by diocesan chapter, thereby reviving the law of Edward VI. The reason for the deviation from the law in this case of Armagh " may be conjecturally traced to the weakness of the Government, a compulsory compliance with inevitable prejudice, and instant forgetfulness of the act of abolition, or the absence of an intention to execute it strictly and generally ; but it is not recorded." [1]

---

[1] Leland, ii. 227.

Owing to the difficulty [1] of assembling the chapter of Armagh, through the opposition of Shane, the election did not take place. Cecil, however, had informed Sussex by a letter, 28 November, 1561, that the Queen had promoted Loftus, [2] but by another letter of 13 December the appointment was stayed. Chagrined at the delay in the appointment of his friend, the Deputy wrote, 25 December, 1561, [3]

I know not who hath informed that he is not worthy of that place, but if a vehement zeal in religion, good understanding in the Scriptures, doctrines, and other kinds of learning, continual study, good consideration of life, and a bountiful gift of God in utterance, be sufficient to enable him, I undertake I have better ground to enable him than any man of that land or this, or what vocation so even he be, hath to disable him ; which I wish he might by commandment show before the Queen's Majesty, in the presence of all the bishops of that realm. And then I doubt not it would appear fitter to entreat him to receive it than to reject him, when not by himself but by others the place was sought for him, I ensure you neither doth he affect that or any other place of himself, neither have I for blind affection but for very duty sought his placing there. And if any man have other opinion of me God keep his head from aching till my doings approve his opinion ; I will not trouble you long in this matter. The name [of Armagh] is great, the living very small. I have these three years sued for a fit man to be placed here, and hitherto could get none. The Queen at my departing as you know willed me to seek some fit person ; I recommended this man as fit, he was allowed, and now thought unfit, and I will provide none other [who] shall by my means sustain like reproach hereafter. God send you as well to do as I would myself. From Kilmainham the xxvth of December 1561.

Elizabeth had evidently let it be understood that her reason for not promoting Loftus was that in some way

---

[1] It will be seen later how this occurred.

[2] Loftus was the youngest son of an ancient and wealthy Yorkshire family. At a public act at Cambridge he appeared before the Queen who was as much struck by his beauty as by his oratory and learning. She encouraged him to proceed in his studies and promised him early promotion. On his coming to Dublin as chaplain to Sussex he took up his abode with Bishop Craik at St. Patrick's Deanery, and on 8 October was presented by the Crown to the rectory of Painstown in the diocese of Meath.

[3] *S.P.I., Eliz.*, iv. 83, P.R.O., London.   Shirley, 98.   Sussex had written in similar terms on 29 November.

he was not considered a fit man for the position. Later, however, Sussex granted him a commission for the ordering of ecclesiastical causes in the diocese of Armagh of which the Queen approved, and directed the necessary writings to be given to him granting him " full authority and due allowance of the revenue of the See " (6 October, 1562).[1]

The real reason, however, of the delay in promoting Loftus seems to have been Elizabeth's desire to placate the Dean and Chapter by her condescension to recognise their privilege, and at the same time to secure her own selection. But it was unsuccessful. A year passed before the consecration of Loftus was proceeded with. Meanwhile the delay led to misgivings on the part of Craik, who wrote to Cecil, 2 January, 1562,[2] recommending Loftus for Armagh :— " that he is fervent and zealous in religion, setting forth the Queen's Majesty's proceedings, and is learned to defend the same accordingly, and is not only wise and discreet, but also of a sincere and pure conversation, as I would wish that the Queen's Majesty and her honourable Council should not refuse the willing service of such a fit man, as I do wish likewise that more plenty of such like preachers were placed in this realm of Ireland."

Politics Enter into Religion.

One of the greatest difficulties in the writing of the history of Elizabeth's reign is to separate politics from religion. The difficulty increases with the years. The Queen was only a few years on the throne when these matters became involved. As early as 5 September, 1561, in a letter [3] to Charles Cardinal Borromeo,[4] Commendone shows how they were being considered at the papal Court :—

I learn from the Court of Denmark that the King has got a suspicion that the match with the Queen of Scotland, which he designs for himself, is to be concluded with one of the sons of the Imperial Majesty, in regard to which I would respectfully suggest to you that perchance it would be most expedient to hinder the one and promote the other, for that besides the kingdom of

---

[1] *P.C.R.I., Eliz.,* i. 472.
[2] *S.P.I., Eliz.,* v. 3, P.R.O., London.   Shirley, 101.
[3] *C.S.P., Rome,* 1558-71, no. 102.   [4] Afterwards canonised.

Scotland the Queen of that country has perhaps a better title
to the kingdom of England than Queen Elizabeth herself, so that,
in the event of the match with the King of Denmark coming
about, not only would Scotland be quite lost to the Catholic Church,
but some day one of her bitterest enemies might gain a signal
accession of strength : if the match were made with a son of the
Emperor, not only would Scotland be retained by the Church,
but there would be hope of yet more, Queen Elizabeth being in
ill odour with the grandees by reason of the extraordinary favours
conferred on Milord Robert [Dudley] ; and the people beyond
the Trent being all still Catholics, as also in Ireland, the condition
of which island I learned from Irishmen in Flanders to be such
that, were there such a King in Scotland, a great revulsion might
be expected to the service of God ; and were there no other result
either in Ireland or England, there would at least be a curb set
upon Queen Elizabeth, that she should no longer coerce her people
into heresy, and these Princes would be deprived of much of the
boldness and confidence which they owe to the adhesion of such
great a realm, which would be of no little importance in regard
to French and Danish affairs alike. Nor only so : the Pope might,
if occasion should serve, confer upon such a King of Scotland
the investiture of Ireland, which fief the present Queen of England
has forfeited,[1] whereby the Pope would maintain his feudal overlordship ; and in like manner, should occasion serve, he might
grant the investiture of England itself, thus recovering the rights
acquired by the Apostolic See in the times of Kings John [2] and

[1] According to mediæval polity the Pope was the overlord of Ireland. He
had conferred it on Queen Mary, but had not conferred it on Elizabeth. Therefore, according to this theory, Catholics were not bound to give obedience to
her. But even the Irish chieftains did not always adhere to the theory, e.g.
Shane O'Neill, Desmond, etc. But the point is worth remembering, especially
in relation to the Bull of Pius V in 1570.

[2] On the death of Hubert, Archbishop of Canterbury, in 1205, King John
refused to accept the papal nominee, Stephen Langton, and Pope Innocent III
refused to recognise the royal nominee, John de Grey. Moreover, John wreaked
vengeance on the monks of Christ Church, Canterbury, by driving them from
their monastery and taking possession of their property. Innocent placed the
entire kingdom under Interdict, 24 March, 1208. When this proved of no avail
and the King committed acts of cruelty against the clergy, the Pope declared
him excommunicated in 1209, and formally deposed him in 1212. The Interdict,
however, did not apply to Ireland as John was only lord of that country with
the Pope as his overlord. The King, at last repenting of his opposition to the
Pope, and having been reconciled to him through the Bishop of Tusculum,
Papal Legate, granted a charter of 3 October, 1213 (with the King's golden
Bull), whereby, of his own free will and by counsel of his barons, he offered
and freely granted to God and His Apostles Peter and Paul, to the Holy Roman
Mother Church, and to Pope Innocent III and his successors, all the kingdom

Henry II, doing God great service, and no less augmenting the power of the Apostolic See, as well in temporals as in spirituals, succouring three realms and curing in great measure the disorders and disquietude of Germany, whence as from the prime and original root of the present poison the other provinces have derived and still derive their infection.

For many years this matchmaking for the Queens of England and Scotland caused flutterings and much anxiety in continental courts as the years advanced, and served to embroil the religious question with the question as to who were to be the consorts; the question of the consorts was subservient to the religious question. No doubt the whole matter was the preservation of the Catholic faith in these islands, but the introduction of the consort question was to have a far-reaching influence on the course of history in these countries.

SHANE AT THE COURT OF ELIZABETH; SIGNS HIS SUBMISSION.

Returning to the chief disturber of the Queen's peace in Ireland, whose submission was essential to any progress in pacification, the services of Kildare were now requisitioned to induce Shane to cross to England. After much conversation in which Kildare yielded to his terms, Shane agreed to go to the Queen's presence, but his passport for safe conduct was to be signed by the five Irish Earls, and a sum of money was to be provided for his journey. There was little goodwill or sincerity on either side. Shane, however, was persuaded to allow the garrison of Armagh remain; £500 were paid over to Shane before starting, £1000 awaited him at Chester, and a second £500 in London. Shane came to Dublin, not unfearful of Sussex, and, in spite of a letter from Mary Queen of Scots, took ship, insisting on the company of

of England and all the kingdom (realm) of Ireland; and taking back these kingdoms as fees, swore fealty for himself and his successors to the Pope and his successors. In token of this the King willed to the Church of Rome a yearly grant, in lieu of service, of 1000 marks sterling, namely 700 for the kingdom of England, and 300 for the kingdom of Ireland, exclusive of Peter's pence, and swore to defend against all men the patrimony of St. Peter, and especially the kingdom of England and the kingdom of Ireland. (*Chart.* 15 John, M. 3 and 2.)

Kildare and Ormond.[1] Thus the uncrowned monarch of Ulster set out to meet the Queen whose authority he was ever ready to acknowledge upon the sole condition that she should never exercise it.

Shane was presented to the Queen by Kildare early in January, 1562. " The bare rough heads of his galloglasses, who did not lay aside their axes, their long curls, their wide-sleeved saffron shirts, their short tunics, and their shaggy cloaks of fur or frieze, which in Ireland covered a multitude of sins, made Englishmen stare ; not less, says Camden, than they now stare at Chinamen or American Indians. . . . Shane prostrated himself before the Queen, and then on his knees ' confessed his rebellion with howling,' and made his submission in Irish, which few or none could understand." [2] It was translated into English, and two days afterwards (6 January) was signed and sealed by Shane.[3] " For lack of education and civility," he is made to say, " I have offended." He thanked the Queen for his pardon, promised to deserve well for the future, begged her favour for the gentlemen of his company, his kinsmen and friends, and admitted in writing that he had done homage on his knees to Elizabeth as Queen of England, France, and Ireland. Shane's pretensions, it is said, were so extraordinary that the courtiers, " noting his haughtiness and barbarity, devised his style thus ; O'Neale the great, Cousin to St. Patricke, friend to the Queene of England, enemy to all the world besides." [4]

Shane was acknowledged by the Queen as actual captain not only of Tyrone, but of the greater part of the present Co. Antrim, with a proviso that he should not levy Irish exactions outside his own proper district. He promised to do his best to persuade the chiefs under him to come to Dublin and do homage, to attend all general hostings in Ulster, and to keep the peace with O'Donnell, O'Reilly, etc. He agreed not to molest the garrison of Armagh, on condition that

---

[1] *S.P.I., Eliz.*, iv. 69, 78. Ware says that Shane sailed 3 December, 1561. He was in court by 6 January, 1562.

[2] Bagwell, ii. 34. Machyn's *Diary*, 4 Jan., 1561-62. See also Camden and Campion.

[3] *S.P.I., Eliz.*, v. 5, P.R.O., London.   [4] Campion, 189.

they were victualled from the Pale. The retention of the garrison in Armagh was as a support for Elizabeth's bishop there. Shane left three hostages in London, but they were all persons of no importance. Good faith existed on neither side. Elizabeth dismissed Shane with honour because she knew not what else to do, and Shane agreed to her terms because he was in the net and saw no other means of escape. A sum of £300 certainly, perhaps more, was lent, or rather given, for the return journey, and the Queen issued a proclamation declaring Shane's virtues, and appointing Commissioners to determine his controversies with the Pale. Shane was back in Ireland by the end of May.[1]

DESMOND PETITIONS ELIZABETH FOR AN ECCLESIASTICAL FAVOUR.

Whilst the negotiations with Shane were being conducted, Munster was disturbed by the chronic jealousy between Butlers and Geraldines. Ormond had been ordered by Elizabeth not to come over with Shane but to remain in Ireland in order to be a watch over Desmond, who was carrying on a petty warfare with all the gentlemen of the west, burning towns, and carrying off plunder. Ormond complained also of his invasion of his own country. But the Corporations of Cork, Kinsale, and Youghal declared that Desmond was their only defence. They preferred him whom they knew, with all his shortcomings, to the Government in Dublin whom they had no reason to like. Even the Lord Deputy had no desire to waste men in endeavouring to subjugate people so far away from Dublin. FitzWilliams had to be content with Desmond's promise to go to England at Easter. Like Shane, Desmond was willing to keep order provided his own freedom was not interfered with.[2]

Meanwhile he desired to have a part in ecclesiastical affairs. At this time, according to memoranda in the State Papers,[3] the dioceses of Armagh, Cashel, Meath, and Cork were vacant, as well as " divers small bishoprics in the Irishry."

---

[1] " In May, George Elcock, Mayor of Drogheda, was brought before Sir Wm. FitzWilliams upon suspicion of holding correspondence with the rebels, and was committed to Dublin Castle." (Loftus, *Annals*.)

[2] *C.S.P.I., Eliz.*, v. 11, 27, 50, 92.   [3] *Ib.*, vi. 18.

It was considered " needful to place bishops presently " who should be " well chosen," and a commission was to be appointed " to receive surrendered bulls and to grant letters patents." It was ordered that Roger Skiddy who had been originally recommended by Queen Mary in 1557 for the diocese of Cork and Cloyne and who had not been appointed by the Pope, should be made bishop of that See by Elizabeth's letters patent, and Hugh Lacy, of Limerick, who had been appointed by the Pope in Mary's reign,[1] was recommended now for deprivation. But this deprivation did not take place immediately. For the Archbishopric of Cashel Desmond had a nominee whom he recommended to Cecil, 18 February, 1562 :—[2]

I commend me very heartily unto your worshipful Mastership, having sent my very loving chaplain and friend Sir Edmond Hiffirnan, Chancellor of Cashel [3] (of whom passing good opinion is conceived among us of civility and good manners) to be suitor to the Queen's Majesty for the archbishopric of Cashel now void, and have written to my friends in his favours, of whom I reckon you (although I be not yet acquainted with your mastership) as any other, these shall be therefore most heartily to beseech you to show yourself my good friend, in presenting my said chaplain's letters, and moving his purpose to her most excellent Majesty and the Council, whereby I doubt not (your Mastership standing my aid) to have good success in my attempts, knowledging me bound to acquit your goodness with any pleasure I can, when occasion serve, thus resting your own assured friend, I take my leave with your Mastership, from Cork, this 18th of February, 1561 [*i.e.* 1562].

Your very loving friend,

GEROT DESMOND.

---

[1] Bishop Casey was deprived by Mary. When Lacy was deprived in 1571, he was succeeded by Casey.

[2] *S.P.I.*, *Eliz.*, v. 34, P.R.O., London.

[3] The See was vacant, from the death of Roland Baron or Fitzgerald on 28 October, 1561, until 1567 when James MacCaghwell was appointed by Elizabeth, and Maurice MacGibbon by the Pope. Heffernan, therefore, was not appointed. His death occurred sometime in 1563, as on 15 June of that year (5th Elizabeth), " the presentation of John Wale to the vicarage of Killenaule, vacant by the decease of Edmund Hiffernan " was directed " to the vicar-general or keeper of the spiritualities." On 21 July his dignity of Chancellor was bestowed upon John Archdeacon. (*P.C.R.I.*, *Eliz.*, i. 478-9.)

Desmond's submission having been communicated to Elizabeth, she received him into her favour at the intercession of Her Majesty's Privy Council and the Earl of Sussex. In articles drawn up and sent to the Queen (28 June, 1562), Desmond states :—[1]

I do firmly vow and promise that I will, to the uttermost of my power, aid and assist the Bishop and all other spiritual Ministers, to cause the honour and divine service of Almighty God to be maintained, furthered and established in all churches and parts of the realm of Ireland, and specially in your Majesty's counties of Cork, Limerick, Kerry as is, and shall be, ordered and limited by the laws, statutes, and orders of the realm of Ireland, and to punish the offenders thereof, according to the qualities of their offences.

He likewise promised to be answerable to the laws ; not to aid pirates, outlaws, rebels, or traitors ; not to make war on the Queen's subjects ; to suffer the Lords Fitzmaurice of Kerry, Great Barry, Lord Roche, Young Barry, Red Barry, Courcy, Sir Maurice Fitzgerald, etc., to remain upon the Queen's peace, and to repair to parliaments.

Desmond thus pretended to acknowledge Elizabeth's spiritual supremacy in the Church. But, as in the case of many others, his intention to carry out his promises was quite another matter. Indeed, as will be seen, he was by no means a believer in or supporter of Elizabeth's " reform." His petitioning of the archdiocese of Cashel for his friend Heffernan was inspired, doubtless, with the object of paying a compliment to Elizabeth and at the same time of securing a Catholic bishop who would be left in peace by her officials. However this may be, this procedure on the part of a Catholic nobleman can be regarded only as extraordinary, and would not be considered by the Roman authorities as justifiable. One must take into account, however, the amount of deception which was practised on both sides, by Irish chiefs and by Elizabeth and her officials. It was an age of deception, and promises and oaths were good only as long as they were convenient.

---

[1] *S.P.I., Eliz.*, vi. 30, P.R.O., London. Shirley, 116.

THE BISHOP OF KILDARE COMPLAINS OF WANT OF PREACHERS AND OF POVERTY.

The diocese of Kildare seems to have been as great a thorn in the side of the Government as that of Armagh. More than a year had now passed since Craik was consecrated for it and he still preferred to remain in his deanery of St. Patrick's, Dublin, excusing his incompetence in the bishopric on the ground of ignorance of Irish. This state of affairs evidently induced Elizabeth to look out for some other post for him. Meath which was vacant by the deprivation of Walsh, seemed to him more " comfortable " and " acceptable " to a " man fearing God." On 10 January, 1562, Craik wrote to Cecil [1] stating that Sussex had informed him at last Christmas that—

the Queen's Majesty's pleasure is that I should take upon me the bishopric of Meath, unto whose highness's ordinances I am obliged and most addicted, being a foreigner, and received by favour, notwithstanding my late suit to come into England in these my sickly days ; and what I shall do therein, I most instantly desire to know the Queen's Majesty's pleasure by your worship, and that I may have the assistance of preachers if I tarry here, which I would be loth to do, if that should so stand with the Queen's Majesty's pleasure . . . from Saint Patrick's by Dublin, the xth of January anno 1561 [*i.e.* 1562].

As we have seen, the " reform " during the early years of Elizabeth's reign was mainly confined to the endeavour to obtain suitable bishops for a few important Sees, to procure their acceptance by the chiefs, and to induce them to remain there. It was as difficult to find preachers, or clergymen, of the " reform " as to find bishops. And so Craik was asking a practically impossible favour for the administration of his diocese. It will appear later how the Government was at its wit's end to secure preachers from England. But Craik had other troubles. He probably received little or no revenue from his diocese, and he had to pay to Elizabeth the first-fruits of the deanery of St. Patrick's which he had held only for a little over a year. Accordingly he wrote to Cecil, 5 February :—[2]

[1] *S.P.I., Eliz.,* v. 7, P.R.O., London. Shirley, 104.
[2] *S.P.I., Eliz.,* v. 17, P.R.O , London. Shirley, 106.

I have been sued of late both in the Exchequer and Common Pleas, since his lordship's departure out of Ireland. In the Exchequer I am sued for not compounding for my first fruits, which I thought had been long since remitted and forgiven me of the Queen's Majesty, as I was credibly informed, else I would not have incurred the danger of the Queen's Majesty's laws. Further, one William Basnett [1] prosecuted the law against me for my deanery, claiming the same in farm by a lease granted by the late famous prince of memory King Henry the Eight, which troubles doth not a little grieve me, not only interrupting me of my study, but also augmenting my late sickness that I have gotten in this country since I did here arrive, most humbly desiring you to be a mean unto the Queen's Majesty for me, as well for the remitting of my first fruits as also I be not thus troubled in the law for my deanery, considering that I am a poor man having no other substance nor friends to be bounden for me, being also as yet much indebted for my charges and furniture to come over into this realm of Ireland. Which considered, I most humbly desire you to speak to my Lord Lieutenant for me that it would please his honour to direct his highness's letters unto the Lord Justice here, and to Mr. Baron Bathe and other the officers of the Exchequer and Common Pleas, that I might be thereby remitted and discharged of my first fruits, and from the suit of the Common Law, or else that I may be removed from hence into England to some poor quiet living that is out of trouble of the law, for surely this trouble will more abbreviate my days, if you be not a means to the Queen's Majesty for me in my aforesaid petitions and suits. Thus most instantly desiring you to procure and solicit for me licence to come over into England, for the recovery of my health, with your good remembrance and furtherance in all my suits, as my sure expectation is in you, and as I have heretofore at all times experimented. And thus I most humbly bid you well to fare in the faith, fear, and love of Jhesus Christ, with much increase of worship, from my poor house the Deansrath, [2] the 5th of February, 1561 [i.e. 1562].

Postscripta. I beseech you that there may be more preachers sent into this the Queen's Majesty rude realm of Ireland.

---

[1] Dean Basnett (d. 1553) bequeathed to his children—of whom William was one—property of the deanery lying at Kiltiernan, Co. Dublin. (See Ronan, *The Reformation in Dublin*, p. 334.)

[2] Deansrath, Clondalkin, Co. Dublin, part of the possessions of the deanery of St. Patrick's.

Shortly after this a friend of his came over to help him in the preaching of God's word, but evidently in St. Patrick's, Dublin, and not in his diocese of Kildare. His friend, however, was soon in trouble with his bishop in England for non-residence, and Craik wrote another letter [1] (18 February) to Cecil to set this matter right :—

Right worshipful, my duty not forgotten, these are to certify you that I being sickly and not able to endure such labour in preaching as I have done heretofore since my arriving in Ireland, I wrote to one of my old acquaintances David Padye parson of Compton Westeleys in com. South [County of Southampton] to come to assist me in preaching of God's word, which he doth here at this present to God's glory, yet I am certified that my Lord Bishop of Winchester hath cited him intending to deprive him for not resident, may it therefore please your worship to direct your letters to my Lord of Winchester willing him to stay in this matter, seeing he [Padye] is my friend and is occupied here for a time in setting forth of God's glory, confounding his enemies, wherein he doth both advance the truth and the Queen's Majesty's proceedings. And thus most humbly desiring you to have me in memory for my former suits in my late letters, and to have conference therein with my singular approved good Lord, my Lord Lieutenant, for I have no friend in whom my trust is reposed under God, and the Queen's Majesty, as in his honour, with my Lord Robert and my L. Ambrose Dudley, and also in your worship, whose friendship I have experimented [experienced] ; and thus most humbly I bid you well to fare in the faith from the love of God, with much increase of worship. From St. Patrick's by Dublin the 18th of February, anno 1561 [i.e. 1562].

Craik wrote again to Cecil, 23 April, 1562, asking leave to cross over to England on urgent affairs and for the sake of his health, and reminding Cecil that the latter had not replied to any of his letters.[2] Cecil, no doubt, was wearied by letters from Craik about his inability as a bishop and a preacher, and about his poverty.

CIVIL AND RELIGIOUS LAW SET AT NOUGHT.

FitzWilliams took a very gloomy view of the country committed to his charge in the absence of Lord Deputy

---

[1] *S.P.I.*, *Eliz.*, v. 35, P.R.O., London. Shirley, 111.
[2] *S.P.I.*, *Eliz.*, v. 91, P.R.O., London.

Sussex. The English Pale was in a deplorable state, every one expecting a total change of policy, and refusing to obey any law.[1] Pirates blockaded Cork and Kinsale, even lying openly under Lambay in Dublin Bay, while the Queen's ships were nowhere visible. Lawyers and judges simply administered justice as they liked, and Crown business was deliberately delayed. The difficulty was aggravated by the sending over of English officials who were much inferior in ability to the Irish-born.[2]

On account of riots and other offences committed, to which " notable and public " punishment is allotted, the Queen sent (3 July) instructions to Sussex that " a place might be appointed for the open hearing and determining thereof, like to our Council Chamber commonly called the Star Chamber at Westminster, and with like authority and jurisdiction." [3]

The Protestant religion was not any better respected by the people than was the civil law, and this, as Sussex wrote to Cecil (22 July),[4] is due not only to papists' dislike of it but also to the worthlessness and greed of the Protestant ministers. Sussex proceeds :—

Our religion is so abused, as the papists rejoice, the neuters [neutrals] do not mislike changes, and the few zealous professors lament the lack of piety. The people without discipline, utterly void of religion, come to divine service as to a May game. The ministers, for disability, incompetence, and greediness, be had in contempt, and the wise fear more the impiety of the licentious professors of the new religion than the superstition of the erroneous papists. These matters be so far come, as they be not, I think, to be helpen by private commissions, but rather by parliament wherein limits in religion and discipline may be appointed, with such severe orders for punishment of the breakers thereof, as men may fear to go beyond or come short. God hold his hand over us that our licentious disorders, and lack of religious hearts, do not bring in the meantime his wrath and revenge upon us.

The male heads of Catholic families in Dublin, forced to attend Protestant service in order to avoid the enormous

[1] Bagwell, ii. 44.   [2] *S.P.I., Eliz.,* vi. 8, P.R.O., London.
[3] *Ib.,* 41, P.R.O., London.
[4] *Ib.,* 57, P.R.O., London.   Shirley, 117.

fines for non-attendance which were extorted from them, went to the churches, but such was their contempt for the service that they behaved as they would round the May-pole. For some years many of those who heard Mass in private houses on Sunday mornings, persuaded themselves that they were guilty of no great sin in complying with the law by attending Protestant service later in the day. All that the law required was their presence in the church during Protestant service. As explained by the law-givers them-selves, the people were not bound to give internal assent; they were not required to receive communion in the new way, or even asked to listen to the sermon. Mere presence was, therefore, as they were told, quite sufficient; no one troubled about internal assent. Partly for this reason, and partly because the new service was largely copied from Sacred Scripture and from the old Catholic Missal and prayer-books, and accompanied by Mass vestments,[1] even good Catholics for the time being had little scruple in attending Protestant service, thus escaping the pains and penalties laid down for non-attendance.

The law exacting fines for non-attendance at the law-established churches on Sunday was sometimes enforced in a few towns during Elizabeth's reign, but the law prohibiting the public Mass was always enforced whenever the Govern-ment had the power. The new Oath of Supremacy, however, was not admitted by the towns or boroughs during Elizabeth's reign at least down to the year 1601, and the old Catholic oath was retained. The report made by the commissioners for ecclesiastical causes, 16 March, 1564,[2] deals with this subject. It states: " concerning religion and the favourers of it, we are sorry to say that we find blind ignorance, the leader to superstition, so set by, as it is hard to persuade willingness to hear the truth soberly taught, and yet there appeareth in this people fear to offend, wherefore they be not to be despaired but to be hoped of ; *for those we have to*

---

[1] Although Elizabeth ordered the Second Book of Common Prayer of Edward VI to be followed, yet she allowed the rubrics of the First Book to be put in practice in the use of the Mass vestments so as not to disturb the conscience of those assisting at the service.

[2] Shirley, 140.

do with we find conformable to the laws, and the judges with other of the lawyers, ready, as they seem to us, to execute the laws for religion, and accordingly have promised us now in the assizes and sessions to inquire specially of defaulters against these laws for religion yet with this caution, as we thought good that they meddle not with the simple multitude now at first, but with one or two boasting massmen in every shire ; that it may be seen that the punishment of such men is meant" The boasting "massmen" are presumably the Mass priests. The last clause in italics confirms the traditional account of a general impression that the penal laws were not to be enforced rigorously for the present except as regards Mass priests. The other clauses in italics are directly contradicted by Brady, the Protestant Bishop of Meath, writing two days before. He complains of the obstinacy of the clergy, lawyers, and people ; and both speak of the same district, for at that date Brady's diocese was almost the only place where the commissioners were authorised and had the real power to execute the laws.

An interesting entry in the State Papers in regard to the upkeep of St. Patrick's Cathedral may be conveniently inserted here. On 8 July, 1562, the Queen sent an order requiring all persons to assist the proctors of the Cathedral " in collecting honey, fruit, and other things, which had been paid, from the earliest period of time, from all parts of the province, to the Dean and Chapter, for the use of this Cathedral ; these, being either duties reserved in their leases or benefactions of the pious in ancient times, were to be applied to the repair of the church, which, during the suppression [of religious houses], had fallen much into decay : the proctors, however, were strictly prohibited from carrying about with them any pastoral staff, cross, Mass-book, or other ensign of popery." [1]

SHANE FRUSTRATES APPOINTMENT OF LOFTUS TO ARMAGH.

Not many months had passed since Shane returned from London and conducted himself with " civility," when, having

[1] *P.C.R.I.*, 4 *Eliz.*, 8 July, 1562.

again asserted his authority over the northern chiefs, he was strong enough to oppose any innovation in religion in the country under his sway. Almost a year had elapsed since the Queen recommended Loftus to the Chapter of Armagh for that archbishopric, and Curwen was commanded to consecrate him, but neither order was carried out. It was given out at the time that the cause of the remissness of the Chapter was the difficulty of assembling it. That was only half the truth.[1] The whole case is stated in a letter from Sussex and Council to Elizabeth, 2 September, 1562 :—[2]

It may please your Highness to be advertised that having given order according to your pleasure and commandment for the electing of Mr. Adam Lofthowse to be Archbishop of Armagh, we have received answer from the Dean of Armagh that the Chapter there, whereof the greatest part be temporal men,[3] and Shane O'Neill's horsemen be so sparkled [on the alert] and out of order, as he [the Dean] can by no means assemble them to proceed to the election of him according your Majesty's nomination in your letters to the Dean and Chapter, and the *congé d'élire* granted to them from me by your Chancellor, by your Highness's command-ment. Whereupon we have taken order for the stay of the fruits [profits of the See] in the tenants' hands until your Majesty's pleasure be further known, and do think the best way to proceed herein will be to deliver unto him by your Majesty's warrant the possessions of the archbishopric *absq computo* [without account] from the date of your letters, as in like cases hath been used, and thereupon to grant unto him commission here to order causes ecclesiastical within that diocese, according the statutes of the last parliament, whereby the place may be sufficiently supplied till your Majesty may take further order therein. The people in those parts be far disordered in religion [i.e. opposed to the Reform], he is discreet, well learned, and hath a goodly gift of utterance in the pulpit, which moveth us the rather to beseech your Highness's speedy resolution herein, and so we shall pray

---

[1] Donat O'Taig, papal archbishop, did not die until towards the end of the year 1562. Very little, however, is known about his occupancy of the See. According to Lynch he was compelled in 1561 to flee from his diocese, went to Munster, was captured at Adare, was imprisoned, and escaped to Killaloe where he died.

[2] *S.P.I., Eliz.*, vii. 2. Shirley, 119.

[3] From Celtic days the lay hereditary patrons had a voice in the election of the abbot and bishop of Armagh.

to God long to preserve your Majesty in prosperity. From Dublin the second of September 1562.

Your Majesty's most humble and faithful
Subjects and Servants

T. Sussex.	H. Dublin, Canc.	James Bathe.
W. Fitswylliams.	Jo. Plunket.	Henry Radeclyff.
John Chaloner.		

The Queen, in a letter of 11 October, to the Lord Lieu-tenant,[1] acceded to his request, and ordered the necessary writings [2] to be made for their performance, as well as for a grant of money which she especially warranted for Loftus, " and so to continue until he may receive his establishment in the bishopric by such ordinary means, as in similar cases hath been accustomed." The Queen here refers to the time when the election of Loftus by the Armagh Chapter should be accomplished.

In granting permission to the Armagh Chapter to elect a bishop of her own choice, Elizabeth, doubtless, wished to show that she was conferring a privilege on them and paying them a compliment. But the hardy Northerners who in-herited the right of voting for St. Patrick's successor were not deceived by her act of grace and resented this intrusion on their ecclesiastical privileges. What was Loftus, they might say, to them, or they to Loftus ?

One point in these letters calls for comment, namely, as to the profits of the See of Armagh. FitzWilliams, in a letter of 30 June, to Cecil [3] states : " I saw a letter from the Queen Majesty's Council unto the Barons of the Exchequer to call in the revenues of the bishopric of Armagh as well the spiritualities thereof, as temporalities. I humbly beseech you if [that] there may be another to the same effect for all bishoprics likewise void, but for the spiritualities chiefly, which by no mean they will let come to the Queen's Majesty."

---

[1] *S.P.I.*, *Eliz.*, vii. 25, P.R.O., London.

[2] Loftus related in his *Annals* how Hugh O'Neill, cousin of Shane, drinking at Drogheda, fell in with the Archbishop of Armagh's (Loftus) collector of revenues, and said that " his cousin and all his ancestors were patient fools for taking an earldom from Kings of England." The servant reported the matter to Loftus who reported it to Sussex. This, it was said, roused a suspicion about Shane's intentions.

[3] *S.P.I.*, *Eliz.*, vi. 36, P.R.O., London.

A few months afterwards Elizabeth, seeing the opposition in Armagh, had been quite content if Loftus could gather in any of the revenues without giving an account of those who supplied them or without her exacting of the first-fruits of the See. The revenues of the spiritualities, namely, from the office of bishop, as distinct from the possessions in lands, were of more importance in the eyes of the Government than the temporal revenues, as they would indicate an acceptance of Elizabeth's Supremacy. FitzWilliams was forced to admit that in the vacant Sees of Armagh, Cashel, and Meath the people would not allow the spiritualities to be paid into the Exchequer. This admission, side by side with Shane's opposition in Armagh, shows the temper of the people in face of the " Reform " that was being thrust upon them even in a half-hearted manner.

THE DEAN OF ARMAGH AND THE ARCHDEACON OF MEATH ; COMMISSIONERS FOR ECCLESIASTICAL CAUSES.

Terence Daniel or Donnelly, Dean of Armagh, was one of those elusive persons who played a double part, for which this period is remarkable. He acted so cleverly as intermediary between Shane and the Government that sometimes he seemed to favour one party and sometimes the other. In May he was one of those appointed to hear and determine controversies between Shane and the gentlemen of the Pale.[1] A few months later (31 July, 1562) [2] Sussex requested Shane to send Daniel and John Garvey,[3] Archdeacon of Meath (appointed by Elizabeth), to confer with him about the execution of Shane's articles of indenture, and about the place where Shane and the northern chiefs would meet Sussex. The Lord Lieutenant commended Daniel for his part in the negotiations, but he was forced to admit to Cecil that little hope was to be expected that Shane would continue in obedience. Shane had his own grievances, and Daniel was one of those appointed by Sussex to decide the spoils done by the English on Shane while he was in

---

[1] *C.S.P.I.*, *Eliz.*, vi. 6, P.R.O., London.   [2] *Ib.*, 60.
[3] Garvey, as early as 14 July, 1560, had been appointed by Elizabeth as Archdeacon of Meath, with the rectory of St. Columba of Kells, vacant by deprivation of Robert Luttrell. (*Fiants*, no. 262.)

England. Shane informed the Queen that only 40 out of
the 3880 kine taken from him were restored, and that goods
of the value of 2000 marks were also taken. He sends presents
of two horses, two hawks, and two greyhounds to Dudley
to obtain favour for him with the Queen. Meanwhile, Shane
was preying on the northern chiefs exacting recognition of
him as their overlord, whilst Sussex was endeavouring to
win them to the Queen's side. Sussex was especially anxious
to win over the O'Donnell family, the second strongest in the
North, and to proceed to Armagh to discuss the situation
with those chiefs. His task at this time was particularly
difficult as he found the people on all sides " stirred to hate
the English and procured to exclaim against disorders without
seeking amendment." [1] When all else failed the Government fell back upon commissions by which it was thought
that the people of the North might be brought into line with
the " reform."

The commission for ecclesiastical causes already referred
to by Sussex and the Queen, was directed to " Adam
Loftehowse, Archbishop of Armagh ; Sir George Stanley,
Sir Thomas Cusack, Terence, Dean of Armagh ; [2] Sir John
Garvey, Archdeacon of Meath ; and Henry Draycott, Chief
Remembrancer, to exercise ecclesiastical jurisdiction in the
province of Armagh, to visit, reform, redress, and correct
all errors, heresies, schisms, contempts, and enormities,
which may or can be restrained or corrected, for the pleasure
of Almighty God, setting forth of His word, increase of virtue,
and the conservation of the peace and unity of the realm " [3]
(6 December). This was followed (18 May, 1563) [4] by another
commission to Loftus, Garvey, and Draycott, Chancellor of
the Exchequer, to administer to all ecclesiastics, to all the
officials of the Crown, and to all in the pay of the Queen, an
oath couched in these terms : " I do utterly testify and declare
in my conscience that the Queen's Highness is the only supreme governor of the realm, and of all other Her Highness's

---

[1] *S.P.I.*, *Eliz.*, vii. 6, 39, 40, 55, P.R.O., London.
[2] Although Daniel's name is inserted in the commission, it does not follow
that he acted on it. These commissions were loosely drawn up and presumed
consent when sometimes it was not warranted.
[3] *P.C.R.I.*, *Eliz.*, i. p. 479, no. 59.   [4] *Ib.*, no. 60.

dominions and countries, as well in all spiritual or ecclesiastical things or causes, as temporal, and that no foreign prince, person, prelate, state, or potentate, hath, or ought to have, any jurisdiction, power, superiority, pre-eminence or authority, etc."

And following the early policy of her father and her brother, Elizabeth had a form of declaration drawn up which every Archbishop and bishop was required to take at his consecration :—

I, N. . . ., elect and consecrated, profess that I have and hold all the temporalities and possessions of the said bishopric from the hands of Elizabeth, Queen of England, and so forth, and her successors, as in right of the Crown of her kingdom of Ireland ; to her, and to her successors, kings of England, I will be faithful. So help me God and the Holy Gospels.[1]

In this oath, however, there is no mention of the Queen as the Head or Governor of the Church. It was thus an oath similar to that usually taken in Pre-Reformation days by Catholic Bishops to the Kings of England, and which those of Elizabeth's time would in general agree to take.

Irish Bishops at the Council of Trent.

One of the most important duties of Father Wolf, papal commissary in Ireland, was to recommend to the Holy See those priests whom he considered most fit to fill the vacant Sees. It was thus that, 17 December, 1561, Thomas O'Herlihy, a secular priest, was appointed to Ross, and on 28 January, 1562, Donald McCongail,[2] also a secular priest, was appointed to Raphoe, in the room of Art O'Gallagher ("greatly lamented" according to the *Four Masters*), Eugene O'Harte, a Dominican, to Achonry, in the room of Cormac O'Coyne, a Franciscan, his uncle, and Andrew O'Crean, a Dominican, to Elphin. As to the church of Achonry, Wolf says it was used (1561) as a fortress by the gentry and had not a vestige of religion. He recommended

---

[1] Mant, i. 270.

[2] McCongail had been Wolf's companion in his travels through Ireland and the bearer of the letter to Rome recommending the above ecclesiastics for bishoprics.

O'Harte as likely, by his good life and by aid of his friends, to take back the Church and restore it to its proper uses " as Dr. Christopher did in Tuam." Crean of Elphin, McCongail of Raphoe, and O'Harte of Achonry, having been despatched to Rome, and consecrated, repaired to Trent for the final sessions of the Council in 1562. They joined in many discussions, such as on the Pope as the source of episcopal Jurisdiction, the Mass, Holy Orders, Matrimonial impediments, etc., and their names and votes are handed down in the Acts of the Council in graceful verse.[1]

Whilst present at the Council their poverty was a matter of much concern, and Cardinals Mantua, Seripando, Ermland, and Simoneta wrote (3 December, 1562),[2] to Cardinal Charles Borromeo [3] in their favour :—

Your letter of the 25th of last month received to-day and perused by us with the Cardinal of Lorraine and the French ambassadors.

The three Irish bishops that are here with nothing to live on but the trifling allowance of 20 crowns a month a-piece, granted by his Holiness, make great complaint, that living being so dear, they cannot subsist, and crave and supplicate that their allowance be raised to 26 crowns a month, since many less needy than they have as much. Should it seem good to you to speak to his Holiness on this matter, we are of opinion that you will do that which is well pleasing to God.

Nine days afterwards (12 December) the Legates at Trent informed Cardinal Borromeo [4] that " His Holiness is well pleased that the allowance to the three Irish bishops be raised to 25 crowns a month."

---

[1] Theiner, *Acta S. C. Trid.*, ii. 53, 136, 228. Bellesheim, ii. 142-4. Moran, *Abps. of Dublin*, 89. See for *Wolf's letter I.E.R.*, i. 215 ; ii. 155, 458 ; iii. 147. Hogan, *Hib. Ignat.*, 12, 13.

  " Post hos, tres juvenes quos frigida Hibernia legat,
  Eugenium, Thomamque bonos, justumque Donaldum,
  Omnes ornatos ingens virtutibus orbis,
  Misit ut hanc scabiem tollant morbumque malignum,
  Sacratis omnes induti tempora mitris."

[2] *C.S.P., Rome*, 1558-71, no. 201.
[3] I.e. St. Charles Borromeo, Archbishop of Milan.
[4] *C.S.P., Rome*, 1558-71, no. 203.

The Archbishop of Tuam and the Bishop of Clonfert.

As Archbishop Bodkin's name has just been used in reference to his recovery of the Cathedral of Tuam for religious purposes, it is important to get his position at this time quite clearly. In an official letter in Italian to Rome, 12 October, 1561,[1] Fr. Wolf states :—

In Connaught we [himself and MacCongail, his companion] have together seen, but not visited, the Archbishop of Tuam and the Bishop of Clonfert, *worthy men according to the standard of the world. Both are adherents of the Queen, as,* I have already informed you, *are all the rest of Munster.*[2] This Archbishop of Tuam, Christopher Botteghin by name, got his archbishopric, according to common report, by force of arms and the royal authority. He would not tell me how he got it, save that by means of Cardinal Pole a composition was made between him and one Arthur O'Frehir [O'Frehil], the true and lawful archbishop, who is still living and was ousted from the See by the said Christopher, who holds also the Sees of Kilmacduagh, Enaghdune, and Mayo, which Sees, he says, were many years ago united with that of Tuam, which others deny, alleging that it was he himself of the royal authority that first united Kilmacduagh and the

[1] *C.S.P., Rome*, 1558-71, no. 108.

[2] The italics are ours, for the purpose of drawing attention to Dr. Moran's translation (*Abps. of Dublin*, 85-7) of the same which differs considerably from that in the *Calendar of the State Papers*, Rome. In both cases the words are given in inverted commas. Dr. Moran's translation reads : " We saw there (though we did not visit them) the archbishop of Tuam and the bishop of Clonfert, *who in the ways of this world are good and honest men. Both of them have taken the oath of allegiance to the Queen, as I have already written about others in Munster.*" These translations of Dr. Moran convey quite a different meaning from those in the text above, and are certainly not verbatim. The Italian text as given by Moran (*Appendix*, p. 416) says of these two bishops : " li quali secondo il mondo sono uomini dabbene. Tutti due hanno dati suoi voti alla Regina come gia ho scritto delli altri di Momonia." The first idea Wolf means to convey is that they are worldly men but otherwise good. Unfortunately we have not the letter that Wolf wrote about the bishops of Munster, otherwise we should be able to know what was the nature of the oath referred to. The only two bishops of Munster that certainly went over to the " reform " are Walsh of Waterford and Skiddy of Cork, and presumably it was of these that Wolf wrote. If that be so, then Bodkin and Burke are to be put in the same class, and for a mere oath of allegiance must be substituted an Oath of Supremacy. As Moran had adopted the theory that only one of the Marian bishops (Curwen) had gone over to the " Reform " he was over anxious to remove any suspicion about the orthodoxy of Bodkin and Burke. In the Vatican list of 1580 Burke is entered as a schismatic, and we have already seen that Bodkin had taken the Oath of Supremacy.

other Sees with the archbishopric. He told me that he had the archbishopric by Arthur's resignation ; and indeed if that were accepted by the Supreme Pontiff, I should deem him much fitter for the place than Arthur, because he is a man that knows how to govern, and is in good repute with the magnates of the country. The church has been for three centuries garrisoned as a fortress, Mass and other divine offices utterly disused. He has now recovered it by force and at great personal risk, and rededicated to its proper uses ; and where of yore there were but horses and other beasts now Mass is sung and said, and he himself is daily in the choir, though in Tuam there are not more than twenty or thirty houses. *He is in good repute with all, even with his enemies, the former possessors of the church.*[1]

It is well to point out at once that Bodkin and Burke were five years later pronounced schismatics by three Connaught bishops. But, taking Wolf's letter as it stands, it shows that he misjudged the situation. He did not visit the Cathedral, neither did he, as it appears, hear the other side from O'Frighil. Bodkin's antecedents should have made Wolf rather sceptical about his story. Bodkin, on 15 February, 1537, had been promoted by Henry VIII from Kilmacduagh to Tuam. But the Roman authorities ignored him, and appointed, 7 October, 1538, Arthur O'Frighil. Bodkin's story about a composition with O'Frighil is probably true. And, though Wolf admits O'Frighil was the lawful archbishop of Tuam, yet he recommends the usurper Bodkin, because he had administrative ability and was esteemed by those in power. Wolf's statement that Bodkin was " in good repute with all, even with his enemies, the former possessors of the church," from whom he recovered it by force, is probably true. He and the Bishop of Clonfert, uncle to the Earl of Clanricard, were able to hold their Sees simply through that magnate's power, and the Marian bishops of Kilmacduagh, Anaghdune, and Mayo were nobodies. But the story, swallowed by Wolf, that the Cathedral of Tuam had been, for three hundred years, in the Middle Ages, used as a stable for horses is impossible to believe.

Although Wolf succeeded in finding excellent men for

---

[1] Again Dr. Moran gives a very free translation. He says : " *His morality is unimpeached*," etc.

some of the vacant Sees, and in putting new life into the Catholic Church, yet in many respects his work did not meet with the success expected from it, and principally in regard to the schismatic bishops.

Sussex's Plan for the Rule of Ireland.

By the middle of the year 1562, Elizabeth and Sussex were quite convinced that they saw a way of subduing the whole country, reducing it to permanent obedience, and thus making the spread of the " reform " a simple matter. The correspondence between Queen and Lord Lieutenant went into the details of their schemes. On 4 July, Elizabeth wrote to Sussex [1] evincing great expectation of the civilising effect of the royal presence on the Irish chiefs :—

Sundry captains of the Irish countries having heretofore seemed desirous to receive their countries of us and to make the same inheritable according to the English manner, you shall endeavour to further that purpose, confer with the said captains, and advertise us of your opinion. You shall animate as many of the great persons as shall be inclined to come over next winter to see us, and to take degrees of honour of us.

In reply to this Sussex sent the following report :—[2]

Ireland is to be divided into six parts, viz., Ulster, Connacht, Upper Munster, Nether Munster, Leinster, Meath. The people inhabiting the whole be governed either by English laws, or by the Brehon law, which is a corrupt kind of civil law, or by Irish customs grounded on the will of the lord ; that is to say, the English people by English law, except where great lords, to maintain their extortion, use the other ; and the Irish people by the Brehon law and customs. The Brehon law doth admit th' eldest of every nation to be by election captain of his nation, which by custom hath of late been so abused as for the most part the strongest of every nation is chosen to be captain ; which kind of election causeth great numbers of idle men of war to be maintained, who bring coyne, livery, bonnaught, and all other kinds of exactions. And although the English people ought not to use any such election, yet the same is in many places used, and no part in effect is free from coyne, livery, and all Irish exactions to maintain idle men

<hr>

[1] Carew, no. 235.   [2] *Ib.*, no. 236.

of war, under colour that without such maintainance the Irish would be too strong for the English.

To devise how the English may be governed by English law without the use of these extortions, and the Irishry induced to leave their election, and, upon states granted them from the Prince, to be governed by the same law, or by certain constitutions to be made by their own assents (which I take to be the easier to be compassed at first) is the matter I mean to take in hand. No government is to be allowed in Ireland where justice is not assisted with force.

He then goes on to show how the captainry of the ruling families may be settled :—

The Irish election to the captainry of their nations is the chief cause of all their disobedience, rebellion, and other enormities. The hope that every Irishman hath to come in time to be elected captain of his nation is the cause why every of them keepeth idle men of war, that thereby he might be the stronger, and so thought the worthiest to be elected upon the next vacation. . . . Therefore every person now possessed of the captainry of his nation should be induced to leave that tenure, and to take the same from the Prince to him and his heirs male. The captain may then be persuaded to keep no more men of war within his country than are needed for his ordinary defence, and to convert the rest to a reasonable penny rent to his own commodity ; and the freeholders, answering him after that sort, may also raise an ordinary penny rent to themselves of such things as before they did wastefully consume.

Marrying or fostering with the Irish is treason which is to be qualified with loss of goods and lands during life.

Many persons within the English Pale set their lands to tenants of Irish birth and blood, to enhance their rents, whereby the English people decay and the Irish increase. This is to be remedied by Parliament.

He has some encouraging news to communicate to the Queen about various parts of the country, especially about the ruling families of Leinster.

In Upper Munster the Prince never had any duties leviable in those parts, neither have they seemed to acknowledge any duty to the Prince till of late.

The Kavanaghs being heretofore the strongest nation in Leinster . . . have of late submitted themselves in such sort as they live

6

in obedience, and answer every term to all the Queen's courts at Dublin, and be there impaneled upon quests and juries as other freeholders of English blood be. To continue this it will be necessary to continue them under the government of an England born captain, as they now be, who for his better maintainance must have the use and custody of the Queen's castle of Leighlin, Ferns, and Enniscorthy, and their territories, with the allowance of twenty harquebuziers to guard them and twenty horsemen to attend upon him, with certain kerne to be found upon the country ; which force will be sufficient to direct those people in all ordinary causes ; and if any extraordinary cause arise, he is to be further aided from the principal governor as occasion shall serve.

The Byrnes and the Tooles be in like sort reduced to come termly to Dublin to answer all the courts. Similarly for them an English captain is to be appointed.

As to Shane O'Neill, after the recent failure of the royal presence to placate him, he urges :—

It will be necessary to expel Shane O'Neile out of Tyrone, who usurps all rights belonging to the crown and the earldom of Ulster, and by spoil and rapine keeps the most part of the Irishry of Ulster in his subjection and in rebellion against the Queen. He molests all others that acknowledge their duties to her, and seeks to join with the Scots and to procure aid out of Scotland, contemning to observe the indentures made between the Queen and him at his late being in England.

DESMOND AND O'NEILL DEFIANT.

In pursuance of her policy of the beneficent influence of the royal presence to heal the many wounds in the body politic of Ireland, Elizabeth summoned Desmond and Ormond to repair to the English Court to have their controversies settled by her. But encouraged probably by the success of Shane, Desmond behaved in London very much as he had behaved at Waterford. Answering his questioners contumaciously, and refusing to apologise, he was committed to the custody of the Lord Treasurer. Elizabeth wrote to the Countess of Desmond hinting that a little gentle imprisonment would do him good, and charging her to keep the peace between her son and Ormond.

Meanwhile, Shane had returned to Ireland, having taught

Elizabeth to see Ireland partly with his eyes. Except in the matter of persuading the principal chiefs to take their land and titles from her and in establishing a Star Chamber, Elizabeth was at issue with Sussex. Sussex wished to expel Shane from Ulster, encourage the Scots against him, and then drive them out. Elizabeth wished to make the best of Shane and allure him, if possible, to keep his promises. Sussex saw in the administration of justice in the Irish parts by Brehon law a difficulty in the ordering of the country as he would have wished it. His plan was to accept the Brehons not as arbitrators but as counsel, and, by empanelling juries to find the facts, he hoped to fuse the Irish and English systems.

Shane was as troublesome as ever, and refused to meet Sussex at Dundalk, declaring that he would deal directly with the Queen. He wrote letters in plenty, sent the intriguing Terence Daniel, Dean of Armagh, to Sussex, and cleverly put the blame for his warlike action on the hurts done during his absence by the chiefs who owed obedience to him. He especially demanded the withdrawal of the garrison from Armagh. He would on no account allow this danger to his complete sovereignty over Ulster. His claim was certainly distasteful to many of the chiefs who earnestly prayed for help from Elizabeth. They resented Shane's overlordship as much as they did the Queen's. Latin was the usual language of correspondence between the English Government and the northern Irish chiefs, but Sussex was requested by Maguire to write in English, as clerks, " or other men of the country," might know his mind if he used Latin.[1]

Towards the end of the year 1562 the south of Ireland was in no more peaceful state than the north was, notwithstanding Sussex's previous report. According to his letter to the Privy Council, 28 December :—[2]

Thady O'Bryne [Brien] since his breaking out of prison with Shane's pledges,[3] hath joined with old Sir Donald O'Bryne that

---

[1] Latin seems to have been commonly understood by the educated Irish-speaking people, and English not generally known. Shane's correspondence with the English Government was either in Latin or Irish.

[2] *S.P.I., Eliz.*, vii. 58, P.R.O., London.

[3] The hostages given by Shane on his going to London.

usurped against the Earl of Thomond, and so they both assisted by some of Desmond's men begin some disorders in those parts ; for redress whereof I have sent the Mr. O'Connor with commission to assist the Earl with the Queen's Majesty's ordnance at Limerick for the taking of certain castles where they be now maintained, which I trust will ease those troubles, and if there appear further cause I will send further aid in time lest by supportations of neighbours the matter grow more perilous to him.   Some attempts have been made of late to procure certain of the Mores to join with Lynagh McShane and certain of the Byrnes and Tooles, and so rebel.   Upon persuasion that I would cause them all to be killed in their beds this Christmas, upon knowledge whereof I have so wrought with every of them as they know the untruth and remain satisfied, some disorders were of late like to have grown between O'Reilly and the English border upon him, which is staid by Sir G. Stanley and Sir G. Cusacke, and those parts remain in quiet.

Desmond Ratifies Treaty with Elizabeth.

The indefatigable Cusack, whose great idea was the conciliation of Ireland by arrangements with the native nobility, was as anxious to obtain terms for Desmond as for Shane.   Tired of his detention in England, Desmond agreed to be responsible for order in Munster.[1]

Among other things the Treaty (22 February, 1563) deals with the controversy between himself and Ormond, whereby the countries under their rule have been disordered, wasted, and spoiled in their private quarrels, arising from titles of lands, liberties, and such like.   The chief grievance seems to be against the number of hangers-on, harpers, and the rest who attended the native chiefs.   The Treaty lays down that—

All Irish laws, called " Brehon Laws " are to be abolished within those shires ; and the Earl and the Lords should be bound in penalties for the performance of this condition.   And as no small enormities occur by the continual recourse of idle men of lewd demeanor called rhymers, bards, and dice players, called " carroghes "[2] who under pretence of their travail, bring privy

---

[1] *P.C.R.I., Eliz.*, i. 485-7.
[2] I e. who profess to play at cards all the year round and made it their only occupation.

intelligence between the malefactors inhabiting those shires, to the great destruction of all true subjects, care should be taken that none of those sects, nor other evil persons, be suffered to travel within their rules ; and that proclamation be made that whosoever should maintain any such idle men within their territories should pay such fines as the President or Commissioners should think fit. And as those rhymers, by their ditties and rhymes made for divers lords and gentlemen in Ireland, in commendation and high praise of extortion, rebellion, rape, rapine, and other injustice, encourage those lords rather to follow those vices than to abandon them, and for the making of such rhymes, rewards are given by the gentlemen ; for the abolition of so heinous an abuse, order should be taken with the said Earl, the lords and gentlemen, that henceforth they do not give any manner of reward for any such lewd rhymes, under pain of forfeiting double the sum they should so pay, and that the rhymers should be fined according to the discretion of the Commissioners.

It is probable that neither Cusack's intercession nor Desmond's promises would have prevailed, had not the Earl's enforced absence left Munster in confusion. Desmond (20 December) suggested to the Privy Council that the Munster Chiefs would not consent to the civil life proposed, and desired them to furnish him with ordnance and skilful gunners to batter the strong forts and castles of the said Chiefs.[1]

The Queen was silent on these points, but urged Desmond to put down private war, and to stay in Dublin until Cusack should decide what was necessary for peace between him and Ormond.[2]

Whether we take the Government's complaint seriously about the demoralising influence of the Irish bards or rhymers, this much may be admitted that they were very useful in carrying despatches from one chieftain to another, and, when necessary, were adepts in the art of improvising verses to communicate their news, allegorically if necessary. An interesting feature of the *Fiants* of Elizabeth is the number of harpers who sued for pardon so that they might unmolested carry on their occupation.

[1] *S.P.I., Eliz.*, ix. 77, P.R.O., London.
[2] *C.S.P.I., Eliz.*, x. 8.

ANOTHER EXPEDITION AGAINST SHANE.

Although Sussex saw too clearly that the Irish problem was beyond his powers, yet he made another attempt to subdue Shane and began his preparations early in the year 1563. A general hosting was ordered, and some of the northern chiefs promised to do their best against Shane. Five hundred labourers were taken out of the Pale to cut a pass in the woods between Dundalk and Armagh, and a commission was issued [1] to help Sussex. This was directed to Hugh, Archbishop of Dublin, Primate and Chancellor, and Gerald, Earl of Kildare, for the martial government of the counties of Dublin, Kildare, Meath, Louth, Westmeath, Carlow, Wexford, Kilkenny, Tipperary, and the King and Queen's County, in the absence of the Lord Lieutenant (who was about to proceed to the North, to chastise the rebel and traitor O'Neill, to reform those parts, and reduce them to obedience) ; to take and survey the muster and array of all the inhabitants, as there should be occasion ; to cause them to be assessed and arrayed to horses and arms of light cavalry, horsemen and footmen, according to the quantity of their lands ; to cess the men in every barony for the defence of the country, and to place them to serve in such places as should seem most expedient ; to fine, chastise, and imprison such as were negligent, remiss or rebellious, and certify the amercements into the Exchequer ; to treat and parley with the King's enemies or rebels of the province ; to grant safe conduct to all who might come to treat and to return to their country ; to make and establish ordinances and agreements with them, and compel them to observe same ; to resist and punish, with fire or sword, or otherwise those enemies and rebels who should attempt any evil against the Crown or people ; to levy and enlist in the Army the people of those districts for the defence of the faithful subjects thereof ; and authorising them (the Commissioners), in the absence of the Deputy-General, to lead and govern the array of the army, and to do all things belonging to the office of general or lieutenant of the Army, so long as it should remain in the field.

[1] *P.C.R.I., Eliz.,* i. 475.

Similar commissioners were issued to the Anglo-Norman Lords and Magnates of various counties.

The overtaxed and desponding Pale scarcely answered the call to the general hosting. In the meantime Sussex collected a small force at Armagh (6 April), fortified the churchyard and advanced to Dungannon. Tirlogh Luineach, " the second man in Tyrone," and Maguire, could do nothing to help Sussex who just escaped Shane's ambush and returned to Armagh, and afterwards fell back on Drogheda. The same night Shane plundered Dundalk. Thus, this expedition, like so many others, came to nothing. Ormond and Kildare were now ordered to try negotiations with Shane, who again demanded his full rights over the northern chiefs. Shane also hinted at some understanding with the southern Geraldines, and that he might be worth conciliating.[1]

While Shane was defying the Government, Cusack was at the English Court advocating a conciliatory policy. In desperation Elizabeth sent him back with large treating powers. She was humiliated and told Sussex plainly that he had failed. A mere form of submission was the best that could be looked for from Shane, and by the Treaty concluded he gained everything and yielded nothing. He was acknowledged as The O'Neill with all the powers ever exercised under that name, and was released from all obligation of appearing before the Lord Lieutenant, and from his former promises to the Queen.

Shane's Bond ; Armagh Cathedral Restored for Divine Worship.

In his petitions of 11 September,[2] sent by Sir Thomas Cusack and Robert Flemyng,[3] Shane begged the Queen to restore the church of Armagh to its former state so that prayers might be offered there as well for her happiness and prosperity as that divine worship might be carried on there and the dead be buried, and earnestly requested that the large bell of the said church be preserved without injury

---

[1] *S.P.I., Eliz.*, viii. 58, P.R.O., London. Shane was evidently in communication with the Desmonds by friars or by rhymers.

[2] *Ib.*, ix. 7, P.R.O., London.   [3] Flemyng was Shane's secretary.

as the Lord Deputy commanded, and that all the ornaments
and furnishings of that church wherever they may be found
be restored, and thus it may be that for all time prayers may
be offered to God in that church for Her Majesty, and principally for this he advises her usual clemency, for there is
no church of any worth or decency in the northern part of
Ireland, but this alone.[1]

This simply meant that the Cathedral, instead of being
used as an ammunition depot should be restored for the
worship of God according to the Catholic Faith.   On 16 November, Shane entered into a solemn bond for £1000 to
the Queen's use [2] to carry out the above promise which he
will " strive to perpetrate."   This bond was signed in Irish
by O'Donnell, Maguire, and James Caragh O'Donilagh.
Two days later the articles of indenture were signed and sealed
by O'Neill, with a paper seal bearing the hand of Ulster,
and signed by Cusack for the Queen.   On the same day,
from his camp at Benburb, Shane sent four letters of petitions, two to the Queen, one to Cecil, and one to Cusack.
In his first letter to the Queen,[3] he thanks Her Majesty for
her goodness in pardoning him, and promises to be a faithful
subject and to allow the Cathedral to remain for divine
worship according to the direction of Her Majesty.   He
binds himself and all the chief men of his country under
oath and many penalties to carry this out, " for nothing could
be more pleasing to them than this most holy restitution,
as all the forefathers and renowned men of Tyrone are buried
there."

Shane still professed much anxiety to live clearly after
the English fashion.   An English wife was the best means
to that end, and of all eligible persons he preferred Sussex's
sister, Lady Frances Radclyffe.   An English wife would,
he said, increase his civil education and make his followers
acknowledge their duties to the Queen.   He asked Elizabeth
to give him, as a dowry, the lordship of Mellifont Abbey,
and of St. John's, Ardee, and the customs of Drogheda, and
that he might dwell at Mellifont as all his mansions were
destroyed.   Shane would thus have a powerful stronghold

---

[1] *Appendix VI*, A, B, C.   [2] *S.P.I., Eliz.*, ix. 59.   [3] *Ib.*, 62.

on the borders of the Pale and strengthen his position as overlord of the North.   But Elizabeth met this clever move by a cleverer one, that the question of an English wife must be adjourned until he had proved his love of civilisation by deeds as well as by words.[1]

Thus the fencing of these two wily rulers went on.

O'Tooles and O'Byrnes Reported Obedient.

About the time that Shane was concluding his peace with Elizabeth, Sussex and Council reported good news from the country of the O'Tooles and the O'Byrnes (22 September).[2]

The Byrnes and Tooles (saving such as were at the killing of the Talbots) do at this present live in obedient order and do termly [at stated times] repair to Dublin to the sessions and be impanelled in juries and live as other subjects of that country, and they that were at the killing of the Talbots do offer to abide our order in all disputes [?] and contentions between the Talbots and them ; the cause of their contention is Talbot, since he recovered Talbotstown in Ui Mail of your Majesty, claimeth certain rights upon them and hath made a lease of all Ui Mail binding the lessee to expel the Tooles out of the lands which they say they have ever had since the beginning, hereupon Talbot took stresses and they meant in revenge thereof to take stresses again, in the doing whereof fell out the killing of the Talbots. The Kavanaghs do live in like obedience as the Byrnes do.

Somewhat later, however (3 July, 1564), the report [3] on these families was not favourable : " The Tooles and the O'Byrnes upon the mountains here not far from Dublin, which lately were in good obedience, will not even to answer the law here but upon protection." As a matter of fact, the above episode led to very unpleasant results, of which later.

Irish Ecclesiastics Forge Papal Letters.

Even during periods of her greatest trials the Irish Church has had to bear many troubles caused by her own sons who not only forged papal dispensations but forged letters of

[1] *S.P.I.*, *Eliz.*, ix. 63-6.   [2] *Ib.*, 17, P.R.O., London.
[3] *Ib.*, xi. 21, P.R.O., London.

recommendation to the Holy See for bishoprics. In the letter [1] already referred to (12 October, 1561), sent by Fr. Wolf to Rome, the papal commissary relates :—

Malachias O'Moloney, canon of Kilmacduagh, has given false dispensations, as you will see by the copy which I send and has inculpated Christopher [Bodkin] in the practice, saying that he had seen and approved the rescript ; but Christopher has sworn in my presence upon the Gospel that he never saw or approved any such Apostolic rescript ; *and I find many reasons for holding that he would not have seen it, though, it had been a true Apostolic rescript.*[2]

And this Malachias I hold to be a forger of Apostolic letters ; nor has he dared to present himself before the Archbishop when summoned. Therefore, I desire to know how we should deal with this Malachias, rebel as he is, and unable to produce any original rescript, to which he can give credit.

Again, we confess our inability to understand Fr. Wolf's procedure. Christopher Bodkin, he admits, was a schismatic, intruded into Tuam by Henry VIII, and at this time also an adherent of the Queen, and he admits that the lawful Archbishop was Arthur O'Frighil, and yet he acquiesces in O'Moloney's summons before the intruder. At the same time Wolf also admits that Bodkin would be a most unlikely man to see any papal rescript, as a royal bishop. With all Wolf's anxiety to secure efficient and suitable bishops for Irish Sees, there is something suspicious about his dealings with Bodkin. Wolf was discredited some years later, and retired from the Society of Jesus.

Another case of those troubles caused by ecclesiastics

---

[1] *C.S.P.*, *Rome*, 1558-71, no. 108.

[2] The italics are ours. Again we must draw attention to Dr. Moran's suppression of facts (*Abps. of Dublin*, p. 86). He omits the above passage in italics, manifestly because it shows that Bodkin, a royal Bishop, dare not receive any papal rescript. But in the *Appendix* (p. 418), in which he gives the Italian text of Wolf's letter, he gives portion of the passage thus : " allegandomi molte ragioni," (alleging to me many reasons), but omits the remainder of the sentence. He inserts these three words rather to fit in with the preceding phrase and as it were to give the reasons why Bodkin never saw or approved of the rescript which Molony had in his possession, but in reality they should be taken with the omitted passage that follows, giving the reasons why Bodkin would not have seen any rescripts at all sent by Rome.

proceeding to Rome to seek bishoprics without commendatory
letters is given by Wolf in the letter referred to.   He states :—

Fourteen persons have left Ireland for Rome without letters
from me ; one of them is the Dean of Raphoe, his purpose being
to solicit that bishopric [1]

He is, as I am informed by persons worthy of credit, *a very
rude, coarse man*, fitter to be a soldier than a Churchman, *and his
appointment to the See would be the very ruin of that Church.   And
being informed that for going to Rome he needed a testimonial from
me, he said that he would leave my testimonial out of account, and
so he went.* [2]   Believe him not if he say that he knew not of my
visit to Ireland, for there is no one either heretic or Catholic that
knows it not, seeing that I caused it to be published in every part
of the country.

On this subject of bishoprics it may be interesting to recall
the stand taken by the Bishops of Ross and Raphoe at the
Council of Trent in the session dealing with Holy Orders.
During the debates they lamented that many persons in
Ireland when nominated to benefices neglected to receive
ordination, whilst they seized on the fruits and revenues
attached to these benefices ; and also that too many bishops
were appointed, receiving their title *in partibus infidelium*, and
hence often occasioned annoyance to the bishops in whose Sees
they resided.   A remarkable case of alleged deception occurred
in 1563 in the diocese of Clogher.   It is set out at length in
a letter [3] (1 September 1563) of Pope Pius IV to Fr. Wolf :—

The pope is informed by Odo Icearballan [Hugh O'Carolan],
Bishop of Clogher, that, whereas he had been appointed by Apostolic
Authority to the then in a certain manner vacant See of Clogher
and been duly consecrated thereto, and had gotten possession,
or what was tantamount to possession, of the governance and
administration of the said church, and had continued to hold

---

[1] Wolf had recommended Donald MacConigail who was the bearer of
his letter to the Holy See, and who was appointed to the See.

[2] Once more we have to draw attention to Dr. Moran's suppression of
disagreeable facts.   He omits the passage in italics altogether in his English
translation (*ib.*, p. 86) and in the Italian Appendix (p. 419), because it would
show the Dean of Raphoe in an unfavourable light, namely, going to Rome
in a spirit of disobedience to the papal commissary without whose letters he
should not depart.

[3] *C.S.P., Rome*, no. 275, *Four Masters, ad an.*

the same in peace for the space of 28 years one Remund Mamathunian [MacMahon], who passed for a clerk, addressed himself to the Apostolic See, and alleging the said Church to be void, and omitting all mention of him Odo, the bishop in possession, did by suggestion of falsehood and suppression of the truth procure of the same authority his appointment, or at least a commission, by Letters Apostolic to the Archbishop of Armagh, for his appointment to the said See,[1] which Letters he presented to the said Archbishop, who because they omitted all mention of the said Bishop Odo, pronounced them to be surreptitious, against which pronouncement the said Reimund, having, it is said, appealed, died pending the appeal, and thereafter Cornelius Macardile, who likewise passed as a clerk, procured of the same authority his appointment to the said church [2] as void by the death of the said Reimund, still without mention made of him Bishop Odo, though he was still living and in possession, or at least the said Cornelius procured a commission for his appointment by Letters Apostolic to the said Archbishop, which letters were presented to the then living Archbishop of Armagh Donat Otayg [O'Taig, 1560], who being unable to pronounce for, would yet not pronounce against, his intimate friend the said Cornelius, and therefore bade the said Bishop Odo and Cornelius to address themselves to the said Court for the decision of their claims, but the said Cornelius, rather than come to Rome for the investigation of his pretended right, did not scruple to use the temporal power forcibly to oust and despoil the said Bishop Odo of his Church and his long occupancy thereof.[3]

And whereas it is stated at the close of the said information that a matter of this nature may more readily be investigated in those parts of Ireland where a sufficiency of witnesses to the facts may be found than in that Court at which, as above set forth, the said Cornelius is not disposed to present himself, for which cause the said Bishop Odo has made humble supplication to the Pope, that of his Apostolic benignity he would deign to remit the trial and decision of the case to some just man in the said parts ; the Pope therefore, assuming that the state of the case is substantially as herein set forth, hereby refers the causes that are or may be between Bishop Odo and the said Cornelius and all others, jointly or severally, to the said David Wolf or his

[1] O'Carolan was appointed in 1535, but took the Oath of Supremacy in 1542. MacMahon was appointed in 1546.

[2] Appointed 29 May, 1560.

[3] Odo is careful to omit that he himself had been deposed for heresy in 1557.

deputy or deputies, to be decided summarily, quietly and without judicial forms etc.

The usual formula, dealing with the trial, pains, and penalties, follows.

The diocese of Clogher provides another instance of this unworthy struggle for episcopal honours and possessions in the year 1568. It was an extraordinary state of affairs in view of Elizabeth's efforts to find bishops for some of these dioceses. The Holy See, taking for granted, on the authority of MacMahon, that the See was vacant through the verting of O'Carolan, appointed him. MacMahon, dying at Rome *c.* 1557–1560, McArdle was appointed to succeed him. O'Carolan, having then probably returned to his allegiance with Rome, resented the intruder. McArdle, however, continued to act as bishop, and was granted bene-fices for his support. One conclusion seems clear from all this, namely, that the diocese of Clogher must have been in an otherwise settled condition, from the Catholic point of view, to have been able to bear such a contention. Both O'Carolan and McArdle were in other respects unworthy of the epis-copate ; they were denounced as " simoniaci et concubinarii."

THE EMPEROR PETITIONS ELIZABETH FOR TOLERATION FOR CATHOLICS.

So far the " reform " was only a half-hearted affair ; some Acts of Parliament, fines for non-attendance at Pro-testant service, and the appointment of a few Protestant bishops. There is now evidence of increased activity in religious matters on both sides. A few letters will show the procedure adopted and incidentally how Elizabeth's mind was hardening against Catholics. On 2 September, 1563, Cardinal Charles Borromeo wrote to Bishop Crivelli, Nuncio in Spain, telling him that the Pope is much affected by the pitiable plight of the Catholics of England caused by persecutions, and considers that the best means of aiding them is to solicit the Catholic King's intervention to induce the Queen of England to allow the Catholics in that kingdom the use of churches in which they may celebrate and hear the Divine Offices and the Mass, and further to release those poor bishops and other Catholics whom she has now for so long a time kept in prison on the score of religion.[1]

And the Emperor Ferdinand I wrote to the Legates at the Council of Trent, acknowledging their letter of 23 August in which they solicited him to intercede with the Queen for a partial toleration of Catholic worship. On the same day he wrote to the Queen acknowledging the clemency which in deference to his previous letters she has shown to the imprisoned prelates, and craving for the Catholics at large the indulgence suggested by the Legates to the Council, namely, the use of at least one church in every city in which without molestation or hindrance to celebrate the Divine Offices and Sacraments.[2]

On the 3 November, the Queen wrote to the Emperor that it was indeed a matter of no small moment to treat so leniently men who had so insolently and openly put themselves in opposition to our laws and the peace of our loving loyal subjects, chief among whom were those who during the reigns of those most noble Princes, our father and brother, set mind and hand to work openly by speech and by writing, and that though they were not private persons but magistrates, to commend to others that very doctrine which they now so obstinately reject. Yet these are the men whom we, in deference to your request, have by our grace, but certainly with no small offence to our people, spared.

Now, as to your Majesty's further intercession in their behalf, to wit, that there be certain churches assigned to them in their several cities in which, safely and without let, to celebrate by themselves their divine offices; this request is of such a kind and beset with so many difficulties that we cannot without hurt alike to our country and our own honour, concede it. And therefore, we . . . can now in no wise foster and nourish by excessive indulgence the perversity of the same men, and the no less or yet greater presumptuousness of their likes.[3]

According to Elizabeth it was no crime on her part and her father's and brother's to impose on Catholics the acceptance of the State religion, but it was for Catholics to worship according to their conscience and for bishops to warn their flocks against the lately-introduced service drawn up in England and imposed on an unwilling people. Elizabeth's

---

[1] *C.S.P., Rome*, no. 148. [2] *Ib.*, no. 278. [3] *Ib.*, no. 287.

reasons for not allowing public worship to Catholics are that it was " in opposition to our laws and the peace of our loving, loyal subjects." The first reason may be allowed, but the second does not bear examination. Her " loving, loyal subjects," i.e. Protestants, were a very small minority, and Elizabeth as a ruler of a nation took no account of the peace of the majority of her people. The request of one church in every city for Catholic worship was indeed a very modest one.

Both Sides Move in Religious Matters.

Cecil himself was not idle in endeavouring to find ways and means of pushing on the " reform " in Ireland, for a Minute in his handwriting in the State Papers, and dated Windsor, 7 August, 1563, shows his scheme to be : " That the Dean of Armagh [Terence Daniel] may be Primate. That the Primate [Loftus] may be Bishop of Kildare and Dean of St. Patrick's [Dublin]. That the Bishop of Kildare [Craik] may be Bishop of Meath. The Chantor of Armagh to be Dean." [1]

It does not appear that Terence Daniel had applied for the post, but it is not improbable that he was a party to the proceeding, and that he had been consulted by the Lord Lieutenant, whatever his motives may have been. He was as mysterious as Shane in his dealings with Elizabeth and the Government. On 15 October, Elizabeth wrote to the Earl of Sussex [2] (the draft being in Cecil's handwriting) stating her pleasure on these points :—

We are moved to allow that the Dean of Armagh should be made Archbishop there, and the Archbishop [Loftus] there to be Archbishop of Dublin, and the Archbishop of Dublin, now being our Chancellor there, to be eased, as he hath often times desired and as his great years do require, of the burden both of the bishoprick and of the Chancellorship, for which purpose we would he were so friendly used by you, or some other, that his said suit might be renewed, and to have a pension during his life of £200 by year, as Sir Thomas Cusake shall devise with you. And for the bishopric of Meath we have determined to bestow

---

[1] *S.P.I., Eliz.*, viii. 63.   Shirley, 124.   [2] *Loc. cit*

the same upon a honest learned man of that country named Brady, whose learning and sufficientry is here so well recommended upon proof, as we think him very meet for the same ; and upon communication with the Chancellor there, and knowledge from himself of his contentation to leave the same, we mean to appoint Sir Tho. Cusack to be our chancellor there.

Later (23 July, 1564), Sir T. Wrothe wrote to Lord Robert Dudley in reference to Terence Daniel : " The Dean of Armagh to be Bishop of Armagh would promise to do much with Shane O'Neill, and some think he would perform it." [1]

A week after her letter to Sussex on the bishoprics she again wrote to him (21 October) " that upon good report and proof had of the good zeal, learning, and ability to preach " of Hugh Brady, she preferred him to the bishopric of Meath " being presently void," " where he may yield good fruit to that his native country." Sussex is to have the requisite letters " issued for the election and admission of him orderly thereunto," and similar letters for the restitution of the temporalities. On account of his poverty the payment of first-fruits is not to be demanded of him until he has been twelve months in his bishopric. [2]

The word " election " in the letter refers, of course, to Elizabeth's own election of him, and not to any procedure on the part of the Chapter of Meath. Walsh, the Catholic bishop, was still at large, and presumably looking after his diocese. Brady did not delay in coming to Ireland, and, 10 December, wrote to Cecil :—[3]

After a long and troublesome passage (thanks to God) I arrived in Dublin in the 3 of December, where delivering the Queen's Majesty letters and your honour's to the Lord Lieutenant, he comfortably and friendly received me, whose great wisdom mixed with much humanity I cannot but commend, and if I have not hereafter a great comfort and stay of him, in my opinion it shall be my own default. . . . The day of my consecration is appointed the 19 of this month, the charges is very great, besides that I tarried at the waterside 19 days for passage, I assure your honour it hath and will beggar me, *sed quorsum haec.* I leave to trouble

---

[1] *S.P.I., Eliz.,* xi. 35, P.R.O., London.
[2] *P.C.R.I., Eliz.,* i., 484-5.
[3] *S.P.I., Eliz.,* ix. 69. Shirley, 130.

your honour any further at this time, purposing hereafter if God
permit it, to write at large from Dunboyne the town where I
was born, this 10 of December, your honour's continual orator.
—Hughe Bradie.

The See of Down and Connor had been vacant since
1562 by the death of Eugene Magennis. Although he had
become King's bishop in the reign of Henry VIII, and
returned to his allegiance to the Church in that of Mary,
shortly after his death, as it would appear, a petition [1] was
sent to the Queen, apparently by William Piers, Constable
of Carrickfergus, asking her to prefer " some worthy learned
man to the bishopric of Down within that Pale (a goodly
benefice) to the intent that he being assisted by certain Irish
prelates near adjoining who are very zealously affected,
may with special severity establish order in the Church."
The most that can be said about these unnamed Irish prelates,
is that they were willing to show allegiance and fealty to
Elizabeth as their Queen. The northern bishops, generally,
were willing to show the same fealty to her.

In other directions also Elizabeth was displaying religious
activity. Between April and October, 1563,[2] she presented
no fewer than twenty-four clerics to vicarages, rectories,
prebends, and dignities in the dioceses of Dublin, Meath,
Cashel, Ossory, Waterford and Lismore, Ferns, Emly, and
Ardagh.[3] Dublin and Ferns were held by Protestant bishops ;
Meath, Ossory, Cashel, and Emly were vacant, the two first by
royal deprivation, the third and fourth by death ; Waterford
and Lismore, and Cork, were occupied by " reform " bishops.
Thus, Elizabeth found it possible to promote men, some of
them bearing Irish names, to Cathedral and parochial positions in which she expected them to garner the fruit of her
" reform." This action was probably the result of certain
decisions come to by the Privy Council (noted October, 1564)
for the ordering of the Irish people ; " to cause the people
to resort to Common Prayer and to be instructed to understand the articles of their faith and commandments of God,
and to place convenient ministers for this purpose in places

---

[1] Shirley, 132-3.   [2] *P.C.R.I., Eliz.,* i., 477-81.
[3] See *Appendix III.*

convenient." [1]   On the other hand, Fr. Wolf, papal Nuncio in Ireland, was endeavouring to provide for the Catholics of the Pale.   In a commission, dated Limerick, 7 December, 1563, to Thady Newman, priest of the diocese of Dublin, he tells how he is prevented from visiting Leinster on account of the dangers of the journey.   His movements throughout the country were well watched by Elizabeth's spies.   He gives Newman power to absolve in all cases, no matter how enormous and grave, of heresy and schism, having exacted private or public adjuration and imposed a salutary penance. All cases were to be absolved gratis and without hope of any payment.[2]   Thus ended the fifth year of Elizabeth's reign.

COMMISSIONERS REPORT ON STATE OF RELIGION.

On 20 October, 1563, Sir Thomas Wrothe and Sir Nicholas Arnold, appointed commissioners for Ireland, were instructed by Elizabeth to take the muster of the garrisons, and remedy all abuses and disorders there.   They were especially to take care that in no company should there be more than five or six Irish soldiers ; that limit had been laid down in previous orders.   On the same day a second memorial was issued to them as follows :—[3]

To our other instructions it is requisite you make [privy] those whose names are expressed in your commission. We now give you apart further instructions, not to be imparted to others.

1. You are to enquire " in what sort our laws are there observed for the orders of religion, and what disorders you find therein, and by what causes the same do arise, and to note well who be of our nobility and Council therein conformable, and who not."

2. " Because it hath been always required by our good subjects there, to have some university erected in that realm," we at this time intend to take in hand the erection of some public schools of learning in Dublin, " for the maintainance both of teachers and readers, and also of some numbers of learners and scholars, to be chosen of our natural subjects of that realm." We understand " that the college of St. Patrick's in our said city, whereof there lacketh now a dean by the death of the late Bishop of Kildare,

---

[1] *S.P.I.*, *Eliz.*, ix. 51, P.R.O., London.   Loftus, *Annals,* 1563.
[2] *S.P.I.*, *Eliz.*, ix. 68.   Shirley, 128.   [3] Carew, nos. 240-1.

might be well converted to be a place of public teaching, reading,
and learning ; and the revenues thereof, being well ordered, might
well sustain a sufficient number of readers, teachers, preachers,
and of a competent number of scholars." At your first coming
there you shall communicate with such as you find favourable
thereto how the house and possessions may be converted to such
a good purpose, " and how the prebendaries and others having
interest, and being not meet to be continued there (for teaching
or learning), may for the present time be recompensed." " We
would also know how the cathedral church of Dublin is endowed
in possessions, and what number and sorts of persons are maintained therewith, and how the foundation thereof is maintained
and kept ; because, if anything were therein necessary to be
reformed, upon knowledge we might give order thereto."

We have ordered that one—Bradby [Brady], one of that nation,
a graduate in Oxford, being a Professor of Divinity, and well
recommended for his conversation, shall be Bishop of Meath.
You shall see him furthered with such credit as shall be requisite,
and we think him not unmeet for you to confer withal in the
matter of St. Patrick's.

When the Commissioners arrived in Dublin in February,
1564, they found Leix and Offaly again in rebellion, not a
groat in the Treasury, and the £11,000 that they brought,
quite inadequate for the carrying on of the Government.
Sussex resented their interference in matters of the army.
Wrothe, rather nervous about his duty, and anxious to deal
out justice even-handed, was consequently unpopular. Arnold, a rougher type, had little respect for Wrothe's finer
feelings, and a coolness sprang up between them. Wrothe
was thus early anxious to be recalled, but had to continue
his unlovable task.[1]

Their letter to the Privy Council, 16 March,[2] is worth
recording in full :—

Concerning religion and the favourers of it, we are sorry to
say that we find blind ignorance, the leader to superstition, so
set by, as it is hard to persuade willingness to hear the truth
soberly taught, and yet there appeareth in this people fear to
offend, wherefore they be not to be despaired but to be hoped of.
For those we have to do with, we find conformable to laws, and

---

[1] Bagwell, ii. 68.   [2] *S.P.I., Eliz.*, x. 34. Shirley, 139.

the judges with others of the lawyers ready as they seem to us to execute the laws for religion, and accordingly have promised us, now in the assizes and sessions to inquire specially of defaulters against those laws for religion ; [1] yet with this caution, as we thought good that they meddle not with the simple multitude now at first, but with one or two boasting mass men in every shire—that it may be seen that the punishment of such men is meant.

The Lord Lieutenant hath willed the Bishops here to agree upon injunctions which his Lordship will set forth with authority, they will surely do much good. Here are two good Bishops of Armagh and Meath, their lives be unblamed and their diligence in preaching worthy to be commended especially Meath. The Chancellor is civil and conformable, and will do as he seemeth what authority shall command. The rest of the Bishops as we hear be all Irish, we need say no more. Here is also one Beard a preacher who seemeth honest and preacheth well, and finding this country so far backward in religion, we somewhat doubted even amongst our companions in commission, whether the offer of the altering of Saint Patrick's would be so accepted as it ought for there be amongst us few earnest favourers of religion but the Master of the Rolls [John Parker], we therefore so used the matter amongst them by occasion offered by them that they have desired us to be humble suitors to the Queen's Majesty that the said College may be altered to the same that her Majesty hath appointed, and have entered into device how the prebendaries that will not be conformable may be without wrong by law compelled. So as now her Majesty may choose whether she will do it at their humble suit and request or of herself ; and if her Majesty meaneth to proceed upon their suit, that we may have letters accordingly. If we had commission by special words to visit, it would, as well for Christ's Church, as Saint Patrick's, have furthered very much. The time till we hear by your Lordship's, her Majesty's pleasure concerning these things, we trust shall not be much hindrance, as we hope to use it, for we will be doing as other things will give us leave.

In one sentence they summed up the whole episcopal situation, that is, as far as they were aware : " The rest of the bishops be all Irish, we need say no more." On Loftus and Brady alone could they rely for any real " reform " work. In St. Patrick's Cathedral they feared opposition

[1] I.e. the law of compulsory attendance at Common Prayer.

from the prebendaries. As will be seen later, these ecclesiastics, with the exception of a few appointed by Loftus, were all Catholics even in the year 1574. As to the people the Commissioners found them confirmed in Catholicism and unwilling to listen to the " reform " tenets, but ready to obey the ordinary law. They were not to be molested in their religious practices for the present, but a Mass-priest could not be tolerated in public. Even the lawyers and judges could not be relied upon to urge the " reform "; they, with the gentry of the Pale, were still faithful to the Catholic Church, very few of them having either taken or observed the Oath of Supremacy. So far, the " reform " was a crude, uninspiring affair. There was nothing of the missionary spirit in its bishops. Their work should be " comfortable " and " acceptable " as to " a man fearing God," as Craik expressed it. And when it was not agreeable they petitioned for translation. Loftus and Brady alone showed any spirit of adventure. No doubt, Elizabeth succeeded in getting a number of clerics to accept benefices, but these were mere jobs. It did not mean that thereby they were accomplishing any great work for the " reform." For the most part they were " unprofitable workmen " like Curwen.

Thomas, Earl of Sussex, set forth a proclamation about the end of the year 1563 against the meetings of the Friars and Popish priests in Dublin and that none should lie within the gates of the City : also a tax upon every housekeeper that missed coming to Church on Sundays, and had it collected. How much the sum was does not appear, but being exactly gathered in his time many came to Church rather than pay that tax. At first they would go to Mass in the morning and to Church in the afternoon, but to prevent that, a roll of the housekeepers' names was called by the wardens of each parish. This was special legislation for Dublin City where friars and priests could not be tolerated, but outside the city the simple people were not to be molested as at the assizes verdicts could not be obtained against them for their non-attendance at Common Prayer. An example, however, made of a Mass-priest might, it was thought, provide a very salutary lesson.

Elizabeth Appoints Irish-Speaking Bishop to Kildare.

Alexander Craik, appointed by Elizabeth to Kildare, 21 August, 1560, died early in 1564.[1] He had spent little time in his diocese, and found his deanery of St. Patrick's a more congenial living. During his short occupancy " he did more mischief to his See than his successors have been ever able to repair." [2] By the consent of the Dean and Chapter of Kildare, 2 June, 1561 (whatever that may mean in reality), he exchanged almost all the manors and lands of the bishopric with Patrick Sarsfield, for some tithes of little value.[3] " By this exchange the very ancient See of Kildare was reduced to a most shameful poverty."

As Loftus of Armagh and Brady of Meath were the most active of the " reformers " they considered themselves time and again bound to advise Cecil on Church matters. Now that Kildare was vacant, and as they were evidently looking after the " reform " in Dublin, Curwen being of little or no account, they addressed a letter from that city to Cecil, 3 March, 1564,[4] informing him that on St. Stephen's Day Mr. Beard, vicar of Greenwich, had arrived and had joined them " in preaching of the Gospel, to our comfort and furtherance of our business." It is to be presumed that the preaching took place in Dublin, and possibly in Meath, but certainly not in Armagh. " As there is great need of such " preachers, but lack of living, they beg Elizabeth to bestow on Beard the bishopric of Kildare, vacant by the death of Craik. But as the bishopric is worth only about £100 a year [about £1200 *1914 value*] something *in commendam* [5] would be useful. Rather, however, than be deprived of his

---

[1] He was buried in St. Patrick's Cathedral, under the altar at the north side.

[2] Harris, *Ware's Bishops*, 391.

[3] The lands he gave in exchange were: the manor of Bishop's-Court near Oughterard, Bishop's-Court near Ana-Liffey, Carne, Ballbrindan, Clowan-Curry (Cloncurry), Killieghmore, Killcrants, Ballyloghglass, Bellachstown, and Clonangory, for which large estates he received back in exchange the Rectories, Churches or chapels of Disert-dermod (Castledermot), Kynnagh, and Bally-Cutland in Co. Kildare (in the diocese of Dublin), with the tithes thereunto belonging. (*Loc. cit.*)

[4] *S.P.T., Eliz.*, x. 25. Shirley, 133.

[5] A benefice to be held conjointly with another for a period for the purpose of increasing the revenue of the holder.

services, they were willing to grant him some of their revenue until he should be provided for.

Elizabeth did not see her way to comply with their wishes, the chief reason being that she had found one of the prebendaries of St. Patrick's, Robert Daly, was well able to preach in the Irish tongue. It will be remembered that Craik's complaint of his failure to " reform " in Kildare was his inability to preach in that language. Accordingly, the Queen directed letters [1] to be made out for Daly's installation, and, as the bishopric was only worth about £50, " as we hearsay," he was to have the deanery of St. Patrick's, and the vicarage which he already held in Dublin diocese. [2]

THE SEE OF MEATH A SEA OF TROUBLES.

Nothing shows more vividly the abhorrence of Irish Catholics for the Protestant bishops thrust upon them than a letter of Brady of Meath, 14 March, 1564, to Cecil. [3] Scarcely three months in his diocese, yet he feels constrained to write this gloomy but illuminating letter, one of the most important on the whole subject of the " reform " at this period :—

My humble duty with like humble thanks for your goodness, I now, right honourable, by experience find that whereof perhaps I have doubted, *episcopatum potius esse onus quam honor* [the bishopric to be a burden rather than an honour], If I should respect quietness of life and contentation of mind, I had rather be a stipendiary priest [4] in England than Bishop of Meath in Ireland. O what a sea of troubles have I entered into, storms rising on every side, the ungodly lawyers [5] are not only sworn enemies to the truth [" reform " tenets] but also for lack of due

---

[1] *S.P.I., Eliz.,* x. 49.   Shirley, 149.

[2] He was prebendary of Clonmethan and held also the vicarage of Swords. During his eighteen years' occupancy of the See, Daly was " three times turned, in a manner almost naked, out of his house and plundered of his goods by the rebels.   It was thought that the third outrage was the cause of his death, for he died in 1582 soon after it happened." (Harris, *Ware's Bishops,* 391.)

[3] *S.P.I., Eliz.,* x. 30.   Shirley, 135.

[4] The term " Priest " was still used by Protestants of this period as a fit one for their ministers.

[5] In this, Brady differs from the Commissioners, but, it may be presumed, that he knew more about the lawyers than they did

execution of law, the out-throwers [disturbers] of the country ;
the ragged clergy are stubborn and ignorantly blind, so as there
is left little hope of their amendment ; the simple multitude is
through continual ignorance hardly to be won, so as I find *angustiae
undique* [troubles everywhere] ; my Lord Chancellor [Curwen of
Dublin] preacheth now and then, primate [Loftus] diligently,
Mr. Beard is a good helper in this business, for whom I beseech
your honour provide some stay of living, the lack of him would
much discourage us, the great gravity and zealous wisdom of
Sir Thomas Wroth and Sir Nicholas Arnold [Elizabeth's Com-
missioners] shall, and doth, further much God's cause here, whose
diligence and uprightness in the service they be sent for, shall
better appear hereafter than now I can write of ; for my own
diligence I have rather others to speak, than myself, and yet this
far I dare presume, by God's help to do as much good as any other
[who] could be sent hither, for a great number of the simple people,
and specially where I was born [Dunboyne] are greedy hearers,
and such as I trust will be unfeignedly won ; there is not much
done concerning St. Patrick's, and yet I fear not the good success,
if it be not hindered thence, which God defend [forbid] it should.
The state here, I may say to your honour, is both fickle and strange,
the malefactors increase and are boldened, and the chief ministers
discouraged, and in effect unabled ; let it be looked to betime,
for else there may follow that [which] I would not see ; of the
rebellion late attempted by the O'Moores I need say nothing,
for that the Queen's Majesty is sufficiently instructed of the whole
proceedings thereof, I trust it will be soon ended.

Such was the state of religion " in the best peopled diocese
and the best governed country " in Ireland ; " the ragged
clergy " stubborn in their profession of the Catholic faith,
the people " hardly to be won " over to the " reform," the
lawyers by their regard for justice a stumbling block to
any advance, and all this in a diocese where so much was
expected to be accomplished.

Brady's reference to St. Patrick's Cathedral has to do
with the scheme for transforming it into a University. This
had been attempted on various occasions in many reigns.
The present scheme, which Brady approved of, provided for
a principal or provost, two preachers, a reader or professor
of divinity, a reader of philosophy, twelve fellows, forty
scholars, a master of the grammar school, etc. This scheme

was endorsed in Cecil's hand, October, 1563.[1] But in the following February, on account of the disturbed state of the country, Cusack recommended to Cecil that the scheme should be suspended.[2] Meanwhile, there was no sort of education for the Protestant clergy to whose ignorance and inability to preach the *State Papers* abundantly testify. Indeed many of these clerics who conformed were sent to Oxford or Cambridge for three and four years, enjoying the revenues of their benefices at the same time.

The Mr. Beard to whose diligence in preaching the Gospel Brady testifies was the Vicar of Greenwich who arrived in Ireland on St. Stephen's Day, 1563. The " reformers " around Dublin relied on an obliging English minister to help them in their preaching. Craik had already brought over one Ledwich. " For as there is great need of such " preachers, wrote Brady and Loftus to Cecil, 3 March, recommending Beard, " So we would be right sorry, that for lack of [a] living, we should be deprived of his help."

Curwen Desires an English Bishopric.

Curwen, the compromiser in many reigns, and an " unprofitable workman," was likewise tired of the business of " reform," because he could accomplish little or nothing, but more probably because he had not set his heart in it. In a letter,[3] 3 April, to Elizabeth, he pleaded : " I am insufficient and not liable to serve your Grace in the office of Chancellor of this realm and to accomplish the ministry belonging to the Archbishop here." He sees nothing incongruous in pleading that he had served Her Highness as well as her sister Mary for eight years and a half. In recompense for this service he besought Her Majesty to bestow upon him some bishopric in England, " to spend the rest of my life in the service of God, . . . where I trust I should recover better health than I have had in this realm." But if there was no suitable bishopric, the Queen might give him some " other spiritual promotion " to the yearly value of his archbishopric, so that he may be able to keep

---

[1] *S.P.I., Eliz.,* ix. 49. Shirley, 126-8. [2] *C.S.P.I., Eliz.,* x. 12.
[3] *S.P.I., Eliz.,* x. 43. Shirley, 142.

his old servants, and " continue some part of the hospitality which hitherto I have ever kept." If, however, Her Majesty cannot accede to this request, then he would beg to be relieved of his Chancellorship, and receive instead " some pension or other living *in commendam* to supply the small value of my said bishopric, which was well helped by the fee of the office of Chancellor." He is afraid that Her Majesty has heard some evil reports of him,[1] and consequently if he left the archbishopric and was not rewarded by another, it would " engender slander against me that I was deprived of it."

On the same day, he wrote to Cecil [2] in identical terms, but added some items that are worth recording. He assures Cecil that he would be pleased to have a pension of £200 yearly (about £2400, *1914 value*), being more in need of an augmentation than a diminution of his income, and that he spent every penny of his revenue as Archbishop and as Chancellor in serving Her Majesty. His petition did not succeed in its objective until three years later. In the meantime he was continued in the archbishopric, was deprived of the Chancellorship, and received no prebend *in commendam*.

CURWEN DISAPPROVES OF SUPPRESSION OF ST. PATRICK'S.

As Curwen was foiled in his attempt to get clear of Dublin and the troublesome " reform," he was determined to get his own back on his enemies in his own church. The idea of suppressing St. Patrick's and converting it into a University had been put aside on account of the disturbed state

---

[1] Strype, *Life of Parker*, i. 221. Strype, in his life of Archbishop Parker, tells that he met with a letter written about 1562 by Adam Loftus and addressed to the Archbishop of Canterbury, wherein Loftus " hinted how his grace of Canterbury had promised to aid him in all church causes of Ireland, especially for removing the Archbishop of Dublin " ; and Strype adds, that Curwen " was, as described by the Archbishop of Armagh [Loftus], a known enemy, and labouring under open crimes, which although he shamed not to do, I am almost ashamed to mention." From this passage Mant concludes that " Archbishop Curwen's character suffered under some heavy moral imputations, as we have already seen his unsteadiness as to religion " (i. 282).

[2] *S.P.I., Eliz.*, x. 44. Shirley, 145.

of the country. Curwen now sums up courage to write to the Earl of Pembroke [1] telling him that " the notion of the change cometh of certain greedy persons which hath repaireth out of this realm to the court, which look more for their own gain than any profit to the contrary, thinking at the dissolving thereof [of St. Patrick's] to have the prebends to farm at a low price, as divers of them have made their boast here." He then continues :—

A University will be but of small profit for here be no promotions to bestow upon clerks when they be learned, which is requisite of necessity, and an university here were unprofitable, for the Irish enemies under colour of study would send their friends hither, who would learn the secrets of the country, and advertise [acquaint] them thereof, so that the Irish rebels should by them know the privacy of the English Pale, whereof we are like to grow no small hurt, and besides these the prebends be parochial churches, having cure of soul, and therefore needful to be bestowed upon ancient men, and not amongst young scholars, the whole profit of them standeth in tithes, without any temporal land, which now, corn being extremely dear, be somewhat worth, but if the price of corn shall fall, they would be of no small value to help any number of scholars ; moreover the change of the church would be a destruction to the Archbishop here who hath not one benefice within the English Pale to bestow upon learned men, but only the prebends of St. Patrick's which be in number not past 24, so that if they be altered, he shall not be able to have one learned man to preach God's word in his diocese, and where the deanery being now void and they prohibited to elect them a new dean, according to the ordinance of that Church, it may please your honour to be a suitor for them to her Highness to license them to proceed to the election of a new dean wherein ye shall do a meritorious deed to Godward, and bind the poor company of that church, and me and all other successors to be your daily orators. Thus being bold to trouble your honour with my poor suits I humbly take my leave, committing your good Lord to Almighty God who long preserve the same in health, with increase of much honour. At Dublin the 21st of June 1564. Your honour's to command—H. Dublin, Chanc.

---

[1] *S.P.I., Eliz.*, xi. 13. Shirley, 151. Pembroke was one of the Lords of the Privy Council, to whom the settlement of the " Reformation " was particularly entrusted by the Queen.

The underhand work that was engaged in by the supporters of the " reform " is not very edifying. In the event of the suppression of St. Patrick's Cathedral a profitable business might be done in the matter of securing the revenues of the prebends and paying a certain sum to Elizabeth towards the upkeep of the University that was to take its place. Who the supporters of this scheme were we do not for certainty know. It is clear, however, that Curwen was not anxious to see his old friends, the Catholic prebendaries, now old men, deprived of their incomes ; also he pleads the harm that would be done to the people who would then not have pastors to minister unto them, and the indignity offered to an Archbishop of Dublin who would have no prebends to bestow on his friends. Curwen was no stern " reformer " ; he was anxious to let matters slide, or get away from the troublesome diocese.

PAPAL LETTER TO SHANE O'NEILL ; COMMENDS HIS STEADFASTNESS IN THE FAITH.

Although Loftus had been consecrated Archbishop of Armagh, 3 March, 1563, by Curwen in Dublin, he had not dared to present himself in his episcopal city. The diocese was bereft of its Catholic primate by the death of Donat O'Taig or O'Tighe sometime before the August of 1562, and Fr. Wolf, papal commissary, thought it important to have the vacancy filled without delay. He found a worthy man in Richard Creagh or Crevagh, the son of Nicholas Creagh, an extensive and respectable merchant of Limerick. Richard received a classical education in his native city, and was particularly skilled in Spanish which was to be useful to him as a trader with Spain. On one occasion, having laden his ship in a Spanish port with merchandise for the Limerick market, he retired to a church to pray. On his return to the harbour he found the ship's sails had been hoisted in the meantime, but, to his utter consternation, he saw it struck by a " sudden gust of wind " and buried in the waves. Returning to the church he gave thanks to God, and resolved to devote himself to His services.

From Spain Richard repaired to the University of Louvain,

where after a distinguished course, especially in the Scriptures, Ecclesiastical History, and Theology, he received his bachelorship of Divinity, and was ordained priest. Having returned to his native city, he edified all not only by his deep learning, but by his zeal for religion and his deep humility, and was commonly engaged in teaching children.

During the reign of Queen Mary he refused the See of Limerick, and later that of Cashel. When Fr. Wolf, during his stay in Limerick in 1562, met him he at once marked him out as the proper man to succeed either O'Taig in the archdiocese of Armagh or Roland Baron in the archdiocese of Cashel. Accordingly, he sent him to Rome, August 1562, with the necessary recommendations for a bishopric. Creagh admitted that he left Ireland with 40 crowns from Wolf, 12 marks from the Bishop of Limerick, Hugh Lacy, and 20 crowns of his own. At Rome he was forced by obedience to accept the See of Armagh, 22 March, 1564, was consecrated on Low Sunday in the Papal Chapel, and received the pallium on 12 May.

Meanwhile, Shane had sent messengers to Rome with letters to have his younger brother appointed to a northern See. In reply to this, Pius IV entrusted Creagh, the new Archbishop, who was then leaving for Ireland, with a letter to Shane, the " Prince of Ulster," 14 July, 1564,[1] in which the Pope commended his indefatigable zeal and steadfast courage in defence of the Catholic faith, exhorting him to persevere therein to the end. There is nothing in which the Pope would not gladly gratify him so far as he might with a clear conscience. He is, therefore, the more distressed that his petition for the preferment of his brother to the episcopate cannot be granted by reason that he has not yet attained the lawful age according to the decree of the recent Council, whose decrees it would be the more scandalous to violate because the Pope has confirmed them and ordained them to be everywhere observed. Pending the minority of the Prince's brother a pension has been reserved for him out of the fruits of the void Church, that he may have the means to fit himself for future preferment.

[1] *C.S.P., Rome*, 1558-71, no. 34.

As to the Prince's claims of ecclesiastical patronage [evidently to benefices under his jurisdiction], the Pope has no information upon which to decide the question, the Prince's messengers reporting that the letter on that subject was intercepted by the heretics. This defect will doubtless be supplied by Richard, Archbishop of Armagh, the bearer of this letter, upon his return to Ireland, and upon receipt of his advice the Pope will, so far as he lawfully may, study the Prince's interests. This Archbishop, chosen as he was for his exemplary life, the soundness of his morals and doctrine, and his extreme zeal for the Catholic faith to be pastor of so noble a Church, is also well known to the Pope to be very well affected to the Prince, both by the zeal which he displayed that the Prince's desire should be gratified, and by his eloquence in extolling the Prince's merit. He therefore desires the Prince's counsel, aid, and countenance both to assure him possession of his See, and to support him in the governance of it. Respect for the Pope and the Apostolic See, and regard for the public weal of the kingdom, should induce the Prince with unremitting zeal so to do ; and thereby he will greatly gratify the Pope, who is confident that the Princes and Catholics generally will recognise that the best interests of the Church have been consulted in the appointment. The Archbishop will upon his arrival convey to the Prince the Pope's salutation and Apostolic blessing, and will declare his paternal mind at large. May God grant the Prince increase of grace, preserve him, His trusty and well approved champion, for the defence of holy religion and the Catholic faith, and protect him against all his enemies.

From all this it appears that Shane O'Neill, besides exerting supremacy over the northern chiefs, was anxious to have a voice in the appointment to northern benefices. He seems also to have been opposed to the appointment of Creagh to Armagh, as will appear by his later attitude towards him, and the Pope was aware of this and was careful to remind Shane of Creagh's goodwill towards him. Moreover, Shane considered that he could legitimately present a bishop of his own choice, his own brother, to the Pope for a northern See, that of Down and Connor. This difference of view between the Pope and Shane was to lead to unpleasant results between Shane and Creagh.

PAPAL COMMISSION FOR CREAGH AND WOLF.

Besides the foregoing letter to Shane, Creagh was the bearer of a papal commission,[1] 13 July, 1564, to himself and Fr. Wolf for the amendment of the morals of the clergy throughout Ireland, the abatement of prevalent abuses and the promotion of the salvation of the faithful. There seems little doubt that discipline among clergy had become considerably relaxed, and that the people resorted on slight provocation to brutal measures ; this was especially the case in the Irish parts of the country, and particularly in the North.

The powers and duties of the commissioners are set out as follow :—

(1) To absolve from excommunication even the greater suspension, and all their ecclesiastical sentences, censures, and pains, subject nevertheless to the imposition of salutary penance, the descendants of those who were guilty, either as principals or as accessories, of the murder of Cardinal Ruffus and of the capture of Donat MacTaig, late primate of Ireland, and also all such as have since laid violent hands, even to the effusion of blood, upon priests and other clerks.

(2) To delegate to ordinaries faculty to grant to parish priests resident within their dioceses in places remote from the sea, or where there is scarcity of fish, licence to eat cheese, butter, and other such food in Lent and other prohibited seasons and times without scruple of conscience and to authorise the use by priests of portable altars on which, while in fear of the heretics and no longer, to celebrate Mass with due reverence and solemnity in suitable places outside their Churches.

(3) To institute to Cathedral, even Metropolitan Churches now void or hereafter to become void *extra Romanam Curiam,* such of the neighbouring bishops as they may deem meet, provided the Pope for the time being be first by their letters notified of the vacancies and the persons whom they deem meet for preferment, and he or the Apostolic See have appointed them, as administrators in spirituals and temporals, with all the power pertaining to such administrators ; so nevertheless that after the

[1] *C.S.P., Rome,* 1558-71, no. 313.

deduction of a meet and modest portion of the fruits, rents, and issues of the void Church, or its episcopal or archiepiscopal table, to be assigned to the administrator, all the residue of the said fruits etc. be applied to the restoration of the church and the upkeep of its ornaments.

(4) The Archbishop carefully to consider and report to the Holy See with all speed by particular information under his seal when and where outside the churches he may be able to celebrate Mass, and what relics of the Saints lawfully to be granted to him, and by him to be held in due reverence, and holy oil he may be able to transport from Rome to Ireland. The Nuncio in like manner is to consider and report as to the transfer, so far as he shall deem it expedient, of Cathedrals oppressed by heretics, or otherwise deserted by Catholics, to neighbouring towns or other places where Mass and the other Divine Offices may be more conveniently celebrated.[1]

(5) Jointly or severally to proceed by inquisition in a simple, summary and informal manner, against all and each of whatever dignity, station, rank, order or condition though of episcopal or even higher dignity, who are tainted with simony, openly keep concubines, or unlawfully usurp and retain the fruits of ecclesiastical benefices, even though under pretext that they are due to them as first fruits or by right of patronage, or otherwise, and also against regulars of dissolute and scandalous life, to whichever of the mendicant orders they may belong, the process, so far as it may relate to bishops to be sent in the usual way, duly closed, to the Holy See for more mature consideration, all offenders of a lesser degree to be sentenced and punishment to be invoked according to the canons of the Council of Trent and other canonical regulations.

(6) To prohibit, under sentences, censures, and pains ecclesiastical, and even by public edict, the granting by any Irish priest, whatever his dignity, rank or order, of absolution to anyone from sentence of excommunication whether incurred *simpliciter* or *ad cautelam*, for laying violent hands upon clerks, and also to prohibit as aforesaid the presuming to go to the Roman Curia with intent to obtain churches or other benefices ecclesiastical, without prior attestation by the said commissioners, or one of

---

[1] Here we have an important contribution to the question as to how the ancient Catholic Cathedrals became Protestant property. The Cathedrals, in places where Protestants were in supreme power, and which in consequence of the persecution and penalties of the law, were unwillingly deserted by Catholics were to be canonically transferred to the nearest town or place where Catholics were unmolested and free to attend Mass in their churches.

them, of the Catholic faith and probity of those for whom such churches are solicited, and that the incumbents are dead and the said churches and benefices really void.[1]

(7) In reinforcement of sentences of excommunication to cause the decrees of the Council of Trent to be observed *in judicio et extra.*

(8) The Nuncio in amplification of his faculties in matrimonial cases to have power for just and reasonable cause to dispense with the impediment of the fourth degree of consanguinity or affinity etc.[2]

THE RELIGIOUS DUEL BEGINS.

The difficulty of educating Catholic priests in Ireland was long felt, and candidates found a welcome in Continental colleges, especially in Louvain and Paris. The departure of these youths from the coasts of Munster came to the knowledge of Elizabeth, and so, for the first time, the system of espionage on sea merchants and their ships comes into prominence. Memoranda in the *State Papers,* 23 August, furnish evidence of the recruiting and the espionage.[3] Sir Thady Newman, the papal commissary's representative in Dublin, who apparently was exerting himself in the diocese in this business of recruiting priests, was to be examined and inquiry was to be made at Waterford for Denis McVard, probably a scholar, who would give information as to what " priests " were being shipped to Antwerp for Louvain. Mr. Wingfield, the master of the Ordnance, should " apprehend Malachi O'Quin and Sir Richard, the clerk [curate] of Wicklow Church." These were apparently on their way to Waterford. Sir Thady Newman and Sir Edmund Quin [4] had made themselves responsible for sending the money for the journey and the education of the student after them. Inquiry was to be made about a " Thomas Fitzgerald that

---

[1] This article seems purposely aimed at the state of affairs referred to in Fr. Wolf's letter of 1561 (see p. 91).

[2] This impediment was evidently considered most important as the Irish did not consider it an impediment at all.

[3] *S.P.I., Eliz.,* xi. 81, P.R.O., London.

[4] The title " Sir " was given to those ecclesiastics who had graduated in Theology. Sir Richard was probably bringing Malachi O'Quin, a candidate for the priesthood, to Louvain, or seeing him safely shipped at Waterford.

had written unto his brother Sir Peter Fitzgerald who is at Paris," what are his benefices, " and who is this Oliver Fitzgerald who should be sent to the said Sir Peter." It is also asked " who is the archdeacon that provides for John White, scholar, at Louvain, that provides for James White."

These memoranda show clearly for the first time that some of the parochial clergy were sending aspirants to the priesthood to the Continent for education and paying for them out of their slender resources. Finally, the memoranda mention that a James Quemerford (Comerford) of Waterford had written to his brother Nicholas Quemerford at Louvain, 14 August, and had professed himself to be " of the old religion." The duel had now begun between Elizabeth and her spies, and the Catholic clergy, in this matter of sending aspirants to the priesthood abroad for education, and a new epoch in the " Reformation " was ushered in.

Elizabeth's Orders to Proceed with the Reform.

Having started the campaign against the education of Irish priests on the Continent when they were deprived of such in their own country, Elizabeth now proceeds on a more drastic one which concerns the faith and practices of those at home. So far the work of administering the Oath of Supremacy had been chiefly confined to the home counties, Dublin, Meath, and Kildare. The area of such operations was now enlarged, and a commission of 9 June, 1564, was issued to Ormond, Desmond, Barrymore, Roche, Patrick, Bishop of Waterford and Lismore ; Roger, Bishop-elect of Cork and Cloyne ; Hugh (Lacy), Bishop of Limerick ; John, Bishop of Ossory ; Thomas, Bishop of Leighlin, etc., to exercise Her Majesty's ecclesiastical jurisdiction in the counties of Carlow, Waterford, Kilkenny, Cork, Kerry, Limerick, and Tipperary, with power to correct heresies and other offences and to administer to all persons there, as may seem good to them, the Oath of Supremacy.[1]

A more important step was taken on 6 October when Elizabeth wrote to the Lord Deputy [2] nominating Loftus, Archbishop of Armagh; Brady, Bishop of Meath; Fihil, Bishop

---

[1] *Fiants*, no. 666.   [2] *P.C.R.I., Eliz.*, i. 489-90.

of Leighlin; Daly, Bishop of Kildare; Terence Daniel, Dean of Armagh; the Earl of Kildare and lay members of the Council as commissioners,

to inquire into any heretical opinions, seditious books, conspiracies, false rumours, tales, slanderous words or sayings, published or invented by any person or persons against Her Majesty or the laws or statutes of the realm, their coadjutors, councillors or abettors; of any disturbance or misbehaviour committed or perpetrated in any church or chapel, or against Divine Service; and to enquire, order, correct, all such persons as should obstinately absent themselves from Church and Divine Service, as by law established; authorising them to visit, reform and redress in all places, all errors, heresies, schisms, spiritual or ecclesiastical, by censure or ecclesiastical deprivation; for the increase of virtue, the pleasure of God, the preservation of peace, and unity of the realm; to enquire and search out all masterless men, quarellers, vagrant and suspected persons, and all assaults and affronts perpetrated in the Kingdom; to hear and determine all causes and complaints of those who, in respect of religion or lawful matrimony, have been injuriously deprived, defrauded or despoiled of their lands, goods, possessions or livings; to ensure their restoration and the removal of the usurpers with all convenient speed; to hear and determine all manifest and notorious avowtries, fornications, and ecclesiastical crimes; to devise politic ways and means for the performers of this duty, and, upon due proof, to award such punishment, by fine or imprisonment as to them should seem expedient; to summon all offenders or suspected persons before them, and all necessary witnesses for trial, and commit to ward all obstinate and disobedient persons not conforming to these rules, orders, and commandments; to take recognizances or obligations from all offenders and suspected persons for their personal appearance and for the due execution of their commands; permission to appoint Geoffrey Penchebecke to be Register [1] of all decrees and proceedings under this commission; to appoint an officer to receive all such sums of money as should be assessed or taxed upon offending persons; and assign and appoint such fees to him for his pains and charges, as should be expedient; to certify to the Exchequer a note of all fines imposed; and as there are still in the realm divers perverse and obstinate person, who refuse to acknowledge Her Majesty's prerogative

[1] The Register of Penchebecke has never come to light, as far as we are aware.

8 *

and to observe the ceremonies and rites in Divine Service, established by law, Her Majesty directs the Commissioners to cause all archbishops, bishops, and other ecclesiastical officers or ministers to subscribe the oath contained in the statute, for restoring to the crown the ancient jurisdiction over the state, ecclesiastical and spiritual, and abolishing of all foreign power repugnant to the same, and if any of the clergy peremptorily and obstinately refuse to take the oath, their refusal is to be certified into Chancery without delay.

Three days later, the Queen wrote to the Lord Justice, the Council, and the Commissioners for ecclesiastical causes, informing them that nothing should be more regarded than that the people should be instructed to live in the due fear of Almighty God and in conformity of religion without falling into sects and errors in contempt of God and the peril of their souls (for which purpose laws were established giving Her Majesty supreme prerogative, under God, to govern all states, temporal and ecclesiastical) ; and committing to them the charge and direction of such causes, by letters forwarded by the Bishop of Meath, with whom Her Majesty had full conference, touching the weal of the realm, and who, Her Majesty hoped, would prove a faithful minister in his pastoral office ; wherefore Her Majesty desired the Lord Deputy and Council to assemble immediately and proceed with the performance of this duty.

This grandiosely-worded fulmination, like that of so many other commissions, looks all very well on paper, but it is more formidable in that setting than it was in reality. One will look in vain for any report of or reference to the result of the commission in the *State Papers*. Like other commissions it set out with the best of intentions, and the commissioners travelled from town to town, attended assizes and sessions, punished or fined offenders, and delivered addresses to the court on the duty of good and godly living and the observance of the Queen's laws and due loyalty to her supremacy and religious service. In this way it was considered that the people would be induced and encouraged to accept the " reform," but as this history proceeds it will be apparent what little success attended the sittings of the commissioners.

STATE OF IRELAND : O'NEILL PEACEFUL : REST OF
IRELAND DISTURBED.

The year 1564 had opened with Ireland in a disturbed
state.   Cusack, the new Chancellor, informed Cecil, 2 February,
that the agreement with O'Neill was concluded in an opportune
time as there are now " stirs risen in the English Pale by the
Geraldines, Conors, and Mores." [1]   On 16 March, Wrothe
and Arnold, the commissioners, informed the Privy Council
that on account of want of payment to the soldiers the expedition against the Mores and Conors will " neither be honourable nor profitable to her Majesty." [2]   The Queen, not pleased
with this gloomy report, informed the Council, 9 April, [3]
that she " liketh not toleration in rebellion, and that the
rebels are to be subdued and oppressed by force."   Accordingly, stern and determined measures were adopted, and Sir
Edmund Butler was able to report, 11 June, [4] his victory
over the Mores of Leix.   For this service he was " suitably
thanked by the Council who promised to report him favourably
to the Queen."   This improvement, as usual, was only
temporary, as Arnold, 3 July, [5] was forced to complain of
the unsettled state of the country through the Tooles, Byrnes,
O'Reilly, the Mores, and " other loose people."   A governor
was recommended for Leix and Offaly.   This was followed
up in August, [6] by commissions to the sheriffs and magnates
of the counties bordering on Leix to cess and levy the inhabitants for the maintenance of the soldiers, and " to provide
the horses and men that by their tenures they are bound to
keep, for the suppression of the O'Mores and O'Connors."
Even this cessing did not work the miracle expected, [7] for
16 August, [8] Wrothe reported that : " The O'Mores and
O'Connors are out killing in a cruel manner.   The Kavanaghs
and Byrnes are preying on others.   The whole country is
unsettled and even the cesses due to the Queen are badly

---

[1] *C.S.P.I., Eliz.,* x. 12.   [2] *Ib.,* 34.   [3] *Ib.,* 47.
[4] *Ib.,* xi. 4.   [5] *Ib.,* 21.   [6] *Ib.,* 58.
[7] On 18 June, Wrothe informed Cecil of the poverty of the English Pale and
recommended the forfeiture of the leases of parsonages, by which means the
rent corn may be reserved to the Queen, and a commission to make new leases.
(*C.S.P.I., Eliz.,* xi. 12.)
[8] *Ib.,* 73.

paid by the people, 13,000 pecks of corn being now unpaid." [1]
Wrothe wishes to quit this lawless land, and return home.
On the same day, the Lord Justice and Council issued a
proclamation [2] against the rebels of the O'Connors.

Two months passed and still no progress had been made
against the rebels of Leix and Offaly, and the expedition had
become so expensive that the Queen decided to discontinue
the action and recalled Wrothe. [3] But on 31 October Arnold
and Council were able to report to the Queen that they had
reduced the O'Connors and the O'Mores, ninety of the former
and thirty-five of the latter being slain and executed. [4] And,
three days later, Wrothe informed Cecil that the Mores had
desired peace through Francis Crosby, but the Council rejected their request. [5] On 21 November they sent a commission to Ormond to pursue the proclaimed rebels, for the upkeep
of 200 kern, and tell how the force is to be disposed. [6]

While these troubles were occupying the attention of the
Council in Ireland, Cusack was able to tell Cecil in February, [7]
that O'Neill was still persevering " in his good conformity."
And O'Neill himself boasted to the Privy Council, 29 February, [8]
of his integrity, and intimated that he wished to be created
an English Earl and to have a more ample fortune.   Terence
Daniel, the Dean of Armagh, informed Cusack of the " conformable proceedings of O'Neill relative to the trial of certain
malefactors."   This means that O'Neill, according to Daniel,
was carrying out the procedure of English law, as requested
by Elizabeth.   Daniel, evidently, acting on a request of
Cecil, informed Elizabeth's Secretary, 10 March, [9] that he
was remaining in Ulster looking after O'Neill, and that the
latter intended to keep the peace.

On 25 May, [10] he followed this commendation by another
in which he set forth the results of Shane's loyalty : " quietness of the North under his rule ; all kinds of husbandry and
sowing of wheat ; " and that, whilst in the O'Donnell's country,
Shane abstained from doing any harm.   But Shane, fearful

---

[1] William Dyke, in a letter to Cecil (17 Aug.) gives the amount as 14,900
pecks of corn, besides beeves.
[2] *C.S.P.I.*, *Eliz.*, xi. 74. " Imprynted at Dublin by Henry Powell, the
16 of August, 1564."
[3] *Ib.*, 90.   [4] *Ib.*, 97.   [5] *Ib.*, 98.   [6] *Ib.*, 105.
[7] *Ib.*, x. 14.   [8] *Ib.*, 20.   [9] *Ib.*, 28.   [10] *Ib.*, 69.

of the galloglasses who had been serving with O'Donnell, reported to Cusack [1] that he was ready to support forty men to aid in the expulsion of those Scots out of Ireland, and to show his regard for the Queen he offered to restore to her the fishing of the Bann and Lough Foyle. Needless to say, Shane was playing his own game, and offered to get rid of the mercenary Scots when it suited him. As the result of some dispute he was not above taking Calough O'Donnell prisoner, and, in order to settle the controversy, Terence Daniel, Patrick Dorelle, Chantor of Armagh, and Simon Barnewall were appointed to decide the controversy. As a further proof of Shane's good intentions towards Her Majesty, he conformed to what was evidently a request of the Queen for horses and hawks as presents from Her Majesty to the King of France. Accordingly, 8 August,[2] Wrothe informed Cecil that those presents from " the Great O'Neill," or the Earl of Desmond, were to be carefully conveyed to the French Court.

The position of Loftus as Archbishop of Armagh evidently appealed to Wrothe as an anomaly, for, 23 July, he recommended Terence Daniel for the See.[3] Daniel had shown himself a very useful intermediary between the recalcitrant Shane and the Council of Ireland. Daniel would be a Catholic Archbishop giving allegiance to Elizabeth as temporal ruler of the country, for it would be absurd to expect Shane to recognise him in any other capacity, and Wrothe must have been aware of this. Meanwhile, Shane had appealed to Rome for the same purpose, and probably Wrothe was aware of this also at the time he wrote approving of Daniel. So that Daniel would have papal and royal approval. But neither Queen nor Pope approved of his appointment. The Queen appointed Loftus, and the Pope selected Creagh.

Other matters now occupied Shane's attention. The Scots had usurped some of his territory, and, as he intended to proceed against them, as soon as the waters of the Bann had subsided, he thought that he was entitled to aid from Kildare and others.[4] The Queen, " not without compassion for him," and anxious about his present position against

---

[1] *C.S.P.I., Eliz.*, xi. 1.   [2] *Ib.*, 68.   [3] *Ib.*, xi. 35.   [4] *Ib.*, 83.

the O'Donnells, directed Arnold, 3 December,[1] to make him " some allowance to keep him from penury, till it may appear what shall become of his causes."

In the extreme South of the country the only notable attempt at pacification was made by Ormond who issued a proclamation taking away " the mischievous custom of coyne and livery " in the Co. Tipperary, with orders necessary for the preservation of the country.

Thus the year 1564 ended with storm clouds in the religious atmosphere ; Elizabeth's commissioners sent afield, orders given to proceed with the " reform," and, on the other hand, students going abroad to prepare for the priesthood, and a Catholic Archbishop of Armagh coming from Rome with papal Bulls. The arena was being prepared for a clash of forces.

CREAGH, ARCHBISHOP OF ARMAGH, A PRISONER IN THE TOWER.

In July, 1564, Creagh started from Rome on his journey to Ireland, riding on horseback first to Augsburg, attended by an Ulster student. At Louvain he first appeared in his episcopal robes. Sailing for Ireland in an Irish ship, he was driven by contrary winds to Dover, and, proceeding thence to Rochester, found an Irish boy begging (a poor scholar) whom he brought with him to London. He visited St. Paul's, Westminster Abbey, and Westminster Hall without being recognised. Within an hour after he had landed in Ireland, having said Mass in a monastery of his province, probably the Franciscan house at Drogheda, he was taken prisoner by the soldiers of the governor, and afterwards conveyed to London where he was imprisoned in the Tower, 18 January, 1565. A set of questions was drawn up by Cecil, 22 February,[2] with a view to obtaining all the information about the communications that were being carried on between the Pope and Ireland, and about the students, Irish and English, who were being educated on the Continent. To all these questions Creagh truthfully answers, thus painting an invaluable picture of the period :—

[1] *C.S.P.I.*, *Eliz.*, xi. 110.   [2] *S.P.I.*, *Eliz.*, xii. 33.   Shirley, 163-79.

To the questions, what Lords of Ireland and how many were privy to your going out of Ireland towards Rome, and how many Englishmen were privy thereto ?

I answer truly that as I never went about to hide my going away, so in likewise I never, neither by myself nor by any other, by word, writing, or otherwise, made any lord that is, or was living under, privy of my going to Rome, neither also any Englishman that I remember. For going away, I intended, if God would, for to enter into such religion as I should there in Rome see best or most agreeable to my weak complexion, but as I was commanded by obedience to take my way to Rome, so being there ready for to enter to the religion [Order] of the Theatines, otherwise called Paulines, dwelling at Montecavallo, I was commanded by the Cardinal, under pain of obedience, to change nothing about myself till I should know further of the Pope's will, which will by the said Cardinal was afterward declared unto me, and under pain of cursing [excommunication] if I should be inobedient, and so was sent with the same will unto Ireland.

To the questions :—

How many were acquainted with you in Rome being English or Irish, and by whom were you there succoured ?

I answer that I saw and spoke sometimes with divers English and Irishmen, as Mr. Sekwhil,[1] the Earl of Derby's son, the Master of the English hospital called there the Bishop of Saint Asse,[2] and others dwelling in the said hospital, one also of my Lord of Leicester's men, called Edmond, an Irishman, for lack of costs was at my poor table and house, dwelling the space of two months or thereabout ; of Irishmen also I was acquainted with Muiryrtagh and Donough O'Brien, scholars, Diarmaid O'Mady, Knoghour [Connor]og, one Muires, and other scholars whose names I remember not, also a friar of Saint Austin's, and a priest from O'Neill's country, which being sent thither for to procure the bishopric of Down and Connor for O'Neill's brother, as also *jus patronatus* [patronage] of some benefices for O'Neill, would not be so acquainted with me as other Irishmen were. Also one Robert and another called Diego, serving men or soldiers, which, because

---

[1] Thomas Sackville, afterwards Lord Buckhurst and Earl of Dorset, who was detained for a time a prisoner in Rome.

[2] Bishop of St. Asaph, Thomas Goldwell, appointed by Queen Mary. He was deprived by Elizabeth, " and going abroad, made his appearance at the Council of Trent in the year 1562. The remainder of his life was for the most part spent in Rome ; having an appartment in the English hospital, which a few years after was converted into a College or seminary of Missioners." He died about 1582 (Dodd's *Church Hist.*, i. 507 ; Wood's *Athenae Oxon.*).

I have cast them away from all acquaintance for displeasure (of the which, as I heard say, they were partakers) made to Mr. Sekwhil, were about afterward to do me hurt, yea also to accuse me of heresy for favour shown to Englishmen, and chiefly the said Robert, as I think the aforementioned Edmond knows, I mean the Earl of Leicester's man.

At the time that I have been in Rome I was succoured by the Pope both in meat, drink, and house rents, because I was sent thither by obedience towards his messenger's commandment, which for to obey I was bound by mine oath made when I was received to student in the common schools of Louvain.

To the question :—

In your return by Louvain how many English, Irish, or others did you make privy to the cause of your return to Ireland ?

The truth is, that I know none English or Irishman that was so privy, except an Englishman of the Jesuits that dwelt in the university of Dilingua,[1] not far from Augusta in Germany, and two friars of St. Francis (an English and the other an Irishman) in the convent of Antwerp, with another Jesuit an Englishman that I met in Antwerp, as also Doctor Clement (a Physician) there dwelling, and some young Irish scholars heard in Louvain by others (perhaps that came from Rome) that I was appointed to be Archbishop of Armagh, other men by the way knew or heard more about me, as the Cardinal of Augusta (who did hold me the space of a senyght [seven night] to be refreshed and to recover my health of the ague that I caught by the way), divers of the Jesuits in sundry places, and the doctors of [the university of] Louvain, whom I called to dinner once, because of my acquaintance before with them.

To the question :—

How many in England or Wales knew you at your return to Ireland ?

It is so that to never a body in that way I willed myself to be known, yea neither of the scholar that I took for my man at Rochester, although my letters [episcopal Briefs] were seen outwardly by two poor men and a poor woman, which knew not their meaning, but when I was asked sometimes what I was, I told that I have spent a piece of my time with merchandise, which was true.

To the questions :—

To whom was your intent to resort at your landing in Ireland, and whose friendship meant you to have used in Ireland ?

---

[1] I.e. Dillengen, near Augsburg.

As I was sent by obedience from Ireland, and so also to Ireland sent back with loss both of my friends, kinsfolk, and all commodities that I had among them, and sent for to dwell and serve among barbarous, wild, and incivil folks, having nobody before me there that ever before time I was acquainted with (save only that I saw some of the prelates of Armagh [Province] in the English Pale at Queen Mary's time) so the Pope thought convenient to send some kind of letter with me to Shane O'Neill, with the letter also for a pension to be given to his brother on the bishopric [Down] that the priest aforesaid required in Rome for the said brother, which priest feigned to come at once with me to Ireland, but tarried nevertheless there. For a direct answer, I say truly that I intended only to go straight to the place that [I] was by obedience appointed to, knowing not whether Shane O'Neill should repute me for his foe, or for his friend, first because that his messengers both in Ireland (as I heard say) of the Pope's messenger [Fr. Wolf] were desiring letters of commendation to Rome for to have that Archbishopric of Armagh, for (I think) the Dean that is there, which (I ween) is of his fostered brethren ; [1] and also in Rome and Trent were persuasions concerning the same made to the Cardinal Moronus [2] (overseer of such matters) and to others, and therefore were much displeased of my sending [being sent] to Rome. Secondly, because that the messengers have judged that I have made not my devoir in Rome in procuring the bishopric of Down and Conor for Shane's brother, a young man unlearned, not passing 23 year old. If Shane or any other should give some help for erection of some schools wherein youth should be brought up in some good manners and beginnings of learning, I should wish it ; thinking earnestly that long ago they should forsake their barbarous wildness, cruelty, and ferocity, if their youth were brought up conveniently in knowledge of the duty towards God and their princes. As for erection of any university, I am not so ignorant but that I know it cannot be done without the aid and authority of the Queen's Majesty ; for other friendship or conversation with them I intended doubtless to shun it, while they should live that are brought up in such all kinds of iniquities, murders, adulteries, drunkenness, robbing, stealing, foreswearing, and other like, without any punishment to be spoken of.

[1] Terence Daniel was a foster-brother of Shane.

[2] Giovanni Moroni, of Milan, born 1509, Cardinal Bishop of Ostia, Papal Legate at the Council of Trent. These representations were probably made by the three Irish bishops at the Council.

Now be it death or life, prison or freedom, or any other thing, the truth is that I have answered, and although I lost my part of a ship (esteemed to be worth 9000 ducats) by the French galleys in the war at our Sovereign Lord, King Harry's time, and also by the searcher of Dover were taken £32 from my brother, coming with them to Louvain for my help there being at school, at other lands' men's cost, nevertheless, my poor power from my youth hitherto, was (as I thought) always spent for to serve the crown of England, as of nature and duty I was bound, knowing and also declaring in divers places the joyful life that Irishmen have under England (nothing so plucked of their good, as by sundry ways other princes' subjects are oppressed in other countries) if they were good and true in themselves. For a conclusion, as much sorrow as I had for being oppressed or charged with such burden that I was commanded to come with to Ireland, so much perhaps joy I have to be discharged thereof; howbeit, if I should die to-day, and that of my death Ulstermen should know to-morrow, the Archbishopric of Armagh, and such other should be procured from Rome (as I think, and as hitherto it was wont to be) for some other of that country, to whom God give grace to be true to his natural Queen and Crown of England, whom the Lord God maintain now and ever.

A few points in these answers call for comment in view of subsequent history. O'Neill sent a priest to Rome to procure the bishopric of Down and Connor, vacant by the death of Eugene Magennis, for his brother, an unlearned lad of twenty-three years. The Pope refused the request on account of the candidate's youth, but granted him a pension on the bishopric. It does not appear that Shane's brother at the time was in Holy Orders. Shane's messenger, evidently, was not pleased with the result of his mission, and, having pretended he was about to return to Armagh with Creagh, remained in Rome, probably for the purpose of repeating his petition. Creagh was doubtful about a friendly reception from Shane, firstly because Shane wanted the Archbishopric for the Dean, Terence Daniel, and secondly because Shane believed that Creagh had not done all he could to obtain Down and Connor for his brother. It will be remembered that Elizabeth's commissioner, Wrothe, had also recommended Daniel for Armagh. It now appears that about the same time Shane had sent messengers to Fr. Wolf at

Limerick asking him for commendatory letters to Rome in favour of Daniel for the Archbishopric. Wolf's refusal, and his sending of Creagh to Rome, gave great offence to Shane who at once despatched messengers not only to Rome but to the Papal Legate at the Council of Trent who had been appointed to oversee episcopal candidatures. It also appears that Creagh intended to take a firm stand against the brutalities and iniquities which he says were prevalent in the North, and that though he was ready to profess loyalty to Elizabeth as Queen of Ireland, and to preach it to his people, he at the same time would refuse to take his episcopal appointment from other than the Pope, whilst the Catholics of Ulster would see to it that the Pope would appoint a Catholic bishop. Doubtless, Creagh after a short time in prison revised his opinion about "the joyful life that Irishmen have under England if they were good and true in themselves." Elizabeth's treatment of such a saintly man, and a loyal subject of the Queen, whose one object was to accomplish the practice of religion and its virtues by the people over whom he was placed as bishop, was not imbued with a Christian spirit. It was quite clear to Elizabeth that her own Archbishop was unable to get a foothold in the diocese, and she preferred to see a Catholic people live in religious and moral disorder rather than allow a Christian bishop to exercise his zeal for their sanctification. The truth is that she resented the affront to her ecclesiastical dignity by the sending from Rome of a papal archbishop in face of her own appointment. Moreover, she considered the capture of Creagh a splendid opportunity of learning all about the ways and means of Catholic action in Ireland and abroad for the continuation of the Church. It is important to point out that the appointment of Loftus to Armagh meant not only the presence of a Protestant Archbishop in the diocese but the application of the revenues, supplied by a Catholic people, for the support of one not of their faith. On this application of the temporalities, and of the spiritualities, Elizabeth was determined, and she would not admit that Loftus had not as good a right, even better, to them than Creagh had.

CREAGH'S FURTHER EXAMINATION.

On 17 March, 1565, another examination, revealing further interesting details of Creagh's career, was taken of the Archbishop by Richard Ousley, Recorder of London, and Thomas Wilson, Master of Saint Katherine's :—[1]

Being asked divers questions, and first touching him whom he calleth the Pope's Nuncio, doth answer as followeth, that the said Nuncio came from Rome about four years since August last past, and hath made his continual abode all the same time in Ireland, called by name David Wolfe, born in Limerick, where his examinate [Creagh] also was born.   And farther he said that the said David Wolfe hath been about seven years abiding in Rome, and was a Jesuit there professed, and sent from the Pope by obedience into Ireland by commission, to see what bishops did their duties there, and what Sees were void, and touching himself [Creagh] he saith that he hath been most commonly heretofore in the Bishopric [diocese] of Limerick and there taught children.   The occasion of his acquaintance with the Nuncio was that the Nuncio heard of this examinate that he was learned, and so required him to go to Rome to take upon him the Archbishopric of Cashel, and afterwards the Archbishopric of Armagh being void before his departure; he charged him upon his obedience to go to Rome, for the Archbishopric of Armagh or Cashel, the which he could not refuse to be, because that when he proceeded [was promoted to] bachelor of divinity in Louvain, he swore obedience to the Pope, and therefore durst not disobey his Nuncio.   Being asked what instructions he had by the Nuncio at his going to Rome, he said, the Nuncio wrote in his favour to Cardinal Morone the which letter he did read, but did not well remember the contents thereof, but he well remembered that he said he [Creagh] would not willingly take the Archbishopric of Armagh upon him, but rather that he should hear of him to be one of the religion [religious order].   And at his coming to Rome he delivered his letters to the Superiors of the Jesuits, minding to enter into religion, but he was commanded shortly after by Cardinal Gonzaga that had the place of Cardinal Morone when he went to the Council at Trent, that he should not enter into the religion till he knew the Pope's pleasure.   Being demanded what money he had at his going out of Ireland, he saith that the Nuncio gave him 40 crowns, the Bishop of Limerick [Hugh Lacy] [2] 12 marks, the which 12 marks

---

[1] S.P.I., Eliz., xii 51.   Shirley, 171 ff.

[2] This confirms the opinion we have already expressed about Bishop Lacy's orthodoxy.

he had as an exhibition for his finding [upkeep] there, and 20 crowns he had of his own, and more he had not, by credit or otherwise. Being asked where the Nuncio doth commonly keep in Ireland, he saith that he doth secretly come to Limerick and hath been this last Summer [1564] in Tyrone, with Shane O'Neill, as he heard, and the letters that he received were delivered unto him in Limerick in the presence of a priest called Sir Thomas Molam [Motham].

He [Creagh] went out of Ireland in August two years past [1562] and came to Rome in January, and in February next he was commanded not to enter into the religion, and afterwards charged upon the Pope's curse, not to refuse the Archbishopric of Armagh, and about Easter twelve months after [1564] he was consecrated by Lomellinus [1] and another Bishop in the Pope's chapel, and so came from Rome in July last past. In all which time of his abode at Rome, the Pope did bear his charges, after he had warning not to enter into religion, and had daily meat, drink, and wine for himself and his servant at the Pope's cost, paying for his house room 6 crowns by the month, having had at divers times from the Pope to the number of 700 crowns, of the which sum he had at his going out of Rome given unto him by the Pope 300 crowns, and 100 crowns for the Nuncio. He had apparel of three sorts, of blue and unwatered chamlet, and wore the same in Rome, having four or five servants waiting there upon him. And at coming out of Rome he had the Pope's blessing, and Cardinal Moronus told him that he was informed the Queen would turn shortly to the Catholic Faith ; he came from Rome on horseback with a priest and one man, the which servant being a scholar was of Ulster, and went thorough with him, but the priest returned shortly to Rome. At Augusta [Augsburg] he took another servant, where he was well entreated of the Cardinal of Augusta for a seven night space ; at his coming to Antwerp he spoke with D. Clement [2] and told him that he was compelled to receive the Archbishopric of Armagh, but what D. Clement said to him again he doth not well remember. From Antwerp he went to Louvain, and there sent for the doctors of Louvain, and made them a banquet, sitting with them in his Archbishopric's apparel of blue

---

[1] Clerk of the Apostolic Chamber, Bishop of Anagni, etc., afterwards Cardinal.

[2] John Clement educated at Oxford, tutor to the children of Sir Thomas More. In the reign of Edward VI, he, being then one of the College of Physicians in London, left his native land for religion's sake. He returned in the reign of Queen Mary, but finally leaving England, after the accession of Elizabeth, he returned to Mechlin where he died, 1 July, 1572.

chamlet, the which apparel he did not wear in any other place since he came from Rome. He came to Dover by a contrarie wind, in a ship of Ireland, that should have gone straight to Ireland, and so being arrived in England he were unknown and at Rochester he found an Irish boy begging whom he took with him to London, and there lodged at the Three Cups in Broad Street in October last, where he tarried not past three days, and at his being in London, he went to Paul's Church, and there walked, but had no talk with any man, and so to Westminster Church to see the Monuments there, and from thence he came to Westminster Hall, the same time that he heard say Bonner was arraigned, but he did not see him, neither can he tell what he was that told him so. Being asked what he would have done if he had been received Archbishop of Armagh, saith, he would have lived there quietly. Being asked what he would have done if he had been refused, he answereth, that he would have gone to Louvain to his track again, as being discharged of his obedience, whereunto he taketh himself to be bound in conscience.

Also he saith that Goldwell and he dined and talked divers times, and at one time this examinate heard that a Frenchman of the Pope's palace should report that the Frenchmen had entered and invaded England, the which talk Goldwell doubted to be true, and thereupon they sent to the palace to inquire the certainty, and then after, the Frenchman denied it, and so they found it untrue.

Creagh Explains his Answers.

On being asked to explain more fully his answers, Creagh, 23 March, 1565, replied as follows :—[1]

Whereas I was asked whether the religious man or messenger [Wolf] have sent any letter with me for to receive any money in any place, I was not remembered that he have sent a letter to the Rector of the College of his religion [Jesuit Order] in Paris, that if [I] should go that way I should receive 80 crowns sent thither from the Pope to be sent to the said messenger to Ireland, but I passed not by Paris, and yet I received the said 80 at Rome, for they were the 80 that I said I have received from the Pope with the 20 and 100 crowns during my being there. Also where I answered that if [I] should not be received by the Chapter of Armagh, I should go to dwell at Louvain, I was not then remembered [mindful] that I have asked leave of the Pope (when I was com-

---

[1] *S.P.I.*, *Eliz.*, xii. 60.   Shirley, 176 ff.

manded under pain of cursing to take the Archbishopric) for to enter to religion when I should think it good, which leave it is like he should grant in case I were not received there, and to religion in Louvain or other place [I] should enter having that leave. Also where I said that the Cardinal did name that messenger in his letter sent to Ireland—*pater reverende*—my remembrance failed for the letter was written in Italian tongue, and the words that I meant was—*Nosa revontia*.[1] In Italian were written also the letters that the said messenger have with me to his superiors and to the Cardinal, wherefore I would not then understand them, but as he did declare them to me [indifferent] whether I did declare them wholly or not. The said messenger's priest Thomas Motham whom I said he was present when the said messenger did command me in all authority that he could (that were his words as I remember) for to go to Rome, I am not sure whether he heard the messenger so speaking, but as I think he was at least about, or nigh in the place before and after me, he have sent divers with his letters also, as one William Moiryrtagh or Morgan, Brian Tayg Richiblican or Kiblican, also Domigha fr Rickard, Croeun Diarmaid Mady, Richard Ardur (or so), Moris Derby (of the which some were handsomely learned ; also beyond seas, whose names I did not so remember being asked before of the right honourable Mr. Secretary Cecil) with many other of divers parts of Ireland ; of the which aforenamed three or four had of the Pope exhibition [endowment] for themself and their servants (and also the three bishops that were at the Council of Trent) as I had, except that beside the two servants that I had at the Pope's expense, I had also for the space of about 2 or 3 months sometime 2 and sometime 3 poor scholars being content only with some meat and drink. What I have learned at the Emperor Charles and other good men's charges and costs,[2] I have bestowed it to my poor power, for the profit and wealth of the Queen's Majesty's subjects old and young,[3] and thanks be now unto Almighty God and to her gracious Highness for my reward, being here in such poverty (beside divers my poor body's sickness) that I can neither day neither night change apparel, having neither of myself neither of anybody one penny to cause the broken sherth [shirt] that is on my back to be once washed, whose incommodity [discomfort] honesty will not have it declared, beside the misery of cold, and such others, without gown or convenient hose. If it were gracious and merciful pleasure for to

[1] Probably meant for *Vostra Reverentia* (*your Reverence*).
[2] I.e. at College in Louvain.   [3] I.e. taught a school at Limerick.

suffer me to go teach the youth in the arts and some books of manners, I should do it for nought, as hitherto I have done, neither asking or receiving a penny of the Church or Ecclesiastical benefice during my life, which I pray (for the good Lord's sake) that some merciful heart move or speak unto her merciful Majesty, whom the Almighty Lord preserve now and ever.

Creagh was evidently kept in a disgraceful condition, and practically in solitary confinement, the only person allowed to speak to him being one William Bermyngham who was about to return to Ireland. He therefore petitioned the Privy Council to allow him the liberty of the Tower and that some one may have permission to visit him.[1] His escape from the Tower, shortly after the 23 March, looked on by himself as miraculous, took place on Low Sunday, the anniversary of his consecration. Though £100 was offered for his detection, he made his way safely to Louvain. In the summer of 1566 he made his way back to his diocese, where he found everything in disorder.[2]

Elizabeth Appoints to the See of Down.

Eugene Magennis, Bishop of Down, having died towards the end of 1562, a letter [3] supposed to be of the year 1563 was addressed by Pers, the Constable of Carrickfergus, petitioning Elizabeth to appoint a suitable man to the See, and hinted that such a one would be welcomed by some of the neighbouring prelates. Carrickfergus on Belfast Lough was an English stronghold and likely to support a Protestant bishop in Down. Shane O'Neill, as we have seen, desired the See for his brother and sent messengers to Rome to press the demand, which was refused because of the candidate's youth. No papal appointment was made to the See for three years, namely, until 12 October, 1565. Meanwhile, it was understood that Shane's brother, who had been granted a pension out of the bishopric, would be promoted to the See as soon as his age would permit. On 6 January, 1565, Elizabeth wrote to the Lord Justice and Chancellor ordering the usual letters for the election, consecration of, and

---

[1] *S.P.I.*, *Eliz.*, xii. 61.   [2] Coleman, *Stuart's Armagh*, 166.
[3] *S.P.I.*, *Eliz.*, ix. 83.   Shirley, 132-3.

they keep close, who under a form of sound doctrine yet by merry tales and pretty conceits disseminate many and diverse empty and profitless matters repugnant to the Catholic faith and the Christian religion, whereby they lead even good Christians into various errors ; and to such a degree are these evil colloquies multiplied that none fear to utter derisive and unseemly words even against God's holy Church and the Christian religion ; wherefore it would seem to be needful and very meet that an office of the Most Holy inquisition should be established in certain places in the island, for that thereby would ensue not only the destruction or correction of the evil but also the confirmation and corroboration of the good. And especially would this be so under the sway and jurisdiction of the most Illustrious and the Catholic Prince O'Neill, and in other places approved by him and the Nuncio Apostolic and the Very Reverend the Archbishop of Armagh, with the advice of other Catholic prelates and princes, where those who should execute this office would be beyond the power of the heretics to disturb or molest them.

Signed.   Fr. MILERUS, Episcopus de Hibernia.

Loftus, Dean of St. Patrick's ; Question of a University.

Meanwhile Elizabeth, unheeding Curwen's letter for the customary election of a dean for St. Patrick's, sent the following letter,[1] 6 January, 1565, to the Lord Justice and Chancellor, in commendation of Loftus and conferring on him the deanery, of her own pleasure. This she does, as she states, until she can advance him " to some better preferment in the Church," there being at the time no place in England or Ireland " meet for his preferment." Armagh, she admits, was " a place of great charge [burden], and in name and title only to be esteemed, without any worldly endowment of any moment coming towards him." Loftus, as a matter of fact, had so far been unable to set foot in his diocese, or to draw any revenue from it except what might proceed from the district round Drogheda.

Brady of Meath, on the other hand, was strongly in favour of converting the cathedral into a university, and in the following letter,[2] 10 January, 1565, to Cecil he hints at a

[1] *S.P.I., Eliz.,* xii. 3.   Shirley, 158.
[2] *S.P.I., Eliz.,* xii. 7.   Shirley, 160.

state of affairs among the prebendaries and canons which is decidedly interesting considering that five years had now passed since the Act of Uniformity had been passed. He says :—

As touching Saint Patrick's that there is nothing done I marvel, the thing so necessary, so much wished-for here, so well liked-of there, the promise of so noble a prince to perform it, and yet nothing done. I can say nothing, but I know the devil doth envy so godly an act ; there be a sort of dumb dogs maintained, of the living enemies to the truth, and all setters forth thereof neither teaching nor feeding save themselves. I speak generally of them from bishop to petty canon, none but disguised dissemblers, they say themselves they be old bottles, and cannot away with [take in] this new wine : for God's love, let there be new gotten [they] that may away with it. The tender thought [young intellects] of this land placed in their room, and brought up in learning, will make this land flourish, happy and twice happy shall the bringers hereof to pass by,[1] their names shall be registered in the book of perpetual memory ; and as I said, I am glad that her Majesty was not prevented of any of her noble predecessors, but that she may perform so noble an act. I have forgotten myself to trouble you so long, I pray God bless you, and make you an instrument to further this common commodity for this poor land. Your own with prayer as long as life lasteth.—H. MIDEN.

And, in a letter,[2] 28 February, to Sir N. Arnold, Cecil adopts the opinion of Brady when he says : " I am sorry to hear no good done in the survey of St. Patrick's, how it might serve for the commonweal, which now serveth for lurking papists."

Brady here accuses Curwen, prebendaries, and minor canons of St. Patrick's of being papists in disguise, and these excuse their inaction in the matter of " reform " on the ground of their old age, comparing themselves to " old bottles " into which one cannot put " new wine." Brady's accusation was perfectly true, and some years later Loftus dolefully remarked that, except for the few Protestant prebendaries he had promoted, the remainder (about twenty) of the chapter were all papists. They outwardly conformed by their presence at the services in the Cathedral, drew their

---

[1] Be those who bring it to pass.   [2] *S.P.I., Eliz.*, xii. 50.

stipends, paid their Catholic vicars, where possible, to conduct Catholic services in the churches of their prebends, and presumably said Mass themselves in houses in some back-streets in the neighbourhood of the Cathedral. If such things could be done in Dublin, at the centre of the Government, it is no matter for surprise that the rest of the country continued practically on its old Catholic lines. The appointment of a few Protestant bishops was a matter of small importance, and had little or no influence on the faith of the people, as these bishops often confessed.

The last word was not yet heard about the deanery or the appointment of Loftus to it. Brady in a letter,[1] 3 April, to Cecil while admitting that his " workfellow " Loftus deserved a secure means of livelihood, yet he thinks it false economy to starve a nation for the sake of one man. By this he means that the university should have been established as of more benefit to the country than the deanery. Brady would have bet his " best gown " that Loftus had not been appointed, and if he had, that he would not have accepted it. He marvels that " so noble a prince " (Elizabeth) would have broken her solemn promise made in the presence of so noble personages. Is all the work of Sir Thomas Wrothe for the advancement of God's work come to this ? He then continues :—

O unfortunate realm, unworthy of so great a blessing : O Satan, old enemy of all godly proceeding, how hast thou prevailed in stopping a work so necessary for this poor country, so famous for the prince, so honourable for her councillors' memory, the one and the other could never by time be forgotten, nor age wear out of memory ; thus (right honourable) when I had awhile with some passion of mind passed over and digested as I could these so sudden news unlooked for, I began at length to bridle and bring under my own rash and unskilful judgment, and to refer all to God's will and your godly wisdoms, whom I know in his fear carefully to seek His glory and the profit of this wretched country.

Brady asserts that when he was last with Cecil a promise had been given him that the deanery, if it were continued, would not be given to one who already had a benefice, for

<hr/>

[1] *S.P.I., Eliz.*, xiii. 5. Shirley, 180.

he would rather add to the number of those, who are very
few, who would not only " further God's cause but also give
sound and wise counsel to the well-ordering of the State
here." He dolefully confesses that " small fruit are we too
able to bring forth in this so barren a ground." But he does
not envy Loftus, for he thinks him worthy of a good position,
provided Loftus was suited elsewhere, as he had agreed with
Brady he would seek to be. Brady then apologises for his
bold and frank speaking, declaring that it " proceedeth not
of a malicious spirit, but of a spirit zealous of God's glory
and furtherance of his true religion."

This was the beginning of a serious estrangement between
Loftus and Brady. Meanwhile, Loftus was eager, while
retaining his nominal archbishopric, to have a valid excuse
for remaining in Dublin. As to Craik, so to Loftus, the
deanery of St. Patrick's was a welcome oasis. He quickly
presented himself before the Chapter as their dean and then
returned for a while to his safe archiepiscopal residence at
Termonfechin, near Drogheda. In a letter [1] thence, 8 April,
to Cecil and the Earl of Leicester, he complains that the
Barons of the Exchequer have charged him with the first-
fruits of the deanery whereas the Lord Chancellor and Council
by deed released him from the obligation. He understood
that, as the benefice was granted *in commendam*, the Queen
meant that he should have it gratis. Then he reveals the
real reason of Elizabeth's grant of the deanery to him, namely
that, under a bond of £1000 he should resign it " whensoever
the Queen's Majesty should convert the same [St. Patrick's]
to a school or house of learning." But, he states, he " thought
good for certain respects not to declare " to the Chapter this
arrangement. He therefore begs his friends to plead with
the Queen that he may compound for the first-fruits.
Elizabeth, acceding to his request, issued a discharge, 11 June,
1565. Loftus and Brady had been considering together the
question of St. Patrick's as a University, " a common place
of learning in this rude and ignorant country," the want of
which " hath brought a general disorder in this land." This,
of course, is a mere dealing with generalities ; neither of them

[1] *S.P.I.*, *Eliz.*, xiii. 8.　Shirley, 184-7.

gets down to the fundamental question, how is a University in Dublin to alter the faith of the people throughout the country ? Who are the young intellectuals who are to frequent its halls, where are they to come from ? They, perhaps, convinced themselves that as a gesture of Protestant organisation in Dublin it might overawe Catholicism in the rest of the country. They both felt that the area of their influence was narrowing rather than enlarging. Loftus was unable to officiate in Armagh, Brady was useless in Meath, Walsh was despised in Waterford, Bodkin in Tuam, and Burgh in Clonfert were hemmed in under the protection of Clanricarde, Daly was laughed at in Kildare, Curwen was " unprofitable " ; not one of Elizabeth's bishops was able to accomplish anything of real practical value for the furthering of the " reform."

However, Loftus now agrees that St. Patrick's is the " fittest place in the land " for the University and that he is willing to further the work. He tells this to Cecil in a letter, 10 October,[1] but states that " the old Bishop," Curwen, " is as unwilling to this, as to further any other our business." Curwen was certainly a stumbling-block to the " reform," whatever may have been his motives. Loftus recommends that he be provided for in England, and that some one be placed in the bishopric " as willing faithfully to join with me, as I with him ; both we shall procure the voluntary resignation or just privation of all the Gainsayers," i.e. the prebendaries of St. Patrick's. To put it plainly, the main reason at the back of the heads of Loftus and Brady seems to have been to get rid of these Catholic prebendaries at any cost.

Loftus then recommends the resignation of the Bishop, the Dean, and the Chapter into the Queen's hands. But the Queen is to be careful to see that, whoever is appointed Archbishop of Dublin, the prebends may be wisely distributed by him. He states that he or Brady would have gone over to the Queen to put this matter before her, " were it not for very poverty."

[1] *S.P.I., Eliz.*, xv. 12. Shirley, 225-8.

Loftus Confesses that the Nobility and Gentry of the Pale still Attend Mass.

As little or no progress was being made in inducing the people to accept the tenets of the State religion, much faith was placed in the ability of an ecclesiastical commission.   In October, 1564, Loftus held the chief place in the commission. To aid this body in its work of compulsion of people's consciences in the direction of the " reform," a proclamation was issued which imposed a fine of 12d. (about 12s. *1914 value*) to be levied by the churchwardens, for the use of the poor, on those who, not having reasonable excuse omitted to resort to their parish churches on all Sundays and Holidays.   A memorandum in the *State Papers* likewise shows that this subject was receiving the serious attention of the Government.   It consists in an advice :   " to cause the people to resort to Common Prayer, and to be instructed to understand the articles of their faith and commandments of God, and to place convenient ministers for this purpose in places convenient."   As a piece of advice it was all very well, but as to where the " convenient ministers " were to be obtained, the commission was left in the dark.

Even this special commission, to inquire into the way in which the law for attendance at Protestant service was being observed, was not a great success.   Loftus, as the head of the fifteen commissioners, saw clearly that sterner measures should be adopted to compel the people, and especially the nobility and gentry, to attend.   In a letter, 17 May,[1] Loftus tells the sorrowful tale to Elizabeth :—

It may please your most excellent Majesty, whereas your Highness hath given commission and authority to me and other your faithful servants and subjects here, for the ordering of all causes ecclesiastical within this your realm : I have thought fit (for as your Majesty hath placed me Chief in commission, so indeed the rest are contented to put the chief care, and, in a manner, the whole burden on me) to signify to your Highness the manner and order of our proceedings, that thereby I may both render an account to your Majesty of our bounden duty and service, and humbly crave your Highness's resolution and special instructions

[1] *S.P.I., Eliz.*, xiii. 42.   Shirley, 194-7.

in certain causes concerning our commission, wherein I thought not fit to further to proceed until your Majesty's pleasure were therein specially known. Immediately upon my arrival here, after I departed from your Highness, I called together as many of the commissioners as conveniently I could, and by their advices determined to inquire by the oath and verdict of certain juries, chosen out of all the several parishes within the English Pale, to inquire of, and present, all manner disorders and offences committed against your Majesty's laws and injunctions, that concern causes ecclesiastical. And upon return to their several verdicts, we found many and great offences committed against your Majesty's laws and proceedings. All which we are about presently to reform with such diligence and speed, as by any lawful means we may. But among all their presentments they brought nothing against the nobility and chief gentlemen, which yet have contemned your Majesty's most godly laws and proceedings more manifestly than any of the rest, and therefore we determined to call them before us, and to minister unto them certain articles, unto which we required the nobility to answer upon their honours and duty to your Majesty, without oath ; the rest of the gentlemen answered upon their oaths. And when they brought unto us their several answers, we found by their own confessions, that the most part of them had continually since the last Parliament frequented the Mass, and other service and ceremonies inhibited by your Majesty's laws and injunctions, and that very few of them ever received the holy communion or used such kind of public prayer and service as is presently established by law. Whereupon I was once in mind (for that they be so linked in friendship and alliance one with the other, that we shall never be able to correct them by the ordinary course of the statute), to cess [tax] upon everyone of them according the quality of their several offences a good round fine and sum of money, to be paid to your Majesty's use, and to bind them in sure bonds and recognizances, ever hereafter dutifully to observe your Majesty's most godly laws and injunctions. But for that they be the nobility and chief gentlemen of the English Pale, and the greatest number too, I thought fit not to deal any further with them, until your Majesty's pleasure were therein specially known, which I humbly crave with such expedition as conveniently may be. And verily in my opinion, if they were once brought to some good order and dutiful obedience somewhat sharply dealt with all now, it should be no small furtherance to your Majesty's proceedings and their example should be a great cause to bring the rest and meaner sort to a godly reformation. And thus I humbly commit your Majesty to Almighty God, who send your Highness a long and prosperous reign over us.—From Dublin, 17 May 1565.

Loftus, thus, in most unmistakable terms, confesses the failure of the " reform " within the Pale and among the very gentry and nobility who were expected to provide an example " to bring the rest and meaner sort," namely, the poor denizens of the city and the poor farm labourers in the country, " to a godly reformation." The names of the Nugents Scurlocks, Nettervilles, Cusacks, Eustaces, FitzGeralds, Suttons, etc., are to be found among the Catholic gentry. The vast majority of the gentry had been hearing Mass as if they had never heard a word about " reform," and not only allowed their mansions to be used as Mass-houses for the Catholic people but gave bed and board to the Mass-priests who were forbidden by law to say Mass in a public church. And all this was done, not spasmodically, but by a certain arrangement for each district. Loftus says they were " linked in friendship and alliance one with the other." Even as late as 1630, Launcelot Bulkeley, Protestant Arch-bishop of Dublin, in his visitation of the diocese, confesses that certain of these houses were recognised as the Mass-houses of certain districts. So that, even seventy years after the Act of Uniformity had been passed, the haunts of Catholics for almost public worship were well known. It is worthy of note that Loftus, in the above report, refers to the jurors at these sessions of ecclesiastical inquiry as unwilling to give evidence against the gentry, and he also states that he did not force the nobility to reply on oath, but that all came forward boldly, and confessed that the majority of them had been attending Mass, since 1560, as before, and had not attended Protestant service.

Brady Complains that " All Things Waxeth Worse than Otherwise."

The payment of first-fruits was ever a source of complaint on the part of Elizabeth's bishops. Having seen the success of Loftus's petition for the remission of first-fruits on his deanery, Brady now pleads with Cecil,[1] 16 May, to induce the Queen to confer a similar favour on him. He had been charged with the first-fruits of Aldermary Church, London, which he had not been able to enjoy, as before he received any revenues he was appointed to Meath. He does not, therefore, see how in conscience he should be charged to pay first-fruits for Meath and Aldermary, particularly as the next incumbent of the latter had to pay similar charges on it. The amount was only a matter of £23, yet he protests that were he able to pay it, he would willingly do so. He then proceeds :—

I am at this present very poor, charged with a great house, driven to large expenses, or else infamy and discredit, for these people will have the one or the other, I mean they will either eat my meat and drink, or else myself : and that I may speak of it without vaunt [boast] or comparison, I feed as many continually as any bishop in England doth, and have not as yet provision toward the same, but all of the penny ;[2] and to do otherwise I cannot, unless I should utterly discredit both myself and my doctrine, which both maketh me to have often an heavy heart, and an empty purse ; and to help me forward to more grief I am presently compelled to go into the Earl of Desmond's country, leaving my own function and business behind me undone, to my great charges and some hazard, amongst so untamed a people ; and yet I speak it not as to spare either charge or life to do her Majesty's service according to my bounden duty.

Brady then speaks of his former application for a favour for one Leech, and continues :—

To say anything farther of the state of the country at this present I will not, only this, all things waxeth rather worse than otherwise, and, as I said before, I fear me, without some speedy redress, the whole body [politic] will be so sick as it shall with difficulty recover, so frowardly be men here disposed, I pray God you will dutifully look unto it. This poor man, Robert Gorye, having a custodian upon the place of a gaol in Westmeath, hath already bestowed a good piece of money of the same. No man can tell better how necessary it will be than I myself, that is within

---

[1] *S.P.I.*, *Eliz.*, xiii. 42. Shirley, 187.
[2] I.e. he has to pay for all out of his own pocket.

my diocese, and [I] have of late travailed [worked] there myself, and therefore require your honour to further the same. I wrote unto you for the office of the Remembrancership for Jeffrye Pintchbacke,[1] a poor kinsman of your own. Death had rid both you and me from farther trouble of that suit ; God send him a joyful resurrection. As for the matter of Saint Patrick's [University], I am afraid to say any more, and yet more afraid to keep silence ; if you will say there is already done as . . . done, I say there is to hinder it and to further it ; and if you will ask me how to further it, I can tell you how to perform it, whereof I will say no more, till I hear from you ; thus leaving at this time further to trouble you, desiring God long to continue your health, and to increase your honour and virtue : from my house at Ardbrachan.[2]

Before the sealing hereof, the news of O'Neill's victory against the Scots is come ; he giveth fair words, attributing the glory thereof to her Majesty. Of my part I can say little, but I pray God he may prove so faithful as he saith of himself : surely he hath done good service, if he employ all to the furtherance of her Highness' service, and if he do not, he was never so much belooked unto. What I shall learn or hear I will certify your honour if [I] may be so bold. Once again I say, if her Majesty will not let a Governor be known, before God I speak it, you will all repent it : here is nothing goeth forward, for God's sake look to it. From Dublin, this 16 of May. Yours in his prayer so long as life endureth.—H. MIDEN.

Brady received a letter from Cecil of 24 May releasing him from the charges on Aldermary Church, and thanked him profusely in a letter of 23 June.[3] Again he harks back to the question of St. Patrick's Cathedral, and makes suggestions on other matters. As far as one can gather he seems to favour himself for the See of Dublin, his own diocese of Meath being undesirable. " Call home," he says, " the old unprofitable workman [Curwen], and give him some living, he may in his old days live at home quietly ; and place another to join him with my Lord Primate." So, he did not favour Loftus for the See of Dublin. But he wished him to be provided for elsewhere, " which will be hardly done in this land." But as Loftus has been granted the deanery of St. Patrick, then

---

[1] A relative of Cecil, who had been registrar of the ecclesiastical commission.
[2] Thus far in a secretary's hand : the rest holograph.
[3] *S.P.I., Eliz.*, xiii. 74. Shirley, 200.

his whole scheme is upset, for he [Brady] wishes St. Patrick's to be converted into a university. He says :—

The erecting of a college in Oxford or Cambridge hath deserved just commendations to the founders, what shall the erecting of a whole academy in this so barbarous and ignorant a country deserve ? This is the way to extirp ignorance, the only mother of murder, robbery, adulteries, with vices infinite, which daily we have perpetrated without check. It is the only way, right honourable, in place of wilful stubbornness to bring civil obedience with commodities more, too many now to rehearse ; whereof though we for our time do not so plentifully reap the fruits, yet let them that cometh after be cared for.

It is the same old story, the failure of the " reform," nothing succeeding, and the only hope to bring " so barbarous and ignorant a country " to reformation is to be centred in the creation of a university in Dublin.

Irish Protestants Fear Innovations in Ritual.

About a week after Brady's last letter, Robert Daly, Bishop of Kildare, wrote to Cecil,[1] 2 July, reminding him that when he was at Court he got leave to write to him about Irish affairs, but that he abstained from doing so until he had something of importance to tell him.

But now (he says) the bruit of alteration of religion in England is so talked of here amongst the Papists, and they so triumph upon the same that it would grieve any good Christian heart to hear their rejoicing in that behalf. Yea, in so much that my Lord Primate, my Lord of Meath and I, being the Queen's Majesty's commissioners in ecclesiastical causes, with others our associates, dare not be so bold now in executing the said commission as we have been unto this time ; to what end this talk will grow unto I am not able to say, but only by conjecture, I fear it will grow to the great contempt of the Gospel, and of the ministers of the same, except that spark be extinguished before it grow into a greater flame. The occasion of this bruit is nothing else but that certain learned men of our religion are put from their livings in England as it is reported here, but upon what occasion it is not known here as yet. The poor Protestants, being amazed

---

[1] *S.P.I., Eliz.*, xiv. 1. Shirley, 203.

at the talk, doth oft resort towards me to learn what the matter means ; whom I do comfort with the most fruitful texts of Scripture that I can find, willing them to put their trust in God, who promised that the faith should not decay in His elect, and that he promised never to leave His flock comfortless.   Now, good master Secretary, because I would not be tedious unto you, I most humbly beseech your honour, for God's sake, to accept my poor request, and my bold enterprise, sending me some comfortable words concerning the establishment of our religion, wherewith I may both confirm the wavering hearts of the doubtful, and also suppress the stout brags of the sturdy and proud Papists ; and thus I pray the living Lord to be your shield and buckler for ever.—Written at Kildare, the 2 July, 1565.

To understand the nature of the conflict as to ceremonial in the English State Church, it will be useful to summarise the main points.   On the breaking up in disorder of the Conference of Westminster, 31 March, 1559, between the Catholics and the Reformers, a committee was appointed to prepare the Prayer Book.   There were two Prayer Books in existence, the First and Second Prayer Books of Edward VI, of the years 1549 and 1552 respectively.   The Book of 1549 had been arranged with the express object of not offending too glaringly Catholic sentiment, and although Transubstantiation was acknowledged, yet the Mass was not recognised as a sacrifice.   The Second Book of 1552 was made in deference to the wishes of those who thought the First Book savoured too much of unreformed doctrines and ceremonies.   It removed all that could form an acknowledgment of Transubstantiation.   This was done under the influence of foreign reformers, such as the German, Martin Bucer, the Italian, Peter Martyr, and the Pole, John Laski, who had taken refuge in England.   The Queen and Parker, Archbishop of Canterbury, and also Cecil, preferred going back to the First Prayer Book, and to remodel it with a tendency towards Catholicism. But her Council were guided by the consideration that whilst it was impossible to satisfy the Catholics, it was politic to consult the wishes of the foreign theologians. They therefore proposed that the Second Book should be selected as the one to be presented to Parliament to be attached to a new Act of Uniformity.

The Second Book was the one adopted by the Committee, and no vestment, except the surplice, was to be allowed at any of the services ; and the communicants might stand or kneel as they thought fit.

The Queen was unwilling to consent to so simple a procedure. If not very particular about doctrine, she was at any rate fond of a high ritual. " Her taste revolted from the bareness of Protestant ritual, and above all from the marriage of priests." [1] A compromise was effected. The Queen was willing to accept the Second Book so long as the ornaments that had been prescribed in the First Book, but omitted in the Second, were allowed.

As to the Ornaments of the Ministers, the Rubric of the First Book of 1549 ordained :—

1. " In the saying or singing of Matins and Evensong, Baptizing and Burying, the Minister in Parish churches and chapels annexed to the same shall use a surplice."

2. " And whenever the Bishop shall celebrate the Holy Communion in the church, or execute any other public ministration, he shall have upon him, beside his Rochette, a surplice or albe, and a cope or vestment [chasuble], and also his pastoral staff in his hand, or else borne by his chaplain."

" Upon the day and at the time appointed for the ministration of the Holy Communion, the priest that shall execute the Holy Ministry shall put upon him the vesture appointed for that ministration, that is to say, a white albe, plain, with a vestment or cope," and the assistant priests or deacons " shall have upon them likewise the vestures appointed for their ministry, that is to say, albes with tunicles."

In the Second Book of 1552 all this had been changed and the following substituted : " And here is to be noted that the Minister at the time of the Communion, and at all other times in his ministration, shall use neither albe, vestment, nor cope, but being Archbishop or bishop, he shall have and wear a rochet ; and being a Priest or Deacon, he shall have and wear a surplice only."

The Act of Uniformity, therefore, of 1559 contained the clause which was according to the Queen's wishes that all

---

[1] J. R. Green, 371.

the Ornaments of the Book of 1549 were to be retained.   So
that although the doctrines of 1552 were adhered to, the
ceremonial of 1549 was preserved.   There were a few slight
alterations which are not necessary to mention here.   One
point, however, is of importance, namely : " morning and
evening prayer [is] to be used in the accustomed place of the
church, chapel, or chancel," that is, that the priest stood at
the upper end of the choir, at his stall, and nearest the altar,
towards which, whether standing or kneeling, he turned his
face in the prayers.   That was according to the Rubric of
1549, which had been altered by the Book of 1552 into ordering
that the minister " shall so turn him as the people may best
hear."

After a general visitation of the country was determined
upon, a body of Fifty-three Injunctions was published for
general guidance.   In accordance with these : images, though
not ordered to be removed (and the Queen still retained the
Crucifix in her own chapel) should not be restored in places
where they had been already removed ; no altars were to
be taken down except by the curate and churchwardens ;
the holy table was to stand in the place where the altar had
usually stood, except during the Communion, when it was
to be so placed within the chancel that the minister might be
best heard.

The Archbishop of Canterbury, though less attached to
the higher ritual than the Queen, was too timid, and always
in fear of offending the Puritans.   This party was composed
of those who had taken refuge on the Continent during Mary's
reign, and who on their return showed themselves a party of
malcontents within the Church, who thought that the Reformation had not been carried far enough.   Others there
were who thought that it had been carried too far.   Between
these two parties stood Elizabeth and Parker.   The State
Church, however, became swamped during Elizabeth's reign
with anti-ritualistic bishops through Parker's fear of offending
the Puritans and through his influence over the Queen.   And
so during his primacy and owing greatly to his own action,
the Vestiarian contest gained strength.

These bishops, returned from the Continent, and restored
to their Sees, disliked all ornaments and vestments, and any

Pope with all his ? . . . O what inconvenience were it to thrust out of their livings and ministry so many godly and learned preachers, only for this that they will not be like the papists, the professed ministers of Satan and Anti-Christ, in superstitious and wicked order of apparel and outward show ? . . . so long as these things were indifferent, and left at liberty [free choice] for a time to win the weak they might be worn ; [1] but now, being urged, and compelled of necessity, I cannot perceive (to write to you my conscience freely) how they can be safely used. . . . Nay, I myself have felt, and that to my grief, how the using of it hath encouraged the adversaries and hindered the course of the true and sincere religion . . . the true and sincere ministry of the Church of Christ ye shall never [restore], unless ye remove and quite take away all monuments, tokens, and leavings of papistry ; for as long as any of them remains, there remains also occasion of relapse unto the abolished superstition of Anti-Christ.

Having thus endeavoured " to unburden my conscience of a matter that troubles it not a little," Loftus relates a much more important matter :—

The 13th of this month, by virtue of our commission for causes ecclesiastical, we committed to the Castle of Dublin Doctor Walsh, late Bishop of Meath,[2] there to remain until the Queen's Majesty's pleasure were known ; he refused the oath, and to answer such articles as we required him ; and, besides that, ever since the last Parliament, he hath manifestly contemned and openly showed himself to be a misliker of all the Queen's Majesty's proceedings ; he openly protested before all the people the same day he was before us, that he would never communicate or be present (by his will) where the service should be ministered, for it was against his conscience, and (as he thought) against God's word. If it shall seem good to your honour, and the rest of her Majesty's most honourable Council ; in mine opinion, it were fit he should be sent into England, and peradventure by conferring with the learned bishops there, he might be brought to some conformity ;

[1] Loftus evidently believed that the end justifies the means. So long as vestments, which he considers the inventions of man through the inspiration of Satan, might be instrumental in deceiving Catholics who were forced to attend Protestant service, it would be quite lawful to use them. Edward VI used a similar method with the Mass and the Sacrament of Penance before they were completely abolished by him.

[2] Since his release from Dublin Castle the bishop had been in his diocese ministering openly to his flock, for which, according to the powers of the ecclesiastical commission he was liable to arrest.

he is one of great credit amongst his countrymen, and upon whom (as touching causes of religion) they wholly depend. I beseech you let me understand your mind here in (and of another letter that I wrote to the Queen's Majesty concerning proceedings with the lords and gentlemen here) with such expedition as conveniently may be. The God of heaven long preserve your honour, and stir up a diligent care in you to help and comfort [this] afflicted Church. I have sent your honour a goshawk and a tiercel [1] [by] this bearer, if these do like you, I mayhap another year help you with more. —From St. Patrick's this 16 of July, 1565.

The sympathies of Loftus with the Puritan party here appear without disguise in its opposition to the surplice and other Popish apparel, as he terms the authorised dress of the clergy of the English Church. Later it will be seen how, when he became Archbishop of Dublin, he had the Communion Table removed from its customary place to the centre of the church, a characteristic Puritanical device.

Unrest in the Country ; Desmond and Ormond Feud.

After his return from England, Desmond kept quiet for a time. The indefatigable Cusack visited Waterford for the purpose of settling his dispute with Ormond, but had to leave his work unfinished so as to proceed with the more pressing business of O'Neill. On 12 January, 1565, he informed the Queen that he had concluded all matters satisfactorily with Shane whom he praises for dealing with the Scots.[2] But, a fortnight later, FitzWilliams had to complain to Cecil of Shane's late disorders at Carlingford and of the violence of his men.[3] The heads of the Government in Dublin were at the time carrying on a personal warfare among themselves, which was well bruited abroad. Brady, in a letter to Cecil, 29 January,[4] states that " there hath been some jarring betwixt my Lord Justice [Arnold] and Mr. Marshal [Fitz-Williams]. I am sure the whole court ringeth of it there, or this time." He hears that Sussex is returning shortly, and assures him how welcome it will be to himself. Sussex himself

---

[1] *Goshawk* was the short-winged hawk, as distinguished from the *falcon* or long-winged hawk ; the *tiercel* was the female of the *goshawk*.

[2] *C.S.P.I.*, *Eliz.*, xii. 9, 10.   [3] *Ib.*, 18.   [4] *Ib.*, 21.

complained to the Lords of the Council, 29 January, of Arnold's misgovernment, of subverting the English Government of the country, and that £40,000 will not be sufficient to restore Ireland to the tranquillity it was in two years ago.[1] On the same day Arnold wrote [2] to Cecil a " general discourse on the state of the country," assuring him of what he thought would be welcome news, that he acts with the wild Irish as with bears and bandogs ; so that he sees them fight earnestly and tug one another well, he cares not who has the worse. Cecil, a month later,[3] reminded Arnold that he is not to con- sider what the world only will judge, but what God sees, and that he (Cecil) as a Christian man cannot without per- plexity contemplate the wild Irish set to fight as bears and bandogs.

As to the old feud between Desmond and Ormond, the latter reported to Cecil, 8 February,[4] that he was attacked by Desmond whom he overthrew and took prisoner. He now desires the Queen's letters to bring Desmond prisoner to England. FitzWilliams recommends Ormond's policy, but the Council ask Ormond to draw up a statement as to this conflict, and to present questions to Desmond. These the latter answers at Waterford, 18 February.[5] Ormond then charges the Desmonds with treason,[6] and the Queen in reply [7] states that she mislikes the hostility between the two Earls, and commands Ormond to come to the royal presence. In similar terms she writes to Desmond, McCarthy More, O'Sullivan Beare, Roche, Barrymore, Fitzmaurice, Power, and Dunboyne, the lords of Munster, and to Sir Maurice Fitzgerald. Later, however, she changed her mind and wrote strongly to Lords Roche, Barrymore, Power, and Dunboyne to maintain order during Desmond's absence.

On 23 April, Arnold was able to inform the Privy Council that Desmond, McCarthy More, and O'Sullivan Beare were repairing to England.[8] FitzWilliams represented to Cecil, 3 April, that Arnold was responsible for this most unsatis- factory state of the country, and that he had spent seven weeks at Waterford investigating the dispute between Ormond

[1] *C.S.P.I.*, *Eliz.*, xii. 19. [2] *Ib.*, 20. [3] *Ib.*, 50.
[4] *Ib.*, 28. [5] *Ib.*, 31. [6] *Ib.*, 37.
[7] *Ib.*, 39-46. [8] *Ib.*, xiii. 23.

and Desmond, and had made no progress.[1]   He complains likewise that as Treasurer for War, he has disbursed by order of Arnold upwards of £33,000.   This expense for war in Ireland, without the excuse of any progress made, was most distasteful to the parsimonious Queen.   Brady, likewise, informed Sussex, 4 April, that Arnold had become discredited through bad management, and that much harm had been thereby caused, and that he had advised the Earl of Leicester to recall him.[2]

THOMAS STUCLEY APPEARS ON THE SCENE.

There now enters on the Irish stage one of those hectic characters who set events marching at a great pace for a time, but who, after a sequence of success and failure, end their lives in tragedy.   This was Thomas Stucley,[3] a bold buccaneer, who very seriously, if indirectly, affected by his strange career the fate of Ireland.   The younger son of an old English family in North Devon, he began his career by attaching himself to the party of the Duke of Somerset ; and, on the execution of the latter for conspiracy against the State in 1552, he managed to make his escape to the Continent, joined the armies of France, won his way to the confidence of the King of that country, learned, according to his own story, of a design that His Majesty was forming for the invasion of England, and communicated his information to the Privy Council.   He was next heard of in the army of Charles V. Returning to England on the accession of Queen Elizabeth, he dedicated himself to the then fashionable profession of piracy, was imprisoned for spoiling the Queen's friends on the high seas and obtained his release through the intercession of influential friends.   He afterwards won the hand of the only daughter of the wealthy Admiral Curtis, soon ran through her immense fortune, deserted her, returned to his favourite practice of piracy, and attracted the notice of Elizabeth, who rather favoured pirates on her own side.   She warmly received his plans, and even issued a licence authorising him to found a colony in Florida, using the Irish ports

---

[1] *C.S.P.I.*, *Eliz.*, xiii. 6.   [2] *Ib.*, 25.
[3] See *Catholic Bulletin*, April, 1929, pp. 344-5.

as a base for his small fleet of privateers, in the year 1563. The havens of Cork and Kerry were the happy hiding-places of English pirates at the time, and they did a roaring trade with the Irish chiefs, who, unlike Elizabeth, were indifferent whether the goods exposed for sale had been taken from her friends or foes, and who gave a ready welcome to Stucley's bounding barque.

On 17 November, 1564, Wrothe wrote to Cecil [1] that Stucley was upon the west coast of Ireland with a ship of four hundred tons and a hundred " tall soldiers beside mariners," and is now in Kinsale and remains there. He is afraid that he will keep to the sea ; efforts have been made to catch him but they have not yet succeeded.

The next time we hear of Stucley is in a letter of his, 22 April, 1565,[2] to Cecil in which he declares :—

Pleaseth your Honour the 9th of March last I came unto Waterford in the company of the Lord Viscount Barrymore unto the Lord Justice of this realm who hath commanded me to attend upon his Lordship until he know the Queen's Majesty's pleasure what I shall do, which I have and will most humbly obey. His Lordship telleth me that he hath written unto the Queen's Majesty how I came unto him and to know her Highness's pleasure. I shall most humbly desire your Honour of your accustomed good-ness towards me as this is not the first good turn which I have sought and have received at your hands, so shall it not be the last as I may have occasion to use your honourable goodness, even so I pray your Honour to think that if ever it shall please God to send me ability I will never be unthankful to do you service in anything I can or may to my life's end. I assure your Honour I have little left at this present but mine honesty which I shall most humbly desire you to think well of, not doubting but when I shall by your good means be heard I shall be better judged of than I am at this present. Fearing to trouble your Honour with so long a discourse by writing, I have sent unto my cousin Mr. John Pollard [blank] pleasure [?] to inform you of my doings and also how my ship and goods was taken away being before delivered unto the Queen's Majesty's use for the trial of my doings. I pray Almighty God to preserve you with my good lady your wife and of yours, from Dublin the 22 April, 1565.

[1] S.P.I., Eliz., xi. 101, P.R.O., London.
[2] Ib., xiii. 19, P.R.O., London.

Stucley had one friend in Ireland, Shane O'Neill, and to him he applied to make a petition to the Queen in his favour. Accordingly, 18 June,[1] Shane wrote to say that when it pleased Her Majesty to call him to the royal presence, many of the nobles and magnates of that kingdom showed him great friendship, and in particular a gentleman, Master Thomas Stucley, showed him every kindness. And Shane says that he recognised that all this attention and kindness shown to him manifested the magnificence and honour of Her Majesty and her kingdom. In a similar letter to Leicester he avows that Stucley treated him in a more friendly manner than did anyone else, although he (Shane) was a stranger to him, and he asks Leicester to show Stucley every possible favour, so that the Queen may not only condone what he has done but send him back to him.[2]

The charge against Stucley, given in a letter of the Privy Council to Arnold, 22 June,[3] consisted in piracies committed against Spanish subjects against which the Spanish ambassador complained bitterly. The Privy Council deplored that he was still at large when other pirates had been punished. Arnold himself was to bring him over to London or to send some one else with him with a proper guard. To this command Arnold answered[4] that he was sending Stucley who was, however, "prevented by disease from putting to sea." He inquired what he had been doing at sea but "cannot find that he committed any piracy in any coasts of this land." In fact Stucley " used himself so liberally and so courteously with Viscount Barrymore, Barry Oge, McCarthy Ruadh, and others, the lords and captains upon the countries of the West Coast, and with O'Neill in the North, that he may be able when it shall please her Majesty to pardon him his former faults (if there be any) to bring to pass any service which her Majesty would have at any time practised with him as soon as any man I know of his vocation, and have thought it my duty to signify to your lordship this much as I have heard of him."

The next day Arnold wrote to Cecil[5] that when Lord Barrymore brought Stucley to him, Barrymore swore on the

---

[1] *S.P.I., Eliz.*, xiii. 65, P.R.O., London.   [2] *Ib.*, 67.
[3] *Ib.*, 69, P.R.O., London.   [4] *Ib.*, 72, P.R.O., London.   [5] *Ib.*, 73.

Gospels that Stucley came to him willingly, praying that he might have his aid against the City of Cork, which did him great wrong, and that Stucley was willing at all times to serve Her Majesty. Stucley was at liberty to go where he wished, and yet he made no attempt to escape which " doth argue plainly if he had known any fault in his life . . . he would have sought some mean to have kept himself out of danger." Brady [1] also sends his recommendation of Stucley to Cecil stating that " since his hither coming he hath behaved himself very courteously, neither can I find any man complain of him at any time." Finally, O'Neill writes to the Queen, 28 July,[2] soliciting pardon for him, and does not think " such a prudent man as Stucley would do anything against the Queen or her laws."

O'Neill Professes Loyalty ; Sydney Suspicious.

Having witnessed Shane's anxiety to have the adventurous Stucley sent to him, to find out in what ways the buccaneer would be useful to him, it is important to see how he deals with adventurers of another kind, the bold Scots who came to Ireland to sell their military services.

Terence Daniel, Dean of Armagh, and intermediary between the Government and Shane, informs Cusack that he has read the contents of the Queen's letters to Shane who promises to follow Cusack's advice, and who would be glad if a Parliament were held. Terence then adds an item which he expects will be of great interest, if not of pleasure, namely, that the Scots send all the hawks of the North to the Queen of Scotland every season. Shane and the Scots were at daggers' drawn again, and after Easter Shane attacked James McDonnell's castle on Red Bay and Sorley Boy's at Ballycastle. Having inflicted a heavy defeat on them he took McDonnell, who was wounded, and Sorley Boy prisoners.[3] Shane quickly informed Cecil of his victory over the hated Scots (2 May) and bragged about the obligations under which he had placed the Queen. He also informed Cusack that he was sending a horse to England for the Earl of Leicester. Cusack was much delighted at Shane's services against the Scots, and continued to write

---

[1] *S.P.I., Eliz.*, xiii. 74.　　[2] *Ib.*, xiv. 32.　　[3] *C.S.P.I., Eliz.*, xiii. 34.

in glowing terms of his good conformity. But Brady and Loftus could tell that Elizabeth's Bishop for Down dare not present himself there for fear of bodily harm from Shane who had had his own brother (as was said) appointed to the See by the Pope.

The Queen had already decided that Ireland could not be governed any longer by accommodation, and had determined to send over Sir Henry Sydney, cheaply if possible, but if necessary, at any expense. Sydney's advice was plain. Leix and Offaly must be pacified by a general pardon, followed by gentle dealings, or else the people must be extirpated. Munster might best be managed by keeping the nobles at Court, and by appointing a President and Council to rule it ; 200 foot and 100 horse would be a sufficient force. Thomond should be divided among as many men as possible, supreme military command being given to the Earl. The Scots should have no grant of land, but be expelled when the Government was strong enough. As for Shane, he was a common robber, never to be reformed unless by force. Shane knew that he could neither hoodwink Sydney nor hope to defeat him openly, and he began a new correspondence with Scotland. He refused to give up his prisoners to the Queen of Scots or to the Earl of Argyle, until he knew the will of his " own Queen." And his secretary, Gerot Fleming, informed Cusack [1] that Shane refused McDonnell's offer of all his property in Ireland and Scotland for his liberty, on the ground that Shane was the Queen's officer, and that the quarrel was none of his. [2]

O'NEILL SENDS THE DEAN OF ARMAGH WITH PRESENTS TO ELIZABETH.

Cusack writes to Cecil, 23 August, [3] that the Dean of Armagh, a wise and discreet gentleman, has been sent by O'Neill to the Queen with presents, and to inform her of the state of the North country. There is no ecclesiastic, he states, in the North so able to serve the Queen in the affairs of that part of the land. In matters of dispute between the North

---

[1] *C.S.P.I., Eliz.*, xiii. 82. [2] *Ib.*, 46. Bagwell, ii. 91-2.
[3] *S.P.I., Eliz.*, xiv. 46. Shirley, 222-4.

and the English Pale, and in Cusack's proceedings with
O'Neill, the Dean showed himself " a wise, faithful, and true
subject." For this he deserves thanks and reward ; and if he
were appointed to the Archbishopric of Armagh, the whole
North would rejoice greatly.[1] Cusack asks Cecil to use his influence to this end. And if O'Neill were created Earl of Tyrone,
and granted his other requests " then assuredly he would
prove as dutiful a subject as any in Ireland of like calling
in all services." It would be well if the Queen sent " a letter
of thanks to the said O'Neill for his good service with reward,
and then her Highness may trust assuredly to have him
at commandment, to yield all things that shall be required,
which is greatly to be considered." Cusack tells how he has
taken great pains to bring Shane to show devotion to the Queen
" a thing easily done," as far as he could perceive. The
sooner the Dean returns the better, for his presence with
O'Neill not only reminds Shane of his duty to the Queen
but also all the rest of the gentlemen of the country. He
preaches with " good and virtuous exhortations, to whose
preaching and talk they give great faith, grounding himself
therein upon the Gospel and the Epistle, reproving sin . . .
and to live in the fear of God and obedience of their prince "
(Elizabeth). Because of the Dean's preaching that part of
the country " is much the more reduced to good order " so
as no other part of the country " is so well at this present,
whereby every man may by his own in such sort as merchant-
men and all others, as well foreigners as countrymen, may
pass through the country with their merchandise, or any
other thing, without fear of robbing, by day and night, which
is very rare to hear the like."

A few days afterwards, 25 August,[2] Shane wrote to the
Privy Council describing his victory over the Scots, and that
all their towns and castles are in the Queen's possession—
nominally, of course, but really in his own hands—and that

---

[1] Shane had already, according to Archbishop Creagh, sent messengers
to Wolf to obtain the Archbishopric of Armagh for Daniel. In this he was
disappointed. It now appears that Daniel was quite ready to accept the
Archbishopric from Elizabeth and thus acknowledge her supremacy. It
may be that Shane had consented to this, and it may be that it was on account
of this Wolf called Shane an " heretical " tyrant.

[2] *C.S.P.I.*, *Eliz.*, xiv. 50.

all the Scots are expelled from the kingdom. He praises
Arnold—an opponent of Sussex—and hopes that Sydney will
be as good, namely, that he will not interfere with himself.
But Arnold, not knowing of Shane's commendation, reported
to the Privy Council [1] (31 August) that Shane was jealous
of him and had put his own soldiers in guard of the castles
of Newry and Dundrum. He thinks that O'Neill is likely
enough shortly to take more into his hands than the Queen
will approve of. In this he was quite correct for (22 October)
the Earl of Clanricard [2] reported to FitzWilliams that O'Neill
invaded the country of O'Rourke and O'Conor Sligo, spoiled
the whole country, and carried away 3000 cattle, requiring
the tribute due in old time to Kings, and would have it paid
yearly. Clanricard offers his services against O'Neill.

About 27 October [3] Shane wrote to the Queen requesting
that all the articles of peace concluded with Cusack be observed
and that the Earldom of Tyrone be conferred upon him. He
asks that an Irish Parliament be held at which his claim should
be considered, and that the town of Belgriffin in North Co.
Dublin be granted to him with maintenance within the Pale
when he comes to attend Parliament. On 4 November [4]
Cecil wrote to Sydney that the Dean of Armagh would shortly
return with instructions for Shane, and on 10 November [5]
the Privy Council wrote similarly to Shane. Finally, 12 November,[6] the Queen wrote a strong letter to Sydney bidding
him command Shane to repair to him and answer for his
conduct against the Scots in the North and for his expedition
into Connacht, where Shane was " doing all things as though
the countries and subjects were his own." If O'Neill does
not appear dutiful, then Sydney is to have no parley with
him, but to leave him so to receive what he deserves.

[1] *C.S.P.I., Eliz.*, xiv. 57.   [2] *Ib.*, xv. 15 (1).   [3] *Ib.*, 28.
[4] *Ib.*, 37.   [5] *Ib.*, 39.   [6] *Ib.*, 42.

PART II.

"THE HOUR HAS NOW COME."

SYDNEY, THE NEW LORD DEPUTY.

FOR the first half-dozen years or so of the reign of Queen Elizabeth her Irish policy was generally of an indefinite and haphazard nature. She allowed most things to drift, and, on the whole, avoided energetic measures that would have cost money, and which were, therefore, abhorrent to her parsimonious soul. For this reason, much as she disliked the doings of Shane O'Neill, she preferred to keep him in tune by soft words, and even by treaties. But the state of the Pale, where reigned unrest, army disorganisation, and financial confusion, the armed conflicts between the Geraldines and the Butlers, and certain victories of Shane, led Elizabeth in 1565 to revise her policy. Her advisers had been representing to her that she must either make up her mind to lose Ireland or meet force by force, no matter what the cost. Foremost among her influential advisers was Sir Henry Sydney.

The chosen companion and bed-fellow of Edward VI, he was regarded as "the most complete young gentleman" in the court of the youthful king. Under the Catholic Queen Mary, he was no less appreciated, and was made Vice-Treasurer and General-Governor of Ireland in 1556. In military and diplomatic affairs he was equally skilled. Doubtless a staunch Protestant under Edward, he could be an equally staunch Catholic under Mary, and once again a Protestant of a certain brand under Elizabeth. Like most English officials in Ireland he took his religion from his Sovereign, change in that matter not weighing heavily on him. Having on one occasion, during his term of office as Lord Justice in Ireland, reduced Shane O'Neill to something like submission, he was considered the best man to reduce the intractable land to obedience.

Though he did his best to act up to the instructions Elizabeth had given him to promote Protestantism in Ireland by word and work, he had little but contempt for the Protestant ecclesiastics whom he met there. He was ready to discuss theology with Catholic Bishops, and he would have been satisfied to leave them unmolested in their Sees, or even avail himself of their assistance, if they would only consent to recognise the Queen's supremacy. In the same way, he had little love for Her Majesty's favourites, the Ormonds (Butlers), and took sides with their enemies, the Geraldines, as far as he dared. He even won a certain amount of respect from the haughty Shane, who saw something to admire in his off-hand, dashing, rough-and-ready methods of settling difficulties. On taking office, " he found the Kingdom almost ruined by intestine feuds and dissensions." As for the Protestant religion which he had to promote, he admits that " there was but small appearance of it, the churches being uncovered, the clergy scattered, and scarce the being of a God is known to those ignorant and barbarous people." For the next fifteen years, the destinies of Ireland are largely in his hands.

Sydney, partaking of the nature of the period in which he lived, was a strange mixture of contradictory qualities, of kindness and cruelty, of generosity and meanness, of rough justice and sharp practice, of strong impulse and cool deliberation, of unbounded self-conceit, and of deep distrust of his subordinates.

Instructions for Ecclesiastical Government.

The general voice both of England and Ireland had pointed to Sydney as the fittest man to govern. But he knew well that he was more likely to lose a great reputation than to gain fresh laurels, and he determined not to go unless treated fairly. By serving the Queen he complained that he was £3000 poorer, and he suggested various ways to stave off financial ruin. " If you will not grant these things," he said to the Queen, " give me leave to serve you anywhere except in Ireland." But his demands were only partially granted. Some of the ruined castles were to be restored— Kilmainham, at the expense of the lessees, Dublin and Carrickfergus at that of the Government. The military force was not to be increased, and Sydney was expected to heal the distracted land with 882 soldiers and 300 kerne. It was even supposed that he could put down piracy, for though the Queen was willing to lend a ship and a pinnace, she refused to give a single sailor, and coolly told him that he might man them out of his ordinary garrison. He was allowed to retain the presidency of Wales, but his salary as Lord Deputy was the same as his predecessor's. He was not dignified with the title of Lord Lieutenant which had been a special compliment conferred on Sussex, but his powers were almost identical. The finances were to be reformed, if possible, without further charge to the Queen, and with greater ease to the subject, an impossible task, which Sydney knew well that he could never perform.[1]

He received minute instructions as to the principles on which he was to conduct the Government. These are dated 4 July, 1565,[2] although his patent was not made out until 13 October.[3] They are sufficiently important to quote in full :—

1. Item, the principal and first care which her Majesty committed to the said Lieutenant and Council is that they have regard to the due and reverent observation [observance] of all good laws and ordinances established in that realm for the maintenance of Christian faith and religion, and that all means be used as well by example as otherwise, that devotion and godliness may increase from the highest to the lowest, and errors and evil opinions may be *restrained*,[4] suppressed, and abolished ; and because one of the principal means to further this is to have the clergy well instituted [established] her Majesty requireth the said Lieutenant by the advice of the said councillors to inquire of the state

[1] Bagwell, ii. 94-6.
[2] *S.P.I.*, *Eliz.*, xiv. 2, P.R.O., London. Shirley, 206-9. The document in the P.R.O., London, under date 5 October, is an abridgment of that of 4 July.
[3] *C.P.C.R.*, *Eliz.*, i., p. 493.
[4] The italics are corrections by Cecil of the original draft.

of the clergy of that realm, in what parts the same is defective, and by what means it may be repaired and amended, and as much as in them shall be to apply themselves thereunto, and wherein they shall find lack of their own power, to advertise [inform] and show their advices.

For the matters of Religion.

5. Her Majesty, understanding that the Archbishopric of Cashel and the Bishopric of Ossory [1] have been long void, whereby hath grown lack to the ecclesiastical government there ; would have it considered whether, because these two livings are very meanly endowed, it were not meet to unite these two together, so as the living might be meet for some person of such behaviour, as being bishop thereof, might serve as a councillor there in Munster hereafter, when *a council* should be there established *for governance of the same parts.*

Inquisition also would be made of the bishopric of Limerick,[2] whether it be void, or that by some means some person were placed there to serve for the like purpose in such a council.

6. There was also charge given to Sir Tho. Wrothe and Sir Nicholas Arnold, at their going over thither in commission, to cause the college and revenues of St. Patrick's to be surveyed to the intent the foundation of the same might be reformed and reduced to the more profit of teaching and learning for the subjects of that realm. But because, as it appeareth by reason of the multitude of other matters committed to the said commissions, little hath been done therein, therefore to the intent the same may be with more ease converted to the good purposes intended, it is necessary, and so her Majesty willeth and commandeth the Archbishop of Dublin, Chancellor there, to forbear to put any hereafter to any prebends there, when the rooms shall become void, until her Majesty's pleasure shall be further determined ; and that as soon as possible may be, the state and survey of the same college may be made and sent over with advice how the same may be reformed and newly erected to a more public benefit for the service of God and the realm than now it is ; wherein the advice of the two Archbishops of Armagh and Dublin, and the Bishop of Meath would be had, and a good establishment hereof would serve to bring up the youth of that realm to increase knowledge and

---

[1] Cashel was vacant since October, 1561, by the death of Roland le Baron, but neither Pope nor Queen appointed until 1567. Ossory was held by Thonory, who did not die until 1565. According to the above it had been long vacant, thus confirming our view that Thonory was deposed in 1561. Elizabeth appointed Gaffney, December, 1565.

[2] At various times the deprivation of Hugh Lacy, Bishop of Limerick, had been suggested.

civility in sundry parts of the same, where now nothing but barbarous *and savage conditions* remaineth.

7. It would be foreseen that no alienations were suffered to
be made by the clergy *of any of their possessions*, nor impropriations
of their benefices ; for the let [prevention] whereof, if there be not
sufficient law, you shall do well to have at the next Parliament
some special law provided for the same.

8. There was of late a commission sent thither for the governance of the state ecclesiastical, according to the statute giving her
Majesty authority so to do ; the execution whereof would be so
used within the English Pale, as there should not be suffered in
such open sort, as is reported, the use of things manifestly in the
Church *and in other obscure places*, contrary to the laws *of the realm*
established. And whatsoever hath therein negligently been
lately by suffrance passed over, would be from henceforth more
severely *reformed*, and the bishops *and other the ordinaries* would
be moved to visit their cures, *without burdening of the curates and
the people*,[1] and to see the laws and injunctions heretofore published,
duly kept and observed.

According to the eighth instruction, Catholics, who were
forced to attend Protestant service under penalty of fine, were
to be no longer allowed to make a May game of that service,
or to carry out their own services in " obscure places." Up
to the present these had taken place " by suffrance," as
Elizabeth did not wish to antagonise the Catholic nobility
and gentry who were her main support for the maintenance
of law and order within the Pale. As to Limerick, Elizabeth
was unable to see how she could deal with the Catholic bishop,
Hugh Lacy. That city was so remote from Dublin, and
English power was so weak there, that any attempt to meddle
with that bishop might prove disastrous. Not for six years
(1571) more did she actually appoint William Casey, who
had been deprived by Queen Mary, to that bishopric and
granted him the temporalities. Lacy, however, continued
his pastoral office in his diocese until his death in 1580,
occasionally having to retire elsewhere for safety.

" Sir H. Sydney's opinion upon the minute of Instructions
first devised for him." [2]

---

[1] I.e. the fees usually paid to a bishop on the occasion of his visitation
of parishes and churches were no longer to be exacted.

[2] *S.P.I., Eliz*, xiv. 3. Shirley, 210-11.

1. The estate of the clergy as it is, and the defects thereof, shall be certified, and how the same may be repaired, as the Council there shall think meetest ; but the only way is by sending learned pastors from hence [England], and by giving them competent livings there [Ireland], for which there is presently a good opportunity offered by the vacancy of the Sees of Cashel and Ossory, which joined together will make a sufficient living for a sufficient man to be an Archbishop there.

5. My opinion for Cashel and Ossory is before written : nevertheless I will, God willing, certify the opinion of the Council there, as well touching those bishoprics, as the bishopric of Limerick.

6. For the survey of St. Patrick's, and all matters, contained in this article, as the order in the same is very good ; so shall it be by me (as near as I can) observed.

7. To prevent alienations and impropriations,[1] I will confer with the judges, and what may be done lawfully shall be attempted ; but to do it without a parliament I think it impossible.

8. I desire to know where I may have the copy of the commission mentioned in this article, and for other matter contained in the same, shall be executed as it shall seem expedient unto me.[2]

On 9 July, 1565, amended instructions were drawn up, the original draft being altered by Sir W. Cecil. These were repeated under date of 5 October of the same year. They are nearly to the same effect as the original instructions of 4 July. Some extra points may be set out here. In reference to St. Patrick's College they mention :—

The same hath not been prosecuted to effect by reason (as it is thought) that the said commissioners were otherwise occupied : her Majesty chargeth the said Lieutenant and Council without delay to give *commission and* order *to the Master of the Rolls*, the *Auditor*, and *Surveyor that for the time shall be, with any others to be named by the said Lieutenant,* for the survey thereof, and willeth and commandeth the Archbishop of Dublin, Chancellor there, to forbear from the presentation of any person hereafter to any prebend there ; and that he, with the Archbishop of Armagh, and Bishop of Meath, and such others as the said Lieutenant shall adjoin to them, do well and speedily consider the best means

---

[1] *Impropriation* is the annexing of a benefice to the use of a lay person or a corporate body. The term came into use after the " Reformation," when many benefices, that belonged to monasteries, passed into *improper* hands.

[2] *S P.I.*, *Eliz.*, xiv. 7.   Shirley, 211-13.

for " reforming and reducing the said college to the public benefit of learning of that realm."

As to the commission for ecclesiastical causes they state :—

4. Item, the commission which lately was sent thither to the Justice, the Archbishops, and Bishops, and sundry others, for the government of the state ecclesiastical, is *to be considered* by the said Lieutenant now being, *and upon certificate made from him, using therein the advice of such of the Bishops as he shall think meet, what they shall think meet to be further done for the renewing of the same, there shall be sent thither such commission without delay.*

" LAWS AND ORDINANCES FOR MAINTENANCE OF THE CHRISTIAN FAITH."

On 5 October, 1565, " A Brief Declaration of Certain Principal Articles of Religion " was drawn up to be set out by the order and authority of Sydney and Council, the Archbishops and Bishops, and other High Commissioners for Causes Ecclesiastical.[1] This was printed at Dublin by Humfrey Power, 20 January, 1566. It is as follows :—

For the Unity of doctrine to be holden and taught of all parsons, vicars, and curates, as well in testification of their common consent and full agreement in the said doctrine, as also necessary for the instruction of their people in their several cures, to be read by the said parsons, vicars, and curates, at their possession-taking, or first entry into their cures, and also after that yearly at two several times by the year, that is to say, the Sundays next following Easter-day and St. Michael the Archangel ; and this upon pain of sequestration, deprivation, or other coercion, as shall be imposed upon such, as shall herein make default.

Then follows the declaration of assent to be made by each minister in the presence of his people.

Forasmuch as it appertaineth to all Christian men, but especially to the ministers and pastors of the Church, being teachers and instructors of others, to be ready to give a reason of their faith, when they shall be there-unto required : I, for my part, now appointed your pastor, vicar, or curate, having before me the fear

---

[1] *S.P.I., Eliz.,* P.R.O., London, xv. 4. Mant, i. 271.

of God and the testimony of my conscience, do acknowledge for myself, and require you to assent to the same.

The Articles are twelve. The first asserts the Trinity of Persons in the Unity of the Godhead.

The second sets forth the sufficiency of the holy canonical Scriptures to salvation : and confesses all the Articles contained in the three Creeds.

The third is as follows :—

I acknowledge, also, the Church to be the spouse of Christ, wherein the word of God is truly taught, the Sacraments orderly ministered according to Christ's institution, and the authority of the keys duly used. And that every such particular [national] church hath authority to institute, to change, clean to put away ceremonies and other ecclesiastical rites, as they be superfluous, or be abused ; and to constitute other, making more to seemliness, to order, or edification.

The fourth Article confesses that

it is not lawful for any man to take upon him any office or ministry, ecclesiastical or secular, but such only as are lawfully thereunto called by their high authorities according to the ordinances of this realm.

The fifth Article acknowledges

the Queen's Majesty's prerogative and superiority of government, of all estates and in all causes, as well ecclesiastical as temporal, within this realm.

And the sixth denies

the authority of the Bishop of Rome to be more than other bishops have in their provinces and dioceses.

The seventh confesses the Book of Common Prayer to be

agreeable to the Scriptures, and Catholic, Apostolic, and most for the advancing of God's glory, and the edifying of God's people, both for that it is in a tongue that may be understood of the people,[1] and also for the doctrine and form of ministration contained in the same.

---

[1] The Government had previously admitted that English was not understood by the people and had recommended translation into Latin.

The eighth asserts the perfect ministration of Baptism, although there is in it

neither exorcism, oil, spittle, or hallowing of the water now used ; and for that they were of late years abused, they be reasonably abolished.

The ninth condemns " private Masses " or a

public ministration and receiving of the Sacrament by the priest alone, without a just number of communicants.

It also condemns the doctrine of

the Mass being a propitiatory sacrifice for the quick and the dead, and a mean to deliver souls out of Purgatory.

The tenth affirms that the

Holy Communion ought to be ministered to the people under both kinds.[1]

The eleventh

utterly disallows the extolling of images, relics, and feigned miracles; and also all kind of expressing God invisible in the form of an old man, or the Holy Ghost in the form of a dove, and all other vain worshipping of God devised by man's fantasy, besides or contrary to the Scriptures : as wandering on pilgrimages, setting up of candles, praying upon beads, and such like superstition : [and] exhorts all men to the obedience of God's law and to the works of faith.

The twelfth article is a general acknowledgment of the preceding.

These things, above rehearsed, though they be appointed by common order, yet do I without all compulsion, with freedom of mind and conscience, from the bottom of my heart, and upon most mature persuasion, acknowledge to be true and agreeable to God's word.   And therefore I exhort you all, of whom I have cure, heartily and obediently to embrace and receive the same ; that we, all joining together in unity of spirit, faith, and charity, may also at length be joined together in the kingdom of God, and that through the merits and death of our Saviour Christ : to whom with

---

[1] One of the Irish bishops at the Council of Trent defended Communion under both kinds, but expressed his readiness to abide by the papal decision.

the Father and the Holy Ghost be all glory and empire, now and for ever. Amen.[1]

INSTRUCTIONS AS TO CURWEN.

In the same instructions to Sydney he is informed that Curwen is sick, impotent, and not meet to continue as Chancellor. Curwen's place is to be given to another and he is to be notified that Her Majesty " hath always had good opinion of him and never had heard any report made but to his commendation, and so would have him hold himself well assured, and for that of late his health is decayed and is likely to decay more and more by continuance in so painful an office as the Chancellorship is." No doubt the " unprofitable workman " appreciated Elizabeth's kind consideration of him. But she informed Sydney that she was pleased " to let him remain Archbishop and one of the principal of her Privy Council, hoping he will continue a careful councillor as he hath always been, and so manifest that her Majesty doth not deliver him from his other office but for his service and his own commodity [well-being]. He shall have an annuity of £100 by year assured to him during life." In other words, Elizabeth is not prepared to relieve him of his archbishopric, on account of the scarcity of suitable men for the office of bishop in Ireland. She was unable to get anyone for Cashel or Ossory, and she did not wish to be burdened with another vacant See. To appease Curwen she granted him £100 a year in lieu of his fee as Chancellor. Such was the state of the Elizabethan establishment after six years of " reform."

SYDNEY RECOMMENDS LOFTUS FOR CASHEL AND OSSORY.

Cashel and Ossory were important Sees for the " reform," lying as they did on the main road to the cities of the South, but they were difficult to control on account of their distance from Dublin. A move, however, must be made if the South

---

[1] This declaration seems to be the same as one, of which a summary is given by Strype (*Life of Abp. Parker*) and published in England in 1561. under the title *Metropolitans and Bishops*, probably Parker's own work (vol. i. 182-3). (Mant, i. 275.)

is to be brought into line with the new establishment through the institution of a governorship.

Loftus had warned Cecil against one Johnson who had been recommended for the See of Ossory. Sydney also heard of this, and, on his way to Ireland, thought it well, from Chester, to write to Cecil, 24 November,[1] and give him his opinion about the disposal of the vacant Sees. He says :—

Sir, I hear that earnest suit is made to her Majesty for the bishopric of Ossory and Cashel, I beseech you most heartily, and that for the service of the Queen, that you will procure the stay of it until you shall hear from me out of Ireland ; my concept and intendment is this, to remove the Primate of Armagh to those Sees, and to place the Dean of Armagh in it, by the translation the Primate shall lose nothing, but enjoy like dignity in effect which he did, more living, and in a more civil place, and a greater flock to understand him than he had before ; and on the other part, the Dean greatly pleased, who is as able to direct Shane as you and all the Council are to direct me : and I believe he will do well, and verily think while I govern there he will do no evil. Sir, trust me this is a matter of great consequence, and therefore I beseech you, either send me authority thus to dispose and place, if I shall so think good, and can, or at least stay the grant to any, till [you] eftsoons hear from me ; believe me, Sir, much by this means may be wrought with Shane, for God's love stay at least. I tarry here only for wind, which, God once sending, I will not be willing [to] omit to go to the sea. I have no more but my most hearty commendations and my wife's done to you to my lady your wife, and to my Lady Bacon. I wish to you all a long, quiet, and happy life.—From Chester this 24 November, 1565.

Cecil on 23 December, 1565, namely a month afterwards, assured Sydney that " he would never advise any resolutions in matter of moment without his advice." Other influence prevailed, and the changes contemplated here never took place. It is important, however, to notice the reasons for the translation of Loftus to Cashel and Ossory, that he would have as dignified a title, more income, and more people to preach to than he had in Armagh. In truth, he had never preached in Armagh, but such trifles of accuracy did not weigh heavily on Sydney when a disagreeable situation

[1] *S.P.I.*, *Eliz.*, xv. 51. Shirley, 229-30.

presented itself.   He too, like other officials, thought that the
only way of pacifying Shane and the North was to allow Terence
Daniel as Archbishop of Armagh.

Sydney Seeks Conference with O'Neill ; Stucley as Intermediary.

Sydney was wind-bound for nearly two months in Wales
and Cheshire.   He and his wife were forced to flit about
the coast, in places where food, drink, and lodging were alike
bad.   He lost all his wine and other property, worth £1500.
Elizabeth afterwards expressed sorrow for his losses, but
it does not appear that she did anything in the way of com-
pensating him.   At last, the wind changed, and Sydney
found himself in charge of a country as restless as the sea
that washed her shores.

His first care, 21 January, 1566, a week after he landed,
was to let Shane O'Neill know of his arrival, and so urge him
to appoint a meeting at Drogheda or Dundalk.   He enlisted
the service of the Dean of Armagh for this purpose, and
afterwards that of Stucley.

Shane O'Neill had made the acquaintance of Stucley at
the English Court, and was quite captivated by the bold
buccaneer.   When Stucley, after his capture at Kinsale, had
been brought to the Tower of London, he found no warmer
intercessor for his release than Shane who pleaded to the
Queen that Stucley was not the man to do anything against
her laws.   Not only was Stucley released, but he was sent
back to Ireland with letters of recommendation to the Irish
Council from Cecil, Leicester, and Pembroke.   By his winning
ways he captivated Arnold and Brady, and soon won over
Sydney to his side.

Shane himself was anxious to befriend Stucley and requested Sydney [1] to send him as intermediary in their negotiations.   Sydney agreed to this,[2] and sent Stucley with
Justice James Dowdall, who were to give Shane " full satisfaction," and hold the bait of an earldom to him if he but
showed himself amenable to English law.   The negotiators
were sent back to Sydney who was requested to give credence

---

[1] *S.P.I., Eliz.*, xvi. 20, P.R.O., London.   [2] *Ib.*, 27.

to their report. Shane's reply lost nothing in the telling of it by Stucley : " ' What,' said Shane, ' is an earldom to me, who in blood and power am better than the best of them.' You have made an earl of MacCarthy Mor, yet better man than he yield obedience to me. I admire your Queen, and ' I confess she is my sovereign lady, yet I never made peace with her but by her own seeking.' As for obeying the summons to appear in person in the Lord Deputy's camp, ' whom would you have me trust, Mr. Stucley ? See what happened when I trusted the Earl of Sussex and went on a safe-conduct to London. The Queen herself told me that indeed safe-conduct I had to come safe and go safe, but (she added) she had not told me when, and so she there held me till I had agreed to such inconveniences to my honour and profit as I would never perform while I live, and that made me make war. If I were to do [the same] again, I would do it, for my ancestors were Kings of Ulster—Ulster was theirs and shall be mine. As for O'Donnell, he shall never come into his country if I can keep him out of it, nor Bagenal into Newry, nor the Earl of Kildare into Dundrum or Lecale.[1] They are mine : with this sword I won them, and with this sword I will keep them. This is my answer. God be with you, my masters.' "

Although Stucley had made two journeys to Shane, the latter was intractable, and would never come to any governor. This was the report of Bagenall in February,[2] who concluded by confessing that he has " known the country for over 20 years and never knew it so much out of frame ; for there was robbing, stealing, and killing throughout the English Pale. The countries of the Walshes, the Byrnes, and the Tooles within four miles of Dublin, by robbery one of another almost throughout waste." Bagenall, of course, refers to the efforts of the Irish in South Co. Dublin and present Co. Wicklow to recover lands that had been forcibly taken from them by the Government and granted to the latter's supporters.

Sydney himself had a similar doleful report to make to Leicester (1 March),[3] and stated that Shane made peace with the Queen only when she sought it, that he (Shane) can bring

---

[1] Kildare claimed Lecale. [2] *S.P.I.*, *Eliz.*, xvi. 33, P.R.O., London.
[3] *C.S.P.I.*, *Eliz.*, xvi. 35.

1000 horse and 4000 foot into the field; that he has agents abroad, and that he is able to burn and spoil to Dublin gates and return unmolested.

STUCLEY BEFRIENDED BY SYDNEY, BUT OUT OF FAVOUR AT COURT.

Stucley was playing his cards well. Although he failed to induce O'Neill to meet Sydney, yet the latter believed he could be useful to him in a very important position. Bagenall had agreed with Stucley to sell him his office of Marshal of the Army and his whole estate in Ireland for £3000 *Irish*. Accordingly Sydney wrote to Cecil, 7 March [1] informing him of this, and that Stucley had the Queen's favour and Cecil's good opinion. And he gave his own opinion of him : " I judge him an apt man in the execution of the office," and when stationed in Navan he will be a " neighbour to O'Neill," and in time may be " a good instrument " for preserving O'Neill's friendship. " And in wars a lusty plier to defend his own and his neighbours. And albeit I never had cause to doubt of Stukley's sufficiency in discretion, saving that his lease dealing for his own commodity was some mean to his credit ; [2] yet have I found in his late service with O'Neill such honesty and deep judgment and such care of the prince's [Elizabeth's] love and my place, as giving me a new opinion farer different from mine olde. And, therefore, have thought good to desire your helping hand to this his purchase."

Evidently according to pre-arrangement with Sydney, Stucley wrote on the same day to Cecil to continue his goodness to him as mediator for him with the Queen. [3]

The response from Cecil (27 March) was not encouraging. [4] He relates how the Queen made " strange speeches " of Stucley's appointment, and did not think that Stucley was seeking chiefly the success of her government. The whole court spoke strongly against Stucley when they became aware of Sydney's letter, and would by no means have him appointed to a place of trust. As usual Cecil is most anxious

---

[1] *S.P.I., Eliz.*, xvi. 52, P.R.O., London.
[2] I.e. Stucley had made a bargain with Bagenall advantageous to himself.
[3] *S.P.I., Eliz.*, xvi. 53, P.R.O , London.   [4] *Ib.* 67.

to be on the best terms with Sydney, and advises him not to waste time with Stucley and not to be deceived by him. A few days afterwards (31 March) Cecil in another letter to Sydney [1] informs him that the Queen is much annoyed at Stucley's remaining in Ireland. He is sorry for Stucley who, in Ireland, " might percase have begun to turn upward in Fortune's wheel, but here [in England] I think he shall not be able to stir the wheel."

The purchase of the important office of Chief Marshal of the Queen's forces in Ireland from Sir Nicholas Bagenall carried with it an estate that the latter had obtained in the Magennis country about Greencastle in Co. Down. But it does not appear that the exchange was ever sanctioned by Elizabeth. In the meantime, Sydney had promoted him to be Seneschal of Wexford and Constable of Leighlin [2] to which were attached monastic lands at Leighlin and other lands in the vicinity.[3] This taking over of monastic lands was to cause him trouble later with the Pope. His position of

---

[1] *S.P.I., Eliz.*, xvi. 71.

[2] Commission to Thomas Stucley, seneschal of Wexford, to execute martial law in the county and liberty of Wexford, Cavanagh's country Idrone, and that part of the county Catherlough, late under the rule of Sir Nicholas Herne (24 Aug., 1567). (*Fiants*, no. 1119.)

[3] Lease, 26 September, 1567, of the site of the house of friars of Innescorthy, a ruined castle, land, and a weir there, lands of Garran, Kylkenan, Loughwarch, Karrickerowe, and Ballyneparke, customs of boards, timber, laths, boats, bearing victuals, lodges during the fair, things sold there, and fishings, belonging to the manor; the fourth part of Deinge, the sixth of the fourth part of Kylmaloghe, and land in Garryheste, in O'Moorrowe's country, C. Wexford; also the manor of Cloghamon in O'Morrowe's country, an old bawn of lime and stone, an old town towards the water of the Slane, another town by the gate of the manor, the lands of Cloghamon, Balluibege, Kyltilt, Ballycoddan, Burgeshamon, Ballyhamyn, Kylrushe and Ballybreny, both Grages, Ballygowne, Boleghorche and Ballyvangan, Ballypark and Cahirusuyne, Kulmylaghe and Ballyvicwalter, in the O'Morrowe's country. Also the site of the abbey of Downe, in O'Morrowe's country, the land extending from the ditch by the little stream to the mountain, and all other appurtenances, to hold for twenty-one years, at a rent of £72 3s. 8d.; maintaining two English horsemen in the friary, and not levying coyn or other impositions. (*Fiants*, no. 1129.)

Lease under commission at Dublin, 26 September, 1567, to Thomas Stucley of the moiety of the rectory of Donnahannoke and Ballegmone and the rectory of Tankerstown, Co. Kildare, the rectories of Strabo, Rathmore and Moyactone, Co. Carlow, and Kilcurrie, Co. Kilkenny, possessions of the late monastery of Thomascourt, Dublin, the tithes and altarages to the vicar of Rathmore excepted. To hold for twenty-one years at a rent of £24 13s. 4d. Not to levy coyn. (*Fiants*, no. 1265.)

trust, however, brought him into close contact with the Earl of Kildare, the Desmonds, the Butlers, the O'Neills, and others, and he came to learn of the plot that was being hatched, for a struggle, with the help of Spain, against Elizabeth. This plot revived an old dream of his that he had communicated to the Spanish ambassador in London some years previously, and he at once took an active interest in promoting it.

REFORM " GOETH SLOWLY FORWARD "; " CHURCHES IN RUINS."

Sydney, having gathered his Council around him, considered the various points of Elizabeth's instructions of 5 October, 1565, as to the ecclesiastical state, and sent the following reply to the Privy Council, 13 April, 1566 :—[1]

And for the residue of her Majesty's said instructions digested into four principal parts ; it may like your lords to be advertised ; that as to the first article of the first part, I her Majesty's deputy, and the residue of her Council here, which are laymen, can no less than (as truth is) declare for the Archbishops of Dublin and Armagh and the Bishop of Meath, that they are diligent in the function of their offices pastoral, as well in often and fruitful preaching, and setting forth of God's glory and true Christian religion themselves, as also in the earnest calling on and looking to the other pastors and ministers within their provinces and dioceses to do the like ; and are earnest and careful exhorters and overseers over the residue under their charge, to reduce them by all good means out of error and contempt of godliness, unto right belief and true devotion ; and likewise on the part of me her Majesty's deputy, with the rest of her Council here our best endeavour (by God's grace) hath been, and shall be, both by good example and earnestness, and by all other good means, to maintain and further the same there, and throughout all this realm universally.

Howbeit that for all this, it goeth slowly forward, both within their said three dioceses (by reason of the former errors and superstitions inveterated and leavened in the people's hearts ; and in want of livings sufficient for fit entertainment of well chosen and learned curates amongst them, for that those livings of cure being most part appropriated benefices in the Queen's Majesty's possession are let by leases unto farmers with allowances or reservation

---

[1] *S.P.I., Eliz.*, xvii. 8.   Shirley, 233.

of very small stipends or entertainments for the vicars or curates besides the decay of the chancels, and also of the churches universally in ruin, and some wholly down) and out of their said dioceses. The remote parts of Munster, Connacht, and other Irish countries and borders thereof (saving the commissioners for the ecclesiastical causes have travelled with some of the bishops and other their ministers residing in the civil and nearer parts) order cannot yet so well be taken with the residue until the countries be first brought into more civil and dutiful obedience. I, the Deputy, have given charge to the said bishops to make diligent, search, and to certify me in the next term of every the said decayed chancels and churches in their dioceses, and also of the want and vacancy of curates, upon which certificate the parties faulty therein shall be called before us, and straight order taken with them for the re-edifying [rebuilding] of them, and also for the supply of the want and vacancy of curates, and so (as we may) we shall proceed for the rest of the realm.

To the second article thereof, a survey was taken of the foundation and state of the College of St. Patrick's by Sir Thomas Wrothe and Sir Nicholas Arnold, and (as Sir Nicholas Arnold saith) was carried over by Sir Thomas Wrothe to be showed unto your lords with their opinions, certified according the charge of their commission, for the best means of reforming thereof; and I, the Archbishop of Dublin shall according her Majesty's commandment, forbear from the absolute presentation of any person to be prebend there until her Highness's pleasure further known. The livings of the prebends are most part in benefices with cure [of souls], and they for the more part aged men, who, with the rest of the ministers of that college, according the rules of the same, give their due attendance on that collegiate church, daily doing divine service, and devotion with due reverence and harmony convenient, and some of them do preach also. Nevertheless, they have been treated with by us, the Archbishop and Bishop of Dublin, Armagh, and Meath, and are found conformable to depart with such portion of their livings as shall be thought fit by her Highness for the setting forth and maintenance of learning and teaching for this realm. And for that the survey and opinion of the former commissioners aforesaid is already there to be showed to your lords and related to her Majesty, we have stayed off proceeding further therein, until thereupon it may like your lords to procure her Highness's further pleasure to be signified unto us.

To the third article thereof, we know not as yet of any alienations or wastes suffered to be made by the clergy, nor of any appropriations of benefices by them put in use, nor that the clergy of this realm are greatly inclined to offend in that part, except the alienations or waste done by the Bishop of Ferns [1] who to the use of his sons hath put away the most part of the living of his bishoprick; for the which, and other the like which might hereafter happen, remembrance for remedy and provision shall be had against the next Parliament.

To the fourth and last article thereof, the commissioners for the causes ecclesiastical do (as they may) proceed therein, howbeit slowly for the causes aforesaid.

H. Sydney.	H. Dublin Canc.	Ad. Armachan.
Jo. Plunket.	Nicholas Bagenall.	
Francis Agarde.	W. Fitzwilliam.	Robt. Dillon.
James Bath.	Henry Draycott.	

This document of the Council of Ireland in the year 1566 is a clear confession of the failure of the " reform " even in the dioceses of Dublin, Armagh, and Meath where at least some success might have been expected. The chief result was the decay of churches and chancels,[2] " universally in ruin and some wholly down," and the miserable wage to vicars or curates some of whom had three or four cures to make up a decent living. The Queen had most of the benefices in her hands and leased them out to " farm," sweeping the money into the royal treasury, neither she nor the " farmers " of the tithes going to the least expense to keep the churches

---

[1] Alexander Devereux, Bishop of Ferns, died at Fethard in 1566, having been bishop of Ferns almost twenty-seven years, and was buried there in the chancel of the parish church. The following entry shows the extent to which the bishop favoured his relatives : " Licence to John Deveroux, dean of the cathedral of S. Edan of Ferns, William Deveroux, clerk, treasurer of the same, and William Deveroux, clerk, rector of Tamon in the church of Ferns, that, having no residence within the precincts of the catheral, they may for three years absent themselves from it, remaining in any other part of the county Wexford for study (20 July, 1566)." (*Fiants*, no. 918.)

[2] In the year 1531 and up to the year 1560 there were in the diocese of Dublin 273 churches. In 1630, namely, 70 years after Elizabeth's Parliament, the Protestant Archbishop of Dublin, Launcelot Bulkeley, drew up an exhaustive report on " The State of Most of the Parishes and Churches in the Diocese," and counted not more than 37 churches in repair, the rest having gone to ruin. These parishes were in charge of 55 Protestant clergymen, one of whom had six curacies, six had five, two had four, several, three and two. Only eight parishes had a Protestant population of over 100 persons, six had less than eighty, ten less than forty, twelve less than twenty, twenty less than ten, ten had a few, and nineteen apparently had none at all. (See Bulkeley MS., F. 3, 17, T.C.D.)

in repair. In the areas under English power, as priests and people were forbidden to have Mass in their churches, they were no longer allowed to use those churches for the purposes for which their Catholic ancestors had built them and provided lands and tithes. Elizabeth's secular and ecclesiastical officials by the arm of the law were granted those churches, lands, and tithes for the support of her ministers and religion, and yet Sydney had to confess the disgraceful state into which the churches were allowed to fall. The few Protestant worshippers and the few Protestant ministers were totally inadequate for the number of those churches. The State Church was, therefore, entirely wanting in the essential and principal part of a church, namely, people to be ministered to. To state then that "most of the bishops in Ireland"[1] accepted the "reform" and that, therefore, the cathedrals and churches became Protestant property is pure fiction. The Council's letter totally disposes of such a notion. Sydney confesses the want of ministers for those churches, but the Catholic priests were in the country as they had been in Mary's reign. Clearly a very small percentage had gone over to Elizabeth's reform. The Council distinctly state that with the "remote parts of Munster, Connacht, and other the Irish countries and borders thereof, order cannot yet so well be taken until the countries be first brought into more civil and dutiful obedience."

The work of destruction was chiefly confined to the parishes within the Pale—Louth, Meath, parts of Dublin and Kildare —where the authorities had it in their power to prohibit the Mass in public. Outside that area the people had been but little affected by the attempted change of religion, and carried on in the old way, using their churches for Catholic services. In cities and towns as Waterford and Youghal,

---

[1] Dean Kennedy says that "the Archbishop of Dublin and most of the Bishops in Ireland accepted the changes consequent on the Reformation in England, when the Supremacy of the King was established in place of that of the Pope, and they therefore retained possession of their Sees and Churches." (*Christ Church Cathedral* [*sic*], p. 11.)

He omits to say that Mary came along and upset the Edwardian system. And certainly it is not true that in Elizabeth's reign, which is the point that matters, most of the Irish Bishops accepted the Supremacy. The churches, therefore, did not come into Protestant hands by that means.

where a garrison was temporarily stationed, the priest might be driven out for a time, but seldom hesitated to return the moment the soldiers had taken their departure for other fields of activity. This is what happened even after Sydney's grand tour of north, west, and south, and sometime afterwards. It was only a temporary subjection to English rule ; permanent force would be necessary to achieve a lasting success, and without such a force anything like a " reform " was out of the question. Sydney himself confessed this much. But with the advent of the new and energetic Lord Deputy, with his clearly defined programme for the diffusion of English sway over the land, for the curtailment of the power of the great chiefs and nobles, and for the introduction of planters from England, the people of Ireland found themselves united by the common interest of self-preservation.

The Lord Deputy (15 April) informed the Privy Council of his journey in Leinster, Meath, and Westmeath, that not an O'Toole, O'Byrne, Kavanagh, Kinsella, O'Morrough, or O'Doyle refused to repair to him. He took their sufficient sureties and pledges. The Walshes', Archbolds', and Harolds' countries he committed to the charge of Thomas FitzWilliams of Merrion. All the coast under the Red Mountain, being the west part of the Tooles' and Byrnes' countries, bordering on the Co. Kildare he committed to Robert Pheybo. The O'Mores were tractable, but the O'Conors were waiting to do mischief. He held sessions, executed fifty notable offenders, and twenty more by martial law. Not a bad beginning for Sydney ! Kilkenny was also in disorder, and he desired Ormond to return in order to bring that portion of the country to civil obedience.

New Bishop for Ossory ; Star Chamber to be Erected.

Cecil (1 March) desired Sydney [1] to set about immediately to fill the vacant Sees, " to the intent there might be some good done in those parts, that the people might be taught and instructed better than I think they be." Sussex, when Lord Lieutenant, had requested that his chaplain, Christopher

---

[1] *S.P.I*, *Eliz.*, xvi. 34. Shirley, 231.

Gaffney, an Irishman, should be appointed to Ossory, but, although Cecil considered him fit for the post, Sydney was to use his own judgment, as in all such cases. This letter appears to have crossed one from Sydney to Cecil, Dublin, 3 March, 1566,[1] in which he says : " The Primate of Armagh would fain be Archbishop of Cashel with Ossory, sure, Sir, both for Church and country causes, he shall be able to do much more good there than where he is. I beseech you, let me know your opinion in it, for I will no further persuade it till I know it, but this I know, both God's cause and the Queen's shall much be advanced by it." Loftus did not receive the desired change, and the promotion of Gaffney to the See of Ossory did not take place until May, 1567, when he was consecrated in St. Patrick's, Dublin.

In another letter of the same day (3 March) to Cecil,[2] Sydney wrote about the Star or Castle Chamber that had been set up by Sussex, and from which he saw " no great effect follow." He continues :—

Nevertheless, I find it a court so necessary and of so great consequence here as I must allow and greatly commend the erection, and also desire you that it may be further established by sending us hither the orders of the Star Chamber especially that which is to be observed by the clerk, and the order of the processes, and the form of the seal thereunto belonging together with such authority as the court hath there for the accepting of recognisances and cancelling of bonds, whereof if advertisement [instruction] might come before the next term that court should be fully established, which, being yet but in his infancy was worth to the Queen this last term about £100.[3] (About £1200 *1914 value.*)

[1] *S.P.I., Eliz.,* xvi. 41, P.R.O., London. [2] *Ib.,* 42.

[3] The Star Chamber was a room in the old House of Lords, so called from its ceiling being adorned with gilt stars, or, according to some, because it was originally the place of deposit of the Jewish stars, *starra,* or covenants. The despotic tribunal that sat here was also called the Star Chamber. It was under the direction of the chancellor, and had jurisdiction of forgery, perjury, riots, maintenance, fraud, libel, and conspiracy, and in general of every misdemeanour, especially those of public importance, for which the law had provided no sufficient punishment. It was this criminal jurisdiction (its civil having gone into disuse) that made it so powerful and odious an auxiliary of a despotic administration. Its process was summary, and often iniquitous, and the punishment which it inflicted, often arbitrary and cruel. The court was at liberty to adjudge any punishment short of death. Evidently, Sydney saw in it a magnificent weapon in Ireland for the profit of the Queen's Exchequer as it afterwards became in England for Charles I.

12 *

Vacant Bishoprics : Sydney's Recommendations.

At last Curwen's request was granted, and Elizabeth informed Sydney, 28 March, that she was translating him to Oxford.[1]   He was unable to do anything for the " Reform," if he was ever really keen on doing it.   He was in the way, and he knew it, and so did Loftus and Brady know it.   His palsy provided a reason why he should seek a more genial climate.   Sydney then (23 April) [2] recommended Brady for Dublin as " the fittest to succeed both for his sufficiency in preaching, wherein he is equal to the best of the Bishops here, and for his grave judgment in Council, wherein he far exceedeth the rest."   He is also exemplary in life and hospitality.   Loftus would be a meet successor to Brady in Meath, and would not object to lowering his status—from archbishop to bishop—as he would thereby increase his revenue.   Sydney then wished to touch a tender cord in Elizabeth's heart by pointing out to Cecil that by the three new appointments to Armagh, Dublin, and Meath, she would gain the first-fruits of the three bishoprics.   Curwen's translation, however, did not take place until the following year, when Loftus, and not Brady, succeeded him.

Meanwhile, Curwen, 24 April,[3] thanked Elizabeth profusely for her favour, though he says he did not " deserve the hundredth part," but did his duty to the best of his power, " with which (I thank God) I pleased the country here indifferently."   That is, the people did not like his " reform."

Loftus,[4] too, agreed with Sydney that Brady was the fittest man for Dublin, and assured Cecil that, with himself as Dean of St. Patrick's, and Brady as Archbishop, there would be good hope of the reformation of the Church of Dublin.   Loftus preferred to be Dean of St. Patrick's, a nice, comfortable position, than be Bishop of Meath, subject to the vagaries of fortune.

There was no mention as to how the Church of Armagh was to fare.   The show of success was to be made in Dublin.

---

[1] C.S.P.I., Eliz., xvi. 69.   [2] S.P.I., Eliz., xvii. 31.   Shirley, 238.
[3] S.P.I., Eliz., xvii. 33.   Shirley, 240.
[4] S.P.I., Eliz., xvii. 39.   Shirley, 242.

There was about this time also a vacancy in Leighlin by the death of Thomas O'Fihil.[1] Sydney recommended to the Privy Council, 18 May, Daniel Cavenagh, " a gentleman of those parts, and a professor of divinity." As the benefice is so small, not £100 a year (about £1200 *1914 value*), " few would have accepted the dignity with so small commodity ; yet finding this gentleman, enabled by the wealth and strength of his friends in those parts, to be a good servant to the Queen for the preservation of justice, whereof that country hath great need," he earnestly recommended him. He had been well recommended also by the Archbishops of Armagh and Dublin, and by the Bishop of Meath, as well as by the Chapter of Leighlin, of which he was a member, for " his learning, ability, and honest conversation," and for " his sufficiency and ability to preach." [2]

Cavenagh was, however, not appointed for a year, 10 April, 1567, and was consecrated by Curwen in St. Patrick's, Dublin. Meanwhile, Elizabeth was able to appropriate the revenue of the bishopric, such as it was.

Curwen, himself, although appointed to Oxford, 24 March, had not received his patent. He requested Cecil,[3] 21 May, " so move her Majesty," that he " might come hence before the winter next ; for I am here in the winter so sick and likewise weak, as heretofore I have been scant able to pass it over with life ; and very glad would I be if it might stand with her gracious pleasure, to come away in such time as I might provide fire for winter, and hay for my horses." And he adds another reason, no doubt one that would appeal to Elizabeth, why his successor in Dublin should be speedily appointed. It is to the effect that " if the See stand vacant much of the lands will be pilfered away by Irishmen, and the houses spoiled, which now I shall leave in good estate."

Curwen enlisted Sydney on his side to secure his speedy departure to his own country and to more friendly surroundings, urging " his infirmity of the palsey, and thereby his

---

[1] Ware says he died the Friday before Palm Sunday, 1567 (Harris, *Ware's Bishops*, 461). Others have followed Ware in this. The date should be 1566.

[2] S.*P.I.*, *Eliz.*, xvii. 53. Shirley, 246-7.

[3] S.*P.I.*, *Eliz.*, xvii. 63. Shirley, 248.

disability to travel towards winter." He also pleaded for
" the last half-year's rent of the Bishopric of Oxford."
Accordingly, Sydney requested Cecil (23 May) to present
his petition to the Queen.[1]

Meanwhile Brady had conversation about the Archbishopric
with Sydney who promised to write to Leicester and Cecil
in his favour. But he feared that Cecil had heard some
sinister report about him, and might be opposed to him.[2]
He wrote about this to Sussex from Dublin and complained
that he was " shut out at doors." He doubted that O'Neill
will come to Dundalk to meet Sydney, " his pride joined
with his tyranny is intolerable." Finally, he announced
that two young men had come from Cambridge, evidently
preachers, to help himself and Loftus. He was at this time
lodging at the Deanery of St. Patrick's.

On 8 June Sydney wrote to the Privy Council recommending Gaffney for Ossory, and stating that he had had
favourable letters from Curwen and Brady.

Loftus was not satisfied with the state of " the poor
Church of Ireland," and besought the Privy Council, 10 June,[3]
that " such bishops hereafter from time to time may be sent,
as for their learning and zeal in God's Holy Word, may be
bishops indeed." He complained that " there be sent bishops
to occupy almost all the best rooms in the land, of whose
unableness and untowardness, if it might do good, I would
say more." However, anything he could say on the subject
would not change matters. He then recommended that " a
zealous and learned man in God's Holy Word " be appointed
to Dublin, and St. Patrick's to be turned into a college.
" This," he says " is not my suit alone, but it is the earnest
prayer of all those that desire the godly and peaceable subjection to the Queen's Highness. And, my good Lords,
remember also that you shall answer before the tribunal
seat of Jesus Christ, if this land perish for want of faithful
and learned preachers." It is illuminating to see how Loftus
and Brady were playing about with the Archbishopric of
Dublin and the Deanery of St. Patrick's. Neither had a

---

[1] S.P.I., Eliz., xvii. 64.   Shirley, 250.
[2] S.P.I., Eliz., xvii. 40.   Shirley, 246.
[3] S.P.I., Eliz., xviii. 12.   Shirley, 255.

word now as to the progress of the "reform" in Armagh or Meath.

On the same day he wrote to Cecil [1] in similar terms, and reminded him that he (Cecil) had, on another occasion, seemed "to pity the conversion of the tithes, contrary to the institution, from the use of their pastors." Sydney had also complained that the tithes were being swallowed up by the Queen and the lay people, and little or no provision made for the Protestant ministers. "For," continued Loftus, "if your honour understood how simply [badly] they [the parishes] are served now, and heretofore have been, you would rather pity the case of the people much fleeced and nothing at all fed."

Loftus is concerned that the people are fleeced and are not fed with Protestant doctrine by Protestant ministers. He conveniently ignores the point that the tithes of the Catholic people were instituted for the support of the Catholic religion and its ministers, and he took it for granted that it was the business of the people to provide the tithes for the support of the State clergy. Whether their money went to Elizabeth and her lessees or to her ministers was a matter of indifference to them; they were being fleeced in any event and they had no desire to be fed by Loftus, Brady, or any of their clergy, as these reformers readily confessed. It was a family squabble over the distribution of the spoils, and the people no doubt looked on with a good deal of amusement at it whilst at the same time resentment was in their heart. Their own clergy had to eke out an existence as best they could, depending on the charity of those who could afford it. As to St. Patrick's, Loftus says that "the erecting of the college, wherein many godly ministers and learned preachers shall be placed, would discharge them [the cures], for that the benefices are almost all within five miles of Dublin." From this it would seem that the prebendaries of the Cathedral were unable to draw any revenues from their prebends beyond a five-mile radius of Dublin city.

Loftus also gave Gaffney [2] a commendatory letter for Ossory on his departure for the English Court, "for that,"

---

[1] *S.P.I., Eliz.*, xviii. 13. Shirley, 257-8.
[2] *S.P.I., Eliz.*, xviii. 20. Shirley, 259.

he says, " the place is Irish, and none of his country birth
(that I know), meeter than he." And he requested Cecil [1]
that if Gaffney be appointed to Ossory, the livings that he
now enjoys should be given to " Master Lecke, sometime
servant to King Henry the Eight, and now attending on the
Lord Deputy, to whom they are promised upon the preferment of the said Gaffney." Gaffney was prebendary of
Tipper in St. Patrick's Cathedral, besides being Dean of
Leighlin, and in order that Lecke might succeed Gaffney in
the other livings, Loftus adroitly suggested that the bishopric
of Ossory " is a liberal stipend and a living sufficient to maintain the state of the bishop there." It had already been
complained that it was a poor living, worth only £100 (about
£1200 *1914 value*).[2]

Loftus (3 July) recommended to Cecil [3] James MacCaghwell,
who is also going to England, as one fit for Cashel. When
he was last in England, he says, he received commendation
of him from the Bishop of Salisbury and others. The living,
being very small, is not meet for anyone else except a native
of that country birth. Loftus had evidently given up the idea
of taking upon himself the burden of these two dioceses.
He was intent on Dublin.

On 30 May the Lord Deputy wrote to the Privy Council
that Dominick Lynch of Galway desired to build a free-
school there, and would contribute perpetuities towards the
maintenance of a master. The parsonage of Galway and
the site of a ruined house, called Earl's Stone, should be
requested of the Queen towards that good work.[4] Since the
suppression of the Religious Houses the lack of schools was
a serious affair. Dublin also felt that something should be
done to educate youth. Early in 1561 the municipal authorities took the matter into their hands, and " it is agreed that
Mr. Maior shall, by the advise of eight of the aldermen, give
ordre for the scholehouse of the cittie, and to provide a good

---

[1] Shirley, 261.

[2] It had already been reported that Lecke had sustained great losses through
the late Bishop Craik of Kildare. On 9 May, 1567, he was presented to Gaffney's
prebend of Tipper, and on 9 October had licence to hold with it the vicarages
of Dunshaughlin and Donockmashe in the diocese of Meath. All these had
probably been held by Gaffney. (Mason, notes lxxx.)

[3] *S.P.I.*, *Eliz.*, xviii. 37. Shirley, 263.   [4] *S.P.I.*, *Eliz.*, xvii. 69.

lerned maister to teache therin ; and to lymite and appoint to him such yerlie stipend, to be paied of the treasorie of the cittie, such as by them shall be thought mete, provided that they take the said ordre by Shrovetide next." [1]

The scheme hung fire for more than a year, but on the fourth Friday after 29 September (= 23 Oct.), 1562, " it was agreed by thactoritie of this assembly that the master of the grammar scole of this cittie shall have yerely as a sallary or pencion from this cyttye twentie poundes lawfull money of Irelande ; to have and injoy the same sallary or pencion by thandes of the treasorer for the tyme beinge to the said scole master so long tyme as he shall well and diligently attende his chardge in teaching in the said scole." [2]

BISHOP OF WATERFORD ASKS TO BE RELIEVED OF THE DEANERY.

Patrick Walsh, Bishop of Waterford, was one of the seven Marian bishops who had accepted the Supremacy. Like Curwen of Dublin he complained of advancing years and wrote, 15 June, 1566, to Sir Henry Sydney [3] asking to be relieved of the Deanery that he held concurrently with the bishopric :—

I grow now unable to discharge the burden of my functions, finding myself both in body and sense so decayed for age [4] as whereof I conceive the more care, that mine impotence with detaining of those dignities I have from such as shall be thought worthy to supply them, cannot excuse me before God, I am thereby in conscience stirred to wish myself rid of part of them, and although they being united doth scant make a competent living ; and therefore my good lord, I shall most humbly beseech you to accept my resignation of the Deanery of Waterford, to be by your honour commanded to one Peter White,[5] of the birth of

[1] *C.A.R.D.*, II. ii.

[2] *Ib.*, 24. This Dublin school was situated in Ram Lane, afterwards called Schoolhouse Lane, by the side of the present St. Audoen's Catholic Church. It is likely that the premises of the " College " of St. Audoen's, or presbytery of old St. Audoen's which stood here on the site of Blakeney's Inns, was utilised for the purpose.

[3] *C.P.C.R.I., Eliz.*, i. 494.

[4] In those days a man was old before he reached his sixtieth year.

[5] On 22 June the Lord Deputy wrote to the Chapter of the Cathedral of Waterford for the election of Peter White to the Deanery.

this city, a man very well learned, past degrees in schools, and of virtuous sober conversation, by whose industry and travail a great part of the youth of both of this country and of Dublin have greatly profited in learning and virtuous education ; wherein, in my opinion, your lordship shall do a good deed by discharging of me that am far spent, and commendation of him that is so well able every way to discharge the duty of that room.

In November, however, Walsh was appointed one of the commissioners for arbitrating between the Earls of Ormond and Desmond.

O'NEILL APPEALS TO THE CARDINAL OF LORRAINE AND TO THE FRENCH KING.

Sydney had said that O'Neill had agents abroad ; that was quite true. On 25 April, 1566, Shane sent an important letter [1] to the Cardinal of Lorraine in France :—

To the Most Reverend Cardinal Lorentino, We Lord O'Neill, prince of the Irish of Ulster and defender of the Faith in the parts of Ireland, Salute You.

We make known to you by those present letters that we have sent our letters to the Most Christian Prince, the King of France, requesting his Majesty to send us for our aid five or six thousand Frenchmen well armed for the expulsion of the English out of Ireland who are heretics and schismatics and enemies of Almighty God and of the Roman Church, as well as of the French and the Irish. And as we have defended the Catholic Faith [2] in parts of Ireland according to our ability and have followed the maxims of the Roman Pontiffs, we request you, in all becoming reverence and humility, to persuade the most Christian King of the French (since this is the opportune time, and all the Irish are in our council) to send to us the said number of Frenchmen for the expulsion of the said heretics from Ireland and for the union of Ireland to the Crown of France. And so farewell.

From Dungannon, xxv. April, 1566,

MISI O'NEILL.[3]

---

[1] *S.P.I.*, *Eliz.*, xvii. 35, P.R.O., London. (In Latin.) See *Appendix D*.
[2] Hamilton (editor, *C.S.P.I.*, *Eliz.*) substitutes " Romish " for " Catholic." He is frequently guilty of introducing names not found in the original documents.
[3] In Irish characters, i.e. I, O'Neill.

In his letter of the same date to Charles IX [1] he expressed
the desire that the perpetual treaty proposed by the late
King might be concluded, and that he and his successors
would be humble subjects to the Crown of France. He
requested Charles to write to the Queen of Scots in his favour.
He complained that on his late visit to England, notwithstanding the safe-conduct obtained for himself and retinue
from the Queen, the "stupid" Council of England etc.,
some of his gentlemen were detained as hostages and imprisoned as criminals, but that all have now with the grace
of God returned to Ireland. He complained likewise of the
injuries done to himself and of the detention by the Queen
of Desmond, his ally in the Catholic cause, but rejoiced in
the good news that Sir John Desmond was fighting boldly
with great power against the English. He concluded by relating how O'Brien of Thomond, well known to the French
Court, was expatriated, and that he himself had deposed
young O'Donnell for favouring the heretics, and had set up
his brother in his stead.

It is useful to note that at this stage there was some sort
of understanding beteeen O'Neill, Desmond, and Thomond
about the expulsion of Protestants, and that Shane was
regarded as their spokesman in the seeking for foreign aid.
Shane was in reality preparing for what he expected from
Sydney.

Sydney Advises War on O'Neill; Journey through Ulster.

Persuasion had failed with O'Neill, as Sydney doubtless
foresaw, but as yet the latter was in no condition to carry
things with a high hand. He assured Leicester that with
500 well-paid and well-appointed men he would chase Shane
before him within forty-eight hours, or be accounted a traitor.
But he had rather die than have the name of losing Ireland,
and yet he could do nothing without proper tools. Six
thousand times a day did he wish himself in any part of
Christendom, so that he might escape from the Irish Purgatory,

[1] *S P.I.*, *Eliz.*, xvii. 34.

with its endless and thankless toil.[1]   His efforts were thwarted by the Sussex party at Court, including Leicester and Ormond. Smarting under the sense of failure, Sussex was too ready to find fault with Sydney.   Cecil, however, stood staunch friend to Sydney, and the Queen, though angry with Sydney for his coldness to Ormond and for his favour to Stucley, and, above all, for his financial importunities, pacified him with a graceful letter, and re-established his credit at court.

Like every other English ruler before and since, Elizabeth found it difficult to get at the truth about Ireland.   She now sent her Vice-Chamberlain, Sir F. Knollys, with large powers, and with directions to keep the chief part of the information he might acquire for her own ear.   It was a repetition of the system, favoured by Thomas Cromwell, of sending one official to spy on another.

It was now considered that no good could be expected of Shane, and the question was how he could be subdued. Elizabeth was startled by the proposal of a winter war upon which Sydney and Knollys insisted.   Their plan [2] was to begin about harvest, to destroy as much ripe corn as possible, and to drive the Irish herds into flooded woods and bogs. Cecil worked hard to persuade his Mistress, and at last she yielded, ungraciously grumbling at the expense.   An agent was sent to Scotland with friendly messages to Queen Mary and complaining of aid given to Shane.   Shane himself had sent a representative to the Scottish Court, and, as we have seen, also to the Court of France.

The winter campaign was abandoned by the Council, chiefly by the advice of Knollys who now favoured immediate war on account of Shane's arrogance.   But Sydney desired it to be clearly understood that his own reputation should not suffer if any untoward accident should happen in this war for which he felt himself unfit.   Knollys, anxious about his part in the venture, pointed out to Cecil the necessity of two brigantines to keep the Scots from aiding Shane, for 300 Scots are harder to vanquish than 600 Irish.[3]   Moreover,

---

[1] *S.P.I., Eliz.,* xvi. 35, 41, 42 ; xvii. 14, 15, P.R.O., London.   Bagwell, ii. 104-5.

[2] *S.P.I., Eliz.,* xviii. 9, 17, P.R.O., London.

[3] *C.S.P.I., Eliz.,* xvii. 67.

Shane had made a treaty with Hugh O'Donnell, his prisoner, for the delivery of certain castles, had confederated with the Scots, and was actually in Maguire's country, endeavouring to gather the northern Irish together to resist the threatened English invasion.

On 24 June it was reported that Shane had already fortified the castles of O'Donnell and Maguire, Dundrum and Lifford, and the Earl of Argyle would be with him in July.[1] Sydney saw the futility of carrying on an immediate war against Shane who was thus already prepared, and acknowledged that he himself had been put aside as it were in disgrace, and desired to be recalled.[2] On 15 June the Queen assured Sydney of her objection to a winter war, but consoled him with the promise of 1000 men and of ships to guard the Scottish coast to prevent the Scots from coming to Shane's relief.[3] Sydney was to levy 200 horse and 200 foot in Ireland. Accordingly, on 18 July a writ was issued to the sheriffs of the counties of the Pale to summon all lords spiritual and temporal, knights, gentlemen, and freeholders, and others of the counties to attend the Lord Deputy on 15 August with arms and victuals for seven weeks. On this occasion also the Tailors' Guild contributed to the expenses of the weavers and barbers of their " jorney into the northe," and further contributed to a loan to the Lord Deputy thus, " payd over plus to the ses [cess] mony lent to the lord Deputy III *li*. VI*s*. 11*d*." [4] It was one of the rules of these craft guilds that they should provide men for the hostings in the defence of the City and the Pale.

" Upon this preparation here," wrote the Queen,[5] " we think Shane O'Neill will grow into some heat, and percase break his brickle peace, and therefore he is to be seen to for the hurt of the frontiers as though you had open wars with him."

To add to Sydney's troubles, disorders had also taken place in the South, evidently by arrangement with Shane, and the Desmond force had grown in strength, as it was

---

[1] *C.S.P.I., Eliz.*, xviii. 25. [2] *Ib.*, 1. [3] *Ib.*, 17.

[4] Webb, 98-9. In the year 1580 the Accounts show the repayment of a similar loan.

[5] *C.S.P.I., Eliz.*, xvii. 41.

said, by "confederation with outlaws and rebels," even spoiling the Ormond country. To obviate this mischief, assemblies of kerne and galloglasses are to be prohibited, and certain rebels and outlaws to be apprehended.[1]

While a weapon was being slowly forged for his destruction, O'Neill assumed the offensive, refused to come to Sydney at Dundalk, and entered the English Pale with fire and sword. He had, in his passage, burned down the cathedral of Armagh, and all the houses around, which might be used as a garrison by the English in the event of his retirement northward which evidently he contemplated. He had razed many castles in Ulster and Lecale, entered Fermanagh, and expelled Maguire[2] who, with MacDonnell, had refused to join him. On 29 July Shane besieged Dundalk, but was driven off and proclaimed a traitor. He withdrew to the borders of Tirconnell, where he made offers to the Scots, but Sydney had been beforehand with him, and no help came from that quarter. Shane was likewise to be disappointed by the Desmonds. On 9 September he wrote to John of Desmond[3] that now is the time, or never, for them both to set against the English, as he had robbed and burned Meath, and that the English have no other object in mind than to subdue both the English and the Irish Pale. By the "Irish Pale" he evidently meant those parts of Ireland, under the rule of the "degenerate" Anglo-Irish, which would acknowledge Elizabeth as queen, provided those chiefs were allowed to rule as they liked. They desired freedom for the Catholic Church, at least in their own territories, but they desired also their own temporal power over minor chiefs. On the same day Sydney was pleased to be able to report to the Privy Council[4] that Desmond had voluntarily repaired to him, professed loyalty to the Queen, and received a post at Drogheda.

An expedition under Colonel Randolph arrived from Bristol in Lough Foyle, consisting of 1000 men, and Sydney moved forward. In an interesting account given by Sydney of his attack on Shane O'Neill's crannog and of his march northward after leaving Drogheda, 17 September, 1566, accompanied by Kildare, O'Donnell, and Maguire, he states:[5]

---

[1] *C.S.P.I., Eliz.,* xvii. 80.   [2] *Ib.,* 89.   [3] *Ib.,* xix. 7.   [4] *Ib.,* 11.
[5] *His. and Arch. Assoc. of Ir.,* 1870-71, p. 15 *seq.*

" Passing by Ardmach, we found that the rebels had burned the whole town, and the great and ancient church of the same, and all the houses belonging thereunto, and thrown down a great part of the stonework, even as much as it should seem he had leisure to do, and the rest we suppose he will do. . . . The 27th, we encamped within eight miles of Clogher, a Bishop's See, but the Bishop a rebel with her Majesty ; and finding that country so well inhabited, as we think no Irish country in this realm like it, we remained in that camp one whole day, purposely to destroy the corn, whereof we found no small abundance, burning that day above 24 miles compass, saving only the Bishop's church." On the 29th he removed to the castle and monastery of Omagh. In the day's march old Maguire, who had joined his camp, died. His death was unfortunate as had he lived but twenty days longer Her Majesty would have recovered much more land and castles.

On 14 October he encamped in Ochanes' country, over against Derry, but " there came no one unto us but Odighortie and his brother Caheir, with the Bishop of Derry [Eugene O'Doherty] a gentleman of that surname." He was entreated by Odogherty and the Bishop to pass over into Derry. On the 14 October he encamped twelve miles west from Derry at a Bishop's See called Raphoe, and there came to him the principal men of Tirconnell, with the Bishop of Raphoe [Donald MacCongail], " all which recognise fealty and service to your Most Excellent Majesty." On the 21st he encamped in O'Connor Sligo's country " where O'Connor Sligo came unto us with the Bishop of Elphin [Andrew O'Crean] most humbly offering service and fealty to your Majesty and all courtesy to us." On the 22nd he came across the river at Sligo to the town which " hath been a great town full of merchants' houses, all which are now dis-inhabited and in ruin. Therein is a large monastery of White Friars, [*recte* Blackfriars = Dominicans] and a Bishop's house."

In his account of all his services in Ireland drawn up in 1583,[1] Sydney states that on his journey through Tirconnell he made a new fort of an old church. He boasted that a

---

[1] Carew, *Cal.*, 1575-88, p. 334 *seq.*

country of seventy by forty-eight miles was now obedient to the Queen, and the service of 1000 men restored to O'Donnell who agreed to hold his lands of the Queen, the treaty being witnessed by the Bishop of Raphoe. The journey took two months to accomplish without Sydney's having met any of O'Neill's men.[1]

It is important to understand clearly the attitude of the Bishops of Derry, Raphoe, and Elphin in attending on Sydney during his tour through their dioceses and in swearing fealty and allegiance to Elizabeth. In general three things must be clearly distinguished in the attitude of Irish bishops during this period, namely, the adoption of Uniformity of Worship, the taking of the Oath of Supremacy, and the taking of an oath of allegiance or fealty to the Queen as the temporal ruler. It is quite clear that Sydney proposed neither the first nor the second to any of these bishops, but was quite content to receive the third. His object was not to antagonise them but to win them to his side in order to secure the good obedience of their chiefs to the Queen as their overlord, and to bind them in a confederacy against Shane. By this means Sydney saw a favourable chance of overcoming the turbulent northern chief and reducing him also to subjection. The chiefs were only too willing at the time to get rid of the exactions of Shane, and those bishops, except the Bishop of Clogher, were also quite willing to profess obedience to Elizabeth provided they were allowed freedom of conscience, which on this occasion there was no question of taking from them. Thus Sydney went gaily on his way on friendly terms with Catholic bishops, and indeed admiring the bishops' houses, and especially " a large monastery of White Friars " in Sligo which caused him no particular resentment. Possibly he may have been more pleased to see those ecclesiastical establishments in such good order than he was to see the ruined chancels and churches within the Pale. The Pale was the Pale, and in permanent possession of the Government, but Sligo and the North were in the Irishry and not yet in permanent English occupation.

[1] *S.P.I.*, *Eliz.*, xix. 43.   Bagwell, ii. 108-10.

Sydney Deplores the State of the Protestant Church.

While Sydney was in Drogheda (19 August) preparing his attack on Shane he was mindful of the state of the Established Church, and in particular of the diocese of Ferns. His letter to Cecil [1] is pathetic, and shows how he was overwhelmed not only by the secular but also by the ecclesiastical situation :—

Sir, I leave to the report of my Lord Primate in what pitiful estate the ecclesiastical causes in this realm do stand ; where, himself and the Bishop of Meath excepted, I find few or none, either worthily to walk in his function, willing to reform their clergy, or able either to teach any wholesome doctrine, or to serve their country or Commonwealth as magistrates ; such is the imperfection of our Irish [Protestant] Bishops in this time, whereof one [Devereux, Bishop of Ferns], being lately deceased, hath left his See so naked, as his bastards, the tokens of his incontinency, have at this day in manner the whole of his livings, in whose place I have received commendation for one John Devorox to succeed, dean of the same church, whose learning and sufficiency, like as the Bishop of Meath hath commended, so do I think him the best chosen man for other respects that is in this land ; for besides that he is a gentleman of the best house in the County of Wexford, and brought up in the University of England,[2] I find him of good discretion and judgment and able in causes of justice to do her Majesty and this country very good service ; and therefore I heartily require you to procure presentation, wherewith, if it might please her Highness, in respect of the smallness of the living, to grant a toleration for the keeping of his deanery, and to be gracious unto him in his first fruits, in my opinion the benefits were very well bestowed ; and so, recommending him unto you, I bid you most heartily well to fare.

Comment on the early portion of this letter would be superfluous.

[1] *S.P.I., Eliz.,* xviii. 93. Shirley, 264.

[2] It is worthy of note that the Irish ecclesiastics educated in the Universities of England were generally those who were the most willing to go over to the " reform."

ANOTHER BISHOP DEVEREUX FOR FERNS.

Like Curwen of Dublin, Alexander Devereux, the late
Bishop of Ferns, had been a compromiser in religion.   He
was consecrated in St. Patrick's, Dublin, by Archbishop
Browne and other assisting bishops, 14 December, 1539.
Although appointed by Henry VIII, he continued to hold
his See during Mary's reign, probably because he had not
taken a wife, though he had already taken unto himself
a concubine.   He was born at Ballymagir, Co. Wexford,
and was the last Abbot of Dunbrody before the Suppression.
As Sydney pointed out, he made several leases in favour of
his children and others to the great detriment of his See.[1]
Some of these leases were confirmed by Dean Devereux,
evidently a relative, and by the Chapter of Ferns, the
treasurer of which was another Devereux.   It is clear that
the powerful family of Devereux had gone over to the " reform."   One of the family, evidently the Bishop's brother,
asked Cecil to appoint his nephew John Devereux, Dean of
Ferns, to the See, on the death of Alexander.[2]   The letter
was written by Nicholas Devereux [3] from Alexander's own
natal manorial residence at Ballymagir, in the parish of
Old Ross, and now called Richfield.   It declares :—

My bounden duty remembered unto your honour, being so
bold to refresh mine acquaintance, whilom being one of the Earl

[1] " In 1548 he made a fee-farm lease of the town and lands of Sledah, 80
acres and a water-mill, Chermiestown, 80 acres, and Poulemanna, 100 acres
to Philip Devereux and William Devereux, receiving a rent of 31s. Irish money.
In 1549, he leased the island of Begerin to James Devereux, his brother, in
fee at 7s. per annum Irish money ; which lease he procured to be confirmed
by the Dean [Devereux] and Chapter.   The same year he made a lease in fee
of the townland of Balligillan and of 80 acres of land, and 30 acres in Killrane,
to one Turner at the rent of 36s. 8d. Irish money.   The year following he
made another fee-farm of the lands of Slany and Newton, containing 3 ploughlands [i.e. 360 acres] to one Rossiter at the rent of 28s. 8d. Irish money.   And
in 1560 he and his Dean and Chapter joined in a fee-farm lease to his brother,
James Devereux, of the rectory Kinnith, at the rent of 30s. which was then
worth £50 per annum."   He died at Fethard in 1566, and was buried in the
chancel of the parish church.   (Harris, *Ware's Bishops*, 445.)

[2] The Devereux family was supposed to be a branch of the Devereux's
of Herefordshire.   When Robert Devereux, Earl of Essex, was Lord Lieutenant
of Ireland, in 1599, he passed a day at Ballymagir, and knighted his cousin,
Sir Philip, who is said to have sold three townlands to pay for three days' open
house on that occasion.

[3] *S.P.I., Eliz.*, xviii. 95.   Shirley, 267

of Shrewsbury's [1] wards, and your honour's schoolfellow in England, so it is, right honourable, that the bishopric of Ferns, in the County of Wexford in Ireland, is now void by the death of last incumbent, and is come to the Queen's Majesty hands; whereupon I have been a suitor to the right honourable Sir Henry Sydney, Lord Deputy of Ireland, for the commendation of a nephew of mine, Sir John Devereux, dean of Ferns, in whose favour the said Lord Deputy have written unto your honour to see him preferred unto the said bishopric, being all made away for the more part by the bishop that was last, the exiguity and smallness thereof considered being all dismembered, that it may please your honour to be mean to her Majesty to grant him a toleration to enjoy his said deanery with a bishopric aforesaid, which it may please your honour to compass accordingly, to whom I commit Richard Deverox, this bearer, brother and factor of the said dean, whom it may please your honour to accept accordingly; thus most humbly taking my leave, etc.

Notwithstanding the fact that the late Bishop had granted Church lands in lease to his relatives at ridiculously low prices, Nicholas Devereux, evidently a brother of the Bishop, does not hesitate to refer to the fact so that his nephew, the Dean, may have his Deanery as well as the Bishopric.

Six weeks later Elizabeth wrote to Sydney (12 October) [2] that she was well content to bestow the bishopric on John Devereux in respect of the good opinion both he and Brady had of him,

and therefore we will and authorise you to cause all things meet and requisite by the order of our laws for the electioning, confirming, consecrating, and instituting of him in that place and function . . . and further, for his better ability for housekeeping in this beginning, we are pleased that he shall enjoy his said deanery in commendam during our pleasure, or until it shall be found meet by our deputy for the time being to revoke the same. And touching the first fruits . . . ye shall take such reasonable days [respite] with him with sufficient surety for the payment thereof as you shall think meet, in which matter (were it not for precedence

[1] Evidently, Francis (Talbot) Fifth Earl, *d.* 1560. An adherent of the Papal Supremacy during the reign of Mary, he continued this adherence under Elizabeth who still retained him as one of her Privy Council. He and Viscount Montague were the only temporal peers who refused to recognise Elizabeth's supremacy. (Burke's *Peerage*, 915.)

[2] *S.P.I., Eliz.*, xix. 22. Shirley, 277.

sake) we would be content upon your instance to have showed some more favour.

John Devereux was, about the end of the year, consecrated by Archbishop Curwen without any assistants,[1] and was granted the deanery with his bishopric for five years.[2]

Bishops Loftus and Brady Quarrel.

In the preceding reigns much damage had been done to the royal cause by differences of policy and also by jealousy between the heads of the ecclesiastical as well as the secular government. Sydney himself, an instrument of the Sovereign, had very limited powers, and had many spies and enemies in his own camp. Knollys was watching his movements and reporting success or failure, and Ormond, Elizabeth's favourite, was jealous of his friendship for Ormond's enemies, the Geraldines.

Among the Protestant bishops the same suspicion and jealousy of one another, and the same reporting of one another's movements to the Court, manifest themselves. Loftus, like Browne, was in favour of pushing the " reform " ideas to the utmost limit, whilst Brady, like Staples, was inclined to go more slowly. Loftus now wished St. Patrick's to be turned into a university so that preachers of Protestantism might be produced for the country. Although he had recommended Brady for the See of Dublin (as he could not very well ask openly for the post for himself), yet one may read between the lines that he was anxious to obtain it for himself. He was useless in Armagh, and, therefore, some other position must be given to him. His tenure of the deanery of St. Patrick's was only temporary, and he seemed over-anxious about abolishing it, so that a more important post might be given him. He had already shown his dislike for Cashel and Ossory. He and Brady were the only candidates for the Archbishopric of Dublin.

But the breach between these two bishops came at last.

---

[1] Harris, *Ware's Bishops*, 446.

[2] He died in 1578, and was buried in the parish church of St. Mary at Wexford.

Loftus had championed Calvinism, and was on friendly terms with the Earl of Argyle, the patron of John Knox. Indeed, Knox had in a letter to Argyle (13 November, 1565) praised Loftus for his fervency " in suppressing the tyrannical kingdom of the Common Antichrist." Brady had made known his objections to Loftus on this point. And now Loftus, with leave of absence for twelve months,[1] crosses to England to present himself at Court and explain his position. From Lichfield he wrote to Cecil,[2] 3 September, 1566, urging the suppression of St. Patrick's and the appointment of an Englishman to Dublin, so that the number of that race in Dublin may increase. Brady, of course, was an Irishman. Loftus had heard that Brady was spoken of as likely to be sent to Dublin, and he had recommended him, but now he is sorry he did so. " If it would please your honour," he writes to Cecil, " to pause awhile, I could show such matter as I would (God is my witness), except it were for the church of God's sake, be loth to utter by any means, but least of all by writing, upon knowledge whereof, the matter I know should go no further." It does not transpire what charges Loftus had to make against Brady. But the latter's letter to Cecil probably provides the clue. Meanwhile, Loftus disapproved of the appointment to Ferns of Devereux who had been recommended by Brady and Curwen. He says of Devereux: " an unfitter man cannot be ; he is now of late deprived of his Deanery for confessed whoredom." John Devereux seemingly was as good as his uncle Alexander, the late bishop. This, however, if it was true, was not accounted against him, as when he was appointed bishop two months after this letter he was allowed to retain the deanery also, for the purpose of augmenting his revenue, and Elizabeth, were it not that there was a precedent against it, would have dealt more generously with him.

BRADY'S REASON FOR THE QUARREL.

Brady, in turn, reports to Cecil [3] the state of the country, especially of the North, and then craves " patience for a few

---

[1] *Fiants*, no. 928, dated 14 August, 1566.
[2] *S.P.T.*, *Eliz.*, xix. 1. Shirley, 269-71.
[3] *S.P.T.*, *Eliz.*, xix. 13. Shirley, 272-3.

words for myself, my brother and workfellow in the Lord, the Lord Primate." He says that Loftus

before his departure hence hath said to some of his friends and mine, he would complain of small assistance he had in executing his commission for causes ecclesiastical, and therefore would procure to himself a more absolute authority. I would not whether he will touch myself ; if he do, I most humbly require your honour to stop one of your ears till either I answer for myself, or a number of his countrymen and mine both may report the truth between him and me : if he say I have drawn backward, I only say again he hath drawn too fast forward, as the circumstances shall well declare ; and therefore, if he do get absolute power to himself alone, or what else soever he doth there obtain, far be it from me to envy it ; I wish (with all my heart) he use no unhonest means to come by anything he shall demand. I trust your good nature will take in good part, and use discreetly, what I have herein said. Satan, our enemy, is very busy by his instruments to set dissension between my Lord and me : I trust he shall not prevail. The Lord God grant us so to look diligently to our office and function, and common duty we owe to his Church, that we forget our own private quarrels or causes. It had been my special duty to have visited your honour with some hawks, or one thing or other ; the Lord God knoweth it was not lack of good will, neither will I hereafter (by his help and assistance) be so ungrateful ; and so I humbly take my leave, beseeching Almighty God long to continue your health, to the comfort of his Church. From my house of Arbrachan, this 14 of September.

Your honours alway in his prayer,

H. MIDEN.

The customary promise of a hawk was a neat way of securing a good hearing. This much must be said about Loftus that he was over-anxious to have the control of ecclesiastical affairs, commissions, court of faculties, etc., in his own hands. In regard to the court of faculties he had another battle of words later.[1]

LOFTUS DENOUNCES CURWEN AND THE PREBENDARIES OF ST. PATRICK'S.

A month after his last letter, Loftus, who had gone to England because of his " diseases," which were worsened

---

[1] See *Appendix V*.

by his " travail upon the seas," had only reached Cambridge whence he again wrote to Cecil, 5 October.[1] After a long preamble, he says :—

I beseech your honour, for Jesus Christ's sake, that my suits for the Church, and especially for the bishopric of Dublin (because thereof will the rest in a manner depend) may be so furthered of your honour, that they may be finished also, and that with that expedition which the cause requireth . . . for when he [Archbishop Curwen] neither doeth good in preaching, nor reforming his diocese himself, when he placeth in the sufficient livings [2] for able preachers those that he never see, nor never come there, open enemies and such as for want of learning are never able, if they would do the Church any good : when in open judgment (loth I am to say it, and I say it not but constrainedly) ; when I say, in open judgment he [Curwen] will swear terribly, and it not once nor twice, I beseech your honour is it not time, and more than time, that such a one be removed ? And yet I spare him, I assure your honour, that you may understand how far I am from maligning him. I stayed only for the end of these matters, otherwise would presently return : for although I have good will to enjoy my licence of the Lord Deputy and Council, which is for a year, yet I cannot quiet my conscience so ; for I have sought, and do not find, so long a licence given of the Lord God : you marvel, peradventure, why I come not up : I trust your honour will acquit me of that, that it is not for want of good will, of doing my duty to the Queen's Majesty, and your honours all ; and I praise God I may boldly say, that is for no notorious crime that I fear to be charged with ; and yet there are causes, whereof part your honour hath received in my former letters ; and more there are of that nature, that as I had rather any should tell them than myself, so peradventure your honour hath rather understand them of any than of me ; and because I know there is nothing whereof your honour may be certified by my presence but the same I am able to make known by my letters, and such as are as privy to the Church state as myself, therefore I willingly abstain from coming. Recompense at my hands your honour cannot look for ; it is the Lord God's cause ; He will recompense it, and hath already (praised be God) my prayer and service your honour shall be assured of. From Trinity College, in Cambridge, the 5th of October, 1566.

Your honours at commandment,

AD. ARMACHAN.

[1] *S.P.I.*, *Eliz.*, xix. 19. Shirley, 274-6.   [2] Prebends of St. Patrick's.

Here again Loftus speaks, though to us rather obscurely, yet to Cecil clearly enough, of the appointments made by Curwen to the prebends of St. Patrick's and, perhaps, to other positions in his patronage. He calls them absentees, enemies of the truth, and useless preachers, were they ever so willing to preach in favour of Elizabeth's religion. It is a notorious fact, worth repeating, that during those years, and for years afterwards, the prebendaries of St. Patrick's were practically all opposed to Elizabeth's " reform." This state of affairs was undoubtedly mainly responsible for Loftus's recommendation of the suppression of the Cathedral, for his desire to get rid of Curwen, and to have himself installed. It is interesting to note that, according to Loftus, many of these old prebendaries drew their stipends and did not attend choir service at St. Patrick's. Ecclesiastical matters were, indeed, seven years after the introduction of the " reform," in a very muddled condition in Dublin. That being the case in the centre of Elizabethan activity, it was difficult for it to be in any better condition elsewhere.

LOFTUS CONFESSES INABILITY TO DO ANY GOOD IN ARMAGH ; OFFERS TO RESIGN.

About a month later (3 November) Loftus was at Southwark (London), and sent another letter to Cecil [1] describing the state of his diocese of Armagh :—

I have sent your honour herein enclosed a letter I received from a servant I have in Ireland [evidently his collector at Drogheda], whereby ye may perceive how that small portion of my living, which remained at my departing, is now altogether waste and destroyed ; I assure your honour, the whole profits of the bishoprick is not above £22 a year [about £260 *1914 value*] ; for although God send quietness, and that peace ensue the repressing of this rebel Shane O'Neill, yet these wastes will not be inhabited, nor the spoils recovered many years hereafter ; all towns mentioned in this letter were the remnant of the archbishopric and now of the whole revenues there remaineth nothing but the bare house and four score acres of ground at Termonfeghan ; [2] although I know ye are I thank God for it very well inclined to do me good

---

[1] *S.P.I., Eliz.*, xix. 31. Shirley, 278-80.
[2] His Archiepiscopal residence near Drogheda.

yet I doubt not this loss of all (in a manner) that I have, will move you the sooner to forward my suit concerning the remission of that small sum [First Fruits] I stand bound to the Queen's Majesty for ; I would to God I might obtain the Queen's Majesty gracious favour, and your honour's good will, to resign the archbishopric ; for neither is it worth anything to me, nor I able to do any good in it, for that altogether it lieth among the Irish. From my lodging at Southwark, this third of November, 1566.

The rebellion of Shane O'Neill, which had just occurred, was the cause of the loss of the temporalities of the See of Armagh, here described by Loftus. But more serious still was the confession of Loftus that he, the foremost man in the " reform " and in the ecclesiastical commission, was quite unable to promote the State religion in his diocese which was a mere nominal entity as far as he was concerned. The " reform " indeed was going slowly, indeed " waxeth worse."

Four days later (7 November) he wrote to Cecil [1] recommending McCaghwell for Cashel as he knew not where a fitter man might be provided, and the place was suitable " for none but one of Irish birth," and, therefore, not for Loftus. McCaghwell had been previously appointed to Down, but was prevented by O'Neill from occupying the See. The Archbishop of Canterbury, Lord Salisbury, and others also bore testimony to his fitness. McCaghwell himself was the bearer of Loftus's letter to Cecil.

After a week, Loftus again wrote to Cecil [2] beseeching him to have him discharged of the debt of £165 for the First Fruits of St. Patrick's deanery. He asks this " not so much in respect of my ease and benefit, as of the good shall grow of it to the Church of God in Ireland ; for being discharged of this debt, I mind (God willing) to keep still my preachers ; and burthened with it, I shall be constrained to put them away."

Sydney and Loftus Recommend the Calvinist Goodman for Dublin.

Loftus succeeded by his indirect method in convincing Cecil and Elizabeth that he, an Englishman, was the proper

---

[1] *S.P.I., Eliz.*, xix. 35. Shirley, 280.   [2] *S.P.I., Eliz.*, xix. 46. Shirley, 282.

person for Dublin. Accordingly, Elizabeth wrote, 16 January, 1567, to Sydney,[1] that Adam Loftus, much commended for his wisdom and integrity, shall be Archbishop of Dublin, and some other man, of less estimation, may be found out meet to have Armagh. Sydney's letter about Creagh (p. 207) was written on the same day, and was not, of course, in her hands at this time. Another letter of Sydney's, 18 January,[2] also crossed Elizabeth's. In this he had recommended his friend Mr. Goodman for Dublin for his " excellency in learning, and unspotted life and good example." Loftus, also, four days later wrote to Cecil [3] from Dublin, stating that it was on his recommendation that Sydney wrote in favour of Goodman. He is of opinion that he is " the fittest man to profit God's Church of any that I know of the English birth." Probably at this time Loftus had given up all hope of having the See for himself, and was content to be Dean of St. Patrick's. Nothing reveals his Calvinistic tendencies more clearly than this approval of Goodman, who was a violent nonconformist, going beyond even his friend Calvin.[4]

Sydney was so taken with him that, when Loftus was promoted to Dublin, he again wrote to Cecil in favour of Goodman. In a letter written from Waterford, 4 March, he says :—

---

[1] *S.P.I., Eliz.*, xx. 8.   [2] *Ib.*, 12.   [3] *Ib.*, 17. Shirley, 289-91.

[4] " This Goodman being a furious hot spirit, and guilty in conscience of wicked attempts (but especially, as was thought of the conspiracy with Will. Thomas, that would have killed Q. Mary) ran out of England to Geneva, in the beginning of Q. Mary's reign, and there joined with John Knox (as quiet a spirit as himself) that was the firebrand of his country of Scotland. There was no man more ready than he (as Knox was for Scotland) to oppose in the beginning of Q. Eliz. the settlement of the Church in England according to the way used in the time of K. Ed. 6 [i.e. in allowing vestments at the Communion Service]. Sure I am that when Sir H. Sydney was Deputy of Ireland, and had much to do with the Popish rebels there, Goodman showed his faithful diligence in that service. He was the author of several works. ' The First Blast of the Trumpet against the Monstrous Regiment of Women,' printed beyond the sea, 1558, laid down doctrines ' destructive to the sacred persons of Princes, and their State and Government.' They were ' condemned by the episcopal clergy of England in the time of Q. Elizabeth and after when he lay on his death-bed at Chester, in 1602, he was visited by Mr. Jam. Usher (afterwards Archb. of Armagh), at what time he came from Ireland into England to buy books for Dublin [University] Library several of whose stories he heard with great delight, which he would afterwards, when an ancient man, repeat to his friends.' He was buried in the church of St. Werberg in Chester." (*Athen. Oxon.*, i. 314-16.)

If Armagh have Dublin, then I humbly beseech you, Sir, to help Christopher Goodman to the deanery of St. Patrick's, for God forbid that he, Loftus, should be bishop and dean in one church in such a city. Sir, I think you did know this man in Scotland; he hath been in my house almost a year; if ever man on earth, since the apostles' days deserved to be held a saint, he is one. Sir, the whole Church of this realm shall be bound to pray for you if you prefer [him] to that place, and I shall think it a great grace done to myself so to place him.

The See of Leighlin being still vacant, Sydney had written in favour of " Daniel Cavenagh, a priest." The latter was accordingly appointed, but, through some hitch, delay occurred in the sending of the patent. Meanwhile, Sydney informed Cecil, 10 March,[1] " That a young man of the County of Kilkenny is repaired into England to obtain the same by another man's commendation." He, however, renewed his recommendation of Cavenagh " as an apt man, and not uncommended by the clergy here for his learning and conformity in religion." Elizabeth sent the usual letters of nomination, 10 April, and the letters patent, 7 May, and Cavenagh[2] was consecrated in St. Patrick's by Curwen.

Sydney Rejoices at Appointment of Loftus to Dublin.

A week later (11 March) Sydney wrote from Youghal to Loftus[3] expressing his pleasure at his appointment to Dublin, " most because by this means I am in hope, that as the City of Dublin is the chief place within this realm, and most open for any good example, so it will grow (by your good and careful order) to reformation in religion." In a Latin postscript he says : " The hour has now come for reforming the church." (*Nunc venit hora ecclesiam reformandi.*)

Loftus and Sydney were, therefore, of one mind on the lines the " reformation " was to take, and Loftus was, at

---

[1] *S.P.I., Eliz.*, xx. 42. Shirley, 292.

[2] Like Devereux of Ferns, " He made long leases of many parts of his See, reserving only small rents to his successors; and died on the 4th of April, 1587." (Harris, *Ware's Bishops*, 462.)

[3] *S.P.I., Eliz.*, xx. 52 (1). Shirley, 293-4.

last, free to put into practice the Calvinistic principles which had been the secret causes of the delay of his appointment to Dublin since October, 1563. Sydney rejoiced at the prospect of the Church being " reformed " according to these principles. Incidentally, he was convinced that so far there had been no " reformation " in the Irish State Church. On the 21 March, Loftus wrote to thank Cecil [1] as being the " only means " of his translation to Dublin. As usual the money question obtrudes itself, and Loftus has a favour to ask of Cecil :—

The Bishopric of Dublin is so alienated and set out in lease by the bishop that now is [Curwen] that nothing is reserved for his successor, but only £400 Irish [about £3200 *1914 value*], and 12 score acres of ground.[2] I humbly therefore beseech your honour if it be your pleasure to be a means for my preferment to that bishopric, to be a mean also that I may have *in commendam* the deanery of the St. Patrick's in such sort as I have it with the archbishopric of Armagh ; for if I should pay the first fruits of Dublin, being altogether as much as the bishopric is worth now, I should be in a great deal worse case than I am presently ; and whensoever I am discharged of my first fruits and out of debt, I bind myself to your honour by this my letter to keep it afterwards at your devotion, and so resign it whensoever it shall be your pleasure to require me by your letters ; but I beseech you that in this I may stand at no man's courtesy but yours : thus you see instead of some payment, I indebt myself deeper unto you. I beseech your honour let me understand your mind herein by this bearer my servant, whom I have sent to you for that purpose : for I am minded not to change at all, but to continue in this poor estate I am in now, rather than I should leave the deanery [3] and enter into new payments of the first fruits.

Loftus, however, changed his mind, and finding it impossible to retain the deanery of St. Patrick's together with the See of Dublin, was at last content to accept the latter and resign the former, preferring £401 1s. 6½d., the estimated annual

---

[1] *S.P.I.*, *Eliz.*, xx. 52. Shirley, 295-7.

[2] Swords and St. Sepulchre's were probably the only archiepiscopal manors left to the Archbishop, within the five-mile radius previously mentioned as the limit outside which no revenues of prebends could be obtained.

[3] The value of the deanery in 1547 was £240 (about £3600 *1914 value*).

value of the Archbishopric of Dublin, to the £20 per annum which he had from the primatial See of Armagh, with his uncertain tenure of the deanery of St. Patrick's.[1]

His occupation of Termonfechan was as fruitless as his archiepiscopal office. His royal mistress and Head of the Church did not expect him to be a missionary but a bishop with all the comforts and revenues in keeping with the dignity of his office. It was not the fault of Loftus that he was useless in Armagh ; it was just the failure of the " reform."

[1] As to the application of Loftus to have himself removed from Armagh to Dublin, Harris says : " it is not to be admired [wondered] at, that he sought a translation from a primatial See : for the North was then ruined by the rebellion of Shane O'Neill, and Armagh, which with its cathedral had been utterly destroyed, afforded but little profit." (*Ware's Bishops*, 195.)

Mant (i. 280-1) does not agree with this reason for translation from one See to another, and quotes Dudley Loftus's *Annals* on the subject : " At first there were many who wondered at the archbishop, why he should resign his archbishopric of Armagh, for to be translated to Dublin, considering that the primacy of Armagh was not only a higher title, but also had a greater revenue and income belonging to it. So Adam Loftus made answer, he would rather less honour and less revenue in quietness, than to be in danger, and to live within his diocese so far from the metropolis of Ireland, and to hazard himself especially in those times."

This whitewashing of Loftus by his nephew and by Mant is quite out of colour with the facts as given above in Loftus's own letter.

And Strype relates, under date 1561, that " he meets with a letter, without date of year, but supposes near about this time, writ from Adam, Archbishop of Armagh, to our Archbishop of Canterbury, dated from Trinity College, Cambridge, Sept. 27, wherein the Irish archbishop, now not long entered upon his functions, hinted how the Archbishop of Canterbury had promised him his aid in all Church causes of Ireland, at his last being in England ; especially for removing the Bishop of Dublin [Curwen]. He was, as he described him, a *known enemy*, and laboured under open crimes ; which although he shamed not to do, I am, said that Archbishop, almost ashamed to speak. So he desired him, now being in England again, to put to his helping hand, and to recommend some zealous man to succeed in that bishop's place : and that he, the Archbishop of Canterbury, would write to the court of this matter." (*Life of Abp. Parker*, i. 221.) This letter of Loftus to the Archbishop of Canterbury was evidently written when he was at Cambridge in 1566. It shows how anxious he was for Curwen's removal, incidentally pleading his own cause by his display of zeal. Curwen is represented not only as a lewd person but as one not partial to the Reform, " a known enemy."

For causes, not specified, the archbishopric of Dublin was in such an impoverished state in 1572 that " Queen Elizabeth, on account of the poverty of the See, granted him [Loftus] a dispensation to hold any compatible sinecure with his archbishopric, not exceeding one hundred pounds a year in value." (Harris, *Ware's Bishops*, 353.)

ARCHBISHOP CREAGH ASKS SYDNEY IF HE MAY CONTINUE IN ARMAGH.

Sydney, after his bloodless victory or rather circuit of Ulster and Connacht, returned to his house at Kilmainham. Although he did not meet Shane or any of his soldiers, yet he succeeded for the time being in reconciling most of the northern chiefs to his government. As long as they were allowed free control in their own native territories, and were not to be subject to Shane's tyrannical imposts, they were quite willing to remain loyal to Elizabeth in temporal affairs. Some of the northern bishops also had come to pay their respects to Sydney as he marched through their territories, but there was no hint from Sydney that he desired to interfere with them in matters of religion. The Lord Deputy reserved that interference for the dioceses directly under English control, namely, those principally within the Pale.

Archbishop Creagh was at this time with Shane at Dunavally, parish of Loughgall, Co. Armagh. He had escaped out of the Tower in 1565, fled to Spain, and returned to Ireland. "On a certain Sunday," says Stuart,[1] "of the month [of August, 1566], in which Shane was proclaimed a traitor the primate preached before him and six hundred of his soldiers in the cathedral of Armagh, inculcating loyalty. Enraged at this sermon, Shane, five days afterwards, burnt the roof of the cathedral and broke down some of its walls. So dreadful was the havoc perpetrated by this indignant and vindictive chieftain, that Camden [2] describes its effects in the following terms : ' In our memory, the church and city of Armagh were so foully defaced by the rebel, Shane O'Neill, that they lost all their ancient beauty and glory, and nothing remaineth at this day, but a few small wattled cottages, with the ruinous walls of a monastery, priory, and the primate's palace.'

"But Shane asserted that he had burned the cathedral to prevent the English troops from lodging within its walls. Primate Loftus, not satisfied with this pretext, assailed him with the spiritual weapon of excommunication ; but the Irish

---

[1] Coleman, *Stuart's Armagh*, 163.
[2] *Britannia* (Holland's *Trans.*, p. 109).

chieftain, disregarding ecclesiastical denunciations, marched southward, and besieged Dundalk with a considerable corps of horse and foot. Here, however, his efforts were rendered abortive by the valour of the garrison and by the timely arrival of William Sarsfield, mayor of Dublin, who marched against him, with a select body of citizens,[1] and compelled him to raise the siege. Yet the adjacent country was wasted and pillaged by his army. Thus repulsed, Shane retired to his strongholds."

We have already considered the grand tour of Sydney through the North which followed the retirement of Shane. During all that time Archbishop Creagh remained in the company of his chief. On 29 December, 1566, Shane signified by letter to Sydney that he was anxious for peace, and agreed to stand by the articles he had made with Cusack. In a letter of 18 January, 1567, to the Privy Council,[2] Sydney stated that "these winter wars have already daunted his [O'Neill's] courage," and that he has not answered Shane's letter but threatened to extirpate him as the only way of suppressing his insolence and reforming the province of Ulster. Four days previous to Shane's letter, Creagh also wrote to Sydney who forwarded copies of both letters to the Privy Council and also of letters he received from Spain. Creagh's most important letter runs thus :—

Right honourable lord, at our being in Spain, doubting whether the Pope's Holiness should command us to come back again into Ireland, we have written our letters unto my Lord Robert [Earl of Leicester] showing that if we should be by the said Holiness commanded to come thither, we should have none other thing to do but what our Lord and Master Christ have commanded "give Cæsar his own, and to God His own." The foresaid our simple letters, as we think, the King of Spain (because we were his father's scholar at Louvain the space of 7 or 8 years) have directed unto his ambassador in England, willing him to know whether the Queen's Majesty should be content that we should fulfil the office that we should be bound to concerning the Archbishopric of Armagh. Soon after we have received without

---

[1] The weavers, barbers, and other members of the Dublin Guilds.
[2] *S.P.I., Eliz.*, xx. 13. Shirley, 286.

our own procurement from Rome such letters as was necessary
for the abovesaid archbishopric, whereby we were bound by our
catholic religion for to come to Ireland, wherein, being before the
Lord O'Neill's going to Tirconaill, we desired him (according
our letters above mentioned, directed to the Lord Robert) to
provide for all possible means whereby he might be at accord with
the Queen's Majesty and your Lord ; but he was then so busy
about his affairs, that he took not then heed thereto ; and now,
before we should earnestly speak thereof unto him, we thought
best to know of your lord's will ; and what your lord shall will
us to do therein, we shall by God's life do the best we can. The
said Lord O'Neill, for safeguard of his country, have burned the
cathedral church and the whole town of Armagh, although we
have earnestly chided with him before and after he did the same ;
but he alleged such hurts as was before done to his country by
means of that place . . . if it be your lordship's pleasure, you
shall not disdain to write unto us, first, whether you will have us
speak concerning any peace with the said Lord O'Neill, and how ;
secondly, if that peace should be or not, whether it should please
your lord that we should have our old service in our churches,
and suffer the said churches to be up for that use, so that the
said Lord O'Neill should the less destroy no more churches, and
perhaps should help to restore such as by his procurement were
destroyed ; finally, whether your Lord heard anything concerning
our letters sent by the King of Spain unto his Ambassador and
to my Lord Robert ; so we commend your lordship and Almighty
God. From Dunavally, this instant Christmas.

By your lord to command in what we can lawfully execute
Richard Arch. *Ardmagh.*

Sydney did not condescend to reply to this loyal letter
of Creagh in which he asked but for freedom of religion to
come amongst Catholics and the common right to use in peace
the churches built by Catholics for Catholic worship, and at
the same time he promised, as Shane's archbishop, to do all
in his power to keep that prince in dutiful obedience to the
Queen. The Deputy's mind was fixed on the extirpation of
the hated Shane.

As to Loftus's excommunication of Shane, doubtless the
northern chief only laughed at it. He would have remembered
that his own ancestors had been the patrons and had not
asked for English money to build the cathedral or keep it
in repair, and, he would have soliloquised that just as he had,

as he alleged, burnt it for his own safety, as many others, English and Irish, had turned churches into ammunition depots, being safe stone buildings, or had burnt them in similar circumstances, so he could rebuild it when peace came. And, doubtless, he scorned the claim of Loftus to have any say or part in the matter of Catholic churches, as he would have laughed at the antiquarian lament of Camden. For the coming of Loftus to Armagh was to take possession of the Catholic Cathedral and of the temporalities, lands and tithes, which had been provided for the support of the Catholic religion and its priests. It cannot be said in the case of Armagh, at all events, that the Marian bishop went over to the " Reform," and that, therefore, Loftus could claim possession, even if that was considered a valid reason for taking over Catholic property from Catholic people.

SYDNEY'S PROGRESS THROUGH MUNSTER AND CONNACHT.

In the meantime Sydney wished to see the state of Munster for himself. He spent nearly three months on his journey and gave an account of it to Elizabeth, 20 April, 1567.[1] He found the Queen's County and Kilkenny in pretty good order and very prosperous compared with what he had formerly seen there. The O'Carrolls he found quiet, and their chief willing to pay rent to the Queen, and anxious for a peerage. Between the Fitzpatricks, the Desmonds, and the Butlers, Tipperary was in evil case, suffering especially from " the excessive train of horsemen and footmen led and kept there by the younger brethren of the Earl of Ormond, who rather consumed than defended the good of the poor country." Leaving Tipperary, the Lord Deputy proceeded to the city of Waterford, which, he reported, gave him a reception fit for the Queen herself. Most of the lords, gentlemen, and freeholders of the country responded to his summons, " and it well appeared that they had not forgotten the good obedience which they had been taught to observe by Sir Warham St. Leger and the other commissioners during the time of their abode there." All the same he felt that they were not

[1] *S.P.I., Eliz.*, xx. 66. Bagwell, ii. 111. *Catholic Bulletin*, June, 1925, 608-18.

to be trusted "unless continuance of justice was also disturbed by the Power kerne and others, who had been used to live by coyne and livery, and now betook themselves to undisguised rapine." Sir Maurice Fitzgerald's country [1] contrasted favourably both with Lord Power's [Waterford] and with the Desmond territory about Youghal, but the chief was somewhat too ready to take the law into his own hands.

Youghal suffered much from pirates, and in conversation with Desmond Sydney concluded that Ormond was in the right in his controversy with Desmond. "Your name," wrote Sydney to Elizabeth, "is no more reverenced, nor letters of commandment obeyed, within any place within his [Desmond's] rule, than it would be in the kingdom of France." But the greater part of the noblemen and gentlemen of Cork came to Sydney craving justice and protection against the Desmond tyranny, all except the Earl of Glencare [MacCarthy More] and O'Sullivan Beare. "Viscount Barry, the Lord Roche, De Courcy, Sir Donough MacCarthy (Captain of the Carberry), better known as MacCarthy Reagh, Sir Dermot MacCarthy (Captain of Muskerry), Barry Oge, Richard Condon and Barret . . . the greatest, and indeed very great possessioners in that county," [2] who were "or ought to be free subjects, but so injured and exacted upon by him [Desmond] as in effect they are or were become his thralls and slaves—all which, with open mouth, and held-up hands to heaven, cried out for justice and that it might please your Majesty to cause your name to be known amongst them with reverence, and your laws obeyed, offering to submit themselves, life, lands, and goods, to the same. Besides all these lords' and gentlemen's possessions, the Earl of Desmond enjoys under his rule or rather tyranny the third part of this great county [Cork] which I know to be greater than all Yorkshire—in all which his limits neither is your name reverenced or your laws obeyed ; neither does any sheriff execute any part of his office therein ; and yet [all

---

[1] *The White Knights*, in Tipperary, south of the Galtee mountains. (See *Hist. and Arch. Assoc. Ir.*, 1870-71, p. 592 *seq.*)

[2] See *Kilk. Arch. Soc.*, 1858-59, for MacCarthys (p. 139 *seq.*), Desmonds (p. 354 *seq.*), also 1890 (p. 194) ; Geraldine Documents, 1868 (p. 356 *seq.*).

this] is infuriously held by him, by report of the inhabitants, not having anything to show for the same, but by prescription, as he terms it."

Like Clonmel, Cashel, and Fethard, the city of Cork and the towns of Youghal and Kinsale, though of great importance to English rule in Ireland, were "on the highway to utter ruin." This was partly owing to Spanish trade along the coast, which brought the Spaniards into contact with the natives and enabled them not only to take "an incredible quantity of fish which might be turned to the use and benefit of your subjects," but also many other products of the country, such as "hides, tallow, fell, wool, flax, flesh, and yarn," which were formerly disposed of in the towns, but are now carried off direct to Spain, to the impoverishment of these towns. To remedy a mischief that would inevitably lead to the ruin of the English interest in Ireland, the Deputy bluntly stated his considered opinion, an opinion that coloured his whole Irish policy, that it could be done only "by ministering of justice and by planting some civil people upon those barbarous places." Unless this course was soon taken he was convinced that King Philip of Spain could drive the English out of Munster and Connacht with three thousand men and twenty thousand pounds which twenty thousand men and a hundred thousand pounds would not suffice to recover. To obviate this danger the towns must be looked to and strengthened "for the loss of them would be the loss of this your country."

Bad as was the state of the towns, that of the country subject to the Desmond influence appeared a thousand times worse in the eyes of the Deputy, who saw everything through coloured glasses now that the Earl had proved haughty and intractable. "I never was in a more pleasant country in all my life," he continued, "but never saw I a more waste or desolate land, there heard I such lamentable cries and doleful complaints made by that small remnant of poor people which are left, who, hardly escaping the fury of the sword and fire of their outrageous neighbours, or the famine with the same, which their extortious lords have driven them unto, either by taking their goods from them or by spending the same by their extortionate taking of coyne and livery, make

14 *

demonstration of the miserable state of that country. Besides this, such horrible and lamentable spectacles there are to behold, as the burning of villages, the ruin of churches, the wasting of such as have been good towns and castles." Everywhere were exposed " bones and skulls of the dead subjects, who, partly by murder, partly by famine, have died in the fields, as in troth hardly any Christian with dry eyes could behold." Women upon the point of becoming mothers were murdered by one of Desmond's vassals, and the Earl lodged and feasted in the murderer's house. " Surely," said Sydney, " there was never people that lived in more misery than they do, nor as it should seem of worse minds, for matrimony among them is no more regarded in effect than conjunction between unreasonable beasts. Perjury, robbery, and murder counted allowable. Finally, I cannot find that they make any conscience of sin, and I doubt whether they christen their children or no ; for neither find I place where it should be done, nor any person able to instruct them in the rules of a Christian ; or if they were taught, I see no grace in them to follow it ; and when they die I cannot see they make any account of the world to come."

Sydney rather destroys his case by such bigoted and exaggerated account of the natives. Naturally, they did not inform him where and by whom they were educated, or where they followed their religious exercises. But that they were not neglected, Sydney might very well have concluded. It is well to remember that even in the sixteenth century there was such a thing as political propaganda, and that uncomplimentary epithets were mainly reserved for those who were actually opposed to the English, and such language is not to be taken too literally.

Limerick and Clare equalled Cork in " desolation, waste, and ruin," as well as in " the lack of reverence for your name, obedience to your laws, and evil disposition of the people." In all those countries that were subject to Desmond rule and influence, there were just two bright spots, Rochestown and Kilmallock which he found fairly well inhabited.

Meanwhile the Earl of Desmond, who wanted to depart, was forced to remain, " blowing out words of evil digestion," and declaring that he would not disband his men, but would even increase their numbers and continue to exact coyne and livery as before. On Desmond's account the Deputy still kept in his train the gentlemen of the County Cork whose names he had mentioned and whom he had found to be "faithful and assured to your Majesty." He was also joined by Lord Fitzmaurice of Kerry, whom, greatly to his surprise, he also found faithful and assured, while, as for the Earl's brother, Sir John of Desmond, "I found him a ready and an humble subject to serve your Majesty, were it against his own brother or whosoever else." Though full of natural affection for his brother and fearful of the overthrow of their House, Sir John disliked the number of armed men whom the Earl kept about him, for what reason he knew not. Sir John was playing a game, as the Earl afterwards played, although Sydney did not see it. A similar attitude was taken up by Bishop Lacy "who was supposed to be an earnest friend to the Earl." Others whom he interrogated were of like mind ; wherefore he summoned the Earl into his presence at Kilmallock, charged him with the levying of 600 men, and upbraided him "with grievous and weighty words for his rash and doubtful doings." These 600 men were now between Kilmallock and Limerick, whither the Deputy was about to proceed, and he bluntly informed the Earl that if any outrage was offered to him on the way, " he [the Earl] should be the first that should die for it." He then committed the Earl to custody and led him " to Limerick, and from Limerick to Galway, and so to the Castle of Dublin where he yet remains."

Continuing his journey to the good and true city of Limerick, he was met by three hundred well-appointed men, and was received by the Catholic bishop, Hugh Lacy, "in full pontificals, and with much ceremony of an entirely Roman character." That is, the Bishop came with mitre and crozier, with his attendant ministers, cross-bearer and acolytes, and with smoking censer. And, most likely, as was customary, Sydney did not object to his being incensed by the Bishop. At all events, he made no complaint of this Catholic display. The city he found much decayed, partly through the misdeeds of Desmond, but more through those of the Earl of Thomond, who was both incompetent and treacherous. Here Sydney " combined all the forenamed lords and gentlemen in faithful love and amity, confirmed by their promises and solemn oaths, which in all semblance they showed faithfully to keep. All seeming desirous that Sir John of Desmond should be chief in commission amongst them, " he confirmed their choice and placed the counties of Cork, Kerry, and Limerick in care of a commission composed of Sir John, Andrew Skiddy, a lawyer, and Henry Davells, an experienced soldier.

In Clare, where the O'Briens of Thomond held aloof, owing to the influence of the Earl of Desmond, he found all " waste and desolate," but O'Shaughnessey, with whom he lodged one night, proved to be " a very obedient, loyal and civil man," anxious to be delivered from the exactions of the Earls of Clanricard and Thomond, and deserving of every support and encouragement.

Galway, which Sydney next visited, more " resembled a town of war frontiering upon an enemy, than a civil town in a country under the sovereign. They watch their walls nightly, and guard their gates daily, with armed men." " In the churchyard the Bishop of the town received him in his pontificals, accompanied with divers priests and clerks in copes, singing." The Deputy " entered the church of Our Lady, and there remained until the *Te Deum* was sung in Latin," and after prayer went to his lodging. The Deputy did not evince much gratitude for the Bishop's welcome, but was pleased to commend highly the sermon preached a few days later in the same town by " a priest of Ireland, who was sometime a friar," who gave his preface in Latin and afterwards delivered " a godly lesson " to his hearers, and was in consequence recommended to Clanricard in warm terms of approbation.[1]

It does not appear who the Bishop was who thus received the Deputy as if there was no Act of Parliament ordering uniformity of worship, but it is quite probable that he was the Marian bishop, William Mor, ousted by Bodkin. The reader can imagine the feelings of the puritanical Sydney when confronted with all this Catholic ceremonial and

---

[1] *MS., T.C.D.*, E. 3, 18.

especially the singing of the *Te Deum* in Latin, and yet he suffered it all because it was a testimony to him of the fealty shown to himself and the Queen whom he represented.

Clanricard's sons, Ulick and John, by two wives both living, were chief disturbers of the west, and they, too, like Desmond, were sent prisoners to Dublin. The Earl of Clanricard, who is " equal in all good parts with the best of his coat of this country breed," is " so overruled by a putative wife, when he best intended she forceth him to do worst." At Galway he was visited by the new O'Donnell, who offered his services to the Queen, and asked to hold his country by letters patent from Her Majesty, a request which was readily granted. A like request was made by O'Connor Sligo and was granted in like manner.

The town of Athenry was deserted, four families only remaining, who greeted the Lord Deputy with cries of " succour, succour." Clanricard's own country was in pretty good condition, but he was quite unable to keep his sons in check.

Sydney, from his journey, came to the conclusion that Munster and Connacht did not contain the seeds of reformation within themselves. Ormond did not lack ability ; but he was absent, and likely to be absent, and his work could not be done by deputy. He summed up the qualifications of the other great lords in a few pithy sentences. " The Earl of Desmond, a man both void of judgment to govern and will to be ruled. The Earl of Clancare, I suppose willing enough to be ruled, but wanteth force and credit to rule. The Earl of Thomond, the most imperfect of all the rest hath neither wit of himself to govern, nor grace or capacity to learn of others." Lord Roche's country in Cork was pretty well managed, and O'Shaughnessey, the son of him whom Henry VIII knighted, was an exception among the gentlemen of Galway. Sydney again advocated a President and Council for each province severally, and that nothing else would be of any avail. He condemned, " the old and necessary policy of keeping the Irish by all possible means at war between themselves." If this cowardly system of fostering dissensions, lest quiet should bring unknown danger, were still persisted in, informers encouraged, and comfortless silence given to his own letters, then he begged the Queen to choose some other minister. Ireland could only be reformed by justice, and by making it possible to practise the arts of peace.

In addition to this, he desired to see a number of English colonists planted in points of vantage all over the land. As a step in this direction he saw that lands could be made available only by sequestrating the lands of the actual holders, which could be effected by inventing or discovering flaws in the titles of occupation or by inducing the chiefs to abandon the ruling family system, and surrender their lands to the Crown. The chiefs would then receive them back as royal grants, and hold them or a part of them as subjects of Her Majesty, in which case the penalty for disobedience or rebellion would be forfeiture. The Deputy evidently looked on the actual situation of the Earl of Desmond as likely to furnish a suitable opportunity for applying these schemes to the province of Munster. The Earl was safely locked up in Dublin Castle. He was not perhaps guilty of overt treason or even of traitorous intent ; but his attitude had been " so punishable and fineable " as to afford, if properly handled, an excuse for effecting " the reformation of all Munster." He therefore suggested that the Earl should be brought to trial before a competent tribunal either in Ireland or England, according as the Queen should decide ; he earnestly requested instructions on this head.

On his return to Dublin, 20 April, he was able to report that, thanks to " the diligent and painful services of the Earl of Kildare," the English Pale was never, in the memory of the oldest man that now liveth, in greater quiet and obedience.

Murder of Shane O'Neill.

Towards the end of his lengthy report, Sydney had good news of Ulster to communicate to Her Majesty. Shane " is now driven to the woods and almost not heard of where he is, daily spoils and preys [being] taken from him, to the enriching of your Highness's subjects and the impoverishing of him." His principal followers, too, were falling away from him, and some of them had submitted to the Queen

—the O'Hanlons, the MacMahons, and the Maginnesses. Turlough Lynagh O'Neill " showeth himself a devoted subject to your Highness, daily imbrewing himself in the blood of the rebel's followers ; all Clandeboy is wholly at your Majesty's devotion ; the Glynns, the Ardes, the Dufferin and Lecale are now possessed by the right and ancient owners and ready at your Majesty's commandment ; all Tirconnaill together with O'Cahan's country is quite obedient to your Majesty and daily doing annoyance to the rebels ; in Fermanagh the rebel has no footing, the Captain thereof [the New] Maguire, being a devoted subject to your Majesty ; so that the rebel is now, as it were, cooped in Tyrone, neither dare he show himself in the plains thereof, being so greatly distressed by your soldiers, by their daily incursions ; his cattle do daily starve and die in the woods in which, God willing, ere it be long he himself shall be well hunted."

After Randolph's death the settlement at Derry had gone from bad to worse, but the appointment of Edward Saintloo put heart into the garrison. Sickness, however, reduced the number from 600 to 200, but a fire having caught the magazine, once a church, the settlement ceased to exist. Shane now supposed the road into Tirconnaill once more open, and advanced with a large force to the ford over the Swilly, now called Farsetmore, near Letterkenny. O'Donnell was in the neighbourhood, and collecting his men, told them that death was far preferable to the insults that they had of late years suffered at O'Neill's hands. They attacked Shane who was taken by surprise. Shane escaped in confusion, and made his way into Tyrone, leaving a couple of thousand of his men slaughtered. He never collected another army. He thought of appearing before Sydney with a rope round his neck and begging for mercy, but he placed himself in the power of the MacDonnells. These had just landed at Cushendun in Antrim, 18 May, with a large force of Scots under the command of Alexander Oge MacDonnell who had come over from Scotland at Sydney's request. To him Shane now sent proposals for a permanent alliance against the English.

Alexander agreed to a meeting, and Shane, accompanied by the unfortunate Countess MacDonnell, and by Sorley Boy, who was still his prisoner, directed his steps towards Red Bay. His escort was reduced to fifty horse. The Scots made a feast to welcome their visitor, and after dinner Shane's secretary [Neale MacConnor] was accused of circulating a report that James MacDonnell's widow was about to marry the man [Shane] who had killed her husband. The secretary incautiously said that O'Neill was a meet partner, not only for their chief's wife, but for Mary of Scotland, who was a widow at this time. Shane, who had been indulging as usual in strong drink, came up at the moment and took part in the altercation. Alexander and his Scots drew their dirks and almost cut him and his secretary to pieces, 2 June, 1567. The body, wrapped in an old Irish shirt, was thrown into an old chapel hard by, and Captain Piers of Carrickfergus, who had all along plotted for this conclusion, came four days afterwards and cut off the head, which he sent, preserved in salt, to Sydney at Dublin.[1] Piers received 1000 marks, the reward that Sydney had placed on the head, and the ghastly trophy was stuck on a pole over the gate of Dublin Castle, where it was seen by the historian Campion four years later. Shane's entire body had been valued at £1000, £500 being the sum promised by proclamation for simply killing him. The trunk was buried in the Franciscan Monastery at Glenarm, and it is said that the monks from Armagh came afterwards to claim it. " Have you," said the prior of Glenarm, " brought with you the remains of James MacDonnell, Lord of Antrim and Cantire [killed by Shane], who was buried among strangers at Armagh ? " A negative answer was given, and the prior said : " While you continue to tread on the grave of James, Lord of Antrim and Cantire, know ye that we here in Glenarm will trample on the dust of your great O'Neill."

Shane the Proud was perhaps the ablest of Elizabeth's

---

[1] *S.P.I., Eliz.*, xx. 54, 69, 83, 93, 97 ; O'Sullivan Beare, *Hist. Cath.*, iii. 5 ; *Four Masters ;* Campion's and Hooker's *Histories.* " It is thought," says Campion, " that Tirlagh who now usurpeth the name of O'Neale, practised this devise with Agnes [Countess MacDonnell], Alexander, and Torwy [Sorley Boy], when he perceived Shane discouraged, and not able to hold out." It was O'Donnell (to Lord Deputy, 28 April) who said that he treated of marriage with James MacDonnell's widow, who, he said, would willingly be allied to him in order to be avenged of Shane for the death of her late husband. And he desired leave to join the Scots now come against Shane.

Irish opponents. He intrigued at different times with Spain, with France, and with Scotland, but received no foreign help. Neither France nor Spain was prepared to court the hostility of England, and Scotland simply used him as a means against Elizabeth. He posed as the Catholic champion, but this was simply to gain his own ends, principally the overlordship of Ulster, the other chiefs paying him tribute. They were as Catholic as he, but resisted his overbearing claim. Alone, however, he bore the brunt of the contest against Elizabeth, and 3500 soldiers were sacrificed to subdue him. The service cost Elizabeth more than £147,000. His moral character, perhaps no different from others in that rude age, was not beyond reproach. " By far the most remarkable Irishman of his time, he cannot be regarded as in any sense a national hero. His ambition was limited to making himself supreme in Ulster. Had he been allowed to oppress his own province and perhaps to levy some blackmail beyond his border, it is not likely that he would have troubled the Pale, or denied the titular sovereignty of England." [1] Being such as he was, the men of the North rejoiced at his fall, and the *Four Masters* do not pretend that he was much loss, except to his own race.

Few of Ireland's heroes have been painted in such repellant colours as Shane the Proud. This work, done by enemies in his own day, has been continued ever since more or less on the same lines, by unfriendly hands. One point in particular calls for exhaustive inquiry, [2] and, until it is cleared up, the memory of Shane must continue to suffer at the hands of his own countrymen. Was Shane concerned merely with his own supremacy in Ulster ? Or had he all the time before his mind the vision of Ireland a Nation, with no alien foe treading its sacred soil and no alien influence moulding its destinies ?

We have seen how Archbishop Creagh of Armagh thought he was promoting God's glory by excommunicating Shane,

---

[1] Bagwell, ii. 119.

[2] We understand that such an inquiry has been made by an Irish scholar, but as original work in the secular or even in the ecclesiastical history of Ireland has received such scant support, one of the most important characters in Irish history still remains under a cloud.

how he preached to him loyalty to the English Queen, although Creagh's loyalty did not save himself from the rigours of the Tower of London. Again, Father Wolf, S.J., the Papal Commissary, did not hesitate to describe Shane as " a cruel, impious, heretical tyrant," although the same papal representative afterwards threw all the weight of his influence on the side of the Munster confederates. Moreover, those confirmed loyalists, the *Four Masters*, thought they were saying all that could be said in favour of Shane when they recorded in their Annals, " grievous to the race of Owen, Son of Nial, was the death of him who was slain, for Shane O'Neill had been their champion in provincial dignity." Shane, according to them was merely a champion of the rights of the race of O'Neills, whilst they belonged to, and upheld their own clansmen, the O'Donnells.

Whatever verdict may be arrived at as a result of exhaustive inquiry into the policy and motives that governed the earlier part of his career, there is some evidence available to warrant the conclusion that at least towards the end of his days he had made up his mind that no single Irish chief, whether Celt or Norman, whether in Ulster or Munster, was safe as long as there was an English soldier or an English official on Irish soil.[1] Consequently, just when the activities of the new Lord Deputy, Sir Henry Sydney, had indicated a new phase of conquest and confiscation, Shane addressed to the Munster Geraldines an earnest appeal for co-operation. He asked them to remember that the men of Norman blood were exposed to danger no less than the Celtic chief ; he called on them to combine with him in an effort to avert the ruin that menaced both alike, and urged them to recognise that now or never was the time to banish the Sassenach from the land (September, 1566).

That the Munster chiefs were fully alive to the danger is proved by the efforts and sacrifices that they made in the years that followed. But at this time they held back, either believing that the time was not yet ripe, or that they were unable to take prompt action, or that they were contemptuous and jealous of the Celtic chiefs. They adopted the wait-and-

[1] *Catholic Bulletin*, May, 1925, pp. 446-7.

see policy—who was going to win—before they committed themselves irrevocably. But some of them did more ; they threw in their lot with the Lord Deputy, and actually took part in the campaign against Shane. The Ulster chief, rather short-sightedly, played into the Deputy's hands by wasting his forces in war on the rival family of the O'Donnells whom Sydney had cleverly joined in confederacy with himself against Shane.

Sequel to the Murder ; Bishop of Down Submits to Sydney.

All this had taken place in the absence of Sydney, but, on receipt of the good news, he quickly made his way to Ulster. His first thought was to solve the thorny problem of the headship of the O'Neills and thereby ensure perpetual peace for the distracted North. Tirlogh Luineach, tanist of Tyrone, who had supported the English in their wars against Shane, was immediately chosen by the family as the O'Neill. This " title in truth he accepted, it being given him with the brutish ceremonies incident to the same," as Sydney remarked. Shortly after the inauguration ceremony he did homage to Sydney who reported, 18 June,[1] that " in the presence and hearing of all that were in my camp [at Castle Cobra in Tyrone], as well of them who came with me, as those that came with him, and all the other potentates and landlords of Ulster, [I] rebuked him sharply for taking upon him the title of O'Neill afore her Majesty's pleasure was known, affirming unto him that I would not confirm the same, but would write to her Highness to nobilitate him with the title of higher honour and dignity [i.e. Earl of Tyrone], which he seemed reverently to accept, and willingly to expect her Majesty's resolution."

The Deputy then allotted the various districts of Tyrone to those of the chiefs whom he thought most likely to be obedient subjects, " to the great rejoicing " as he said, " and contentment of all the proprietors of that province, saving some particular and peculiar followers of his [Tirlogh's] own, who much repined that the great and regal estate of

[1] *S.P.I., Eliz.*, xxi. 22.

the O'Neill, as they termed it, should be so broken and dismembered." Tirconnaill and other parts of Ulster were similarly settled by him. He then returned to Dublin to perfect the schemes that he had in mind for the final reduction of Ireland to civility—the building of bridges, erection of forts, introduction of colonists, the tenure of lands direct from the Crown, instead of according to the old Brehon Law.

Hemmed in on all sides, as Shane was by his capture, his position was not without its effect on unsuspected quarters. Maguire, " the third beast in all Ulster " who had already gone over to the English Government, and probably acquainted with the fate intended for Shane, brought with him to Drogheda, 29 May, " the feigned Bishop of Down, who of late came from Rome," namely Meiler Magrath.[1]

This occurred three days before Shane's murder and had for its object the presentation of the Bishop to Sydney. Thomas Lancaster (afterwards Archbishop of Armagh), who sent this information to Cecil, rejoiced at the good news but was careful to add, " notwithstanding he [Bishop of Down] surrendered and gave his submission, God grant it be from their hearts as they declare it outwardly." In a " Memorial of things not expressed in the letters brought by Ralph Knight but committed to be declared by speech," [2] Sydney desired to " know the Queen Majesty's pleasure concerning the Bishop of Down who humbleth himself and craveth mercy and restorement to his bishopric from her Highness." Somewhat later (6 July), the Queen assured Sydney, " we like also of the submission of the Bishop of Down and think it good that he, and others whom ye shall not find meet to expel, be induced to submit themselves and to take their bishoprics of us." [3]

Meiler Magrath's position at this time is of special interest.

---

[1] *S.P.I.*, *Eliz.*, xx. 97, P.R.O., London. Conatius Maguire of Fermanagh had to pay a fine of 100 cows for his appointment as captain of the country of Cavan. (*Fiants*, no. 1081, 26 July, 1567.)

On 20 June the appointment was made of Donald O'Madden to be captain of the country of the Longford, he having shown by letters of the bishop of Clonfert and the clergy of the diocese that he was not guilty of the murder of Hugh O'Madden, the previous captain. Fine eighty fat cows. (*Fiants*, no. 1080.)

[2] *S.P.I.*, *Eliz.*, xxi. 22.   [3] *C.S.P.I.*, *Eliz.*, xxi. 49.

Although appointed to Down and Connor, 12 October, 1565, he probably did not make his way back from Rome until the middle of 1566. Having visited Archbishop Creagh, he went with him to Inis Darell in August, 1566, to meet Shane probably with a view to taking possession of his diocese. Neither Creagh nor Shane had any great regard for him, and probably Shane was still hoping to have the diocese for his own brother when he should come of age. During the pursuit of Shane in September by Sydney, Magrath seems to have gone into his people's country of Fermanagh, in the diocese of Clogher, where young Maguire had succeeded to the captainry on the death of the old chief in Sydney's camp. When Shane was surrounded in May of the following year, Magrath saw the chance of getting possession of his diocese by offering submission in company with Maguire to Sydney. Accordingly the chieftain and the bishop came in haste to Drogheda to take an oath of allegiance. That is evidently all that his submission amounted to at this time, for Sydney speaks of him as one " who humbleth himself and craveth mercy and restorement to his bishopric from her Highness." There was no question here of accepting his bishopric from the Queen, but simply that he might be enabled by Sydney's help to occupy his See. Had he accepted the Supremacy Sydney would probably have had little difficulty in arranging the matter for him by receiving from him the papal Bulls. Moreover, in the Queen's reply it is significant that she counsels Sydney that Magrath and others like him who submit might " be induced to take their bishoprics of us."

It is clear then that Magrath still continued at this time as Catholic bishop. But what occurred subsequently is rather obscure. He probably made his way to his diocese and continued to profess loyalty to the Queen, but there was no move on the part of the Queen to make him one of her own bishops. It would seem that the chiefs and people turned against him, perhaps for his too loyal professions, and that he was anxious to be translated to some other diocese. As Clogher, his people's diocese, ruled by his friend Maguire, had had a dispute about the rightful bishop, Magrath evidently considered this an opportunity of applying to

Rome to have himself translated to it, but this new move did not find favour in Rome, and he continued in Down.

ARCHBISHOP CREAGH TAKEN PRISONER.

The most striking contrast between any two men of this period is that between Creagh and Loftus, both archbishops of the same See. Loftus, granted easy life, honours, and wealth, in the midst of a religious warfare, and Creagh, as loyal as Loftus to Elizabeth, yet, banned and hunted, undergoing long journeys and hardships at all seasons, in order, with disinterested zeal, to minister and preach to his people the word of God ; Loftus rewarded by the Queen because he could do nothing to spread her " reform " in his diocese, Creagh imprisoned for years in loathsome dungeons because he preached religion, morality, and discipline to his people who wanted not Loftus's ministrations ; such is the contrast in the light of historical facts.

Creagh's zeal was too efficacious, and his influence too extensive, not to render him an object of jealousy and vengeance to a Government that was ultimately determined on the extirpation of Catholicity. Spies were accordingly set upon him as he was left behind during Shane's forced march into Tirconnaill. On the advance of the English army Creagh retired to Connacht where he was taken by O'Shaughnessey on the last day of April. Thomas Lancaster reports the capture to Cecil, 31 May, from Drogheda,[1] and states that Sydney is ready to send him again to the Tower of London, whence he escaped " trusting he shall be better kept hereafter."

The capture of Archbishop Creagh and the submission of Meiler Magrath may be regarded as the first-fruits of Shane's debacle. Elizabeth, 6 July, sent her thanks to O'Shaughnessey at Sydney's request.[2] Creagh was to be " brought to Dublin and thoroughly examined especially of his aiders to escape, and of such as were thought anywise privy as to his escape as afore." He was to be " indicted and ordered to receive that which in justice he hath deserved for example sake." The Queen was careful not to mention

[1] *S.P.I., Eliz.*, xx. 97, P.R.O., London.   [2] *Ib.*, xxi. 49.

visitation held in St. Patrick's by Loftus, Dean Weston
exhibited the Archbishop of Canterbury's dispensation from
taking holy orders. Nor was the Dean the only lay member
of the chapter. At the same visitation, Thomas Ythel,
prebendary of Castleknock, on being asked why he did not
take holy orders and reside on his prebend, answered, as to
the first, that he had the dispensation of the Archbishop
of Canterbury which he produced and which was read; as
to the second, he pleaded a like dispensation during the time
he should pursue his studies at Cambridge. On 29 September,
1559, license had been granted to Thomas Ithell, master of
Arts, rector of Castleknock, to be absent in England for three
years, for the purpose of study and other business.[1] On
24 August, 1562, a similar license was granted to him.[2]
Again, 20 May, 1565, license was granted to him, now doctor
of laws, and still rector of Castleknock during those six years,
to be absent in England for five years, for study and other
business.[3] Thus, after eight years' enjoyment of the prebend
and University course, he had not yet taken Orders, and
intended devoting another three years to study. About
this time it was a common practice to grant those licenses
" for study and other business in England." On 24 August,
1562, John Standishe, archdeacon of Glendaloch and prebendary of Newcastle, had one for three years.[4] On 16 July,
1565, John Maguyre, clerk, rector of St. James of Uske, and
vicar of St. Edan of Kynneghe, diocese of Dublin, along with
a dispensation to hold a third benefice, had licence to be
absent for five years.[5] George Hopton, rector of Kylcol-
manbane, diocese of Leighlin, had one also for five years.[6]
Geoffrey Crosse, prebendary of one portion of Donaghmore
in Ui Mail, diocese of Dublin, had one for six years.[7] And
yet there was complaint of lack of preachers.

Curwen, now translated to Oxford, begged Cecil[8] " to
hasten Mr. Doctor Weston's coming hither, as I may be
able to take my journey into England in long and warm days
and short nights, for if I should be driven to travel in the
cold weather, I do fear it would put me in danger of my life."

[1] *Fiants*, no. 158.   [2] *Ib.*, no. 446.   [3] *Ib.*, no. 729.
[4] *Ib.*, no. 445.   [5] *Ib.*, no. 740.   [6] *Ib.*, no. 801.
[7] *Ib.*, no. 1091.   [8] *S.P.I., Eliz.*, xx. 29.   Shirley, 304.

Curwen was anxious also about other material comforts, and intimated to Cecil that he understood from his servant, whom he had probably sent over to Oxford to inspect his new quarters, " that there is no house belonging to the bishopric of Oxford which is for the bishop's mansion." He begged, therefore, that he " may have an house for me and for my family, and some land withal to find my cattle and geldings upon a reasonable rent." Curwen was as meticulous about his material comforts as Loftus and Brady.

No sooner had Loftus been informed of his translation to Dublin than he wrote to Cecil complaining of certain things that were on foot for the diminution of his dignity and privileges. The Mayor and Bailiffs of Dublin had for some time looked on the position of St. Patrick's and the archiepiscopal palace of St. Sepulchre just outside the walls of the city and free from the jurisdiction of the city as anomalous. The archbishop's manor of St. Sepulchre and the deanery of St. Patrick's were exempt jurisdictions. It seems that the Mayor, etc., were not imbued with the ancient respect for these ecclesiastical privileges. A few years before this complaint of Loftus they had solemnly drawn up a resolution against alleged infringement of their jurisdiction by the archbishop's court :—

The Fourth Friday after Easter, 1565. . . . Yt is agreed by thauctoritie of the said assemblie that no citizen or inhabitant of this cittie or suburbes of the same shall from this day forthe at any tyme move . . . attempt or bringe or cause or procure to be moved, attempted or brought, eny accion, suyt, querrell or playnt in the faire court of the most reverend father in God the lord archebusshope of Dublin for the time beinge, to be holden within this cittie before his barons, or other his judges of the same court, against eny cittizen or inhabitant of this cittie or suburbes therof, unlesse the matter and cause of the same accion, querell, suyt, or pleint do growe, arise or be givven in the tyme of the faire court to be holden, or within xv daies next before the same court to be holden, upon payne of ten poundes to the offender tociens quociens, and yf the offender be free [man] of this cittie (he is) to lose his fredome. And that no man shall upon the like paine use or practise eny covin, collusion or disseit in fraud of this lawe or of the good meaning thereof.[1]

[1] *C.A.R.D.*, ii. 39.

The court referred to here is the " Pie Powder " Court [1] of the Archbishop's principal manor of St. Sepulchre.[2] It dealt with all disputes, disorders, damages, robberies, etc., that occurred during the days on which the fair was held, usually three days, within the archiepiscopal manor.[3] The court sessions were held in the Tholsel before the archiepiscopal barons who imposed fines and settled disputes.[4] Evidently the Mayor, etc., considered that this court had been usurping the rights of the ordinary civil court by trying cases of dispute, etc., which had not occurred during the time of the fair, and they set forth the limits of the Pie Powder Court.

This was a few years before the translation of Loftus to Dublin. But the Mayor, etc., were now bent on a more serious incursion on the rights and privileges of the archiepiscopal palace and St. Patrick's Cathedral. On 16 July, 1567, Loftus wrote to Cecil [5] that he understood that the Queen's Attorney and one Mr. White were being dispatched with a memorial to London to have these privileges abolished and the palace and cathedral brought within the jurisdiction of the City. Either as dean or as archbishop his position would be affected. He therefore asks that he " be not made inferior to such as hath been before " him, namely, Curwen, and accuses the Mayor and Burgesses of Dublin of presumption, arrogance, and disdain, jealous " that any personage should live so near their nose not subject to them." He is informed, he says, that these parties are well supplied with money for their

---

[1] " Pieds Poudrés," " pedes pulverizati " (i.e. dusty feet), so called from the dusty feet of the suitors engaged in the court of the fair.

[2] The archiepiscopal palace stood near St. Patrick's, in St. Kevin Street, on the site now occupied by the Gardai depot. See *Journal R.S.A.I.*, 1890, pp. 31-41 for *Manor of St. Sepulchre.*

[3] A slovenly, badly written Register of the Pie Powder Court, 1586-87, during the administration of Archbishop Loftus, is preserved in the British Museum (*Egerton MSS.* 1780). It tells that the Mayor and Bailiffs of the City come before the barons or judges of the Fair Court held within the city at the Tholsel in Skinners' Row (Christchurch Place) and deliver up to them the keys of the city gaol and gates to be held and kept in custody according to the custom of the city during the time of holding the court. The gates mentioned are the Bridge, Ormond's, St. Nicholas's, Dame's, and Newgate.

[4] The perquisites of the markets, fairs, and court were a considerable source of revenue to the Archbishop of Dublin, particularly in the days when he had control of his other manors, such as Ballymore, etc. He had tolls of the booths erected, of buying and selling, as well as the fines of the court.

[5] *S.P.I.*, *Eliz.*, xxi. 62. Shirley, 308-10.

venture which is a subtle device, and that their " wise advocates [are] especially chosen as much for private respects as for the public affairs."

Apparently Loftus's pleading struck a tender cord in the Queen's heart for, 20 March, 1568, she directed a conference to be had with the Dean and Chapter, the principal heads, lords, gentlemen, and freeholders of the diocese, for raising a contribution towards the re-edifying of the Cathedral and house for the Archbishop, and ordered a commission to take up timber and stone for that purpose.[1] But the Queen makes no mention of any contribution out of the royal purse.

Brady Complains of Poverty ; The Council Intercede for Him.

Loftus would have been very pleased to retain the deanery of St. Patrick's with the archbishopric in order to keep up the dignity of his office and the conviviality expected of him. The £3600 (*1914 value*) of the deanery or, perhaps somewhat less on account of troubled times, would have been a useful addition to the £4800 or thereabouts of the archbishopric. But that was not to be. He had to be content with the revenues of the See. It was better to be in Dublin with that modest income than to live on £300 a year in Termonfechin. The deanery was accordingly bestowed on Dr. Robert Weston, the new Lord Chancellor, who arrived in Dublin about 8 August and was installed as dean of St. Patrick's before the 24th. Scarcely a fortnight after his arrival he wrote to Cecil complaining of the smallness of his fee as Chancellor (about £5200), and the impoverishment of his deanery. He therefore begged[2] that the Queen would pardon him the 100 marks that she had lent him, the first-fruits of the deanery, and the yearly twentieth part. Whatever the expenses of these men may have been, they were emphatic about the smallness of their incomes, and Elizabeth was not remarkable for generosity. In the same letter Weston reported that Curwen had taken ship, 11 August. Thus the late Archbishop was to be favoured with fairly long days and short nights for his journey to his new diocese.

[1] *C.S.P.I.*, *Eliz.*, i. 511, *note*.   [2] *Ib.*, xxi. 89.

It was now Brady's turn to complain of his poverty. His letter to Cecil, 27 October, 1567, first deals with the charges against him, probably those that Loftus had made as to his neglect as ecclesiastical commissioner. He therefore begged Cecil [1] to let him know what he had heard about him, and continued his letter :—

Since my coming hither, but chiefly the time of this last war, I have spent all I could get upon hospitality, besides the charges of a preacher and of a free school erected upon my own charges, which with the beggary of my clergy not able to pay their 20th part, whereof I am accountable, and brought in the cash of 240 pound Irish, which already I have paid, and resting in debt yet of that 20th part, £70 16s. 10½d. and of my [first] fruits £224,[2] besides that I have already of these first fruits paid £149, which debt, as the Lord God knoweth, I am not able to discharge, if it may please your honour of your accustomed goodness and pity towards me in such misery to extend your goodness towards me, in helping to relieve this my present care-full necessity.—H. MIDEN.

Brady, in a postscript, recommends John Garvey,[3] Dean of Christ Church, and servant and chaplain of the Earl of Sussex, for the Archbishopric of Armagh. He calls Garvey " a man very much travelled amongst the Irishry, grave and well learned, a sharp preacher in the Irish tongue." He also tells Cecil that the new Lord Chancellor is " the patron of virtue and godly modesty," and that from Sydney and him " there is great hope of such reformation as never happened before."

The same day the Council of Ireland, including Loftus, sent a letter to the Privy Council [4] begging to have Brady's debts to the Queen remitted :—

Our most humble duties to your honours premised, being moved with the consideration of the sufficiency of the reverend father Hugh Brady, Bishop of Meath, in the function of his office pastoral, and his earnest and careful setting forth of her Majesty's most godly proceedings, and sincere preaching God's most holy

---

[1] *S.P.I., Eliz.*, xxii. 13. Shirley, 313-16.

[2] Brady was now four years Bishop of Meath and had paid only £149 out of £373, the first-fruits of the See.

[3] Garvey was later appointed Bishop of Kilmore, and eventually (1589) Archbishop of Armagh.

[4] *S.P.I., Eliz.*, xxii. 14. Shirley, 317-20.

gospel, as well in the English, as the Irish tongue, upon the confines here, to the right good edifying of many of the ruder sort, and no less alluring of the residue : among other things he hath erected a school for the better education of the youth within his diocese at his proper costs, besides the entertainment he hath hitherto given to a learned preacher, to help him in the function within his said diocese ; as also with the respect of his disability to maintain hospitality or to repair his decayed mansions or churches which were become very ruinous before his entry to the same, and by reason of the late northern wars [Shane's raids], whereby his Lord's lands for the most part there bordering, were remaining as waste, and of divers other vagrant kern, which have and do still waste divers of his tenants ; and remaining also endebted presently to her Majesty as he hath declared unto us, in certain several sums of money, which chiefly have grown by reason of the inability and evil payment of his clergy, of their twenty part [of yearly income] due to her Majesty, and by him answered in her Highness Exchequer, amounting in the whole to three hundred and odd pounds, and tenpence halfpenny, which payment (as he affirmith) was in a manner made by himself, without any great help of them, by reason of their poverty as aforesaid, and also for parcels of his first fruits of that bishopric, at the feast of the Annunciation, 1567, £74 13s. due already, and at the same feast, 1568, yet to come £74 14s. 0d. and at the said feast 1569, £74 16s. 0½d. amounting for those first fruits £224 4s. 0d. over and besides that for the residue of those first fruits the said Bishop hath already paid to her Majesty said use £149 8s. 0d. grown due for his first two payments at the said feast in the years 1565 and 1566 as he affirmeth. For which respects with divers others overlong to trouble your honours withal : we have thought it not unfitting to our duties to advertise your honours, the said bishop's present poor estate, to be by your honours charitably considered : vouch-safing to stand therein his gracious good lords, and to be means to her Highness of her princely favour and grace therein, to be extended : as it shall be pleasing to her highness, whereby the rather, if it may so stand with her Highness liking, to disburden the said poor bishop of those debts : besides he standeth to her Majesty for her former clemency and goodness most straight bounden, he also may henceforth be enabled the better to serve God and her Highness in his function and calling, and maintain his begun commendable hospitality, and to be encouraged to the persevering of his good proceedings, rather than with con-straint of further disability growing on him, to be (against his own will and good zeal), disenabled from the executing of the effectual ministry of his said function and charge, which amongst this people consisteth not a little in feeding of the poor, and keeping good hospitality. And thus leaving any further to trouble your good lords but wishing to the same all godly and happy honour and prosperity, do humbly take our leave. From Dublin, this 27th of October, 1567.

Your lords humble at commandment,

Robert Weston.	Adam Dublin.	W. Fitzwilliams.
Robert Dillon.	Jo. Plunkett.	H. Draycott.
James Bathe.	John Challoner.	Thomas Cusake.

The first-fruits and twentieth part of income were undoubtedly a heavy tax on the bishops and clergy of the State Church, and it took a deal of pleading to induce Elizabeth to remit them. In dealing with this question, and with these complaints, it is easy to lose sight of the position of the Catholic clergy whose revenues had been sequestrated, and who had, therefore, to live on charity. They had to look on at this fencing with Elizabeth for the support of her clergy, and saw the tithes contributed by the members of their flock augmenting the revenues of the " farmers " of the tithes,[1] Elizabeth's lessees, and swelling the royal coffers. Nevertheless, many of them continued to remain with and console by their ministrations the flock entrusted to their care, regardless of whether a sufficiency would be at hand for their support, or how they should be housed.

New Grants of Monastic Possessions.

In order to confer with Cecil on the state of Ireland, Sydney left from Howth on Thursday night, 9 October, Weston and FitzWilliams having been appointed Lords Justices. He brought with him a sheaf of petitions in favour of the good and loyal men whom he had met on his official journeys through the provinces. Some of them had been already recompensed for their services by grants of religious possessions. Sir Edmond Butler had received the monastery of

---

[1] It must be noted that the " farmers " of the tithes were not always Protestants ; some of them were important Catholic personages, who at the same time lent their houses for the celebration of Mass and, doubtless, contributed to the support of the Mass-priest.

Innistiocke, Co. Kilkenny, the monastery of Cahir, Co. Tipperary, the priory of Connall, Co. Kildare, the monk's land, parcel of the abbey of Baltinglas, and the abbey of Kilkilihine, Co. Kilkenny (12 Nov., 1566).[1] The Lord of Delvin received the abbeys of Inchemor and Fowre (10 May, 1566).[2] James Butler, brother of the Earl of Ormond, was granted the abbey of Duske and the monastery of Fertnegeragh, Co. Kilkenny, with their lands and possessions (15 Jan., 1567).[3] On 10 August following, the Queen, lamenting the death of James, had letters patent passed for these possessions to his son, James Butler.[4]

Others of these notable personages received their grants shortly after Sydney had gone over to the Queen. Viscount Barrymore received a lease of the abbeys of O'Manne and (another, *blank*) in Co. Cork, but with this condition that if these abbeys be situate near any of her Majesty's " strengths " (strongholds), or should be otherwise suitable for her Majesty's service, then the Lord Deputy is instructed to grant him a lease of two of the abbeys of Ballybegg, Buttevante, Castleyehane, or Tymolagye, which he shall select (12 March, 1568).[5] Oliver Grace received a surrender of the abbey of St. John's, in Ormond, Co. Tipperary, and a grant enabling him to make leases of parcels of the premises to such " as shall aid him to inhabit [colonise] the same, lying among disordered persons of the Irish." [6] The Mayor and Commons of Waterford, in consideration of a block house built by them for defence of the haven, and for other good services done by them, were granted the possessions of the nunnery of Killkellinge, wherein they have an estate.[7] The town of Drogheda requested the Queen, November, 1567, among other things that she would grant the abatement or allowance of the rents of the Hospitals of St. Mary de Urso and St. Lawrence, and the houses of the White Friars and Augustine Friars, for the maintenance of a free school.[8] The manor or lordship of Kilheale (Kilteel), Co. Kildare, with the rectory, titles, altarages, etc., were granted to John Alen of St. Wolstan's, finding a competent priest or chaplain to serve

---

[1] *C.P.C.R.I.*, *Eliz.*, i. p. 498.   [2] *Ib.*, p. 500.   [3] *Ib.*, p. 503.
[4] *Ib.*, p. 503.   [5] *Ib.*, p. 513.   [6] *Ib.*, p. 513.
[7] *Ib.*, p. 515.   [8] *C.S.P.I.* *Eliz.*, xxii. p 31.

the cure of the parish of Kilheale. Thus, as rewards for loyalty, as means of supporting English colonies, as means of defence, as support for free schools, and as providing stipends for ministers of the " reform," and in various other ways the religious possessions were a most useful source of supply to the parsimonious Queen.

An interesting case of the loyalty shown by some of the Irish chiefs was that of Lord O'Connor Sligo, of the territory of Carbery, in the province of Connacht. The Lord came to England with Sydney, and presented himself before her Majesty at Hampton Court, 8 November, 1567, and there in the Irish tongue, through her Majesty's interpreter, declared that the principal cause of his coming was to see and speak with her Majesty in person, acknowledging her to be his sovereign prince and ruler, and lamenting the uncivil, rude, and barbarous life which he and his ancestors for a long time had led, unconscious of the divine name and service ; declaring himself innocent of any treason or crime against her Majesty, and asserting that he had for many years resisted the odious traitor and rebel, Shane O'Neill ; and now with great fidelity, prostrate at her Majesty's feet, he implores her to receive his submission, in those terms ; first, he acknowledges her Majesty to be his natural princess and supreme sovereign, and promises obedience and adhesion to her and her successors, and to defend her against all men in the world, as becomes an obedient subject. He submits himself, his lands, and castles to her mercy and prays to be received into her favour, and that hereafter he may be reputed as English ; he prays for a re-grant of his lands and castles to hold of her Majesty by such tenure and service as she may consider necessary ; and that he might be perpetually exempt from the yoke and services imposed by O'Donnell, or any other person, and only serve the Imperial Crown of England. The Queen in her mercy received him into her favour, made him the re-grants at a rent of £100 Irish money or cows to that amount, the Lord binding himself to the performance of the treaty in a sum of £10,000, and swearing on the Evangelists of God faithfully to observe it. 20 January, 1568.[1]

[1] *C.P.C.R.I., Eliz.,* i. pp. 508-9.

In all this humble submission there is not one word either about accepting the Act of Supremacy or the Act of Uniformity of Worship, but simply an act of mere allegiance to the Queen as his temporal sovereign. On account of this voluntary submission O'Connor was allowed by her to preserve the friary at Sligo, in which his ancestors were buried, substituting Secular Canons for Dominicans. This whole episode again shows that in some Irish parts Catholicity was still tolerated, but, doubtless, because Elizabeth and her officials had not yet been able to take those parts into their own hands. The conversion of the Dominican friary into a college of secular canons most probably did not take place as O'Connor Sligo would scarcely create opposition against himself from his people by such a suppression.

Another Connacht chief, the Earl of Clanricard, " of whose fidelity to our Crown," said Elizabeth, " we have always good testimony by the report of all such as have governed there," was anxious to receive some reward for his loyalty and his good civil order. " Requiring to have certain monasteries in the province of Conogh granted unto him, he shall understand that we do mean to have favorable consideration of his requests in that behalf ; so as first we mean to have the said monasteries and the lands thereto belonging surveyed ; whereupon our pleasure is that he shall have an estate to him and his heirs male of such abbeys and the lands thereto belonging as shall be extended to the yearly value of 100 marks sterling. . . . Where the said Erle requireth to have the house of the Friary of Anry [Athenry], in Conogh, reserved for burial of his howse and other the Lords of that province, we are pleased that the said howse shall be preserved to the said uses as the said Erle can devise, and that license of mortmain may be granted for land to be annexed thereunto, for the maintenance thereof, to the value of 100 marks." [1] (20 April, 1568.)

The extensive grants [2] of religious houses, rectories, and

[1] *C.P.C.R.I., Eliz.*, i. pp. 515-16.
[2] Grant to Richard, earl of Clanricarde of the lands of Cowlock (except 30 acres of underwood), Skillenglas, and Ballimone, Co. Dublin, possessions of John Burnell, of Ballgrifen, Co. Dublin, attainted. To hold for ever, by the service of a tenth part of a knight's fee. 25 February, 1569. (*Fiants*, no. 1281.)
Grant, under instructions at Greenwich, 20 April, 1568, to Richard Bowrk

lands made to the Earl would leave one almost to conclude that there was little left for any other loyal lord to obtain. Nevertheless, such grants did not mean that the Earl obtained full possession of them, at least at this time, for that would depend on how far his temporal sway was sufficient to force obedience to the grants.

The fact that Clanricard accepted those religious possessions from the Queen does not mean that he had gone over to the " reform," or that, even, like Bodkin and Burke, he recognised Elizabeth's supremacy. As he was burdened with keeping civil order in the district he probably considered that he was entitled to the possessions, as the houses were suppressed, and that they were better in his hands than

(Burgh), earl of Clanricard, of the site of the priory of Clontoyskerte in Omany in Connacht, with appurtenances and the rectory of the same. The site of the priory of Aghrym in Omany, lands of Aghrym and Kylleglan in Omany, and Ferne prior in Clanrycard, 6s. 8d. chief rent out of Kyllarynyny in Omany, the rectories of Aghrym, Soggan, and Kylcoveryn, and the vicarages of Kylkeryll and Kilclone in Omany. The site of the monastery of S. John the Baptist in Tweme (Tuam), land and tithes in Tweme, 10s. chief rent out of Eagan in the country of M'Coystelaghe, and the vicarages of Kylleare, Began, and Annagh. The site of the house of the nuns of Kylkrenata in Connacht, lands of Kylkrenata Ardover, Urly *alias* Urghly, Leleete lands, Tonmoyll, Irgloune near Tome, Ballane in Clanricarde, Termonkelan in the country of O'Connor Don, Kilghyll in Magherryvagh, Bannabaghe in Omany, Cowllesturny in the country of M'Wyllyam eightery, Oghyllbegge in Shyllanghy, Dromalgagh in Omany; the rectories of Kylkrenata, Khryehe *alias* Khryegh, Taghmaconell, Kyllane, Kylleomer in Omany; Kyltolglagh in Clanrichard, Dromlagh in the country of O'Connor Slygogh, Ardekerane, and Clonmaknoyse in the country of O'Molaghlene. The site of the monastery of friars of Balleclare in Connacht with appurtenances. The site of the monastery of friars of Rosserelle in Moyntermorgho in Connacht, with appurtenances. The site of the monastery of Carmelite friars of Baalyloghryegh (Loughrea) in Connacht, cottages, land, 12d. and 12d. respectively chief rents out of two houses lately occupied by Thomas Colman, and 2s. out of one of James Fonte in the same town. The site of the house of friars of Kylboghte, with appurtenances. The site of the monastery of Anaghdowne in Conncht, land in Anaghdowne, Lysdiche in the country of O'Flaertie, Shankyll and Mukkerys, Owre in O'Flaerte Knockan in the country of O'Flaerty, a ruined chapel in the island of Aryne (Arran) and land there 6s. 8d. chief rent out of Laspydell, the rectories of Ballencourte in Clanricarde, Kylcomen in the country of O'Flaerty, Kargyne in Moyntermorgho, and Lysdiche. To hold the above, together with the religious house of Kylnemanaghe, in tail male, by the service of a tenth part of a knight's fee, at a rent of £68 9s. 6d., being £7 12s. 10d. for Clontoykert, £3 5s. 2d. for Kylnemanagh, £8 10s. for Aghrym, £4 16s. 4d. for Tweme £34 5s. 8d. for Kylkrenata, 25s. 4d. for Balleclare, 15s. 2d. for Rosserelle and Balleloghreigh, 7s. 9d. for Kilboght, and £6 11s. 3d. for Anaghdowne. 18 July, 1570. (*Fiants*, no. 1581.)

in the hands of other magnates. At the same time it must be admitted that he was as capable of playing the game as Desmond, O'Neill, and the rest, when the occasion required it.

Elizabeth Ungrateful and Parsimonious towards Sydney.

When Sydney started for England he was tired of his term of office in Ireland, although he had already received some measure of thanks from the Queen for his campaign against Shane. As a show of his success he brought with him O'Connor Sligo, Ely O'Carroll, the Baron of Dungannon, the Baron of Lixnaw's eldest son (Patrick Fitzmaurice), Brefny O'Reilly's eldest son, and Ross Mageoghegan's eldest son. " All these and many others went with me to surrender to her Highness all their lands, and to receive the same again of her, yielding far greater rent and service." Cecil, however, whilst advising Sydney to have patience in the Queen's service,[1] hoped to see his " recovery of the Crown in Ireland in deed that is only now had in title." Instead of being hailed as a victor and thanked for his achievements, he received little but reproaches from Elizabeth. " When I came to Court," he says, " it was told me it was no war that I had made, nor worth to be called a war, for that Shane O'Neill was but a beggar, an outlaw, and one of no force, but that the Scots stumbled on him by chance."

But Sydney had other troubles. He was Leicester's brother-in-law, and the Leicester party had a powerful opponent in Ormond. Sydney was inclined to lean to the Desmond side in the latter's controversy with Ormond much to the chagrin of Elizabeth. The Queen accused Sydney of culpable slackness in arresting Desmond, and of proposing to confer the Presidency of Munster on Sir Warham St. Leger, an enemy of Ormond. Desmond was in fact a prisoner at this time, and, after he had been two months under restraint, complained bitterly that he expected better usage from Sydney,

---

[1] Sydney was angry with Elizabeth on account of the report that she intended to deprive him of the Presidency of Wales, and Elizabeth was no less sharp in her reply to him that the office and the Deputyship were always held at the royal pleasure. The fact is that it went to the Queen's frugal heart to see even her ablest servant holding two great places at once.

that he was a prisoner [1] for no reason, and that it would be grossly unjust to decide his cause in his absence. His enemy, he added, had already every advantage of favour and education. For some time the Queen insisted that Desmond should be arraigned, and, if possible, condemned in Ireland before being sent over, but Sydney persuaded her to be satisfied with having him indicted only. FitzWilliams, who was a strong partisan of Ormond, wrote at the same time to complain that Sir John of Desmond would not come near the Judges of Assize, and that the Geraldines continued to spoil the Butlers with impunity. Sir John's desire of conferring with his brother, the Earl, in Dublin, was the occasion of his undoing when the Government had almost given up hope of catching him. The two brothers, not having a groat, were, at the Queen's expense, sent over to London where they arrived, 24 December. But Elizabeth commanded that Munster should supply them with money.[2] "And truly," said Sydney, some years later, "this hard dealing with Sir John of Desmond was the origin of James Fitzmaurice's rebellion, and consequently of all the evil and mischief of Munster."

Shane being out of the way, it was possible for Sydney to make some reduction in the military force, but not to do so without money. The Queen owed £41,000 for the war against Shane; £10,000 was grudgingly sent, and after some time £20,000 more was got together, some of it by loan, which the Queen repented of, but fortunately the money

---

[1] The following is a list of the "Irish Lords in Prison" at this time : "McDonnell the gallowglass and his brother Brian, and Donnell, Henry McShane's sons. Doltóye Donallough and his brother Malaghlin Boy (*Buidhe-yellow*), Shane Boy Donlough. Rore Oge McDonnell gallowglass's sons, Kilgrane McColl's gallowglass with his many horsemen and gallowglass with the number of 300 drowned and slain. The Earl of Desmond, Viscount Baltinglass, Lord Donboyne [*d*. in prison, 1567], Lord Power, Lord Burke, Earl Clanricarde's son, Maurice FitzThomas, Knight, Oliver Plunket, knight, Nicholas O'Wogan, Oliver O'Wogan, Davy O'Wogan, James Eustas [Eustace], Maurice Fitzgerrott, Garret FitzPhilip, Christopher St. Michael, Baron of Rheban, Piers Butler, brother to the Lord Doneboyne, The Lady Doneboyne, Piers Butler's wife, Richard Butler, base son to the Baron Doneboyne, Henry Neil son and pledge to the traitor Shane, Kedaly O'Malaghlyn, pledge for the traitor, with divers others to the number of xx." (*S.P.I., Eliz.,* xx. 100, P.R.O., London.)

[2] *S.P.I., Eliz.,* xxii. 25, 39, 45, 58.

had been despatched. As usual Elizabeth expected great things from her Deputy but was not prepared to pay the bill.

New Scheme for Government of Ireland ; Provincial Presidencies.

When Sydney had been some months in England, Cecil drew up an elaborate scheme for the future government of Ireland, probably the result of their joint opinion.[1] It was proposed that a Parliament should be held without delay, which should declare the Crown entitled to Ulster and provide for its divisions into shires. A new local tyranny such as Shane's should be made impossible. Civilised men should be encouraged to settle in the North, especially those of Irish birth, " for it is supposed that they may better maintain their habitation with less charge than such Englishmen as are mere strangers to the land." A residence for the Deputy should be provided at Armagh. Levies that O'Neill formerly commanded might be made available for the Queen. Forts were to be built near Newry, Lough Neagh, and near the efflux of the Bann, and the coast of Antrim was to be guarded against the Scots by forts at Portrush and near Larne. To protect Belfast, a strong post should be placed at Bangor, and another on the eastern shore of Lough Neagh. Bridges were to be thrown over the Blackwater and over the Bann at Coleraine, over the Erne at Ballyshannon, and over the Foyle at Lifford.

Munster was to have a President and Council resident at Dungarvan, the parsonage of which, by a singular provision, was to be attached to the Presidency. A similar Government for Connacht was to be placed at Athlone. Tirconnell was to be treated as in some degree separate both from Connacht and Ulster.

Although Shane was gone, and Sydney's strength remembered, yet the conditions in the North were little altered. Tirlogh Luineach sent a Latin letter, 13 December, 1567,[2] to Sydney requesting the island of Lough Neagh, and the priory

---

[1] *S.P.I., Eliz.*, xxii. 48.   Bagwell, ii. 126.
[2] *C.S.P.I., Eliz.*, xxii. 44.

of the Cathedral church of Down for his priest, chaplain, and secretary, Edmund O'Coine [O'Quinn], which formerly he obtained from the Roman Pontiff in the time of Queen Mary and whose fruits he received from the farmer now for four years past. In this request there was question only of the temporalities : Tirlogh never ceased to be a Catholic.

Tirlogh was showing signs of imitating Shane, and of not acting quite up to expectations. There were ominous signs of an alliance between him and O'Donnell who divided the customs of Lough Foyle and the rent of Inishowen between them. Tirlogh still continued his relations with the Scots, and, like Shane, proposed various marriages for himself. James MacDonnell's widow or her daughter,[1] and Sir Nicholas Bagenal's sister-in-law, were among the ladies he fancied. He was on the best terms with Sorley Boy, and said he would have no mercenaries if only Sir Brian MacPhelim and Art MacBaron would obey him. It was now proposed to send over to Ireland the young Baron of Dungannon, Hugh O'Neill,[2] whose English education might be supposed to have given him a love of order. He had, however, studied the strength and the weakness of England at headquarters, and he was consequently destined to be more formidable than any of his predecessors had been.[3]

As soon as Desmond and his brother were gone, fresh troubles sprang up in Munster. Lady Desmond reported that the country was impoverished by rapine and by the irregular exactions of the Earl's people, that it was impossible to raise even the smallest sum for her husband's necessities. The Earl's cousin, James Fitzmaurice, claimed to have been appointed leader of his people by Desmond, and was thought by the Countess and the Commissioners the fittest person. But the Lords Justices ordered the lady to govern with the Catholic Bishop of Limerick's help.[4] Fitzmaurice was taken prisoner, but, on the arrival of a commission from the Earl and Sir John, he was released. He kept very quiet for some time, waiting until he saw how his cousin's affairs sped in London.

Stucley, although Seneschal of Wexford, could not leave

[1] *C.S.P.I., Eliz.*, xxii. 36, i.-v. [2] *Ib.*, 37.
[3] Bagwell, ii. 127-9. [4] *S.P.I., Eliz.*, 16, i.-v.

16

off his old hankering after the ways of the pirate, and was another source of trouble to Elizabeth. In her letter, 6 July,[1] to Sydney, she complains of Stucley's behaviour as follows :—

Here it hath been lately exhibited unto us a complaint by certain subjects of our brother the King of Spain, inhabitants of the Low Countries against Edward Cook of Southampton a pirate, who they allege invaded them by sea and took their goods being hides and skins, brought from Indies, and a great sum of money, and carrying the same into Ireland, hath made sale to Stucley thereof, which they require to be redressed, and so if it be true that Stucley had bought any part thereof the charge be to give straight order that the same goods be forthcoming to be answered where Justice shall limit. And surely we marvel that Stucley would have such boldness, knowing what he hath escaped, as to deal with pirates and their prises.

Dean of Armagh Desires to Serve Elizabeth in the Archbishopric.

Terence Daniel, Dean of Armagh, friend and adviser of Shane O'Neill, having lost his protector and patron, and having been informed that Elizabeth was anxious to have him appointed to the Archbishopric, sent a letter to Cecil, 5 October,[2] thanking him profusely for his good offices :—

My humble duty premised unto your honour. Since it hath pleased Almighty God of His infinite goodness to appoint your honour in King Edward's reign to show me your good favour and great friendship, which your honour hath always since continued without any my desert, for which I yield unto your honour most humble thanks, not able to requite the same by any means but my poor heart, good will, continual prayer, and daily travail in her Majesty's service, as I have been commanded by your honour, whereof I will never cease whilst I have life and ability of person. For the continuance of my service to her Majesty I refer the declaration thereof unto my Lord Deputy's report, and other the Queen's Majesty governors of this realm for the time being, since the death of King Henry the Eight of famous memory. And for recompense of that her Grace's service and other considerations it hath pleased her Majesty I should be admitted to the Archbishopric of Armagh. And albeit the same is

---

[1] *S.P.I., Eliz.*, xxi. 49, P.R.O., London.
[2] *Ib.*, xxii. Shirley, 310-12.

of great report yet the revenue small, by this her Majesty's most gracious remembrance and other her Majesty's great benefits received, I find myself most happy to be a subject and servitor to so noble a princess, and shall according my duty, faithfully serve her Grace during life, wishing myself, once again young years to serve her Majesty per multos annos.

I have sent by my good Lord, my Lord Deputy, my resolution in the acceptation of the same dignity, whom I have found always my very good Lord, and the rather by your honour's good commendation, for which I humbly beseech your honour to give unto his Lord hearty thanks.

Daniel had accompanied Sydney during the Lord Deputy's late progress in Ulster and Connacht when Shane O'Neill was nowhere to be found. His presence in the Deputy's train was evidently meant to bring good-will to Sydney from the chiefs of the districts through which they might pass.

He mentions the countries of O'Hanlon, Magennis, Macartan, Lecale, Dufferin, the Ardes, Claneboy, Killultagh, and the Route. At Coleraine, he says, Tirlogh Luineach, a " savage and timorous man " submitted, and that all Connacht has been tamed by the building of the bridge of Athlone. He then concludes :—

We take final order and security for their [the Irish Captains] obedience to her Majesty, and restored the bishops and clergy of all that province to their ancient liberty from the tyranny and extortions of the same gent [O'Neill] in such good order and commendable sort as the like was not observed these two hundred years past.

From Rathwyer, this 5th October, 1567,
Your Honour's daily orator,
TERENCE DANYELL, *Dean Armachan.*

The intended promotion of the Dean had been laid aside nearly three months before he wrote this letter, probably on the opposition of Sydney himself, and Lancaster was appointed. It is not at all improbable that Sydney doubted the Dean's profession of loyalty.

Meanwhile Daniel continued his customary correspondence with members of the Government of Ireland. In a letter,

16 *

27 November,[1] to Elizabeth's ecclesiastical commissioners, he complained of Tirlogh Luineach's encroachment on the liberties of the Church of Armagh: " I have promised to proceed against him according to the order of the law of the church if he will not give over his extortion. . . . At length he did sign me liberty for the church for this 12 months to come, and promised to make me satisfaction of all the damages that he did to the church under his own rule, since he took upon him the government of the country."

This letter is an extraordinary commentary on the whole confused state of the North, at a time when the Protestant Loftus could make practically nothing out of Armagh, spiritually or temporarily, and the Government were in difficulties as to whom they might appoint who would be likely to accomplish something. That Daniel was professing allegiance to Elizabeth as Shane had done, there is no doubt. Evidently, he was prepared to go farther and accept the archbishopric at the Queen's hands, but that he intended to adopt uniformity of service in the use of the Book of Common Prayer can scarcely be maintained. Were he ever so willing, he could not hope to carry it out against the will of Tirlogh Luineach.

In another letter, 10 December,[2] to the Lords Justices, the Dean tells of the coming of the Scots to Ireland before the capture of Shane O'Neill. He states: " The Chantor [Sir Pat Dorelle] of Armagh is coming from Scotland and I challenged him for his going thither at the request of Shane O'Neill. He sware to me that it was for very fear of the said Shane that he went there, and the said Shane sware that he would have hanged him if he had not gone there. And at his being in Scotland he did nothing but that the said Shane commanded him to do. And reported to the Earl of Argyle upon whom he waited that he would do nothing contrary to his duty towards his prince [Elizabeth]. . . . I was earnestly in hand with him to know by whose means the Scots came into Ireland," namely whether they came to help Shane or the O'Donnells. The Chantor related that they were coming to O'Donnell and that he himself came in their company. Coming through Cantyre, Sorley Boy would have them come with himself. They were driven by tempest and weather to the island of Rathlin and thought to land in O'Donnell's country. "And after that Sorley followed them to the said island and agreed with them for certain weeks, and so they landed together at the Glynns, at a place called the Market town, and they all be not fully 400."

The Dean here wishes to show his loyalty to Elizabeth and how he had stood against Shane, and that he had threatened the Chantor for, as he thought, going to Scotland to procure a band of Scots for Shane. The Scots, as a matter of fact, came to the support of the MacDonnells, through the efforts of Sorley Boy, and were present at and took a part in the murder of Shane.

LOFTUS RECOMMENDS A CALVINIST FOR ARMAGH.

The struggle for the Archbishopric of Armagh was not yet finished. Elizabeth had favoured Terence Daniel, Sydney recommended Lancaster, Brady praised Garvey as the fittest man, and now Loftus suggests one Mr. Cartwright, a bachelor of divinity, and fellow of Trinity College in Cambridge. Loftus mentions, in a letter to Cecil, 5 December,[1] that some who are labouring for it are unworthy, and have good livings and cures already. He probably refers to Garvey and Daniel. It does not appear, however, why he differed from Sydney's choice, Lancaster, or whether he included him among the number of unworthy seekers after the post. Though he admits "the profits of that bishopric be very small, yet the place and authority is very great." And, ignoring his own reason for seeking to be translated from it —that he could do no good in it, as it lay among the Irish —he believes that "as a godly, learned man in that room might profit and do much good, so an ungodly and ignorant man might hinder and do much harm." Cartwright, a man of "excellent learning and godly life," would be meet for that place and dignity. He "used himself so godly (during his abode with me in Ireland) both in life and doctrine that his absence from hence is no small grief and sorrow to all

[1] *S.P.I.*, *Eliz.*, xxii. 35. Shirley, 321-3.

the godly and faithful here." Cartwright was probably one
of the preachers who had been brought over from England
to help in the " reform." He belonged to the same Calvinistic
school [1] of which Loftus was so great a supporter : hence
Loftus's anxiety to see him promoted and be a helper to him
in his Puritanism.

CREAGH IN THE TOWER OF LONDON : EXAMINATION AND ANSWERS.

Setting out from Rome, 11 August, 1560, Fr. Wolf reached
Cork, 21 January, 1561, after a long and dangerous journey.
At once he entered on his work with such energy and success
that for the next dozen years his word was law in Rome
and his recommendation decisive in the appointment of
bishops. His influence stemmed the tide of prevarication
to a considerable extent in the country. Perhaps it is not
too much to say that to him, more than to any other man
of that age, belongs the credit of bringing back to vigorous
life the dead bones with which the Catholic Church in Ireland
had been strewn in the course of the previous twenty disastrous years. The comparative freedom with which he
was able to move all over the country for a few years was
not to last. His activities attracted the attention and pro-
voked the hostility of the English authorities. Before the
end of the year 1567 he found himself interned in the dreary
vaults of one of Dublin's prisons, where he was to spend the
next five years of his life. At the same time his friend,
Archbishop Creagh, was transferred to the Tower of London,
where he was to die a broken man some nineteen years later.

Creagh, having been imprisoned for some time in Dublin
Castle, " in a subterranean and most obscure cell in which
neither light nor sun ever entered," [2] was indicted. " After

---

[1] Thomas Cartwright, B.D., " a man of noted learning," says Watson
(*Life of Hooker*), was born about 1535, and educated at St. John's College,
Cambridge, afterwards Fellow of Trinity College, and Margaret Professor
of Divinity. In 1570 he was expelled the University for nonconformity, and
became minister to the English at Antwerp. He was afterwards Master of
the Earl of Leicester's Hospital, at Warwick, " where he lived quietly and
grew rich." He died in 1602.

[2] Hogan, *Iber. Ignat.*, p. 17.

suffering much in prison about that time, he was brought
to his trial in King's Bench before Sir John Plunket, then
chief justice of that court, and being there arraigned of high
treason, and enforced to abide a jury of gentlemen of the
Pale, he was found guiltless : but they, for acquitting of
him, were all committed to the said castle, and put to great
fines. When they could get no way by law to make him
away, or that his constancy [in religion] could not be infringed,
he was sent over to the Tower of London." [1] Not immediately,
however, was he sent to London, for after six months in Dublin
Castle, he again escaped. What followed is told in a letter
from Meyler Hussey to the Privy Council, about December,
1567.[2]

He narrates that Sydney issued a proclamation for Creagh's
arrest, and a reward of £40 to his apprehender. Thereupon
the Earl of Kildare " made earnest pursuit after the said
Crevagh by sundry ways with number of people," committing
the charge of these spies to Hussey. " And having sought
all the means possible to find the said Crevagh, with great
travail and hazard of life," Hussey took an oath not to
deliver him up until Sydney and Kildare promised upon
their honour to intercede with the Queen to spare his life.
Hussey also refused to accept the reward offered, in consequence of which and of his true and faithful service to the
Queen, he now asked that Creagh's life be pardoned. " Otherwise," he says, " he [Hussey] shall never have credit in his
said country, nor be well thought of, neither hereafter be
able to serve her Majesty according to his bounden duty
in the like attempt."

Creagh, according to Sydney's advice, was sent to the
Tower of London where, on 22 December, and apparently
before Cecil, his examination took place. A Minute in the
State Papers [3] sets out the questions put to Creagh :—

To examine the bishop that came from Rome now prisoner
in the Tower what confederacy he knew between the Earl of
Desmond and O'Neill or any others being rebels.

In primis. What time he came first to accompany Shane

---

[1] *Theatre of the Cath. and Prot. Religion*, l. xi., c. iii., pp. 576-7 (1620).
[2] *S.P.I., Eliz.*, xxii. 53. Shirley, 324-6.
[3] *S.P.I., Eliz.*, xxii. 8, P.R.O., London.

O'Neill; what letters and messages he brought from Rome and other places. What was the intent and meaning of the said letters and messages.

Item. How often did he speak with Shane O'Neill and of what matters. And whether did he preach in presence of Shane O'Neill and what were the contents of his sermons.

Item. Whether did he extol the authority of the Pope in his presence, and dissuade the hearers from obedience to the Queen's Majesty.

Item. What was the intent of Shane O'Neill to have done if he had not been killed and overcome.

Item. What was the confederacy by messages or letters betwixt Shane O'Neill and the Earl of Desmond or his brother Sir John.

Item. What did he tell Oliver Sutton thereof when he sent him with a letter to the Lord Deputy.

Item. What noblemen or gentlemen in Ireland did he know to have had confederacy or intelligence with Shane O'Neill.

Another Minute in Cecil's handwriting [1] gives Creagh's answers :—

A friar, the Bishop of Down,[2] came to Creagh about August, 1566 ; he, Creagh, went to Shane O'Neill, being in an island called Inish Darell [3] in company with the Bishop of Down, and dined with Shane upon a Wednesday, with whom was Turlough Lennough.[4] He asked of Shane whether he had received the copy of a letter from the Pope and required his favour, which Shane offered to him.

The said Shane was then ready to go with power against Pers,[5] and willed this examinate [Creagh] to subscribe a letter by which the friars of Carrickfergus were willed to depart from Knockfergus, or else they should be spoiled.

He saith that Shane told him that if he should go with power against Knockfergus, then if they would not depart they should repent, and after this Shane made the journey.

---

[1] *S.P.I., Eliz.*, xxii. 50. Shirley, 326-8.

[2] Meiler Magrath.

[3] Probably an island in a fresh-water lake near Clon Darell, Co. Armagh.

[4] Tirlogh Luineach, son of Niall Conallagh, after the death of Shane, styled O'Neill.

[5] Pers, or Captain William Pierce of Carrickfergus, a celebrated " Irish Captain " of the period, from whom Sir John Piers of Tristernagh Abbey, Co. Westmeath, is the ninth in descent. He it was who cut off Shane's head, after his betrayal and murder at Cushendun, and claimed the reward of 1000 marks offered by proclamation to him who should bring up his head.

He saith that the next Sunday following, Shane O'Neill came to Armagh where this examinate preached afore Shane and Turlogh Lennogh and Hugh O'Donnell.

At another time, when Shane had made a journey into O'Donnell's [country ?] and had hanged a priest, this examinate went to Dondavill [1] to Shane, who required absolution of him : but this examinate could not absolve him, for that it belonged to the authority of the Pope.

At another time Shane came to Armagh to bury his brother, where this examinate was ; Shane O'Neill told him that he should be well used, and have his church as honourably as ever any archbishop had. This examinate saith that an Irishman whom he had seen with Shane in household told him that he was sent into Munster because the Lord Deputy was at Limerick, he saith that he heard Shane report that he trusted to have favour of John of Desmond.

It is to be noted that Creagh did not answer the questions as to what he said in his sermons, whether he extolled the authority of the Pope and preached against the authority of Elizabeth, and what letters he brought from Rome. He had, however, on another occasion, answered those questions to the effect that he would accept his bishopric from none other than the Pope, and that he was bound in obedience to do so, but that he was always willing to show and preach loyalty to the Queen as the temporal ruler of Ireland. As Shane was the prince of the territory, yielding submission to Elizabeth, Creagh considered himself free to minister to his Catholic people. There was no proof that Creagh aided him to rebel ; on the contrary, he endeavoured to induce him to be loyal to the Queen.

After eight years' imprisonment, Creagh directed a memorial to Elizabeth [2] as follows :—

First, he is content if her Majesty's pleasure so be to depart her highness's realms and dominions, and not to return again without her gracious leave and license during her reign.

Not to deal or intermeddle with any matter prejudicial to her Majesty's estate, and the quietness thereof either by practise at home or by dealing with any foreign prince abroad, and that neither by word, writing or otherwise he will attempt to procure

[1] I.e. Dunavally.   [2] *S.P.I.*, xl. 87, P.R.O., London.

the disturbance of the same, but by all means he can seek to persuade the obedience of the realm of Ireland to the Crown of England.

That during his life he will seek to live quietly and peaceably, and if any matter be brought unto him tending to the disturbance of her Majesty's quiet government not to enter into it but rather contrariwise forthwith give her Majesty notice thereof and faithfully discover the same.

Humbly prostrate beseeching her Majesty upon his oath taken, or such sureties put in as his poor estate is able to get for the performance of the premises, to cast her eyes of pity upon him being by divers infirmities grievously diseased, by his eight years' imprisonment, and not likely to live unless it please her Majesty to grant him liberty by means whereof he may be able to travel for his health.

Although it could not be shown that Creagh had been guilty of any treasonable act, yet he was still confined to the Tower of London where he died about 1586, after practically nineteen years' imprisonment.

ELIZABETH'S TEMPORISING WITH THE CATHOLIC RELIGION.

One of the most curious examples of Elizabeth's indecision and temporising is in reference to the friary of Sligo. She told the Lords Justices, 25 January, 1568,[1] that it was " to be preserved so as the friars there being converted to secular priests the same there may continue as well for the sepulture of Donald O'Connor's posterity as well for the maintenance of prayer and (service of God) learning." [2] Sir Donald O'Connor had already surrendered his possessions and received from the Queen patent of his inheritance under the seal of England. But a few months later (April), she bestowed on Clanricard practically all the friaries within his rule. On 30 August she rewarded the dutiful Gerald, Earl of Kildare, by a grant under privy signet, of the manor of Geshell, King's County, with the advowson of the church there of the B.V.M., and the whole barony of Geshell con-

---

[1] *S.P.I., Eliz.*, xxiii. 17, P.R.O., London.
[2] " Learning " was crossed out by Cecil who substituted the words, " service of God."

taining thirty-nine carucates of land, also lands in Westmeath, Meath, Co. Carlow, City of Dublin and County, Queen's County, Kildare, and Co. Wexford, and the advowson of the rectory and vicarage of Norraghe, Co. Kildare. To hold for ever, by the service of two knights' fees, rendering yearly to the Bishop of Meath four cows for Bishopscourt.[1]

So far, compulsion in religious matters had not been exercised on the Catholic bishops of Munster, and although there had been a question of depriving Hugh Lacy of Limerick, yet he still continued undisturbed in his See. In January, 1568, Munster was in such disorder, according to the report of the Countess Desmond,[2] that few can trust a father, son, or a brother. None of the Chiefs would come to the commissioners at Cork unless the Countess came.[3] In this state of affairs, the commissioners appealed to the Catholic Bishop of Limerick to assist them in securing the peace of the province. Along with the Countess, the Bishop had been appointed a commissioner to take over the rule of the Desmond country, and was ordered to meet the other commissioners at Youghal. He sent a reply, 23 January, from Kilmallock [4] that he was not able to meet the commissioners at Youghal, " not only for the miserable state of those parts but also for lack of money," and he cannot travel so far. He prays God to witness that he has " more desire to be in their company for accomplishing the expectation therein than you have of my being there." It was a polite refusal, but the commissioners were not to be put off, and they desired proof of his loyalty. Indeed they stated that they thought he was not honest in the excuse he made.

" We require you," they wrote from Cork,[5] " repair unto us with the speed may be upon sight hereof. And if it may be said the Countess [Desmond] will likewise so do, to the intent with God's grace our travail shall not be in vain. Let not money tarry your hither coming, for we will bear your charges to and fro, and despatch you out of hand. We pray you let us understand your resolute determination herein with the speed may be."

[1] *Fiants*, no. 1240. [2] *S.P.I., Eliz.*, xxiii. 16, ii.
[3] *Ib.*, 16, i. [4] *Ib.*, xxiii. 16, iii, P.R.O., London.
[5] *Ib.*, xxiii. 32, vi., P.R.O., London.

Lacy obeyed this threatening summons, as his position would have become unsafe if he continued to plead trivial excuses. His presence was necessary on account of his authority and of his knowledge of the affairs and conditions of the Desmond territory. The point to be noted is that, eight years after the Act of Supremacy had been promulgated in Dublin, the Government officials were pleading to a Catholic bishop in Munster to come and help them in settling the affairs of the province.

The commissioners in Munster, of whom Brady was one, were able to inform the Lords Justices (Limerick, 1 February) [1] that the Bishop of Limerick and the Countess of Desmond came to Kilmallock 21 January, and stayed at Lord Roche's house, Lord Barrymore and Lord Power being in their company. But it does not appear that they went to Cork. [2] The Countess and the Bishop were confirmed in their rule over the Desmond territory. The meeting of Bishops Lacy and Brady must have been an interesting affair. In April, however, the Countess asked that James Fitzmaurice should govern in the absence of the Earl, as the latter and Sir John had given under their seal the rule to Fitzmaurice.

In November, amongst a dozen letters written from the Tower about the rule of his territory, the Earl wrote to the Bishop of Limerick [3] desiring him to " be counsellor not only to his lady but also to James Fitzmaurice, the captain of the country, touching the peace kept in the country, and in executing justice to the poor and in collecting as much money as they can because they may send the same to me to pay my debts and charges which is unknown to any but to myself."   He then complains of the Chancellor of Limerick, Sir Donoghow Cashie, who " received from Lord Roche and others certain sums of money for me and my brother ; he dealt so unkindly towards me that he would not bestow one penny thereof on me."   He threatens that if he were discharged what he would not do to the Rev. Chancellor.

---

[1] *S.P.I., Eliz.*, xxiii. 32, vi., P.R.O., London.
[2] *The Calendar (loc. cit.)* says that they went to Cork 21 January. It was to Kilmallock they went, whence Lacy wrote 23 January, that he was unable to go to Cork.
[3] *S.P.I., Eliz.*, xxvi. 30, 40, P.R.O., London.

Desmond then appealed to the good nature of Cecil, 8 February,[1] to obtain for him furniture for his chamber and table, the charges whereof he will repay to Her Majesty at a convenient time.

The business of the commission having been terminated, the Lords Justices, 7 February,[2] recalled Bishop Brady of Meath and continued Justices Plunket and Fitzsimon in the commission. They desired authority from the Queen to be allowed to the Countess Desmond and Bishop Lacy to continue in their rule of the Desmond country. In letters, 6 February,[3] to the Countess and the Bishop they thank the former for her foresight and good service and the latter for his advice and furtherance of the Countess in the apprehension of James Fitzmaurice and Thomas Roe. Her Majesty will be informed of their good services. As to the Earl, now being in the Tower, he submitted to the Queen, 16 March,[4] and expressed his willingness that Her Majesty should take from him some portion of his land and liberties for the more quiet government of the realm. Later (14 July), the Earl and Sir John of Desmond entered into recognisances in £20,000 to perform the articles of submission.[5]

JAMES FITZMAURICE, CAPTAIN OF HIS COUNTRY.

Meanwhile, James Fitzmaurice, who had been appointed by the Earl of Desmond captain, during his confinement in the Tower of London, was not to be cheated out of his position, and was liberated from custody unknown to the commissioners. Indeed, the Countess and the Bishop of Limerick were quite willing to relinquish their task, and besought the Lords Justices to approve of Fitzmaurice's rule.[6]

The country people would not permit him to appear before the commissioners, saying that the Earl and Sir John were pledges enough for his good conduct. Fitzmaurice was not long in making his authority felt and in exacting tribute from neighbouring clans. On 6 July, Thomas Lord Fitzmaurice of Kerry complained to the Lords Justices [7]

---

[1] *S.P.I.*, *Eliz.*, xxiii. 31.
[2] *Ib.*, 32, vii.
[3] *Ib.*, 32, viii., ix.
[4] *Ib.*, xxiii. 71.
[5] *Ib.*, xxv. 35.
[6] *Ib.*, xxiii. 74.
[7] *Ib.*, xxv. 45, ix.

that James, with all the power of the Geraldines, had entered his country on the preceding Thursday, took all the cattle, burned the houses, and was still there pulling up all the green corn and killing his men. In this campaign James had evidently some approval from Bishop Lacy, for the latter drew up a report which Lord Thomas called " a false book." Lord Thomas asked that an English captain might be sent to Limerick with " 40 pikes and 60 harquebuses," and a letter to the Earl of Thomond to aid him. A week afterwards [1] the Lords Justices commanded James to refrain from encamping in Thomas's country and to make restitution for the spoils. James's answer was his assembling of all the lords and captains, the wasting of Thomas's country for a week, and his encamping right against Thomas's Manor house. In the conflict that followed, Thomas relates (1 August) that at least 300 of James's men were killed.

Matters went from bad to worse during the following few months, embittered doubtless by the treatment of the Earl and Sir John in the Tower, and by the Queen's order that their revenues should be sequestered for their charges and sustenance during their imprisonment.[2] Such was Elizabeth's hospitality to her unconvicted prisoners that the Earl complained of the cold of the Tower and desired " some honest house of the Tower, where he may have convenient lodging under sure keeping." [3]

The situation in the Desmond country reached a climax in November when Jacques Wingfield, Master of the Ordnance, reported to Cecil [4] that the Queen's lands in Cork and Limerick were utterly waste. Extortions were made by James Fitzmaurice who had entered Kerry. " There is neither a quiet Geraldine nor a contented Butler."

Returning to the early part of this year, one notices the anxiety of the Government to implicate the Earl of Desmond in the rebellion of Shane O'Neill by securing some tangible proof. When Shane O'Neill said in his letter to the Cardinal of Lorraine that he was seeking French help on behalf of the Irish princes with whom he was in council, he was somewhat exaggerating his position. The opposition aroused against

[1] S.P.I., Eliz., xxv. 70, iv.   [2] Ib., xxvi. 6.
[3] Ib., 11.   [4] Ib., 22.

him by the Ulster chiefs is sufficient answer to his claim. But he was certainly in communication with Desmond, although the Earl does not appear to have done much except to carry on his own campaign against his hereditary enemy, Ormond. The Government was aware of the correspondence between Shane, the Earl of Desmond, and Sir John of Desmond, and ordered an examination of Jacques Wingfield [1] (February). This concerned the confession of " a little friar " (Friar Minor, i.e. Franciscan) " who was found begging in the camp after that Shane was slain " as to " whether he did carry letters to the Earl of Desmond," and as to " the answers to the letters to the traitor Shane." Sydney and Patrick Sherlock were to be examined together as to this conspiracy against the Lord Deputy. There is nothing in the *State Papers* to show the result of these examinations. Evidently they came to nothing, for if Elizabeth could have satisfactorily proved that Desmond was in league with Shane it would have gone ill with him, and probably would have cost him his head. As has been already pointed out, there was no cohesion between the ruling chiefs, their interests being not the general good of the country but their own local supremacy, although towards the end Shane seems to have had some idea of inducing the South to make a simultaneous move with him for getting rid of Elizabethan rule.

LOFTUS ACCUSED OF CALVINISTIC PRACTICES.

One of the most lengthy and significant letters of this period was that written by Loftus to Cecil,[2] 25 January, 1568, in defence of his religious practices. He had been reported by some of his co-religionists to Cecil who acquainted him of the fact. The letter which is an explanation of his conduct, speaks for itself :—

It may please your honour, albeit I was in mind fully resolved to have continued my suit to your honour for the placing of some godly learned man in the Archbishopric of Armagh (a thing very needful and of great weight) yet now understanding by Sir William FitzWilliams that some man (enemy to God and His truth, and not

---

[1] *S.P.I.*, *Eliz.*, xxiii. 60, P.R.O., London.
[2] *Ib.*, 18, P.R.O., London.

my friend as it should appear) hath informed your honour that
I intend innovations concerning the administration of the
Communion, I am enforced (and that to my great grief) to leave
off that my suit, and first to purge myself of their untrue reports.
I have greatly to praise God, and render unto you most humble
thanks, in that it pleased you to let me have intelligence hereof,
which argueth the friendly care your honour hath of me, and that
those misreports have not estranged your good will for me so far,
but that place is left for my purgation.   Which emboldeneth me
to desire your honour to suspend your judgment, and to continue
that good opinion of my doings, which heretofore you have had
until my cause be perfectly known.   Your honour, I' trust, well
knoweth what a number of enemies I have in this land, who
openly have endeavoured themselves, and gone about to have
discredited and undone me (if God and Right had not sustained
my cause), and therefore no wonder is it, though now secretly
they work against me this mischief.   The ground of whose malice
did arise (I know) for that it pleased God, to make me (though
unworthy) an instrument for the banishing hence of Popery and
setting forth of the Queen's Majesty's most gracious proceedings
in this miserable realm, overwhelmed with idolatry.

Where at my first being Primate there was not so much as
any show of a Reformed Church (the happy success hereof envied
of some men, being so solid [sealed, bound] up in ignorant blindness and not able to abide the light and knowledge of God's Holy
Word and of due Reformation) hath caused them (according the
custom of that brood) to burst out into these open, and manifest,
slanders of the same and the ministers thereof.   For, that neither
I have made innovation nor intended any (as they untruly have
bruited), the daily services used in both my Cathedral Churches
within the city of Dublin and elsewhere in my diocese will report
where no other form of prayer or administration of Sacraments
is used than such as is allowed and appointed by the Statutes
and injunctions usually throughout all England, nor have I in
my sermons either to the clergy or people ever persuaded any
innovation or seemed to mistake of (but wished reverently to
be embraced) that order set forth already by the law.

So that upon what ground or pretence this surmise of innovation should grow I cannot well conjecture except it were upon
occasion of a Communion ministered in St. Patrick's Church about
Easter last (since which time I am sure I ministered no Communion)
then I preached and there were present, my Lady Sydney, Mr.
Agard and others, to the number of four hundred (as I remember)
by reason of which great number of communicants I caused the

Communion Table to be placed in the body of the Church, under the pulpit (as it is ordered and allowed by the Book of Common Prayer), and saving that we had not the curious singing, which at other times is used, we observed in all respects the order therein set forth.

I hope your honour hath other judgment of me, than that I should make innovations or delight in singularity which hitherto hath been so far from me, that I have vehemently detested, and fled all schism and discord in the Church, and endeavoured to my power (as is the duty of my profession and calling) the good quiet order of the same.

If your honour (whom I have always held as only patron of my diligent endeavours to further God's work in cleansing His Church from the filth of idolatry and vain worshipping of God) shall seem to dislike thereof, upon an uncertain and untrue report, what discouragement I may have thereby and what boldening the enemies and papists, I trust you will consider and as heretofore your honour hath been my only stay and credit, and of whose good will and honourable favour I have (to my great comfort many ways tasted), so I doubt not, without just cause, you will not estrange the same, the continuation whereof, I most humbly crave at your hands. I might have procured the favourable letters of the Lords Justices to witness mine innocence in this behalf, and that I am so far from intending innovation, as they are from truth, that made that report, if this were not sufficient for my purgation, but I hope my credit be not so sore cracked and of so small value with your honour but that I will my just defence be accepted and believed and may countervail the unjust bruits of mine adversaries, whereof I trust by your comfortable and friendly speedy answer of this, to be resolved, and I am in the meantime assured to continue in some grief and perturbation of mind. God bless you and send you much increase of honour, from Dublin the xxvth day of January, 1567 [modern reckoning, 1568].

I humbly beseech your honour with the next post to bestow on me two or three lines.

Your honour's most bounden at commandment,

ADAM DUBLIN.

This letter is on a par with the cunning letters of his predecessor, George Browne. Loftus pretends that it was on account of the large number of communicants that he had the Communion Table moved to the centre of the Church. This action for some reason or other was looked upon as

17

savouring of Calvinism. This much must be said that the position of the Holy Table was a debatable question among Protestants at this period.[1] But that Loftus intended by his action to show favour to Calvinistic practices seems beyond doubt. It was in keeping with his other well-known opinions as to the stripping of church services of all papist ornamentation. The " curious singing " he had also discarded. But what is of more importance is his admission that up to the time he became Primate " there was not so much as any show of a Reformed Church." Indeed, with truth, he might have added " up to the time he became Archbishop of Dublin." He had already confessed he could accomplish nothing in Armagh, and even during his short time in Dublin he could not have effected much. He afterwards admitted this. His pleading was mere empty boast, and did not deceive Cecil. Of course he had to make out a case of envy of his success in order to cover up his innovation.

It is of some interest to know that from Easter to the following January he had administered the Communion only on one occasion, namely, at Easter. The whole episode throws light on the bickering and jealousies prevalent among the members of the " Reformed Church " so early in its career. It was a very unhappy family. On 1 May, Elizabeth sent a significant instruction to Sydney [2] that " we cannot allow that any parsons of any sort should by their doctrine, example, or other innovation make any diversity therein."

LOFTUS AIRS HIS GRIEVANCES.

Although Loftus was fond of comfort and an easy life in " civilised parts," yet as he had received little emolument

---

[1] The fourth Rubric of 1552 directs that it " shall stand in the Body of the Church, or in the Chancel, where morning and evening prayer are appointed to be said." " In the reigns of Edward VI after 1550, and of Elizabeth and James I, it was a common practice in parish churches to place the Holy Table lengthwise in the chancel or in the body of the Church, the short ends facing east and west ; but in Cathedral Churches this custom does not seem to have been generally observed." (W. R. Stephens, *Helps to the Study of the Book of Common Prayer*, 140.) There was a want of uniformity, and also of a clear idea as to the exact meaning of the Holy Table, whether it was to take the place of the ancient altar or to be merely a Communion Table to be moved about for convenience of the Service.

[2] *S.P.I., Eliz.*, xxiv. 29, P.R.O., London.

from Armagh, it would be unfair, taking the archiepiscopal position of the time, to blame him for making a stand against Elizabeth's greed for money in the matter of the first-fruits. The letters of the " reform " bishops on their material comforts during this period form a kind of companion picture to those on their failure in the " reform." On the 26 March, namely, shortly after his appointment to Dublin, Loftus begged the Lords Justices [1] to plead with the Queen for the remission of the first-fruits of Dublin (£534 15s. 2d.) as "she had granted in the case of Armagh, a living of no more yearly profit than the one he resigned." FitzWilliams to Cecil [2] gives the reason for the petition ; " otherwise he [Loftus] cannot keep house and maintain his living. He preaches God abroad in the country, and that only he came here, the wicked enemy to God's Church, that subtle serpent the devil " would have worked greater havoc.[3]

Another grievance of Loftus was in respect to the attempt of the City of Dublin to procure a statute to take away the Liberties and Franchises of the Archbishopric of Dublin in the Manor of St. Sepulchre outside the City. The City's statute was sent over under the great seal to Her Majesty and purported to have been " signed by all bishops and earls, except the Earl of Ormonde." " This would mean," writes Loftus to Cecil, 2 April,[4] " no small decay of the patrimony of the Archbishop in time to come as the escheats mean half of their living, and seneschals and constables have fees for life." Loftus considers that this move was " meant chiefly for his discredit and of the whole ministry. They would not have attempted it against Ormond."

The rights and privileges of the Archbishops of Dublin in their manors and courts dated back to the days of King John. No doubt, in this case, Loftus's grievance was of an important and historical nature, not personal, involving the dignity of his successors and burdening Loftus with the payment of pensions to the officials of his court.

---

[1] *S.P.I.*, *Eliz.*, xxiii. 83, P.R.O., London. [2] *Ib.*, xxiii. 84.
[3] On 6 March the Queen commanded Loftus and the Dean and Chapter of St. Patrick's to grant a further lease of the parsonage of Swords to Fitz-Williams. (*C.S.P.I.*, *Eliz.*, xxiii. 66.)
[4] *Ib.*, xxiv. 1, P.R.O., London.

Loftus was so keen on his liberties that he sent his servant, Lewis Chaloner, over to Cecil (27 May) with his petition to have them preserved. Shortly afterwards (13 June), he was in a position to thank Cecil for the stay of the Bill.[1]

Loftus had not confined his complaints to the members of his flock, he included those bound up " in ignorant blindness " who were not able " to abide the light " of the " Reformation," and who " according to the custom of the brood " slandered him. Here, unmistakably, he refers to Catholics, and most probably to some of the municipal authorities. It would be unreasonable to suppose that the " reform " had effected them to any extent, any more than it had effected the people of Dublin in general. It is not at all unlikely, therefore, that the Municipal authorities had very little regard for Loftus, whether from personal or religious motives, and endeavoured to bring his manor under their jurisdiction.

After all, charters counted much in those days. Accordingly, he drew up a petition to Cecil [2] to safeguard the ancient liberties of the manor. It had been mooted that a Parliament would soon be held in Dublin for the purpose of putting the " reform " on a more secure basis than it had so far acquired. Acts were already drawn up by Cecil to be passed in that Parliament. Amongst those English Acts affecting the State Church of Ireland, was one entitled " an Act for resuming of certain franchises and usurped jurisdictions from all archbishops, earls, etc." The Act was obviously directed against the mere Irish, but Loftus, with his Manor of St. Sepulchre, would probably come under it. Accordingly, he petitioned Cecil (2 April) that the Act may not be passed, or, if passed, it may be revoked. This seems to be the meaning of the grievance and the reason for its removal in Loftus's petition to Cecil. In all such matters, the letters sent give merely a general idea of the subject ; it is the verbal report of the messenger which gives the details that the sender did not dare to put in writing lest they might be brought up in evidence against him. The City, however, did not succeed in its petition against Loftus.

[1] *C.S.P.I.*, *Eliz.*, xxv. 4, P.R.O., London.
[2] *Ib.*, xxiv. 1, P.R.O., London.

Lord Chancellor Weston Confesses Failure of the "Reform."

Weston was not long in office as Lord Chancellor and Dean of St. Patrick's when he wrote to Cecil, 3 April, 1568,[1] dolefully but spitefully confirming the reports of Loftus and Brady on the failure of the religious " reform " :—

So blinded through corruption of nature, evil bringing up, continual acquaintance and custom of sin, not only void of all knowledge of God like heathenish people, but drowned in idolatry and superstition with disobedience to their prince . . . a great number of them want all sense and sealing of sin. Ignorance the mother and nurse of those foul babes ; they have no instruction ; their parsons, vicars, and curates, some of whom I examined, be so void of knowledge of God and His Will that they know not His commandments ; no marvel if this blind people led by those blind guides, and being of nature given to sin and bred continually in the same, with no instruction or knowledge, should fall into the ditches or rather into the gulf of infidelity.

He then recommends Her Majesty to have pity on the miserable state of the Church of Ireland, so that the people may be truly instructed in the will of God. He refers here, of course, to the miserable state of the " reform " Church inasmuch as the Catholic people had refused to be instructed according to its tenets. His opinion of the " reform " ministers was by no means complimentary. It was very easy to recommend instruction of the people, but he was no more capable than the other " reformers " to have it carried out. At all events he was more sincere in his admissions than Loftus, who, having pleaded his inability to do anything in Armagh, claimed immediate success in Dublin.

Dean of Armagh Intends to Resort to the English Pale.

Terence Daniel, Dean of Armagh, although disappointed at not being appointed Archbishop of Armagh by Elizabeth, set about to restore order in the North. He reported to the Lord Justices, 22 January, 1568,[2] from Carlingford that he

---

[1] *C.S.P.I., Eliz.*, xxiv. 2, P.R.O., London.
[2] *S.P.I., Eliz.*, xxiii. 20, ii., P.R.O., London.

went to Maginnis's country [Co. Down] and brought Maginnis and Turlough Brasslagh together and took an order betwixt them that I left them friends, and had taken order between Maginnis and the Bishop of Dromore [Arthur Maginnis] who was at variance, and at my return through Maginnis's country being in danger of drowning at divers time I wrote a letter to the said Turlough Lynagh that I made peace between the foresaid parts, and if it should please him to abide mine order I would have proved what order I would take betwixt him and his nation. . . . I intend to resort to the English Pale for I had no kind of living to maintain me in this country for the country is so utterly waste.

Six months had elapsed since Shane's death, and the form of Government outlined by Cecil and Sydney had not yet been put into operation. The North undoubtedly was in a disturbed state, but scarcely so disturbed as to leave the Church or its ministers without the revenues from their possessions. We must look elsewhere to find a reason for the Dean's anxiety about his material comfort. He was probably tempted to hope that eventually some more lucrative position might come his way from Elizabeth's Government. He had been working up favour for himself at the Irish Council. He did not succeed, however, in establishing himself in the English Pale. But between January and June, he continued to send letters to the Lords Justices reporting his mediations between them and Tirlogh Luineach, who was behaving just as Shane had done.[1] A scheme for the Plantation of Ulster (February) was drawn up,[2] and pensioners were found willing to dwell at Carrickfergus and other places in Ulster. Indeed, a device for a general plantation of Ireland with Englishmen had been drawn up in January.[3] Every two parishes were to find a man, and £9 2s. 0d. for his entertainment, and the noblemen and gentlemen of knowledge were to procure that the parishes be contributory. But, above all, it was pointed out to the Privy Council that a settled governor was necessary to keep the North at peace.

Before the end of the year (2 November, 1568), Terence Daniel was appointed commissioner with Sir N. Bagenall, to determine and examine all offences committed by the

---

[1] *S.P.I., Eliz.*, xxiv. 9, vii. ; 45, ii., iii., viii.
[2] *Ib.*, xxiii. 33-5. [3] *Ib.*, xxiii. 26.

captains or inhabitants of Tyrone, MacMahon's country, Ferney, O'Hanlon's country, and Magennis's country, upon any within the Pale, or by the English upon them, and to take pledges for the performance of their orders.[1]

LANCASTER APPOINTED TO ARMAGH; ELIZABETH'S INSTRUCTIONS FOR REBUILDING THE CHURCH FOR PROTESTANT SERVICE.

In accordance with Elizabeth's usual policy of procrastination, the See of Armagh remained without a Protestant bishop for some months, although Thomas Lancaster, Treasurer of Salisbury, had been nominated long since. It was not until 12 March that she directed the Lords Justices and Council to do all that was necessary for his appointment.[2] On 28 March she gave further instructions about him.[3] She styles him Bishop of Kildare, and Cecil adds in a note that " therein for his time served very laudably."

In this Elizabeth and Cecil were mistaken.[4] The Thomas Lancaster whom they appointed to Armagh was not he of the same name who was Bishop of Kildare and who was deprived by Mary. The new Archbishop was Treasurer of Salisbury, January, 1559, and as Elizabeth had a patent made out for his consecration, he could not have been already a bishop. Elizabeth goes on to say that he was " well acquainted with Ulster, lately with the Deputy in all the said realm using himself commendably in preaching and teaching and very faithfully and discreetly in the service committed to his charge."

She then gives directions for nomination and commendation to the Dean and Chapter, and for the ratification and confirmation and giving of the royal assent to his election.

Further : to charge and command such archbishops and bishops as you shall think meet to proceed to his consecration and to do all other manner of things that by law and custom shall be requisite for the full perfecting of this our royal pleasure.

[1] *Fiants*, no. 1226.   [2] *S.P.I., Eliz.*, xxiii. 69.
[3] *Ib.*, xxiii. 86, P.R.O., London.
[4] *Athen. Oxon.*, i. 175, also makes the same mistake. Lancaster, Bishop of Kildare, had been consecrated in Dublin, July, 1550, by George Browne. (*Ware's Bishops*.)

Furthermore where we are given to understand that the Church of Armagh and the house belonging of old time to the Archbishop is decaying, and chiefly by the late rebel Shane O'Neill spoilt and ruined, our will is that speedy conference be had with Dean and Chapter of said Church, and with others, principals heads and freeholders of the diocese, for contribution of money or its value as of the labour, handiwork, timber, carriages, and other stuff in the diocese towards the re-edifying of the church and house of the Archbishop. The work to be assisted by the commissioner royal. Our meaning is to have the service of God hereby furthered and advanced.

Instructions are likewise to be given :—

Within the said parts of Ulster for the repairing of the churches which we hear to be in such lamentable ruin through the late rebellion in those parts as in some places there scantily remaineth knowledge of where the churches were built. And where there do remain any tokens, the ruins be such as in the same scantily is coverture for wild beasts, which is to be grievously lamented ; so we think it most necessary to be first re-covered. The Deputy at his coming will supply the want.

It is clear that Elizabeth's intention at last was to reconstruct Armagh Cathedral and the churches of the diocese for Protestant service. She does not say that the house, when reconstructed, is to be the abode of the Archbishop. On the contrary, she sent secret instructions on the same day stating her will on the matter.[1] The house is to be the residence for the Council to govern those parts, as without this house there can be no such residence. No one but the Archbishop is to be informed of this decision, as otherwise it is likely the people will not be so ready to give their labour for the rebuilding of the church and house. " As the nominated Archbishop," says Elizabeth, " cannot enter there without some monetary help, we have caused to be delivered to him the sum of £200 ; for the repayment, the Archbishop agreed to answer on the profits of the Archbishopric. If any further sum be necessary the Justices are to lend to him secretly any other such parcels exceeding not the sum of [blank],[2] on bond to repay the same in some convenient time, and give an account of the expenses."

---

[1] S.P.I., Eliz., xxiii. 87, P.R O., London.
[2] £50 written over the space.

On 15 June Lancaster wrote to the Queen telling her : [1]
" I was consecrated the 13 June [2] at Dublin and intend by
God's grace the 17th of the same to repair towards Armagh
as far as the Oriel [Louth] there to take order with the Dean
and other officers of the Church, the masters of the Church,
certain masons and carpenters for the cutting of timber and
burning of lime. I would have gone myself to Armagh but
I dare not, because of this broil. As I shall learn further
I will certify your Highness." Though he dare not go to
Armagh, yet he says that " there is not one of any power that
draweth the sword against Her Highness." No Scots have
arrived but those whom " Turlough Lynagh hath taken
contrary to his oath and promise. Con O'Donnell and Sir
Hugh Duff O'Donnell have killed two of Tirlogh's horsemen
and followed him from Lifford as far as Armagh, spoiled
the town and beat the Clergy." So, the O'Donnell-O'Neill
feud was still producing evil consequences.

PAPAL PETITION FOR RELEASE OF CREAGH AND WOLF.

The continued incarceration of Archbishop Creagh and
of David Wolf, S.J., Apostolic Commissary, was the source
of much anxiety to Pope Pius V, who accordingly wrote,
13 March, to the Nuncio in Spain :—[3]

---

[1] *S.P.I., Eliz.*, xxv. 5, P.R.O., London.

[2] Ware says that Lancaster " was consecrated in Christ's Church, Dublin, by
Adam, Archbishop of that See, Hugh, Bishop of Meath, and Robert, Bishop of
Kildare, on the 13th June, 1568 [*and Harris adds*] [the patent for his consecration
and restitution to the temporalities bearing date four days before. On account
of the poverty of his See he had a Licence dated the 26th March following
his Consecration, to hold *in commendam*, the Treasurership of Salisbury, the
Rectory of South Hill, in the Diocese of Exeter, the Rectory of Sherfield, in
the Diocese of Winchester, the Archdeaconry of Kells, together with the Rectory
of Nobber and the Prebend of Stragony [Stagonil] in the Cathedral of St.
Patrick's, Dublin ; all which, at the time of his advancement, he possessed, to
hold during such time as he should continue Primate : but under a proviso,
that the said churches should not be defrauded of their usual services ; but be
supplied by the provision of Vicars and Curates. A.D. 1572, An Act of Parliament passed to enable him to make leases of his lands within the Irish Pale,
without the consent of his Dean and Chapter]." (Harris, *Ware's Bishops*, 97.)
He died in 1584 and was buried in St. Peter's, Drogheda, in the vault of Ottavian
de Palatio.

[3] *C.S.P., Rome*, 1558-71, no. 517.

On behalf of Archbishop of Armagh and David, S.J., in captivity in England.

We are informed that our venerable brother the Archbishop of Armagh, who, as you know, is Primate of Ireland, has been arrested by the English, and is kept in chains in the Tower of London; that our dear son David, of Ireland, S.J., is kept in most close custody by the said English in the town of Dublin, and that both are very harshly treated. Their several woes are a sore grief to us by reason of their singular goodness and many labours on behalf of the Catholic Religion. But while, as in duty bound, we desire to help them as best as we can, we see not how this may be unless our dearest son in Christ, the Catholic King, were to write earnestly on their behalf to the Queen of England. And so we would have you plead with the King for them both, and be zealous and instant with him, and crave of him in our own words that he write, sparing no pains, to the said Queen and his ambassador on their behalf, than which office there is none by which he could at present better please Us.

In reply the Archbishop of Rossano, the Nuncio at Madrid, wrote to Cardinal Alessandrino, Papal Secretary of State, 1 May :—[1]

Touching the affair of the Archbishop of Armagh as to which his Holiness writes me by the brief just received. I suppose it will be in the recollection of his Holiness that the Archbishop of Cashel [Maurice MacGibbon] in Ireland was likewise at his Holiness's feet, and received the pallium in Rome [6 June, 1567].[2] He arrived here some days ago and waited upon me, and told me of the unjust edict of the Queen of England, that he and the said Archbishop of Armagh were to be arrested for being Catholics and having given their obedience to the Pope, and how that it was already carried into effect in the person of the said Archbishop of Armagh, and that he [MacGibbon] for all that was minded to go to Ireland, but desired first to make sure that he could count on the interest of this King.

I took the matter to heart, and wrought so upon his Majesty that he wrote to his Ambassador in England to do all in his power with the Queen for the liberation of the said Archbishop of Armagh, and for permission to the said Archbishop of Cashel to go and

---

[1] C.S.P., Rome, 1558-71, no. 523.
[2] The See had been vacant since 1561 ; neither Elizabeth nor the Pope appointed until 1567.

live in security in his Church, intimating that we would be content that the Archbishop should go to one of the ports of Spain nearest to Ireland, there to tarry until the withdrawal [of the edict] should be obtained from England and communicated to him in writing, and that thereupon he might forthwith make the best of his way to his Church : besides which the King gave him 500 Crowns with a promise of more at his departure : and so he went. Of Father David [Wolf], S.J., I knew nothing and therefore I said nothing about him.

So his Majesty wrote to his ambassador in favour of these two Archbishops in very warm terms : but by what I gather, for methinks he is wont to use a certain caution in dealing with this Queen, he bade the Ambassador in the first instance to feel his way and be circumspect, giving him to understand that to avoid a breach of faith he must promise nothing that could not be performed : that this Archbishop of Armagh was taken under the protection and parole of his Catholic Majesty, which must needs be held a great point of honour ; and again that he must add nought that she might deny him, because many nations, and that nation [England] most of all, seem to become as it were hostile as soon as they refuse aught that is asked of them which, accordingly, is what, of all men, great Princes are careful to avoid.

Pursuant to the brief I have now spoken afresh to the King on his Holiness's part, and his reply is that to his letter touching the Archbishop of Armagh he has as yet received no answer, albeit he thinks he has heard that he is somewhat less closely confined. His Majesty adds that he feels great pity and is sore at heart for the Archbishop and other good and faithful Catholics that are in prison, whom, when he was in that realm, he knew and that he is trying to secure their discharge, to which end there is nothing that he would not now, if he could, do : and that he will at once write again warmly, on behalf of the Archbishop and Father David to his Ambassador there, because with the Queen's Ambassador here it would be inopportune to deal in the matter by reason of the affair which I am about to relate.

This affair was to the effect that the English Ambassador in Spain launched out into some venomous words against the Pope, whereupon the King had him removed from the Court until he should hear from the English Queen. The King wished to avoid a breach with England so as to be able to keep his Ambassador in London, " seeing that the only place left in that Kingdom where seed of religion is still openly sown is the Ambassador's house where Mass is daily celebrated and the Catholic life is lived."

This is the first time we hear of an edict against the Archbishops of Armagh and Cashel. There is nothing in the *State Papers* about it. Elizabeth's grievance seems to have been that a Catholic Archbishop or Bishop should be appointed by the Pope to a See to which she had either appointed or intended to appoint one of her own. The petitions in favour of Father Wolf and the two Archbishops produced no amelioration of their position.

Archbishop of Cashel in Spain ; Arrives in Ireland.

Although Roland Baron, Archbishop of Cashel, died 28 October, 1561, no successor was appointed either by the Pope or the Queen for six years. Maurice MacGibbon, abbot of the Cistercian Monastery of St. Mary of Mayo, was proclaimed at the papal consistory on Wednesday, 4 June, 1567.[1] In the consistorial act there is no mention of Roland Baron or indeed of any predecessor, but the See is stated to have been vacant for sixteen years, namely, since the death of Edmund Butler in 1550. Our view is that Roland Baron was never consecrated. MacGibbon was consecrated in Rome, and, 19 September, received the pallium, after which ceremony he set out for Ireland, calling at Spain on his way.

Elizabeth, probably aware of MacGibbon's appointment, took courage and appointed a royal bishop to the same See in the person of James MacCaghwell, 2 October, 1567. This bishop had been appointed by her to Down in 1565, but was unable to take possession of his See because of Shane O'Neill. Cashel was as difficult a See to hold as Down, and neither papal nor royal bishop expected to be able to carry on his office there. This seems to be the reason of the delay of six years in filling the vacancy.

It would appear that MacGibbon arrived at some port in Spain early in 1568, and sent letters to the Apostolic Nuncio at Madrid in reference to his going to Ireland. He desired him to find out from the Spanish ambassador in London if the Queen would allow him to take possession of his See of

[1] He was allowed to retain his monastery for one year.

Cashel. As Elizabeth had already appointed an Archbishop there, the situation for MacGibbon was one of extreme danger. A bishop coming to Ireland furnished with papal bulls was regarded by her as a sworn enemy to her in her capacity as Queen and as Governor of the State Church.

On the receipt of a reply from London, the Nuncio in Spain, 6 May, wrote to the Papal Secretary :—[1]

The ambassador writes to his Catholic Majesty that he has done his office for the Archbishop of the Cashel, but finds difficulties ; and that he will endeavour to do the like for the Archbishop of Armagh ; but by what he writes methinks he has no good hope.

Secretary Cayas tells me that the ambassador [in England] has it in his instructions that, as the Pope cannot keep a Nuncio in that Kingdom, he must regard himself as there on his Holiness' part also, and act in all matters that he shall perceive to subserve the interests of the Holy Apostolic See, as if he were the minister of that See : and therefore he deems that it would be well that in the matters aforesaid and the like matters his Holiness should direct that everything should be communicated to the said ambassador, because it would not but be helpful and serviceable.

His Catholic Majesty is minded to send another ambassador to England, who will be the same gentleman that he told he purposed to send thither to recount the affair of the Queen's ambassador which I reported in the other letter ; but who that gentleman will be, is, I believe, as yet undetermined. It is settled that he is to bear the King's commission to do all that he can to procure the discharge of the Archbishop of Armagh and Father David [Wolf].

As to the Archbishop of Cashel in Ireland, who is now tarrying in a port, I know not what he will do when he receives this answer. I should think it would not be amiss that I should learn the mind of his Holiness as to his going [to Ireland], for methinks he has no inordinate desire to expose himself to the risk of martyrdom.

The following are the copies of the despatches of the Spanish ambassador in London to the King :—[2]

Diego de Guzman de Sylva to his Catholic Majesty (27 March) : The favour and compassion which your Majesty desires to manifest towards the Archbishop of Cashel and the Archbishop of Armagh accord with all that your Majesty does in what concerns the service

---

[1] *C.S.P., Rome*, 1558-71, no. 524.   [2] *Ib.*, no. 525.

of God and the weal of His Church Universal, and will have a corresponding reward in great felicity and many years on earth, and eternal life in Heaven. As I have written in reference to this prelate [Cashel] to Secretary Gabriel de Cayas, the business at present is one of great difficulty, and a matter of what it seems just now unmeet to speak to the Queen ; for, besides that little good could be done therein, the result, by reason of the wonted suspicions of your Majesty, which the heretics of all parts instil into her, might, as I am advised, be untoward, and little to the advantage of the Church in those parts of this Kingdom in which the Queen has most power, and so, if one would do one's office with success, it would be necessary to consider carefully how one does it, and walk very warily, for one could not succeed unless one kept in a manner covert there among the Catholics, and so that one could not be molested by those that are not Catholics ; for though in effect in certain parts of Ireland they [Protestants] dissemble with them [Catholics] deeming it expedient so to do for the present in order not to disturb the country, they yet display great vigilance in obstructing any provision that may there be made by bull or ordinance of his Holiness. I will therefore give all the due attention and consideration to the case ; and find out what is feasible, and the matter shall be handled in accordance with your Majesty's instructions ; and the like shall be done in regard to the confinement of the Archbishop of Armagh, which gives me great concern, seeing that it is strict and very grievous for one who is, as he is, in ill health. And the worst of our position here in these matters is that your Majesty's favour, instead of helping these good men, rather makes against them ; and for this reason one must needs proceed with great caution.

Other letters [1] passed between the Nuncio and the Papal Secretary in the following two months on the subject of securing at least better treatment for Creagh and Wolf "who now languish miserably in the strictest confinement, solely for holding the true faith of Our Lord Jesus Christ." The new ambassador to London is to be Don Guerau Despes, a Catalan Knight of the Order of Calatrava, who is married, a lettered gentleman, and reputed a very good Christian and a prudent man.

Following on this correspondence, the Nuncio in Spain wrote in May [2] to MacGibbon :—

[1] *C.S.P.*, *Rome*, 1558-71, nos. 535, 537, 541, 543.   [2] *Ib.*, no. 527.

Your letters, the first and second, have been delivered to me. That I deferred answering the first was due to the reason which you yourself assign. Nothing was lost thereby, for the letter from England had not even been delivered. It is now to hand, and from what the Catholic King's ambassador writes to his Majesty one is better able to discern the cruel animosity of the Queen towards the Catholics to hope for that which we desire and crave. Secretary Cayas, your constant patron, and moreover a ready promoter of all good works, will write to you, and more fully expound the answer lately received from the King's ambassador. It will now be your part to submit the question of your going thither [to Ireland] to prudent and conscientious consideration. I am grieved to hear of your servant's death, and of the ill health with which you are troubled at times. Meanwhile take care of yourself, and so love me as I love you : and be not unmindful of me in your prayers.

MacGibbon, seeing it was hopeless to expect a favourable letter from Elizabeth, left Spain on his dangerous mission to Cashel, probably in the month of June. He was scarcely four months in Ireland when Lancaster of Armagh wrote to Cecil [1] 12 November, reporting that he (MacGibbon) had carried off the Protestant Archbishop of Cashel, MacCaghwell, [2] and shipped him to Spain, and that he intended to supply his place there.

Lancaster also gives an account of his own troubles in the See of Armagh. " For my part," he says, " I dare not go to Armagh for fear of the like ; yet notwithstanding somewhat is done towards the Church [of Armagh] for there is a roof cut for the chancel with shingles, [3] etc., and as yet not brought home, and all because of that wicked man, Turlough Lynagh and his followers." Lancaster trusts that next year he " may be able to do something there for the glory of God."

---

[1] *S.P.I.*, *Eliz.*, xxvi. 20, P.R.O., London.

[2] " This year complaint was made to the State at Dublin how Morris Reiagh (MacGibbon), an Irishman, having lately been at Rome and there consecrated by the Pope's Bull, Archbishop of Cashel, arrived in Ireland and made challenge to the same See, which being denied unto him by the Archbishop which was there placed by his [*sic*] Majesty, the said pretended Bishop suddenly, with an Irish skeyne, wounded the Bishop and put him in danger of his life." (Loftus MS., *Annals, ad. an.*, 1567, i.e. 1568.)

[3] Shingles were wooden blocks or tiles, which were fitted into a frame for the purpose of roofing. They were used more commonly than slates.

Thus, Sydney's great progress in the North had accomplished nothing. Tirlogh Luineach, notwithstanding his profession of loyalty, had become as troublesome as Shane, and was in occupation of Armagh. So, all Lancaster's preparations for roofing the Church and preparing the house for the Deputy came to nothing. His hope that next year he might do something seemed rather optimistic. At this time, however, Terence Daniel still continued his office of mediator between Tirlogh and the Deputy. He appears in a note in the *State Papers* of July [1] as a commissioner for ecclesiastical causes along with the Archbishops of Armagh and Dublin, and the Bishops of Meath, Kildare, and Leighlin, and John Garvey, Archdeacon of Meath. This was an old list (before 1567) and was sent to Sydney to be subscribed by him. In it Loftus is mentioned as of Armagh, Curwen of Dublin, and Thomas (Fihil) of Leighlin. Loftus had been changed to Dublin, Curwen to Oxford, and Fihil was dead.

Trouble for Sydney in North and South.

Sydney lost no time in trying to realise his idea of bridging the North with forts and bridges. He met Tirlogh Luineach at the Bann, and thought him inclined to obey. " The Archbishop of Armagh and the Bishop of Meath, with divers noblemen and gentlemen as well of England as the English Pale, lawyers, merchants, and others came from Dublin to Carrickfergus, only for visitation sake, the Bishops riding in their rochets, and the rest unarmed. A treaty was made with Sir Brian MacPhelim to build a proper carriage bridge over the Laggan at Belfast. On his road to Dublin most of the chiefs and gentlemen came to pay their respects to the Lord Deputy." [2] Sydney believed that all Ulster difficulties originated in Scotland. Argyle did not pretend to be guided by any rule but the good of his own country, and he had 5000 men always ready to invade Ireland if he did not approve of Elizabeth's policy. If the Scots were once disposed of, Sydney thought it would be easy to govern Ireland ; the O'Neills would then be shut up in their own province, and would have to work or to starve.[3]

[1] *S.P.I., Eliz.*, xxv. 52, P.R.O., London.   [2] *Ib.*, xxvi. 18.
[3] Bagwell, ii. 149.

In the South matters were as troublesome as ever. When James Fitzmaurice found that Sydney had not brought the Earl or Sir John of Desmond back to Ireland with him, he called a meeting of the Geraldines, and informed them that their chief and his brother were condemned to death, or at least to perpetual imprisonment. He was immediately chosen captain of the country and accepted the position in spite of Sydney's threats. But the Earl of Clancare also put himself at the head of a confederacy. Fitzmaurice was soon afterwards proclaimed a traitor. Edward Butler told Sydney's messenger that no man of Irish birth could be safe since Sir John of Desmond had been sent to the Tower for little or nothing. The Butlers carried on their practices of extortion and spoil on one another, so that the presence of Ormond alone could settle their country. But Ormond still remained in England as much for attendance at Court as out of ancient malice against the Desmonds. Sydney was thus obliged to go to Kilkenny himself, where he hanged several of Edward Butler's men, not by martial law, but " by the verdict of twelve men orderly." A similar example was made at Waterford, and Sydney returned to Dublin to make preparations for holding a Parliament.[1]

STUCLEY, CONSTABLE OF LEIGHLIN; THE BUTLERS RESENT THE COLONISTS.

It has already appeared how Stucley had been brought into contact with Bagenall, Marshal of the Queen's forces in Ireland, who, tired of the work, offered his position and farms to Stucley for £3000. Although this deal had the good will of Sydney the Queen refused to sanction it. Sydney, however, remained his friend, and appointed him Seneschal of Wexford and Constable of Leighlin where Stucley also purchased a couple of farms. The Queen was greatly displeased on learning of Stucley's new office, from which she ordered Sydney to dismiss him and send him to London to answer for his misdeeds. But apparently Sydney thought that he could overcome her opposition by delay, for Stucley

[1] *S.P.I., Eliz.*, xxvi. 22, 59.

was still in residence in Leighlin when Sir Peter Carew arrived to claim Idrone in Co. Carlow,[1] in the autumn of 1568.

Forty-five miles to the south of Dublin the road from Leinster to Munster crossed the River Barrow at a place called Leighlin Bridge. To the Norman settlers the point was one of great strategic importance, for on its safety depended the readiest road of communication between the English of Leinster and their colleagues in the South. Accordingly, as early as 1181, a stronghold, the first of its kind in Ireland, was erected there to guard the pass and protect the King's garrison. Just beside this Black Castle, one of the settlers a little later founded and built a monastery for Carmelites. In 1320 Maurice Jakis, Canon of the Cathedral of Kildare, built the famous bridge, known as Leighlin Bridge, to facilitate communication between the new Carmelite Monastery on the left bank of the river and the monastic establishment in a secluded spot called Old Leighlin, a little more than a mile from the opposite bank, which dated from the sixth century. In the course of time, when the descendants of the settlers had to fly from the wrath of Art MacMurrough and his father, the trouble and expense of guarding castle and bridge against the Irish enemy devolved on the Carmelites, who by way of recompense for many a year received an annual grant from grateful sovereigns. On the suppression of monasteries by Henry VIII, who did not even spare his monastic friends, the Carmelites were evicted, and their monastery was converted into a military barracks by the Lord Deputy, Sir Edward Birmingham. Henceforward it became the residence of the Constable who had the heavy task of keeping the bridge against the Kavanaghs who, from the days of Cathair Mor, King of Leinster, had occupied the district to the south of Leighlin, known as the Barony of Idrone.

For almost two centuries from the day when Art MacMurrough asserted his right as King of Leinster and banished the Carews and other Norman settlers out of the lands subject to his sway, he and his descendants steadfastly defended that right and occupied those lands. Through

[1] See *Kilk. Arch. Soc.*, 1858-59, pp. 400-28; 1860-61, pp. 20-44, 69-80, 144-64.

bloody feuds amongst themselves, and influenced by the strange panic that drove so many Irish chiefs into head-long recognition of Henry VIII, the house of MacMurrough gradually weakened, and renounced the name of MacMurrough for that of Kavanagh. After some years they seemed to have settled down, and John Hooker reported to Sir Peter Carew, 25 May, 1568 : " Your Barony of Idrone is now in the tenure of a certain sort called the Kavanaghs. These do deduce their genealogy and race from the MacMurrough, who, proclaiming himself King of Leinster, did espulse and destroy all the race and nation of the English blood, and invaded their lands and inheritance ; and that which ap-pertained to your ancestors, these Kavanaghs do, with like right, keep and occupy. These men . . . Sir Nicholas Heron [Military governor of Carlow] brought to the Queen's peace ; and Mr. Stucley, now supplying his place and dwelling at Leighlin [Black Castle], doth in like order keep them in subjection and under bond, they being all to his command-ment. . . . This Leighlin was sometimes the house of your ancestors, and by them made a monastery, which, being dissolved, is now in the Queen's hands, and a very strong Castle which Mr. Stucley hath, who hath offered me the same house or any other which he hath to be at your commandment."

The Kavanaghs might have gone on for many a day in the Queen's peace were it not that in the autumn of 1568 they were visited by an English gentleman, who notified them that the Barony of Idrone was not theirs but his. He had come to claim it, he said, and he was their lord, and they his vassals. This gentleman was Peter Carew,[1] one of the colonists who had recently undertaken the task of civilising Ireland, and hoped to enrich themselves incidentally at the expense of the natives.

Carew had befriended Stucley in critical circumstances during his days of piracy, so that when Carew came to claim Idrone, Stucley, who was doubtless aware that he had nothing to gain by opposing him, took the line of least resistance and extended a cordial welcome to the unwelcome guest. Carew

[1] Carew, 1515-74, nos. 257, 260, 264. For Sir Peter's career, see *The Discourse and Discovery of the Life of Sir Peter Carew*, collected by John Vowell, *alias* Hooker. *Ed.* John Maclean, 1857.

proceeded to Dublin to vindicate his claim, and returned with a decree (17 December) from the Lord Deputy and Council that he was the rightful Lord of the barony of Idrone.[1]

As to Stucley, matters were made worse for him by Elizabeth's determination to bestow the Constableship, 4 November, on Sir Nicholas Heron.[2] A short time before (24 October),[3] Cecil reported to Sydney that Nicholas White, in commission in Munster, had asked for Stucley's office and that Her Majesty had readily assented to it. He hopes Sydney is well content. Again, 15 December, Cecil wrote to Sydney [4] that he had appointed White to Stucley's office, and mentioned that he " never deserved evil language from Stucley's mouth." Stucley " must amend his language of me before I advance him to his pleasure. I mean not to make a contented Mr. Stucley." He admits that " White is inferior to Stucley in marshal service, but much superior in civil, and not so ignorant of ordering a ward of soldiers in Ireland as the other of civil controversies." Finally, he is careful to ask Sydney " not to mislike " him for preferring White. (The effect of this casting out of Stucley will appear later.) On 6 January following, Cecil again told Sydney [5] that " her Majesty would no wise endure Stucley to continue ; otherwise he would not have sought to displace Stucley." Accordingly White was appointed.

When this news arrived, angry discussions took place between Stucley, White, and the rest, and White on several occasions gave his own version of what was said, and managed also to keep Cecil informed of other things said about himself. He says [6] that Stucley has incensed Sydney against Cecil and that he himself was appointed because he took side with Ormond against Sydney. " But since I came here," says White (March, 1569), " he has not shown himself abroad in this city [Dublin], but has departed into Co. Wexford where men think my Lord Deputy hath devised some kind of rule for him." White professes that he himself is wholly addicted to the English, and that his countrymen do not trust him. He does not know what harm Stucley will yet do.

[1] See *Catholic Bulletin*, July, 1925, pp. 730-40.
[2] *S.P.I.*, *Eliz.*, xxvi. 13, P.R.O., London.
[3] *Ib.*, xxvi. 8.
[4] *Ib.*, 57.
[5] *Ib.*, xxvii. 2, P.R.O., London.
[6] *Ib.*, 44.

A few months later the expected harm had evidently materialised, for, 10 June, White wrote to Cecil [1] of Stucley's evil practices, " broken out in more heinous sort, more than I expected." He tells him of the accusation made by T. Masterson, sometime servant to Mr. Vice-Chamberlain, and lately placed in the Constableship of Ferns. Masterson charged Stucley openly at the Council Board of raising rebels and conspiring with them in the Co. Wexford to levy war against the Queen's Majesty and subjects. Whereupon " Stucley is committed to close prison, and the Council debated about the manner of trial and the careful ordering of the cause." White also informed Cecil that before Stucley came over to Ireland he had made a grant of all his farms and goods to Mr. Agard and John Thomas. Stucley thus secured his property against confiscation.

Following White's recommendation of an examination of witnesses against Stucley, Richard Stafford of Leighlin Bridge, deposed that Whitmonday, 1568, when he was at Enniscorthy, Stucley began to rail and chide him. William Hore, who was present, took Stucley aside and asked him why he was so offended with the gentlemen of the Co. Wexford. " We hearsay," said Hore, " that Mr. Heron [2] will be here shortly as seneschal and that the Queen hath given him the said office and some other part of your living." Then Stucley said, " I care not a (———) for her (h———) [3] nor yet for her office."

The coming of Carew to Leighlin was to hasten unexpected developments in the bosom of the great Ormond family. The chief opponent Carew had was Sir Edmund Butler,[4] brother of the Earl of Ormond. Edmund complained that Carew was trying to grab some land that had been given to him by the former Earl his father. The land in question was in the north-west of the Barony of Idrone, and was called Clogrennan. Carew held that Butler's conveyance was nothing in law, and not sufficient to bar his own title,

---

[1] *S.P.I., Eliz.*, xxviii. 24.
[2] Heron had been appointed to the office by Elizabeth, but it was White who received it on the recommendation of Cecil.
[3] Here Stucley made a ribald pun on the name Hore.
[4] *Hist. Arch. Assoc. Ir.*, 1870-71, pp. 153-92, 211-31.

as he "had recovered his whole barony against the Kavanaghs." [1] The outcome of all this was "the rebellion named the Butlers' wars, the chief and principal guide whereof was Sir Edmund Butler," who "became not only a mere Irishman, but also an Irish kerne in apparel, behaviour, and all other savage manners of the Irishry ; and being altogether carried and led by them he ranged and spoiled the whole countries with sword, fire, and all hostility." Although Sir Edmund alleged the plea that Carew was trying to grab his lands, the real truth was that "a general conspiracy was made and had been working a long time to prevent and withstand the general reformation which was supposed should have been established throughout the whole land, for the suppressing and reforming of the loose, barbarous, and most wicked life of that savage nation, which, rather than yield unto, they would put the Queen's Majesty's Crown and dignity in peril."

It thus appears that even the Butlers who supported the Protestant interest resented this new parcelling of the country, in the general or civil reformation, amongst colonists. The result of all this will soon be seen in the part that the Butlers took in the Fitzmaurice rebellion.

PARLIAMENT IN DUBLIN ; ACTS FOR REPAIRING CHURCHES AND ERECTING SCHOOLS THROWN OUT.

Elizabeth's second Parliament, summoned to settle the country in the matter of secular and religious reform, began 17 January, 1569, held three sessions, and, 11 March, was prorogued until 10 October. As usual, there is no list of the members who sat in either House. Many Englishmen had, by Government influence, been returned for remote places.[2] From the outset it was clear that matters would not proceed too peacefully. The first difference arose about the appointment of a Speaker. James Stanihurst, Recorder of Dublin, favoured by Sydney, was again chosen by a large

---

[1] Elizabeth issued a commission to Sir Peter Carew and Henry Davells to protect her loyal subjects in the countries of Carlow, Kinsellagh, Kavanaghs, and the Morrowes, 19 July, 1568. (Carew, no. 261.)

[2] Bagwell, ii. 152.

majority over Sir Christopher Barnewall, who was also a lawyer and the candidate favoured by the gentlemen of the Pale. It soon appeared that the House of Commons was divided into two parties bitterly hostile to each other. The Court, or English party, consisted chiefly of officials and of the Lord Deputy's nominees, men who might be trusted not to exhibit too much independence. On the other side were the gentry of the Pale, the burgesses returned by the old corporate towns, and the common lawyers generally, who had been roughly handled by Sydney in Sir Peter Carew's case, and who asserted that some of the English members were returned for towns not incorporated, that sheriffs and mayors had returned themselves, and that others were ignorant of their constituencies and non-resident. The Judges held that the first and second objections were good, but that there was nothing in the third. When the Attorney-General reported this decision, and that the Government had still a majority, the Irish party professed not to believe him, and demanded that the Judges themselves should come down. The Judges confirmed their decision, but the Irish party, headed by Sir Edmund Butler, still obstructed the business and opposed the suspending of Poynings' law and the introduction of Bills that were not first certified under the Great Seal of England. The suspension of Poynings' law was obviously for the purpose of enlarging the Government's jurisdiction, and ultimately was passed. It took a fortnight for matters to settle down in any peaceful fashion, and Edmund Butler, openly censured by Sydney in the Council Chamber, withdrew in disgust to his own country.

The House of Lords was no less mutinous than the Commons. Several Acts, however, of great political importance were passed. Shane O'Neill was attainted, the name of O'Neill extinguished, and the Queen declared entitled to Tyrone. Irish captainries were abolished unless established by patent, and the Chief Governor was enabled, on certain conditions, to make the remaining Irish countries into shire ground. When Sydney came over as Lord Deputy he received certain instructions from the Queen. In one of these it is said: " As for religion, there but small appearance of it, the churches uncovered, and the clergy scattered and scarce the being of a God known to those ignorant and barbarous people." This was probably the foundation of some Acts given in an Abstract of Bills to be passed by this Parliament.

The preamble sets forth the ignorance of the people for want of good school discipline :—

Forasmuch as the greatest number of this your Majesty's realm hath of long time lived in rude and barbarous states, not understanding that Almighty God hath by His divine laws forbidden the manifold and heinous offences, which they spare not daily and hourly to commit and perpetrate, nor that he hath by his holy Scriptures commanded a due and humble obedience from the people to their princes and rulers ; whose ignorance in these so high points touching their damnation proceedeth only of lack of good bringing up of the youth of this realm, either in public or private schools, where through good discipline they might be taught to avoid these loathsome and horrible errors.

It is said that " as instruments well suited for producing this general improvement among their countrymen, regard appears to have been had to the native youth, who, being by the circumstances of their birth acquainted with the Irish language should be trained in a knowledge of English, and at the same time in the sound religious principles and practices of the Church : that thus in due course they might become efficient in disseminating true religion, and social and moral cultivation over the country, through the medium of either the Irish or the English tongue, as occasions might require, and in a way exempt from all offence on the score of national antipathies."

Though Parliament was opened, 17 January, 1569, it was not until its fifth session, 26 May, 1570, that this Bill became law.

In the Abstract of Bills for Parliament [1] two important matters were contemplated, namely, the Reparation of Parish Churches, and the Erection of Free Schools in every shire. As to the first, the " Ordinaries of every diocese shall execute severe and ordinary means as appointed by ecclesiastical laws to compel such persons as are found to repair said parish churches. The Queen's farmers are bound to

---

[1] *S.P.I., Eliz.,* xxvii. 12, P.R O., London.

build up the Chancels by a certain day ; parsons and vicars are to do the like upon pain of deprivation."

As to the second, " the school house is to be made at the charge of the whole shire, and the schoolmaster to be an Englishman. The stipend to be appointed by the Governor ; the Ordinary to pay one-third, the clergy two-thirds ; the schoolmaster to be admittable and removable by the Governor for the time being."

The first was thrown out by the Commons, the Catholics, some of them still farmers of the tithes, not caring to provide for the Established Church, and no one wishing to bear taxation. The second was thrown out by the Bishops,[1] who thought that they and not the Lord Deputy should have the patronage in their own hands, and demurred to the exemption of impropriated lands that were often the richest part of the possessions of the Church. In the end Lord Chancellor Weston summed up : " Churches and schools still find no favour among us, yet, in my opinion, the reformation of Ireland must come from churches and schools." [2] Other drafts in the Abstract deal with the following : On account of the lack of suitable residences for the Governors, the episcopal palaces at Waterford and Cork were to be given up by the bishops to the Queen at a certain rent.

The Governors were to present to the dignities of Deans, Chancellors, Chantors, Treasurers, and Archdeacons of Munster and Connacht for ten years to come, except to the churches of Waterford, Limerick, and Cork, and only those are to be appointed who can speak the English tongue and shall reside within their dignities. The anxiety now about the ability of the dignitaries to speak English was evidently in view of the contemplated plantations.

All leases, grants, etc., made by Purcell, sometime Bishop of Ferns, and Alexander (Devereux), late Bishop of Ferns, by loan or to the use of any their bastards, of any the possessions of the said bishopric of Ferns, shall be void.[3]

---

[1] Mant (i. 287) and Cox (i. 319) are both wrong in asserting that this Act was passed.

[2] *S.P.I.*, *Eliz.*, xxvii. 25, 48, P.R.O., London.

[3] *Ib.*, 14, 15, P.R.O., London.

THE DESMOND CONFEDERACY.

While preparations were being made for the holding of the Dublin Parliament, the south of Ireland was rapidly developing concerted action on the part of the chiefs. One of the first signs was the dislodging of Elizabeth's archbishop from Cashel. MacCaghwell had taken possession of his See in October, 1567, and was opposed the following June by MacGibbon, the papal archbishop. Four months afterwards (November) MacGibbon ousted MacCaghwell, and, it is said, shipped him to Spain. This apparently was done with the aid of the Munster chiefs, but it is not quite clear whether MacCaghwell, seeing he could do no good in the archbishopric, allowed himself to be deported to a land where he could repent at leisure of his part in the "reform." However this may be, the chiefs were dismayed by the imprisonment of the Earl of Desmond and of Archbishop Creagh, as well as by unmistakable signs of an intention to impose the Protestant religion on the country, and, above all, by clear evidence of a project to plant tracts of the County Cork with settlers from England.[1] "To them the struggle was for their lands and lives; and as the colonisation scheme leaked out, it became easy, with such a cause, to unite all Ireland against the invaders. The religious cry and the land cry fell in together. The land was the rallying cry among themselves: religion gave them a claim on the sympathy and the assistance of the Catholic powers. . . . It cannot be said that England deserved to keep a country which it mismanaged so disastrously. The Irish were not to be blamed if they looked to the Pope, to Spain, to France,

---

[1] Froude, in describing the scheme of colonisation of Ireland, tells how a number of English adventurers, chiefly from Somersetshire and Devonshire —Gilberts, Chichesters, Carews, Grenvilles, Courtenays—twenty-seven in all, had volunteered to colonise that part of Munster to the west of a line drawn from the mouth of the Shannon to Cork, and how several of them—Sir Peter Carew, Warham St. Leger, Richard Grenville, Humphrey Gilbert, and others— having advanced some sort of fanciful claim to certain lands in that region, set out to take possession of them without even waiting for permission; how they carried with them, under the name of servants, a considerable number of retainers, how St. Leger and Grenville laid hold of a number of farms and castles in the neighbourhood of Cork which the MacCarthys and Geraldines supposed to belong to themselves, and how Carew laid claim to lands in Idrone then in possession of the Butlers. (*Hist. of England*, c. lix.)

to any friend in earth or heaven, to deliver them from a Power which discharged no single duty that rulers owe to subjects." [1]

The Munster clans caught fire ; MacCarthy More (who had already renounced his English title of Earl), James Fitzmaurice, and the South-Western chiefs, held a meeting (or " parliament ") in Kerry which laid the foundations of the " Desmond Combination." They were determined to use the opportunity of the quarrel between the Butlers and the English for a common rising to save themselves from the impending destruction. Edmund Butler had left the Dublin Parliament in disgust when Sydney had carried the abolition of the Irish captainries and the erection of the Irish countries into shire lands.

It is important to have a clear idea of what was meant by Irish captainries, [2] which were one of the most prominent and indeed essential features of the ruling family system during the first half of Elizabeth's reign. They consisted in the age-old right of every great Irish Lord or Chief to maintain a fighting force for his defence against unruly neighbours, and for the protection of the under chiefs and nobles from whom he received tribute in one way or another. This fighting force was recruited from three classes : (1) the younger sons, brothers, relatives and retainers of the Lord ; (2) hired troops from one or other of the mercenary clans, such as the Sheehys and the MacSwineys, who fought for the highest bidder ; (3) and freeholders and the members of the tributary families.

The members of the first class, " idle men " or " half sirs," as they were called, were young men who did little work, hung on to the big houses, and by long-established custom had the right to quarter themselves on the tributary families at certain times. This right, called coyne and livery, pressed heavily on these families, was open to grave abuse, and was one that members could hardly be sorry to see abolished. This was the permanent bodyguard or standing army on a small scale. The members of the second class— the hired troops—were called in only on special occasions and in times of great urgency, and were paid by the Lord himself, but were quartered, also by coyne and livery, on

[1] Froude, *Hist. of England*, x. 236.
[2] See *Catholic Bulletin*, July, 1926, pp. 745-51.

the tributary families. The third class furnished a quota of men up to a certain extent for a certain period of military service, whenever called on for the " rising out." This period seldom exceeded a couple of months, during which they also were quartered on the members. But when that period expired, and they were free to return to their homes, the chief who had to wage a long campaign soon found his forces diminished.

Had this system been used as a defensive measure, and in the interests of the country as a whole, the English could never have hoped to conquer it. But when used, as it was only too often, for purposes of aggression, jealousy, and vengeance, it led to disunion, dissension, and internecine strife which weakened the country and smoothed the road for the invader. Defective though it was, the English Government in Ireland was quite alive to the fact that it placed in the hands of the Irish chiefs a formidable weapon against their schemes of colonisation and reformation all over the land. Very naturally then, Sydney and Cecil included in their schemes the abolition of Irish captainries and coyne and livery on the ostensible ground that they only fostered discord and strife, and placed an intolerable burden on the rank and file of the people of the ruling families of the country. In reality, they were moved by the desirability of removing the one great obstacle that stood in the way of complete conquest.

When, therefore, towards the end of 1569, the chiefs and lords came to know of the Bill for the abolition of these their rights, they saw that there was not a chief in Ireland who was not affected by the measure. The loyal Ormonds as well as the more independent Geraldines, the Anglo-Normans as well as the Celts, all were opposed to it. Thus, within a few weeks, the foundations were laid of a confederacy that, for the time at least, buried the rivalries and animosities of centuries. In one shape or other this confederacy lasted for almost fifteen years, cost both England and Ireland untold sums of money, and countless lives. Early, then, in the year 1569, the movement among the chiefs had developed into a formidable conspiracy, of which the Government soon became aware.

JAMES FITZMAURICE.

Very little has survived to indicate the origin and growth of the Confederacy. There is practically no record on the Irish side, and naturally the chief confederates took great care that the Council of Ireland in Dublin knew as little as possible of what was going on. But one can picture the meetings of the local chiefs in remote spots, the conferences between the chiefs of one province with those of another, the passing of the messengers, chiefly roving friars, unobserved from house to house, expounding projects and securing signatures. One can picture also, conferences with bishops and leading ecclesiastics, some of whom might give ready acceptance to the projects, and others rather slow in committing themselves on the plea of letting well enough alone. The position, put clearly enough, was that if the old Celtic system was to be saved, if the Catholic Church was to be preserved in Ireland, the whole country must combine, and thus combined must appeal to Spain and Rome for help in the struggle that was now inevitable.

One of the curiosities of Irish history is to be found in the inadequate, or negligent, or even hostile way in which James Fitzmaurice has been treated by writers of all colours.[1]

[1] O'Sullivan Beare's *Catholic History*, so full of detail concerning the period immediately following Fitzmaurice's death, is strangely at fault in narrating the events of his life. Dominic Daly (*Geraldines*), whose work was really a panegyric of the Munster Geraldines, and who wrote some thirty years later than O'Sullivan, leaves much to be desired in the way of accuracy. Subsequent historians, down to our own day, have merely copied their blunders or omissions, or coloured them still more darkly by the additions of one-sided assertions and reports found in the *State Papers* which have become available during the past century. Stranger still, the *Four Masters*, writing at a time when the memory of the events in which Fitzmaurice took so prominent a part, was still comparatively fresh in mind, dispose of him in this fashion : That in 1569 he was " a warlike man of many troops," that he took part in a confederacy of the Munster Irish from the Barrow to Mizen Head, that Sydney was able to crush him completely the next year because " he was opposed by the whole country " ; that while he took Kilmallock in 1571 by the aid of " the Irish soldiers, insurgents, mercenaries, and retained troops of the country," Perrott, the new President of Munster, was joined at once by " the chiefs, noble rulers, lords and dynasts of the province," and how, nevertheless, he carried on the struggle till the spring of 1573, when, his object having been partially attained, he surrendered to the President.

Briefly, the reason for this is to be found in the accession of James VI of Scotland as James I of England after the death of Queen Elizabeth. The Catholics of Ireland never lost sight of the fact (?) that he was son to Mary Queen of Scots, whom many of them regarded as a martyr for the old faith. They knew, too, that he was said to have leanings towards the Catholic Church, and that on this understanding he had been in receipt of subsidies from the Pope. They had reason for believing that more than once he had favoured or connived at the forces that had occasionally been supplied from Scotland to the Irish chiefs in their struggles against Elizabeth. The advent of such a man was hailed with delight and hope by the beaten ruling families and crushed chieftains. James, the descendant of Edward Bruce, the last-crowned Celtic King of Ireland in the fourteenth century, was regarded as an Irish King as well, and could, therefore, be regarded as rightful sovereign of the Kingdom of Ireland.

One of the first to turn this pleasant fancy to account was Archbishop Lombard of Armagh, agent for the Irish chiefs in Rome, but who never saw his diocese from the day of his consecration in 1601 till that of his death in 1625. He took, however, an active part in Irish affairs, and for some years at least his word carried great weight both in Ireland and in Rome. Like most of the Anglo-Irish, he cherished hopes from the beginning that James I would become a Catholic, but, when these hopes had proved vain, he directed all his efforts to softening the sovereign's heart, and thus secure a tolerable measure of freedom for the Catholics of Ireland. This, he thought, could best be done by claiming or recognising the Stuart King as lineal descendant of the last-crowned King of Ireland, and therefore rightful wearer of the Irish crown.[1]

Ere many years had passed, the legend had been elevated

---

[1] This line of reasoning was eagerly grasped by the Anglo-Irish chiefs and nobles who came out of the struggle against England with increased if not preponderating influence in Irish politics. In their efforts to play the game and to please the new-found Irish King, they stopped short at nothing, not even at voting for the confiscation of Ulster, thereby enabling the Stuart monarch to plant the broad acres of the O'Neills, O'Donnells, and allied clans with his countrymen and adventurous colonists from England, whose descendants remain in possession to this very day.

to the rank of a national tradition.[1] Under its influence
Irish historians no less than Anglo-Irish writers were anything
at all but ready to emphasise the struggles that had been
waged against Queen Elizabeth for more than half a century.
They were, therefore, driven to gloss over or explain away
the deeds that in normal times would have immortalised the
men who led the movements against her Majesty. The
Four Masters, for instance, refer to Fitzmaurice's efforts as
directed against " the Queen's Parliament," rather than
against the Queen herself. If we were to take their pages
at their face value we should be forced to conclude that
they were altogether unaware that the movement of which
Fitzmaurice was the life and soul had the sympathy and
sometimes the active support of practically every chief and
ruling family in Ireland. Nay, more, one might conclude
that they were unaware of the cordial co-operation of the
Irish bishops, the zealous help of the whole Franciscan body,
the connivance or open assistance of the Courts of France,
Spain, and Portugal, with copious supplies of the " Wine
from the Royal Pope."

As a consequence of this coldness or neglect or downright
suppression on the part of Irish historians, the deeds of
James Fitzmaurice have been allowed to be unrecorded in
the achives of Europe, his memory to be consigned to practical
oblivion, and the way left open to the enemies of his country
to paint him in dark colours.[2]

[1] Those who desire to see the lengths to which it was carried have but
to glance through the pages of two of the most influential Irish writers of this
and the succeeding reign, David Rothe, Bishop of Ossory, and Archdeacon
Lynch of Tuam. Its effect in moulding the destinies of the nation throughout
the seventeenth and eighteenth centuries may be seen in the insane feeling
and affection for the Stuarts which was the main cause of the collapse of the
Confederation of Kilkenny and paved the way for Cromwell's march through
Ireland, and finally committed vocal Ireland to the cause of James II and the
pretenders, thus affording the Williamite settlers a specious excuse for the
penal code that disgraced English rule in Ireland and made the man of Irish
blood a serf on his own soil.

[2] Even Thomas Russell, probably a friar, in his " Relation of the Geraldines,"
drawn up in 1638 (*Hist. and Arch. Assoc.*, 1868-69, p. 361 *seq.*), whose father
had served in the Fitzmaurice Confederacy, although he takes a pride in the
House of Desmond and shows a personal admiration for James, yet carried
away by the legend, he does not hesitate to characterise him as " a scourge "
responsible for " the final overthrow and last downfall of the famous house
of the Geraldines of Munster." Russell, however, is careful to insist that

In the name of religion and country Fitzmaurice succeeded in uniting all Ireland in a solemn confederacy against Elizabeth in 1569, took the field against her forces, and laid the foundations of a spirit of resistance which was to survive for many generations. He made his country known and respected in many lands, and was welcomed in many foreign Courts, and won the confidence of Pope and Cardinal. His steps abroad were dogged by spies and informers who more than once were Irishmen in the pay of England. For the space of ten eventful years his name was a nightmare and his deeds a source of constant fear to English officials who saw in him the incarnation of all that was bad, just as his own countrymen looked to him for inspiration and direction in the dark days through which they moved.[1]

PARLIAMENT OF THE IRISH IN MUNSTER ; TWO BISHOPS SENT TO SPAIN FOR AID.

Sir Warham Sentleger, President of Munster, wrote from Cork, 14 February, to Sydney [2] that on the previous day, Sunday, Cormac, the brother of Sir Dermot MacTeig, came to him. Cormac had been " with the Earl of Clancarty, James Fitzmaurice, McDonough [MacCarthy], and the rest of the Irishry of the south-west parts at the Parliament that they held. The whole effect of the assembly, as Cormac credibly informed me, was to resist the Deputy's devices, and resolved to send messengers to the King of Spain for

Fitzmaurice " stood out to re-establish the Roman religion in Ireland, which then began to be mightily oppressed." But he says nothing about the Pope, probably because it was not just then considered right and proper to recall the fact that the Pope of the day had extended help and encouragement to Irish rebels against the English Crown. In " The Pedigree of the Geraldines," where he is less constrained by political expediency, Russell gave free vent to his feelings of admiration for Fitzmaurice. He tells how he had travelled much in France, Spain, Flanders, Germany, and particularly in Poland, where he had won fame and promotion for his services against the Turks, and how the common soldiers in the Turkish army " were wont to say that the God of the Christians had raised up [another] Scanderberg to be revenged on them," so great was the terror his name inspired as a warrior in the Christian armies. (All this, of course, was pure fiction.)

[1] See *Catholic Bulletin*, August, 1926, pp. 834-40.
[2] *S.P.I.*, *Eliz.*, xxvii. 23, P.R.O., London.

aid to help them in this their lewd interprise." Sentleger was informed by Cormac and others that " those vile traitors have despatched into Spain to be practised in their villainy the Bishop of Ross in Carbery [Thomas O'Herlihy], the papist traitor in Ireland,[1] and also the usurped Bishop of Cashel [MacGibbon] whom traitors use as though he were a god." There was " great gossip between these two and great confirmation of friendship. These two devilish prelates be by James Fitzmaurice conveyed into Kerry, the Earl of Desmond's liberties, whence they are to be shipped, or else shall depart this land when wind serveth."

Sentleger considers that it is necessary to inform Her Majesty of all this, and suggests a plan for the plantation of Kerry. " Well-minded gentlemen should be sent who intend to venture their lives and livings in these parts ; if there should happen wars between her Majesty and the Spanish King it would be great danger to have the southmost parts unguarded ; chiefly, because the people of these parts of the country have a great liking for the Spanish people on account of their trafficking. The coming hither of those gentlemen with such force as they can bring preventeth all these mischiefs."

The project was evidently worth considering, and expert advice worth having, for, 21 March, one John Corbine reports to Cecil [2] that these harbours should be fortified, namely, Bear Haven, Crook Haven, Baltemor, Ogglevance River, Balinaskelligs, and Valentia. He assures him that " no shipping hurt them, and by land no man can come at them ; these are already fortified to the Spaniards, for every year 200 sail fisheth there, and carrieth away 2000 beeves, hides, and tallow." These places at present pay no dues to the Queen, and, a most important consideration for her, would be no charge upon her if they were in her hands. He advises that the McSweeneys' galleys should be destroyed, and reports that there is coin in MacCarthy's country.

It was not long until Sydney became aware that the Fitzmaurice conspiracy had the support of the most in-

---

[1] He had been at the Council of Trent ; hence the above description.
[2] *S.P.I., Eliz.*, xxvii. 57.

fluential chiefs in the land [1]—the Geraldines, the Butlers, the MacCarthys, the O'Sullivans, the Burkes, the O'Briens, the O'Rourkes, the O'Connors, the O'Mores, the Kavanaghs, and last but not least, Tirlogh Luineach, the head of the O'Neills. Though the English were not aware of the fact at the time, the episcopal envoys from Cashel and Ross brought with them to Spain an important document signed by twelve archbishops and bishops, six earls, and nineteen heads of ruling families (of which later).

CONFEDERATE WAR IN MUNSTER.

An alliance, somewhat unnatural, between the rival Butlers and Geraldines made a formidable insurrection possible. Only a couple of years previously the armies of these two houses had met in bloody battle. Further trouble had been summarily stopped by the energetic action of Sydney who had both Earls conveyed to London. Desmond was in the Tower, paid an enormous fine, and surrendered many acres and castles to the Queen. Ormond was a favourite at Court, but one could never tell how long Elizabeth would continue her good graces. In any event the House of Ormond was as closely affected as that of the Geraldines by the abolition of the system of captainries and of coyne and livery.

On the departure of Ormond for London in 1565 his brother Sir Edmund Butler had been made Captain of the Ormond clans, assisted by his two younger brothers, Edward and Piers. Edmund could not shut his eyes to the danger that confronted his House as long as its head was detained in London, exposed to the same pains and penalties as those inflicted on Desmond. His desire to raise and maintain an

---

[1] " James Fitzmaurice was joined in an unanimous and firm confederacy against the Queen's Parliament [*sic*] by the English and Irish of Munster, from the Barrow to Carn-Ui-Neid [near Mizen-head, S.W. Cork]. While Thomas, Earl of Ormond, was at this time in England, his brothers Edmond and Edward joined forces with James Fitzmaurice. These two went to the fair of Inis-Corr [probably Enniscorthy, Co. Wexford] on Great Lady-Day ; and it would be difficult to enumerate or describe all the steeds, horses, gold, silver, and foreign wares, they seized upon at that fair. The Earl [Ormond] returned to Ireland the same year, and his brothers were reconciled to the State." (*Four Masters.*)

armed force was fortified by the refusal of some of his tributary families to submit to the customary exactions of coyne and livery. Sydney had indeed prohibited such tributes and had forbidden Edmund to exact them, a command that the loyal Sir Edmund flatly refused to obey. In ever-increasing numbers Edmund marched his retainers into the territories of the refractory chiefs.[1] The gentlemen of Tipperary reminded Sydney in a haughty letter that " we and our ancestors acknowledged him [Ormond] as our Lord and Captain, and indeed know no other sovereign but him whose lieutenant is Sir Edmund Butler, his brother and heir-apparent."

It was not until towards the end of 1568, however, that Edmund's vision and interests travelled outside the borders of the Ormond Palatinate and were turned in the direction of a league with other Irish chiefs for the defence of their rights on something like a national scale. In this he was considerably influenced by the order awarding possession of certain lands of Idrone to Sir Peter Carew [2] which Edmund held and believed to be his own. " None but fools and slaves would sit still to be robbed," was the prompt comment of the Brothers Butler. Before many weeks had passed, they were in conference with the southern chiefs and particularly with James Fitzmaurice, the acting head of the Munster Geraldines.

The Captainry of the Munster Geraldines had been bestowed on James Fitzmaurice by the Earl of Desmond, a choice that had the cordial assent and approval of the Geraldines as a body. In this he was opposed by Thomas Roe Fitzgerald, who, though the eldest son of the late Earl of Desmond, had been excluded from the succession. On James Fitzmaurice fell the task of maintaining the absent Earl's rights against the claims of Thomas Roe and his English supporters. As happened in the case of the Butlers some of the tributary families of the Geraldines took advantage of the abolition of coyne and livery and refused to pay the customary exactions to the head of the House of Desmond. One of these was Lord Fitzmaurice of Kerry against whom

[1] *S.P.I., Eliz.,* xxix. 56, 57.   [2] *Ib.,* 60, i., iii.

James Fitzmaurice, as we have seen, led a punitive expedition right up to the door of the Kerry chief's castle at Lixnaw.

The signal for further trouble to the Butler-Geraldine alliance was evidenced in the departure of Richard Grenville, sheriff of Cork, for England. Grenville had made a beginning of colonisation by seizing lands to the west of Cork harbour. MacCarthy More and Fitzmaurice, with the seneschal of Imokilly, the White Knight, and other chiefs, and 4000 men, took Tracton Abbey and the country in charge of Sentleger. Fitzmaurice declared that help was coming from Spain, that Edmund Butler was on his side, and that he could take the artillery at Kinsale when he pleased. He vowed that he would never depart from Cork until Lady Sentleger, Lady Grenville, with the rest of the English, and Barry Oge, Cormac MacTeig, with all other prisoners, were delivered up to him. It was reported to Sydney that all the country between Cork and Kinsale is destroyed, and that unless the Deputy come with a main army, the whole country is likely to be overthrown. It were better to the Queen to spend £40,000 than that Cork should be lost.[1]

About the same time Sir Edmund Butler, with his brothers, Piers and Edward, devastated the eastern part of Queen's County. The sheriff of Kilkenny had called a general hosting for 15 July, but Butler's " rage and tyranny " prevented that service. MacCarthy More and Fitzmaurice had meantime left the Butlers and proceeded to Kilmallock which they attacked, extorting a ransom of £160. At Limerick Fitzmaurice met the Earl of Thomond and John Burke, the Earl of Clanricard's son, and held a Parliament at Blackstones. At Waterford, reported the Mayor and Corporation, the Geraldines burned and slew where they listed, forced " good subjects to become partners of their confederacy, or else to end their wretched lives by famine." They further stated that the rebels stripped honest men and women naked, and tormented them with more cruel pains " than either Phalaris or any of the old tyrants could invent." But even before the open rebellion great disorders had been caused by the general poverty.

[1] *S.P.I., Eliz.*, xxviii. 37, 38, 43, 44.

Briefly, the situation was thus : Waterford was a stronghold for its own people, and a refuge for many others, but the confederates held the open country. Edmund and Piers Butler devoted themselves to the district between Waterford and the Pale. North of the Pale was held by Tirlogh Luineach. Edward Butler was busy south-west of Waterford. Fitzmaurice preached a crusade in the Desmond country, calling on the citizens of Cork and the clergy of the diocese to "abolish out of that city that old heresy raised and invented," and to send away all Protestants by the next wind, "namely, Barnaby Daly and all them that be Huguenots,"[1] and Grenville's wife and children. "The Queen," he said, "is not satisfied with our worldly goods, bellies, and lives, but must also counsel us to forsake the Catholic faith by God unto His Church given, and by the See of Rome hitherto prescribed to all Christian men. . . . If you follow not this Catholic and wholesome exhortation, I will not nor may not be your friend."[2] Viscount Decies, Lord Roche, and Lord Barrymore sent answer to the confederates to do their worst to them for they would be true servants to the Queen.

Sydney left Dublin in July, rebuked Kilkenny, was snubbed by Tipperary, and received no help from Waterford, the citizens claiming exemption under their charter.[3] Resistance was offered him at Mitchelstown, the garrison stating that they held the place for God and James Fitzmaurice, but the place was taken by assault and Lord Roche's son left in possession. Sydney pushed on to Cork where the wavering citizens were confirmed in their allegiance. Castles in the Mallow district were seized, the chiefs taking the oath of allegiance. Limerick was reached (17 October) where Sydney was joined by Ormond.[4] Lord Fitzmaurice, William Burke of Clanwilliam,[5] and MacSheehy, captain of Desmond's

---

[1] I.e. the colonists.   [2] *S.P.I., Eliz.*, xxix. 8.

[3] "Sir Philip Sydney, having sent to the Mayor of Waterford for an assistance of men only for three days, the said Mayor arrogantly sent him word that he would send him none, pleading this a privilege amongst others granted unto the city of Waterford that they were not at any time compellible to go or send to any hosting except the King or his son were there present in person." (Loftus, *Annals, ad an.*, 1569.)

[4] *S.P.I., Eliz.*, xxix. 68, 70, 78.

[5] *Kilk. Arch. Soc.*, 1858-59, p. 355 *seq.* ; 1890, p. 194 *seq.*

galloglasses, also swore allegiance. Edward and Piers Butler likewise submitted. But Edmund soon afterwards escaped from Dublin Castle and was led safely through the Wicklow mountains by young Feagh MacHugh O'Byrne and others.[1] He reached Holy Cross, Tipperary (25 November), where he offered a thankoffering for his escape. Sydney was highly indignant, and stated that " he has done more mischief than any rebel in the memory of men," and Sydney and Ormond blamed each other for want of loyalty, jealousy, and the rest. Even the Countess of Desmond abused James Fitzmaurice, attributed his rebellion to his desire to usurp the Desmond inheritance, and signified her intention to repair to the Queen to plead for the Earl's release. The destruction of the country was so great, it was stated, that she could get no money.

James Fitzmaurice, closely pursued, withdrew to the glen of Aherlow, Co. Tipperary. Ormond was again abused by Sydney for his slackness, and Fitzmaurice was called an Irish beggar. But Sydney did not care to push Ormond's loyalty too far lest the Queen's favourite might round on him. It was Captain Humphrey Gilbert who, ignoring the charters of the corporate towns in the Ormond country, declared that the Queen had absolute power, and acted fully up to his opinion. Under his drastic treatment all the Geraldines, except James Fitzmaurice, submitted, and the MacCarthy Mores acknowledged their treason on their knees. Gilbert, who was knighted by Sydney, was able to declare that the city gates lay open, and the English name was never so much feared in Ireland. It needed now only a good sour lawyer to manage the escheats of the forfeited estates, and a Council with President in Munster. " These people are headstrong," he wrote to Sydney, " and if they feel the curb loosed but one link, they will, with bit in the teeth, in one month run further out of the career of good order than they will be brought back in three months." On the other hand, Sydney, thwarted at home, and in bad health, begged earnestly for his own recall. All classes were against him, and he felt as if he could not live another six months in Ireland.[2]

[1] *S.P.I.*, *Eliz.*, xxix. 81, 86.   [2] *Ib.*, 78, 81, 83.

Whilst Geraldines and Butlers, for once united by fear of losing their lands, kept the south of Ireland in a turmoil, the Ulster ruling families were unusually quiet. But some intrigues were being carried on between the chieftains. Terence Daniel, Dean of Armagh, sent a servant to confer with the Donnellaghs, his kinsmen, and to make them promise not to join Tirlogh Luineach. Tirlogh, for the present, was busy receiving his new wife, James McDonnell's widow, and daughter of the Earl of Argyle. She brought with her 1200 Scots at least. Tirlogh had now between 3000 and 5000 men under his orders, and was reported by Daniel (to the Lord Chancellor and Council) as intending to attack Newry. Daniel was acting as Government spy on Tirlogh and begged that powder should be sent in haste. Tirlogh Brasselagh also acted the spy and, whilst urging on Tirlogh, informed the Dean that the English army or the force of the orders should be sent against him.[1] The arrival of Ormond in Ireland left the Earl of Kildare free, and the forces of the Pale were drawn northwards. Sydney followed later and found that the Scots had eaten Tirlogh out of house and home who could no longer support them, or make any move. Tirlogh was useless, therefore, to Fitzmaurice. The Butlers having submitted, the confederacy from which so much had been expected fell to pieces.

IRELAND LOOKS TO SPAIN AND ROME FOR HELP.

The fear of losing their lands had bound the Irish chiefs and nobles together. If Elizabeth would not interfere with their land and religion, they asked for no other sovereign. Capable statesmanship on the English side would have brought about a peaceful solution of the land problem. But to put an end to internal Irish squabbles Elizabeth's advisers saw no other means than the sword. In the centuries previous these squabbles were the main components of the Anglo-Irish relations. Now, however, Elizabeth had introduced a sharp thorn into Ireland's side. The Irish chiefs were not only to profess loyalty to her as to a sovereign but to profess

---

[1] *S.P.I., Eliz.*, xxix. 44, 45.

the religion that had lately originated in England.[1] With very few exceptions the Irish chiefs were Catholics. Deprived of their property and power by Elizabeth, not only could the Catholic churches not be supported by tithes as they had been for centuries, but the priests dared not conduct the religious services in public for the people. This was the situation that confronted the Irish chiefs, especially since the scheme of provincial presidencies had been set to work. No one felt its poignancy more than James Fitzmaurice. He was an ardent Catholic and enthusiastic Irishman, and believed that the Queen's misdeeds would bring about a crusade. With this in view he sent Archbishop MacGibbon of Cashel and Bishop O'Herlihy of Ross to Spain to procure the necessary aid. For the next ten years the centre of Irish interest is transferred to the Continent, shifting between Spain, France, and Rome. During those years the fretful form of Eire stands on the southern shore peering into the mists and gazing across the waters watching for the foreign galleys to bring " Spanish Ale " or " Wine from the Royal Pope." What the disappointments were which crushed her soul will be the principal subject of the remaining two periods of this history.

There was much trade between Spain and the rest of Munster, the foreigners carrying away fish, beef, hides, and tallow in exchange for wine and sometimes for arms. It was to these havens on the Kerry coast that Spanish galleys were likely to come. They afforded easy access as well as being secure from the land side on account of the mountains. Constant watch was kept by the inhabitants, and many false rumours only opened fresh sores in the disappointed natives. Irish priests and students were constantly travelling to and from Louvain, Paris, and Rome. Doubtless they lost no opportunity of telling Englishmen and foreigners of the English abuses in religious matters in Ireland. They might tell how Sydney had one archbishopric and two bishoprics in farm for a mere trifle and had Cashel for £40. The revenues of one See supported the grand falconer, and those of another

---

[1] Mr. Baldwin and Sir W. Joynson-Hicks candidly admitted that England owes its established religion to the Reformation (*Prayer Book Debate in the House of Commons*).

the clerk of the kitchen. These two men were said to be " sufficient persons no doubt to have such cure of Irish souls as the English doctrine will permit them to have at this day." By Elizabeth's parsimony the deanery of St. Patrick's was appropriated to the support of the Lord Chancellor, much to the disgust of the Chancellor—Dean Weston—who saw the abuse clearly enough. The parsonage of Dungarvan was assigned for the maintenance of the Lord President. Laymen were appointed to ecclesiastical dignities. All these abuses would be told in the halls of the universities and in the courts of the Continent.

The gentry of the Pale and of the greater part of Leinster were Catholics at heart, only waiting for the opportunity to profess openly. In Ulster all were ardent Catholics, but loyal, when necessary, to the Queen. Connacht, besides being Catholic, was anti-English, although Galway sang the *Te Deum* at the coming of Sydney. In the Desmond portion of Munster all were Catholics and Confederates, daily expecting help from France and Spain. Thomond had done useful work in France for Ireland. Ormond was the broken link in the Irish chain. The bishops of Ulster, Connacht, and Munster were Catholics with a few exceptions. Those of Leinster were, of course, Protestant, all, except one, having been recently appointed by Elizabeth. The northern clergy looked to Raymond O'Gallagher, Bishop of Derry, who had lately returned from Rome. Munster built its hopes on Archbishop MacGibbon of Cashel, who had gone to Spain.

PART III.

" SPANISH ALE."

ARCHBISHOP OF CASHEL IN SPAIN ; LETTERS TO THE KING AND THE POPE.

MacGibbon, the representative of the Southern Confederates to Spain and Rome, set out in February, 1569, along with the Bishop of Ross, and was escorted from Cashel to the sea coast with solemn pomp by James Fitzmaurice and the other leaders of the Confederates. The case of the Confederates is told by MacGibbon in his Latin letters to the Pope and Philip of Spain,[1] in the name of the Bishops and Nobility of Ireland. He began by pointing out the fidelity of Ireland to the Holy See, during the 1127 years since the preaching of St. Patrick in 443 [2] and the " divers schisms, errors, and heresies of the unstable and restless sect and nation of the kingdom of England." He then continues :—

Your Holiness and your Catholic Majesty must know that all the nobility and the entire people of that kingdom [Ireland] wish to walk as usual in the footsteps of their forefathers, and to remain firm, steadfast, and constant in the same faith and unity of the Catholic Church, and to persevere to the death in perpetual obedience and devotion to the Supreme Pontiffs and to the Apostolic See. They hate and abhor sects and heresies so much that they prefer to leave their homes and go abroad rather than to live under heretics, or to acquiesce in the errors and restlessness of the English, who, in the last schism under Henry VIII and Edward VI, plundered and devastated the churches and monasteries of Ireland, proscribed and afflicted Catholic bishops and religious persons, and threw the whole population into the greatest confusion. This Queen Elizabeth has revived the tragedy, and has imprisoned

[1] *Spic. Ossor.*, i. 59.
[2] This was a curious date at which to mark the beginning of St. Patrick's preaching.

the chief bishops and other religious persons of the kingdom for their perseverance in the faith and their Catholic obedience, and throughout the whole island has executed the policy of her father and brother with the greatest determination and vigour, sending new preachers and heretical bishops with great store of heretical books to be circulated among the people.

The Archbishop then prays that the Pope and the Spanish King may make it their immediate care that the Irish people " shall not be contaminated and destroyed by the accursed and contagious heresy which flourishes in England." He then continues :—

Your Holiness and your Catholic Majesty must know that it has long been, and now is, the highest desire of the nobility and all the people of that Kingdom to come absolutely under the patronage and protection of his Holiness, and of the most clement and Catholic King of Spain, to whom all men of position and property in that island look directly for the means of avoiding the affliction and danger of the heresy and schisms in the ever-changing Kingdom of England. They have, therefore, deliberately resolved, with God's help and the favour of the most clement Catholic King, to accept the person of any active Catholic prince of his Catholic Majesty's blood, whether of the Spanish or Burgundian branch, especially appointed by him for the purpose, and to receive him and crown him as their true, legitimate, and natural King, and thus to re-establish in perpetuity the royal throne of that island, and to venerate the presence of one King, one faith, and one kingdom, the donation of that island having been first obtained from and confirmed by the Apostolic See.[1]

Not without cause do all the states of that island most strongly desire this, since that kingdom in extent, in its temperate climate, in its fertility, and in its wealth, might well vie with the kingdom of England, if only it were ruled justly and piously by a religious resident Catholic Prince or royal head. They all in general detest the tyrannous and inconstant yoke of the English State, and still more its heresies, with which they desire to have nothing in common, except neighbourliness and Christian love.

Then follows a list of all the nobles, prelates, chiefs, and towns in Ireland that were prepared to promote Papal and Spanish interests in their country " together with those of many English residents in the island " :—

---

[1] MacGibbon believed in the authenticity of Adrian's Bull.

Archbishop of Armagh.
„   Dublin.
„   Cashel.
„   Tuam.
Bishop of Meath.
„   Kildare.
„   Waterford.
„   Cork.
„   Limerick.
„   Ossory.
„   Clonfert.
„   Ross.
Earl of Desmond.
„   Kildare.
„   Ormonde.
Lord O'Molaghlen.
„   Machartimor.
„   MacWilliam Burk.

Earl of Clanrickard.
„   Thomond.
„   Tyrone.
Lord O'Donald.
„   O'Bryn (O'Brien).
„   O'Rourk.
„   O'Reilly.
„   O'Conor Ruo.
„   O'Conor Don.
„   O'Conor Sligo.
„   O'Conor Assy.
„   O'Carvel.
„   O'Madyn.
„   O'Suyllevan Mor.
„   O'Suyllevan Berre.
„   MacGille-Patrik.
„   MacNemara.
„   MacMorgo (Murrough).

"With all the other bishops, prelates, religious, barons, nobles, knights, cities, towns, and the whole community of this kingdom."

It has been urged that of the twelve archbishops and bishops, six earls, and nineteen heads of ruling families, whose names were appended to the petition, some could not and others would not have signed it. There was, for instance, no Catholic Archbishop of Dublin, no Catholic Bishop of Ossory, no Catholic Bishop of Waterford ; it was not likely that either Archbishop Bodkin of Tuam or Bishop de Burgh of Clonfert would have signed it, and it was certain that the Earl of Ormond would not assent to it. All that is quite true, but the promoters of the petition seemed to have been satisfied with the signature or assent of the acting head of each diocese or ruling family severally concerned in the transaction—for instance of the Vicar of the diocese of Dublin, of Sir Edmund Butler for the Earl of Ormond, and of James Fitzmaurice for the Earl of Desmond.

Whether Archbishop MacGibbon did really get the assent of all these parties, or took for granted their assent with moral certainty that it would have been given, there seems to have been some misgiving in the mind of Philip II of Spain as to the authority behind the petition. The document itself in the Spanish archives has the following note added in Spanish, in Philip II's own hand, for the instruction of the Prime Minister : " I know not the meaning of this letter or who it is that sends it, and I have received no communication about it. It is the same statement which the Nuncio gave the other day. These letters will be considered in Council, but not the others which came with them which my confessor has, and which I will forward before post hour ; you will return them, and advise what answer should be given."

Papal Bombshell ; Archbishop of Cashel's Reply.

Nevertheless, the Archbishop was kindly received, was listened to with attention, and was given to understand that the King was well disposed and was likely to take action in the desired direction. On the strength of these assurances, he sent more than one message to the Irish chiefs assuring them of practical help. Scarcely had favourable news arrived from Spain when Fitzmaurice raised the standard of revolt, as we have seen, and swept down on the lands and towns occupied by the loyal colonists, especially on the City of Cork. To the Chapter and Clergy of that city he sent a message " to frame themselves to honour God as your ancestors have done, and to destroy out of the town all the Hugenots with the first wind."

A veritable bombshell, however, soon burst over MacGibbon's head from the Holy See in reply to the duplicate copy of the petition which he had sent to the Pope (1 March). The Holy Father (wrote the Cardinal Secretary of State, 9 June) [1] is amazed that the Archbishop has promised to the King of Spain, on behalf of the Irish, obedience to anything he may command. It should be remembered that the Kingdom of Ireland belongs to the ecclesiastical dominion under the title of the fief, and so cannot be granted to any other sovereignty except by the Pope who safeguards it, as is his duty, as a right of the church ; the Pope refuses to address to the King any such letters as your request. However, if the King asks that the fief of such a kingdom be granted to him the Pope will not, I think, refuse it to him.

[1] See *Catholic Bulletin*, Jan., 1925, pp. 45-54.

MacGibbon received this letter two months later, and replied to it after three days. He was somewhat upset, he says, that the Pope did not approve of the advice of the nobles of Ireland about bestowing the Kingdom of Ireland on the Catholic King. They did not mean to deprive the Church of its rights in the matter, but rather that they might be released from the tyranny and cruel yoke of the English. He then continues :—

But was not England itself a fief of the church ? And nevertheless according to the decrees of the Pope himself and the Sacred Council of Trent it is permitted to any Catholic prince willing to do so to take by force of arms the whole English power. I always thought that the Supreme Pontiff, as soon as he understood the nature of my embassy would at once wish the Catholic King to be exhorted to undertake such a pious work. Are we then to wait until his Holiness delivers us from the hands of the English ; or until the King of France, who can scarcely defend himself, does so ? Who more powerful, I ask, than the Catholic King of Spain, who more devout, more obedient to the Pope or in a better position to make the attempt ? If Ireland but knew that his Holiness could snatch her from the jaws of the English she certainly would have addressed no other sovereign than the Supreme Pontiff. Who can blame the captive for trying to recover his liberty by the first means that comes to his hand ? Your Eminence may say that the sway of the Spaniards is just as galling as that of any other nation. I am free to confess that if anyone had asked me fifty years ago which rule I would prefer to be under, perhaps I should have answered England ; but as things have turned out in the interval there is all the difference in the world between Spanish and English rule. If in England or Ireland a man now hears Mass or receives the Eucharist in a becoming and Catholic manner, goes to Confession, and receives the other sacraments, or seeks any little favour of the Apostolic See, he becomes at once convicted of the crime of treason. Yet all these are done in Spain with impunity, and there is praise for those who do them and punishment for those who neglect them. Here again, Your Eminence may say that all this is nothing to the point, and that whoever wishes to obtain the throne in Ireland must first ask it of the Supreme Pontiff. This, too, I freely acknowledge, and I doubt not that the Catholic King will do so. But in my humble opinion the Irish should not be accused of want of respect and reverence in offering to come under the Catholic King. How

else could they have hoped to win the ears of one who has so much
to occupy his time and attention ? And, in any event, so great
is his piety that I know he would not listen to us unless we had
the consent of his Holiness. Your Eminence will kindly bear
in mind that unless the King of Spain, or some other Catholic
sovereign, brings aid quickly to our nobles neither the Pope nor
Spain nor France will be able to provide a remedy howsoever
willing they may be. Such are already the preparations and
the power of the English through the recent friendship and the
new alliances made with the prince and cities of Germany, that
the result will be not only bad for Ireland, and such as never before,
but for Scotland, France, Flanders, and the whole of Europe. But
if it pleases his Holiness that I should desist from this embassy,
I shall do so most willingly as becomes a most obedient servant,
return home, and prepare my neck for the axe, as others of us
also must do, unless Divine Providence, from some other source,
provides the remedy. I beg that his Holiness write to me as
soon as possible what he wishes done in the matter, whether he
wishes the Catholic King to lend aid or not, and what I am to
do, for it is necessary that I return home soon to feed the flock
committed to my care. I have already written to his Holiness
how the Lord Deputy of Ireland besieged a certain castle of mine,
and, among other things carried off my Pallium. And I wrote
to Rome that his Holiness would send me another and you replied
that you would do so when I returned to my diocese. His Holiness
must understand that, when I return, I cannot so easily send another
messenger to Rome, nor can a messenger from Rome reach me
easily, for almost all the ports of Ireland are in the hands of the
English. It would be much more convenient to send by a Spanish
messenger to Secretary Cayas, the Spanish King's secretary,
how matters stand, and so I shall be informed before I depart
from this Court.

The Archbishop's advice and vision were sound. He saw
clearly the danger of delay in sending aid, danger not only
to Ireland but to Scotland and Spanish Flanders. Had his
advice been acted upon at the time, the history of the next
ten years, and probably of succeeding generations might have
been quite different. It was a turning-point in the history
of Europe and provides the theorist with one of those big
" If's " of history.

PAPAL POLICY : ENGLISH INFLUENCE.

The Archbishop's letter certainly did not err on the side of mildness. Had he been better acquainted with the ways of diplomatic correspondence he would have taken the Cardinal's letter more calmly. The latter's rebuff was really meant for the King of Spain with whom the Pope was utterly tired because of his toleration of Elizabeth's doings during the past ten years. He had closed his ears to the cry of the English Catholic refugees on the Continent who had been vainly calling upon him for help to secure the removal of Elizabeth from the English throne and the settling thereupon of Mary Queen of Scots. A rising did take shape in England in 1569, with help from Spain, under the leadership of the Duke of Norfolk who was to marry Mary Queen of Scots. The Duke proved a broken reed, and as time went on they had to select another prospective husband for Mary.

Just at this time the English refugees formed an influential band, some of whom were at work in Spain, some in the Spanish dominions of Flanders, and some in the city of Rome. In Rome and its neighbourhood a group of English and Welsh ecclesiastics and laymen surrounded the Pope and dinned into his ears the cry of their persecuted people. Although they would favour the fomenting of trouble in Ireland against Elizabeth, it by no means followed that they would wish to see Ireland separated from the English Crown or that they would welcome a Spanish ruler at their doors just as they were endeavouring to put Mary Stuart on the throne. The Pope was aware of this point of view, and, as Philip had rendered little help to the English, his Holiness administered a gentle and indirect rebuff to him for his remissness. The letter to the Archbishop of Cashel was the means he employed. There was no Irishman of note in the city of Rome at the time, indeed there was hardly an Irishman at all there to say a word for the Irish cause. Accordingly, a policy that was to hold the field for many a weary year was taken up by the Holy See, and formed the groundwork of the reply that so filled the Archbishop with confusion and led to the writing of his outspoken letter to the Cardinal Secretary. This was to the effect that, as Ireland was a

fief of the Holy See, whatever prince went to her help
should have the sanction of the Pope who would lay
down and impose the conditions under which that help
might be given. This, of course, did not mean that the
Pope was not anxious to see Ireland relieved, and at once,
but English influence made him guarded in showing any
favour to any foreign ruler's presumption to take the Crown
of Ireland. Thus the papal letter to the Archbishop of
Cashel reminded him that the Pope was the master, and
intimated to Philip that his assistance should be subject
to papal supervision especially in its ultimate object. In
other words, that although Philip might assist the Irish to
drive Elizabeth out of Ireland he should not expect the
dominion of Ireland without papal sanction. These two
conflicting aims kept Ireland in weary waiting for many
years.

Philip of Spain Temporises.

After the papal rebuff to Philip II of Spain for his inactivity in lending help to the English Catholics, the King
gradually came round to the notion of having Mary Stuart
placed on the English throne. He had been rather averse
from this idea, as the accession of the francophile Queen of
Scots, the widow of a French King, seemed to him to mean
a strengthening of France and a consequent danger to Spain.
But now as France was weakened by internal feuds, and
England had grossly offended him through her pirates and
the confiscation of Spanish gold, he gradually adopted another
line of action. One of the ways in which he could help
English Catholics was by helping and directing an Irish
insurrection which would be most embarrassing to Elizabeth.
He therefore detained the Archbishop of Cashel in Spain,
adopted his accustomed rôle of temporising, made vague
promises of help, and took some steps to ascertain for himself the real position in Ireland by means of special envoys
sent to this country.[1]

In his correspondence (18 November, 1569) [2] with his

---

[1] See *Cal. Spanish Papers* for correspondence with ambassador in London,
1569. See *Catholic Bulletin*, Jan., 1925, p. 53.

[2] *C.Sp.P.*, no. 158.

ambassador in London he confesses his willingness to accept the offer of the sovereignty of Ireland made by the Archbishop, and to give effective help ; " but the noise the thing would create and the jealousy it would arouse in France, not to mention the obstacles it would present to the carrying through of the present negotiations with the Queen of England, have induced me rather to detain the Archbishop with fair words and money for his expenses until I see how these negotiations are going to turn out." Should Elizabeth, he adds, prove amenable to reason, and should the old alliance with her be renewed, he could not, in that case, think of helping the Irish against her ; but he would ask her to allow them liberty in the practice of their religion, and he would then send the Archbishop back to his country as well satisfied as possible under the circumstances. " But if she should be shameless enough to force us to break with her, I think it would be well to seize Ireland, as the Irish are constantly begging me to do—and it would be done easily with troops sent from Spain. If she saw me in possession of that island it would give her something to talk about." In view of that possibility, he therefore requires the ambassador to supply him with " full information with regard to the state of affairs in Ireland, and what forces the Catholics of the country have against the heretic Queen. I also wish to know if they would be parties to expelling them, and what leaders the Catholics have who could be made much of. Make every effort to investigate this thoroughly, and report to me by first opportunity."

A month later (16 December) [1] he was less sanguine of being able to move Elizabeth by persuasive methods alone, and was afraid that force must be used if religion is to be restored, and oppression to be banished out of her dominions. " We think here," he wrote to his ambassador, " that the best course will be to encourage the Catholics of the North [of England] with money and secret favour, and to help those in Ireland to take up arms against the heretics and deliver the crown to the Queen of Scotland, to whom it belongs by succession. This course, it is presumed, would be very

[1] *C.Sp.P.*, no. 165.

agreeable to the Pope and to all Christendom, and would encounter no opposition from anyone. . . . What you say is very true, that we are beginning to lose reputation by deferring so long to provide a remedy for the great grievance done by this woman [Elizabeth] to my subjects, friends and allies." Philip had already lost ten months in suggesting the remedy. Had he acted then, he would have accomplished much, but he was to waste, not ten months, but ten years.

During the following year, 1570, Philip occasionally mentioned the subject in his letters to the ambassador who informed him that the conquest of Ireland would be comparatively easy. Elizabeth, he noted, received but a small revenue from the country, because she purposely kept it uncultivated lest it should tempt some prince or other to enter into possession of it, and because the English feared that, if civilised, it might become more populous and powerful than England.

It was not without good reason, therefore, that the Archbishop of Cashel wrote encouraging letters to Fitzmaurice and his confederates, assuring them of help from Spain in the shape of money, arms, and munitions, if not of men. Without warning, however, he saw his negotiations upset by the advent and machinations of that amazing English buccaneer, Thomas Stucley.

Meanwhile, efforts were being made in Rome to deal with the " presumptions and persecutions " of the " pretended " Queen of England.

Bull of Pius V; Elizabeth Excommunicated.

By the beginning of 1569 all hopes of Elizabeth's conversion had vanished, and the Pope had definitely taken up the cause of the Queen of Scots, who for nearly twenty years was to form the pivot around which papal and Spanish diplomacy revolved in all that concerned the future of the Church in the British Isles. Again, as in 1568, England was disappointed in her expectation of help from Spain, the latter Power being sufficiently occupied with the Moors and the Low Countries. But many English Catholics had openly declared that they had no intention to take up arms in favour of Spain or indeed to have anything to do with that nation. Towards the end of 1569 the appeal to arms was tried, but the revolt of the Earls of Northumberland and Westmoreland failed miserably.   Elizabeth, whose power had become consolidated by a decade of Catholic inactivity, was able to crush it without difficulty, though with much savagery.

English Catholics had conscientious scruples as to whether, without a papal document against the Queen, they could undertake anything to deliver themselves from Elizabeth's tyranny.   In a belated letter of February, 1570, Dr. Nicholas Sander,[1] writing from Louvain to Rome for help for the insurgents, stated that the help the two Earls required was simply that they might be absolved openly of obedience to the Queen and that they might persuade those who took up arms that they were doing so not as revolutionaries, but as sons of the Church.   In this obscure situation, 4000 men had gone to Scotland to await the papal decision, and for three months had been expecting steps to be taken by the Pope against Elizabeth.   If the Pope would sanction the retention of ecclesiastical property by the nobility, this body, with few exceptions, would support the Catholic cause, and the vast majority of the people, which was Catholic, and many schismatics would follow their example.[2]

Pius V had already, in the spring of 1569, sent to England a papal envoy, Nicholas Morton, a former prebendary of York, and then penitentiary at St. Peter's, Rome, to inquire how the excommunication of Elizabeth would be received in England.   Although he told the insurgents what Pius V thought about the Queen, he gave them no intimation of a papal sentence that would have removed their scruples against an armed rising.   But, after his return to Rome, what he had to say about the feeling in England was sufficient to make Pius V decide to proceed against Elizabeth.   He plainly told the Pope that the English Catholics had held back simply because Elizabeth was not declared a heretic and not deposed by sentence of the Holy See.   Pius V no longer deferred the opening of the process against the " pre-

---

[1] Sander was unaware at the time of the failure of the revolt.
[2] Pastor (*It. ed.*), viii. 405-6; Pollen, *The Month, IC.* (1902), p. 140, and *English Catholics*, p. 143 *seq.*

tended " Queen of England, 5 February, 1570. Twelve
refugees in Rome were cited and questioned ; had Elizabeth
usurped the authority of head of the English Church ; had
she deposed and imprisoned Catholic bishops and conferred
their Sees on schismatics and laymen ; had she introduced
an oath and laws against the Holy See. The interrogatories
terminated on the 12 February, and 25 February of the same
year a Bull solemnly pronounced sentence on Elizabeth as
follows :—

We declare the said Elizabeth, heretic and fautress of heretics,
and her adherents, to have fallen under sentence of anathema,
and to be cut off from the unity of the Body of Christ, and her,
Elizabeth, to be deprived of her pretended right to the said realm
and of all and every dominion, dignity and privilege : and also
the nobles, subjects and peoples of the said realm, and all else
who in any manner have made oath to her, to be for ever absolved from such oath, and all duty of liege-fealty and obedience,
as by the authority of these present, we absolve them, and deprive
the said Elizabeth of her pretended right to the realm and of all
else aforesaid, and lay upon all and singular the nobles, subjects,
and peoples, and others aforesaid, our injunction and interdict,
that they presume not to yield obedience to her, or her admoni-
tions, mandates and laws : otherwise we involve them in the like
sentence of anathema.[1]

On many occasions Pius V thought it well to inform the
Spanish ambassador in Rome that the Bull was intended to
settle the consciences of English Catholics and to give them
courage. This accounts for the fact that the Bull was not
published at once with the usual formalities, and that only
by degrees it might become generally known in England.
With a Brief of 30 March, 1570, copies of the Bull were sent
to the Duke of Alva, Philip II's great viceroy in the Spanish
dominions of Flanders, so that he might publish them there,
especially in the maritime towns. Through the English
traders, it was expected, the Bull would soon become known
across the English Channel. At the same time about
eighty copies were sent to the London banker Ridolfi [2] for

[1] *C.S.P.*, *Rome*, 1558-71, no. 649; *Bullarium Romanum ;* Pollen, *English
Catholics*, p. 150; Camden, *Ann. ed.*, 1630, lib. II. 7.
[2] *Bibl. Chigi in Roma. Miscell.*, t. xlviii., p. 39 *seq. ;* Pastor, viii. 414.

tribution in England. Eventually the Bull made its way into England, and on the morning of 25 May, 1570, was affixed to the door of the episcopal palace in London. Suspicion of the audacious act fell on John Felton, a rich and well-known gentleman of Southwark, who immediately admitted his deed, and, on the scaffold, professed his allegiance to the papal sentence. In Rome the secret of the Bull was preserved so closely that even the Spanish ambassador was unaware of it. It was not until May that it was issued for printing, but it was immediately withdrawn from sale.[1]

The means selected by Pius V for the publication of the Bull did not meet with success. Alva objected to its publication, and the King of France politely refused his co-operation. When, for the first time, in April, the Pope informed the Spanish ambassador of his plans against Elizabeth, the ambassador raised serious objections to the effect that such a step should not be taken until all was ready for the execution of the papal sentence, for otherwise the only result would be a stimulus to Elizabeth to annihilate her Catholic subjects. Philip agreed with the ambassador and was very vexed that his own advice had not been first asked as he was best conversant with English affairs.[2]

On 15 July the ambassador was entrusted with the duty of representing to Pius V that the omission of the King of Spain's name, to whom would naturally fall the execution of the papal sentence, would be interpreted as favouring France. He pointed out that the King of Spain would never permit France to set foot in England. Desiring, at least for the present, to retain Elizabeth's favour, Philip wrote to her that no action of the Pope was so displeasing to him as the Bull, and retained his ambassador at London. But the latter was shortly afterwards forcibly expelled by Elizabeth.

Considering the want of co-operation on the part of the Duke of Alva and of France, Pius came round to their view that Elizabeth should be kept in the dark about the excommunication. He did not, however, agree with the other

---

[1] Schwarz, *Briefwechsel*, 160; *ap.* Pastor, 415.
[2] Zuniga to Philip II, 11 Aug., 1570, *Corresp. Dipl.*, iii. 493-99 ; *ap.* Pastor, 416.

proposals that the Bull should be suspended, and Elizabeth's
subjects absolved from their oath of allegiance by Brief
only. Alva, however, was not to be put off so easily. He
wrote to Pius, in August, 1570, that the excommunication of
the Queen had not succeeded in its object ; on the contrary,
it had done great harm to the Catholics. It had given an
excuse for persecution, and, since loyalty to Elizabeth was
threatened with excommunication, nothing remained for the
Catholics but to abandon their country, and this would
mean the end of the Catholic faith in England. The Pope,
however, was of the opinion that, even for these reasons, a
promulgated sentence could not be withdrawn, and that Alva
should make known to the English Catholics that, in case
they remained in the country, they would not be considered
by the Pope as excommunicated. Alva retaliated by declaring
such an expedient as insufficient, on account of the impossibility
of getting into touch with all the English Catholics and of
finding anyone in England who would consider himself bound
to believe in his statement.[1]

About this time a proposal was made by an Italian
merchant as to the means of executing the Bull without
recourse to force. It should be published in Spain, Flanders,
and France, and then on the basis of the Bull all commerce
with England should be forbidden to the Kings of Spain and
France. The mercantile blockade would oblige Elizabeth
to yield. It seemed that these proposals were pleasing to
the Pope who entrusted the Spanish ambassador with com-
municating them to Philip. Both Philip and his ambassador
declared the plan impracticable (10 June).[2]

By mid-summer, therefore, it was perfectly clear that
as far as the main object of the Bull was concerned it was
a dead letter. It was not, however, without its consequences.
Justices of the Peace were obliged to sign a document by
which they pledged themselves to apply rigorously the law
as to the assistance at Protestant worship. In this respect
the Bull had one important result ; it opened the eyes of
the English Catholics to the fact that they had to choose
between the Mass and the Protestant services, that they were

---

[1] *ap.* Pastor, 417.   [2] *Corresp. Dipl.,* iii. 500 ; *ap.* Pastor, 417.

no longer free to assist at the latter, as some of them had been doing in the belief that as long as they remained Catholics at heart it was allowable to escape fines and imprisonment by conforming outwardly to the Queen's religion. The people took the lesson seriously to heart, and manifested openly that their obedience to Elizabeth did not include their attendance at Protestant services.[1]

Although Elizabeth let it be understood that she despised the papal sentence, she made use of the Emperor Maximilian II to induce the Pope to withdraw the Bull (28 September).[2] But Pius would not agree. " If," he replied, " the Queen attaches importance to the Bull, why does she not return to the Church ; if she does not attach weight to it, why make such a noise about it ?—Elizabeth's threats are of no avail." But the Queen now sought to win public opinion against the Bull. By libels, sometimes " in the coarsest and most frivolous tone," she did all possible to drag the Pope and his Bull into ridicule and down into the mud.[3] Parliament, summoned 2 April, 1571, enacted a series of laws that were directed partly against the revolts of recent years, but partly also against Catholics as such.[4]   " The disaffection of the Catholics

[1] Bishop Grindal of York lamented that " the greatest part of our gentlemen are not well affected to godly religion," namely, Protestantism.   In southern England there were not ten nobles " that do favour and allow of Her Majesty's proceeding in the cause of religion." (*Frere*, 151-2.   See Green, 383 ; Lingard, vi. 11-16 (ed. 1854).)   " In Lancashire the people openly welcomed and entertained priests from Louvain ; in most places the people fell from their obedience and utterly refused to attend divine service in the English tongue." (Pastor, 418.)   Especially in Lancashire did the people, aware of the Bull, restore Catholic worship in their own houses and in their parishes.

[2] Schwarz, *Briefwechsel*, 159 *seq.* ; *ap.* Pastor, 418.

[3] Meyer, 69 *seq.* ; *ap.* Pastor, 418.

[4] Lingard, vi. 120-3.   Seventy years afterwards, when the Spaniards sought from Pope Urban VIII the excommunication of Richelieu and of Louis XIII for their league with Protestants, the Pope, mindful of the inefficacy of such proceedings against Henry VIII and Elizabeth, rejected the appeal.   Henceforth, the Holy See would never pronounce sentence of deposition against a reigning prince.   Whilst Catholic writers defend the Bull as according to ancient legislation (see Hergenröther, *Staat und Kirche*, 679), Protestants have instituted a violent polemic against it.   These polemists have done much to embitter the relations for centuries between Catholics and Protestants in England.   It was quite easy for them to pretend to fear a renewal of the threat against the security of princes by the issue of a Papal Bull.   But they did not allow that circumstances had changed in the centuries that followed, or that a Pope who claimed a right in the Middle Ages, with the approval of

was met by imposing on all magistrates and public officers the obligation of subscribing to the Articles of Faith, a measure which in fact transferred the administration of justice and public order to their Protestant opponents." [1]

OFFICIAL OPINIONS ON THE BULL.

When Gregory ascended the throne it seemed that the fate of the Catholic Church in England was sealed. Newly-ordained priests could not in future enter the country ; those already there could not remain much longer. The Catholics, and particularly the younger generation, deprived of their teachers, and forced by the law to attend Protestant sermons, began now more and more to embrace the new religious doctrines. Burghley and Elizabeth had reason to believe the moment near when with the last Catholic of the hitherto ultramontane faith might be extinguished in England. English Catholics began to ask whether in the circumstances they were bound to obey Elizabeth in civil matters, and if they did, were they excommunicated. On this point it will be useful to give here the following opinions on the Bull taken from the diplomatic correspondence between the Holy See and Spain :—

Questions touching the Bull of Pope Pius V against the Queen of England :—[2]

It may be argued that the Bull is no longer binding upon Catholics because it has failed of its purpose, since, instead of

the nations, might not consider it his duty to exercise it in the intervening period since the sixteenth century. For more than a century the Bull still served as an excuse for Protestant polemics and as a pretext by which every violation of right against Catholic subjects was justified. (Meyer, 70 *seq.* ; Pastor, 419.) In January, 1815, when there were still grounds for grave anxiety that the Veto Bill was being favoured by Rome, Daniel O'Connell stated at a meeting in Clarendon Street : " Let our determination never to assent reach Rome. It can easily be transmitted there. But even should it fail, I am still determined to resist. I am sincerely a Catholic, but I am not a Papist. I deny the doctrine that the Pope has any temporal authority, directly or indirectly, in Ireland. We have all denied that authority on oath, and we would die to resist it. His Holiness cannot, therefore, be any party to the Act of Parliament we solicit, nor shall any Act of Parliament regulate our faith or conscience." (Denis Gwynn, *The Struggle for Catholic Emancipation*, 203.)

[1] J. R. Green, 383.

[2] *C.S.P.*, Rome, 1572-78, no. 266 ; about the year 1573-74.

helping the Catholic cause, it has damaged it, and a law that has proved futile is no longer binding.   On the other hand defective publication of the Bull is not alleged, and apart from the Bull every Catholic is bound to hold the Queen illegitimate and excommunicate.

Nevertheless, Catholics may with a clear conscience obey the Queen in civil matters.   They may even with a mental reservation acknowledge her as head of the Anglican Church.   They may defend her against those who attack her unlawfully.   They may not, however, defend her against those who attack her *vi bullae* or *studio religionis*, and with reasonable hope of victory, but in such a case are bound to co-operate against her.

The Queen, though the Bull had not been published, might lawfully be dethroned as a perturber of the peace of the Universal Church.

In a letter of 25 October, 1574, to the Cardinal of Como,[1] the Nuncio in Spain mentions that—

in the course of a recent conversation which I had with His Majesty of [Spain] as to these matters [conversion of England] and especially as to the affairs of Ireland, which realm His Majesty said was very dependent upon the Apostolic See, I answered that England also was very dependent thereon [2] and that I had seen many writings bearing upon this matter ; and as we conversed of the deprivation of the realm of England made by Pius V in the person of this lady [Elizabeth] for that she is a heretic, I said—and truly—that the deprivation was of the realm of England and not of that of Ireland, and that these realms being distinct, the deprivation of the one did not include the other ; to which His Majesty subjoined, that His Holiness might yet make deprivation of that realm [Ireland] keeping the deprivation most secret in his own possession for use in due season.[3] Pius V, as you doubtless know, for the most part kept his own counsel as to his doings ; so that it is no marvel if, being perchance ill informed of these matters, he omitted the deprivation of the realm of Ireland, as I afterwards explained to His Holiness [Gregory] when he adverted to the subject, being desirous that a remedy should be found for some untoward consequences of

[1] *C.S.P., Rome*, 1572-78, no. 358.

[2] On account of the excommunication of King John and his resignation of the Kingdom of England as a fief to the Pope.

[3] Until the Pope had deprived Elizabeth of the realm of Ireland, the King of Spain did not see how he could attempt to take it for himself or Don John.

that Bull of deprivation, which ought never to have been published until an army was on the way to England upon that enterprise, so that in one hand there might be borne the Keys of St. Peter, to wit, the deprivation, and in the other the sword of St. Paul; for the publication of the Bull of deprivation unaccompanied by the conquest of the country has done much harm, causing the death of many Catholics, and making that lady much more hostile to the Apostolic See. However, seeing that that Bull left no manner of abuse of her [hers] unsaid, I would not refrain from entering upon some discourse of the matter for what it may be worth.

From the scope of the Bull it seemed clear that the pro-hibition against the allegiance of Catholics to Elizabeth held only under certain conditions that now no longer existed. But in order to allay any conscientious anxiety of scrupulous Catholics, Campion and Parsons begged the Pope to be good enough to declare expressly that the Bull indeed affected Elizabeth and her adherents, but that it did not oblige Catholics to refuse allegiance to Elizabeth as long as the present state of affairs lasted, and not until the Bull could be publicly enforced. Gregory XIII granted this request on 14 April, 1580,[1] and his pronouncement was included in the list of faculties given by him on that day to the two Jesuits.[2]

Papal Overlordship of England and Ireland.

The mediæval view of the overlordship of the Pope in England and Ireland is set forth in the correspondence between the Nuncio in Spain and the Papal Secretary, 19 December, 1575.[3] The Nuncio writes :—

As to Ireland, the Apostolic See granted the government and dominion of that island to the King of England, and if my memory

[1] It seemed, however, that Gregory XIII somewhat earlier had been of a different opinion. According to a *Newsletter* from Rome, 20th February, 1580, Bonelli had more than 500 copies of the Bull printed to distribute in the papal Court and amongst the foreign ambassadors. (*Urb.* 1048, p. 24; *Bibl. Vat.*)

[2] The scruples of the English Catholics were clearly seen in the questions that were sent to a theologian (Creighton, Bishop of Peterborough) and in the replies to them. This theologian wished for a papal declaration on the Bull, and was of the opinion that without it the Bull placed no burden on Catholics. (*English Hist. Review*, 1892, p. 84.)

[3] *C.S.P., Rome*, 1572-78, p. 462.

is accurate, the grant was by Alexander III [an error for Adrian IV] to King Henry II, and the concession was made without reservation of right to the Pope; but this will more clearly appear in the briefs of the concession that will be found in the Roman Archives.[1]

I remember seeing this Bull in England, and I think that there was no reservation whatever therein, though the Irish say openly that that island *est juris Sedis Apostolicae*. It may be that there is something which I have not seen, but experience shows that it makes no difference, seeing that there has been such a long succession of Kings of England in that island without recognition of the Holy See. Afterwards in the time of the Schism, Henry VIII raised that dominion to the rank of a Kingdom; and where as aforetime the Kings of England styled themselves Lords of Ireland, he was the first to call himself King of Ireland; and his successor Queen Mary and the King, her husband, having a scruple about using that title assumed by a Schismatic King, obtained from Paul IV the erection into a kingdom.

As to the realm of England, there is the so-called Blessed Peter's penny, which occasions no difficulty because it has always been levied by the Apostolic See, and there have been many collectors of this penny, which was wont to yield 700 or 800 ducats, as may be seen in the books of the Chamber. After the reconciliation of the realm Pope Paul IV deputed me collector, but I made no use of my powers as I quitted the realm, and there ensued that which ensued.

King John of England yielded the realm into the hand of Pandolf, Legate Apostolic in those realms, promising that neither he nor his successors would ever take that realm save from the hand of the Pope, and I have seen the writing whereby he did so, and another touching the same matter, on the strength of which it has sometimes been pretended that the Apostolic See has the lordship of England; as to which I was at one time at pains to inform myself, and found that this right does not exist because John had no power to transfer any right or alter the laws or the succession in the kingdom without the consent of Parliament,

---

[1] See *Gir. Camb.*, i. 61-2, who alleges the Bull was granted by Hadrian IV. Capgrave (*De Illustribus Henricis, Rolls Ser.*, pp. 71-3) mentions its confirmation by Alexander III. The text of the Bull as printed (from *Cotton MSS., Claudius E.* viii. 13*b*) in Rymer's *Foedera* (*Rec. Comm.*, i., l., p. 19) and by Baronius (*Ann. Eccl.*, 1159, xxi.) does not differ materially from that of Giraldus. A late manuscript of the Bull is preserved at the Vatican (*Misc. Arm.*, i., vol. 17, f. 129). The grant is presupposed in Alexander III's Bulls to Henry II and the Irish princes and bishops, printed in Rymer's *Foedera* (vol. i., l., p. 45). See Martin Haile, *Life of Card. Pole*, 1911.

of which there is no evidence : besides which there was no exercise of such right, for none of John's successors received the kingdom from the Pope's hand.

One thing I observed in England that makes much in favour of the Pontifical authority, to wit, that when the two houses of the White and Red Roses were united by the marriage of King Henry VII with Elizabeth, daughter of Edward IV, whereby an end was put to the great and ancient rivalries of those two houses, King Henry and his Queen procured a declaration of the Pope touching this matter and his confirmation of this union, whereby the authority of the Roman Pontiff is manifest even in temporal matters such as the succession to States.

I procured a copy of that Bull and of many other like matters concerning these two realms, which together with the registers of the legation I lost on the death of the Cardinal [Pole] as I was not then in England.

Cardinal Cervino, afterwards Pope Marcellus [1555] a great and diligent investigator of matters pertaining to the Apostolic See, made a collection of all the pretensions of the Holy See in that realm and of the Bulls relating to them, if my memory serves me well, and sent it to Cardinal Pole, which book came to my hands, and is, I think, at Padua among my papers : and though I believe that you will have found all that there is in the Roman Archives, nevertheless, if you believe that there is some light to be had from this writing, you can write to Galerio to send it you under obligation of silence and secrecy.

The Kings of England claim the *jus Supplicandi* for persons meet to rule churches ; they administer temporalities *sede vacante*, and require bishops to swear fealty to them for the temporalities. They have, moreover, laws most prejudicial to the Apostolical authority and the liberty of the Church, and among them one called *premoneri* [*praemunire*] which is most bestial ; to which laws they hold on tooth and nail, as the saying is, and I can bear good witness thereof, for there was daily to do about the matter. If these laws could be abolished when by God's grace we get the upper hand, it would be a most holy thing : we did indeed at the time of the reconciliation [under Queen Mary] procure the abolition by Parliament of all laws prejudicial to the authority and obedience of the Apostolic See made at the time of the Schism, all of which were specified ; and an authentic catalogue of them was made and sent to Paul IV, and placed in the Castle [of S. Angelo] among the other documents of the Apostolic See.

Sovereign Right of Rulers.

In defending Dr. Nicholas Sander, the companion of James Fitzmaurice on his expedition to Ireland in 1579 (of which later), Knox in his introduction to the *Letters and Memorials of Cardinal Allen* writes :—

" *It would be easy to defend him on principles very generally assumed as true at the present time. Subjects, it is said, have an indefeasible right to rebel against their sovereign whenever they judge his rule to be oppressive, and they may call in foreign powers to aid them in their attempt.* The right of revolution has now become part of the common code of modern Europe. Now, what treasure is there dearer and more precious to a true Catholic than the Faith ? A sovereign, then, who like Elizabeth made the exercise of the Catholic religion in England impossible, has thereby lost all claim to the obedience of her subjects, and they may justly depose her by themselves or with the help of foreign princes. I do not see what answer can be given to such a defence of [Sander] on modern principles, except to deny that the Catholic Faith is a treasure the loss of which would justify rebellion. But surely on these same principles it is for the person concerned, not the bystander, to determine the nature and degree of the oppression which warrants him to revolt. He is the judge and executor of the judgment in his own cause. This answer would be sufficient, *ad hominem* in a controversial dispute. The subject, however, must be examined more closely in serious history ; for though there is a certain amount of truth, or rather of truth perverted, in these modern principles, it would be unfair to [Sander] to rest on them his justification."

Knox then turns to discuss the principles of the natural law on which civil power is based : " According to the teaching of the Church and the principles which prevailed during the sixteenth century, the sovereign's title to govern his subjects comes in ultimate analysis from God. . . . God gives the authority, but He does not designate the person of the recipient. . . . The natural law, from which the sovereign derives his right to rule, prescribes also the end at which he should aim in ruling. His sovereignty exists because it is indispensable to his people's good ; the end thereof of the exercise of his sovereignty, must be his people's good likewise. To use his power merely for his own private good would be to rule as a tyrant, not as a sovereign. Hence, if he should enact anything plainly contrary to God's law, and to the state's injury, his enactment would be without binding force.

He would no longer command in this point as God's minister in virtue of the power God has given him, and to disobey him therein would not be to disobey God, but on the contrary to disobey would become a duty. . . .

So much for the bearing of the natural law on the problem under discussion ; now for the teaching and practice of Christianity on the same subject. The subjects of a Christian State (notes Knox) are also

"members of a supernatural polity instituted by God to enable them to attain [their] higher end ; [and therefore] the Christian sovereign cannot duly exercise his authority as God's minister in the temporal order without taking into account the supernatural polity, or the Catholic Church, and the acts of its rulers, and regulating his own mode of government so as to be in harmony with them . . . first by not opposing what the Church enacts for the eternal good of his subjects ; and secondly by using the temporal power which God has given him in her service when she calls on him for aid in carrying out the work which God has entrusted to her. . . . Human frailty and the decay of Faith may impair the harmony and set the temporal ruler at variance with the spiritual one, but they cannot render untrue the divine ideal or make that praiseworthy which contradicts it."

These principles were universally admitted and acted on in the Middle Ages, " when the Catholic Church had remoulded on a Christian pattern and vivified with a Christian spirit the whole fabric of political, social, and domestic life, so that the Catholic Faith extended as a living power into the every-day actions, views, language and customs of men. During this time the States of Europe were knit together into a kind of Christian Common-wealth under the headship of their common spiritual father, the Roman Pontiff. It was then that the temporal authority of the Pope over Christian States and their rulers was most fully exercised and freely acknowledged. How far this sprang indirectly from his spiritual office of Christ's Vicar and how far it has had its source in what may be called the international law of an undivided Christendom may be disputed. . . . But, whatever the source of this power, it was acknowledged by all men, and its decrees were regarded as valid and binding, just as treaties between States are held to bind now. The highest exercise of this power was when the Sovereign Pontiff solemnly deposed an offending sovereign and absolved his subjects from their oath of allegiance to him." Heresy was then looked on as one of the great crimes that called for deposition ; " and men greeted as an act of supreme justice the solemn deposition of an heretical king."

The common law on the subject is laid down in the Fourth Lateran Council of 1215, which was attended by four hundred and twelve bishops, eight hundred abbots, and many of the sovereigns of Europe. Its decrees, therefore, " must have been in perfect harmony with the common sentiments of Christendom." The decree concerning the deposition of heretical rulers thus " became part of the ordinary statute law of the Church. It had not been abrogated by desuetude in the sixteenth century ; for Allen and Parsons appeal to it as in full force in a memorandum drawn up for Philip II ; and St. Pius V acted in accordance with it when he issued his Bull deposing Queen Elizabeth [in 1570]. . . . There was nothing startling in an assertion of a power, which his predecessors had claimed and used for centuries without reclamation from the European commonwealth of Christian States. The Pope's prudence in thus acting might possibly be questioned ; his right to act thus was unquestionable.

" This Pontifical act was not a mere empty protest. Its effect was that Elizabeth ceased to be Queen *de jure*, while she remained Queen *de facto* as before. . . . It was far from the desire of [his successor] Gregory XIII that the Bull should remain without execution. He saw too clearly the ruin to innumerable souls which resulted from Elizabeth's continuance on the throne. As spiritual pastor of these souls, he was bound to use all lawful means to save them from perishing. Hence, not content with aiding by his munificent gifts the purely spiritual work of conversion which was carried on by the colleges of Douai and Rome,[1] he left nothing undone to impel Philip of Spain to overthrow Elizabeth by force of arms."

To sum up then ; the viewpoint of Catholics at that time was :—

That this exercise of papal authority by Pius V was not only in accordance with the received maxims of that age but in no way opposed to the principles of civil liberty. It existed, was recognised, and appealed to, not only by one

---

[1] On 28 March, 1577, the Cardinal of Como wrote to the Chancellor, Doctors, and Masters of Faculties of the Academy of Douai, commending to them at the instance of the Pope the many pious Irishmen, who, his Holiness knows, are wont to have recourse to the University of Douai to study letters and the good arts, that by the favour, tutelage, and aid of the said authorities they may with less anxiety and more zeal devote themselves to their studies, and enjoy the privileges of scholars. (*C.S.P., Rome,* 1572-78, no. 585.)

sovereign against another, but by the people against their rulers. The supremacy of the Pope was felt to be the mainstay of all authority and the bulwark of popular liberty. At all events it was the manner of the age : the nations would have it so. The Popes found themselves invested with an office, which was none of their seeking, but which they saw it was salutary for them to discharge at the united bidding of kings and people. Such so to speak was the international law of Europe.

Again, Catholics considered that, as in Christendom generally, so in England and Ireland in particular, up to this time, none but a Catholic prince was considered capable of reigning. Such was the understood law of Europe ; and such was the custom in these kingdoms of Europe, when it had but one faith, was as one religious confederation, with the Pope at its head ; and the laws of each kingdom severally were in accordance with this fundamental principle. The prince who broke the unity of Faith, or failed to protect his people in the exercise of their religion, was considered to have, *ipso facto*, forfeited his crown.

Catholics could point out that at that time Protestants had claimed that very right for themselves. They saw how Luther absolved the Germans from their obedience to the Emperor Charles V. Calvin and Beza had called on the Huguenots of France to rise against their sovereign, and were aided and abetted by Elizabeth. John Knox and the Presbyterian clergy of Scotland thundered out their anathemas against the Queen Regent, and against the unfortunate Mary. They declared that " no oath or promise can oblige any man to obey or give assistance to tyrants against God."

In those cases Catholics recognised that the minority religion of Protestantism was raising itself up against the recognised religion of the State, and that it was not for the mere exercise of religion that they strove but that they incited rebellion against Catholics to the destruction of civil order. English and Irish Catholics also recognised that Elizabeth's imposition of her religion of a small minority on the mass of Catholics in those kingdoms was not a mere claim of the exercise of that religion but was a destruction of the civil order which she as sovereign was bound to see preserved.

They recognised that as Protestants on the Continent were the aggressors, so in these countries were they also. They felt that no earthly power was justified in depriving them of what was their dearest and most valued heritage, their Faith, their Mass, their Sacraments, their churches, their shrines. Ireland and England had been their Catholic home ; and what were kings or queens that they should ravage and lay them waste ? [1] Such was the situation that they envisaged, and such was that which Pius V saw. If one may regard his action as imprudent and impolitic, as indeed it was regarded by theologians and statesmen of the time, one must consider the provocation he received and the position of authority in Europe which he held by the will of princes and people.

MEILER MAGRATH PETITIONS ELIZABETH FOR A BISHOPRIC.

After his submission to Sydney in 1567, Meiler Magrath, the papal bishop of Down, disappears from the scene for two years. He seems, however, to have remained during those years a Catholic bishop. Matters altered when Elizabeth feeling herself strong enough appointed a bishop to Down in the person of John Merriman about January, 1569.[2] What happened to Magrath in consequence is obscure, but this is what seems to have occurred. In order to secure Merriman in his See it would seem that Magrath was taken into custody, shipped off to England and placed in the keeping of the Protestant Bishop of London.[3] This took place in July, 1569. Magrath was evidently given to understand that it was hopeless to expect Elizabeth to recognise him as a Catholic bishop in Down, and pressure was evidently brought to bear on him to change his coat completely. After some months' hesitation or initiation into the ways of the State Church he decided to conform to Protestantism, and to petition for a Protestant bishopric in his native land. Early in the year 1570, he sent several letters to Cecil informing him of all the benefices that had been conferred on him by the Pope, and that now

---

[1] *Clifton Tracts*, vol. i., no. v. 2.
[2] Harris, *Ware's Bishops*, 205. Merriman was a native of England and chaplain to Elizabeth.
[3] *C.S.P.I.*, *Eliz.*, xxix. 26. "The Irish Bishop at the Bishop of London's."

he was prepared to renounce them all and to receive a bishopric from the Queen " in some place where her rule is observed," for obviously he could not be expected to show himself as an Elizabethan bishop in any of the dioceses where the Irish were in control. The Queen, with her usual hesitancy, kept him waiting for months until he was worn out with anxiety and fever. The fact that the See of Down had been granted by the Deputy to Merriman did not prevent him from sending in a formal memorial to the Privy Council,[1] 11 April, 1570, asking for that bishopric and giving all the reasons in cocksure fashion why he should be appointed to it. The Latin document states :—

After waiting so long and being so long excluded from the presence of your most illustrious Council, I dare not depart without having some information as to my affairs, and so I beseech both your lordships to be so kind as to tell me what Her Royal Highness and your Lordships have decided to grant me, namely, whether you will bestow on me that dignity [Down and Connor] which formerly I obtained, or some other, or none at all. For if there be any difficulty as to the dignity that I formerly obtained, and which (as is said) had been already granted to another [John Merriman] by the Lord Deputy so that it may not be granted to me again by Her Highness, the reply to that is easy. The Lord Deputy, without any difficulty, indeed with the same ease, can transfer to another dignity him who was granted my place, and myself in this latter, especially, as I understand that he has not received any letters patent from her Majesty. There is a reason why Her Highness and Your Lordships might grant that dignity to me rather than to another, for being settled in that diocese [2] I can serve Her Royal Highness much better and more effectively there than in any other part of Ireland ; and he who has been appointed by the Deputy cannot offer such service as I can, as the said Deputy and those who know us both can testify. But if it should happen that Her Royal Highness cannot revoke the grant of the Lord Deputy, I beseech her Majesty that she grant me what she thinks meet for me in some safe place and where her rule is observed, for I have no desire to live among those rebellious and vulgar Irishmen among whom I was born. But, in order that her Majesty may provide me with some special place in the English portion of Ireland I may point out to Her Highness

[1] *S.P.I.*, *Eliz.*, xxx. 41, P.R.O., London.   See *Appendix VI (e)*.
[2] He expected that English power would succeed in settling him.

21 *

and your Lordships that the diocese of Cork and Cloyne has been long vacant : this I would gladly accept unless I could recover the former [Down] that would be more pleasing to me, for I could much better and more easily serve her Majesty there than elsewhere. For, I have there, and in the neighbouring districts, many friends and kinsmen some of whom were sometimes rebellious but, with my counsel and persuasion, I should hope to bring them back to the peace and jurisdiction of her Majesty ; and, moreover, in that same diocese I could speak the doctrine of truth (as far as it in me lies) in public, and neither monk nor other Papist could prevent me. Many other things I might point out which I omit for brevity sake. Further, I beseech Her Majesty to grant me once more those smaller benefices namely, priories, simple rectories, and chapels which I formerly obtained from the Bishop of Rome for myself and my brother, along with his letters to Lord Maguire in whose country [Fermanagh] they are situated ; that an order may be made making over those same benefices to me and securing them to me. The names of the said benefices appear clearly in the letters that the Lord Secretary has,[1] and these might be sent to the Lord Deputy so that after perusal these grants might be more expeditiously made to me. For indeed all these have been usurped by Papists and by the Queen's rebels, but by the favour and help of friends and relatives I could collect some of the fruits, provided I had the royal grant which I could show to them.

Finally, I beg your Lordships that you constrain me not longer to wait, lest falling again into a fever I may be a further burden on her Majesty and your Lordships. May the Eternal Father, the Lover of Pure Counsel, govern and direct your counsel for His glory and the public good. Amen.

Postscript.—I beg your Lordships to consider that I am bereft of all human help in this renowned kingdom, so that there is no one from whom I can or hope to obtain money by gift or loan unless from Her Highness and by your favour. Hence I earnestly beseech you that you request Her Highness that she grant me in some manner the necessary money for my journey.

Your Lordships most humble servant,

MEILER MAGRATH, *Irishman.*

To the noble Counsellors of the Kingdom of England.

{ Memorial of Meiler Magrath, Irishman sometimes called Bishop.[2]

---

[1] He had evidently yielded up his papal Bull to Cecil.

[2] Magrath does not like to call himself " Bishop " plainly ; that would mean a papal one.

The bishopric of Cork and Coyne was vacant since 1567 by the resignation of Roger Skiddy who had been nominated by Mary in 1557,[1] but who received from Elizabeth in 1561 the mandate for his consecration. It is remarkable that during those ten years (1557-67) there was no papal appointment to the See, and when Nicholas Laules was appointed by the Pope in 1568 there is no mention of his succession to Skiddy but to Skiddy's predecessor John O'Heyne (*d.* 1557). Thus, Skiddy was not regarded as a papal bishop.[2]

Cork and its county had just before this time received Protestant colonists from England who were called by the wrathful Fitzmaurice " Huguenots." Accordingly, in recommending a man for the See, Sydney [3] says, December, 1569, " it is fit to be bestowed on an Englishman by reason of the places there frequented with our nation and speech as scarcely better a bishop may be employed." It was to this place of English manners, speech, and religion that the fastidious Franciscan friar, Meiler Magrath, asked to be appointed. But Sydney appointed him neither to Down nor to Cork and Cloyne. He recommended for the latter his " chaplain, Richard Dixon, M.A., of Cambridge, who lived with the Bishop of Norwich, who will certify of his learning. He is content to take it, shows himself honest, sober, of very good government, diligent in preaching, with modesty and good grace to edify." Dixon was a canon of St. Patrick's, Dublin, and prebendary of Rathmichael. He was appointed by patent to Cork and Cloyne, 6 June, just two months after Magrath's petition, and was consecrated the same year. He was deprived, however, the following year, for reasons that will appear later.

Magrath, however, was promoted by Elizabeth to Clogher, 18 September, 1570, and, 3 February following, was translated to Cashel, having received little or nothing in temporalities from Clogher, the northern Irish chiefs having turned against him for his acceptance of the " reform."

---

[1] It is morally certain that Skiddy had never been consecrated.

[2] After his resignation he was appointed warden of Youghal until his death in 1587.

[3] *S.P.I., Eliz.*, xxix. 84, P.R.O., London.

PARLIAMENT FOUNDS A SYSTEM OF NATIONAL EDUCATION.

When the rebellion in the South had died down, Sir Edward Fitton, appointed President of Connacht, set to work to bring that province into English order. The townsmen of Galway he found loyal and peaceable enough, but the people of the province were cold in religion, and inclined to superstition. He committed the statues and images in the churches to fire, expelled sundry friars from their convents, and, as he narrates, "reformed some churches, procuring the clergy to put away their concubines, or else to marry them." A kind of census was taken of the province, malefactors were executed, and a provost-marshal appointed to hang out of hand all who could find no one to answer for them. As a final indignity, "such as do come unto us," says Chief Justice Ralph Rokeby, "we cause to cut their glybbes [long hair], which we do think the first token of obedience." [1] A commission had been appointed as justices and commissioners of Connacht, 24 July, 1569, consisting, among others, of Loftus, Bodkin, Roland de Burgh, and Brady. [2]

Clanricard and O'Connor Sligo seemed to agree with Fitton's course, but Thomond and Clanricard's son, John Burke, offering opposition, Fitton was shut up in Galway. In the South, on Gilbert's departure, Fitzmaurice gathered a new force to attack the "Huguenot" colony, and spoiled Kilmallock. Sydney had now to fall back on the proferred friendship of Ormond to put down the fresh disturbance. Later, Thomond found it impossible to carry on his opposition and boarded a French ship in the Shannon. He received monetary help at the French Court, but advised to seek pardon from Elizabeth, he made his submission to the Queen, and was sent back to Ireland. Edmund and Piers Butler also submitted and awaited the Queen's pleasure in Dublin Castle. But their brother Edward could not be caught. Elizabeth approved of Sydney's fortifying policy in Ulster. Irishmen were to be encouraged to take estates of the Crown, and Englishmen to settle in Ireland. [3]

Parliament reassembled, 26 May, and, after the unsuccess-

---

[1] *S.P.I.*, *Eliz.*, xxx. 4.   [2] *Fiants*, no. 1417.
[3] *S.P.I.*, *Eliz.*, xxx. 12, 40, 48.

ful rebellion, the Irish Party was in more submissive mood. An Act was passed in this session for the erection of a free school in every diocese at the cost of the diocese, with an English master appointed by the Lord Deputy, except in Armagh, Dublin, Meath, and Kildare, where the bishops were made patrons. The foundation was Scriptural and Protestant, "for the Elizabethans could not understand the possible permanence of any but the State religion." [1]

Henry VIII's system of parochial schools having never come into being, this must be considered as the first attempt at national education. Salaries were to be fixed by the Lord Deputy, but paid by the clergy, one-third by the bishop, and two-thirds by the general body. Some measure of success attended this scheme—unlike the mediæval attempts at Irish universities—but it is more than probable that in many dioceses the schools were never founded at all. A Bill to compel the residence of spiritual persons was thrown out by the Commons, evidently for the reason that residence of such persons in the places of their cures from which they drew their revenues was found impossible.

Clancare, Fitzmaurice, and Ormond's three brothers, were attainted by name as "vile and ingrate traitors." Ormond objected to this stigma on his own house. He had before pleaded that his brothers took up arms against Sydney for his part in the confiscation of Odrone country by Carew. Ultimately the Butlers were pardoned, and Fitzmaurice was reduced to carry on as best he could with a few followers.

Lack of Protestant Bishops for Irish Seas; Lawyers Thwarters of the "Reformation."

A few ecclesiastical matters may be dealt with here in a summary manner. Christopher Bodkin, Archbishop of Tuam, acted as interpreter for the President and commission of Connacht [2] at Galway during Fitton's campaign. "The Bishop of Killaloe, i.e. Turlough [Terence], the son of Mahon, son of Turlough O'Brien died, 1569." [3] He had obtained it

---

[1] Bagwell, ii. 176.   [2] *S.P.I., Eliz.*, xxx. 31.
[3] Annals, *Four Masters.*

in the reign of Queen Mary, in 1554. His sons, Mahon and Donough O'Brien,[1] are mentioned as outlaws in the Patent and Close Rolls, 25 October, 1569, probably because they had taken the side of Thomond. On 26 December Sydney asked Cecil " for the bearer Morgan, the son of Mac-I-Brien Arra,[2] to have the profits of the Bishopric of Killaloe to keep him at Oxford, that he may be more fit to enjoy the place. Otherwise they will be utterly converted to temporal uses for want of men to serve as bishops."[3] On 17 May, 1570, the Queen replied to Sydney [4] "that she was pleased that Morgan, the son of MacBrien Arra,[5] shall be allowed for his maintenance and sustentation in learning the profits of the bishopric of Killaloe which no person could enjoy without the good will of the said MacBrien Arra ; so as when he should arrive at maturer years, if he be found meet to have the said bishopric, he might be admitted thereto." He was not consecrated until six years later. Meanwhile, the Pope appointed, 10 January, 1571, Malachy O'Molony [6] to the See vacant by the death of Terence or Turlough.

Loftus, apparently deprived of his palace of St. Sepulchre, had to fall back on his residence at Tallaght as his chief house. Even of this he was not allowed peaceful possession. A Mr. Brereton (19 March) had a suit against him for the house, but the nature of the complaint does not appear. Loftus intended to repair to England to fight his case and bear with him a recommendation from his supporter FitzWilliams to Cecil. Back in Tallaght he wrote to Cecil [7] (2 July) thanking him for the remission of the first-fruits of his archbishopric. He had now a report to make about Dr. Weston, the lay Dean of St. Patrick's and Lord Chancellor. " A new chancellor," he says, "should neither be a dissembling papist nor cold or carnal Protestant." Evidently Weston was not

---

[1] *S.P.I., Eliz.*, xxx. 56, iii.

[2] Arra is a barony in Co. Tipperary, whence the bishop's family took the name for the sake of distinction.

[3] *S.P.I., Eliz.*, xxix. 85.   [4] *C.P.C.R.I., Eliz* , i. p. 539.

[5] MacBrien Arra had submitted to Sydney and received a patent for his estates from Elizabeth (*ib.*, p. 534).

[6] For some reason Malachy O'Molony, clerk, was granted a pardon, 6 August, 1572. (*Fiants*, no. 2129.)

[7] *S.P.I., Eliz.*, xxx. 64.

sufficiently militant in his Protestantism for one of Loftus's kidney, and he may have come under the influence of the papist prebendaries of St. Patrick's. Loftus does not like a lay Dean, and suggested that the deanery should be " conferred on a preacher." He cunningly gave a reason that he expected would appeal to the Queen : " Pitiful to see how the poor people give their tithes to be instructed, and for want thereof continue in ignorance." The Catholics had indeed to provide the Dean, lay or clerical, with tithes, but that they wished to be instructed in his religion or that they remained in ignorance of it is rather fanciful.

Mr. Cartwright of Cambridge, a preacher who had been with Loftus for a year, and had been recommended for a bishopric, was now recommended (26 October) by him to Cecil's favour as he " will prove a rare and a singular ornament to the Church." [1]

Brady of Meath now gets a respite of five years for the payment of his fruits in consequence of his great losses in the rebellion of Offaly. On the death of Chief Baron Bathe he wrote to Cecil [2] (6 February) in favour of Second Baron Cusack who " of long time, both painfully and faithfully, by all men's report, is the only man of his profession that favoureth religion in this land and therefore in my opinion the fitter for that room. The number of lawyers is great and beareth no less sway. So are they, for the most part, nay, I might say all, thwarters and hinderers of matters that should tend to the reformation of religion." One of the most remarkable features of this period is the steadfastness of the lawyers and gentry of the Pale in their profession of the Catholic Faith.

The See of Cashel being vacant by the sudden abduction of MacCaghwell, the Protestant incumbent, by MacGibbon, the Catholic Archbishop, a note in the *State Papers* [3] avers " the necessity of English officers " in places " where English is spoken, and so an English bishop for Cashel and Emly now united." It would appear that English colonisation was now being carried out also in Co. Tipperary.

---

[1] *S.P.I., Eliz.*, xxx. 88.   [2] Brady, *State Papers*, pp. 8-9.
[3] *S.P.I., Eliz.*, xxx. 103.

Stucley Sets Out for Spain.

Philip of Spain was being led by a train of events to take more than a passing interest in the Catholics of the British Isles, though in his own wavering, uncertain fashion. As a devout Catholic, and one keenly interested in the welfare of the Church, he could not shut his eyes to the fact that, if Elizabeth were allowed to go on her way unchecked, the Catholic Church in England would be a thing of the past. His Ambassador in London, Don Guerau de Spes, assured him that the Catholics of England, who were the majority of the country, only needed a favourable opportunity and a little outside help to place Mary of Scotland on the throne and to restore the Catholic religion. This advice was given about the time of the Irish Confederacy early in 1569, with which doubtless he was in touch. On the other hand, Philip's viceroy in Flanders, and influential adviser on all English affairs, the Duke of Alva, counselled the King to be cautious in his dealings with the English Catholics, in whom he had little confidence. As to Ireland, Alva warned the Ambassador " on no account in the world are you to listen to any proposals about Ireland or other parts, as I can assure you that such a course might ruin everything." He was strongly in favour of peace with the English Queen. Philip, however, was more amenable to the Ambassador's advice, and was not averse from creating trouble in England, if only this could be done without having to show his hand, and particularly without having to incur responsibility for whatever might happen as a result of veiled intervention.

Dejected but not dismayed by the failure of the rising in the North of England, the Ambassador, while keeping an eye on the collusion between Elizabeth and the Protestants on the Continent, was gathering the threads of another movement. His chief helper was Ridolfi, a Florentine banker in London, and secret papal agent, who linked up the insurgent element with Rome. In Ireland the Ambassador made use of a Spaniard and two Italians, namely Mendoza, Lottini, and Alexander Fideli. Mendoza, a West Indian trader who had been captured by English pirates, and cast adrift on the Irish coast, made his way to Dublin and lodged a

complaint with the Deputy. Mendoza, who was imprisoned
for some time in Dublin Castle, turned his enforced leisure to
account by probing the state of feeling in Ireland and ascer-
taining the possibilities it afforded for a Spanish invasion.
One of the Italians, Lottini, a ship captain, was in close
touch through his nephew in London with the Spanish
Ambassador and his plans. The other Italian was Alexander
Fideli who became Stucley's confidential servant. In his
report (May, 1569) to the Spanish King, the Ambassador
stated that an Italian (probably Fideli) then in Ireland had
conveyed to him that there was in that country an English
Catholic named Stucley who proposed that, in case the King
of Spain wished to take possession of Ireland, he, Stucley,
would undertake that it should be done, if only he was provided with twenty armed ships and some weapons for the
natives. A few weeks later the Ambassador informed the
King of the widespread indignation in Ireland created by
the colonisation scheme. He added that Stucley and some
of the chiefs were thinking of sending an envoy to Spain
to hand over the country to the King, and that Stucley
would make Waterford harbour ready for the landing of
10,000 men who would be sufficient for the purpose.

Stucley, who had been deprived of his seneschalship
of Ferns because, as it was reported, he had favoured the
Catholics, now undertook a new rôle and started a new phase
of his adventurous career. Hatred of Elizabeth and her
government, as well as the spirit of adventure and material
profit, turned his eyes towards the land of Spain, Catholic
in religion and a field for the adventurous. Before he left
Enniscorthy he applied for a pardon which was granted and
in which he was styled " late seneschal and constable of the
Castle of Wexford, late captain of the people called the
Cavenaghes, and late constable of the Castle of Laghlyn,
Co. Carlow." [1] Spanish spies made their way to Dublin as
well as to London, and Stucley made the acquaintance of
Don Jhoan de Mendoza in Dublin, who was evidently an
accomplice of the Spanish Ambassador in London. Mendoza
later found himself suspected of complicity in this affair

---

[1] *Fiants*, no. 1444.

. and accordingly wrote a skilful letter to Cecil (9 November, 1570) :—[1]

Likewise for that it is reported and believed in that Court that I was a mean and a persuader of T. Stucley to go into Spain, and that I had practise with him. But I swear that I never knew of Stucley's going there. If I had known his going, I would have dealt therein with some wiser and better staid man than I think Stucley to be. (This without prejudice to his estimation, if he have any left, for [he] that worketh against his prince I take him to be void of all honour.) The truth will be known before I leave these countries.

This, of course, was a piece of arrogant bluff which very probably did not deceive Cecil. However this may be, it is difficult to understand how Sydney was not aware of Stucley's activities after the latter had left Wexford. What these were is told in the report of the English Ambassador at Madrid :—[2]

Stucley did buy in Ireland his ship called the "Trinity of Bridgewater" the first of February, 1569, by the means of Alexander Fideli an Italian, and now his servant. Thomas Stucley came to Waterford to prepare the same ship to be in readiness for his voyage the 13 of March, 1569, at the which time he laded in his ship 4 ton of water ; 15 pipes of wheat, and 8 pipe of beans. The 25th he shipped his mariners [28 men, English and Irish] [3] and in the same ship 14 horses the 28 of March. On the 17th of April, 1570, Stucley departed from Waterford haven, and none of his company did understand of his pretence towards [intention to go to] Spain saving one Robert Kene of his ship, and Alexander Fideli.

Thomas Stucley landed at Vivero in Gallicia, 24 April, 1570, and sent to the Court of Spain, the 25th, Alexander Fideli and Renold Digbye : the same two messengers returned from the King the last of May, his Majesty being then in Cevyllia [Seville], presenting them with 200 ducats. The King sent, 12th of August, a pursuivant to Vivero for to call Stucley into the Court, presenting him a 1000 ducats to bear his charges. He took his journey from Vivero towards Madrill [Madrid] the 18 of August. The King

[1] *S.P.I.*, *Eliz.*, xxx. 92, P.R.O., London.
[2] *Ib.*, xxxii. 20, P.R.O., London.
[3] They included two O'Neills, a Geraldine, a MacMahon, a MacPhilip, "Murty Paddy," and a Kavanagh (Donal Spainagh).

willed him for to send for William, Stucley's son, and therewith gave him 3000 ducats, Stucley was lodged and had his diet defrayed by the King for the space of 22 weeks, being accompanied by a Knight of the Order of Calatrava called Don Francis Merles of Catalonia.

As the rest of the English Ambassador's letter deals with later events in Stucley's career, we defer it for the present in order to see the relations between the Archbishop of Cashel and that adventurer.

Archbishop of Cashel's Appeal to the King of Spain.

For a year and three months the Archbishop of Cashel toiled night and day to obtain help from Spain for the Confederate Chiefs in Ireland, interviewing Cabinet Ministers, writing memorials to the King, receiving little real sympathy, and many rebuffs. But, as he had the active support of one of the two active parties in the Cabinet at Madrid, he felt justified in encouraging the Munster chiefs to keep up the fight until reinforcements should arrive from Spain. In the other party of the Cabinet he had to reckon with active opposition. Lead by the Duke of Feria, the husband of Lady Jane Dormer, a pious and influential English refugee in Spain,[1] this party favoured the English refugees and adopted their view that while it was right and proper to try to remove Elizabeth, there could be no question of severing Ireland from the English Crown. The Archbishop's proposals, then, for this separation, met with but scant courtesy from the Duke, who even went so far as to display open contempt for the Irish, whom he described as " a sort of beggarly people, great traitors to one another, and of no force."

At this juncture there arrived in Spain the renowned Thomas Stucley who posed as the Duke or Marquis de Stucley of Leinster, whose advent was to be the means of upsetting the Archbishop of Cashel's plans. One, Hogan or Huggins, then resident at Madrid, a spy in the pay of the English Government, sensed this new opposition and related to his paymasters (August, 1570),[2] that he was encouraged to hope

---

[1] See *Cath. Bulletin*, Feb., 1925, pp. 143-54.
[2] *C.Sp.P.*, nos. 247, 260, 273, 275.

that the chasm between English and Irish would now be widened by Stucley's arrival. This hope he believed all the more reasonable as Stucley claimed to have come on the same mission from the Irish chiefs, and he (the spy) hoped to be able to set Stucley up against the Archbishop, so as to counteract his efforts by accentuating national jealousies and antipathies.

When MacGibbon heard that Stucley had fled from Ireland in indignation at the treatment meted out to him by the Queen because, as the messengers reported, he had favoured Catholics whilst holding an official position, he welcomed such a loyal son of the Church. And when he learned that Stucley was a man of great military experience, of wide influence, on intimate terms with the Irish chiefs, and determined to bring England's unholy rule over Ireland to an end, he at once wrote a long letter in Spanish to the King, 20 July, 1570 :—[1]

Encouraged by the confidence I have in your Catholic Majesty, I have dared to speak more freely than perhaps I should have done, but I trust your Majesty will excuse me, as the business is of such importance.

I understand that the English, after having done all the harm they could, wish to make peace with your Majesty which is with no other intention than that they may be able, after the peace is concluded with your Majesty, to treat us more freely by doing all the mischief they wish against us. These injuries, which will be felt by all in general, will be more terrible for myself,[2] because our chieftains have had great confidence in your Majesty, and I have written many times encouraging them to resist the English, assuring them that your Majesty would not fail to send assistance, as I was told by the Cardinal and other men of high position in the name of your Majesty. We have refused on this account, many times, the pardon the English have offered us for the past, telling us to enjoy our goods and lands as before, on condition we would be of their opinion, and recognise Her Majesty as Sovereign and Queen.

Neither can your Majesty conscientiously refuse to send us

---

[1] *Spic. Ossor.*, i. 62.

[2] The Spanish Secretary was of the opinion at the time that MacGibbon was not one who relished a martyr's crown. This opinion does not coincide with MacGibbon's own profession at the end of this letter.

some assistance in virtue of the promises made through me by your Majesty, and that without delay, as we have already been kept in suspense for one year and three months; for, you must hold in mind that your Majesty is the Catholic King, having received that name from your ancestors for the increase of Catholic faith, by favouring the cause of Catholics. In the same way as the Queen of England has favoured and favours the rebel heretics in France, your Majesty can, in an underhand manner,[1] send some assistance to our chieftains, in arms and men, under pretence of their going to Holland, who, contrary to your will, or for some other cause, should go to Ireland.

Your Majesty has now a good opportunity for so doing, by taking advantage of the arrival of that Englishman, Thomas Stukely, who has received such insults from his own countrymen that he will not fail to do them all the harm he can. He is a very daring man, clever in war matters, in which he has been engaged most of his life. He is well acquainted with our own country, its forts, its harbours. I have been informed that he has brought with him experienced mariners from all parts of Ireland. This is the most favourable season in the year, because now our land abounds with good corn and meat, much more than at other seasons of the year; besides if your Majesty does not send some succour within three months, the English will take such hold of our forts and harbours, that even if your Majesty were to make use of all your power, you would not overcome them. I mention this, because I have been informed that the English are making great preparations,[2] and are endeavouring to take possession of the whole country, and to keep it in such subjection that the natives shall no longer be able to make any resistance as they have hitherto done in some places. If the English succeed in their plans (which God forbid), your Majesty will have the worst enemies whom you have ever known. All this your Majesty can prevent now, with the assistance of a few men, by being the first to take possession of the ports and fortresses. The whole success depends on celerity, for your Majesty will be able to do with 10,000 men, and a little expense, what you will not afterwards be able to accomplish with 100,000 men and all available power. If perchance your Majesty is not satisfied with my embassy, or doubts

[1] Elizabeth had been, in underhand manner, aiding the Protestants in France, Holland, and Belgium. MacGibbon regarded those Protestants as rebelling against the peace of those countries as Elizabeth's government was a menace to the peace of Ireland.

[2] Under the presidency of Perrott in Munster.

lest perhaps those who sent me should not keep their word, let your Majesty send some one with me to my country, and I shall make those chieftains place their fortunes and estates under your Majesty's jurisdiction by oath, or give any security required by your Majesty until they fulfil what they have promised. If it does not please your Majesty to send prompt assistance, as I was promised by the Cardinal and other noblemen in your Majesty's name, I request your Majesty to grant me the favour of allowing me to return to my native land, that thus I may discharge my conscience of the great weight I have from the Church, and apologise to my brethren for my delay, by testifying my willingness to die for the Catholic faith, and for the liberty of my country,[1] as much as each of them does. My remaining here would only serve to increase the expenses of your Majesty, without any benefit to myself or any country.

The humble servant and chaplain of your Majesty

MAURICE CASHEL, *Archbishop.*

True, there might be strong reasons against sending help openly to Ireland, and thereby breaking with England, but Philip could easily imitate Elizabeth who was known to be contributing secretly but actively to the support of the Protestant cause in Flanders. Philip could similarly and easily send help in men, money, and munitions to Ireland under the pretence that they were ordered for Holland, but which through error or perversity had made their way to Ireland. Here it was that Stucley, in the Archbishop's eyes, would come in useful. A few thousand men might be placed at his disposal, with sufficient ships, for some imaginary expedition, and once they were on the high seas, Philip could not be held officially responsible if they made their way to Ireland. Although the Archbishop did not express precisely what he had in his mind, it is safe to assume that he had his eyes on a large Spanish fleet that was being got ready just at that time to convey Philip's fourth bride from Flanders to Spain. It is equally safe to conclude, from the anxiety manifested in England on the subject of this very fleet, that Elizabeth was quite alive to the possibility or imminent danger that that fleet might be utilised on the

[1] Henceforth, this was the Irish war-cry.

return journey in some such way as that suggested by the Archbishop.

Stucley Seeks Absolution from Heresy.

In the month of June (some weeks before MacGibbon sent his letter to Philip) the Ambassador in London, influenced by the reports of Ridolfi, the Italian banker in that city, and of the Italian spies in Ireland, assured the King that the sight of a Spanish fleet off the English coast would rouse the hopes of English and Irish Catholics. At that moment the greater part of Ireland would rise up against England, except fortified places like Dublin and a few others, which did not boast of more than 1500 men, as Stucley had informed him. He even threw out the suggestion, hinted at by MacGibbon, that the fleet that was to conduct the new Queen from Flanders to Spain, might be used against the English on the return journey. Philip gave the Ambassador to understand that he was considering steps in case Elizabeth meant war on him, but he would not move until he was sure of her intention. That he was considering those steps is evidenced by the fact that a couple of months later (in September) he summoned Stucley to Madrid from Vivero in Galicia where he and his companions had been detained since the landing in Spain.

Stucley obeyed the summons, proceeded to Valladolid, where he was royally received by Don Francesco de Merles in the King's name. Provided with every luxury, splendidly apparelled, furnished with plenty of money, and attended by a brilliant train, he made his triumphal entry into Madrid. Here he was received by the King with princely honours, as the Duke of Ireland, and flattered by the Duchess of Feria and her influential friends in Church and Court. Handsomely housed, and provided with a splendid allowance for his expenses, this gifted adventurer, with his imposing title and magnificent figure, attracted universal admiration. There was just one fly in the amber at this happy time. Though he attended Mass, and was to all outward appearances a pious Catholic, he did not venture to deny that he had been identified with heretics, and had lived as one for

22

many years.[1] Before he could appear in the eyes of all, without any stain, in his other Catholic practices he should be absolved from the crime of heresy. To achieve this desired object he put his case before the Papal Nuncio at Madrid, who wrote to the Cardinal Secretary in Rome, 24 September,[2] as follows :—

An English gentleman resident in Ireland, who gives himself out as sent by those gentlemen who are in arms for the Catholic religion in their kingdom of Ireland, to crave aid of the Catholic King, has laid before me the enclosed memorial, which you will do me the favour to submit to His Holiness : apprising him at the same time that, although he has already given me by private letters of Cardinal Alessandrino faculty to absolve and dispense in certain cases not expressed in my faculties, even in cases of heresy, nevertheless, as this case is so grave, I did not venture to touch it, and accordingly determined to communicate with his Holiness after making inquiry as to the qualities of this gentleman : and in brief I find, and the Archbishop of Cashel, who is of that country and is here, attests, that the said gentleman was in those parts [Ireland] deemed Catholic at heart, albeit his deeds belied it : and at present he lives here as a Catholic, going to Mass, and observing the fasts and other Catholic usages, so that in regard to this matter I desire to know what his Holiness bids me do. And if he should direct that absolution be given him, you will be good enough to let me know what form his Holiness would have it take, and what penance should be laid upon him, and to take care that the answer reach me as soon as possible, that the gentleman be not disheartened, and that he be comforted by reception into the bosom of holy Church, and not abandoned to despair, since he is now penitent. And in the meantime I will make as if I answered him, and keep him in play with good words. I know not as yet whether, evincing as he does such a desire for this absolution, he may not, to save so much delay, seek it meanwhile of the Cardinal Inquisitor Major. But in any event I desire his Holiness' commission in the matter.

The following is the enclosure referred to, containing Stucley's memorial :—

I have heard that the Archbishop of Cashel gave your Lordship a petition of mine in the Latin language, in which I said that I

---

[1] *Cath. Bulletin*, Feb., 1925, p. 151.
[2] *C.S.P., Rome*, 1558-71, no. 707.

had sworn allegiance to the Queen of England as head of the Church and that I had lived for eleven years in her religion, and that I had destroyed monasteries : no part of which is so : neither did I ever swear allegiance to the Queen save as queen and sovran lady, nor live in her religion, for I was ever in spirit a Catholic, and kept in my heart the faith and religion of the Holy Mother Church of Rome. That which I did was to live among the heretics of my country, not separating myself from their life or society, and eating meat on forbidden days, because I could not do less while I was in my country, where I must needs hazard my life, or do as the heretics did. Outwardly I was consentient with them, but not at heart. I hold the property of an abbey,[1] which I am ready to restore : and I have already built a very good church, and were it possible, and permitted by the Queen and her ministers, I would place religious therein, and give them their own. I have left substance and land and wife to come to crave succour for the Catholics of Ireland, England, and Scotland, and to effect the complete restoration of religion in the three realms, that I may be quit of the excommunication which I have incurred and may confess and communicate as a true Christian.

I humbly entreat your Lordship as Nuncio Apostolic with faculty from his Holiness to grant me absolution, or else for the love of God to obtain the same faculty from his Holiness, that I, as his obedient son, may have dealings with my brother Catholics, and manage the business of the Church with which I am charged, and present myself before his Holiness and kiss his feet as it behoves me, true vicar of Christ that he is, and head of His Holy Church.

On 31 October the Papal Secretary [2] replied as follows :—

The absolution craved by that Irish [*sic*] gentleman [Thomas Stucley] has been considered by the Pope, and definitively it is decided that it ought not to be granted.

Stucley, however, renewed his request early next year, when he had made up his mind to proceed to Rome, urging as an additional reason that it would never do for an unabsolved heretic to venture into the presence of his Holiness.

ARCHBISHOP OF CASHEL TELLS THE STORY OF STUCLEY.

In the meantime, the Archbishop of Cashel had come into contact with some of the Irishmen who had accompanied

---

[1] Evidently in Wexford.   [2] *C.S.P.*, *Rome*, 1558-71, no. 727.

Stucley to Spain, and who supplied him with information about that gentleman's career. So much in dread were they of Stucley, that they assured the Archbishop that if Stucley knew that they had been talking about him they would not count their lives their own. MacGibbon considered that it was his duty to communicate to the King the information he had received before he took his departure for Ireland where he had to report himself. We shall omit the portions of the document the substance of which has been already given in preceding sections.

The document, handed in to the King and Nuncio, and dated 16 December, 1570,[1] continues :—

having learned that some of the principal lords of Ireland had rebelled against the Queen, and knowing the ill-will the Queen bore to him, feeling at the same time his impossibility to take revenge, he [Stucley] sent word to the Spanish Ambassador in England, entreating him to arrange with the Spanish King to send some men to Ireland in order to conquer it, promising at the same time that protection or favour would not be wanting to them. This he [Ambassador] would not do because he was a Catholic ; and it is plain that no protection could be hoped for from Stucley who had destroyed so many churches, monasteries, and images ; and what favour could he promise to give, who was a native of England, who was hated by his own people, and much more hated by the Irish, as well on account of the natural and common hatred they bore him, for having purchased and occupied those lands,[2] which most of Ireland well knew neither belonged to the Queen nor to him, who had no right to them. Being thus in prison, as we have said, he asked leave of the Viceroy, through the medium of some friends, to go to England to ask the pardon of her Majesty. This permission the Viceroy granted, to prevent the envy he might have caused were he to execute justice in his regard. Having obtained this permission, he publicly announced that he was going to England, and took out a passporte to bring with him some horses which had been given to him by Irish gentlemen, as well as others which he had bought ; he also took on board some men, sent by their Irish masters to ask forgiveness for certain things of which they had been assured, and to implore pardon of the Queen ; others of their own free will, who had business in England,

[1] *Spic. Ossor.*, i. 66-70.
[2] The monastic lands in Wexford.

got into the same vessel. All were deceived, for after sailing from Waterford harbour with the intention of going to England, he brought them here to Spain, and now they do not dare to return to England or Ireland, and seeing themselves deprived of all resource, they are almost in a state of despair, principally on ac- count of the fear they have of him, for he threatens them, in case they attempt to return to their country, or to go elsewhere, to put them in prison, or something worse, that is, to throw them into the sea, for they are in his ship, as he did on another occasion with others. Your Majesty can be well informed of all this by the same Irishmen who are here, or in Galicia on this condition, that the same Thomas Stucley be never told who gave the in- formation, for if they suspect this they will never tell the truth, fearing, as it has been said before, this man, who has always been most singularly revengeful in his wickedness. As he is merely a private individual, it cannot be imagined that the Lords of Ireland should place in his hands a business of such importance, above all, as they have not given notice of it to me. They sent me here, and they know it is for their sakes I am at this Court ; neither can I believe that the Irish princes would wish that a private English gentleman should have command in the slightest degree in their kingdom, whilst they with such obstinacy resist the Queen of England, who has so often offered them peace on good con- ditions.[1] Therefore, I consider his coming as a matter of deception, or an act devoid of common sense, for as far as I understand, he has received no commission from the princes of Ireland for your Majesty or anyone else. My opinion has also been confirmed by the arrival of a Franciscan Friar [Patrick O'Hely] [2] with certain despatches for me, the same whom I had formerly sent to Ireland, and who has also been in Cordova with your Majesty ; neither did I receive any intimation by letter of the said Thomas Stucley, nor did the friar hear anything about him, except that there was a report that a certain famous Englishman had gone out to sea, and that it was feared it was with the intention, as formerly, of robbing. It seems to me your Majesty should inquire from the said Thomas Stucley by whose order, and for what purpose, he came to Spain ; for if it be a scheme of his own mind, it is clear

---

[1] As long as Elizabeth was allowed to rule as temporal sovereign and as Head of the Church, she cared little what form of worship was adopted, although she was personally inclined to ritualism, elaborate ceremonial. She evidently would have allowed Catholicism without the Supremacy of the Pope, as her father Henry had followed it. That seems to be the meaning of the phrase " peace on good terms."

[2] Appointed by the Pope to the diocese of Mayo, 4 July, 1576.

he will be able to do but little, neither should he be permitted to
go off at his pleasure, because, now that he has men and other
preparations made for sailing, and not having his country to live
in, he will go about plundering as before, and the King will have
to give an account to God, if, having it in his power to prevent so
much evil, he should not do so.[1]

In an interview with the King, about the same time, the
Archbishop laid stress on what was probably well known
to His Majesty, namely, that Stucley was "a pirate, of life
dissolute, of expenses prodigal, of no substance, or of any
account in his country." In reply to a remark that Stucley
claimed to speak in the name of the Irish chiefs, the Archbishop asserted that so far was this from being true, they
held him in no esteem, and even looked on him as "a shifter
who sought to abuse all men."[2]

The Archbishop's attitude soon became known to Stucley,
who, supported by the English refugees and their friends
at the Spanish Court, set himself deliberately and systematically to discredit him by depicting him as a man of no account.
He called him "a bastard of the Geraldines," a mere
"Dominican friar," who had secured the mitre by intrigue,
who had really been banished from Ireland for his want of
prudence, and who, instead of helping him (Stucley), had
actually "defaced him." To save his own character, therefore, and prevent his mission from being ruined, he (Stucley)
said he was reluctantly compelled "to discover the Archbishop's dissolute life."

After the Archbishop's departure for France, Stucley and
his supporters freely spread abroad that he had been sent
away in disgrace. This was not the case. It would appear
that the real object of his visit was to ascertain whether it
was possible for France and Spain to unite in lending a helping
hand to the Catholic cause in England and Ireland. France

---

[1] If a balladmonger of the day may be believed, Stucley squandered £100
a day, selling at last the blocks of tin with which the Alderman (his father-in-
law) had paved the yard of his London house. When all was gone he deserted
his wife.

> "Make much of me, dear husband," she did say.
> "I'll make much more of thee," said he,
> "Than any one shall, verily":
> And so he sold her clothes, and went his way.

[2] See *Cath. Bulletin*, Feb., 1925, p. 153.

and Spain were watching each other like cat and mouse, and neither would allow the other to move in that direction. As a Spanish expedition to Ireland might be less objectionable from a French point of view, leaving England out of the question, the Archbishop doubtless wished to put that aspect of the question before the French Court. Just at the time of the Archbishop's departure for France, Philip had begun in his own hesitating way to amass on the Spanish coast a force destined for the relief of Ireland. It is now necessary to return to Ireland and see how religion and fatherland were faring.

SUBMISSION OF IRISH CHIEFS.

Although the year 1570 came to a close with peace in the provinces, yet Tirlogh Luineach let it be known that he demanded all the lords, dignities, and titles any O'Neill before him ever had.[1] James Fitzmaurice was reported as keeping company with Edward Butler, but Sydney relied on the presidencies in Munster and Connacht as panaceas for all ills. On 13 December [2] the Queen appointed Sir John Perrott to the office of Lord President of Munster, and besides the archbishops, bishops, and nobility, there should be joined with him in Council a Chief and Second Justice, and suggesting the Castle of Dungarvan with the parsonage annexed ; a house in Limerick, such as the Friary ; a place in Cork, and another in Kilmallock, as suitable places for meeting. The castle of the Earl of Desmond in Kerry, he having violated his obligations and recognisances, was to be seized for the use of the President and Council ; likewise the Liberty of Kerry was to be seized, which Desmond claimed as a Palatinate.

In this year the following Irish chieftains made their submissions by indenture, namely, Brian, son of Cahir, son of Art Kavanagh of Ballyanne, Co. Wexford ; MacVaddock, who was head of a sept of the MacMurroughs ; MacEdmond Duff ; MacDamore, or MacDavid More, head of another sept of the MacMurroughs seated in the barony of Gorey, all of the Co. Wexford ; and O'Farrell Bane and O'Farrell Boy, of the Co. Longford. The terms of the indentures were

[1] *S P.I.*, *Eliz.*, xxx. 73.   [2] *C.P.C.R.I.*, *Eliz.*, i. p. 546.

similar in all cases, and were to the effect that they agreed " to surrender and give up in the Queen's most Honourable Court of Chancery of Ireland, all such manors, castles, lands, tenements, rents, reversions, and all other hereditaments that they and every of them have within the same country, the same to be given back by letters patent to be held by them and their heirs for ever, at the yearly rent to be reserved in the said patents, but to be free from the Bonnacht accustomed to be paid to the Queen's Galloglasses in discharge of which they are to pay" so many marks yearly. Brian MacArt Kavanagh agreed to pay 52 marks yearly ; MacVaddock, six score marks ; MacDamore, 40 marks ; O'Farrell Bane, 200 marks, or for lack of money, the same to be paid in kine, according to the price in the markets of Athboy and Navan ; Faghnie O'Farell, 200 marks.[1]

So badly had the provinces of Munster and Connacht suffered from the scarcity of food that a commission was issued, 27 April, 1570, to John Tickpenny, victualler of the garrison in Munster, with licence for two years to contract with any Frenchman, Spaniard, Portingall, Scot, Fleming, or any other stranger, and to import, in foreign ships, corn, grain, wine, salt, hops, and other merchandise not prohibited by the laws, the merchants and crews of these ships to be protected and permitted to trade in unforbidden goods, in consideration that " whereas the provinces of Mounster and Thomond are of late both by reason of the sturres and rebellions in these parts, the passing of the armie in the midest of theire last somer harvest, the burninge and destroyinge of theire corne, the continewance of our garrison for the maintenance and defence of our good subjects, and the universall lacke of good industrie of the inhabitants, are for the greatest parte growen so barren, wasted, and desolate, that verie slender and allmoste no provicion at all may for the presente be had in those countries for the victualling of our said garrison." [2]

Fitton Subdues Connacht.

While Ormond was reducing the rebellious O'Briens, Fitton was practically shut up in Galway. With a force

---

[1] Annals, *Four Masters, n. ad an.* [2] *Fiants,* no. 1519.

sent by Sydney, and with Clanricard's help, he was able to besiege Shrule Castle, the key of Lower Connaught. After a skirmish with the youth of Mayo and Connemara, under Shane MacOliver Burke, the castle was taken. Here also arose the difficulty of maintaining an army without cessing the people. And both sides had to feed Scotch auxiliaries. Burke was honest in confessing that the Scots were as burdensome to the country as subjection to the English nation would be. Even Fitton could not deny its truth, and yet he thought the presence of the soldiers of some use in keeping the peace. The country was as safe to travel, he said, as the English Pale.

The O'Connor Don, having escaped from the castle of Athlone, was indicted with MacDermot, Clanricard's sons, and all the gentlemen of Mayo with the view of entitling the Queen to the northern (lower) half of Connacht. According to the Annals of the *Four Masters :*—

On the festival of St. Patrick in this year [1571], the President of the province of Connaught, Sir Edward Phiton (Fitton), issued a proclamation for holding a court during eighteen days in the monastery of Ennis,[1] (to devise measures) to set to rights and reduce the Dal-Cais and [the inhabitants] of Upper Connaught.[2] The President . . . was occupied for the eighteen days before mentioned in establishing laws and regulations, and abolishing injustice and lawlessness. The Earl of Thomond gave up his country and his lordship to the President, as an atonement for the lawless act which he had formerly committed against him, and gave up to him Magh O mBreacain,[3] the only one of his (former) towns then in his possession ; so that the towns of Magh [O mBrecain], Bunratty, Claremore, and Clonroad, were in the possession of the President, on his leaving the territory ; and he carried hostages from every chieftain in Thomond along with him to Athlone. It would not be easy to enumerate all the hundreds of kine that were given to the President during the two years that he remained in Thomond.

To improve the position of Galway as a centre for the advancement of English rule in Connacht a license was

---

[1] Co. Clare, which the English made at this period a part of the province of Connaught.

[2] I.e. of South Connaught, i.e. the Earl of Clanricard and his adherents.

[3] I.e. the plain of Ibrickan, now Moymore, a townland near Milltown-Malbay, Co. Clare.

granted for three years to John Crofton to trade with any Frenchman, Spaniard, Portuguese, Fleming, or Scot, and import to Galway in foreign ships, wines, salt, iron, hops, grain, or other merchandise not prohibited by the laws, and to send return cargoes of unprohibited goods. With protection for the foreign merchants and crews. Recites the impoverishment of Galway through the stoppage of trade with strangers who were accustomed to come to the town, as its townsmen went abroad, that it is the only " norrice and place of civility and good order " in the province of Connacht and the necessity of supplying the garrison there. 24 February, 1571.[1]

The sons of the Earl of Clanricard having promised to be good and dutiful subjects of Her Majesty with the customary ease, and little heed as to how long they would consider themselves bound to abide by their promise, a grant was made to John Bourke of Deremicklaghlin of the office of seneschal of the barony of Clare in the province of Connacht. To hold during good behaviour with all profits belonging to the office. With power to assemble the inhabitants for defence of the barony, to attack and punish by all ways malefactors and their adherents, rebels, vagabonds, rhymers, Irish harpers, and idle men and women, and to hold a court baron. The grant not to prejudice any rents or customs of the Earl of Clanricard. 30 November, 1570.[2]

Pardon to Richard, Earl of Clanricard, John Bourke and Ulick Bourke, his sons. 20 March, 1571.[3]

On leaving Ireland, 25 March, 1571, Sydney had not the satisfaction, however, of seeing his favourite project of presidencies entirely successful.[4] But before he left he arranged affairs of the North that was under his special charge. Tirlogh Luineach entered into a treaty of peace with all the Queen's subjects until Her Majesty's further pleasure should be known. Tirlogh's wife had something to do with the treaty and begged support for her husband's messenger at the English Court. The Dean of Armagh was also a party to the treaty. The Scots, with Sorley Boy, in the Glens of Antrim, were thus held in check for the time, and Sydney

[1] *Fiants*, no. 1711.   [2] *Ib.*, no. 1634.
[3] *Ib.*, no. 1757.   [4] *S.P.I., Eliz.*, xxxi. 6, 14.

further secured peace in the Pale by agreement with the O'Farrells of Longford.

PERROTT'S CAMPAIGN IN MUNSTER.

Sir John Perrott, of an ancient Pembrokeshire family, but a supposed son of Henry VIII, was selected for the task of reducing Munster. His demands on going into Ireland included provision of a preacher, post-horses, grain, butter, cheese, beer, etc. Judging by his delay, he was neither anxious for the honour nor in a hurry to begin the work. His salary was fixed at £133 6s. 8d., but he was allowed thirty horse and twenty foot in the Queen's pay. The Council consisted of the Archbishop and Bishops of Munster, and the Earls of Ormond, Thomond, and Clancare, with additional members at the Deputy's pleasure. The First Chief Justice was James Dowdall, the Second was Nicholas Walshe, and Thomas Burgate was first Clerk of the Council. The Council had all the judicial authority of a Court of Assize. The " liberties " of Tipperary were not to be needlessly infringed, but those of Kerry were declared to be null and void. The President and Council were to assist all officers, civil and ecclesiastical and to maintain their proper authority.[1] The President was allowed to " retain one chaplain or minister that shall and can preach and read the Homilies," and the preacher was to receive entertainment in the house of the President, who " shall cause due reverence to be given [to him], in respect of the office that he shall have for the service of God."

MacBrien Arra in Tipperary,[2] and the Kavanaghs, surrendered their lands and received them back by grant, and Perrott was installed in the Presidency. Sydney, having thus provided both a scourge for the rebels and a counterpoise for Ormond, sailed for England and left the government in the hands of Sir William FitzWilliams. Perrott landed at Waterford, 27 February, 1571. About this time Fitzmaurice, who had been lurking about Tipperary with less than 120 " naked villains afoot," suddenly appeared at the head of a considerable but almost unarmed force, surprised

---

[1] See Bagwell, ii. 180.
[2] *Kilk. Arch. Assoc.*, 1858-59, p. 346 *seq.*

and burned Kilmallock. The *Four Masters* (A.D. 1571), give an interesting, detailed account of the engagement :—

James MacFitzMaurice took Kilmallock, not from a desire of [obtaining] its riches and various treasures, though its riches were immense, but because it had always been the rendezvous and sally-port of the English and Geraldines [in their contests] against him. Before sunrise in the morning those who had gone to sleep happily and comfortably were aroused from their slumber by a furious attack made by the warlike troops of the Clann-Sweeny and Clann-Sheehy, who were along with James MacMaurice; and they proceeded to divide among themselves its gold, silver, various riches, and valuable jewels, which the father would not have acknowledged to his heir, or the mother to her daughter, on the day before. They were engaged for the space of three days and nights in carrying away the several kinds of riches and precious goods, as cups and ornamented goblets, upon their horses and steeds, to the woods and forests of Etharlach,[1] and sending others of them privately to their friends and companions. They then set fire to the town, and raised a dense, heavy cloud, and a black, thick, and gloomy shroud of smoke about it, after they had torn down and demolished its houses of stone and wood; so that Kilmallock became the receptacle and abode of wolves[2] in addition to all the other misfortunes up to that time.

There was some suspicion of collusion between the townsmen of Kilmallock and Fitzmaurice, for only two of the former were killed, and against these Fitzmaurice is said to have had a personal grudge. However this may be, Edward Butler is reported by FitzWilliams,[3] 15 March, to have recovered great part of the cattle. Eager to earn his pardon, he pursued Fitzmaurice, and " killed one of his dear foster brethren." Ormond himself travelled on foot all over the glen and forest of Aherlow, but none of the rebels would even skirmish, and it was evident that Munster could only be reduced by the steady pressure of a regular force.[4]

---

[1] Aherlow, a beautiful valley situated between Slievenamuck and the Galtee mountains, and about four miles to the south of the town of Tipperary.

[2] Wolves, literally " wild dogs, or dogs of the wood." Wolves were very numerous in Ireland at this period, and for more than a century later. The last native wolf of Ireland is said to have been seen in the mountains of Kerry in the year 1720. (*Memoirs of the Life and Writings of Charles O'Conor of Belanagare*, p. 450.)

[3] *S.P.I., Eliz.*, xxxi. 21, 33, i.   [4] Bagwell, ii. 184.

Having taken the oath before Sydney in Dublin, Perrott went to Cork where he found himself at the head of about 700 men, 200 of whom were Irish. From Cork he went to Kilmallock, ordered the inhabitants to rebuild their houses, pursued the insurgents as far as Knocklong. The Irish fled into the bogs pursued by Perrott's soldiers, carrying lances, who returned with a trophy of fifty heads. The President decorated the market-cross at Kilmallock with them for the edification of the people of Limerick. This city having been taken, he went to Cashel where he hanged seven merchants for supplying Fitzmaurice's men with provisions. Fethard, Clonmel, Carrick, Lismore, and the strong castle of Mocollop were entered in triumph. At Cork he was attended by Clancare [1] and Thomond (because he was the superior force), by Lords Barry, Roche, and Courcy, and by MacCarthy Reagh and Sir Cormac MacTeig. The White Knight's country was again invaded, his castles taken, and himself driven into the woods. Perrott then marched against the MacSwineys, " slew many of the rebels, and

[1] Perhaps the most important submission was that of the Earl of Clancare, called the MacCarthy More, who described himself as the most unworthy and unnatural Earl, who " with inward sorrow of mind and most hearty repentance, recalling the great benefits and exceeding bounty he received from her Majesty, and the degree of honour and pre-eminence he had been most unworthily called unto, far greater than ever he, a cursed creature, could have deserved, with bitter tears and great compunction of mind, most humbly confesses, which the more aggravates the enormity of his offences, and heaps upon him more abundantly her Majesty's most just indignation, that being seduced by that most pernicious rebel, James Fitzmaurice, and the Geraldines, upon a false pretence, to have a parley with him, and to conclude a peace between James and Richard Grenville, Sheriff of Cork, when, forgetting his duty to God and her Majesty, he was, by subtle inticements and most wicked persuasions induced to take an unadvised and rash oath ; which done, he entered into that fury and madness of unnatural rebellion against his sovereign, confederating with Sir Edmond Butler and the rest of his principal rebels, whereby he swerved and declined from his allegiance, by traitorously raising her Majesty's subjects, besieging her towns, shamefully murdering and destroying her subjects, burning houses and castles, and sundry other grievous offences and heinous and detestable treasons, deserving extreme punishment and sharp correction." He now, most penitent, submits his body, goods, life, and lands to the disposition of her Majesty, and begs the Council to intercede with the Queen for his pardon, as he has now resolved to dedicate " to her Majesty the last drop of his blood." This humble submission was, of course, written out by the Council, and Donyll Clancare had to affix his signature. It was the only thing that he could do in the circumstances, if he wished to keep his lands. But how far he bound himself by it is quite another matter.

hanged as many as he might take, whom the Marshal executed always as he went along ; so that they took a great prey, spoiled all the enemy's country, and with continual travel wore out all their provisions, having no corn in the country left to make their bread, which the President himself wanted for divers days, their chief sustenance being the milk of those kine that they had taken." Want of provisions was the great difficulty ; all peaceable men having been robbed of their cows and horses.

Fitzmaurice suddenly managed to collect a strong force of the MacSheehy and MacSwiney kerne whose maintenance was provided by the men of Desmond. The *Four Masters* relate the next movement of Perrott :—

In the spring of this year an English President, Sir John Perrott, was appointed over the two provinces of Munster. He had many ships and barques, companies and captains. The chiefs, noble rulers, lords, and dynasts of the country joined him at once ; but the soldiers, insurgents, the mercenaries and retained troops of the country sided with James [FitzMaurice], though, of [all] his fortified residences, he retained Caislen-na-Mainge [1] only. The President commanded the men of Munster to muster all their forces, and, providing their own provisions, to come to him on the ensuing festival of St. John [24 June], for the purpose of besieging Caislen-na-Mainge. They did so at his command, and continued besieging the castle from the festival of St. John to the middle of autumn ; but their efforts proved fruitless, for they did not take the castle that year. The President [upon this] went to Cork, and the men of Munster departed for their respective homes.

The *Four Masters* are not quite accurate in saying that the siege lasted into the autumn. It lasted from 21 June to 27 July, namely, five weeks. Perrott attached great importance to the taking of Castlemaine. But the cannon were delayed by storms in their passage from Limerick, and there was a dearth of powder and of almost every requisite for successful war. The castle, standing on arches, and very small, judging from its remains, proved stronger than was supposed. The famished army had to withdraw, after wasting all its powder, without making a breach.

---

[1] I.e. the castle of the river Mang, now Castlemaine, in the Co. Kerry.

Fitzmaurice, strange to say, had not been at Castlemaine, but had been doing other work in Cashel and Cork.

COLONISATION OF ULSTER A FAILURE.

After his failure at Castlemaine, Perrott confessed that the work of " Trotting the mountains " was not suited to English soldiers. Men, munitions, and food were scarce. Kinsale and Youghal complained of their ruinous condition and of the daily dread of being attacked. The return of the Earl of Desmond and of Sir John of Desmond, who " in their time did right well govern these parts," would alone send James Fitzmaurice beyond the seas, and free them from the fate of Kilmallock. Perrott foolishly conceived the idea of ending the war by challenging Fitzmaurice to single combat. The latter suggested fifty aside. It was finally agreed that each party should consist of twelve horse and twelve foot. Knocklong was the appointed place, but " God be praised," said FitzWilliams (25 November), " the rebel chief did not appear." [1] Fitzmaurice had good reasons for not keeping his tryst, fear of treachery being clearly uppermost. But the reason he gave through his Irish rhymer was to the effect : " If I should kill Sir John Perrott, the Queen of England can send another President into this province ; but if he do kill me, there is none other to succeed me, or to command as I do, therefore I will not willingly fight with him, and so tell him from me."

The colonisation of Munster by " Huguenots " or imported Protestants was a failure. It was one of Fitzmaurice's avowed objects to make it so, for the scheme stung him to the quick. But this failure did not deter Elizabeth from lending her aid to a similar project in the North. The Ards of Ulster (east Co. Down) were a suitable place for the experiment, almost surrounded as they were by the sea. Sir Thomas Smith, whose idea was to reconquer the Queen's land without burden to her or to the English State, made an offer that was accepted by Elizabeth.[2] According to his

---

[1] *S.P.I.*, *Eliz.*, xxxiv. 29, iii.

[2] A pamphlet published in London at this time set forth the historical reasons why the English power had waned in Ireland, and advocated colonisation as the real remedy.

plan, a permanent garrison was to be established, " and every soldier to be made master of his own land, to him and his heirs for ever." It was supposed that 600 or 700 men would be enough, and that the penniless younger sons would seize upon this golden opportunity. The pay of the 300 horse and 400 foot would amount to £10,000 a year, and for the first three years they were to pay no rent for their holdings. Smith's plan took no account of how a loan of £10,000 was to be raised free of interest for three years on the security of Irish land still unconquered, or of the fact that although 700 men might take land at a given time it might take 7000 men a very short time afterwards to retain it. Nor did Smith reckon with MacFelim O'Neill, lord of South Antrim and North Down, and the Clandeboye O'Neills. FitzWilliams' pretence that the intruders were brought in entirely against the Scots did not convince the Irish chieftains. He, in fact, reported that the immediate effect of the pamphlet fathered by Smith was to strengthen the Scots whose alliance was now sought by the Northern chiefs. The colonisation project, however, was a complete failure, and great hordes of Scots, introduced by Tirlogh Luineach and his wife, or seeking settlement for themselves, kept the scanty English garrisons in constant alarm.[1]

In the meantime, Ireland lay at the mercy of a foreign enemy. Elizabeth had reduced the army in Ireland, and 6000 Spaniards would have caused as irrevocable a loss as that of Calais, and the Narrow Seas would be no longer safe. Elizabeth's ill-judged parsimony was probably due to the great difficulty of getting money at this time. The breach with Alva had destroyed the credit system of the Netherlands, and English finance had not yet become sufficient to itself. But the Queen took care that Spain should be fully occupied, and the capture of Brill, which coincided with the discharge of the troops in Ireland, made a Spanish descent on that country exceedingly improbable.[2]

---

[1] *S.P.I.*, *Eliz.*, xxxiv. 41, 42, 52 ; xxxv. 2.
[2] Bagwell, ii. 216. Burgeon, *Life of Sir Thomas Gresham*, vi., vii.

Meiler Magrath Imprisons Two Friars in Cashel.

Meiler Magrath did not succeed in his petition to the Privy Council for the diocese of Down and Connor which was granted to John Merriman by Elizabeth, 19 January, 1569. It was not until 18 September, 1570, that the Queen rewarded him for his patience and loyalty to her " reform," by granting him the diocese of Clogher, in which the country of his patron Maguire stood. But, meeting with a hostile reception from the natives, and unable to receive any of the temporalities, he once more petitioned Elizabeth to remove him to a more peaceful and lucrative post. As Cashel was bereft of a royal bishop since the abduction of MacCaghwell, Elizabeth transferred Meiler to it, 3 February, 1571. Not many months elapsed before he was involved in a trial of strength with the Butlers and Fitzmaurice. He was ever on the watch for the coming of emissaries from the Pope, and from the Court of Madrid to which Archbishop MacGibbon and Bishop Herlihy of Ross had gone to seek help for James Fitzmaurice in his single-handed fight for religion and land. He tells the story of a capture in a letter to Weston, 25 July :—[1]

Advertising your Lordship that I have taken prisoners two friars for preaching against the Queen's proceedings, whereof one of them [Edward Cackyrythe] was late at Rome and brought Bulls and other letters with them which I hand your Honour, with this bearer ; and having the said friars five days in my keeping, James Fitzmorris, the rebel, wrote unto me threatening words for their enlarging [release], at whose instance I did not set them at liberty. Yet, being from home where the said friars were kept, Mr. Edward Butler came and with force them take away from thence, and being requested by me to restore the said friars again, he refused to so do, and did set them at liberty.

One of the Bulls referred to was probably that of Pius V, releasing Elizabeth's subjects from loyalty to her, which Fitzmaurice had posted [about January] on the gate of Limerick.[2] Fitzmaurice was at this time lurking in the Glen

---

[1] *S.P.I.*, *Eliz.*, xxxiii. 15, i., P.R.O., London.
[2] Letter of Mayor of Limerick to Ormond. A copy of the Bull was enclosed but is not at present among the *State Papers*. (*S.P.I.*, *Eliz.*, xxxii. 57, i., P.R.O., London.)

of Aherlow, and, hearing of the arrest of the friars, wrote to Magrath, 19 July :—[1]

My friend as you deserve, I have me commended unto you etc. As I am informed that you have taken prisoner the poor friars for preaching the word of God to the poor people whoso are blinded with ignorance those many years for lack of good preachers that would show them their duty. Wherefore I do require you to enlarge at full liberty the said frairs that we may receive good fruit thereby and illumineth our hearts receiving from their mouths the just way of our salvation, the which we need very much by reason of a long continuance in obscurity, and in granting me the said request at this my contemplation, you bind me so [to] do your friendship and pleasure otherwise ; if you do it not, do not only take heed of your own proper body, but also of your goods, your adherents, and all that will be obedient to pay you any kind of rent or duty, without fail to the less [least] coal of fire in their houses and buildings. I will with the permission of God see them brought all to ruin and destruction, so that my power may stretch thereunto. Therefore, choose to take wise and sober counsel in your proceedings.

Your friend as you merit.

In omni tribulatione
Spes nostra Jesus, Maria.[2]

JAMES FzMORISHE *of Desmonde.*

To Meolmorye McCrache
at Casshell or elleswhere.

Fitzmaurice's letter was clever and bold. Loftus, Sydney, and the rest made the want of religion and ignorance among the Irish a constant theme in their condemnation of the natives.[3] Fitzmaurice now shows the dishonesty of the plea,

---

[1] *S.P.I., Eliz.*, xxxiii. 15, iii., P.R.O., London.

[2] " Jesus, Mary, our hope in every trial."

[3] FitzWilliams at this very time (July) complains of the " lamentable ignorance of the people of Ireland. In divers counties not one preacher." Indeed, about this time an entry in the *State Papers* gives the Causes why Ireland is not reformed. " Religion hath no place, men have no fear nor love of God, they regard not faith nor oath, they murder, ravish, spoil, burn, commit whoredom, break wedlock, change wives, without grudge of conscience. They have no regard of churches, nor of the ministers of them, they usurp the church livings, and suffer the churches so to decay as in the most part of them, the priest [Protestant] hath no place to stand in, for defence of the weather. Justice nor law taketh not much better place, for few of that country birth do

for when these friars have come to preach to the people they are thrown into prison. It was bold in its terrible threat that he would leave those who paid tithes to Magrath without even as much as coal in their grate.

Magrath also tells (to FitzWilliams) that when afterwards he met Butler, the latter said he did no harm in taking away the friars as they were only poor men who would do nothing against Elizabeth, and then boldly asked Magrath to write secretly to the Deputy and Council to grant him protection.[1] Of course this was part of Butler's strategy, and he was the only leader who stood out to lend a helping hand to Fitzmaurice.

Magrath was, according to FitzWilliams, endeavouring to the best of his power, faithfully and diligently, to further " religion and other part of your Majesty's service," as might be seen in his sending letters about Fitzmaurice and Edward Butler. FitzWilliams, however, mistakes Butler's request for protection as an offer of service against Fitzmaurice, but thinks " Butler's offence worthy of ten deaths." Magrath inadvertently wrote six capital letters among some Latin lines in his letter to FitzWilliams, and these became the basis of much suspicion against him. Were they some title he was assuming in his writings to his superiors ? After much heart-burning on the part of Magrath and deception played on him by FitzWilliams, Magrath not venturing to explain their meaning in a letter for fear of spies, and FitzWilliams not allowing him to come to Dublin to explain, FitzWilliams suddenly hit on the solution. The capital letters represented men's names, and in particular that of the friar, Edward Cackyrythe, which Magrath wrote down for his own information and as a reminder to deal with these men on a future occasion. It was a way Magrath had of innocently writing Latin lines and inserting capital letters to remind him of some important personages and their meetings, in the hope of explaining them orally later. But FitzWilliams did not

---

so continue their study, as they become learned, and yet of them as they are, be made as the judges of the land. . . . No man need to marvel why that realm groweth daily from bad to worse." (*S.P.I., Eliz.*, xxxii. 65, P.R.O., London.)

[1] *Ib.*, xxxiii. 15, P.R.O., London.

think these people of much importance and boasted that he knew all about their meetings.

It is clear that Fitzmaurice was preparing another *coup*, and his supporters who had gone back to their homes rallied again to his call. It seems extraordinary that Edward Butler, who had pursued Fitzmaurice from Kilmallock and taken some of his cattle and killed some of his men, should have released the friars from Magrath. An explanation is given that he wished to show his power, establish communications with Magrath, and then offer to pursue Fitzmaurice with all his might upon condition of pardon. Magrath, indeed, mentioned the offer to FitzWilliams, which the latter recommended Burghley to accept. But on returning to Cork, Perrott found that Fitzmaurice had not been idle in his absence. The latter had caught English sailors along the shores of the harbour, away from their boats, and driving them, it is said, into a ruined church, overwhelmed them with showers of stones. Thirty-three were slain, and the only prisoners taken, two in number, were sent back. In consequence of this disaster, the ships that should have supplied Perrott's besiegers of Castlemaine, lay idly at anchor.[1]

Elizabeth was determined to bring Munster into civil conformity and, 11 November, 1571, she issued a commission to Sir John Perrott, Lord President of Munster; the Earl of Ormond; Meyler, Archbishop of Cashel; Donyll, Earl of Clancartie; Patrick, Bishop of Waterford; the Bishop of Corke; William, Bishop of Lymericke, etc., to be commissioners in the counties of Waterforde, Tipperarie, Corke, Lymericke, and Keary, and the countries of Desmond, Beantrie, and Carbery, and all countries south of the river Shannyn in Munster, to make the country of Desmonde one county and to divide the rest into such counties, as may be convenient, to ascertain the number of acres in the counties and countries, to extend them in ploughlands and divide these into baronies.[2]

In the preceding year (30 November), a commission was issued to Patrick, Bishop of Waterford and Lismore, to make inquisition of the number of acres in the Co. Waterford,

---

[1] *S.P.I.*, *Eliz.*, xxxiii. 15 ; i., ii., iii., v., 16.   [2] *Fiants*, no. 1846.

to find what places are cessable, and to divide the county into cantreds.[1]

Protestant Bishop of Cork Deposed for Adultery.

Dixon, Sydney's choice for the diocese of Cork and Cloyne, and recommended for his " modesty and good grace to edify," proved himself as great a scandal to the Protestant Church as Devereux of Ferns. His story is told to Burghley by Weston, Loftus, and FitzWilliams, 16 April :—[2]

Richard Dixon, Bishop of Cork, less than twelve months in the bishopric, who has a married wife, has, under colour of matrimony, taken another woman of suspected life in the city of Cork as his wife ; and thereof by public fame and crying out of that misdeed, the matter coming to our ears, he being called and summoned to appear before us to answer thereunto upon examination, by virtue of his oath, confessed the same, and we, considering the heinousness and turpitude in sin, the great exclamation of the whole realm against him, the great offence and slander in general by that his fact against the professors of God's word, namely, Bishops and marriage, to no little glory of the adversaries,[Catholics] and the grief of the godly [Protestants], thought meet not only that he should do public penance for the same, but also as well for the desert of the said offence, as to remove the public slander which otherwise could not be appeased, to depose him from the bishopric. The first whereof is done already, wherein he like a penitent came to the Cathedral church of Dublin [Christchurch] and there standing under the pulpit two several Sundays in the time of the sermons made there by the preachers thereunto appointed, and acknowledged his offence though in not such penitent sort as was thought meet to put away the offence of so grievous and public a crime. But for the other part, we considering the words of our commission, and desirous to do as much as we have there by authority and commandment, and leave no part thereof undone, and yet not to encroach further upon the Queen Majesty's authority than we have warrant in the same, doubting [not daring] to exceed the commission, desire you will send us instruction as to depriving him, having no trust in the consciences of the lawyers [3] here.

[1] *Fiants*, no. 1635.   [2] *S.P.I., Eliz.*, xxxii. 10, P.R.O , London.
[3] The lawyers being practically all Catholics, the Commission had no confidence in their findings.

Whatever Elizabeth may have thought about the question as to whether the ecclesiastical commission had power to depose a bishop, she set the matter right by deposing Dixon. It took her some months to make up her mind, and, 26 November, no doubt shortly after the deposition, Loftus [1] hastened to recommend a friend of his own. Matthew Seyne or Sheyne, he says, is " a man in the judgment of the godly there [Cork] that know him for his sound religion, honest life, and good learning most meet for that dignity. I have known him seven years, and think him the fittest for the place, as he is acquainted with the country's language."

It was not until 29 May, 1572, that Elizabeth appointed Sheyne. He was evidently a man after Loftus's own heart. " He was a great enemy to the superstitious veneration paid by the people to images ; and as an instance of it, in October, 1578, he publicly burned St. Dominick's image at the High Cross of Cork, to the great grief of the super-stitious people of that place." [2]

A few months after Dixon's trial, the bishopric of Down was vacant by the death of John Merriman, who had been recommended by Sydney to the See to the great disgust of Meiler Magrath. Captain Piers of Carrickfergus recommended (6 July) [3] that " some zealous and learned man may be sent hither as in both the languages may instruct the people of the North ; here is great need." On all sides there was much anxiety to secure Irishmen, especially those who knew Irish, for the Sees.

Magrath was not happy in Cashel ; it was not sufficiently bred in English manners and not near enough to his own people. He evidently had a heart-to-heart talk with Fitz-Williams who accordingly wrote to Lord Burghley (Cecil), 24 August :—[4]

The bishopric of Down is void, and the Archbishop of Cashel, a natural man [native] of that soil, is most desirous to remove thither if so it may stand with her Majesty's good pleasure. In which, be such his one earnest request, the Lord Chancellor, the

---

[1] *S.P.I.*, *Eliz.*, xxxiv. 30, P.R.O., London.
[2] Harris, *Ware's Bishops*, 564.
[3] *S.P.I.*, *Eliz.*, xxxiii. 2, P.R.O., London.
[4] *Ib.*, 43, P.R.O., London.

which [1] Bishop of Dublin and the Bishop of Meath earnestly
desired me to commend to your good favour for Cashel one Matthew
Seyny [Sheyne] a natural [native] of this country [Tipperary],
and a fine Latinist and of no young years. The man is very well
recommended to me for an honest man and an earnest Protestant,
and spoke very good English, and of his life I hear no other than
good, and labours in teaching of children, a godly exercise.

What with the uneasiness of some of the Protestant
bishops in their Sees, desiring peaceful abodes in order to
have secure temporalities, and the unexemplary lives of
others, either in selling See lands or leading lewd lives, the
" reform " church was indeed finding it difficult to carry
out " reform " even within itself.

Prebendaries of St. Patrick's still Catholics.

If there was one place in Ireland where the " reform "
might be expected to make some progress it was Dublin,
and especially Dublin's Cathedral, St. Patrick's. Elizabeth's
own treatment of that cathedral could not be taken as in
any way exemplary. Her bestowal of the deanery on a
layman in order to augment his salary as chancellor, and her
bestowal of some of the best prebends also on layfolk, were
not conducive to command respect from the other prebendaries.
Even Loftus was scandalised. He wrote to Burghley,[2]
26 September, 1571, that the deanery of St. Patrick's should
not be made a fee for the Lord Chancellor, and that the
cathedral and seven parishes [3] should be served with vicars.

---

[1] FitzWilliams' letters are very crudely written—both as to caligraphy
and composition.

[2] *S.P.I., Eliz.*, xxxiv. 13, P.R.O., London.

[3] Loftus had already referred to these prebendal parishes as within about
five miles of the city. We do not know for certain where these lay, but if we
take those that fulfil the condition of distance, it will be interesting to see how
these parishes stood sixty years later as to the number of Catholic and Protestant
inhabitants. The figures are given in the Visitation of 1630 made by the
Protestant Archbishop Bulkeley who had the heads counted.

St. Audoen's (in the city). " There are but sixteen Protestant houses in
the parish, all the rest, being above three parts, are recusants " [Catholics].

Swords. " . . . the gentlemen of that parish who are recusants . . .
there is a great concourse of people on Sundays and holydays " at Mass " in

" If your Lordship did know of the number of poor souls that live in those parishes even as sheep without a shepherd without any doctrine and preaching of God's word you would, I am sure, lament their case and be earnestly moved to procure with speed the redress thereof."

Browne,[1] he says, assisted by Sir Val. Browne, sent letters to the chapter to elect him [Browne] to the deanery. " In that case things will be in far worse state than they are. Browne has no sense of true religion, and is void of any learning, and therefore so unmeet for such a great charge that he is scarcely thought worthy of what he has." (Browne had been recommended by the Lord Deputy for the See of Down.)

Loftus then gives us an illuminating piece of information as to the failure of the " reform " after a trial of eleven years. He states :—

And although all the old prebendaries be ignorant Papists, yet there be some procured hither and placed there by me, as Mr. Bukeley, Mr. Kearney,[2] and others, which for virtue and

the house of Michael Taylor of Swoordes. . . . There useth to come to church there about threescore to hear Divine service and sermon."

Clonmethan. " There are not above ten or twelve in that parish that come to hear divine service."

Howth. " There come hither, to hear Divine service, thirty persons or thereabouts."

Saggart. " There are about thirty of that parish who come to hear Divine service to the parish church of Rathcoole, because the parish church is down : all the rest of the parishioners are recusants."

Castleknock. " The most of the parishioners are recusants, yet the last Easter there were about twenty communicants."

Kilmactalway. " There are not above twelve in that parish that frequent Divine service : all the rest are recusants."

As this was the state of the Catholic and Protestant population in 1630, what must it have been in 1571 ? A similar condition Bulkeley observes in the other parishes in the diocese. The only parishes that can boast of a fair Protestant population are those in the city which are adjacent to Dublin Castle or are in the suburbs.

[1] A Christopher Browne was prebendary of Wicklow in 1566, and still held his prebend in 1581. At a visitation of the Cathedral in 1569, he was objected to in an official capacity as he was charged with " divers crimes."

[2] In this year " two dignitaries of this cathedral, Nicholas Walsh, Chancellor, and John Kerney, Treasurer, distinguished themselves by the introduction of Irish types ; they procured an order from the Government for printing the Common Prayer in that language, and, likewise, that a church should be set apart in the chief town of each diocese, where the liturgy should be read

learning are very worthy of that room, but it is to be feared lest the others, be left to their own arbitrament without such admonition from your Lordship as I have spoken of, would choose one of their own Popish faction.

Thus scarcely more than six out of the number of prebendaries belonged to the Established Church. Loftus was in a peculiar dilemma. He resented Weston's (the lay Dean's) authority over the Chapter, he complained of Browne's attempt to have himself elected Dean, and he feared the Catholic prebendaries would elect a Catholic and asked Burghley to interfere in the freedom of the Chapter.

STATE OF THE IRISH CHURCH IN 1571.

Many Government officials have already given their report on the state of religion in Ireland. And one may be pardoned for being somewhat sceptical about the portions of those reports which deal with the social and moral conditions of Catholics. But when a Catholic describes those conditions one cannot withhold acceptance of them unless some sinister motive can be imputed to him. In the letter now to be considered there seems no sufficient reason for imputing any such motive. It seems a sincere statement of fact. The letter was written at Rome, 26 October, 1571,

in that language and a sermon preached, by which means many persons were converted to the established church : the first book printed in this language, with Irish characters, was a catechism, written by this Kerney " (Mason, 170). The same two men were employed to translate the New Testament into Irish. In August, 1587, they seem to have had the translation finished, but an order of the English Privy Council stated that the reason why it had not been printed was the lack of the native Irish printers. The letter further stated that the MS. was in the hands of William Kearney, a relative of the Treasurer. It seems probable that it was this William who had printed the Catechism. He spent fourteen years abroad as a printer, and, having returned to England in 1591, he was permitted to cross over to Ireland with his printing presses for the purpose of printing Irish Bibles, there being no other printer in Ireland who knew Irish and who could manipulate the fount sent over by Elizabeth. Kearney set up his press in the new college [Trinity] sometime about 1593, and had the type of the Irish Testament actually set up in 1595 up to the sixth chapter of St. Luke's Gospel, when he suddenly left the College. The work was not published until 1602 (1603 according to modern dating). This was the third specimen of printing in the Irish language, the earlier specimens being Kearney's Catechism and a poem. (Only one copy of this poem is extant, namely, in Corpus Christi College, Cambridge.)

by Edmund Tanner to Cardinal Moroni, Protector of Ireland.[1] He describes himself as " an exile for religion's sake for more than twelve years from his native country Ireland," and offers his services to the Protector.

He is assured by grave men that during all this time not a hundred Irishmen in all Ireland have been infected with heresy, though not a few, for fear of penalties and confiscation of goods, attend the profane rites of the heretics, and the demoralisation of the people is such that a pious Catholic is hardly to be found ; and no wonder since the clergy are the most depraved of all. Moreover, there is little instruction to be had in the Christian faith that few can so much as repeat the Lord's Prayer, the articles of the faith, or the commandments, and still fewer understand them.[2] Sermons are so uncommon that there are many that have never so much as heard one ; the Sacraments are so rarely administered, so much more rarely understood, that the ignorant people know not whether they were appointed by God or by men. In fine, so gross is the ignorance of the people that there are many who, passing all their lives in the grossest sin, have grown so accustomed thereto that they dare to say that it is just as lawful for them to live by theft or rapine as for him that worthily serves the altar to live by the altar.

And nevertheless, so well inclined are they, or rather prompted by the Holy Spirit, to a good life, that it needs but the admonition or reproof of a good man and forthwith they are dissolved in tears, lamenting that they knew not that such things were sins, or contrary to the commandments of God.

Touched by a sense of their woeful plight, the writer has come from Louvain to Rome to offer his services, such as they are, in that deserted field. As to his qualifications he refers the Cardinal Protector to the Bishop of St. Asaph, and the Bishop of Emly,[3] both of whom are in Rome, and the " London " Prior of the Knights of Malta who will soon be there ; and for fuller information to Father Natalis, Vicar of the Institute of the Society of Jesus, and Father Everard, of the same Society, Alan Cope, Cardinal Hosius' theologian, and the Warden of the English Hospital at Rome, and other priests of the said hospital.

---

[1] *C.S.P.R.*, 1558-72, no. 845. Tanner was afterwards Bishop of Cork.
[2] Fitzmaurice had already expressed the same view (see p. 354).
[3] Maurice MacBrien.

Such a state of affairs is not to be wondered at. Indeed, it would be a miracle of the moral order were it otherwise, considering Elizabeth's prohibition of Catholic practices and the perpetual civil strife throughout the land.

Briefly, the conditions are these : Presidencies are set up in Munster and Connacht, and commissions are appointed to administer the English law and to punish severely all evildoers, to break down the whole traditional system of Irish rule and law. Where there is any opposition, or a chief like Fitzmaurice insists on preserving the ancient customs he is followed up with all the force the Deputy can muster. The crops are either destroyed in wholesale fashion, or gathered when possible for the support of the army. The Irish, on the other hand, consider themselves justified in spoiling and destroying those who should give them the ancient service or who aided the English army. Connacht and Munster and Ulster are thus reduced to a deplorable state of destruction and famine, whereby the English themselves are also the sufferers, for there is insufficiency of provisions for all. And yet English colonists of the Protestant religion are induced to come and take up their abode on forfeited estates, and trading with foreign countries is encouraged to help the seaports under English rule. To carry out the scheme of plantation the countries of the ruling families are to be surveyed and divided into shires for their better plantation, and the new inhabitants, and the old ones who show loyalty, receive their leases from the hands of the Queen, to be dispossessed at the first moment of disloyalty. The Irish ruling families are induced, indeed forced, to receive their castles and lands from the Queen, and when they are so minded to take leases and grants of the ancient monastic possessions. Fatherland is thus to be a thing of the past, and the whole country is to be thus made a happy English colony. With the Acts of Supremacy and Uniformity, and the obligation on the heads of families to attend Protestant service with sufficient use of the old Mass vestments to make it appear not so heretical as they are taught to believe it is, familiarity with the worship, it is considered, will in time bring Catholics round to tolerate it and perchance to adopt it. Grammar schools in the principal towns will provide the necessary instruction in Protestant tenets, as well as in secular matters, so as to achieve a twofold object. The Catholics who refuse to conform or refuse to be educated according to this system must perforce remain ignorant, and deprived of the ministrations of their own clergy and of the Sacraments must become demoralised to a great extent, at all events, taking the weaknesses of human nature as they are. By this constructive and destructive policy faith and fatherland are thus in danger of annihilation, but one chief at all events is fully aware of what the future is to bring— James Fitzmaurice. To frustrate this plan he has given up his whole life, sacrificed ease, family comforts, and lands, and gone into voluntary exile to save Catholic Ireland.

France and Spain ; Mutual Jealousies.

To understand the part played by France in the Irish negotiations it is necessary to survey briefly the condition of that kingdom at this time.[1] For ten years previously, two great parties, the Bourbons and the Guises, had contended for power. The Bourbons, who were Huguenots or Calvinists, hated Spain, envied her possessions in Flanders, and counted on Protestant England and Germany to help them against the Catholics at home and the Spaniards abroad. The Guises, the larger party, were professedly favourable towards the Catholic Church and Spain. Without sacrificing their own interest, they would work for the removal of Elizabeth and the substitution of Mary Queen of Scots. The latter had been Queen of France, was sister-in-law to the young King, and niece of the heads of the House of Guise. She was regarded by them as the rightful heir to the English Crown.

Each party strove to acquire control over the young King, but Catherine de Medici, his mother, was the real ruler of the country as Queen Regent. She used the Guises against the Huguenot Bourbons whom she detested, but she was equally ready to make use of the Bourbons when the Guises became too powerful. As with Elizabeth, so with Catherine, religion was a secondary consideration, subservient to policy

[1] See *Cath. Bulletin*, March, 1925, pp. 246-56.

and ambition. Catherine nursed a deep personal hatred for Philip of Spain, the devout Catholic and the powerful monarch, who was a check on her ambition. All France still felt bitter towards Spain on account of the recent wars. Elizabeth cleverly played on France's feelings, and secretly encouraged the Huguenots by financial aid.

After the peace of St. Germains, August, 1570, the King of France was free, however, to take an interest in the fate of Mary Queen of Scots, then a prisoner in England, and to put an end to English piracy and its baneful influence on French commerce. As a small trial of strength, Captain de la Roche was allowed by France, and apparently with the connivance of Spain, to fit out a couple of ships at Brittany. Bringing arms and munitions and men he landed at Dingle (December, 1570), and entered into some kind of alliance with Fitzmaurice and the Confederates. As a pledge he brought back with him to France Fitzmaurice's son.

" The impunity," says Froude,[1] " with which Elizabeth's Government was able to insult and provoke the Catholic Powers of Europe is the most anomalous phenomenon in modern history. The population of England was less than half the population of either France or Spain." Everywhere, indeed, says Froude, there was paradox ; everywhere contradiction and inconsistency. The Court of France was one month the ally of the Papacy and the irreconcilable enemy of heresy ; in the next it was seeking alliance with England. From Philip, the most orthodox of princes, and the Spanish nation, the most passionately Catholic in the world, some kind of principle, some uniformity of action, might have been looked for with certainty ; yet Philip was compelled to be the chief supporter of a heretic Power [England], by which he was himself insulted and despised. If he attempted to interfere to change the Government in England, France stepped to Elizabeth's side and threatened him with war. If he stood aside to let the Catholics rebel, the Catholic element in France was ready, with its offers of help, to secure the profits of the anticipated revolution. Thus Philip, through fear for his Netherlands, was forced back upon

[1] *Hist. of Engl.*, c. liv.

his sister-in-law's side, was obliged to stand between her [Elizabeth] and the Pope, and to perplex the whole Catholic world by an irresolution not less marked and far more mis-chievous than the vacillation of Elizabeth herself. Had there been no France, the English Catholics would have found an instant ally in Spain, and Mary Stuart would have found a champion. Had Mary Stuart been unconnected with France the difficulty would have been greater, but still not insurmountable. And, again, had there been no Spain, the French would never have submitted to be driven out of Scotland, or would have found an easy means to revenge themselves in the intestine divisions of England. The mutual jealousies of the two Powers left Elizabeth more free to settle her own difficulties than if the " ditch " which divided England from the Continent had been the Atlantic itself.

Confronted by the avowed embarrassment of the English Catholics, privately instigated by the Cardinal of Lorraine, and perhaps believing that by the open exercise of his authority he might put an end to the vacillation of the Great Powers, and unite France and Spain upon what, by the voice of their Church, would be consecrated into a crusade, Pius V determined to wait no longer for Philip's approbation. On the 25 February (1570), therefore, suddenly, that there might be no remonstrance, he drew up a Bull, by which he declared Elizabeth to be cut off, as the minister of iniquity, from the communion of the faithful. He released her subjects from their allegiance, and he forbade them, under pain of incurring the same sentence as herself, to recognise her any longer as their sovereign. The Bull was carried to Paris, and lay waiting for the moment when it was hoped that a war would break out between France and England, and that Catherine de Medici and the King would give their sanction—without which even the Cardinal of Lorraine was afraid to act—to the publication of it before the world.

The Guise influence was at the moment in the ascendant, and Catherine leant as usual to the policy of the predominant partner. " The open talk at Paris," wrote Sir Henry Norris in his despatch from Paris, in the first weeks of the year 1570, " was of war with England, for the release of the Queen of Scots and the toleration of Papistry." An army was to be thrown across the Straits, which the Duke of Anjou was to lead, and the Duke was to be rewarded with the hand of the Queen of Scots. Unfortunately for Mary Stuart's prospects, she had too many friends. France and Spain both wished her well, but could not trust each other, and neither would trust the Pope.

The English admirers of Spain were " dismayed by the careless regard " with which Philip looked upon their sufferings, and were beginning to think that they had no refuge but in God. " The Spaniards," said Sir Francis Engelfield, " dwelt and busied themselves so long in deliberation that the opportunity was gone before they could resolve to act."

In France, too, the stir among the exiles was great. Elizabeth informed Francis Walsingham, her Ambassador at Paris, that certain savage Irish rebels of no value had gone to Spain nominally for conscience sake, whereas they were of no religion, but wholly given to bestiality.[1] Stucley had joined them, and tried to make himself important by superfluously spending other men's goods, he being in fact not worth a " marmaduc." She marvelled that the King of Spain or his Minister should be taken in by such a fellow. Neither could she believe that Julian Romero, an old soldier, had been despatched to Ireland with 3000 men. Walsingham was instructed to complain about the French captain who brought away Fitzmaurice's son, and he was not to be put off with evasive answers either from the French King or from the Spanish Ambassador at Paris. The Spanish Ambassador, with a proud and disdainful countenance, denied all knowledge of Stucley and Romero. " There were no Spaniards who had that enterprise in hand." The French King promised to punish Mons. de la Roche and the other officers who had meddled in Irish plots. Walsingham believed neither of them, and advised the Queen to revenge herself by giving trouble in Flanders. The Netherlanders, indeed, tied Philip's hands, and it was impossible to break conclusively with England until French influence in Flanders should be no longer feared.[2]

[1] *C.S.P., Foreign*, 11 Feb., 1571.   [2] Bagwell, ii. 201.

While Pius V delayed in giving a decision on the question of Stucley's absolution, that gentleman swaggered about in Spain, and affected to take the interests of English Catholicism under his protection. He almost had one Oliver King, a soldier of fortune, at Madrid, dragged before the Inquisition for heresy. King eluded Stucley and, having crossed the Pyrenees in the snow, wrote to Cecil (18 February, 1571), giving an account of Stucley's proceedings. Traitors, he said, abounded who gaped for Elizabeth's death, and Stucley boasted that he would give Ireland to Philip. Some 4000 desperadoes had been got together, rascally ill-armed Bezonians, but officered by old beaten men of war such as Julian Romero. An expedition was expected to sail almost immediately from Vigo, and King, who had a knowledge of military matters and mining, eagerly offered his services, provided the Queen would pardon him. Another Englishman, Robert Huggins, wrote to Walsingham (25 January), and told how he had been imprisoned for forty-seven days on suspicion, and nearly died of ill-treatment. On being released he was ordered to quit the kingdom. He agreed with King that a descent on Ireland would take place in March or April, 1571, and added that Alva had a plan to occupy Caistor and Yarmouth.[1]

THOMOND AND MACGIBBON IN PARIS.

Just when the war spirit was stirring in France, and when the English Catholics were striving to interest that country in their favour, Fitzmaurice and his confederates decided to take a hand in the game. Accordingly, they sent to the French Court Connor O'Brien, Earl of Thomond, as their envoy. Thomond had been a loyalist and had served against Shane O'Neill, but Fitton, President of Connacht, treated him as if he had been a rebel. In disgust he turned to Fitzmaurice, and in July, 1570, was in Paris, urging the Queen-Mother to send a number of gunmen to the help of the Confederates, and offering to hand over to the French certain Irish harbours and strongholds, particularly that of Limerick. All the time, however, he took care to keep

[1] *C.S.P., Foreign*, 25 Jan., 18 Feb., 1571, nos. 1515, 1560.

in touch with Norris, the English Ambassador, who easily took his measure. Though Thomond was simple in appearance, yet, Norris saw, he was full of vanity and deceit, and would abandon his treasonable practices if he could but secure his own property and position in Thomond. Accordingly, Norris advised Elizabeth to grant him what he wanted. This was done, and Thomond set out for England, helped the English against Fitzmaurice, and for the rest of his life remained loyal to the Queen.

The next important event in this chapter of intrigues was the arrival in Paris in January, 1571, of Walsingham as Ambassador. Though the young King wanted peace with England, the Queen-Mother was conferring with the Cardinal of Lorraine, the uncle of Mary Queen of Scots. The Cardinal had already taken a prominent part in Irish negotiations, especially with Shane O'Neill. Walsingham was suspicious of the Cardinal's conferences, kept an eye on Stucley's doings in Spain, and reported minutely to Elizabeth. Evidently he believed that an expedition was being got ready in Spain, and that something similar was taking place in France. He kept a close watch on all the movements of the Queen-Mother, the Duke of Anjou, the Papal Nuncio, the Cardinal of Lorraine, Captain de la Roche, and young Fitzmaurice. De la Roche was watched by Walsingham's spies, and reported to the King and the Queen-Mother for his treaty with Fitzmaurice as to the relief expedition which he was then organising on the Breton coast. The King and the Queen-Mother, of course, denied all knowledge of the matter and promised to punish de la Roche if it was true. But Walsingham was not deceived. He reported to London that the Cardinal of Lorraine and the Papal Nuncio were behind the project and were urging the Duke of Anjou to take it up on the ground that it would open the way to a splendid career not only in Ireland, but in England as well. " At this time," wrote Walsingham, 8 February, 1571,[1] " surely there are great practices in hand for the invasion of Ireland, wherein the Pope and Spain are joined ; and as for the Cardinal of Lorraine, he fails not to further the same to

[1] *C.S.P., Foreign,* no. 1545.

his utmost." At this point Archbishop MacGibbon came from Spain into France.

As no expedition left Vigo, and as Philip trusted Stucley more than him, MacGibbon decided to go to France and see what he could do there. He set out towards the end of January, 1571, was received with honour at Bordeaux by the Bishop, who gave him a horse for his journey. At Nantes he interviewed some people of political importance, and then probably moved on to visit Captain de la Roche, Governor of Morlaix, not far from Brest. On arriving at Paris he was at once waited on by Captain Thomas, a native of the Pale in the French service, who offered him such courtesies as were in the English Ambassador's power. He asked and received an introduction to the Cardinal of Lorraine, to whom he manifested his own importance and the weakness of Ireland.

It transpired that it was the Cardinal who really originated the de la Roche expedition to Ireland. The Archbishop called on Walsingham on 25 March, and explained his reasons for leaving Cashel and Ireland.[1] Another, he said, had been intruded into his See by the Queen's authority, that he had "outraged" the intruder (i.e. carried him off), and that he had been forced to flee in consequence. Walsingham assured him of pardon from the Queen as he seemed to be sorry for his fault. MacGibbon did not hesitate to tell him of his own doings and those of Stucley in Spain. Walsingham in turn denounced the tyranny of Spain, and extolled the benign rule of Elizabeth in Ireland, whose people "enjoy as great liberty as any nation, and if there be any defect it proceeded from themselves," inasmuch as they refuse "to embrace such good orders as Her Majesty carefully for their benefit has sought lately to place there amongst them, to reduce them from barbarousness to civility."

MacGibbon Desires Elizabeth to Restore him to his See.

MacGibbon does not seem to have made any protest against the treatment meted out to prelates, priests, and

[1] *Compleat Ambassador, Letters of Sir F. Walsingham. C.S.P.F.*, no. 624.

churches by the Elizabethan method of reducing the country to civility. His reply was confined to a confession of readiness to do his best, and to a hope that Her Majesty would restore him to his country and his See, in return for which he would tell all the news he had of the conspiracy and of the means to cope with it. He added that the Stucley expedition was likely to sail in April, and that it was to be accompanied by Julian Romero as commander. Walsingham did not know what to make of the Archbishop and his offers, but in general he was inclined to suspect that his real object in asking to be restored to his See was in order to be enabled to complete the negotiations between Spain and Ireland. Walsingham reported: "To suspect that he meaneth no good faith I have these causes: First, I am informed that two Irishmen, sent by him out of Spain, were the cause of [de la] Roche's enterprise; secondly, I am also informed that he was sent for out of Spain by the Cardinal of Lorraine; thirdly, that he wishes the young boy, James Fitzmaurice's son [to be] in Spain, that is now in Brittany; lastly, I do not forget his nation and religion."

Walsingham now determined to leave no source of information untapped and had MacGibbon well watched by spies. In particular he employed one, Captain Thomas, who appears to have been the son of Bath, the Recorder of Drogheda, and who had evidently been supplying the English Ambassador in Paris with information for some time. Acting on a hint from Walsingham, Captain Thomas, who evidently posed as an Irishman and a good friend, took the unsuspecting Archbishop under his wing, and even presented him to the Cardinal of Lorraine and others about the French Court. The Archbishop had a long conversation with the Cardinal, who gave him some encouragement, which he duly detailed to the Captain, who, in turn, retailed it to Walsingham, and between them they concocted a scheme to discredit the Archbishop in the eyes of the Cardinal.

Walsingham now felt that he had little to fear in that direction, especially as the Archbishop called on him later and offered to tell all the news he had if he was pardoned and restored to his See. It is clear that MacGibbon was jealous of Stucley, or perhaps did not believe in him, and

24 *

was ready to inform on him, and upset his schemes in Spain. But when Walsingham, acting on orders from Elizabeth, told MacGibbon, that before he could be pardoned and restored he must reveal all the " secret " information he possessed, he was met by what was equivalent to a blank refusal. A few days later MacGibbon sought an interview with the Duke of Anjou, but here Captain Thomas was before him, and told the Duke that Ireland was poor, and only an expense to the Queen. The Archbishop, he said, was of small credit, having been banished for brawling. Anjou sent MacGibbon two hundred crowns and pleaded want of time to see him. The Archbishop at once left Paris for Brittany. Probably he saw that there was little use in expecting France to come to the rescue of Ireland until it was decided whether or not Elizabeth would marry the Duke of Anjou. This was an affair that might take years to settle, and so the Archbishop sought other fields for his activities. When next he is heard of he is in Scotland, and eagerly sought for by the Government who would confine him to the Tower and by torture force him to reveal the secrets of the negotiations between the Confederates and their agents abroad.

MacGibbon's negotiations were a failure both in Spain and France. He was considered a person of little importance, and Elizabeth, having been informed by her spies of the fact, felt easy in her mind. The probability of a French or Spanish expedition was indeed very remote.

Stucley Honoured in Spain.

MacGibbon's negotiations having turned out a fiasco in Spain and France, it is important to see how the other negotiator, Stucley, fared in Spain. Continuing his account of this adventurer (p. 332), the English Ambassador at Madrid states :—

Stucley was created knight, the 22nd of January, 1571, by King Philip of Spain.

Stucley made offer first to invade Ireland and conquer the kingdom with 10,000 Spaniards, after he demanded but 5,000 so as he might have Julian Romero to govern them.

Stucley hath received at sundry times of the King 10,000 ducats.

There is now delivered unto him as I am credibly informed a warrant or schedule signed with the King's hand for to receive 10,000 ducats.

Stucley hath no pension yet granted him. The falling out of Stucley with the Bishop of Cassell [Cashel] did rise upon this occasion that the Bishop did hide two Irishmen which were fled from Stucley; whereon Stucley came to the Bishop, and finding his men in the Bishop's chamber threatened the Bishop. The Cardinal of Sequenza, Rugomes, and Secretary Cayas began to mislike of Stucley for his evil behaviour towards the Bishop which lessened his credit.

Stucley hath sold his ship to Robert Borne of Vigo who is bound to pay Stucley £200 in two years.

The Duke of Feria, Don Antonio de Toledo, the Bishop of Quenca; these were and are great preferrers of Stucley to the King.

Stucley professeth that he hath good means to land with a small number in Waterford Haven.

Stucley instructed his servants that, if they did meet with any of my men, for to answer upon any question made, that as I served the Queen of England, so he did obey and do service to the Pope and King Philip.

Afore I came to the Court at Madrill, Stucley had taken a house 3 leagues from thence in a village called Arosso.

Stucley 2 years past [1569] sent one Sutton into Spain about this practise.

Stucley had allowed him of the King 50 ducats for the expenses of his house during the 22 weeks he kept house by the King's appointment.

They have an intention in Spain to take the Isle of Sylle [Scilly] to have a harbour for the ships upon any occasion. The means should be to take it by stealth on the sudden.

On the coast of Bysca [Biscay] there is put in a readiness xii great ships and ii Assaveras.

The King of Portugal prepareth an army by sea to the number of xxiii sail and 5,000 soldiers to man those ships.

Stucley's last petition to the King was that he might have his Majesty's license to report to the Pope, to the intent for to make declaration in what state these parts of Christendom remained in, and for to procure his holy help for his enterprise. The King's answer then was he should not depart without his own contentation [gracious permission].

Juan de Castro, a merchant of Burgos in Castyll [Castile], went into Ireland about the suit of Spanish wools which Woofall had taken on the seas, Stucley being then prisoner [in Dublin] did practise with this Spaniard for his going into Spain, and Battist St. Victorye was made privy hereof. One Christopher, an Italian, and now yet in England, being nephew to Fidele and servant to Ragasoni, was a dealer [intermediary] to the Ambassador of Spain [in London] for Stucley.

Pedro de Soubyor, servant to Pedro de Gurto of Bylbo [Bilbao], he useth to [be at] the Ambassador of Spain's house [in London], and writeth matters concerning the State very maliciously.

Robert Jaques, merchant of London, draper, conveyeth letters for the Ambassador legate of Spain, and when he [ambassador] was most straitly kept [watched] he served the Ambassador's turn therein.

STUCLEY'S PROPOSALS FOR THE EXPEDITION.

Now that the Archbishop of Cashel was out of the way, Stucley grew bolder in his plans and demands. Early in the year 1571, he put the following proposals before the Spanish King :—

That there be given him four well equipped ships and a foist and two barks and therewith 3,000 foot and 500 horse, which he will undertake to raise without, for the present, any payment on that account ; and with that force he will go to Plymouth and burn and take the fleet of Aquines [Hawkins], and thence he will go to Ireland and make himself Master of Waterford and Cork.

He craves that there be allowed him as his helper and associate Maestro de Campo Julian [Romero].

With the said succour he will reduce the realm of Ireland to the service and devotion of his Majesty, and defend it against all enemies : his Majesty, on receipt of advice that the design aforesaid is accomplished, to be under obligation to make good to him the pay of the horse and foot aforesaid from the day of their putting out from the port of Santander to the end of the time during which they shall be in his Majesty's service.

He likewise wrote to the Papal Secretary of State, Cardinal Sinigaglia, who reported to the Nuncio of Spain [1] as follows :—

Mr. Thomas Stuckle, an English gentleman, makes the following offer to the Pope and the Catholic King, to wit, that, being given the command of ships of war to the number of twelve, with 3,000

---

[1] *State Papers, Rome,* 1558-71, no. 745.

soldiers aboard, he will within a few weeks bring the whole of the island of Ireland into subjection to the King, as he holds the threads of an important conspiracy in that country, which will assure him a welcome and liberty, to fortify himself in whichever of the best ports of the island he may choose. This affair, he thinks, had better be managed covertly and with dissimulation, it being given out that the ships were being equipped in Spain for the enterprise against Algiers, or else for the purpose of chasing pirates.

The said Stuckle likewise makes this further offer to the Pope and the King, that if they be pleased to put him in command of two ships of war and two armed barks in one of the ports of Flanders, he will either himself go in person, or send his master pilot with them, to burn and sink all the galleons that the Queen of England has in the river Thames ; and this enterprise he deems so certain of success that, for further assurance of the Pope and his Majesty, he is willing to surrender himself as a prisoner to the Duke of Alba, that, if the enterprise fail, his life may be at the Duke's discretion ; and if it succeed, as he makes no doubt it will, he craves of the Pope and his Majesty, that he be assured of maintenance and support for his own life and his son's.

The two said proposals the Pope has left wholly and in all respects to the judgment of his Majesty ; and therefore has bidden me to write to your Lordship, desiring you, on the arrival of the said Stuckle, to do your best endeavour to induce his Majesty to be pleased to put the latter proposal as to the ships to the proof by bidding the Duke of Alba to cause the two ships to be privily made ready, and also the two barks, and to use whatever expedient may seem best to cloak the affair until the result be known ; and then it will be more to the purpose to consider the other proposal ; and your lordship will report what resolution has been arrived at.

Stucley Intends to go to Rome.

Stucley, encouraged by the former grandiose promises of Philip of Spain, was anxious to receive a mandate for his expedition from the Pope. But, as he had not yet been absolved for his commerce with heretics, he apparently impressed upon the Papal Nuncio in Madrid the advisability of having his excommunication removed before he should venture to throw himself at the feet of His Holiness. On this question of absolution, the Papal Nuncio wrote, in February, 1571,[1]

[1] *C.S.P.*, *Rome*, 1558-72, no. 749.

to the Cardinal Legate in Portugal, stating that Stucley denied he was ever a heretic and that the Archbishop of Cashel had drawn on his imagination. " If he were minded to be a heretic, there is no honour or profit that he would lack at home and among his people." As to the design on England the Nuncio states : " I do not believe that his Majesty is likely to engage " in it. It was this design, he says, that Stucley had in mind, " though he speaks only of Ireland." " The Archbishop of Cashel quitted the Court, he, too, by what he told me, *re infecta ;* and rather came to some sort of rupture with this gentleman. I know not the cause, but it is not surprising that ill will should arise between an Englishman and an Irishman, for it is instinctive between these two nations."

Stucley did not, however, expect the rebuff from the King which was communicated to him (8 February) by Secretary Cayas :—[1]

Your last proposal having been laid before the King, he has bidden me to communicate to you his answer, which in sum and substance is as follows :

That though his Majesty knows your spirit and zeal to be very good and of a very Catholic Knight, yet for the present it is not expedient to undertake the affair of the ships, or any other sort of hostilities, until we learn the result of the negotiations for peace, as you have on divers occasions been informed : That as you are determined to go to Rome and Venice, you are quite at liberty to do so, for his Majesty is agreeable thereto, and will be happy to give you the needful passports and the licence for the two horses which you desire to take or send to Italy ; That there be delivered to you here in aid of your expenses the 2,000 ducats which his Majesty has granted you, and that there go forthwith to Bivero [Vivero] a commissary, who will pay all that he shall find to be justly due on account of your ship and the pilots, mariners, and fighting men that you have kept there since the day you put in to Bivero : and so Alexander [Fideli, his servant] may come hither, that the 2,000 ducats may be paid forthwith, so that all else will be completely settled there in the manner I describe : and so you will be able to depart without this burden on your mind : That Master William [Stucley's son] will proceed forthwith to Alcalá, and there make his abode with Parsons [?], who will instruct him with as much care as if he were the son of the Duke of Feria.

In the matter of the licence for the discharge of the ship that is in Bayonne, there has been no opportunity of doing what you craved, for which delay certain weighty causes are adducible : and so you must be satisfied with his Majesty's good will, for that you certainly have, and you depart much in his favour, which is the chief matter to be considered by a person of your quality ; and as this is his Majesty's final decision, and admits of no reply, I have seen fit to apprise you thereof, that, having learned it, you may depart as soon as ever you please. God be gracious to you etc.

In a further letter [1] (13 February), Cayas announced to Stucley, that the King is pleased to grant him besides the 2000 ducats for expenses another 4000, to be paid at once to him, on account of the ship, pilots, mariners, and soldiers in Vivero, from the day of his departure from Ireland to Spain, namely, the 4th of April, 1570. Stucley is also granted licence for the discharge of the ship from London that is at Bayonne (probably captured by Stucley on the high seas), so that he may depart at once. Cayas reminds him how grateful he should be to so benign a King.

The real motive behind the King's action was his desire to avoid any break just then with the English Queen. Such were the consequences in London of the Stucley intrigue that Philip thought it better to pacify Elizabeth by means of a letter from Secretary Cayas, and to allow Stucley to depart for Rome or Venice.

STUCLEY'S BOASTFUL NARRATIVE.

In a long, boastful, and not always truthful, narrative (15 February) [2] of his great deeds for the Catholic religion in Ireland, and a fanciful account of his own importance, claiming to be " of the blood royal of England," Stucley admits that " he has had dealings with the heretics, as likewise all the Catholics that are in that realm [England] have done and do." He boasts that it was at the instance of the Irish Catholics that he went in person to the Spanish King

---

[1] C.S.P., Rome, 1558-72, no. 752.   [2] Ib., no. 750.

to seek for help ; that he pretended to the Lord Deputy he would treat Catholics " as his chiefest foes," and that he wished to bring his son, then in the Deputy's custody, to Elizabeth as evidence of his good behaviour. By large bribes to the Castle officials he had got possession of his son, sailed from Waterford, under pretence of going to England, for the port of Vivero. As to the sons of the Irish chiefs who joined him on the understanding that he was going to London, Stucley now mendaciously asserts that they came with him " by way of hostages " " that the said Catholics [of Ireland] would not fail " to keep their promises to the Spanish King. As to the treaty of peace between Elizabeth and Philip, Stucley says " that that heretic [Elizabeth] will keep none of her promises ; it is only the dread that she entertains of the said nobleman's [Stucley] valour, which she well knows, that has induced her to talk of peace and make it, if indeed she purposes to make it." He was in hopes that the fleet, that was to bring the new Spanish Queen from Flanders, two months previously, would have been given him, and so he was disappointed, " and almost all the fleet is lost." He then pretends that he received letters from Ireland urging him to wait no longer, and recounts the honourable posts offered to him in Milan and in Flanders, but these he refused as his purpose was " to do all the harm he could to the heretics." He believes that his name is included in the treaty of peace, but peace or no peace, if Elizabeth could lay hands on him she would have him beheaded. He narrates how Philip would allow him secretly collect about 3000 men so that he might occupy an Irish port for three months, when Spanish aid might openly and quickly follow, as Ireland was but a passage of two days and two nights from Spain. But when the king refused him artillery, munitions, and victuals, as the peace treaty was expected within forty days, he consented to wait for that time on the understanding he should receive powerful aid if the peace was not made. In any event, he decides to depart from Vivero with his men and two ships, capture some English ship so as to keep his men in hope, and make for Rome " to kiss the Pope's feet, and entreat him by the mercy that is characteristic of his Holiness to have special regard to so great a number of Catholic Christians." He expects then that the Pope will direct a Brief to the Spanish King to lend him about 3000 men " in an enterprise so pious and so Christian." He refuses the King's offer of a pension as " he neither can nor will serve one who keeps at peace with the heretics." He is grateful, however, that the King has adopted his son as his own.

About the same time (February) he wrote a final letter to the Cardinal Nuncio in Spain, John Baptista Castagna, Archbishop of Rossano.[1] " I am about to depart," he says, " and in ill health and great straits and anxiety, whereby I am harassed enough, but by no adversity more than to know that I go with so little relief for my soul, unless this letter shall bring relief." He once more requests the Nuncio to obtain for him the papal absolution from excommunication that he may go among his brethren, sons of the holy Roman Catholic Church.

Apparently there had been great doubt about Stucley's sincerity, and the Archbishop of Cashel's report had had telling effect on the Pope and his Nuncio. Stucley did not, however, depart from Madrid as early as he intimated— probably because he was still in hopes of the papal absolution —and he continued hanging round the Spanish ports for several months.

Elizabeth's Spies Report on the Foreign Negotiations.

While the Archbishop of Cashel's negotiations and Stucley's intrigues were being carried on, Elizabeth's spies were quite active reporting the very details that were being settled, although not always accurately, depending as they did on sailors' gossip over their wine in the foreign ports. These spies were all or nearly all Catholics, and mostly Anglo-Irish.

The going of Stucley to Spain had an irritating effect on the Government. They knew him to be a powerful personality, a clever diplomatist, and one who could command sympathy inasmuch as he had lost heavily on account of

---

[1] *C.S.P., Rome,* 1558-72, no. 753.

his religion. And though Nicholas White,[1] who succeeded him in the seneschalship of Wexford, said he had " more malice than power to do any hurt here, and do not believe that any great prince would venture such a great enterprise on so slender a warrant and so ill a quarrel," yet he advises Burghley to prepare for the worst, and that everything depends on the success of Fitzmaurice. White is going with Ormond and the President of Munster to take a strong castle called Mocollop within eight miles of Youghal which Fitzmaurice has in hand. For his pains he asks for the farm of Enniscorthy and the Murroughs which Stucley had and " which should not remain in the hands of Stucley's friends."

Henceforward a system of espionage will be in full working order along the south coast of Ireland, especially at Cork and Waterford, watching all the havens for merchant vessels and others coming from Spain and France. The coast of Kerry was not so easily watched. The mariners are to be interrogated on all they have seen and heard in the Continental ports and towns about Stucley and the Archbishop of Cashel and the preparations being made for sending aid. The examinations of these mariners provide us with most intimate details of the workings of the envoys. The Anglo-Irish lords as well as the Government officials almost vie with one another in their efforts to extract information and send it to headquarters. One of the first of these reports was sent by Viscount Decies from Waterford, 28 March, to FitzWilliams.[2] He tells how—

certain merchants of Youghal were at Bordeaux within these fourteen days, spake there with one Maurice Reagh [MacGibbon], pretended Archbishop of Cashel, which told them that he came from the King of Spain to the French King to have aid of men to come into Ireland, and reported there that the same was granted unto him, and that he would come into Ireland with a great navy of Frenchmen and Spaniards with the first convenient wind and weather that would serve ; and the merchants did see him rigging of ships, and pressings of men there for that purpose as they said, so as they fear their coming to be at hand, if their wicked attempt

[1] *S.P.I.*, *Eliz.*, xxxii. 6, P.R.O., London.
[2] *Ib.*, 2, iii., P.R.O., London.

be not speedily attempted, which I thought likewise expedient to advertise your honour of. The pretended Archbishop was sent by the archrebel James Fitzmorris to the King of Spain for aid as is reported.

From Limerick was sent a letter to Mr. Carney, Treasurer of St. Patrick's, Dublin, about Stucley. Immediately FitzWilliams, Weston, Loftus, Justice Plunkett, Baron Alymer, and Agard put their heads together, and devised a scheme which they told (7 May) to no man except Burghley.[1] They hired a certain man, a kinsman of Mr. Barron, about fifty years of age, " well languaged in the Spanish, French, Flemish, and a little of the Italian," and provided him with a barque of St. John Dolme. He is to be out of Ireland by 7 June, and is to go to Spain " to learn both at Vivero and those other parts on the coast about the ships, whether Stucley be there or not, and if he be there, then in what sort he is ; whether with any company of soldiers about him or not, and to see if any provisions of shipping be in hand, and to learn if he came, and when Mr. Stucley was last at Vivero or in any of the creeks or ports."

On 13 May, one John Morgans, just arrived at Cork, reports to FitzWilliams [2] that he was—

sent by the Queen to sea with two ships, to repair to the west parts of Ireland, thence to Galicia, to find what ships of war were already furnished at that coast to annoy any of her Majesty's dominions, and certify the Council. So sailing from the Isle of Wight, 8 April, to Cape Finisterre and the Pleas of Bayonne, and so returned along the coast of Biscay where I learnt at once a band of men, 12,000, was granted by King Philip to follow Thomas Stucley, whom they called Duke of Ireland, to land in Ireland, but afterwards they were withdrawn from him ; and himself sent for to the Court, being then at Maydrill [Madrid], Stucley came there to Vermoeney 17 or 18 days since [i.e. about 25 April], where, discharging most of the men he brought with him from Ireland, was fully determined to repair to Rome to the Pope, and returned to the Court to take his leave, but in no such estimation as he was in at his first coming. From which coast diverting my course towards France, anchored at Conqueste in Brittany, where finding a

---

[1] *S.P.I., Eliz.*, xxxii. 28, P.R.O., London.
[2] *Ib.*, 30, P.R.O., London.

Biskayne bound for Flanders that had two of Stucley's men, made my abode there three days thinking to allure the said two men, being Irish, to take ship with me for this realm of Ireland, but missed of my purpose, although I am certain they will take passage hither, and so there hence arrived at Cork this 11 May, where making ready to your Honour to do my duty was dissuaded by Mr. Horssey not to travel for that the way was dangerous, and that your Honour minded to be here very shortly.

The next report comes from Wexford from Nicholas White,[1] 15 May, after his return from the South. He tells Burghley :—

I took a mariner of this country lately returned from Stucley, and sent him to the Lord Justice, by whose examination as also by report of others lately arrived here out of Spain and St. John de Luyce [Luz], I find that Stucley is now out of that credit in Spain to hurt Ireland by way of invasion, and that the King did grow weary of his expenses ; he hath gotten, as they say, a certain collectorship of the Pope in Spain, and like to take his journey to Rome.

FitzWilliams also has something interesting to say about Stucley. After informing Burghley (24 May) that " Stucley was denied his request by the King of Spain," he goes on to say :—

The Pope cannot for honours' sake but reward Stukley, Duke of Ireland, with a red hat at the least, for so I will be envied his Holiness to reward and cherish men of his practise, and great reason to look to this man of all other, who left Florida Kingdom and now the Dukedom of Ireland only for holiness sake, to be a Cardinal, and in Waterford chief sherecke, him by reason of his so often going barefoot and beleaguered up and down, they saith ; and churches, in the same, lent in which he built and furnished his barque and went away in ; but if any change be for the governor [Duke of Alva] in Flanders the practise of the Duke [Stucley] and John de Mandoça may in their passages to and from [Flanders] best be executed.

FitzWilliams had already warned Burghley (7 April) about dealings between these two men, and that Mendoça was on familiar terms with Stucley [2] in Dublin. On 7 May

---

[1] *S.P.I., Eliz.*, xxxii. 31, P.R.O., London.
[2] *Ib.*, 3, P.R.O., London.

he told Burghley [1] about information he received from Mr. Barron, that he had learnt that Mendoça had been " a very busy man to search into the state of Ireland ; for a time he learnt all the news in Dublin ; he would pay and quietly inquire of all the parts of the country : he had been a diligent writer into Spain and Flanders, which now many speak of as he [Barron] saith, and thought he was the worst man that came into Ireland since he was born ; and very great was Stucley and he. I find Mr. Barron sober, wise, and a willing servant."

He surmises that if a new Spanish governor go to Flanders Stucley will go with him, and it will be well worth watching them.

Redmond Stackbold's Answers to Interrogatories Concerning Fitzmaurice.

One of the most important witnesses to the preparations in Spain was Redmond Stackbold, the Dean of Cashel's son. In his examination before Ormond he answers twenty-eight questions put to him, which throw new light on the negotiations. Omitting the questions, which are embodied in the answers, the following is the reply :—[2]

The answer of me Redmond Stacbold to the Right Honourable Earl of Ormond's interrogatories containing 28 articles, written the 16 of October, 1571.

To the first article I answer that the said Bishop [of Cashel] was gone [on] the seas by the persuasion of James FitzMoryse to seek aid of the King of Spain to further the said James in his rebellion.

Concerning the second article, the occasion of my friendship with the said Bishop was for that the late deceased Archbishop [3] deprived me of a poor benefice which I had under patents of her Majesty ; he granted the same to another, and for the deprivation of the same, youth and rashness hath compelled me to join with the other Bishop [MacGibbon], being enemy to the first, seeking a revenge of my quarrel.

---

[1] *S.P.I.*, *Eliz.*, xxxii. no. 28, P.R.O., London.
[2] *Ib.*, xxxiv. 32, i., ii., P.R.O., London.
[3] Elizabeth's Archbishop of Cashel, MacCaghwell, abducted by Archbishop MacGibbon, died in 1570. Nothing more is known about him after his deportation.

Concerning the third article, their meaning [i.e. of his conference with MacGibbon and Fitzmaurice] was in diverting [sending] their letters both to the King of Spain and the King of France to seek their aid for to resist her Majesty in this her realm of Ireland.

To the fourth I answer that I was sent from nobody into France, but shunning to be partakener with the said Bishop [MacGibbon] in his proceedings, understanding my duty unto her Majesty, caused one Mr. Robard Hugayns [Huggins] to write unto her Majesty of the privities between the King of Spain and the aforesaid James, and by a chance afterward I was driven in France to do an undutiful service as in the fourteenth article I will declare.

To the fifth article I answer, the said Bishop [MacGibbon] had too [as] his friends to further him in his suit, the King of Spain's Cardinal, the King's Confessor that is Bishop of Medina del Campo, the Secretary Cayas, and Secretary Grasso.[1]

To the sixth I answer that he [Fitzmaurice] asked 10,000 men, and the King promised 5,000 so that [i.e. in case] he or her Majesty could not agree for the money [2] which was taken from him in England.

To the seventh article : first O'Neill, McWilliam, McCarthy More, O'Sullivan More, O'Sullivan Beare, had knowledge of the said James's mind, and consented thereunto.

To the eighth his [Fitzmaurice's] enterprise was to turn all Ireland into the use of the King of Spain or France or to him first that should come.

To the ninth article, they determined to land at Limerick.

To the tenth article I answer they determined to attempt to join Limerick, Cork, and Waterford.

Concerning the eleventh article, they intended to make a fortress at Ballintimore [Baltimore], at Dangles [Dingle], and the ylle of Wheyne [3] upon the river of Limerick [Shannon]. Of the rest [of the fortresses] I know not.

Concerning the twelfth article, I answer that from Spain there was promised to be sent 5,000 men of arms and the Marquis of Salsas, the captain of the King's Gallaryes [galleys], and the old captain that served in the Newfoundlands should have had the leading of the said army.

Concerning the thirteenth article there was promised to be sent with them eight double cannons royal, six demy cannons,

---

[1] In opposition to the English party headed by the Duke of Feria.
[2] Spanish gold taken by English pirates.
[3] Foyne Island in the Shannon.

and twelve culverins with all their appurtenances, wine, money and corn for a twelvemonth.

To the fourteenth article,[1] the knowledge that I have thereof this is, I have served Monsieur du Bollyn governor of Brittany then, and the said Bishop [of Cashel] sent letters from Spain into France to the Cardinal of Lorraine wherein he advertised him that I served the said Bollyn, he perceiving the same letters of commandment to my master and lord to send me unto him [the Cardinal], there and then [he] demanded me of the state of Ireland before part of the Council, and there commanded me to service, and [I] could not deny him for fear of my life. Then a commission was given to Monsieur la Roche, Knight of the King's Order and gentlemen of his chamber, to come into Ireland to speak with James FitzMorise to the intent that they might have had him to submit himself subject unto the King of France for to resist her Majesty, the which he had submitted by letters under patent.

Concerning the fifteenth article, the compositions between them [the French and Fitzmaurice] was this that the said James should have had for recompense of his submission and service, done unto the King of France, the Earldom of Ormond and Ossory.

To the sixteenth article, the Frenchmen's promise made to bring 10,000 men well harnessed to assist the said James. Victuals for aid, 12 cannons royal, 12 demy cannons with divers and sundry munitions, and small artillery.

Concerning the seventeenth article, he [James] both received letters from Spain by one Edmond Daniel of Limerick, student, and sent letters with him again, and received letters from the Cardinal of Lorraine after this last Easter [1571], promising him succour and aid from the King of France, if the marriage that they pretended to be between his brother the Duke of Anjou and her Majesty [Elizabeth] may not be ended.

To the eighteenth article I answer that the said James sent letters both to the Cardinal of Lorraine and to the Bishop of Nantes ; moreover, his letters into Spain were sent unto Secretary Cayas and to the Bishop of Medina de Campo by the said Edmond Daniel.

Concerning the nineteenth article, the said Monsieur la Roche carried the said James's son with him to be presented before the King for the performance of the said James's promise made to the King ; and the said Monsieur la Roche, upon his oath and

---

[1] This was : " What moved the Frenchmen that landed this last winter at the Dangle [Dingle], to come thither, at whose procurement and commandment they came, and what credit themselves were of in France."

honour, promised to send the child again at the said James's calling.

To the twentieth article. At the beginning of the said James's rebellion I was not in Ireland then, and of such as did consent before him unto his purpose I have declared in the seventh article, and I know that every nobleman of all the West doth favour him by reason they do not resist him, but for the private assistance that they do unto him I am not privy thereof.

To the twentieth-first article I answer that I have no private knowledge of the Earl of Desmond, nor of his brother in procuring the said rebellion, but that the common report of all the said James's men was and is that the said James had word from them to hold [defer] his rebellion unto such time as they should be enlarged [released].

Concerning the twenty-second article, I have not seen any letters but I have heard that Ranell Oge O'Hurley brought letters from the Earl of Desmond unto the said James and also that it was, by the exhortation of the said Ranell, Edmond MacSheehy's sons rebelled with the said James.

To the twenty-third I may answer nothing.[1]

To the twenty-fourth, I know not who brought the said Bulls [to James, which he nailed on the gate of Limerick].

To the twenty-fifth article, one Gerode FitzCalloghe, priest, and Harry Ryan, student, and Geffrey Fitz Myles Burke, horseman, has nailed up the said Bulls.

To the twenty-sixth article I answer that he [Fitzmaurice] takes meat and drink from Muskerry, and is revived from them with victual when he is at Aherlow.

To the twenty-seventh article I answer that as oft as please the said James he taketh meat and drink with the said Walter [FitzJohn of Muskerry] and with all other gentlemen of the County of Cork, Limerick and Kerry.

To the twenty-eighth article I answer to my knowledge, his mother-in-law and his sister-in-law has the custody of the said James's plate and jewels.

A little more than a month after this examination, Ormond wrote to Burghley[2] (26 November) that Fitzmaurice had sent his servant, Denis O'Dussane, about fourteen days ago, to the French Court with letters to Cardinal Lorraine and Monsieur Cendall. He took ship in McCarthy Reagh's country. Messengers were constantly coming and going

---

[1] It was already answered in no. 22.
[2] *S.P.I., Eliz.*, xxxiv. 31, P.R.O., London.

between Spain and Ireland, and spies on both sides were numerous. Patrick Gough, a merchant of Dublin, is reported as having " a Spaniard as servant who is a spy ; he was sent over into Spain in February and March last." [1] FitzWilliams was able to report to Burghley [2] (4 January, 1572) that he hears

from merchants from Limerick, Galway, Waterford, and Chester, that come out of Spain, and some that arrived in Dublin, that there is great preparation in Spain for the sea, and numbers of new barques made in kind of pinnaces, and other sorts capable of carrying 40 or 50 persons. What these sorts of vessels should serve for, unless to enter some straits or barred havens with, and to pass where diverse flats and shoals be, I know not. Such [are] fittest to come along between Ireland and England, but the voice goeth that they be to attend upon the Duke of Medina into Flanders who is going thither, and the other great hell-hounds return.

MATCH-MAKING FOR ELIZABETH ; DISASTROUS FAILURE.

In his answer to the seventeenth article, Stackbold refers to the promised aid from France in the event of the failure of the negotiations then being carried on for the marriage of the Duke of Anjou, the heir-apparent of France, to Elizabeth. This match-making was not taken seriously by either side, and was really intended by England to keep France in good humour.[3] But it opened up possibilities of a far-reaching nature. For many a long day it ranged the French Crown on the side of England and of Protestantism for all practical purposes. By keeping the Catholic Guises from Court it convinced the Irish and English Catholics that no French help was to be expected. The Anglo-French entente was to Philip of Spain like the death-knell of his wide-flung Empire. Not only would England, France, and Germany combine against him, but they would attack him on his weakest side, Flanders. As for the Queen of Scots—as well as for the Irish and English Catholics—this match-making would throw her into the arms of Spain as the only Power from which help

[1] *S.P.I.*, *Eliz.*, xxxiv. 44, P.R.O., London.
[2] *Ib.*, xxxv. 4, P.R.O., London.
[3] See *Catholic Bulletin*, April, 1925, pp. 346-57.

could now be expected. Mary Stuart now entered into a conspiracy organised on an extensive scale by the Catholic peers of England under the leadership of the Duke of Norfolk, to remove Elizabeth from the English throne, place Mary on it, marry her to the Duke of Norfolk, and restore the Catholic religion. By April, 1571, the plot had made such headway that the conspirators were able to send to the Continent a confidential envoy, in the person of the Italian banker in London, Ridolfi. He carried with him letters of authorisation to the Pope, the King of Spain, and the Duke of Alva, Spanish Viceroy in Flanders, on the subject of a proposed Spanish expedition with the co-operation of the Catholics in Ireland and England.

Ridolfi's request to Alva was for " money, arms, ammunition, and troops with an experienced commander at their head." The English, on their part, undertook to have 20,000 foot and 3000 horse in readiness, and expected from the Pope and the King 6000 musketeers and 3000 horse, with 4000 additional muskets, 2000 corslets, and some twenty-five pieces of artillery to arm their own people. In addition, it was considered advisable to send 2000 men direct to Ireland, and 2000 to Scotland so that Elizabeth would have to divide her forces. Alva expressed grave doubts about the feasibility of the project, but the Pope, whom Ridolfi saw next, was delighted with it, and sent the Italian banker to Philip with letters urging the King to seize this most favourable opportunity.

Although no moment could have been more opportune for such a request to Philip, yet as usual he fiddled. He was in constant communication with Alva upon whose word the fate of the expedition depended. Alva did not believe that the English Catholics meant business with Spain, and pointed out that until Elizabeth was first put out of the way nothing could be done. By 11 September, however, Ridolfi was able to report to Rome that Alva had withdrawn his opposition, and had called him to Brussels to make final arrangements. But again, after Ridolfi's arrival in that city, Alva was in opposition. The details of the plot, he remarked, had become known to the Government, and the chief conspirators, including the Duke of Norfolk, had been arrested. Besides, he himself was tired of his post and was anxious to return to Spain, whereas this enterprise would necessitate his prolonged stay in Flanders.

On learning of the discovery of the conspiracy, the Papal Nuncio in Spain wrote to the Pope, 18 October, that this was the ruin of "the goodliest enterprise that could ever have been imagined." His Majesty's grief knew no bounds as he had had at last his heart fixed on the expedition. Likewise the new Governor of Flanders, the Duke Medina Celi, shortly after he arrived there, lamented the mischief caused by Alva's delay: "I am inconsolable that so goodly and important a plot should have come to grief."

Philip had other cares and anxieties to distract his thoughts from the English and Irish enterprise. He had to face the Turks who were making a bid for the control of the Mediterranean, if not for eventual predominance in Europe. The naval battle of Lepanto, the greatest the world had yet seen, had to be fought and won by his half-brother, Don John of Austria, and the Turks driven for ever from European waters, before he could devote serious attention to the interests of the Church in Ireland or in England. Amongst those who served in that battle was Thomas Stucley.

STUCLEY IN ROME; RECOMMENDS PAPAL EXPEDITION TO IRELAND.

Up to 8 July, at least, Stucley was still in Madrid,[1] but he seems to have gone to Rome shortly afterwards, as, before he joined Don John's expedition to Lepanto, he caused a long document addressed to Pius V to be drawn up by his trusty friend Alexander Fideli.[2] It admits Stucley's commerce with the Protestants of England and Ireland, but points his steadfastness now as a most faithful servant. He has quitted country, kinsfolk, friends, and his own state, and hazarded his life and that of his only son. As Stucley is being sent against the Turks with Don John of Austria, Elizabeth rejoices. While he was in Spain she was in dread, but now she is persuaded that Philip will never attack her. She has little dread of the Pope as he is too far away to hurt

---

[1] *C.S.P., Foreign*, 1569-71, p. 448.   [2] *C.S.P., Rome*, 1558-71, no. 754.

her. She has withdrawn the 6000 soldiers that were sent
to Ireland for fear of Stucley, and left there only about 1000.
If His Holiness contemplates reducing both his realms (England
and Ireland) he should attend to the following :—

You will cause ten or twelve ships to be with all possible
diligence equipped and excellently well armed, and have them
brought to the port of Spezia, for there will be no lack of ships
at Genoa and along that coast ; and with the same diligence you
will cause to be embarked upon the said ships 3,000 Italian soldiers,
arquebusiers all ; and with all possible secrecy your Holiness
will cause our master [Stucley] to be recalled, and to embark upon
the said ships, giving out that the ships and men are going to
join the fleet of Don John of Austria, so that neither Elizabeth
of England nor anyone else may have any suspicion of the enterprise ; but the ships, as soon as they are on the high sea, will
with all possible diligence make for the straits of Gibraltar, and
thence straight to your Holiness' realm of Ireland, which passage
with a favouring breeze they will make in twelve days ; because
that sea of Spain is navigated much more speedily in winter than
in summer by reason that, whereas in the summer northerly winds
prevail off the coast of Portugal and prevent progress, in the
winter the contrary is the case ; and as soon as our master shall
have set foot on land and displayed his holy standard, he will
have but to publish your Holiness' excommunication, and without
bloodshed all the island will go over to your devotion, and the
few English soldiers that are there will go over, if not all, at any
rate the more part, to your service, for their chief captain is a
Catholic ; and the rest will deem themselves lucky to be able
to escape to England ; nor will they find it difficult, because the
chief cities, as Cork and Waterford and Ross and Wexford, are
all Catholic, and stand with folded hands waiting to see a captain
of your Holiness and your most holy standard ; and if the city
of Dublin, where the Viceroy resides, should make or attempt
to make any resistance, it will not be for many hours ; for most
of the citizens are Catholics, and will surrender it to our master ;
but I hold it for certain that England will acquiesce therein.

And it will be much the better that this enterprise be of your
doing and with Italian troops by reason that the ancestors of the
Earl of Gildara [Kildare] is descended from the Florentine house
of the Giraldi, and the Earl is not only a Catholic but is lord
of a great number of vassals. His father was beheaded by
Henry VIII ; whereupon the son fled to Florence, where he resided for many a year, as also in the time of Pope Paul III here

in Rome, where he was succoured with money and what else such a lord had need of, until good Queen Mary came to the throne, when he returned to England, and was reinstated by the Queen.[1] And he has ever favoured the Italian nation, insomuch that your Holiness' soldiers will be better seen and welcomed than those of any other nation. And so if the favourable season be chosen, to wit, the winter, Elizabeth of England will not be able, however much she may desire, to afford succour, because her fleet is already in the river Thames in London, and were it ready in the said river, yet the distance is great; but in fact it is altogether dismantled, and were she minded to equip it, there is not time enough, as also there are many other hindrances. Meanwhile our master will build two forts, one in the port of the city of Waterford, the other in that of the city of Cork, in which places there is ready to hand all the apparatus for such a purpose since the time of Henry VIII, who gave much forethought thereto; and had he carried out the work, they would now have little to fear from any fleet, no matter how strong: so that, the forts being built, no fleet will be able to enter that kingdom save at the will of those that shall be in command of the fortress, more especially since the other ports of that region cannot be entered save by small craft, and they must await the tide or they would be stranded and in no little jeopardy; so that there will no longer be reason to apprehend any great force, or that they can do any damage of consequence.

Our master with the forces of his vassals and others of your Holiness' realm of Ireland, leaving for greater security the soldiers and others that he will bring with him to guard the cities and fortresses, will with all possible diligence cross to England, which is reached in a very few hours from the neighbouring coast of Ireland; and will land in Cornwall, and will there make a fort and a levy *en masse* of the Catholics of that and the neighbouring provinces of Devonshire and Somersetshire, which three provinces are Catholic and most loyal subjects of your Holiness. At the same time he will get a footing in the Province of Galia, i.e. Wales, which is the stronghold of the Catholics and the ancient enemies of the English, and operating as abovesaid will draw together the Catholics of that province. He will do the like in the province of Chester, where the people are still Catholics; and thus he will be master of these five Provinces, so contiguous one to another and to the coast of Ireland that in a very few hours one can cross from one side to the other; in which Provinces there will be three

---

[1] It was Edward VI who reinstated the Earl of Kildare.

camps, and distributed between them 25 or 30,000 Irishmen folk most warlike and able to bear any fatigue, whom our master will bring over upon this holy enterprise and at your Holiness' devotion ; and they will on every occasion be of force sufficient to repulse any army that Elizabeth of England may oppose to them.

Furthermore it will be necessary that on receipt of intelligence that our master has set foot on land your Holiness cause some succour to be forthwith given to the English Catholic nobles that are in Flanders, that they also may enter the country by way of Scotland, and with the aid afforded them by the Catholics of that kingdom invade the north of England in force ; and that likewise the Duke of Alva give signs of mustering troops and ships, and also in Spain his Catholic Majesty make a show of great preparations ; so that Elizabeth, finding herself assailed on so many sides at once as to know not whither to turn for very terror, and still less whom to trust, may be fain to betake her to the feet of your Holiness, there to receive the reward of the many outrages which she has done against the Catholic faith.

It is necessary that all these operations and holy enterprises be made in the name of your Holiness and of no one else ; otherwise they could not so readily be accomplished, for many reasons which for the present need not be assigned, and for this reason in particular ; to wit, that if Catholics and heretics alike should think or see that a foreign prince was addressing himself to the conquest of one of those kingdoms, they would set about banding and confederating together to prevent such a thing, and would suspend their particular quarrels rather than suffer themselves to become the subjects of a foreign prince ; but this difficulty will not arise if the operations be in the name of your Holiness, for the Catholics are most faithful, and all they desire is to see your most holy banners displayed, and to see and obey the captains that you will send them upon this most holy enterprise.

And as to the subjects and vassals of our master's State, which he bought of Elizabeth of England with his own moneys, your Holiness will grant him a confirmation of his titles and the name of duke in this duchy [Leinster], so that his subjects and others, marking this, may observe more respect and obedience towards him ; which will be of the utmost importance to this holy enterprise, and the rest of the island will be more prompt to aid and succour your Holiness.

In that your Holiness' realm of Ireland there are two earls [Desmond and Kildare], Catholics and most loyal to your Holiness. Our master humbly entreats your Holiness to grant him authority to create them dukes of their States. The said two Earls command very great forces and numerous vassals, and very great is their authority, and if your Holiness shall accord them this grace, they will have the best possible cause to serve God and your Holiness.

Your Holiness may be assured that at my time of life I am prompted by no private interest, but solely by my desire to set forth the mere and pure truth touching so holy an enterprise for the service of God and your Holiness. And as perchance you may deem I [Alexander Fideli] am an Englishman or an Irishman, and that love of country has induced me to slur some matter over unduly, I assure your Holiness that I am an Italian and a native of the city of Pesaro, a vassal of the Duke of Urbino. True it is, however, that for many and many a year I have served my master [Stucley], and that I know his policy and procedure, which are solely directed to the service of God and your Holiness, otherwise I would not have served him ; and I came to know both the one and the other kingdom, as well by sea as by land, during the long tract of time I spent in them, ever waiting for the grace of God, that after so many perils I might in this most holy enterprise, do most goodly and holy service to God and your Holiness ; and by the space of twenty years I have served this my master, not for wage or other private reward, but solely to this end : and waiting till God should be pleased to inspire your Holiness to give effect to this most holy enterprise which is proposed to you, thereby at so little cost, compared with the greatness and extreme importance of the enterprise, to abase the greatest enemy you have and reclaim three realms to your most holy obedience ; and this especially you should bear in mind that it will be accomplished with so little expenditure and effusion of blood.

And I at your Holiness' command will lead fifty gentlemen, all near kinsmen of mine on the father's or the mother's side without any pay whatsoever, the sole reward which they will look for being the exertions they will make in the service of your Holiness under my master's leadership in this most holy enterprise ; to which I most humbly pray God by His spirit to guide you, and to grant you long life and health and a most happy victory over all your enemies.

As to the fertility of your said realm I suppose your Holiness has already full information. By reason of the good climate, and the kindliness and fertility of the soil, the country, if cultivated in the way practised here in Italy, would suffice to supply England, France and Spain with bread, and yet have enough for itself. Cattle, such as cows, oxen, sheep and goats abound ; horses are there of a kind much better suited to war than those of the English, and in great number. There are most beautiful rivers affording excellent harbourage and abounding in fish, and especially in salmon ; most beautiful woods whereby ships and galleys can be built in plenty : these fringe the principal rivers of Cork and Waterford and Wexford : and on any occasion the vessels could be built in large numbers.

The mines of gold, silver, lead, tin, and iron are of recent discovery : a mine of alum is of extraordinary richness.

These mines are owned by Irish gentlemen who do no sort of obedience to Elizabeth, and will hear of no name but that of your Holiness, to whom they do all obedience and service, as our duty is much rather to your Holiness. [1]

Some years afterwards (probably about 1578), Stucley drew up a confession, which he presented to the Pope, of a long course of disobedience to and misfeasance against the Roman Catholic Church by sworn submission to Queen Elizabeth, and by complicity with the Viceroys in Ireland in the spoliation of churches and destruction of monasteries, banishment, incarceration or slaughter of the religious and priests, and confiscation of revenues, with profession of penitence and a desire to be reconciled with the said Church.[2]

PHILIP OF SPAIN TURNS IT DOWN.

Having distinguished himself as a daring and capable leader at the successful battle of Lepanto against the Turks, 20 October, 1571, Stucley returned to Rome whither the fame of his exploits had already gone before him. The

---

[1] It would appear from this description that the old pirate had heard in his native Pesaro, while still a youth, the Latin verses in which the Irish Saint Donatus of Fiesole, not far from Pesaro, had sung the glories of his own country nearly a thousand years before :—

> " Far westward lies an isle of ancient fame
> By nature blessed, and Ireland is her name,
> Enrolled in books—exhaustless is her store
> Of veiny silver and of golden ore :
> Her fruitful soil for ever teems with wealth,
> With gems her waters, and her air with health ;
> Her verdant fields with milk and honey flow,
> Her woolly fleeces vie with virgin snow ;
> Her waving furrows float with bearded corn,
> And arms and arts her envy'd sons adorn."
>
> *(Catholic Bulletin*, April, 1925, pp. 353-4.)

[2] *C.S.P., Rome*, 1572-78, p. 569.

Eternal City appeared to him a field of labour easily cultivated. There he made pilgrimage in bare feet to the principal shrines, and, although at first he besought Pius V in vain to absolve him from the excommunication incurred by his earlier life, yet in a short time he became in that city as important a personage as he had been at the Courts of Elizabeth and Philip. He cleverly gained the confidence of the English exiles through whose influence he got into touch with the Pope. The scheme that his henchman, Fideli, had already put forward impressed his Holiness, as nothing could have pleased the Pope better than that Elizabeth should be put in her place. But Pius was not in a position to finance a contingent of papal troops, as his resources had been crippled by his contributions to the expedition against the Turks. He very readily, however, directed the Cardinal Secretary [1] (1 December) to recommend Stucley to the King of Spain as worthy of the King's favour. At the same time he added that, if the King desired to embark on the Irish expedition, and did not wish to do so under his own name, he might have it placed under the banner of the Holy See. Further praise of Stucley was sent (6 December) from the same source to the Nuncio in Spain, accompanied by a plea of help for him. [2]

Stucley, however, wanted his pound of flesh for whatever bond he entered into, whether papal or Spanish. Before his departure from Rome, he requested that the Pope should grant him the titles of the estates that he said he possessed in Ireland. But Pius, having no knowledge about the matter, considered it better to wait until he should hear from the Spanish King what he thought about it. [3] Philip rejected the papal proposal. The Nuncio in Spain informed the Cardinal Secretary, 11 January, 1572 :—[4]

As to Thomas Stuclhe [*sic* Stucley]'s offer I have spoken with his Majesty who has known that gentleman for many a year and understands quite well what use can be made of him ; and these same proposals of his have been on the *tapis* here for a long time, and are not new to the King, but they are matters which he would not address himself to undertake without a surer basis.

[1] *C.S.P., Rome*, 1558-71, no. 855.   [2] *Ib.*, no. 858.
[3] *Ib.*, no. 859.   [4] *Ib.*, 1572-78, no. 6.

The plot devised by Ridolfi was a matter of importance and substance, had it not been discovered, which causes the King infinite mortification ; and were there a main enterprise like that of Ridolfi in hand, his Majesty would perchance avail himself of the aid of Thomas Stucley, as subsidiary to the main enterprise, for what it might be worth ; but to his Majesty it seems not well to essay the subordinate scheme before he has resolved upon the main one, because to make an attempt upon Ireland, for to try to burn the English fleet, would not only, it is thought, be more easily said than done, but would be making open war upon that realm, which would excite many humours which would not be easy to digest at this time ; and if it produced no other effect it would at least hasten the death of the Duke of Norfolk, and of all the other nobles that are prisoners, if they are not by this time dead. Ridolfi's conspiracy was in effect completely discovered at the critical point, as you may learn from the writings touching that matter sent by the Legate Cardinal Alessandrino ; and the King has the same report in writing, and I have it likewise from the Nuncio of France. So we must wait to see the fate of the prisoners, for if by good grace they should succeed in so defending or screening themselves as to be acquitted and released (which is not expected), we might revert to our original hope ; and in that case I find the King well disposed. But if they should be put to death, as it is expected, there is no more to be done but to have patience, because to make war and attack those realms deliberately without a rising of the Magnates of the said Kingdom is no enterprise for these times, nor would the King so much as think of it at present ; and this is the answer to the two ciphers received touching this matter.

A Memorial for the King of Spain, June-July, 1572, states :—[1]

As Ireland as well as England is concerned there would be especial reason to begin in the name of the Pope. As regards Ireland it is manifest that it must be so done, seeing that the island is within the Pope's jurisdiction, and he alone has the power to dispose of it, and upon him falls the burden of recovering it from the powers of the heretics, especially at a time when in that country they so rigorously oppress the Catholics, who have recourse with such piteous appeals to the feet of his Holiness.

The same reason is valid as to England, seeing that there is the same and even greater persecution there than in Ireland ;

[1] *C.S.P.*, *Rome*, 1572-78, no. 45.

and such as was never yet seen perpetrated by any heretic prince ; for they are minded to eradicate the Catholic worship by edicts and the last resources of violence, enacting to that end most ruthless laws, each containing an express repudiation of the authority of the Apostolic See ; to which it accordingly belongs to seek a remedy for such grievous evils and give the island security in the service of God by temperate government, making an end of the depredations that they perpetrate on all the world, and dispersing the horde of Malefactors, Apostates, heretics, rebels, robbers and pirates ; so that it would be for our Lord the King to undertake this enterprise at the instance of his Holiness, notified by ambassages and a special brief ; and given such a title, it would seem that the King of France would not dare to make a *casus belli*, for the Apostolic See is respected in France.

On 5 December, 1572,[1] the Nuncio in Spain informed the Cardinal Secretary of State that he discussed with the King the question of utilising the Spanish troops in Flanders as an expeditionary force against England, provided the expedition was supported by the leading Catholics of that country and by a simultaneous rising in Ireland. Philip thus subordinated all to the chance of success of a rising in England, paying little or no attention to Ireland, except as a pawn in the game. For the time being he seemed to think that little could be done without a previous understanding between the Catholic Powers, particularly those of France and Spain.

Archbishop of Cashel in Scotland.

After the Archbishop of Cashel left France about May, 1571, nothing more is heard of him for nearly a year. He probably returned to Ireland, and having received some papers from the Irish Confederates regarding their relations with Spain and Rome, he was on his way back to the Continent when he was taken prisoner in Scotland. In a letter from Berwick, 23 April, 1572, Lord Hundson informed Burghley, that an Irish Bishop, with four or five companions, had been arrested and detained at Dundee, on the west coast of Scotland. They had been, he said, on their way to Flanders and Rome, and the Bishop possessed papers that doubtless

[1] *C.S.P., Rome*, 1572-78, no. 124.

contained all about the conspiracy in Ireland, and the arrest had been effected through the good offices of one of the Stuarts, who had, moreover, relieved the Bishop of 300 crowns. Hundson attached great importance to the capture, believed that if brought to England, the Bishop could be forced to reveal much the Government wanted to know, and advised the Queen to call on the Regent of Scotland to send him to England, where, of course, he could be dealt with in the way best calculated to make him open his lips.   It soon transpired that the Bishop was MacGibbon, a fact that made the English authorities all the more eager to get hold of him. Almost daily despatches passed between Scotland and England, all going to show the anxiety of the English Government to secure him at all costs.   Pressure was brought to bear on the Regent Marr, who was asked to surrender him, or, at the very least, to give up the Archbishop's papers.   Marr, whose wife was " a furious Papist," made one excuse or another, but did nothing beyond informing Elizabeth that he had gathered from the Archbishop's words that a Spanish force was being concentrated in Flanders, and that the large sum of 60,000 crowns had been provided by Spain to meet the cost of an expedition, which was to sail the moment an insurrection took place in Scotland in favour of the Queen of Scots.

Meanwhile Hundson reported that the Archbishop was safely under lock and key, first in the castle of Leith, and then in another fortress, probably Dunbar, but that as far as his papers were concerned, " the varlet had thrown them into a privy."   Although Marr about this time had surrendered the Earl of Northumberland in similar circumstances for a bribe of £2000, yet he would not surrender the Archbishop, evidently because the bribe was too small compensation for soiling his hands in such a transaction, and Elizabeth was tired paying out money.   Accordingly, he sent various excuses to her as he was anxious to stand well with her. In particular he urged that the Archbishop was a Spanish subject, an excuse that the Queen brushed aside with the remark that his only connection with Spain was due to the fact of his being a Papist, and, therefore, an enemy to the Church of England and Scotland.   But the bribe she eventually consented to offer was insignificant, and the Archbishop remained out of her power. Renewed pressure was brought to bear all through the months of June, July, and August, until on the 4 September, Killigrew, another of the English agents in Scotland, reported that the Archbishop had succeeded in effecting his escape with the help of a Papist. This malefactor, he related, conducted him to Aberdeen, where he was at that moment engaged in securing a passage on one of the vessels bound for Flanders or Spain. MacGibbon's mind at this time may be gathered from a reply that he made to the Laird of Clyshe, who had urged him to make his peace with Elizabeth, on the ground that he would lose nothing thereby, and might easily find submission very much to his advantage. The laird duly translated the Archbishop's words into the tongue of the Scot : " He had rather that any nation be their king, yea rather the muckle devil, than her Majesty." [1]

SOME ECCLESIASTICAL AFFAIRS.

Turning our attention to home affairs, a few are not unworthy of passing notice. On 2 January, 1572, the Queen wrote to Sir William FitzWilliams, Lord Deputy, directing the appointment of Matthew Seain or Sheyn to the Bishopric of Cork and Cloyne, vacant by the deprivation of Richard Dixon.[2] The Letters Patent were dated 29 May, and he was consecrated the same year.

The complaints against Loftus had not borne fruit, for, 4 January, news was received in Dublin that he was not to be removed as " he is a wise and good counsellor." [3]

Lord Chancellor Weston, the lay Dean of St. Patrick's, feeling his " conscience grieved at enjoying spiritual livings for temporal service," wished (17 June) to resign his deaneries of St. Patrick's and Wells.[4]

In the North a battle of letters was waged between Terence Daniel, Dean of Armagh, and Lancaster, the Protestant

---

[1] See *Catholic Bulletin*, April, 1925, pp. 355-7.
[2] *C.P.C.R.I.*, *Eliz.*, i. p. 547. Ware says of the deprivation : " I do not find for what cause." (*Bishops*, 564.) We have seen the cause.
[3] *C.S.P.I.*, *Eliz.*, xxxv. 4.
[4] *Ib.*, xxxvi. 42.

Archbishop. Daniel had complained, 21 February, 1572,[1] to Burghley that Lancaster had not delivered to himself or to the master of the works the money for the repair of the Cathedral. Lancaster reminds Burghley that it was never meant to be sent to the Dean for that purpose, but was originally intended for the repair of the archiepiscopal palace as a residence for the Deputy. Lancaster then informs him that the soldiers are going this week to be upon the borders, and so will be always ready to march upon the enemy. The poor country is very glad of this, and has freely remitted all the debt due unto them for all the soldiers since the beginning of Her Majesty's reign unto this day, which would amount to no small sum. He ends this letter on the personal note. As in the case of his confreres the first part of the letter is usually an introduction to the asking of a favour. He bewails his inability to pay his debts on account of the repairing of his ruinous house at Termonfeckin, and desires the remission of the first-fruits.

DIFFICULTY IN FINDING PROTESTANT BISHOPS.

Elizabeth and her Government were in dire straits to obtain " fit " candidates for four dioceses. In 1572 Tuam and Kilmacduagh [2] became vacant by the death of Christopher Bodkin, and Down by the death of Merriman. Ardagh was still, in 1572, in the possession of MacMahon who was a Catholic Bishop, but a move was being made to provide it with a Protestant incumbent. On 1 October [3] the Lord Deputy and Council reported to the Queen that " Ardagh and Down are vacant ; Ardagh, long vacant, of no fruit at all, Down, a year or two void, not much better." Both are said to be important " for the furthering of obedience." In Ardagh, on the edge of Meath, in Co. Longford, " the people are not yet well reclaimed " to Protestantism. John Garvey, Dean of Christchurch and Archdeacon of Meath, is recommended for the bishopric as " a very fit man to go

[1] *S.P.I.*, *Eliz.*, xxxv. 15, P.R.O., London.
[2] In the appointment of O'Molony to Kilmacduagh in 1576 by the Pope, he is mentioned as successor to Cornelius O'Dea. There is no mention of Bodkin. The Holy See did not recognise him as the lawful bishop of that See.
[3] *S.P.I.*, *Eliz.*, xxxviii. 1, P.R.O., London.

amongst them to give them godly exhortation." But he should be allowed to " enjoy also his other spiritual livings (i.e. deanery and archdeanery) as otherwise he will be in worse state. . . . Down lies on the verge of Tirlogh Luineach, but hardly any man can be found for it except one Christopher Browne, prebendary " of Wicklow in St. Patrick's Cathedral.

Although the Queen wrote to the Lord Deputy, 4 November, directing the appointment of Garvey to Ardagh, nothing was done in the matter. A year elapsed before the Deputy and Council took up the question again, and, this time, in their letter to the Privy Council [1] (23 November, 1573), they declare that " the Dean of Christchurch for his calling and otherwise is unfit. But truly, my Lords, I must commend him for his willingness to do any service he can, without the sparing of his purse or body, into what border soever he is sent." He says that Ardagh is " but in title and worth 20 marks a year in living."

No appointment, however, was made to Ardagh for ten years (i.e. 1583), when Lisach Ferral was promoted to it. As to Tuam a letter from the Earl of Clanricard to Burghley, 15 August, 1572, throws important light on the somewhat bewildering condition of the Archdiocese. Through the influence and power of Clanricard, Bodkin had been able to hold Tuam, as well as Kilmacduagh, against the rightful Archbishop O'Frighil. Roland Burke, Bishop of Clonfert, had likewise, as King's bishop, held his See against priests and people through his nephew, the Earl of Clanricard. We have already shown that Bodkin in 1560 had taken the necessary Oath of Supremacy, and had put his finger in the eye of Father Wolf, the Papal Commissary, as to his orthodoxy. That Clanricard had outwardly accepted the Supremacy seems to be the legitimate conclusion from his letter to Burghley.[2]

He informs him of the death of Christopher Bodkin, Archbishop of Tuam, and recommends " Edward Browne, son of Dominick Browne of the town of Galway, Alderman, and now a student in the University of Oxford for the last

---

[1] *S.P.I., Eliz.*, xlii. 86, P.R.O., London.
[2] *Ib.*, xxxvii. 39, P.R.O., London.

7 or 8 years, kept there by his father until he was able to preach and teach the word of God and to be a good assistant to the civil regiment of this province, for reducing the ignorant to the knowledge of their duty to God and the Prince." He laments the " want of learned men not only in Connacht but generally throughout Ireland," and says that Browne " is the fittest in the province." He asks for " letters patent for him to enjoy the temporalities so that he may complete his studies and be better able to become a necessary instrument for the reformation of this his native country."

The Earl of Clanricard granted to Darby McCrahe, priest, vicar of Kilconickny, a lease of the monastery of Loughrea, for seven years (19 September, 1572).[1] In his report to Burghley[2] (26 August), the Lord Deputy states that " to Tuam from ancient times[3] are annexed the Bishopric of Mayo and Anaghoyne [Anaghdune] and the Bishopric of Kylmacowe [Kilmacduagh] called in Latin, Duacens; " " For the better promoting of religion in her Majesty's proceedings," he recommends two fit men to be placed in them. " Having rejected a number of simoniacal suitors, we have made choice of a couple of worthy men, partly against their wills to go thither ; they are fit in learning as in life." He recommends Mr. Carne (Kearney), Treasurer of St. Patrick's, a man of Connacht birth, for the Archbishopric, and Mr. Walshe,[4] a divinity reader, born in Waterford, for Kilmacduagh.

On 21 October,[5] however, the Lord Deputy informed Burghley that Carne and Walshe, " afraid of the unquiet state of these places, are unwilling to go there. We had a couple recommended by the Lord President and the Bishop of Clonfert (Roland Burke). The first is William Lealy, Dean of Tuam, Bachelor of Civil Laws in Oxford." He is fit for the Archbishopric, and a like choice cannot be made

---

[1] C.S.P.I., Eliz., xxxvii. 56.

[2] S.P.I., Eliz., xxxvii. 43, P.R.O., London.

[3] Evidently he looked upon the reign of Henry VIII as in " ancient times."

[4] Nicholas Walshe, son of Patrick Walsh, Bishop of Waterford, was educated at Cambridge, became Chancellor of St. Patrick's, Dublin, was joined with Kearney in the introduction of printing in Irish and in the translation into that language of the New Testament, and afterwards became Bishop of Ossory (1577).

[5] S.P.I., Eliz., xxxviii. 17.

elsewhere. He sustained great loss through the rebels. The other is Stephen Kervan (Kirwan) who was trained in England since his infancy. He was Master of Arts in Oxford, and recently returned from Paris on account of the disturbances there. He is of good parentage, and no one fitter can be found for Kilmacduagh. The temporalities are very small and difficult to collect in Connacht.

On 11 November the Queen decided that Tuam should be given to Lealy, Kilmacduagh to Kervan, Ardagh to Garvey, and Down to Browne, unless the Deputy knew some one better. The Deputy, in reply, states that Ardagh is only worth £10 a year; " the use of an English preacher is not so necessary in these places as a discreet man versed in the language of the Irish. Such a one is Browne, and of English race."

Ultimately Lealy (Laly, or Mullaly) was appointed to Tuam and Kervan to Kilmacduagh (both Connacht men), but Garvey was not appointed to Ardagh, or Browne to Down,[1] and Walshe was reserved for Ossory.

---

[1] William Laly, a native of Galway, educated at New-Inn, Oxford (*Athen. Oxon.*, 716), was appointed Dean of Tuam, 7 November, 1558, namely in the reign of Queen Mary. Consecrated Archbishop of Tuam in April, 1573, he held the See of Anaghdune along with Tuam. Not content with these he applied to Elizabeth in 1584 and was granted also Kilmacduagh and Clonfert. But the Lord Deputy, Sir John Perrott, stayed the warrant. Stephen Kerovan, or Kirwan, a native of Galway, and Archdeacon of Anaghdune, was educated at Oxford (*Athen. Oxon.*, 719) and Paris, and promoted to Kilmacduagh on 13 April, 1573. On 24 May, 1582, he was translated to Clonfert, and Kilmacduagh then remained vacant for five years until Roland Linch was appointed to it. As to the Diocese of Down, Browne was not appointed to it. Elizabeth had left his appointment to the discretion of the Lord Deputy, so that the new Deputy, FitzWilliams, felt himself justified in withholding the confirmation. On 21 November, 1573, a year after Elizabeth's appointment of Browne, she wrote to the Deputy, reciting her former instructions, and added : " that she had since understood that one Hugh Allen, a good preacher, and a zealous man who went with Sir Thomas Smith, as one of the colonies [colonists] to the Ards, was very much commended both by Captain Malby and the said Smith, and therefore, as Down is in Lecale, and the most part of the Bishop's living is in the Ards, she commended that (if Browne had not been already placed there) that he should promote Allen, and provide Browne to some other spiritual living." (*C.P.C.R.I.*, *Eliz.*) Allen was thus promoted to Down.

MERCHANTS BRING NEWS FROM SPAIN.

The reports from merchants trading abroad were being systematically taken, and though not always trustworthy, they show the gossip current though stale, among the sailors who visited foreign ports. These were sent on to FitzWilliams, who speedily despatched them to the Queen or her Council. On 27 February he reported to the Queen :—[1]

" News from Spain by Merchants, and of late by Roger Winston of Taunton ; he heard in September last when he discharged a ship at Sant da Luz (of merchandise) on the borders of Spain that at St. Panderos the boats are 15 leagues to W. of Bilbao, 15 great ships and numbers of small vessels on that coast were ready made for the Duke of Medina Celi to repair as Viceroy into Flanders, and 6000 to be sent out of Castile, etc., and this spring more likely to be more preparations." He also states that a Spanish ship was captured by Captain Malby, and that the Spaniards had been sent into England.

On 12 February Martin de Guerres, Master of the "Trinity," of Bilbao, reported that a common messenger from the Court of Spain said that two months ago Stucley had returned from the Court of Rome, and was seen there with his son. On 5 March the new English Ambassador in Spain reported to his predecessor that Stucley wished him to help him to " Phelim and Cahir O'Reilly the two Irishmen that the Bishop of Cashel and the [*blank ;* probably the Bishop of Ross] [mentioned] for to take letters to the Earl of Kildare on Stucley's arrival in Ireland. Phelim is now in Ireland with O'Reilly of Kildare, but had been recently in Spain with Friar John. He had been an outlaw for many years not only from Englishmen but from Irishmen." [2]

From the examination of Walter French, Merchant of Galway, who arrived at Kinsale, it was learned (30 March, 1572) :—[3]

Spaniards use more cruelty in matters of religion than they [English] were accustomed to. Stucley is returned to the Court of Spain at Madrill from Don John of Austria with whom he was

---

[1] *S.P.I.*, *Eliz.*, xxxv. 23, P.R.O., London.
[2] *Ib.*, 29.   [3] *Ib.*, 46, P.R.O., London.

this last skirmish against the Turks, and that he commonly doth call himself Duke of Ireland, having of the King of Spain towards his housekeeping 1000 ducats a week, and that Rory O'Ruirke in Connacht told W. French, requiring him and the rest of the company to let him [Rory] have passage with them which they deny [refuse] whereupon the said Rory returned to Spain, and was entertained by the King for 40 men, as a friar of Ireland, who called himself Provincial of Ireland [1] told him. Examined [as to] what became of the friar, he said he [friar] requested the Frenchmen who came with him hither [to Spain] to give him his passage, and when the Frenchmen denied [refused] him, saying they had rather be burnt than to have a friar at sea with them, the friar showed letters he had from the King of Spain to the Bishop of Cales commanding him to stay [arrest] and punish any that should be coming [going] into Ireland that would refuse to bring him [friar] over. Whereupon the Frenchmen said that they were bound to Flanders, not Ireland, upon which the friar turned to a portingale of a ship bound for Waterford wherein was a merchant of that city called James Fagan, and by means of the Bishop [of Cales] which threatened the portingale, with whom James Fagan bargained, the loss of his ship and goods, he [friar] was conveyed towards Waterford. And this he [Walter French] said there was one of Limerick [name unknown] who last year returned in the Bishop of Galway's [2] company which wrought the examinatee [Walter French] and many of this Country [Galway] much woe, for he certified them in Spain who of Galway were of their religion, and who otherwise. The said man of Limerick [3] keeps [lives] now in Lisbon in an abbey.

John Crofton, Athlone, reported, 13 April, as follows :—[4]

Received a letter from my servant at Galway of the arrival of a ship laden with wines (40 or 50 tons), wherein arrived merchants of the town who reported that King Philip (to whom lately Th. Stucley by means of great deeds done in the Levant, in company of Don John of Austria, is reconciled) doth prepare a great Armada to pass the seas under the leading of the said Stucley, some say against the Moors, others say hither to Ireland, but whithersoever the army goeth this is certain that all Englishmen and Irishmen, which were permitted as being hitherunto

[1] Probably Bishop Donough O'Gallaghair.
[2] Probably William Morius, the Marian Bishop of Anaghdune, which diocese included Galway.
[3] Probably Edmund Daniel, Jesuit student.
[4] *S.P.I.*, *Eliz.*, xxxvi. 7.

[to] remain and dwell there peaceably notwithstanding any stay or arrest betwixt our Government and the Spanish King, are now imprisoned, and all their goods taken up. And in fine such cruelty showed towards these two nations [English and Irish] as hitherunto during this restraint hath not been accustomed. And the more common report in Spain is that the said army is meant to invade this realm withal. And to this voyage, as it is said, the King of Portugal doth give a great number of men, and so doth the Pope also, but the assured intent of this their purpose is not otherwise known by the common bruit and report in that country in the opinion of most men. And the said merchants affirm that Stucley hath allowed him of the King a thousand ducats weekly (I rather think monthly).

To Kian O'Gara of Tirawley, Connacht, were submitted certain questions to which he answered. The questions and answers are as follows :—

Questions :—

1. Shall declare how many passengers to Spain and back to Ireland ; the landing places.
2. What they heard of the Archbishop of Cashel, Stucley, and others who fled from the land.
3. Their practices against the quiet rule of Her Majesty.
4. What letters from people to these parties ; the bearers ; to whom sent.
5. What Bulls, pardons, indulgences, absolutions, curses [excommunications] brought from Rome.
6. What Books, printed or written, brought by ships to this land. (29 May, 1572.)

Answers :—

1. Only knows Merchants of Waterford, and one John O'Grady, brother to Sir David Wolf [Fr. Wolf, S.J.], now prisoner in Dublin.
2. First they [Merchants] cast anchor at Smerwick, and there landed none ; thence they came to Tarbert on the Shannon (27 March, 1572), and there landed John O'Grady.
3. The pretended Archbishop [of Cashel] is gone to Paris upon the breach between him and Stucley. Stucley is with the King of Spain who giveth him great living, and that Edmund O'Donnell [Daniel], scholar, is in Lisbon.
4. Stucley is daily craving men at the King of Spain's hands to invade this land, who refused him because he is other-

wise vexed with enemies, or else he heareth nothing [i.e. otherwise he, O'Gara, has heard nothing more].
5, 6, 7. Knows nothing.
8. Heard Spaniards speak against Her Majesty.

William Bonffield of Limerick, also examined, differed in some particulars from O'Gara. George Harold FitzPiers of Limerick adds that John O'Grady went to Coimbra for money to release his brother Sir David Wolf before setting out for Ireland. He states that the King of Spain did not like either Archbishop MacGibbon or Stucley on account of their quarrel, and that Edmund O'Donnell, who seems to be a person of some importance, was leaving for Ireland by the next passage. A great prelate, he says, came from Rome to Spain and Portugal and was well received, and that great armies were prepared on his coming, but he knows no more about the matter.

Maurice Brown, merchant of Limerick, has more important information. He answers that a friar and a boy and John O'Grady came to Ireland besides the merchants of Waterford and Limerick. The friar (Bishop O'Gallagher) is an Irishman, and the boy called Felim of Ulster. Both these landed at Smerwick, and John O'Grady landed at Tarbert at the south side and said he would go and see the sons of Ch. Creagh, at Askeaton. Brown says that he heard that the King of Spain was ready to furnish Stucley and Archbishop MacGibbon with men, but, on account of their falling out, he broke off the project. A friar (Bishop O'Gallagher) and one of Stucley's men intended to come with him, but the friar fell sick at Castile. The friar, mentioned above, had a barrel in the ship but he did not know what it contained.

Richard Walsh of Waterford and Nicholas Rice of Limerick, were better informed about the passengers in the ship. They state that they heard in Spain that the friar who came with them was a bishop, Donough Oge O'Gallachowe (O'Gallagher), a Friar Minor out of Galway. Stucley was a captain of three galleys under the King of Spain's brother. The Friar Bishop had a barrel of books. The Spaniards will make war on this land. John O'Grady had a butt of wine, and had gone over to Spain for comfort for David Wolf, and but for the Friar Bishop they would have been stopped in Antelscy (Andalucca?) and Bayonne.

James Traunte, examined before President Perrott, stated that the Cardinal of Lorraine, the Bishop of Nantes, and the Lieutenant of Brittany (de la Roche) were advancers of the expedition to Ireland. De la Roche excused himself to James Fitzmaurice's messenger, and said that the blame for the failure of the negotiations was with Fitzmaurice because he sought aid from the King of Spain and did not rely on the French King.

These reports throw some light on the difficulties attendant on the coming of an Irish bishop into his own country, and at the same time on the constant communication by means of friars and students between the Irish negotiators in France and Spain and the Confederates, especially Fitzmaurice, at home. One name in particular among the intermediaries stands out, namely, that of the student Edmund Daniel or O'Donnell, S.J., who was regarded abroad as a person of no small importance. We shall shortly see more about him. The picture of the Franciscan bishop embarking for home with a barrel of books is distinctly quaint. No doubt the peculiar luggage caused some curiosity and talk among the sailors over their wine in the taverns on the eve of their departure. Only one witness, however, seems to have discovered that the barrel contained books, the library of a bishop of the sixteenth century. The reference to Fr. Wolf is quite fresh. He was at this time imprisoned in Dublin Castle, and his brother had undertaken the perilous journey and the difficult task of raising money for his release. The more money available for the bribery of the Castle officials the easier would be the task. Excuses were easily made by the custodians, and besides there were doubtless many of the Old Faith still within the Castle walls.

SERVICE AGAINST O'TOOLES AND O'BYRNES.

To the south of Dublin lay two important regions that were occupied by warlike and unruly " ruling families," and which were a perpetual danger to the safety of the city and the peace of the whole Pale. One of these regions was the long mountainous range, covered with venerable trees, stretching from Rathfarnham, about four miles outside the city, in a southerly direction, by Glencree and Calary, through the present Co. Wicklow and Wexford down almost to New Ross. This was the territory of the O'Tooles, O'Byrnes, and Kavanaghs. The other, stretching from Sallins and Athy on the east almost to the banks of the Shannon on the west, was the land of bog and moor and pathless forest, the country of the O'Mores of Leix and the O'Connors of Offaly.[1] These wedges, driven by nature into the flanks of the Pale, almost to the City Gates, cut off the loyal subjects of South Wexford and Kilkenny from communication by road with Dublin Castle. Difficult passes and fords had to be negotiated, at Newcastle, Rathdrum, and Aughrim. The narrow neck of land between Kilcullen and Leighlin Bridge, which was practically the only land passage connecting Dublin with Waterford and the south of Ireland, was usually guarded for the King by the Eustaces in their fortified castles of Kilcullen, Blackrath, and Baltinglass, and by the Earls of Kildare from the Keep of Kilkaa.

During the early days of Elizabeth's reign little is recorded of the O'Tooles, O'Byrnes, and Kavanaghs. But when the Butlers had submitted in September, 1569, the South Leinster " ruling families " kept up the fight. In 1570 it was reported that Nicholas Whyte, the Seneschal of Wexford, had given the Kavanaghs " a push in the field." In May of that year the Lord Deputy was able to report that " execution had been done " on these warriors of Wicklow and Wexford. Towards the end of that year, when an expected Spanish expedition was bruited, the head of the O'Mores, Rory Oge, was reported to have leagued himself with the O'Byrnes, and " had done much mischief."

Early in May, 1572, FitzWilliams referred in his reports to his services against the O'Mores, adding that Rory Oge was to be " beset on all sides." A like " service " was done on the O'Byrnes among whom Feagh MacHugh was rising into distinction as a guerilla chief. The occasion of the

---

[1] *Kilk. Arch. Soc.*, 1858-59, p. 339 *seq.*

trouble was the murder by the O'Byrnes of a Wexford gentleman named Browne. Agard, the Seneschal of Wicklow, took
immediate vengeance of some of the mountaineers, but was
inclined to hold out hopes of mercy as the best way to catch
the guilty parties, Matthew Furlong, and others, who had
employed the O'Byrnes. Nicholas Whyte, however, the
Seneschal of Wexford, went " thundering " about saying that
the Queen would never pardon anyone who had a hand in
Browne's murder. FitzWilliams wished devoutly that Whyte
had stayed in England.[1] What followed is described by
Froude [2] from the records left by the chief English actors in
the tragedy. Sir Humphrey Gilbert had done his part in
repressing the rebellion in Munster, " putting man, woman
and child to the sword." But this " Gilbert method of
treatment," remarks Froude, " has this disadvantage, that
it must be carried out to the last extremity, or it ought not
to be tried at all. . . . In justice to the English soldiers,
however, it must be said that it was no fault of theirs if any
Irish child of that generation was allowed to live to manhood."
In May, 1572, a report was sent to Dublin Castle by Mr.
Agard, the sergeant-major, or officer in command.[3] At this
time there was no open rebellion ; the Wicklow marauders
were simply stealing cattle in the Pale, but it was thought
desirable to read them a lesson. In the eyes of the Government they were robbers ; in their own eyes they were patriots ;
just as Drake and Hawkins were pirates in the eyes of the
Spaniards, but to the English they were champions of the
righteous. The principal offenders were the families of the
MacHughs (O'Byrnes), the Eustaces, and the Garralds
(Fitzgeralds).

Having burned sixteen hamlets in the Barony of Shille-
lagh, a party of soldiers next day entered the Glen of
Uí Mail, between Baltinglass and Blessington, where, says
the sergeant-major, " they killed a foster-brother of James

---

[1] *Catholic Bulletin*, May, 1927, pp. 532-9.

[2] *Hist. of England*, x. 254-7.

[3] Commission to Francis Agarde to execute martial law in the Birnes
country, Coulranell, Silelaghe, Omaile, the Fertrie, Fercolyn, and Glencapp,
excepting persons having land worth 40s. a year, or goods to the value of £20,
and with power to treat and conclude terms with rebels. 27 April, 1572
(*Fiants*, no. 2100.)

Eustace, Pat Fallon, and his brother David, whose heads were sent to the Lord Keeper." Having despatched another fellow, and taken much spoil, the soldiers swept round the base of Lugnaquilla to the upper waters of the Avanagh, and fell upon the MacHughs. As Feach, the leader, was not at home, they contented themselves with slaying " two of his foster-brothers, four or five kerns, and as many others as were in five cabins." Having accomplished a good day's work, they turned homewards, and, on their way, picked up a woman whom Agard carried to his station, meaning, as he said, " to execute her unless she served his purpose." A Captain George, with a scouting party, had another form of amusement, for, having encountered a party of Tallons, and killed one of them, he had the rest stripped naked, and " put in a bog."

Their next march was to Glenmalure, where, 24 May, their spy informed them they could have five hundred kine or " some killing." They preferred the latter. " At break of day," reports Agard, " they entered in and had the killing of diverse. . . . They slew many churls, women, and children." " Such," concludes Froude, " and so related, was a week's service of a detachment of English police. Agard was casually alluded to afterwards by the Deputy as an able and zealous officer, and this was all the notice that was taken of his performances. The inference is but too natural that that work of the kind was the road to preferment, and that this or something like it was the ordinary employment of the ' Saxon ' garrisons of Ireland."

In August, 1572, the Lord Deputy and Council considered the state of Ireland so dangerous that they suggested that the defence of the country should be committed to the only force and power there, namely, the native Irish. At the same time FitzWilliams requested Burghley to preserve him from beggary and help him out of his office of Deputyship.

Clanricard, being of no assistance in suppressing the rebellion in Connacht, the Earl of Ormond was appointed to the task, and with the Earl of Kildare, to proceed against Rory Oge O'More. On 26 August the report was sent to the Queen that Rory Oge had submitted, but at the same time the unpleasant news was also forwarded that the Kavanaghs, the MacHughs (O'Byrnes), and the Furlongs had broken out into open rebellion. In October the Lord Deputy reports that the land is in a rebellious state, and that he fears God will demand at his hands the shameful effusion of innocent blood. The names of England and English are hateful to the Irish who seek to expel them. He has had an arrogant letter from Tirlogh styling himself O'Neill. He would rather " accompany the loss of Ireland with his death than live in England to bemoan it." We shall see how the task was accomplished.

Plantation Scheme Causes Disorder in Ulster.

With the subjection of Leinster and Connacht, and the plantations of Munster and Ulster, the conquest of Ireland, it was thought, would be very far advanced. Early in 1572 the news travelled to the North that Sir Thomas Smith was coming over to make a Protestant plantation in the Ardes of Ulster, a peninsular district of the County Down. On 8 February Captain Pers of Carrickfergus was able to inform the Lord Deputy that the country was in an uproar at the news, and that Sir Brian MacFelim O'Neill was likely to revolt. Sir Brian himself complained that his lands had been granted to Smith, and asked to have the grant of these lands of his inheritance, namely, Clandeboye, in consideration of his long and painful service always since his childhood (27 March).[1] Pers then forged a letter, as from the Lord Deputy, declaring that there were no such grants to Smith.[2] While Smith was issuing his " printed books " on the plantation scheme,[3] the Lord Deputy wrote to the Queen

---

[1] *C.S.P.I.*, *Eliz.*, xxxv. 44-5. A Pardon was granted to him (17 May). Fine, 400 good fat cows. (*Fiants*, no, 2106.)

[2] *C.S.P.I.*, *Eliz.*, xxxv. 2.

[3] Grant to Sir Thomas Smythe, principal secretary of England, and Thomas Smythe, his son, to be colonels over all soldiers maintained at their cost, and over the territories and inhabitants of the great and little Ardes, and such other territories as are mentioned in their letters patent. To last for seven years, unless revoked in the meantime, with power to enter the great and little Ardes with an army, and expelling all rebels and seditious persons to possess and inhabit the same, to govern the soldiers and inhabitants, to determine all civil causes except pleas of land, and punish all criminals except traitors and coiners, and to assemble the inhabitants for the defence of the country. 29 Sept., 1572. Recites English Patent, 5 Oct., 1571, and order to Deputy, 16 July, 1572. (*Fiants*, no. 2149.)

denouncing them as the cause of the unrest, and sought to touch Elizabeth's mind through her pocket, by informing her that the soldiers could not be discharged while this commotion lasted (27 June).[1] To add to the disorder Tirlogh Luineach was on the march again. Early in June he encamped near Armagh, and was in touch through emissaries " with all the rebels in Ireland." The Dean of Armagh, who continued his sinister office of intermediary between Tirlogh and the Council in Dublin, reported (3 August)[2] that "knaves from Munster and Connacht entice him to evil." Brady, Bishop of Meath, fearful of the impending invasion, wrote to the Chief Baron (2 August)[3] that he has received news by messenger that Sir " Leynaghe " O'Neill " with a great force is in readiness to invade us this night. The place we should repair to is Moynalty. I have written to the Sheriff, so have I to the Portriff of the Navan. I have sent for Michael Cusack or his son. I will make what numbers I can ready. I pray you, send what numbers you can out of Trim and elsewhere, that they may be with the rest at least in the morning before day. I wish you would take pains yourself to be here very early. Our rising out will be very vain else."

It was at this juncture that the Lord Deputy declared that without the help of the native Irish princes it was impossible to govern Ireland. This was the result of the concerted action of the Irish to help the Munster chiefs by drawing off the English soldiers. But there was nothing constructive about their plan. It was more in the nature of sniping. There was a lack of generalship and of clearly-defined objective. Tirlogh was reported (25 September) as having made peace with O'Donnell and MacFelim who had undertaken the wages of 600 Scottish mercenaries.[4] Quite innocently Tirlogh informed the Lord Deputy that the Scots will do no harm to the English, but will act against the Irish who do not fulfil the peace. He demanded all his " Urraghs," that Smith be not permitted to occupy the lands of MacFelim, that Sorley Boy be not harmed, and that he be addressed not as Tirlogh Luineach but as O'Neill. It was now MacFelim's turn to profess repentance and to blame Smith's

[1] *C.S.P.I.*, *Eliz.*, xxxvi. 46.   [2] *Ib.*, xxxvii. 20, ii.
[3] *Ib.*, 20, x., P.R.O., London.   [4] *Ib.*, 59, i.

scheme for all the trouble.   On the other hand, Smith blamed the leaking out of the scheme for its failure, and endeavoured to persuade the Lord Deputy that the colonies were not intended to destroy the Irish race, but to teach them virtuous labour " and to leave robbing and stealing and killing one of another " (8 November).[1]   FitzWilliams, who had not been consulted in this plantation business, told the Queen that the chance of success had been immeasurably lessened by the sounding of Smith's trumpets beforehand and by the singular ignorance that had been shown of the jealous Irish nature.   The enterprise of the Smiths, from which so much had been expected and which had been so much advertised, had utterly collapsed in less than a year.   Thus, while the Northern chiefs succeeded in defeating the scheme and showed loyalty to the Queen in a humble petition for mercy, they still continued to govern their province in the old Irish way. But their idea of Fatherland and nationality was as un-developed as that of the Lords of Kerry and Cork.

Fitton's Failure in Connacht.

Connacht was in no better state than Ulster.   The Presidency had not flourished greatly under Fitton.   He could secure neither peace nor respect for the common law, and he dared not, while he remained in the province, leave the Brehon law in undisputed possession.   By the ordinary civil and canon law a man was held liable only for his own acts, but by the Brehon law the liability extended to des-cendants and collaterals.   Fitton seemed to have thought it possible to play fast and loose with the two systems, and so use their own customs against the Irish, though contrary as he believed, to all law, human and divine.[2]

The Earl of Clanricard's two sons were in open rebellion, and he was bound to answer for both of them by Irish law, of which he had accepted the liabilities, and by agreement under his own hand.   The Earl was loyal enough during his whole career, but he was unable to control the members of his family, and, to get out of a difficulty, surrendered himself

---

[1] *C.S.P.I., Eliz.*, xxxviii 30.   [2] Bagwell, ii. 216-17.

to Fitton.[1] The President seems to have had no other charge against him than that he levied exactions as his ancestors had done, a charge that came with remarkably bad grace from Fitton. Shut up in Dublin Castle, Clanricard was charged by Fitton with having been an aider and abettor of his sons' doings. With this, Deputy FitzWilliams did not agree, and thought that the Earl could be badly spared from his country. The Queen thought so too, rebuked Fitton, and sent the Earl back to Connacht with a general commission to grant pardons. Later he was able to boast : " After being set at liberty, I did within one twelvemonth hang my own son, my brother's son, my cousin-german's son, and one of the captains of my galloglasses, besides fifty of my own followers that bore armour and weapons ; which the Archbishop of Tuam, the Bishop of Clonfert, and the whole corporation of Galway may witness." [2] He thus rigorously carried out the Brehon law for the advantage of those who despised and tried to destroy it.

Whilst Clanricard, however, was undergoing his six months' imprisonment in Dublin Castle, his sons continued in the field. The *Four Masters* give the following graphic description of the campaign :—

A proclamation was issued by the President of Connaught, Sir Edward Phiton, about the festival of St. Patrick, respecting a court to be held at Galway of all those who were under the authority of the Queen, from Limerick to Sligo. At this summons came the Earl of Clanrickard and his sons, Ulick and John, with the " chiefs of their people." The two sons, hearing an adverse report of the President, and fearing him, fled secretly from the town. The President, likewise afraid of the sons, took their father prisoner and proceeded to Athlone, and then to Dublin. Afterwards he returned to Athlone and proceeded to Galway, demolishing castles on his way. But the Earl's sons gathered their followers also, and not only destroyed their own castles, but plundered the districts of all those in league with the English. They burned part of the town of Athlone [3] crossed the Shannon, and destroyed

---

[1] *C.S.P.I.*, *Eliz.*, xxxv. 12.   [2] *S.P.I.*, *Eliz.*, 8 March, 1578.

[3] In spite of the guns in the castle and the musketeers on the steeple of the church of Athlone, James Fitzmaurice with the young Burkes' forces, approached and " the body of the Church where the malt, biscuit and beer, and all brewing and baking vessels were stored were consumed." (Fitton to FitzWilliams, 16 July, 1572. *S.P.I.*, *Eliz.*, xxxvii. 11, i.)

the walls and castle of Athenry. Finally, they returned to Galway in despite of the English soldiers left there by the President to defend the town. The sons of the Earl continued from the end of spring to the middle of autumn thus injuring the merchants, and destroying whatever they were able upon the English, and upon all their English and Irish adherents. The Council of Dublin and the chiefs of the English at last resolved to set the Earl at liberty, on terms of peace and friendliness, over his territory and lands [on condition] that he should pacify his sons. The Earl accordingly returned to his country in the autumn of this year, and pacified his sons, who dismissed their hired soldiers, after having paid them their stipend and wages.

During these enterprises, James, the son of Maurice [Fitzmaurice] son of the Earl [of Desmond], was along with the sons of the Earl of Clanrickard, awaiting to bring the Scots with him into the territory of the Geraldines ; and it is impossible to relate all the perils and great dangers, for want of food and sleep, which this James encountered (he having but few troops and forces), from the English and Irish of the two provinces of Munster in this year.

The President [Perrott] of the two provinces of Munster laid siege to Caislen-na-Mainge in the summer of this year, having with him the forces of the two provinces of Munster, both English and Irish, and of the large towns, with their powder and lead. In this encampment were the muster of all the race of Eoghan Mor,[1] also MacMaurice of Kerry, i.e. Thomas, the son of Edmund, also the Barrys and the Roches. This whole army [English and Irish] continued besieging the castle for the space of three months, and finally took it, through the want of provisions, not at all for want of defence ; and it was for the purpose of bringing Scottish auxiliaries to relieve the town that James was along with the sons of the Earl [of Clanrickard], as we have before stated.

Perrott in a letter to the Lord Deputy, 16 September,[2] boasted that the above-mentioned chiefs of Munster accompanied him on this journey, and that Fitzmaurice had not above 600 foot and twenty horse. These chiefs of Munster, jealous of the Fitzmaurice leadership, were ever willing to show submission and prove their loyalty to English force. As Confederates they were weaklings.

---

[1] Race of Eoghan Mor, i.e. of the eldest son of Oilioll Olum, King of Munster in the second century. The chief of these were the MacCarthys, O'Sullivans, O'Callaghans, O'Keeffes, O'Mahonys, O'Donovans, O'Donohoes, etc.

[2] *S.P.I.*, *Eliz.*, xxxvii. 60.

Fitton lingered at Athlone for a few weeks after the Connacht men with their Scots mercenaries had retired, and then repaired first to Dublin and then to England. Fitz-Williams announced to Burghley (25 September) that Connacht would soon be quiet, for there would be no one left to resist the rebels.[1]

FITZMAURICE HUNTED DOWN.

Fitzmaurice had joined the Burkes in their rebellion in the hope of drawing off Perrott's forces from the siege of Castlemaine before which the President of Munster had sat down. His pursuit was a wild-goose chase, and every now and then some new Geraldine partisan arose and gave local trouble. Early in June Perrott had besieged Castlemaine, aided by the MacCarthies, O'Sullivans, Barrys, and Roches. After three months the fortress surrendered. Towards the end of August, William Casey, Protestant Bishop of Limerick, reported to the President the movements of the " traitor " James in the neighbourhood of Limerick, and that 1000 Scots were waiting to enter Munster. But Fitzmaurice, accompanied by the Burkes and Scots, was too late. Perrott advanced and drew the enemy between Limerick and Pallas, but was too weak to follow up the disorder he created among the Scots who fled towards the Glen of Aherlow. Edmund and Edward Butler, who had renewed their loyalty to the Queen, rendered good assistance to Perrott and brought in fifty heads.

Perrott, in his report from his camp near Emly (12 September), announced that he intended to pursue Fitzmaurice on the morrow. The Irish lords of Kerry, who in their soul hated the Desmonds, were accompanying the President who asked the Lord Deputy for more soldiers, corn, lead, and match.[2] Perrott, whilst careful not to arouse religious animosity, was in agreement with the Deputy as to the necessity of enlisting Irish chiefs on his side.

Heartened by the submission of the Earl of Thomond, who promised to assist in quelling all rebellions, and in furthering the Book of Common Prayer, Perrott prepared

[1] *S.P.I., Eliz.*, xxxvii. 59, v.   [2] *Ib.*, 59, iv., v.

for a grand attack on Aherlow, with the help of the Butlers. But the garrison of Kilmallock caused some trouble for a while by refusing to march as they had got no pay. Whilst this difficulty was being surmounted by the assurance that pay was coming, Perrott consoled himself at the Cork Assizes where he indulged in some hanging when he found the juries ready to convict. The attacks of the Kilmallock garrison and of the Butlers on the cabins and camp at Aherlow accounted for nearly 200 of Fitzmaurice's men.[1] That was the last important success of the campaign, which had proved beyond doubt that the Munster men had no chance in the field against English soldiers, or even against the Butler galloglasses ; but it had also proved that the success could not be followed up with advantage, and that the problem of Irish Government was as far from solution as ever.[2]

CLERICAL STUDENTS AS FOREIGN EMISSARIES ; EDMOND DANIEL EXECUTED.

In his seventeenth article Stackbold had mentioned " one Edmond Daniel of Limerick, student," as one of James Fitzmaurice's emissaries to France and Spain. The sending of Irish ecclesiastics who were studying on the Continent with letters to and from Ireland was a common affair in those days. Perhaps the most important of them was Edmond Daniel or O'Donnell, a Jesuit student. He was a relative of Father Wolf, S.J., the Papal Commissary, and, with Father William Good, an Englishman, opened a Catholic school in Limerick in ·the year 1564, " so that he might confirm his fellow countrymen in the path of faith and instruct the Limerick youth in the rudiments of the Catholic faith and the rules of Ciceronian eloquence." [3]

At the time of Fr. Wolf's arrest, Edmond Daniel had to flee from Limerick, but he was foremost amongst those who laboured to effect his release by bribery or ransom. Between 1567 and 1572 he was untiring in his efforts to raise money in Spain and Portugal for that purpose, and

---

[1] *S.P.I.*, *Eliz.*, xxxviii. 46. Lord Deputy and Council to the Queen, 1 Dec., 1572.

[2] Bagwell, ii. 224.

[3] Hogan, *Iber. Ignat.*, p. 20.

was evidently in league with John O'Grady. He also acted, as Stackbold told, as courier for James Fitzmaurice in his negotiations with Rome, Madrid, and Lisbon. One of the merchants examined about May, 1572, had stated that Daniel or O'Donnell, " a person of some importance, was leaving for Ireland by the next passage." It would seem that the government officials believed that it was Edmond Daniel who had sent or conveyed to James Fitzmaurice the Bull excommunicating Elizabeth.

Daniel was not long in Ireland when he was arrested by the Catholic Mayor of Limerick, led to Cork, handcuffed like a robber, and thrown into the public prison with the lowest criminals. He was amongst those tried by Sir John Perrott, and was hanged, drawn, and quartered at Cork, 25 October, 1572, on the ground that he was guilty of high treason in refusing to recognise the Queen's supremacy in matters of religion, in upholding that of the Pope, and in carrying letters from the Holy See to James Fitzmaurice. He may be regarded as the first Irish victim of whose martyrdom it is possible to produce direct contemporary evidence.[1] " He died," wrote Father Wolf to the General of the Jesuits, in a letter dated 7 May, 1574, " in the City of Cork on the 25th of October, 1572, for the Catholic Faith and in the Catholic Faith, to the great edification not only of the Catholics, but even of the heretics." In a petition to the Holy See, 7 July, 1575, Thomas Arthur set forth how, being Mayor, or Recorder, of Limerick, he had been constrained to arrest certain persons who appeared to be opposed to the Queen, and amongst the rest Edmond Daniel who, he afterwards discovered, was a Clerk in Minor Orders. He told how he handed him over to the State authorities some months later ; how the cleric was tried for treason ; how he was convicted without very convincing evidence, and how he was eventually executed. Finally, Fitzmaurice himself, in a letter to the General of the Jesuits, 31 January, 1576, in which he gave expression to the gratitude he felt for the many favours he had experienced at the hands of the Society of Jesus, went on to add that " the only return I have made

---

[1] " primus ex omnibus veritatem Catholicæ Religionis sanguinis profusione in Hibernia asseruit." (Tanner, 1675.)

for all your kindness is that one of your body has been cut off by a violent death on my account." [1]

FRANCISCAN COUNCILS IN GALWAY, DONEGAL, AND ADARE.

The net result of the recent campaigns was the defeat of Fitzmaurice, with the usual assizes and hangings. Ulster, following the failure of the plantation scheme, had settled for a while to rest and was left to carry on as of old, and O'Donnell was on friendly terms with the O'Neills. In Connacht, Clanricard's sons, aided by the Scots, had matters their own way also, after the failure of Fitton. Thus from Armagh, on to Donegal, through Sligo to Galway, and as far south as Limerick and Adare, the country was undisturbed by English officials and their armed forces, so that Irish life went on as it had gone in times past. Catholics were able to practise their religion in peace, and priests and friars were able to pass from county to county with impunity for the better government of the Church in those parts. This state of affairs was the matter of some reports which furnish new light on the situation.

On 7 December, 1572,[2] the Lord Deputy informed Burghley that it was " no new thing to have friars gad up and down in Ireland, but we mislike the time, place, and occasion of their meeting." Edward White, Clerk to the Earl of Clanricard, is somewhat perturbed about the same affair, and writes (November) to the Lord Deputy :—[3]

The detestable murder of the godly [Huguenots] in France [4] was soon known to all friars and priests in Connacht and openly

---

[1] *Catholic Bulletin*, Feb., 1927, p. 308.
[2] *S.P.I., Eliz.*, xxxviii. 52, P.R.O., London.
[3] *Ib.*, 52, i., P.R.O., London.
[4] According to a News Letter, dated 29 Oct., 1572, Rome : " Letters are to hand from France by which it is understood that 2000 Huguenots have just been slain, and that tidings thereof being brought to the King while he was at Church, he devoutly gave thanks to God that it has so befallen, and announced that he was firmly resolved to tolerate no religion in his realm save the Catholic." (*C.S.P., Rome*, 1572-78, no. 106.) This was the Massacre on the Eve of St. Bartholomew. Elsewhere has been shown the political and revolutionary movement that was at the back of this massacre and which is admitted to-day by competent and impartial historians. (*Clifton Tracts*, vol. ii., 1854.)

spread abroad through Ireland. A General Council of friars
assembled in the Abbey of Galway on St. Francis day last
[4 October] which was attended by Bishop O'Gallagher. The
godly [Protestants] can scarcely show their faces, as though the
kingdom of Antichrist were erected again ; speaking words against
the State ; threatening Spanish inquisition ; but also defiances
against professors of God's word as it would pity all Christian
hearts to hear, so as for anything I can hear, there is a foul sink
of rebellion breeding in that town. Since which Council, the
friars, yea of Ulster, are so open in Galway as sometimes they
go 10, 14, 16, yea 20 in a company, and so range abroad in the
country sowing the seed of that wicked doctrine. So as the poor
countrymen seeing them so embrased [embarrassed] in the town
dare say nothing, nor the Earl [Clanricard] himself. After this
Council it was concluded another Council should be held at Donegal
in O'Donnell's country where after long conference the same is
removed to Adare [1] in Munster, but 7 Irish miles from Limerick
where said frairs will be very shortly. What may come of it
I know not ; but their devices is all how to subvert the English
Government and set up their own wickedness once again. They are
so bold as though the Pope were king of England and Ireland. All
Hallows' Day last [1 November, 1572] there has been 14 friars in
Galway and there preached in the Abbey there ; whither came
unto them divers Aldermen of the town amongst them one Denis
Kerwan, Mayor, 1570-71 ; the preacher a friar of Ulster ; doctrine
rebellious. So daily to Galway where they behave themselves
like princes. Out of the Council of Donegal 3 or 4 friars went
into France, and took ship at Galway, and thither came a priest
very late out of France named Theg O'Farrelly. There came
from Spain 5 weeks ago a friar Dominican called Cormac appointed in Rome provincial of the Black Friars [Dominicans]
in Ireland.[2] His helping hand with the rest must tend to wickedness ; he brought indulgences and the rest from the Pope and
published the same in Sligo.

FITZMAURICE'S SUBMISSION.

On the strength of the promises held out by Spain to
Fitzmaurice through the emissaries sent by the Confederates,

---

[1] Adare contained an important Franciscan house founded in 1464 by the
Earl of Kildare and his wife, the daughter of James, Earl of Desmond. The
ruins of the friary stand in the demesne of the Earl of Dunraven. (*Kilk. Arch.
Soc.*, 1856, p. 61 *seq*.)

[2] He had been mentioned in Walter French's report of 30 March.

all Munster, much of Connacht, and parts of Leinster had rushed to arms. For a time it seemed as if victory was going to crown their efforts, but the promised aid did not materialise, and, one by one, the chiefs began to desert Fitzmaurice, the leader of the Confederacy. Hoping against hope, he still held out for nearly four years, until early in 1573 a commercial treaty between Spain and England showed him that Spanish aid was out of the question for the time being.

After his last defeat by Sir Edmund Butler, Fitzmaurice no longer attempted to make headway with his opposition to Perrott. He had still 80 kerne with him and found no difficulty in feeding his men either in Aherlow or in the wild district between Macroom and Glengariffe. Perrott, who wished to hunt out rather than pardon him, watched the ports so carefully as to frustrate any attempts at escape. Fearing, however, lest he should escape to Spain, Perrott thought it desirable to accept Fitzmaurice's submission at Kilmallock.[1]

Writing from Limerick, 3 March, 1573, Perrott informed the Privy Council of the whole proceeding :—[2]

The 21 February, being at the Viscount Roche's house, the late seneschal of Imokelly and Onye MacRichard, came, two of the chief men of James, and presented his son to me, desiring in James's behalf that he would accept the child as pledge of the father's repentant mind for his great disloyalty used towards the Queen's Majesty, and on my word alone he asked his life. The next day he was to come to me in the highway on his knees to crave her Highness's mercy. I received his son and appointed

---

[1] Kilmallock (Co. Limerick), the Church of St. Mocheallog of the seventh century, was little known until the Geraldines, at the Anglo-Norman invasion, made themselves masters of the South of Ireland, and particularly of that tract known as the Golden Vein. The position of the new town was well chosen, standing as it did in the midst of one of the most fertile plains of Munster. It lay on the road between Limerick and Cork, and in such a position as to command the important Pass known as the Red Gap. The two great natural strongholds of the Glen of Aherlow and the wooded mountains of Upper Connelloe were on either side, and these same fortresses, which afforded protection to the expelled Irish of the thirteenth century, also gave security to the Geraldines of the sixteenth century. Kilmallock was a walled town from the thirteenth century and closely connected with that branch of the Desmond family known as the White Knights. (*R.H.A.A.I.*, 1889, pp. 204-6.)

[2] *S.P.I., Eliz*, xxxix. 40, P.R.O., London.

him to come to Kilmallock within 2 days when I would hear what he could say. He came to the parish church of that town, he confessed his former lewd and ill life, and acknowledged his duty to her Majesty humbly. I was furnished with victuals and munitions in case James would escape to the wastes and the mountains. I had secret intelligence that unless he had some hope of mercy from the Queen he would fly into Spain. I protected James for 13 weeks conditionally, so that if the Queen did not grant him pardon, then he and his pledges would be set at liberty. . . . I caused some of the chiefest of James's men to yield themselves in certain good towns with halters about their necks, and such like punishment for terror's sake.

The following document [1] was drawn up for Fitzmaurice to read aloud and sign :—

The humble submission of James Fitzmaurice, Gerald and other his associates before the right honourable Sir John Perrott, knight, Lord President of Munster and others of that state, and in the presence of a multitude of people at the Church of Kylmallock, the xxiiird of February, 1572 (i.e. 1573).

The said James Fitzmorrice, the seneschall of Imokelly, and others of his confederacy kneeling on both their knees, and holding their hands joined and cast upward, and with countenance bewraying their great sorrow and fervent repentance for their former life : James in the behalf of himself and the rest spake first in English and after in the Irish in effect as followeth.

I, James Fitzmorrice, first caused by error and lack of the knowledge of my duty, and allured by the company of the Earl of Clancare and Sir Edmond Butler, to whom for their favour, policy, and greatness I yielded, began to make rebellion against Her Majesty and her good subjects, together with the said Earl and Sir Edmonde, in the xith year of Her Highness reign, and when too late I understood how far I had waded in disloyalty, that I with the rest was in the Cities and towns of the land proclaimed traitor, I sought to void the realm, and being by good keeping of the ports debarred of passage, was so void of friends as when the rest were received into mercy I could not at that time have any that either for my good or stinting of evil be mean for me unto her Majesty or the governors of this realm, but rather as a destitute person left to maintain the quarrels of the rest, and desperate and hopeless of all favour, have devilishly followed my wickedness, and being in heart full of anguish and sorrow for the mischief

[1] *S.P.I.*, *Eliz.*, xxxix. 40, i., P.R.O., London.

that I heaped upon mischief could never have bewrayed the same or receive the favour to be but once heard until this present time. And now, therefore, with the eyes of my heart, sore weeping and bewailing my most devilish life past, I knowledge myself to have most wickedly rebelled against God and most undutifully against my prince, and most unnaturally against my native country. The rehearsal whereof in particular were needless in this audience to be made, which are witnesses of them all, and which (woe worth the chance) have and might condemn me as the rankest traitor alive. This sword that I wear (which by God's appointment) should be used in the service of my prince or in my lawful defence and not otherwise, I yield, as abused from his [its] proper course, unto her Majesty, and do bereave myself from the use thereof, until it shall please Her Majesty for my farther trial to commit unto me any piece of service, wherein I vow so much faith and earnestness so any man can have. Her Majesty's word, I cannot but acknowledge, hath wearied [sorrowed] and overcome me, and unto the same I humbly and willingly do yield, and under the same I vow to fight all the residue of my life, if it may please your Lord to draw your sword, that I may kiss the same as a token of Her Majesty's sword, and also to be a mean unto Her Highness to vouchsafe to accept me as her most miserable vassal. And now this garth of Kilmallock which town I have most traitorously sacked and burnt I kiss, and on the same I lie prostrate overfraught with sorrow upon the present view of my most mischievous fact.

And so (right honourable) as my most dread Sovereign Lady the Queen's Majesty hath throughout the world most amply spread her glory and mercy. So prostrate here, I beseech your good Lord to be a mean unto Her Highness rather to have eye unto that mercy which hath made her most honourable than to her justice, wherewith I confess I have deserved a thousand times to be destroyed.

JAMES FITZMORISH DE GERALDINE.

About five weeks after Perrott's last letter he thought it well to send (12 April) a further account of the hopes entertained of Fitzmaurice's loyalty. He wrote to Burghley [1] that he thought

James Fitzmaurice will become a second St. Paul. He hath one, two or three places whereunto I have appointed him, wherefore, and for his submission, he is the most quieted man that may be amongst divers of the lords of Munster. As before their faces he lately now did declare, saying farther that those, which in his time of rebellion did by all means secretly aid him, will not now seem to be acquainted with him. He offereth to serve against Turlough Lynagh, Sir Bryan McFelim in Ulster, the Moores of Leix, the O'Moores of Offaly or any in Connacht, requiring only but meat and drink for him and his company to regain thereby Her Majesty's lost favour. He begs me to be a means to Her Highness for his pardon, which is requisite lest he should be driven to fly beyond the sea and to cause some foreign invasion against Her Majesty here. Travail has brought the country to quiet since the writing of my last letters.

[Perrott then adds :—]

Forty-five notable malefactors were put to death at the sessions at Limerick, some for treasons, some for murders and felonies.

He has now come to Cashel " for the like redress," and will then go to Clonmel " for the better reformation of Tipperary for the four points exempted out of the Earl of Ormonde's patent." He will then go to Cork and expect orders of the Lord Deputy and Council touching the Earl of Desmond and his brother.

FITZMAURICE STILL LOOKS TO SPAIN ; GREGORY XIII'S INTEREST.

Though James Fitzmaurice seemed to be beaten to the ropes, though he had accepted the hard conditions imposed on him, and though for a time the victor was satisfied that the repentance of the rebel chief was profound and lasting, he still continued to look abroad, to France, Spain, and Rome for the help of which he stood in need, and without which he saw it was useless and even harmful to continue the struggle. He had correspondents all the time in those countries who pleaded his cause, which they emphatically represented as that of the Catholic Church. They pointed out to King and Pope that the interests of Christendom could be promoted in the British Isles only in one way, namely, by the establishment of a Catholic State with a Catholic Sovereign in Ireland.[1] Their efforts were supported by the circumstances of the time. A new Pope was now seated on the papal throne in the person of Gregory XIII, who

[1] *Catholic Bulletin*, April, 1928, pp. 414-20.

not only listened with sympathy to their representations, but heartily agreed with the view that "the salvation of Christendom depended on the stout assailing of England." With remarkable energy he tried to interest the King of Spain in their cause, which, in season and out of season, he exhibited as the cause of God and of His Church. He was not long seated on the papal throne when tangible signs of his interests in Irish affairs began to manifest themselves in the diplomatic correspondence that passed between the Papal Court and the Papal Nuncio in Spain.

On 25 April, 1573, the Nuncio in Spain wrote to the Cardinal Secretary of the Pope :—[1]

I have not failed in the office which the Pope bid me do with his Catholic Majesty in aid of the Catholics of Ireland against the heretics, in order that his Majesty may at any rate be now pleased to send thither some force, as he has every reason for not deserting these good men, who for the holy Catholic faith hazard all their substance and their very lives. His Majesty's answer is that he will do all that he can, but at the same time he lets me know the great expense in which he finds himself involved in defence of the cause of God and the faith, intimating that he cannot meet all demands, but that still he will see what can be done. This business got wind some days ago, and there are men here that concern themselves with it ; and just now an Irish friar has arrived.[2] I shall miss no good opportunity of doing all that is possible in aid of this pious and holy work, for if the business goes no further, it will be but a sorry defence this King will make of himself in regard of the realm of Ireland.

As there was little hope of a rising in England, and as Spain's subjects in Flanders were up in arms against the King, the Duke of Alva thought it madness to meddle with England. In those circumstances, and in view of the treaty between Spain and England, Fitzmaurice saw it was hopeless to expect Philip to come out openly in favour of Ireland, and advised his negotiators to confine themselves to securing some secret help in the way of money, arms, and munitions.

The Pope now turned his eyes to Don John of Austria, the hero of Lepanto, and regarded favourably the Irish

---

[1] *C.S.P.*, *Rome*, 1572-78, no. 186.
[2] Evidently as a result of the Franciscan Councils in Adare, etc.

solution that Don John should be crowned King of Ireland. He even suggested to Spain that Don John should also become King of England by marrying Mary Queen of Scots and ousting Elizabeth (January, 1574). Mary, the Spanish Ambassador in London reported, was not averse from the proposal, and neither were the English Catholics, and it was supported by Dr. Sander, the ablest of the English refugees then in Spain.

Notwithstanding fresh appeals on the part of the English Catholics, the Duke of Alva's reluctance to interfere in the affairs of either Ireland or England was intensified by the revolt that had just broken out in the Spanish provinces of the Netherlands, subject to his rule. With French encroachments on Flanders, he was convinced that the one way of coping with all this trouble was to be found in an alliance with England. Elizabeth, on her part, was not slow to recognise the advantages of some such understanding. The " Massacre of St. Bartholomew " and the curt way the Duke of Anjou had put an end to the match-making, taught her that France was not to be trusted too much. Accordingly, she was soon corresponding with Alva, and holding out the olive-branch to Spain. Alva did not see why Spain should risk the loss of Flanders for the sake of the English Catholics ; such a religious crusade by the King " was simply a temptation of the devil." By April, 1573, Philip had accepted Alva's plea for peace, and had consented to some sort of treaty with England.

Yet, always apprehensive of trouble with Elizabeth, Philip kept Stucley about his Court, supplied him with funds, and held out from time to time promises of help. Keeping in touch with the Irish chiefs and bishops, and sending them occasionally financial help, he gave them to understand that they might expect substantial help as soon as he was free to send it.

A few letters in the diplomatic correspondence of the time show how earnestly Gregory XIII had taken up the affairs of these islands. In letters to the Nuncios of Spain and Portugal (7 April) the Cardinal Secretary informed them that the Bishop of Emly (Maurice MacBrien) " having been expelled from his See by the heretics, has repaired to Rome, and there been graciously received by the Pope. He is now returning to his See, by way of Portugal; and the Pope, who deems him a good man, commends him to the Cardinal's especial charity and good offices."[1] On the 17 June the Nuncio in Spain wrote to the Cardinal Secretary[2] that " the Irish Bishop of Emly has arrived here and has given me your letter of the 7th of April, in answer to which I have no more to say than that I shall not fail to afford him all the aid I can with his Catholic Majesty in conformity with the instructions that you sent me in His Holiness's name."

This formal letter clearly did not hold out much hope on account of the mind of the King at the time for the reasons already stated. In accordance with this new phase of Philip's mind the Cardinal Secretary wrote to the Nuncio, 12 July,[3] that " as to the reduction of the Lady [Elizabeth] of England [to the obedience of the Church] all the offices that are being done are good, and must be continued, although there is little or no hope that good results are likely to ensue."

In June letters arrived in Rome from England to the effect that Ireland was in rebellion against Elizabeth; " which rebellion," wrote the Nuncio in France to the Cardinal Secretary, 8 June, " if such there be and well sustained, would be of the utmost importance, and would deprive the Queen of the means of fomenting sedition in France or Flanders."[4] Ireland ever a pawn in the game as far as Spain and France were concerned!

On 16 August the Pope wrote a personal letter[5] to the Duke of Alva " commending to him the cause of the oppressed Catholics in Ireland, which, he understands, has already been laid before the Duke by the Bishop of Casale " (*sic* Archbishop of Cashel).

On 24 August the Cardinal Secretary wrote to the Nuncio in Spain,[6] enclosing a memorial to the Pope by the Irish Bishop of Meath (" Mendense "), to which the Nuncio is directed to give effect in one or other of the ways therein suggested, so as to relieve the bishop's poverty and deliver him from the woeful plight in which he is.

---

[1] *C.S.P., Rome*, 1572-78, no. 174.   [2] *Ib.*, no. 205.
[3] *Ib.*, no. 223.   [4] *Ib.*, no. 202.
[5] *Ib.*, no. 237.   [6] *Ib.*, no. 240. Enclosure missing.

The Bishop (Walsh) likewise called on the Nuncio (14 September) in France who recommended his case to the Cardinals there, but held out little hope that he would be relieved of the straits in which he found himself, on account of the poverty there.[1]

DESMOND'S RETURN ; FRESH ACTIVITY.

For two years the Earl of Desmond and Sir John Desmond had been prisoners in England in the keeping of Sir Warham St. Leger. There the Earl was joined by the Countess. By the beginning of 1573 the restraints on them were gradually relaxed, and there was much talk of sending them back to Ireland. Desmond begged that Ormond might be sent to Ireland with him as he did not desire to leave the field clear for his rival at Court.

After much writing and talking the terms of Desmond's return were at last settled (6 January, 1573).[2] He accepted the Established , Religion, renounced foreign jurisdictions, and promised to assist all (Protestant) bishops, ministers, etc. He undertook to keep the Queen's peace and not to molest the lords of Kerry, as well as the other chieftains who had taken up arms against Fitzmaurice. He bound himself to put down Fitzmaurice's rebellion as soon as possible, to apprehend those who had fled to foreign countries, and to leave such castles in the Queen's hands as she might think necessary for the public peace. In general he was to hold the same position as Kildare or Ormond, and he agreed not to exercise the palatinate jurisdiction that he claimed in Kerry until that claim should have been legally determined in his favour. He further promised to pay the debts he had incurred in England as soon as money could be gathered. The document was signed by Desmond, 21 January, 1573, and witnessed by Sir John. The Queen's desperate resolve to pacify Munster by sending home Desmond was somewhat marred by his detention in Dublin for some months. Though Fitzmaurice promised to be a loyal subject he was merely gaining time to prepare for the great struggle to come. He had accomplished the ostensible and more immediate

---

[1] *C.S.P.*, *Rome*, no. 246.   [2] *S.P.I.*, *Eliz.*, xxxix. I.

object of his campaign, namely, the liberation of the Earl
of Desmond, or rather the agreement to liberate him, and
the recognition of his rights as head of the Munster Geraldines.
Elizabeth herself had grown tired of the Munster struggle
as it was costing her so much money. Perrott's pride was
also satisfied. So, it seemed that everybody was pleased.
One important conclusion was that Fitzmaurice was the
acknowledged leader of the armed forces of Ireland and could
now appeal to all for support. He was therefore in a better
position to proceed with his preparations for the life and
death struggle that he knew he must wage sooner or later
against English rule.[1]

About a month after Fitzmaurice's submission, Fitton
and Desmond arrived in Dublin (25 March), but the Earl
was interned there until the arrival of Perrott. The
President had some hanging to do at Cork, Limerick, Cashel,
and Clonmel. At Cork, sixty, and at Limerick, forty-five
" malefactors " were executed, and no fewer in the other
two towns. Apart from what the Butlers had accomplished
(twenty-one executions), Perrott could boast that he had
killed or hanged 800 persons with the loss of only eighteen
Englishmen.[2] The wonder is that between sword, halter,
and starvation, there was any able-bodied men left in
Munster. But not content with taking off heads, he endeavoured to induce the Irish chiefs to cut off their raven
locks, and the Irish ladies to discard their ornamental but
voluminous linen head coverings (16 June).[3]

On the arrival of Perrott in Dublin, Desmond was called
upon to agree to new conditions ; " to dispense with the
retinue that formed the usual bodyguard of the Irish chiefs,
to undertake to disarm his castles, and leave the English
undisturbed in possession of Castlemayne and Castlemartyr."
Coyne and livery was to be allowed to his rival, the Earl of

---

[1] *Catholic Bulletin*, Feb., 1927, p. 309. Froude sums up the situation
thus : " Fitzmaurice was satisfied with conditions which were a confession of
a want of power to punish him further, and the President had the satisfaction
of seeing the Earl of Desmond's (representative) on his knees in the mud at
his feet. . . . So ended the first Presidency of Munster. It would not support
its cost, and, unless some plan could be found to govern Ireland which would
pay its expenses, Elizabeth seemed contented that Ireland should not be
governed." (*Hist. of England*, x. 290-1.)

[2] *S.P.I., Eliz.*, xxxix. 65 ; xl. 6, ii. ; xli. 43.   [3] *Ib.*, xli. 43.

Ormond, but none to Desmond. There were to be no more armed assemblies in Desmond territory, no Brehon law, and justice was to be administered according to English forms by judges under the writs of the Viceroy. Excellent regulations, all of them, comments Froude, if introduced by England with a strong hand, or if sanctioned by Desmond from a conviction of their inherent fitness. But, as the matter stood, the Earl was required to do everything that England had struggled to do by force, and had failed. The Irish chiefs were to subdue their own people by means of English laws.[1]

Perrott had grumbled at Desmond's return, and now besought the Queen to have him taken back to England, for he could do nothing but harm in Munster. To give colour to his accusation he assured Elizabeth that the plough already laughed the unbridled rogue to scorn, and daily improvement was visible. The poor prayed for the Queen. The 8000 or 9000 men capable of bearing arms honoured Elizabeth's name, and their hands began to wax hard in labour as their feet once did in running to mischief. The revenue might soon be expected to increase. " If the Kings of England," he said in language that must have appealed very strongly to Elizabeth, " have any one thing heavier upon their souls than others, it is that they have not made a thorough conquest of this realm." [2]

In the autumn Perrott sailed for London, with really nothing to show for his Presidency but gibbeted corpses. Evidently quoting some local authority, the *Four Masters* announce his departure as " lamented by the poor, the widows, the feeble, and the unwarlike of the country." Scarcely had he departed than Desmond set about to effect his own escape from his rather loose confinement. This took place between 28 October and 20 November.[3]

---

[1] *Hist. of England*, x. 300.   [2] *S.P.I.*, *Eliz.*, xli. 76, ii.

[3] Ware's *Annals*, Harris's *Dublin*, and Smith's *Kerry*, vary as to the precise date. The *Four Masters* are altogether wrong in dating it St. Patrick's Day. See *C.S.P.I.*, *Eliz.*, xlii. 60, 84. On 28 October, Desmond asks for his freedom. On 20 November, the Lord Deputy writes to him about the rashness of his escape. Loftus (*Annals*) places his escape on 16 November, and gives the name of the Mayor, into whose custody Desmond was given, as Christopher Fagan. That is quite correct. He first appears as Mayor on 29 September, 1573. (*C.A.R.D.*, ii. 83.)

According to Ware : " The Earl of Desmond having promised upon his oath to be faithful to her Majesty, was by the Lord Deputy put into the hands of the then Mayor of Dublin. After a fortnight he was granted leave to divert himself by hunting, and as soon as he got to Grangegorman, on the north side of the River Liffey, he changed his course and escaped to his own territories. He was thereupon proclaimed traitor, with a promise of £1000 and £40 pension to anyone who should bring him in alive, and £500 and £20 pension to him that should bring in his head." [1]

Escorted through Kildare by Rory Oge O'More and Piers Grace, Desmond arrived in Limerick where he was received by James Fitzmaurice and the Countess Desmond. The Earl and Countess lost no time in showing themselves in " the hated Irish apparel " and were joyously received. Having proclaimed that no minister of English law should execute office in Munster, he expelled the English soldiers from Castlemaine and Castlemartyr. On Christmas Eve Adare Abbey " was stored again with friars," and Hugh Lacy, Bishop of Limerick, deposed by Perrott, was re-installed in his cathedral. [2]

The *Four Masters* state that " he ordained that the Church and the men of science should be restored to the possession of their privileges ; and he re-established the [religious] orders to the law of the Pope, as was right." Desmond declared that " as long as he was allowed to rule his own country in peace, he would do no hurt to her Majesty's subjects."

In every part of Ireland there was a decided disposition to question England's right to meddle in the internal affairs of the ruling families. " The Irish nation," wrote one of the English garrison towards the end of this year, " is more engaged with the fury of desperation than ever I have known heretofore. . . . They say they are no rebels, and do but

---

[1] *Annals.* O'Daly (*Hist. of the Geraldines*, c. 18) asserts that the Earl of Desmond, on his arrival in Dublin, was informed by a member of the Council that a plot was laid for the ruin of the Geraldines, and that thereupon the Earl sent word to John and James, cautioning them on no terms to leave their territories, and that having despatched this message, he himself soon after escaped from Dublin.

[2] *Catholic Bulletin*, xviii., 1927, p. 311.

defend their lands and goods. Our own people have lost the minds of soldiers, and are become [too] weak in body to endure travail and [too] miserable in mind to sustain the force of the enemy. . . . This people [the Irish] begin to know their own force and strength, and have learnt the use and sort of weapons, their places of strength and advantage." [1]

On the 30 November, 1573,[2] Justice Walshe reported to Burghley that the news of Desmond's escape reached Fitzmaurice at Limerick. Probably as a sequel to the news, the house of the Protestant Bishop of Limerick (William Casey) was taken and handed over to Hugh Lacy, the Catholic Bishop, lately deposed. The Chantor of Limerick's possessions were taken by force and occupied by one Pursell (probably the Catholic Chantor) who had been deprived by the Ecclesiastical Commissioners. The Abbey of Adare is again stored with friars, the chief strongholds of the countryside are fortified by the Earl, and many of his subjects have responded to the call to join him.

Justice N. Walshe wrote to Burghley, 3 December, 1573,[3] that "the old Bishop of Limerick," Hugh Lacy, who was then at liberty, is reinstated in the See and now and then comes to him. Desmond is in power again in Kerry, and Fitzmaurice makes war so as to have the Earl of Desmond set at liberty. Fitzmaurice wrote to Casey and Walshe to have protection for himself and his men for one month, and to have leave to take meat in the country for himself and his men. He would not come into the city of Limerick, but came across the Shannon with 200 able fighting men, galloglasses, kerne and Scot and eight or nine horsemen, and disposed his men about the country.

Essex's Plantation in Antrim.

Another hardy adventurer now decided to risk his reputation in the government of Ireland. This was Walter Devereux, Earl of Essex, who offered to conquer the province of Ulster

---

[1] Thomas Wilsford to Burghley, 1 Dec., 1573, from Knockfergus. *S.P.I., Eliz.*, xliii. 1.

[2] *S.P.I., Eliz.*, xlii. 88, P.R.O., London.   [3] *Ib.*, xliii. 5.

for Her Majesty, and required a grant from the Crown of
the whole of Clandeboy (Antrim and N. Down). He further
asked for authority by martial law over the race of Hugh
Boy O'Neill and his Scots who held the territory. After some
haggling Essex received a grant of all Antrim except the
lands belonging to the chartered townsmen of Carrickfergus,
the town and castle, and 1000 acres for their support. He had
unlimited power of alienation to men of English birth, and
authority for twelve years to make new subdivisions or to
rename old ones. He had power to give leave of absence
to English tenants for twelve years on the appointment of
a substitute, and to admit 100 foreigners as denizens. He
was freed from all cesses for seven years, and none of his
tenants was to be obliged to serve in war beyond the limits
of his grant.[1] He had all manorial rights except pleas of

[1] The following were the powers and appointments made to Essex :—
Commission to Walter, Earl of Essex, to raise the inhabitants of Clandeboy,
Kilultagh, the Duffren, the Rowte [Route] and the Glynnes, and to lead them
against the rebels and enemies within those countries or any other part of the
province of Ulster with power to punish by fine and imprisonment any who
disobey his authority. To resist him in recovering those parts of Ulster granted
to him by the Queen and now occupied by rebellious Irish and Scots. 23 Sept.,
1573. (*Fiants*, no. 2325.)
Commission to same to execute martial law within the same. 24 Sept.,
1573. (*Fiants*, no. 2326.)
Appointment of Essex, Captain-General of the Queen's subjects of the Irish
nation and of her forces in Ulster, and commission to, among others, Adam,
Archbishop of Dublin, Thomas, Archbishop of Armagh, Hugh, Bishop of
Meath, John Garvey, Dean of Holy Trinity, to take the muster and array,
to cess and dispose the Irish for defence of the country, to punish the disobedient, and do all things for the good government of the province, to treat
with enemies and rebels, give safe conduct, and conclude terms at discretion,
to raise the inhabitants and punish enemies and rebels with fire and sword,
and do all other things for the Queen's honour and the peace of her subjects.
20 Dec., 1573. (*Fiants*, no. 2349.)
Authority to Walter, Earl of Essex, Captain-General of the forces in Ulster,
to take up for his household and for the garrisons at Knockfergus and elsewhere
in the province, wheat, malt, bere, rye, beans, oats, beeves, bacons, butter,
cheese, wine, sack hops, salt, saltfish, herrings, and iron, leather, wood, coals,
straw, and hay, and all manner of victuals, also requisite artificers and means
of carriage by sea or land, paying ready money at reasonable prices. 1 March,
1574. (*Fiants*, no. 2362.)
Various commissions issued to take the muster and array of the inhabitants
of the several counties. 1573. (*Fiants*, no. 2345.)
Authority to Francis Lanye, surveyor appointed by the Earl of Essex
to victual the soldiers in Ulster, to impress bakers, coopers, masons, carpenters,
millers, tilers and all other artificers, and also post-horses, ships, barques,

the Crown, and the freedom of all markets in Ireland for himself and his tenants. Free trade was granted with all lands in amity with the Queen for seven years. The Queen agreed to furnish 200 horse and 400 foot, the Earl providing a like number ; and each party was obliged to keep up those numbers. Among the few things not granted were gold and silver mines, and the right to coin money. The consideration offered for this enormous grant consisted of the services to be rendered and of property amounting to 800 marks.

Speed and secrecy were essentials for the success of such a huge undertaking ; neither, however, was acquired. Essex had no ready money, and preliminaries for the repayment of a loan of £10,000 from the Queen had to be arranged. Further information about the district had to be obtained, and companies had to be sent thither to satisfy Burghley about the feasibility of the project. Moreover, munitions of war had to be collected and commanders to be selected. Essex made light of all opposition and was cheered by the friendly attitude of Perrott and FitzWilliams who were not, however, in love with the chivalric interloper and courtly amateur. The Queen was all smiles and promises, and advised the Earl " to have consideration of the Irish there, which she thought had become her disobedient subjects rather because they have not been defended from the force of the Scots, than for any other cause." She impressed on him not to seek too hastily the conversion of a people who had been trained in another religion. Essex's answer was to the effect that he " would not willingly imbrue his hands with more blood than the necessity of the cause requireth," and that when once the Irish had been brought

---

hoys, boats, lighters, cables, anchors, ropes, masters, pilots, mariners, carts, garrans, and other necessaries, paying ready money at reasonable prices. 11 July, 1574. (*Fiants*, no. 2431.)

Commission to Walter, Earl of Essex, Captain-General of Ulster, to compound with the Irish of the province for taking their lands from the crown under rent in cattle or money, to appoint captains to make truce and peace, to grant pardons, and do all things expedient for the good government of the province. Such grants and pardons to pass the great seal on authority of his letters. In consideration of his diligence in dealing with O'Donell, Tirrelagh Lenagh, Sir Brian m'Phelym and others. (Privy Signet, 13 July, 1574.) 30 Sept., 1574. (*Fiants*, no. 2462.)

28 *

to due obedience, " they would be easily brought to be of good religion."

Having taken leave of Elizabeth, 19 July, 1573, Essex sailed from Liverpool, 16 August, and after a stormy passage, arrived at Carrickfergus, his men and provisions scattered in various parts. He put on a bold face, and told Tirlogh Luineach that he had come to free the Irish from the tyranny of the Scots. Brian MacFelim and the Irish inhabitants were also impressed by the strict orders issued by the Earl against injuring them or taking their goods without full payment. But it was not long before Essex and Captain Pers of Carrickfergus were caught napping, and although orders had been issued to drive the cattle to the vicinity of the Castle, and trusty Scots put to watch them, MacFelim had withdrawn the 10,000 head of horned hostages. In his rage Essex professed to be glad that MacFelim had thrown off the mask, and that now he had " no occasion to trust the Irish."

MacFelim hastened to join his forces to those of Tirlogh Luineach and to the 500 Scots who had landed at Lough Foyle. Essex's force, collected at Carrickfergus, consisted of 600 foot, 200 horse, 100 labourers, and 200 kerne. After a not very glorious foray against MacFelim, a prey of 400 cows, Essex returned to find Smith, his precursor in the plantation scheme, slain, 200 of his kerne in mutiny, Comber in ashes, and his men unable to hold the place.[1]

In a letter to the Queen, 2 November,[2] Essex attributes his failure to the dislike on the part of his adventurers of the hardships necessary for war in Ireland, and of their dissatisfaction with the pay. They allege that as they joined up, not through commission, but permission, they should not be detained in this service longer than they like to stay. " This," says Essex, " is not hidden from the Irish, who also are fully persuaded that this war is altogether mine, alleging that if it were your Majesty's, it should be executed by the Lord Deputy, being your chief general here ; and therefore thinking that I must be in a short time wearied with the charge, have confederated to stand in arms,

---

[1] *S.P.I., Eliz.*, xlii. 33, 34, 55, 58.
[2] *Ib.*, 64. Bagwell, ii. 258-9. Carew, *Cal.*, no. 305.

which they would never do with your Majesty unless it were in respect of me, whereby I must acknowledge the weakness of myself, and so consequently of any subject that shall attempt any great service, and therein part with his prince either honour or profit. Therefore, my humble petition is, that, albeit the moiety of the charge be mine, according to my covenant with your Majesty, yet some means may be devised that all the officers, soldiers, and dealers in this war may seem to be your Majesty's, and I only the instrument and executor of this service ; whereby all men shall either put on better contentations and new courages, or else I with better warrant may punish the mutiny and the base ignobility of the soldiers' minds."

Others reported that the Irish affirm that they are no rebels, that it is not the Queen's wars, and that they do but defend their own lands and goods. Moreover, the English were unwarlike, whereas the Irish had become skilled in the use of weapons. Essex could do nothing against the enemy, and there were traitors in his own camp. Desmond's escape from Dublin was calculated to put hope of relief from the Pale out of the question, and an estrangement between FitzWilliams and Essex made the hope of relief from the Deputy's scanty forces still more remote.[1]

Just before Essex's departure for Ireland, namely, in the month of May, Antonio de Gueras, the Spanish Commissioner in London, had thought that Essex's expedition might be turned to good purpose. Rowland Turner, calling himself Lord Audley, an English priest from Louvain, was sent to Ulster with letters from de Gueras to Sir Brian MacFelim, informing him that Essex was about to land in Ulster to exterminate the O'Neills. In order to frustrate this plan, Sir Brian was advised to put himself under the direction of Turner, a prudent, worthy and faithful Catholic gentleman, with 500 splendidly armed men awaiting his orders in England. Turner, who had lately been in Spain, Scotland, and the Isle of Man, was well known to the English Government ; and his foolish boasts about hanging all Protestants were not likely to enhance his reputation for

---

[1] *S.P.I., Eliz.*, xliii. 1, 10.

ability or discretion.[1] Sir Brian, though very willing to keep off Essex, had no intention of directly opposing Queen Elizabeth, or of engaging in plots for the extirpation of Protestants. Like Archbishop MacGibbon, he feared that the English Catholics would make a tool of him and throw him away when their turn had been served. He received Turner very coldly, who bitterly complained that he was not believed, though an exile for God's sake and for that of the Irish. Notwithstanding all Turner's denunciations of English force and fraud, the people refused to listen to him, and he at last shook the dust from his feet.

" THINGS NEVER SO BAD IN THE COUNTRY."

The state of unrest was no less apparent in the other two provinces than in Munster and Ulster, and the general course of the government was neither smooth nor glorious. There was little force in the country, and whatever there was, was unwilling to serve against the chiefs. Leix and Offaly were almost as bad as they had ever been, all the castles of Offaly being in O'Molloy's hands, and the English planters being burnt out of their homes.[2] The miserable town of Athenry had been plundered and left utterly desolate by Clanricard's sons. Ormond's country in his absence was scarcely better than the rebel district. The general opinion was that the Queen meant to allow the Irish themselves to settle their own affairs.[3] Even the efforts of the Government were futile. On a motion of the Council to send one of their number to go to Cork to call the Lords there together, not one was found willing to go.[4] The promoters of the Protestant religion, having no security or efficient aid in English forces, were unable to have their way outside the walled towns. A letter from Archbishop Loftus[5] to Sydney, 11 May, from his Tallaght residence, a few miles outside the city of Dublin, shows how matters stood even adjacent to the city's walls. " Things," he says, " have never been so bad in the country since the Irish

---

[1] Bagwell, ii. 257. *S.P.I.*, *Eliz.*, xl. 80 ; xlii. 38.
[2] *Ib.*, xlii. 45, i.   [3] *Ib.*, xli. 80.
[4] *Ib.*, xlii. 86.   [5] *Ib.*, xl. 36, P.R.O., London.

Conquest. Murders, burnings, and robberies never more common than now in the English pale." His nephew and others of his men have been slain at the gates of Tallaght. He therefore asks for help this summer to suppress the rage of the Irish, who were never prouder and more insolent than they are at present, before next winter. " It were better for us to be beggared in England than to see the mischiefs that are like to happen in Ireland."

FitzWilliams could do very little. His forces were in-adequate to control Desmond, to aid Essex, or to punish the rebellious sons of Clanricard. Old Cormac O'Connor was again at the head of a Scotch and Irish band that hovered between Leinster and Connacht, and with Clanricard unable to restrain his sons, Connacht was left to its own devices. Fitton, the late President of Connacht, thought his former subjects might, perhaps, by good management be persuaded to stay quiet as long as they liked, " which kind of quiet is no new thing in the politics of Ireland." Like everyone else, he attributed all to the Queen's ill-judged parsimony, " sparing too sparely I fear will cost more spending." [1]

Perrott,[2] on the other hand, stated that the custom of Thanist, namely, that the eldest of the house shall inherit, is the chiefest cause of the disorders of the Irish.[3] At this critical time death deprived the Irish Government of Lord Chancellor Weston's services (20 May, 1573). He was sincerely religious, not without a tinge of Puritanism, and was filled with anxiety at the condition of the Protestant Church in Ireland. Non-resident clergy of that persuasion (with long leaves of absence for study in English Universities), and desecrated churches were the rule. He had felt accordingly that he was a bad example by holding the temporalities of two deaneries, St. Patrick's and Wells, and had offered to resign them. His daughter was married

---

[1] *S.P.I., Eliz.*, xli. 70.

[2] Commission to Sir John Perrott, president of Munster, to sell a great Spanish ship and its lading of rich merchandise, valued at £15,000 sterling which had arrived in Youghill. Power is given to treat similarly any vessel belonging to any Spanyard, Portyngall, or Flemynge, arriving in his province. 3 Feb., 1573. (*Fiants*, no. 2192.)

[3] *S.P.I., Eliz.*, xlii. 57.

first to Brady, Bishop of Meath, and afterwards to Fenton. Loftus was appointed Keeper of the Great Seal, 25 May.[1]

PAPAL AND ROYAL BISHOPS CONTEST KILLALOE.

Morgan O'Brien Arra, who had been appointed by Elizabeth to the See of Killaloe,[2] requested (December, 1572) the Lord Deputy to send him letters to maintain him " in his bishopric against one Malachias O'Mollowney that claims the same by the Pope's Bull." O'Mollony had been appointed by the Pope, 10 January, 1571. Morgan was not yet a consecrated bishop ; in fact there is no record that he was ever consecrated.[3] In January, 1573, he wrote to Burghley [4] that he had not these three years which he continued in Oxford and Cambridge " received any profits [of the bishopric] on account of the rudeness of the people and the disorder there, that for the most part they covet to be fed with Pharaoh's fleshpots then to taste the heavenly Manna, I mean, the comfortable bread of the Gospel." He asks that Her Majesty direct letters to the Government there that he may have some relief towards his going there. He wrote a similar letter to the Privy Council.[5]

The people of Killaloe doubtless thought it presumption on the part of this youth, who was spending his years in the halls of English Universities, to expect them to pay for his education and maintenance. Though he was nominated by Elizabeth as bishop to occupy the See when he should come to the required age, and though his father was given charge of a district, as he had verted to Elizabeth's religion, yet the people preferred to pay for the support of O'Mollony, the bishop of their own faith.

FitzWilliams had sympathy for the youthful bishop-elect, as he had but the custody of the bishopric, and (3 May, 1573) asked the Queen for the warrant for his consecration as was expected.[6] The Queen, in reply, told FitzWilliams that

---

[1] *Fiants*, no. 2281. [2] *C.S.P.I.*, *Eliz.*, xxxviii. 66.

[3] Ware says : " He received the profits of this See six years before his consecration ; but being at last consecrated he sat about thirty-six years after." (*Bishops*, 595.) Ware gives no particulars as to date of consecration and as to the consecrators.

[4] *S.P.I.*, *Eliz.*, xxxix. 18, P.R.O., London.

[5] *Ib.*, 19. [6] *Ib.*, xl. 25.

Morgan had a mind to return to Killaloe, and, as he had
" no fruits on account of trouble in those parts," she commanded FitzWilliams to aid him in obtaining possession of
his bishopric.[1]

Morgan returned to Killaloe, but evidently was not
very comfortable in it. On 22 December [2] he thought it his
duty to report the state of the district to the Lord Deputy,
and the " conspiracies against her Majesty " :—

She deserved loyalty from me because she had sent me to the
Universities of Cambridge and Oxford to be trained in letters,
and had bestowed a good living on me ; but I have little profit
of it because of the wars in those quarters, yet will I be faithful
to her for life. The Earl of Desmond is to assemble next Thursday
in my father's country to meet the Earl of Clanricard and Thady
McMurough O'Brien, and the adherents of Thomond and Clanricard,
of both sides of the Shannon at Thady O'Brien's town called the
Bridge [O'Brien's Bridge] to send some of their messengers with
their letters signed and sealed to Philip [of Spain] desiring him
to send them aid. My father offered him [Earl of Desmond]
£20 if he should not make that assembly by his own country,
and he refused it. We know not what is best for us to be done,
for if we do not meet him and suffer him to come into our houses
he shall spoil all the country. He is [has] above a thousand
rascals, I think he is not past five hundred men well armed.
Therefore, I thought good to desire your Honour to write your
best advice unto my father and unto me what is the best way to
do, or whether it were any harm unto us to meet the said Earl
to know his mind both unto your Honour's and also unto ourselves.
Also, my lord, it is hard to trust any man in those quarters for
they do but rob, steal, burn, and kill every night, happy is he
that is out of their fight. It were better to be in prison in England
than to be here amongst them.

Loftus and Brady had uttered similar lamentations, but
their services could not be dispensed with on account of
the difficulty of getting others to take their places. Ireland
was by no means a pleasant place for Elizabeth's bishops,
presidents, and deputies, and they were all anxious to get
out of it. Meanwhile, another vacancy had occurred.

[1] *S.P.I., Eliz.*, xl. 25, i., P.R.O., London.   [2] *Ib.*, xliv. 3, i.

The Lord Deputy and Council (10 May, 1573) inform the Queen of the vacancy in the See of Kilfenora through the death of the Marian bishop, John O'Niallan (1572),[1] and that they had granted custody of it to Murtough O'Brien, son to Sir Donnell O'Brien (brother to the Earl of Thomond), who was certified by the Archbishop of Dublin and the Bishop of Meath as the worthiest man for the post.[2] The House of Thomond,[3] with at least two of its branches had accepted the Supremacy as a condition of the re-grant to them of their lands and titles from the Queen.

Essex's Disastrous Expedition.

Whilst Munster was at rest because of Elizabeth's inactivity, the situation of Essex in the North aroused some feeling of sympathy in her heart. The recitals of Essex's two trusty messengers opened her mind as to the actual state of Ulster and its prospects for the future. Accordingly, positive orders were sent to FitzWilliams to treat him with more consideration, to appoint him governor of Ulster, with the same power as a President, and to give out that the expedition was not intended against the natives, but against the usurping Scots. In practice, of course, no such distinction was or could be observed.

The English Government was convinced that nothing could be done in Ulster without great expenses, but it saw clearly that the Queen was most unwilling to incur them. The easiest way out of the difficulty would be to make Essex Lord Deputy. He was quite willing to accept the post as it would give him the means of reducing Ulster.[4] But Elizabeth positively refused to make anyone Deputy who had a landed estate in Ireland, so Essex became merely

---

[1] The *Four Masters* state : " The Bishop of Kilfenora (John Oge, the son of John, son of Auliffe O'Niallain), teacher of the word of God, died, and was interred in Kilfenora itself."

[2] *S.P.I., Eliz.*, xl. 30, P.R.O., London.

[3] Commission to William, Archbishop of Tuam, Richard, Earl of Clanricard, Conor, Earl of Thomond, Roland, Bishop of Clonfert, and others to be justices and commissioners in the counties Roscommon, Galway, and Clare, to take recognisances and do all other things contained in the instructions of the lord deputy of 6 June. 18 June, 1573. (*Fiants*, no. 2296.)

[4] *S.P.I., Eliz.*, xliv. 51.

Governor of Ulster, and in less than a month longed to be rid of the office.

An expedition against Tirlogh Luineach fell through on account of the refusal of the gentlemen of the Pale, and of the Louth people to join in it, and also on account of the scarcity of provisions. The timely arrival of fifty barrels of herrings prevented universal desertion on the part of the garrisons of Dundalk and Newry. The soldiers refused to continue in the service unless they were better victualled. Essex did his best to assure them of better victualling, but was in despair as to where the money was to come from. His expenses were over £10 a day, and he had to keep 160 men and 80 horses, and to draw all victuals and forage from England. He made various proposals to Burghley, Sussex, and Leicester, the chief being that Elizabeth should bear the charge of 100 horse and 600 foot. He would then make a last effort with the adventurers, and engaged to make the North profitable to the Crown, either by rents from the natives or by English settlers.

Although Elizabeth had made up her mind to recall Essex as soon as he had " lapped up " all matters with the O'Neills, this letter touched her heart. She resolved to give another chance to the adventurous cavalier whose loyalty and constancy were well known to her. She agreed for a time to maintain the required force, and promised to grant him Island Magee.[1] But royal words, however sweet, could not conquer Ulster. Sweet words, indeed, passed between them, " to which our eyes and the fire only have been made privy." Heroic as was Essex's character in many ways, he had not the gifts necessary for a great general. He could not infuse courage into a starving garrison or endurance into soldiers worn out with disease. The supplies only lasted half the time and fed less than half the number for whom they were intended. The powder was one-quarter coal dust, and not worth firing. The " belly-fed ministers " who accompanied him northwards liked the fare and the hardships no better than the soldiers, and neglected the services of religion.[2] The reinforcements asked for and sent

---

[1] *S.P.I., Eliz.*, xlv. 6, 8.   [2] Essex to Elizabeth, etc., 13 May, 1574.

from various parts of England were only fit for field labour. Veterans avoided the service as much as possible as the name of the pest-ridden Carrickfergus was well known to them. The wretched lads died like flies, and only 300 out of 600 reached the Pale after Essex had been convinced of his foolhardiness.

A gracious letter from the Queen caused hope to spring once more in the Earl's breast, and he mustered a force against MacFelim. The northern chief, regarding Essex as the Queen's governor, and no longer as a private adventurer, agreed to be loyal to Her Majesty, yielded up Clandeboy, and offered to pay a rent of 1500 kine for the first year and to increase it afterwards.[1]

ELIZABETH'S OVERTURES TO DESMOND.

The escape of Desmond had made a great impression on the Irish chiefs, and made a great difference in the state of Ireland, especially as at the time English power scarcely existed. Desmond had nearly 1000 men at his command, and was in touch with the O'Neills in the North, the Burkes in the West, the O'Mores, O'Connors, and O'Byrnes in Leinster, who could draw the whole country at a word, if they had a formula on which they could agree. He desired a conference at Christmas with Clanricard and Thomond at O'Brien's Bridge, and Clanricard informed the Government that he would, if possible, persuade him to conformity. Edmund Butler likewise advised him to make his peace with the Lord Deputy,[2] but Desmond's answer consisted in showing him his patched hose and shoes which he had been forced to wear continually in England. Desmond refused to reduce his followers as long as Captain Bourchier, one of Elizabeth's most capable officials, remained in garrison at Kilmallock.[3] Cork refused to support the soldiers, and the townsmen of Kilmallock connived with Desmond, who took Bourchier prisoner. On reaching Castlemaine, Bourchier found that the fortress had been taken by the Geraldines on Christmas Eve through the strategy of the porter who

---

[1] *S.P.I., Eliz.*, xlv. 66; xlvi. 12   [2] *Ib.*, xliii. 20, viii.
[3] *Ib.*, xliv. 3, i.

handed out to the besiegers the impression in dough of the keys.[1] Castlemartyr was likewise taken over by the Seneschal of Imokelly. To make matters worse, rumours of rebellion and foreign invasion filled the air. Thus, Desmond had broken every promise that he had made while a prisoner in the Tower of London. Instead of maintaining the Protestant religion he had restored the friars to the monasteries and had conferred with other chiefs for the purpose of sending emissaries to Philip of Spain for help to drive Elizabeth's forces and religion out of the country.

The importance of Desmond's escape was not lost on the English Government, and, on account of their slender resources, it was resolved to send a semi-official messenger, Kildare's loyal brother Edward, to remonstrate with him in a friendly way. Desmond refused to go to Dublin for the conference and suggested a meeting at Clonmel on 31 January.[2] Every one knew of Edward FitzGerald's mission, but his unostentatious method of travelling gave an excuse for not treating him with much respect and for not giving him livery for his horses. Seven articles founded upon the instructions of the Irish Government were propounded to Desmond, but while he was lavish enough in his general profession of loyalty he was less compliant when it came to material guarantees. He was ready to give up his castles to his cousin, Edward FitzGerald, who had no warrant to take them and no means to hold them, but he refused to yield them to Captain Bourchier.[3]

Whilst Desmond's followers advised him to accept a general pardon for their own safeguard, as a new English invasion was threatened, Elizabeth blamed FitzWilliams for his slackness, and failed to induce Perrott to return to the country. Elizabeth had to be content with Desmond's recognition of her sovereignty in some fashion and with his yielding up of Castlemaine and Castlemartyr.

NEWS FROM SPAIN; EXAMINATION OF MERCHANTS.

Desmond and Fitzmaurice were made aware of all that was going on in Spain through their emissaries who found

[1] S.P.I., Eliz., xliv., 4, i. 8.   [2] Ib., 20, i., ii., iv., v.   [3] Ib., 37, 42.

means of bringing in the news. But the Government were also on the alert in the southern ports tapping the sources of information in the merchants who came from the Spanish and Portuguese ports with their merchandise. Although many of these pieces of information are fantastic, betraying a feeling of panic, and perhaps intended also to paint a lurid picture of Spanish atrocities against Elizabeth, they furnish some items of importance.

On the 25 April the Lord Deputy informed the Privy Council [1] of the results of the examination of certain merchants who had just arrived from Spain on the south coast. The Mayor of Waterford tells that an English dweller at the Port of St. Maria averred that there was more cause to fear Stucley than the King of Spain, and that Stucley was preparing shipping to come to Ireland, whilst the Spanish navy was bound for elsewhere. Roger Winston and Thomas Colman reported similarly. [2]

Robert Wise, a merchant of Waterford, states [3] that on 6 July in Bilbao, Spanish soldiers told him that there were there 150 new galleys and ships under Pedro Mohendes, an Asturian, and as many more ships expected from Spain and Portugal. He saw a barque of twenty tons laden with pickaxes, swords, and crowbars, and that the report was they were bound for Ireland. " Certain Englishmen, lodgers there, charged him to despatch homewards to tell that that navy was for Ireland, and that a charge was given by P. Mohendes that no ships not of the fleet be suffered to come out of the river." He heard that " Morish Rioghe, the pretended Archbishop of Cashel, was at St. Anderose ready to go with the navy, and that Stucley was a great procurer of the setting forth of the ships." It was rumoured that three Portuguese, who were skilful on the coast of Ireland, were chief pilots for this navy. Pedro Mohendes was determined to go towards the Court of Spain on 13 July, and that on his return the ships were to set out on their journey. There were fifteen great hulks laden with salt, wheat, and other necessaries for the navy. The Captain,

---

[1] *S.P.I.*, *Eliz.*, xlv. 82, P.R.O., London.
[2] *C.S.P.I.*, *Eliz.*, xlvi. 41, xiii.
[3] *S.P.I.*, *Eliz.*, xlvii. 18, P.R.O., London.

who was lately at Dungarvan, went to Bilbao with them, and rode to the Court of Spain.

The late Bishop of Meath (Walsh) was at Bilbao, and before he (Robert Wise) left, was at the Court of Spain. Don Juan of Austria has gone to Flanders by land with 50,000 men. William Gall, Christopher Tieue (?), and John Hannigan of Waterford, mariners, agree to every point with Wise. Gall says that one priest born near Dublin, Sir Simon Connell, had made him good cheer, treated him courteously, and offered him wages to be pilot of one of the ships in which he was to go to Ireland.

Henry Ackworth [1] tells how some of the citizens of Waterford are much beholden to Stucley, and that there are conspiracies amongst them, partly because they are papists and partly through hatred of the English Government. " It is hard," he says, " to trust any papists, because there is a new doctrine taught among them that there is no duty or promise to be kept to princes or others." This was evidently an echo of the excommunication of Elizabeth and of the prohibition to yield her obedience. But even before that event the Irish chiefs considered obedience to the Queen a mere temporary expedient and their promise of momentary account.

Another of these witnesses examined was Meiler Husye. He states :—[2]

(1) He remembereth well that Thomas Stucley came to the Earl of Kildare's house at Kilka, and take his leave of my Lord, and had talk with the said Earl about an hour or two a little before his departure out of Ireland, and whether he tarried at Kilka all night or no, he doth not well remember.

(2) . . . he saith that he, this examinate, was present when Thomas Stucley did talk with my Lord in his great chamber, and my Lord brought Thomas Stucley to his house, but what the talk was he knoweth not, saving that it was thought then that Thomas Stucley made his voyage for England, and he heard the Earl require Thomas Stucley to do his hearty commendations to the Earl of Pembroke when he take his farewell.

(3) . . . he saith that the said Earl did send a horse to Thomas Stucley being a sorel curtal as he remembereth, but whether

<hr>

[1] *S.P.I.*, *Eliz.*, xlvii. 22, P.R.O., London   [2] *Ib.*, liv. 3.

Phelim O'Connor was sent with the horse or no, he cannot tell, and whether my Lord did give unto Thomas Stucley any other horse or no, he knoweth not, but he saith that one Kerlie being a horse-boy but not belonging to my Lord, did go with Thomas Stucley at the self same time, but what horse he had he knoweth not, and whether the sorel curtal was given or sold he cannot tell.

(4) . . . that when Phelim returned from Stucley he complained grievously of Stucley's hard dealing with him, saying that he did cast him off as a salvagios, and would not relieve him, whereupon the Earl said that he looked for no better at Stucley's hands towards any of his, and, therefore, willed Phelim to be of good cheer. . . . But for any message or letters sent by Stucley, he doth not remember any at all.

(6) [He does not know of any message sent by the Earl to James Fitzmaurice at any time. Neither does he know that] ever he did send Teige Ui Hickey in any message to James Fitzmaurice.

(7) . . . and touching Matthew Seyne, now Bishop of Cork, he saith that he heard he was in prison at Divelyn [Dublin] a long time for bringing over of letters, but whether the same came from Rome or from any King, he knoweth not.

(8) . . . that both Laurence and John Walshe went out of Develyn with Cruaghe [Creagh] but which of them was the cause of his escape, this examinate knoweth not, but for himself he was never privy to that escape, and thinketh verily that either one of them, or they both, did seek his enlargement, to have a reward for him in Spain, being counted a very holy man throughout Ireland, and he utterly denieth that either he willed Laurence Walshe to go with Creagh or John Walshe to stay.

(9) . . . touching the Bull or dispensation for my Lord's daughter with the Baron of Delvin, he never heard speech of any such thing before this time, much less is he privy to it.

ARCHBISHOP OF TUAM AND BISHOP OF CLONFERT ATTEND SESSIONS AT ATHLONE.

If anything shows clearly the defection of the Bishop of Clonfert, Roland Burgh, from the Catholic Church it is his joint letter (5 March) with William Lealy, Protestant Archbishop of Tuam, to Treasurer Fitton. He and the late Archbishop of Tuam, Christopher Bodkin, had accepted the Supremacy, and held their Sees and received their temporalities by means of the strong arm of Clanricard who, although supporting Elizabeth's bishops cannot be taken as having really accepted the Supremacy.[1] His defence of those bishops was part of his policy to retain his possessions. He, too, like Desmond, was playing a game, and he had no desire to be hunted from post to post as Shane O'Neill was. He simply wished to be left in peace. Lealy had been appointed to Tuam on the death of Bodkin, and was leagued with Roland Burgh. Their episcopal presence was required at the sessions at Athlone not only to punish malefactors but to strike terror into others. But before undertaking the journey they required their bodies and goods to be safeguarded. This they tell in their very interesting letter to Fitton :—[2]

To the Illustrious Lord Edward [Fitton] Treasurer of this the Kingdom of Ireland, health and the consolation of the Holy Spirit. We have received your letters with all good will, by which we are summoned to Athlone for the sixth day of this month of March. But as lately it is so dangerous to journey from one place to another on account of the coming and staying of the Scots in Clanricard and especially in our dioceses, since they know that we favour your government ; and not content with the Scots now present, other Scots to the number of 700 are to come shortly with John son of the Earl [of Clanricard], as we have heard from many, and likewise between the Suck [River] and the Shannon, there the highway is, such are the perils and dangers, that some men from Kylkellay, who waylay all travellers, as we have heard, are guides of the Scots to those parts ; so that we cannot go to the stated place, Athlone, except by Clonfert and that not even without a safe conduct. And so we earnestly pray your Lordship, as we seek no other place of refuge under God, that you do not defer sending Edmond Offalluyn [O'Fallon] [3] and other faithful subjects

---

[1] Kelly, *Dissertations*, 359. Fahey, *Kilmacduagh*, 207.

[2] *S.P.I.*, *Eliz.*, xlv. 15, i., P.R.O., London.

[3] Lease, under commission, 26 September, 1567, to Edmund O'Fallone, Athlone, merchant, of a messuage in Athlone with gardens, two houses on the south side of the castle there occupied by the present lessee, an eel weir on the river Shynnen in Connacht, of the possessions of the late monastery of S. Peter of Athlone, also the site of the cell of friars of the order of S. Francis of Bealaneny in Omany in Connacht with appurtenances. To hold for 21 years, rent 17s. 11d. Lessee within two years to erect a substantial corn mill of stone, roofed with tile or slate, upon the weir of the river Shynnen at such place as the lord president shall think fit so that it be not prejudicial to the river of Athlone and the new bridge there, maintaining one archer. The upper part

with a safe boat to the harbour of Clonfert on Tuesday next, and, God our Guide, we shall be at Clonfert unless your Lordship desire otherwise, but indeed not without danger to our possessions which we shall leave behind, as happened to us before, as you know. We have nothing else this time than that the Good God may preserve you and bring you to higher things, and so farewell.

From Kilconnel : 5th March,

WILLIAM TUAM.

ROLAND CLONFERT.

On the same day they further write :—

We exhort you in the Lord that, as soon as you have read our letters, you write to us by the bearer of these presents, whether immediately or later we are to repair to the stated place of Clonfert, as the occasion requires, and what other things may be necessary for the safety of our journeys, since the danger to our lives is very great, as we shall relate more fully when we meet.[1]

Although President Fitton wrote (20 March) to the Earls of Clanricard and Thomond, as well as to the Archbishop of Tuam and the Bishop of Clonfert, it was only the bishops who came to the sessions at Athlone.[2]

DEAN OF ARMAGH PROFESSES LOYALTY TO ELIZABETH.

Another dignitary who accepted the Supremacy was Terence Daniel, Dean of Armagh. As an intermediary between Shane O'Neill and Elizabeth and her Deputy he professed much loyalty towards Her Majesty but had not always been true to his word. No doubt he was circum-scribed in his actions by his chief, but the latter having been put out of the way, Daniel found his position precarious, and concluded an arrangement with the Deputy. It seems

of the stone house of the said cell reserved to the use of the lord deputy or president when required. The president of Connacht to have grist ground toll free, and the use of the weirs two nights every month. 12 December, 1570. (*Fiants*, no. 1650.)

O'Fallone also received a grant of a castle in Athlone called the east gate, near the churchyard of the parish church, and a parcel of land adjoining the said castle. 5 August, 1578. (*Fiants*, no. 349.)

Besides the foregoing he received a lease of a mill upon the river of Clonekill, Co. Roscommon, parcel of the possessions of the abbey of Athlone, and two water mills upon the bridge of Athlone.

[1] See *Appendix VI, F.* [2] *S.P.I., Eliz.*, xlv., P.R.O., London.

clear that he was no longer Dean in the eyes of the Catholic people of Armagh, and as he had no other support he made the following appeal, 7 April, 1574, to Burghley :—[1]

I am many days named dean of Armagh which is but a small living, is the country very inhabled. And since the beginning of the rebellion of Shane O'Neill I had no profit by it, for then I left my living and all the goods that I had, and came under the tuition of the governor according to my duty, and so I am dean in name but not in reality, but always I am a painful travailler for the quietness of the places, that I was appointed [2] Commissioner for the which travail and pains I had certain allowances granted to me by concordat by the governors and Council here for the which I am not yet paid. Therefore, I am so bold as to crave your Honour's friendship for the payment of the said concordat of the which I have sent one to your Honour by Mr. Gerete [Geraghty] and shall humbly pray your Honour not only to show your friendship for that concordat but for the rest that I have which are allowed by the auditor Janison, and do refer to the testimony of all governors, councillors, captains, and all other gentlemen of this realm what pains and travails I take in Her Majesty's affairs for the quietness of the north part of Ireland wherein I do intend to continue during my health, and with myself to be able to do more for Her Majesty, but where I can do it, it shall be at the commandment of these that are governors under Her Highness. And so humbly I take my leave from Drogheda, 7 April, 1574.

DEANERY OF ST. PATRICK'S ; CHAPTER CLAIM RIGHT TO ELECT.

The old, unprofitable, time-serving prebendaries of St. Patrick's did not take kindly to the idea that the revenues of the deanery should be diverted from their spiritual object and bestowed upon the Lord Chancellor, a layman, to supply for the Queen's parsimony. They appealed rightly to their time-honoured charter, and to strengthen their case painted a picture of the souls that were neglected because of the lack of a clerical dean. They also referred to those clerics who usually supplied for the Dean in his capitular and

[1] *S.P.I.*, *Eliz.*, xlv. 59.
[2] Ecclesiastical Commissioner to correct heresies, etc. *P.C.R.I.*, *Eliz.*, i. p. 479, no. 59.

parochial duties and who were thus deprived of their stipends. As the deanery was now vacant nearly a year they gave notice that they intended to proceed with the election. Their letter reads thus :—[1]

20th day of March, 1573, in the Chapter House. Within the day and place upon long deliberation had, the President and Chantor of the said Church, being by the space of ten months destitute of a dean, for lack of government is grown into main and great disorders for lack of a dean, contrary to the statute and foundation of the said Church.

Secondly, for that the manse of the said dean together with the living of the said deanery is foully spoiled and wasted to the great hindrance of the successor of the said deanery to the value of £10 current money of England.

Thirdly, since that the ministers of the said Church depending upon the said dignity are unpaid of their wages and stipends to them belonging and know not how to come to the same.

Fourthly, because the said chapter hath by the space of ten months aforesaid expected her majesty's commendation of some worthy to the same dignity and as yet have received nothing to the same effect.

Fifthly, for that a great lordship belonging unto the said deanery, called Kilberry [Co. Kildare] to the value of an yearly rent of £40, is entered upon and seized by the Earl of Kildare and claimed by him as his own inheritance, and thereby not unlike to grow to the great hindrance and decay of the said dignity.

Sixthly, and especially, for that divers parishes belong to the said deanery wherein are many thousands of souls who do daily perish for want of government and instructions of the dean aforesaid their pastor ; [2] [President and Chantor] have decreed according to the foundation and statutes of the said church to proceed to the election of a dean between ninth day of this instant March. And, therefore, have decreed the citation to be set upon the chapter door against the day aforesaid.

Having elected a Dean, of Irish birth, they made known their choice and sent him to Archbishop Loftus for confirmation. On this point Loftus wrote to Burghley, 23 April,[3] as follows :—

---

[1] *S.P.I., Eliz.,* xlv. 81, i., P.R.O., London.
[2] The Dean's extensive possessions lay in Clondalkin, Eskar, Rathcoole, Tallaght, and Kilberry, with a net value of £240 (about £2880 *1914 value*).
[3] *S.P.I., Eliz.,* xlv. 81, i.

The Deanery of St. Patrick's void for almost 12 months,[1] and the church meanwhile governed by a president, the Chantor of the Church [2] (a man of this country birth, well spent in years and corrupt in religion) by the advice of the said president and others of the chapter, thought therefore being stayed for Your Majesty's nomination (as they said) of some worthy man for that room, " Advised by the learned that the right of election was usely and effectually in themselves by the grant of their majesties [Philip and Mary] they have proceeded to an election of a dean and elected one of their own company a man of this country birth, and have presented him to me according to the law for confirmation, giving all the causes that moved them to the election." Loftus stayed to confirm the Dean-Elect, and asked counsel. He thinks some one of his own country [England] should be made dean.[3]

Loftus Confesses Failure to Reform a Stubborn People.

Loftus did not find Dublin an easy and comfortable place to live in. He had been ill-treated by the Irish from the mountains in his palace at Tallaght, he was slighted by the prebendaries in St. Patrick's whom he could not control, and encroachments on his liberties had been attempted by the municipal authorities. Besides all this, he found he was making no headway in his attempt, whatever it was, to reform the inhabitants of his much restricted diocese. Like

[1] Weston, Lord Chancellor and Dean, died 20 May, and was buried in St. Patrick's, under the communion table, in the same vault where his granddaughter, the Countess of Cork, was afterwards entombed. Weston's daughter, Alice, married, first Hugh Brady, Bishop of Meath ; she had, for her second husband, Sir Geoffrey Fenton, Secretary of State, whose only daughter, Catherine, was married to Richard, first Earl of Cork. (*Fasti Oxon*, 151.)

[2] Thomas Crief was nominated to this dignity upon the restoration of the cathedral in 1555. In the year 1569 he was cited by the chapter to purge himself from the scandal of adultery, of which he was accused by the dean, and was required to exhibit six compurgators ; those he produced, but four were excepted against, being themselves charged with crimes ; he required a longer day. The issue of this business cannot be traced further, on account of the imperfect state of the documents which remain. In the year 1579 he was aged 88 years. (Mason, lxxi.) At the time of the complaint in the text he was therefore 83 years of age.

[3] The deanery remained void until 28 Jan., 1577, when William Gerrard, the new Lord Chancellor, was appointed. He presented the Queen's letter, 23 April, 1577. The deanery was granted to him " *in commendam* towards his better entertainment, and to enable him, the more, to do us service in that office, as we did to Mr. Doctor Weston."

his predecessor Curwen, he found an excuse to be rid of all this annoyance in a plea of ill-health ; the Irish air did not suit English lungs, so he petitioned Sydney to be a good friend to him and use his influence with Burghley to have him translated to an English See.

Sydney writing to Burghley,[1] states that Loftus through " want of health and other infirmities of his body [is] not so fit for Her Majesty's service here which requireth a strong and more able body " the air of this country " agreeth not the best for the state of his body." " He is fit," however, for " contentment " elsewhere as he " is a man both well learned, and of good conversation of life, a godly preacher, and plentiful in hospitality." " Her Majesty hath been moved already for his translation (as I take it) by my Lord Chamberlain, whose chaplain he was, and who preferred him to this living."

Loftus himself now appeals to Burghley [2] for his translation, and, in giving his reasons, adds his voice to the chorus of Elizabethan bishops on the failure of the " reform." This, it is to be noted, occurred nearly sixteen years after Elizabeth's accession.

Loftus's reasons for desiring translation are : " love of his natural country " (England) from which he had been " now 16 years a pilgrim " ; weakness of his body " worn with long sickness " ; also he hopes to make his old age, which he feels fast approaching,[3] " more profitable to the Church of God amongst the well affected people of England than the rest of my time hath been here amongst this stubborn and obstinate generation, where men of far greater perfection than myself have long and vainly employed both doctrine and good examples." He confesses that his " disability and insufficiency " deserve to be hidden in the obscurity of Ireland than exposed to the light of learning in England. If he obtain the proposed translation to England, " he shall think those many and troublesome days spent in Ireland, both in my function and in matters of the state, rightly considered."

---

[1] *S.P.I.*, *Eliz.*, lv. 59, P.R.O., London.   [2] *Ib.*, lvi. 27.
[3] Loftus was little beyond forty years of age at this time. He lived for thirty-one years afterwards.

ARCHBISHOP CREAGH'S PRISON LIFE ; UNSWERVING LOYALTY TO ELIZABETH.

Archbishop Creagh had been a prisoner since 1565 with the exception of a short interval after his escape. He returned to his diocese in the summer of 1566 in which year occurred most of the incidents narrated in the following letter. Arrested in Connacht (30 April, 1567), he was again thrown into prison.[1] In the year 1574 he wrote this letter evidently as a defence against calumniators. It is clear that his continued incarceration was the subject of much comment even in Dublin, and tended to embitter the Catholics against the Government through the profound reverence they had for him. Loftus seems to have experienced the ill effects of this revolt of the people against the treatment of Creagh, for he induced the Lord Deputy to write to the Privy Council to have Creagh sent out of England, presumably abroad, where he would be incapable of any harm. The Deputy quoting the words of Loftus stated : " One Creagh, a Romish thing that wonderfully enfaitheth this people and hindereth the Archbishop of Dublin's godly endeavours to promote religion, which hath enforced him [Loftus] to be importunate unto me for the sending of him away." [2]

It is impossible to understand the savage treatment of Creagh except on the ground that Elizabeth would allow no Catholic bishop in any diocese in Ireland to which she had appointed one of her own even though her own bishop could obtain no footing in his diocese, a circumstance that made matters worse for the Catholic Bishop. Added to this was the fact that Creagh was held in special reverence by the people. Although, as she well knew, Creagh had endangered his own safety by withstanding Shane O'Neill's confiscations of Church property and hatred of her and had endeavoured to bring him to a sense of loyalty to her as the legitimate Queen of Ireland, his unpardonable sin was that he had been appointed to an Irish See by the Pope.

---

[1] In July he was in prison in Dublin ; in October he escaped, was re-arrested and sent, 17 October, to London. On 6 November he was lodged in the Tower. He was alive on 30 November, 1586, when he was ordered to be further detained. His death was probably about 14 December, 1586.

[2] *S.P.I.*, *Eliz.*, xlix. 65, P.R.O., London.

Nothing else mattered; she would brook no opposition in that department, and Creagh's case would be an example for others. Worn out by his treatment he wrote the following pathetic letter to the Lords of the Council, explaining his dealings with Shane, the sufferings of his prison life, and his unswerving loyalty to the Crown in which he had been brought up since childhood :—

Right Honourable Lords.

Whereas I have been sundry times charged with many lies as well against my bounden duty to my natural prince [Elizabeth] and country, as also contrary to that I was sworn to in my youth (according the custom of Limerick) [1] to behave myself as my said duty requireth ; I trust your Honours shall well accept to be here truly informed concerning such reports, not only for that all honesty doth require me so to do (though hitherto I have hold my peace therein chiefly for avoiding suspicion of catching vain praise and other the like things), but that also no mean [ordinary] man would gladly be or remain misinformed herein than discharging once my conscience in telling, as aforesaid, the truth, my long silence shall be no further occasion that any others should from henceforth through such tales offend God.

But where as commonly chances that each one esteems his own doings (*nam suum cuique pulchrum*) better or less ill than they be, I humbly crave your Honourable Lords' patience both in hearing and forbearing with my rude writing (which yet shall be as brief and plain as possibly I can) so that your own wisdoms, and not any of my corrupt favour towards myself, may esteem thereof as your Lordships will think best, for though my great sins otherwise committed against God's exceeding Majesty have deserved often, also eternal punishments, yet touching my behaviour concerning my prince and country, with all reverence I can, I take God to witness (esteeming those words an oath) that to my remembrance I will here write nothing but the truth (though the self things for the most part be manifest other by reason or else by experience and witness) ; and if the contrary will be at any time truly known, I am fully content to be, without further ado, therein dealt withal as the Queen's Majesty and your right honourable Lordships will have it.

First then, your Honours may know that for no presumption of myself against her Majesty's proceedings I was made bishop. For before her reign I refused to be made bishop of the city

---

[1] I.e. Limerick was a loyal city.

[Limerick] I was born in, and also archbishop of that province, viz., of Cashel, but at last being strictly commanded I did, for discharge of my conscience, obey, being afore sworn in Louvain to such obedience ; the inability of Irish Scholars being causer of such commandment, rather then any ability that in truth I do or did see in myself for las [? this] Office. Being then in Rome, offered also then the Archbishopric aforesaid of Cashel (where my kinsfolk and native country is) I yielded rather to be sent to Ulster (a barbarous and bare country and I having never a living body there of mine acquaintance) wherein cannot or at the least could not then, any appointed bishop by the Queen's Majesty remain or yet out of it receive any profit, Shane O'Neill spending with his rebellion all that did belong there to the archbishop, yea almost to all other prelates and curates, causing also the self churchmen and priests to help him with their weapons in the field.[1] Wherefore, guessing what indeed might fall out at last of my coming to the country [Shane] desired the very first day he saw me that I should make me ready to go with his errand beyond seas,[2] to whom when I answered I came for no such purpose to the country, [Shane] told no further what that errand should be, but taking another way for keeping to himself the aforesaid aid of Church lands, prayed I would preach the next Sunday and encourage his men to fight against his enemies. All the lord's maintainers and about 600 of his war men being present, straightway after preaching was ended, Shane rose up and, in a very rage among other his treating and most angry loud talk, did swear or affirm to destroy that Cathedral Church of Armagh, which thing he made to be performed within five days after, causing all the roofs to be burned, and some of the walls to be broken ; but perceiving that neither for that, nor for fear of any other things threatened by him in despite and revenge of that preaching, I did shrink from doing my duty owed to God and sworn to my prince (but also I wrote to my Lord Sydney requesting his Honour to command me any service I might with conscience do, of the which letters Shane did know), but also I came to the open field to curse [excommunicate] him [Shane], then began he to try me with gifts promising or also swearing afore the like company aforesaid, that for mine own houses and men I should enjoy more of Ulster commodities than ever did any Archbishop there since St. Patrick's time, if I would be content he might keep for his aid the helper [3]

[1] This strong indictment of Shane must be taken for a fact.
[2] Probably to the Court of Spain.
[3] I.e. The revenues of the Church lands.

aforesaid which when I did utterly refuse, he sought an earnest way to undo me as an heretic,[1] whereof I being privily warned [2] both for letting [depriving] him from [of] aid to war (as he did pretend . . . be against heretics so naming the Queen's subjects), as also for refusing to set my hand to his letter, which he said he would cause to be written to the Spanish King, but I, being soon after privily warned that he sought thereby only means to undo [kill] me as aforesaid, departed privily out of the country, all also Church and churchmen being sorer by Shane oppressed for my being there. For I was yet moreover warned that going to bed he swore that there was none living he hated more than the Queen of England (said he), and our Primate, meaning my poor body.[3] For the which his hate towards me, he would never, from that first preaching, hear any other of my preachings afterwards, though I preached once in his own house, and he absented himself, but not so O'Donnell which soon after that first preaching left Shane (giving high thanks to the preacher), and held with the Queen's subjects. The more I tarried in mentioning [4] this preaching, that also clean contrary to all expectation, I was burdened blamed here in England (but never in Ireland I heard of), that I have cursed [excommunicated] therein the Queen's Majesty's. To the which tale being rehearsed by my Lord Treasurer's careful wisdom (who was then Mr. Secretary) in her Majesty's affairs, I answered that his Honour, receiving all my letters and writings, knew I had no delegative authority thereto, or of my ordinary power I could curse [excommunicate] none that was without [outside] Ireland, or also Ulster, and he that curses without any of those authorities doth fall himself in the curse rather than any other body ; but for conclusion remembering my oath and offer made in this writing's beginning it is sure I did neither so, nor yet said in any of my preachings in Ulster (to my remembrance) any word that perhaps by any of your own Honour's might be misliked of.

Wherefore, your noble wisdoms may also by consideration of the premises perceive what tale was it that I have conspired with Shane at Lefir, the fifteen of December as mine indictment in Dublin did contain, and also her Majesty's letter at my said trial, partly read, did seem to mention some the like thing. So that I wen [ween] nothing now needful to rehearse how Captain Herne told me the Lord Deputy Sydney to have been well informed of

---

[1, 2] Crossed out in text.

[3] It was through fear of Shane that Creagh left Armagh.

[4] I.e. The more he neglected to defend his sermon, the more he was accused in England of having excommunicated Elizabeth.

the contrary things, or also how the Lord Chancellor, Chief Justice, Chief Baron, and others in that trial, sitting in Commission, would not have the Quest to pass for that part of the indictment, for thereto I have also myself then largely answered, showing moreover that within Lefir I was never twenty or also thirty miles, and saw not Shane six weeks afore that fifteen day of December nor after till Christmas Eve, when being warned of his purposed enterprise to begun (according his cursed custom) on Christmas day (viz. : to go kill, burn, and spoil the English pale), I did by God's assistance stay him thereof, so that also neither afterward (as I am remembered) he took any such enterprise in hand during my being in the country. I omit the rest of such my dealings with Shane. To some witness I come touching briefly some other my behaviour. For my preaching done afore my Lord of Sussex (being her Majesty's worthy lieutenant) and Sir Henry Sydney, treasurer, (if remembrance fail not) going by Limerick upon Sir Donnell O'Brien, as I had many thanks of his honour's gentlemen, so I lost for ever after a certain Irish lord's great favour, which being then present did, till that preaching, favour me still.

At my coming to Ireland bishop to Ulster, and hiring a ship at mine own charges so that they [the mariners] should be bound so deal but as I would, I was poisoned by them twice for withstanding and staying them from invading at seaboard Englishmen, and so might take therefore such stuff as I had in the ship myself and also the gold which they supposed I had ; and thinking nothing but I should die, they brought me to Blavet in Brittany, there to have a testimonial (as I ween) that I should be there buried, or otherwise having no such witness, nor yet that I landed in Ireland, they should set themselves in present danger, chiefly by reason of country men that knew and saw me shipped with them in Biscay. When I came to Ulster (hiring thereto another ship and foregoing the other with giving them whole payment) I wrote according my duty to the Lord Deputy Sydney requesting his Honour to command me any service as aforesaid, doubting also nothing at my departure from Ulster but his Lordship would grant me a protection to live among my friends her Majesty's subjects, seeing I have been so sore persecuted for doing my duty against her enemies. Mr. Tremayne may declare further of my dealing which [who] took a very exact examination in writing of perhaps all my doings straight after I went out with the keepers of Dublin Castle, which my going away [escape] I think no man would wonder that should know well how I was dealt therein withal, first in a hole where without candle there is no light in the world, and with candle (when I had it) it was so filled with the smoke thereof (chiefly in summer) that, and had not been a little hole in the next door to draw in breath with my mouth set upon it, I had been perhaps shortly undone. But the two gentlemen that have chiefly elected me to go out with themselves and the said keeper thought I should be much sooner undone in the second lodging with cold, being thereto toward winter removed, where scant was light, and could be without hindrance, no fire. My dwelling in Alesboure (in this over the first time) for more than a month's space might, maychance, make a strong man to wish liberty if for his life he could, though God's witness that I did not by myself or other procure that escape, but rather much grudged at it the self hour, till a little upon mine unworthy prayers (desiring God to give the best) my mind was clean changed, as I have often afore in sundry examinations showed it, but foregoing further rehearse of bearing, almost this eight years, irons with one of my legs (to the beholder's judgment) lost by the same, of my manifold sickness (colics, stones of the reins, such breaking down as Latins called Ernia, and also *exitus fundamenti*, lose all of my big teeth, save two, and daily sore rheums etc.) and many other like miseries as also how I was accused in Rome by Magrath (now appointed by her Majesty Archbishop of Cashel) and by other also in Spain of heresy and other the like things and inobedience and rebellion against the Pope in any foresaid dealings with Shane,[1] this I say and many the like mine unhappiness, miseries, wretchedness, foregoing to rehearse larger : seeing (as I said first) that my private affection toward myself may make me to think better of my dealings and care more for my griefs than in truth they be (my sins undoubtedly deserving sore punishment of God whom I thank most humbly for not reserving them to everlasting pains) I commit, with as good will I can, all to your Honours wisdom and discretion : beseeching with all the veins of my heart the goodness of God to forgive if I have or shall further be dealt with otherwise than I have deserved. And thus wishing Her Majesty, your Honours, and all the realm as much wealth and prosperity of soul and body as ever had any prince, lords, or realm, I take my leave as humbly as I can.

Your said honourable Lordships' unprofitable and unworthy servant in Christ,

RICHARD CREAGH, *prisoner.*

To the right honourable the Lords and others of the Queen's Majesty's Privy Council.

[1] Because he preached obedience to the Queen as the legitimate Sovereign of Ireland.

DESMOND'S SUBMISSION.

The Queen blamed FitzWilliams for idling in Dublin while Essex struggled in Ulster, Desmond lorded it in Munster, and Connacht practically threw off loyalty to her. The Lord Deputy, in all sincerity and truth, pleaded that to take the field without proper forces would be to risk Her Majesty's honour. On all sides slanderous tongues wagged about his lack of zeal, so that his credit was at the lowest ebb. He had indeed issued a few commissions [1] for the purpose of keeping Leix and Offaly quiet, and trusted to their efficacy by granting power to seize goods and by putting a premium on hanging. Elizabeth, however, rebuked him for allowing Edward FitzGerald to treat with Desmond in her name, whereas the conference should have been conducted as between kinsmen. She was piqued because it had been a failure, and, as she said (30 March), " we think ourselves touched in honour." [2] The harassed Deputy, with no great opinion of Desmond's intentions, sent Sir James Dowdall, second Justice of the Queen's Bench, to remind the Earl that there was a Government in Ireland, a fact or a fiction that Desmond had utterly ignored. [3] Desmond gave out (20 May) that there should be no law but Brehon law between Geraldines. [4] The apprehension of Captain Bourchier by James Fitzmaurice showed how

---

[1] Commission to Edward Moore (Mellifont) to make war upon such of the nation of the O'Connors as are proclaimed traitors, or have appeared in rebellion, to punish with fire and sword all Irish persons who help them, and to put in gaol and seize the goods of any English inhabitants of the English shires who help them, with power to treat with the rebels and grant protections, and to raise and lead the queen's subjects. 28 May, 1574. (*Fiants*, no. 2403.)

Grant to Conley M'Geoghegan, chief of his name, of the office of seneschal of the country of Kenaleagh *alias* M'Geoghegan's country, Co. Westmeath. To hold during life. All Irish jurisdictions, usages and lawful customs are abolished. Conley is to apprehend all traitors, felons and other malefactors and commit them to the county gaol to be dealt with by law ; and is to receive half the goods of every felon of his country executed by the order of the law. He shall have all frays, batrees, and bloodshed happening in his country with all other lawful perquisites as any other seneschal in the realm has ; the sheriff of the county shall not execute writs in the country except on default of Conley but shall send his warrant for doing so to the seneschal. Conley may assemble the freeholders and other inhabitants, and command them for defence of the country, the public weal of the inhabitants, the suppression of rebels and punishment of malefactors. 18 June, 1574. (*Fiants*, no. 2415.)

[2] *S.P.I.*, *Eliz.*, xlv. 30.   [3] *Ib.*, 82 ; xlvi. 1.   [4] *Ib.*, 26.

little was thought of Elizabeth's Government. So keenly had the English failure been felt that English Colonists in Munster wrote (29 May) lugubrious and provocative letters to Walsingham and Burghley,[1] some of a classical and others of a Puritanical turn, to the effect that long immunity had introduced universal laxity, and that the Irish could be starved out by taking or destroying the herds upon whose milk they fed, than which no greater sacrifice could be offered to God.

FitzWilliams, almost in despair at the taunts of Her Majesty and the inadequacy of his forces, badly fed and paid, sent for Essex. The Earl who had probably become acquainted with Desmond in London wrote (10 June) to him from Dublin,[2] asking him : " What do you desire or what is the mark you shoot at ? . . . What should move you, then, to seek war, when in peace and with honour you may enjoy all that is your right ? . . . Surely in my opinion Her Majesty had rather to erect many such houses as yours is, than to be the overthrow of yours, although it be through your own default and folly." After a conference at Kilmacthomas, Co. Waterford, with Essex and Kildare, Desmond agreed to go to Dublin on safe conduct. Being called upon to perform the articles concluded in England, Desmond said these had been extorted from him under restraint, and that he was willing to be bound, but only as part of a general settlement. Otherwise he would be the one unarmed man in Leinster, Munster, and Connaught. As to giving up his castles to the Queen, he would give no pledges beyond what he had before agreed to. He could not believe that Her Majesty desired it. As a matter of fact the Queen, writing to FitzWilliams,[3] acknowledged that it was hardly fair to ask Desmond to disarm when others did not. Essex had no part in the conference as oddly enough Elizabeth had not made him a member of the Irish Council.

The meeting having proved abortive, Desmond begged to be allowed to return to Munster on his safe conduct, and was conducted thither by Essex, Kildare, and Ormond.

---

[1] *S.P.I., Eliz.*, xlvi. 32. [2] *Ib.*, 57. [3] *Ib.*, xlvii. 35.

Notwithstanding this, a proclamation was prepared declaring him a traitor, and offering £500 for his head, and £1000 and a pension to anyone who would bring him in alive. Meanwhile, Desmond had arrived in his own country. In answer to FitzWilliams' request for a high military officer Elizabeth (15 June) sent him Sir William Drury.[1] This "express gentleman" was to be consulted by FitzWilliams in all material affairs. Desmond's reply (20 June) to all this was to call certain of his followers together and ask their advice.[2] The result was the famous "Desmond Combination," a document signed by twenty Munster chiefs, 18 July, 1574, which declared: "We . . . do advise and counsel the said Earl to defend himself from the violence of the said Lord Deputy. . . . We renounce God if we do spare life, lands, and goods . . . to maintain and defend this our advice against the Lord Deputy or any other that will covet the said Earl's inheritance."[3] Desmond's brother John was one of the signatures, but James Fitzmaurice's name is absent. It was in contemplation at this time (20 August) to buy them both off with some portion of the Earl's lands,[4] but it cannot be said that this had anything to do with the absence of Fitzmaurice's signature.

FitzWilliams and Ormond[5] attacked the castle of Der-

---

[1] *S.P.I., Eliz.*, xlvi. 65. [2] *Ib.*, 73.
[3] *Desid. Cur. Hib.*, i. 5. [4] Carew, *Cal.*, 1515-74, no. 333.
[5] Commissions were issued in July to the bishops and gentry of the various counties to muster and array the inhabitants. The commissioners shall assemble and divide into companies, appointing a company of not less than two or three for each barony. They shall direct the barony constables to come before them on a certain day with lists of the persons in their baronies between the ages of fifteen and sixty and to command the people to appear at the same time with all such horse, armour, bows, guns, and other warlike apparel as they can put in readiness for the service of Her Majesty. Any able man not appearing shall forfeit 20s. On the day of muster they shall make lists of all men appearing, distinguishing archers, arquebusiers, billmen, horsemen, and kern, also those who have a horse jack, spear, bow, sheaf of arrows, bill, gun, sword, or habergeon of mail. This list, signed by the commissioners present and also the lists of the constables, to be returned by the 20 August following. The musters for the several baronies of the county to be taken on the same day. They shall give notice that all be ready to muster before the Lord Deputy upon six days warning. Any person unprovided with horse or arms such as required by Statute, to be directed to procure them before the Lord Deputy's muster, on the pain in the statute expressed. No man required by law to find horse or armour may be allowed to muster as servant or substitute for another. (*Fiants*, no. 2445.)

rinlaur on the Suir, which, having been mined, was blown up with its garrison. This tragedy had an immediate effect on Desmond who said that he could not hope to hold any fortress against the Government. At Cork, after service in the Cathedral, he submitted in presence of the Munster nobility, and agreed to the modified [1] conditions proposed, " praying [the Queen] for one drop of grace to assuage the flame of his tormented mind." Castlemaine was surrendered, as well as the castles in Kenry, which had been the chief matter in dispute. It was agreed that there should be oblivion as to the other causes of difference.[2] Desmond was thus left undisturbed in his feudal authority, in return for a nominal allegiance. He yielded to superior force, but did not abandon his designs. He was evidently influenced in his submission by the Spanish treaty with Elizabeth, under stress of circumstances, by which even the English and Irish refugees in the Netherlands were refused further asylum there. Of all this he was aware through his many agents in Spain, who, up to the middle of 1574, had been holding out hopes of aid of money if not of men. Foremost among these agents were Maurice MacBrien, Bishop of Emly, Father Patrick O'Healy (afterwards the martyred Bishop of Mayo), and Dr. Sander, an Englishman. They were afterwards joined and strengthened

---

[1] The *Four Masters* are somewhat inaccurate in the following account they give of this episode :—

" The Earl of Desmond was plundering and harassing his enemies in the spring of this year. . . . A son of the Earl of Desmond took by surprise a good and strong castle, called Doire-an-lair [i.e. middle or central oak wood, now Derrinlare, in the parish of Killaloan, barony of Upper Third, County Waterford], and placed in it trustworthy warders of his own people to guard it. When the Lord Justice of Ireland [Sir William Fitzwilliams] and the Earl of Ormond had heard of this castle, it renewed their recent and old animosity against the sons of the Earl of Desmond ; and they summoned the men of Meath and Bregia [N. Dublin], the Butlers, and all the inhabitants of the English Pale, to proceed to devastate Leath-Mhodha. [The summons was obeyed], and they marched, without halting, until they had pitched their tents and pavilions around Doire-an-lair, which they finally took ; and the Lord Justice beheaded all the warders [*sic*]. His people and auxiliaries were so much abandoning the Earl of Desmond, that he resolved upon repairing to the Lord Justice, and making unconditional [*sic*] submission to him ; [this he did], and he was obliged to deliver up to the Lord Justice Castlemain, Dungarvan, and Kenry ; and [thereupon] whatever wrongs had been committed on either side up to that time should be forgiven."

[2] *S.P.I., Eliz.*, xlvii. 47, i.

by Father Wolf. The latter says in his Memorial (p. 475) that " this truce would not have been allowed by James Fitzmaurice Fitzgerald, but that owing to the accord made by the King of Spain with the Lady Elizabeth he was disappointed of succour which he expected from Spain."

To show her appreciation of the loyalty of Clanricard and Thomond, Elizabeth made grants to them of various kinds.[1]

ESSEX'S NORTHERN EXPEDITION; PLANTATION SCHEME.

Having satisfied himself that Desmond would settle down under the new conditions, Essex resolved to make another attempt to conquer Ulster for himself and his Mistress. Elizabeth showed her willingness to help him in the task, provided it did not increase her expenses. Essex, having consulted the Council in Dublin, summoned Tirlogh Luineach to meet him near Benburb on the Blackwater. Tirlogh, even on the promise of safe-conduct, refused to come to any point where the river was fordable (14 June). The Earl, dissatisfied with this state of affairs, continued his march to Lifford, burning and spoiling everything *en route*, but seeing no enemy. Here he was joined by O'Donnell,[2]

[1] Grant under the Queen's letter, 1 March, 1573, to Connor, Earl of Thomond, reciting his surrender, 21 December, 1571, of all his manor and lands in Clonramid, Clare, Bonrattie, Moiaghe, Castle of Banke, Danyngbreake, and elsewhere in Co. Clare, *alias* Thomond, Dryshoke, Kilmacodrike and Newgrange, Co. Dublin (Ballychalmer), and elsewhere in Ireland ; grants all the possessions which he held beyond the river Shenon ; an annual rent of £20 English out of the Exchequer ; with a moiety of the monastery of Eleamaghanaughe *alias* Insula Canonicorum. To hold to him and the heirs male of the body of his father, by knight service, without account. Provided that if he attempt anything against the Crown the grant shall be void. 14 July, 1574. (*Fiants*, no. 2434.) The *Insula Canonicorum* (*Inis-na-g-canánoc* or Island of Canons) in the Shannon is situated at the mouth of the River Fergus, and was rebuilt or founded by Donald O'Brien, King of Limerick, in the twelfth century, for canons regular of the Rule of St. Augustine. To it belonged small parcels of land together with three other islands called Inishorlth, Iniskeirke, and Inistubred, near the said island,

Grant to Richard, Earl of Clanricard, of the seneschalship of Clare *alias* Maghrereogh, in Clanricard, Co. Galway. To hold during pleasure with such lawful profits as other seneschals in the realm receive. With power to assemble the freeholders and other inhabitants, and command them for the defence of the territory, the public weal of the inhabitants, the suppression of rebels, and punishment of malefactors. 14 November, 1574. (*Fiants*, no. 2501.)

[2] *S.P.I., Eliz.*, xlvii. 65.

O'Dogherty and other chief men of Tirconnaill, who saw an opportunity of regaining Lifford Castle from Tirlogh's supporter Conn O'Donnell, who had married Tirlogh's daughter. Conn affirmed " that he had rather live as a felon or a rebel than adventure his undoing for the Queen." Lifford Castle was taken and handed over to O'Donnell. Conn was arrested, escaped, was recaptured, and sent a prisoner to Dublin [1] (8 October).

The expedition now developed into a cattle raid, and though O'Donnell seized upon all O'Neill's cattle at the command of Essex, his men " laid hold on them, and as their manner is, every man carried his booty home." Out of a much greater number, only 1400 head of cattle found their way into the English camp. For this, O'Donnell was forced to provide an extra 600 men and to fight with Tirlogh as long as Her Majesty did. Essex's subsequent burning of all O'Neill's corn, after a bountiful harvest, to the value of £5000, as he boasted, was not calculated to advance friendly relations with the Ulster people. He was sanguine enough to believe that he had broken Tirlogh's strength, and that with the co-operation of FitzWilliams he would preserve Ulster from rebellion hereafter. FitzWilliams thought differently, and no doubt he was right. However, Essex thought he was justified in his boast, and that only a permanent garrison could effect the civilisation of the North. Elizabeth, of course, would derive no benefit from it, but then the garrison would pay itself, and the plantation by Protestants could be accomplished without any expense to her. [2] It did not seem to any official in the Government of Ireland that the country could be brought to accept the " Reform " tenets except by wholesale plantation. And here in Ulster was an object lesson of what might be accomplished in other provinces. No wonder then that Essex was boastful, and Elizabeth was pleased to see how her favourite had succeeded in spite of so much misgiving and so little cordial co-operation from FitzWilliams. She was inclined to favour his plans for the permanent plantation of the North. But her Council, as she was careful to point

---

[1] *S.P.I.*, *Eliz.*, xlviii. 3, 55, 57, i.   [2] *Ib.*, xlvi. 62 (14 June).

out, required information where the colonists should inhabit, whether they should be English or Irish and whether the towns were to be walled with stone or earth. Other details would have to be arranged, as to provisions, maintenance of the garrison, where the labourers and the material were to be procured. To answer all these questions, Essex was summoned to Court (8 November) as soon as he could leave his post. As the choice was left to himself, and as his enemies were thick at Court, he decided to stay where he was. The conditional order, he said, came " either of her Majesty's misliking of the cause, or of me as unable to execute the thing, and so make stay of me there, either by disallowing the work as not feasible, or else to essay as the honour of it should be reaped by another." [1]

ESSEX'S ACT OF TREACHERY.

A most dishonourable transaction disgraced the last days of Essex in Ireland. It is not surprising that Sir Brian MacFelim, a northern Irish chief, should have sought to upset Essex's plantation scheme which he believed was undertaken for the Earl's and the Queen's private interest. He had discovered that Essex had not come as Marshal of Ireland and that his expedition was not in the nature of pacification of the countryside. No wonder then that he showed some hostility to the scheme. But there was no state of war declared by Essex against MacFelim, he was not proclaimed a traitor, and there was no warrant for his arrest. Even if, by a stretch of imagination, he was guilty of treason, how could his wife be considered equally guilty ? Besides, he came in quite a friendly way to meet Essex at Belfast, and brought his wife and other relations with him.[2] It is clear that Essex became panicky and suspected treachery, where there was only friendship without dissimulation. Essex's decision to arrest his guests was unpardonable, and his own account fails to justify him The *Four Masters* seem perfectly justified in charging Essex with the blackest treachery. Their entry reads thus :—

[1] *S.P.I.*, *Eliz.*, xlviii. 45, 46, 47, 51 ; liii. 43, 72-3.
[2] *Ib.*, xlviii. 17.

Peace, sociality, and friendship were established between Brian, the son of Felim Bacagh O'Neill, and the Earl of Essex ; and a feast was afterwards prepared by Brian, to which the Lord Justice and the chiefs of his people were invited ; and they passed three nights and days together pleasantly and cheerfully. At the expiration of this time however, as they were agreeably drinking and making merry, Brian, his brother, and his wife, were seized upon by the Earl and all his people put unsparingly to the sword, men, women, youths, and maidens, in Brian's own presence.

Brian was afterwards sent to Dublin, together with his wife and brother, where they were cut in quarters. Such was the end of the feast. This unexpected massacre, this wicked and treacherous murder of the Lord of the race of Hugh Boy O'Neill, the head and the senior of the race of Eoghan, son of Niall of the nine Hostages, and of all the Gaels, a few only excepted, was a sufficient cause of hatred and disgust [of the English] to the Irish.[1]

It must be noted that Essex's officers made no opposition to the arrest of MacFelim. The O'Neills, however, had defended their chief, but the result is told by Essex in a letter to the Privy Council, in which he boasts that besides arresting MacFelim and his wife, and some principal persons, he " put others to the sword, to the number of 200 in all places, whereof 40 of his best horsemen." He likewise boasted " that this little execution hath broken the faction and made them all afeard." Although there was no official censure passed on Essex, Ormond hinted that he did not like what had been done, and hoped that some worse successor to MacFelim would not arise. If Essex wished to create an Eden for himself in a corner of Ireland he was certainly going the wrong way in taking the lives of his guests and in antagonising his nearest neighbours.

FATHER WOLF'S REPORTS ON IRELAND.

Father Wolf had been Apostolic Commissary in Ireland since the year 1561 for the purpose of supervising the ecclesiastical state of the country and of reporting to Rome. In the year 1566 he was on a visit to Hugh O'Donnell in

---

[1] Camden (*Annals*, A.D. 1574) merely states that Essex slew 200 of the Irish, and took Brian, Rory Oge, his brother, and Brian's wife.

Tirconnaill and there met Sydney, the Lord Deputy, who
was then on his grand tour in the North. It seems that
he was induced by O'Donnell to give his allegiance to the
Queen and the Deputy as the bishops and princes had done.
As has been pointed out this allegiance was concerned only
with temporal matters and had nothing to do with Supremacy
or Uniformity. Sydney accepted Wolf's promise and advised him to go to Dublin under safe-conduct and have his
promise ratified by the Council. Wolf seems to have
journeyed with Sydney to Carrickfergus, but having presented himself before the Council in Dublin he was without
more ado committed to the dungeons of Dublin Castle.
There he lay for five years until July, 1572, when he escaped
by boat and landed at Wexford. He remained in Ireland
until September, 1573, when he set sail for Spain.[1] He went
as negotiator for James Fitzmaurice, accompanied by Father
Richard Corbally and one of Fitzmaurice's sons,[2] a lad of about

[1] Between the years 1561-5 he received back into the Catholic Church
the Protestant Bishop of Limerick. (See the letter of Andrew Trollope,
1587.) The Bishop made the following profession of faith : " I, William
Cahessy [Casey], priest, sometime named Bishop of the Diocese of Limerick,
yet nothing canonically consecrated, but by the schismatical authority of Edward,
King of England, schismatically preferred to the Bishoprick of Limerick aforesaid, wherein I confess to have offended my Creator. I renounce also, if I
might have the same, the Bishoprick of Limerick, the charge and administration
of the said cure. Also other benefits and privileges received from the said
Edward, or other heretics and schismatics. And I draw unto the said holy
and universal church, and do bow myself unto her laws, and I embrace the
Rev. Lord David Wolfe, appointed the apostolical messenger for all Ireland
from the most Holy Lord the Pope [Pius IV]. And I pray and beseech that
as a lost child he receive me again into the bosom of the Holy Mother of the
Church, and that he will absolve me from all the ecclesiastical sentences,
censures, punishments, heresies, rules, and every other blot—dispense with me
and reconcile me again to the unity of the same church." (See Begley, 184-6.)
Casey, however, did not long continue in this frame of mind.

[2] Matthew Shayne, Protestant Bishop of Cork, reports to the Lord Deputy,
October, 1573, about Father Wolf and Fitzmaurice as follows : " The Romish
runagate pardoner, Sir David Wolf, he that forsweared himself and fled from
Dublin, is gone over into Spain, and carried James Fitzmaurice's son with
him the last week, being accompanied with one Sir Richard Corbally, priest,
for no loyal purpose. I dare write, moreover, your Honour shall understand,
that James Fitzmaurice did put away his lawful wife, for that he did intercept
amongst letters written by her to Edward Butler (as he doth allege) and forthwith did marry the O'Connor Kerry's relict, daughter to Sir Donnell O'Brien,
and took possession of the strongest and beautifulest castle in all the west of
Munster, named Carrigfwohill upon the river Synan [Shannon], not far from the
main sea, and combined with Mailles and Flahartes who are notable and seditious

twelve years, who was to be placed in the hands of the Spanish King as a hostage for the faithful performance of any agreement arrived at between the Irish negotiators and the King.

Father Wolf was blamed by his Jesuit Superiors for writing so little about his work in Ireland. In all we can trace only five letters, two of which may be called reports. The first of these reports may be called " An Account of Ireland " and the second " A Description of Ireland." Although written in different years it will be best to consider them here together. The first [1] was written in the prison of Dublin Castle in 1568, and was sent to Bishop Redmund O'Gallaghair of Killala, who was then at Lisbon. This was afterwards amended and presented at Rome some time after 1571. The second [2] was drawn up at Lisbon after his escape from Dublin Castle, and is dated 24 March, 1574. It was the result of conversations with the Spanish Ambassador and for the purpose of enabling the Spanish King to come to a decision in favour of armed intervention in behalf of Ireland.

1. *Father Wolf's Account of Ireland.*

Gerald, Earl of Simonia [*sic* Desmond] and John, his brother, are among the chiefs of the island, and aforetime were heretics, but are now excellent Catholics : they have been in prison in England, but are now free.

James [Fitz] Maurice, cousin german of Earl Gerald, succeeded him as governor in Ireland, and rules Munster in the fear of God : he is a young man, but a good Catholic and a brave captain. He was minded to enter some religious order, or to quit Ireland to live in some Catholic country, but by the advice of the good prelates and Catholic religious he stayed where he was for the good of the country.

rebels, and afterwards went into Connacht to have conference with the Earl of Clanricard's children." (*S.P.I.*, *Eliz.*, xlii. 49, iv., P.R.O., London.) Shayne is entirely wrong in his information about Fitzmaurice and his wife. There is not a shadow of foundation for it. It is interesting to note what he says about the combining of the O'Malleys and the O'Flahertys with Fitzmaurice before the latter's departure, as these two families were the first to come to Fitzmaurice's aid at Smerwick on his landing there in 1579.

[1] Hogan, *Iber. Ignat.*, i. 18, 19. Carew. *Cal.*, 1515-74, pp. 430-8.

[2] *C.S.P.*, *Rome*, 1572-78, no. 293. As this summary omits many important passages, we have translated them from the original Italian document in Begley. *Dioc. of Limerick*, 494-515.

Cornelius [Connor O'Brien], Earl of Tuam [*sic* Thomond] is ever waning in power and losing his men by desertion.

Richard [Clanricard], Earl of Connacht, has trouble with his sons, because the younger by the second wife claimed to inherit, and was countenanced by his mother, and so the state was divided : they are now at peace. The Earl repudiated his first and lawful wife without cause. Both he and his second wife, are, however, well-conditioned Catholics,[1] and readily associate with the religious.

Those of the See of Raimond [Redmund O'Gallagher] of Killala are barbarians untamed and ferocious, and of bestial habits : at one time they pursued the said bishop with intent to kill or take him prisoner ; and he fled to Portugal, and abode some years in Lisbon, whence he went to Rome : he is now in Ireland in another See [2]

Donald Ocnoc Seuez [i.e. O'Conor Sligo], a great friend of the said Bishop Raimond and Father David [Wolf], was in England, and was there received with great honour by the Queen, and returned to Dublin with great power, and promised Father David, who was then in prison in Dublin, that he would procure his discharge by means of the Viceroy. He is a good Catholic.

Lord Oddonel gave up his lands to live in England, professing himself the Queen's perpetual vassal.

John [Shane] O'Neill was a cruel, and impious heretical tyrant ; he burned the Church of Armagh, the Metropolitan church of all Ireland, and all the monasteries of that city, and all that pertained to the monastery of Dunagatil [probably Donegal], the monastery and Cathedral Church of the city of Euse [Derry], the monastery of Valle [Moville], otherwise called in Canoin, and the monasteries of Monicao [Monaghan], Riul [Errigal], Ratain [Fahan]

---

[1] It is quite clear that Clanricard remained Catholic, but his moral character was not beyond reproach. In the *State Papers* is " A Note of the Earl of Clanricard's Wives and Concubines now alive," as follows : " (1) Margaret, daughter to Moroughe, the first Earl of Thomond, and mother to Ullicke Boorke ; she is his only lawful wife, and yet liveth. [He married secondly Catherine, daughter of Donough, second Earl of Thomond, by whom he had issue, John, created Lord Leitrim, and two daughters (*Archdall's Peerage*)]. (2) The Lady Gilles, widow to the old Baron of Dunboyne ; she was married unto him after the death of John's mother, and within three or four years he put her away. (3) Onora, daughter to McBryen Arra, a concubine ; he kept her awhile, and put her away again. (4) Saunyowg, a gentlewoman of Clanricard, a concubine ; he kept her awhile, and again put her away. (5) Julian Browne, a merchant's wife of Gallaway [Galway] ; he married her, and put her away, and then brought home M'Bryen Arard's daughter aforesaid. All these are alive." (*S.P.I.*, *Eliz.*, i. 18 ; *Kilk. Arch. Jour.*, 1858-59, pp. 342-3.)

[2] Transferred to Derry, 22 June, 1569. This portion was inserted afterwards, probably when the document was presented at Rome after 1571.

and Daunes [Devenish] : he kept in prison for six months in a
most pitiable plight the Bishop of Dromore [Arthur Magennis] an
old man of great virtue, now dead ; he caused a priest of holy
life to be hanged without colour or semblance of justice ; he took
away the wife of one of his kinsmen, and had three sons by her,
and being reproved for so doing by the Archbishop of Armagh
[Creagh], he ruthlessly persecuted him and his clergy. He lost
600 men in an engagement with his enemies in a place called
Anselac ; and when he had remodelled his army, the nobles of
Tyrone rose against him, and as he was crossing [1] a river called
Fearzidmor [Farsetmore] he suffered a prodigious defeat at the
hands of Oddo [Hugh] Odaniel [O'Donnell] ; they say that the
dead, including the drowned, numbered 8000 besides 74 of the
bravest and noblest gentlemen of Tyrone. This was on the 9th
of May, 1567, and having sought refuge among the Scottish heretics
[at Cushendun in Ulster], he was cruelly slain on the 2nd of June
in the said year, an event which was predicted long before by that
good and holy old man Richard [Creagh], Archbishop of Armagh,
in the presence of the said David and other persons, the year, the
month, the place, and the persons by whom he was to be slain,
being all specified. They cut off his head, and brought it to Dublin,
where it was exposed in the Castle upon a lance.

To this place succeeded Terence Lunac [Tirlogh Luineach
O'Neill] a man very expert in martial affairs, but very brutish
in those matters that concern the weal of souls. His little finger
is heavier than the fist of his predecessor, and whereas the one
did but persecute the clergy with whips, the other persecutes
them to the death with the most cruel torments.

Oddo Odoneil [Hugh O'Donnell] governs his lands as he can
and has much ado to defend them against his enemies ; there was
a great quarrel between him and his nephew Conal [Conn] but
by the mediation of the Viceroy they were reconciled. Charles
Odoneil and two others were in prison at Dublin, but are now in
liberty.

The bishops of Ireland are hirelings and dumb dogs, and
acknowledge the Queen of England as supreme head of the Church,
all except three besides the said Bishop Raimund, who have been
strong as bulwarks of the Bride of Christ, to wit, Richard [Creagh],
Archbishop of Armagh, William [Walsh], Bishop of Meath, and
Thomas [Leverous], Bishop of Kildare ; they are now either
in exile or in prison. The Archbishop of Armagh was taken
twice and this last time, now in Dublin, now in London, has been

---

[1] Cf. *Annals of Loch Cé*, ii. 393-4.

and is continued in a dark and gloomy dungeon. Bishop William
[Walsh] spent three months in prison in Dublin, and was then
discharged and banished. Bishop Thomas visited Father David
[Wolf] in prison, and, being unable to endure the foul and fetid
stench that issued from the said dungeon, returned without accomplishing anything. The Archbishop of Armagh is kept in
the stocks in a subterranean place, where none can visit him or
speak to him but the warden of the gaol : he has many sores on
his body, and though he is but forty-four years old, he has already
lost all his teeth. He has been many a time brought before the
magistrates ; but neither by threats nor by torments have they
ever been able to induce him to renounce the Catholic faith ; and
when they offered him great honours and dignities, *ipse omnia
arbitratus est ut stercora, ut Christum lucri faciat.* Great is the
amazement of every one and especially of his enemies at his constancy and staunchness in the Catholic Faith. From his youth
up he has made little account of the delights of this world, using
his body very harshly. Much might be said of the upright and
holy life of this great man, but it were not meet at present ; it
will be said in due time and place, for these things cannot remain
hidden, since in him God has shown the world a servant of His
of so grand a type.

2. *Father Wolf's Description of Ireland.*

The writer says he has no ill feelings towards the English
nation or the Lady Elizabeth, but is actuated only by zeal for
the honour of God and the Catholic Church, the weal of souls,
and the extirpation of the Lutheran pest from the kingdom. He
would not have written the description had not the Bull of Pope
Pius V, dated 25 February, 1570, released him from his fealty to
the Lady Elizabeth.

He says (*Cap.* 2) that Henry II was invited to annex the island,
which, as part of the patrimony of St. Peter, could not be annexed
without the Pope's licence. By Bull of Pope Adrian IV licence
was granted to the King to take possession of the Kingdom not
as King but as Lord, and subject to conditions very beneficial
to the inhabitants, alike in temporal as in spiritual matters.

Cap. 3. Gerald, the Earl of Desmond that now is, and his brother
John were by the guile of the Viceroy, Henry Sydney, brought
captives to England on 17 November, 1567, and imprisoned in
the Tower of London. But their kinsman, James [Fitz] Maurice,
whom they had made Captain-General and Governor of Desmond
before they left Ireland, began to defend bravely the Church and

the clergy against the onslaught of Lutheran heretics, then to govern the country of the Earl independent of the neighbouring lords who sought to ruin and waste it according to the custom of the land.

Whilst the Earl and his brother John were in prison in the Tower of London the Deputy Henry Sydney returned to Ireland, and with an army of 6000 English and Irish soldiers went to Munster to drive out the said James and to appoint another Captain-General in his place at the command of Lady Elizabeth ; but having lost several soldiers and horses he returned to Dublin in great dishonour and confusion, and James remained in his post.

There was sent from England into Munster a soldier by the name of John Perrott as president of that country with many captains and soldiers ; and paying their expenses he compelled the lords of Munster to go with him against James who by the assistance of God conquered in such a way that the said John Perrott was forced to continue to remain in the cities and to defend himself there until at last he made a treaty to his greatest shame and dishonour with James, and not being able to do anything in Munster he set out from Ireland for England on the 17 July of last year 1573, and, because of the violence of the war of the said James against the English, Lady Elizabeth was forced to release Earl Gerald and his brother John and to send them back free to Ireland. John Perrott taking ship at the city of Cork for England turned to the lords who accompanied him to the ship, and with great emphasis spoke as follows : My lords, I have been here in Ireland more than three years and I go now to England, and I know not what will come of my deeds, but I state truthfully that never have I seen a gentleman or soldier nobler, more valorous, more experienced and successful in the ways of war than poor James Fitzmaurice, so that I can say and affirm that had he the forces and wealth of the other princes not only would he have driven out us English from this kingdom, but even from England itself, but although I have found him, as I have just said, a man of such valour, yet I find in him two defects unworthy of such a man, which defects, if it were possible by gold and silver, and even by some of my blood, I should take from him, but the remedy for them is solely in the hand of God and of her Majesty (namely Lady Elizabeth), and I shall do my duty in applying it. Of these defects one is that he is a Papist, and the other is that he is not a true subject of her Majesty.

This is the testimony of the greatest enemy of James before many lords who were greatly rejoiced hearing him speak so well of James at that time absent.

The truth is that James would never have made that treaty [at Kilmallock, 1573] with Lady Elizabeth only that he heard that a treaty had been made with the said Elizabeth by the Catholic King, from whom James expected daily help in men as had been many times promised by his Majesty. Now the said James is ill at ease for ever having made a treaty with that excommunicated Elizabeth, and in order not to fail to keep his word he does no harm either to her or to her subjects, and he desires to leave the kingdom in order to live and die among Christians rather than remain there under one who is excommunicated, and a heretical tyrant, and for this reason he has sent his eldest son with me to his Catholic Majesty so that he may send a well-armed ship to take him from that kingdom, and to make use of him in any other kingdom or country, seeing that in that kingdom he cannot live without danger to body and soul.

For this reason he has sent his beloved and eldest son to his Catholic Majesty as hostage and pledge of his fidelity, and having nothing dearer to him than what he has given, he now offers himself to his Majesty, of which I shall say no more but leave all to his Majesty's discretion and wisdom.

Having been sent into Ireland by Pius IV in the year 1560 as Apostolic Nuncio in order to find out if the Catholic lords of that island were well disposed, and to confirm the righteous in their good intentions and to convert the evil doers, and the heretics to the bosom of Mother Church, I have endeavoured to make myself acquainted minutely not only with the state of the hearts of the good and the bad but also (as has been commanded me) with the real state of the towns, cities, seaports, fortresses, and their munitions etc.

Cap. 4. Ulster is in the northern part of the kingdom, and there are most beautiful and safe harbours into which any number of ships can enter safely and be protected from every wind and storm, such as the harbour of Donegal, Keali Beaggthy [Killybegs], Assaruo, Swilly, Lough Foyle, the Bann, Knockfergus [Carrickfergus], Carlingford, Dundalk, Ardglas.

In all Ulster there is no strong city or fortress, except the castle of Knockfergus, which the English hold, and when I was in that fortress before I was taken prisoner I saw no more than two pieces of large artillery (but none of them was demi-cannon) which were fired that day because the Viceroy Henry Sydney entered that castle and they made a great festival.

Ulster has nine episcopal Sees, namely, the archbishopric of Armagh, the bishoprics of Derry, Raphoe, Clogher, Dromore, Down, Conor, Kilmore, Ardagh.

The episcopal cities are neither large nor walled, for in old time the piety of the people rendered walls needless ; but to-day by reason of the sins of the clergy and people it is not only walls that are wanting but also inhabitants, so that the cities are deserted, and all as it were derelict.

There are also in Ulster about 19 great lords besides many untitled nobles, with vast estates but slender revenues, and the names of the lords are these : O'Neill, O'Donnell, the three lords of Clandeboy, O'Ryan [? O'Reilly] O'Rourke, O'Dogherty, O'Cahan, O'Hanlon Maguire, Magennis, MacQuillin, MacMahon, the three MacSweenys [Fanad, Tuath, and Banagh], MacConnell, the three O'Farrells.

There are some castles in Ulster, but most of the people dwell in tents, and migrate frequently by reason of their herds.

Ulster is divided into three parts, to wit, Tirone, Tirconnel, Clanebuy [Clandeboy]. Tirone is held by O'Neyll, Tirconnel by Odoneill, Clanebuy by divers nobles (without the title of Lord) and all of the O'Neyll family. Clanebuy is the fairest and most fertile of all the three parts. All these countries are ever at war with one another, but they always join their forces against the English, and they are always victorious. All the other lords of Ulster obey one or other of these two Lords, to wit, O'Neyll or Odoneill.

Cap. 5. Meath is situated in the east of Ireland, between Ulster and Leinster, and is a most fertile country, rich and most abounding in everything necessary for the life of man.

This Meath is a tract of land of sixty or seventy miles long, and about 20 wide, and I can truthfully assert that I have never seen in Italy (I speak not of the number of cities) or in France, or in any other country, in such a small piece of land, such a nobility of lords, knights, and gentlemen, as in that Meath where there are at least 1500 knights, and as many more officials, and gentlemen because in that kingdom of Ireland no one is a knight who is not a gentleman, and these have their splendid horses furnished with armoury and other things necessary for war at any hour and day that they are called.

There are several large towns in that country, and it seems to me that there is not a mile where there is not a large town, or castle, or lord's or gentleman's palace.

There is no maritime city, but there is a great town near the sea named Drogheda, well walled in the old fashion and containing about 700 or 800 inhabitants, all merchants or artisans, and all Catholics, though perforce they go to hear the Alcoran of the heretics. They have no munitions or artillery, but are armed only with bows, arquebuses and such like weapons.

In all Meath there are six barons of great nobility. Barons in England and Ireland are of greater dignity and rank than those called lords, and they are the Barons of Slane, Delvin, Dunboyne, Skryne, Navan, and Galtrim.

Besides these barons there are gentlemen who are called in English lords, and they are of great authority, as Viscount Gormanstown, Plunkett of Killeen, Plunkett of Rathmore, Plunkett of Dunsany, Plunkett of Louth, Barnewall of Trimlestown, Howth, O'Melaghlin, O'Molloy, MacCoughlan, MacGeoghegain, and many other lords. I have no doubt that there are other lords in Meath, but I mention only those with whom I have practised, and these I know not only personally but I know their very frame of mind. . . . I can affirm with truth that among so many barons, lords, knights, and gentlemen, I know (thanks to God) no heretic except Viscount Gormanstown. These four Lords Plunkett are of the same house, and all in time of war gather under the banner of Lord Plunkett of Killeen, not that he is stronger than the others but because his ancestors are more ancient than all his other brothers, and the Lord of Rathmore (who was my companion for many days in prison) told me that those lords of the Plunkett family can put into the field 500 knights well armed besides as many foot soldiers.

All the above-mentioned barons, lords, and nobles are Catholics except the said Viscount Gormanstown, and are under the Lady Elizabeth for want of a Christian prince who would undertake to govern them and defend them from the heretics, and are always crying out to God to send them some Catholic prince to whom they may yield obedience.

The culture and manner of living of this Meath is neither more nor less than that of France or England, because coming with their King Henry II into Ireland, they have preserved their ancient culture and mode of life and never wish to marry or mix with those who were in the kingdom before them, but the whole of Meath has been and still is united and bound together as if it were a city or republic well governed in love and charity.

In Meath there are under the Archbishop of Armagh two bishoprics, that of Meath and Clonmacnoise. The bishopric of Meath has no city but takes its title from the diocese.

Cap. 6. Touching Leinster—Dublin is a city walled in the ancient fashion, but of no strength, and I should think its population might be about 2000.[1] There is a castle in the city built by

[1] Within the walls and not counting the large suburbs.

John, King of England, son of King Henry II, and in that castle the Viceroy has resided for the last seven years, for fear, some say, of the gentlemen of the country, because in time past the Viceroys used to live in other places outside the city.[1] Five years I have been a prisoner in that castle, in which they keep their artillery, stores of arms and other munitions of war. And many a time I have procured with money permission to see the munitions, which I have minutely examined and tested again and again, and think little thereof, because I have seen but three great pieces of artillery which are called demi-cannon, therein. There are also ten or twelve small pieces such as three or four horses might draw. There are balls without number and of such a size that there is neither in that realm nor yet in England any artillery for which they might serve, and they are rather for show than for use. One of the custodians told me that they had not three pipes of powder in all the castle, and I readily believe it. There are bows and arrows for 2000 soldiers, and not arquebuses for 100. Of equipment for horses I saw no sign, and there is but little for foot-soldiers, chiefly shirts of mail for at most 600 men. I also saw about 600 halberds and about 1000 lances or pikes for horse and foot. Other means of warfare there is none either there or in any of the cities and castles of Ireland except two pieces of artillery which I saw in Cork and other two in Dinghel [Dingle] and a piece in Leglen [Leighlin]. In time past there were many pieces of artillery and much powder in Ireland, but the Lady Elizabeth caused them to be withdrawn from the realm and sent to the Prince of Condé [2] for service against the King of France ; and they were captured by the French at sea and appropriated to the King's use.

Cap. 7. Touching the speech of the Viceroy, Henry Sydney, in the last Parliament of 1569. It seems that for many a year the English in view of the disaffection of the Irish have regarded the realm as lost, especially as they are much afraid that the Catholic League has been formed for no other object than the invasion of England and Ireland ; and for this reason they have denuded the realm of the means of defence, and neither fortify nor build cities or castles therein, knowing for certain that it is already lost.

This is manifest from the words which fell from the Viceroy, Henry Sydney, in the last parliament (to which very few lords of

---

[1] Kilmainham and the Archiepiscopal Palace of St. Sepulchre outside the walls.

[2] For the Huguenot rising.

the kingdom came,[1] knowing for certain that it was summoned for the sole utility of Lady Elizabeth, and not for the glory of God, or even for the common utility of the people) which was in Drogheda in the year 1569, which words are as follow :—

[After declaring the Parliament adjourned and descanting on the benefits received by Ireland from the Sovereigns of England the Viceroy adverted to the insurrection then in progress, in England, of the Earls of Westmoreland and Northumberland, and the risk of the disaffected conspiring to bring a foreign Power into Ireland ; he then proceeded as follows :—]

Therefore her Majesty wills and commands, and I on her part command, that you all be vigilant to watch and guard with all diligence your seaports, especially in the southern part of the realm, such as Cork, Kinsale, Ballatimor [Baltimore] and other ports in that part, and that upon sighting any ships, more than five or six in company, making for the realm, you forthwith give warning to the gentlemen in the neighbourhood, and this under pain of death.[2] I doubt not that there are here, and throughout the realm, vile and thankless persons without number who would rather see this realm under the sway of the Spaniards than under that of England ; but if they knew how the Spaniards treat the Sicilians, the Neapolitans, the Milanese, the Flemings, and the Indians and the natives of all the other regions where they bear sway, I have good reason to say and affirm that this people would not welcome them to the country. So now let each of you, my lords, take heart of grace and publish these my words to your subjects when you go back to your houses ; and so you be loyal subjects to her Majesty, I promise you on her part that you will not lack her favour and her good offices, to each according to his deserts. Besides which you will do a service well pleasing to God, to whom we all pray that He grant her Majesty long and prosperous life and victory over all her enemies. And having ended his speech he said *God Save the Queen*, and the people replied, *Amen*.

This speech of the Viceroy provided the English heretics with much food for thought and occasion to lament that the Viceroy should have so delivered himself in so public a place, as also it gave the Catholics occasion to rejoice in the hope that at no distant time such words must have some good effect but, alas ! that our sins deserve yet more chastisement than we suffer.

[1] This seems a mere boast of Wolf's, as appears from Sydney's appeal to the southern chiefs.

[2] This will explain the reluctance of the Southern chiefs to join Fitzmaurice at his landing in Smerwick in 1579, until they saw hope of success.

I have thus written that it may be understood that the English themselves and their Magistrates have their doubts of the permanence of their rule in Ireland for the reasons aforesaid.

Cap. 8. Touching Dublin and other ports of Leinster. . . . The citizens are almost all Catholics, especially the natives of the city, though they go perforce to the communion and sermons of the heretics.

In Leinster there are other seaports, like Arklow [?Wicklow], 24 miles from Dublin, and a small town, where there is a castle on a rock to prevent enemy ships from entering the port, but that castle has been for many years abandoned by the English, and is almost in ruins, and it is commonly said that the glorious apostle of the country, St. Patrick, entered that town first when he came to preach the faith of Christ Our Lord to that people of Ireland. It is said that the Saint cursed the river of that town as the fishermen knocked out a tooth of one of his companions, and from that hour there has been no fishing for salmon in that river although they may be seen there every day and I have seen them with my own eyes, thousands of them, leaping above the water in front of the town, and yet they cannot be caught. From the hour that the companion of St. Patrick had his tooth knocked out in that town, the place was called in Irish Kilmantayn, namely the church of the Gapped-tooth.

There is also in Leinster the port of Wexford, and that town is large and is walled on one side and protected by the sea on the other, and is a seaport of many ships and barques, and I have heard that it counts about 300 large barques, although the ships cannot be large on account of the bar at the entrance of the river. I passed that bar when I escaped from the prison in Dublin Castle on the 26 July, 1572, but as it was already night when I entered the port I could not see it well or get an idea of the strength of the castle there, but I have heard from others that it has been in ruins and abandoned for many years.

In Wicklow [? Arklow] there is a castle belonging to Lord Thomas Butler, Count of Ormond, and the harbour is very safe, but few ships enter there as it is not a commercial town.

Cap. 9. In Leinster there is an archbishopric and four bishoprics, namely, the Archbishopric of Dublin, the Bishoprics of Kildare, Ossory, Leighlin, and Ferns. All these bishops are heretics or schismatics, for they have received their Sees from the Lady Elizabeth ; nevertheless I know some of them who would much rather be Catholics but that they would lose their Sees.[1]

[1] He probably refers to John Devereux of Ferns and Daniel Cavanagh of Leighlin.

In Leinster there are many temporal lords as well of English as of Spanish [1] descent, as : Gerald Geraldine, Earl of Kildare, Roland of Kilcullen [Baltinglas], Maurice FitzThomas Geraldine, Mountgarrett, Thomas Stucley, an Englishman, Bermingham, *alias* Makeoris, MacMurrough, of the royal blood of Leinster, and a great lord ; O'Toole, O'Byrne, O'Dunn, O'Dempsey, O'More, O'Conor, MacGilpatrick, and many other lords and noble knights, and gentlemen without title of lordship etc.

Of Stuckley the writer says that he is at present at his Catholic Majesty's Court and has purchased very great estates and possessions. He is a very noble person, and in the last few years has sustained immense losses at the hands of certain rebels. He is a man of high spirit, generosity and great valour ; and for his rare virtues and magnanimity and the hatred he bears to the heretic English, and his great zeal for the Catholic faith, the gentlemen of Leinster, who are of the Spanish nation, would fain have made him their captain general, and obeyed him as their superior and lord, but the Lady Elizabeth's persecution of him compelled him to quit the country ; wherefore these lords are ever at war with the Viceroy and those that obey the Lady Elizabeth.

All the lords and gentlemen of Ireland, all the soldiers and all the nobles not of Leinster only but also of Munster, Connaught, Ulster, and Meath await with the utmost anxiety his arrival with a fleet, the good Catholics to aid and lovingly embrace him, the heretics to flee from him in fear. Such is the dread and terror that he implanted in the hearts of the English magistrates of the realm of Ireland that they were at a loss what to do or say, in so much that some said that the Viceroy, Henry Sidney, craved leave of the Lady Elizabeth to quit his office for fear of the said Sir Stukley. I have much to say of his magnanimity, and of what he may do in that island, and of the great esteem in which he is held by the great lords of the realm, and how many there are that would gladly embrace him ; but this I cannot do in writing, nor were it proper to do so at present. . . . As to the large towns in Leinster . . . there is no town or castle that could withstand a company of soldiers with but two pieces of artillery of the demicannon type.

Cap. 10. Munster is divided into three parts, namely, Ormond, Desmond, and Thomond, but Desmond is larger than the other two. . . . Lord Thomas Butler is Earl of Ormond, and portion of his territory is in Leinster, and he has many lords and vassals

---

[1] I.e. Milesian.

in his country who obey him and pay him tribute, as Lord Theobald of Cahir, FitzPiers Lord of Dunboyne, Edmund Lord of Mountgarrett, Edmund Butler, Edward Butler, and Peter Butler, brothers of the Earl Thomas, who have large estates, O'Carroll, O'Dwyer, O'Meagher, O'Kennedy Donn, O'Kennedy Finn, Makeig, with many other Lords etc.   In Ormond there are no cities, but some large towns, walled, such as Cashel, Gowran, Callan, Fegart [Fethard ?], Cnach [Carrick ?], Clonmel, and many other strong castles.

Cap. 11.   Gerald Geraldine, Earl of Desmond, has under his authority many lords and noble knights, who obey him how and when it pleases him ; MacCarthy More now made Earl Clancarthy by Lady Elizabeth.   There are also Lord John [Desmond] brother of Earl Gerald, a great lord ; James Fitzmaurice of Geraldine ; Thomas of Geraldine ; Lord John le Poer of Curraghmore ; Gerald Viscount Decies ; James Lord Barrymore ; Lord Barry Oge ; David Lord Roche ; Cormack MacCarthy, Lord of Muskerry ; Thomas Lord Baron of Lixnaw ; MacCarthy Riagh, MacMahony in the west ; Lord Barry Ruadh ; Patrick Condon ; Patrick de Courcy ; William Burke Fitzwilliam ; O'Driscoll Donn ; O'Driscoll Finn ; O'Donohoe of the Glens ; O'Sullivan Beare ; MacDonoghue ; O'Callaghan ; O'Connor Kerry ; MacBrien Ōgcuanach ; MacThomas of Geraldine ; Lord Roche Ruadh ; O'Driscoll Ruadh ; O'Sullivan More ; MacGillicuddy ; MacEvilly ; Okist ; O'Mulryan ; Mac Y Brien Arra.

The three knights, that is, the Knight of Kerry, the Knight of Walle [= Glynn], and the Knight of Clan Gibbon, which three knights (although called knights) are lords of very large territories, of many castles, and towns.

In Desmond there are three cities, and many safe ports, easy of entrance, that of the city of Waterford, of the city of Cork, of the city of Limerick, of Youghal, Dungarvan, Kinsale, Ballentimor, Cape Clear, Croughan, Dunbuyn, Dunchiaran, Ballinaskelligs, Dingle, Ventry, Smerwick, *alias* Ardchanhy, Byal, [? Tryal or Tralee], and Inis Scattery to enter Limerick.

Cap. 12.   Waterford is in Desmond, a city walled in the ancient fashion and the wealthiest in Ireland.   Its population may be about 1000 ; and all the citizens are Catholics with the exception of four or five young men, and all are merchants or artisans ;   they are given rather to business than to warfare, and have no munitions of war save perhaps four or five pieces of artillery, and these very small, and of little value because they have not men enough to withstand a thousand armed soldiers etc.

Cap. 13. Touching the city of Cork. The city of Cork is in Desmond, and is well walled and strong in the middle of a river called the Lee, and the entrance to the city is by wooden bridges made for the greater safety of the city, but there is a hill above and near the city from which one could not only batter down the houses of the city with artillery but also kill the people in the open square with arquebuses, the hill is so near the city.

The river is so broad and deep that I saw there three Flemish hulks of 1400 and 1600 [pipes] of corn taken from certain English pirates.

The city may contain about 800 inhabitants, all merchants, fishermen and artisans, and all Catholics, though they have a heretic for Bishop, who preaches ever the Lutheran heresy to the people but by God's grace to no purpose, though they are constrained to go to his sermons and other ceremonies that he performs.

The city has no defensive munitions save two pieces of artillery, and neither is a demicannon, nor yet have they powder or balls for them ; and it might be taken without resistance, for well I know the spirit and heart of the citizens who desire nought else in the world than the Catholic religion.

Cap. 14. Touching the City of Limerick. Limerick is stronger and more beautiful than all the other cities of Ireland, well walled with stout walls of hewn marble, and is an island city in the middle of that rapid Shannon river, and there is no entrance except by stone bridges, one of the two of which has 14 arches, and the other 8. . . . For the most part the houses are of square stone of black marble and built in the form of towers or fortresses. The suburb of the city is even better walled than the city, and its wall is 10 feet broad, and in some places 140 [? 14] feet high, and there are ten towers or bulwarks, most beautiful and strong around it, which allow no one to come near the wall.

The population of the city may number 800 or 900 souls ; all Catholics save seven or eight young men who embrace the Lutheran leprosy rather to please the Lady Elizabeth than for any other cause. There is a castle in the said city built by John son of King Henry II and for many years it is disused, and the houses and roof of said castle in ruins, and a part of the wall is already down, but with little expense it can be repaired, and it is in a most beautiful place above the city which it can keep in check, although the people of that city have been always loyal to the princes of England. . . .

Artillery. Limerick has none save two very small pieces, and

31 *

no other munitions of war save a few arquebuses, bows, and cross-bows. I may truly affirm that in all the city there is not half a pipe of powder for the artillery.

Besides these three cities of Desmond there are many other large towns well walled, as Dungarvan, Youghal, Kinsale, Kilmallock, Dingle, Cahir Dunihiesk, Askeaton, Tralee, the so-called Isle of the Earl. There are very many other castles of lords and gentlemen. . . .

Cap. 15. Touching Thomond the third part of Munster. The third part of Munster is called Thomond, and its lord up to our time is called O'Brien. . . . In times past he was always King of all Munster and often monarch of the whole island. Not wishing to allow such a renowned name to continue in that country, Henry VIII, about the year 1540, called over to England him who was then O'Brien, and made him lay aside the name and called him Earl of Thomond. To-day the lord of that country is Cornelius O'Brien, Earl of Thomond, and he has a few lords in his country who obey him, but there are other nobles of the same nation who make continual war on him, and they are : Baron Inchiquin, the two MacNamaras who are great lords, and the two MacMahons also great lords.

There are O'Loughlin, O'Grady, O'Connor Corcomroe, Lord Donald O'Brien, and many other noble knights and gentlemen of Spanish descent, who have not the title of lord although they have large territories, castles, and towns, but the majority of these do not obey the Earl, because he takes the side of the English and they do the opposite.

In Thomond there is no city, or even seaports, although the Earl holds many beautiful castles near the river Shannon, where ships may have safe anchor in any storm, but there is no commerce with those castles or towns.

In Thomond are many mines of metal and silver, and so indeed in the whole Island in abundance, and Earl Cornelius worked them with much profit, but the English do not allow him to work them any longer, and he was exiled from his country by Lady Elizabeth in the year 1571 but was afterwards received back into the Queen's favour through the intercession of the King of France, although he is none too secure in his dominion or safe from the wickedness and perfidy of Lady Elizabeth.

Cap. 16. Touching the Sees of Munster. In Munster there are an archbishopric and ten bishoprics ; the archbishopric of Cashel in Ormond, the bishoprics of Waterford, Lismore, Cloyne, Cork, Ross, Ardfert, Limerick, and Emly in Desmond, and Killaloe and Kilfenora in Thomond.

All these eleven bishoprics are very fine episcopal Sees and so likewise are all the other bishoprics of the island. All the Catholic bishops of Munster have been deprived of their Sees by the Lady Elizabeth, and some have been banished the realm, as Maurice, Archbishop of Cashel, and Maurice, Bishop of Emly, but Thomas Bishop of Ross, is a prisoner in England, true pastor as he of the sheep of Christ, steadfast and strong in the Catholic faith. Hugh [Lacy], Bishop of Limerick, is now old and is a fugitive in the island with some of his kinsfolk and friends. Munster is nearer to Spain than any other part of the realm, and how well affected towards the Spanish nation, I, for good reasons, forbear to write.

Cap. 17. Touching Connacht. Connacht has eight episcopal Sees, namely, the archbishopric of Tuam, the bishoprics of Kilmacduagh, Clonfert, Anachdune, Mayo, Killala, Achonry, and Elphin.

The bishops of those [8] Sees are for the most part Catholic, but some are schismatics, having received their Sees from the Lady Elizabeth, and all those schismatics desire the restoration of the Catholic Church. . . . All the inhabitants [of Galway] are Catholics, except fifteen young men who to please the Lady Elizabeth embrace that Lutheran novelty. Galway lacks munitions of war, artillery and powder alike etc.

In Connacht there is a very strong castle called Roscommon, built by John son of Henry II when he was viceroy to his father. It is built in a most beautiful plain near a great lake [Ree] which almost surrounds the castle, and being built on the territory of Lord O'Connor Don against his will he took it and it has been retained by his successors for 300 years until the present O'Connor in April 1567 under safe conduct from the Lord Deputy Henry Sydney, and suspecting no harm as he was then in Galway, yet notwithstanding the safe conduct (oh, wicked treachery) he was by the said Henry Sydney forced to surrender that castle to the English before the poor old man was set free, he having suffered many indignities with me in Dublin Castle for a year before he gave up the castle. The good old man told me that if he was in his castle again with provisions and some munitions he would defy all the artillery in the world to take the castle. But it is very difficult for the English to hold it for long as it is more than eighty miles from Dublin for which they reserve the few guns they have.

In Connacht there is a well-walled town called Athenry, and James Fitzmaurice with the sons of Earl Richard Burke [Clanricard] destroyed and burned it in the year 1572 with more than

300 villages, castles and towns which were loyal and showed favour to Lady Elizabeth.

James Fitzmaurice crossed the great river Shannon to help the sons of Earl Richard who carried on a most cruel war against Lady Elizabeth because of the said Earl whom Lady Elizabeth kept in prison in Dublin, and having gathered a great army, again crossed the Shannon and entered Meath where they did untold harm and ruined castles, towns, villages, and burned the town of Athlone, where the president of Connacht, Edward Fitton, was who defended the castle but he lacked the courage and the forces to come out against James.

The Castle of Athlone is of great strength. It is held by the English, but by way of munition it has but two very small pieces of artillery, as I am informed by a very reverend person. . . . There is an earl in Connacht named Richard de Burgh [Clanricard], a very Catholic man and valorous, who is, as it were, lord of all Connacht with many other lords under him and obedient to him, such as Lord John Burke, his relation, O'Conor Don, O'Conor Roe, O'Conor Sligo, O'Kelly, O'Dowda, O'Flaherty, O'Shaughnessy, O'Hart, O'Beirne, MacDermot, MacDonough, and MacCostello. There are many other lords, knights, nobles, and gentlemen of castles, towns, and large territories, who are of the same house of Burke, and have no title or name of lord. This house of de Burgh [Burke] is French, and were earls in the time of Henry II who being French brought these MacRichards (as they are called to-day in Ireland) and gave him the most beautiful places in the island, they are men of valour and great bravery, and are almost all ruddy, handsome, and great of stature, and ever ready for war . . . his Catholic Majesty should not let slip the opportunity of taking so good and beautiful a kingdom.

Cap. 18. One thing alone is wanting in that kingdom and that is a Christian King, zealous for the honour of God, who would stay always in the kingdom and compel lazy men to work and chastise the wicked and the bad and reward the good and virtuous.

This is the end of my description and I beg the Majesty of God that He give a King according to His own Heart and not according to our sins. Amen.

Cap. 19. This chapter is here for brevity's sake omitted. [The author therein set forth his reasons for not recording the names of the Catholics of that realm and the several proclivities and predilections of each lord, city and citizen, the reason being that the lords have exacted from him an oath of silence because of the hurt that might result to them, and of the many English spies that frequent the Catholic Court ; but he offers to come in person and discover the matter to his Catholic Majesty alone, upon condition, however, that his Majesty give him succour and help, and undertake his project and protection.]

Cap 20. [The writer mentions that the Pope, having revoked the original grant of Ireland to Henry II, might authorise his Majesty to enter the realm with an armed force not so much to extend his temporal dominion as to extirpate the "Lutheran pest," and plant there the Catholic Faith.]

Again, the Irish lords do not yield willingly to or even obey the Viceroys, for in truth till now the viceroys of that kingdom, and indeed of every other place, as may be seen in the India of Portugal, and elsewhere, do nothing else than strip and take the goods of the kingdom, and at the end of four or five years they depart with full sacks, and then new gifts and presents are necessary for the new viceroys and presidents, so that they have spoiled the kingdom of its goods, thus the inhabitants of the kingdom of Ireland desire to have a king in the kingdom who will defend them and to whom they may yield obedience, and above all wish for their king Lord Don John, having heard of his good fame and fortune, and his zeal for the honour of God.

Besides this, it appears to me that if Don John were created King of Ireland it would be a great scourge and terror to the heretics of England, for there is a prophecy among them that the ruin of England must begin in Ireland, and it runs thus in English : " He that will England win, let him in Ireland begin," which means that he who wishes to take England must begin in Ireland.

Now this creation and coronation of Don John in the kingdom of Ireland will do great harm to the Flemish heretics because the victuals and munitions that Lady Elizabeth sends daily for the assistance of the heretics in Flanders she must keep in her kingdom for fear of being assailed by one army or other of Don John, and by the Irish who will willingly spoil England. The Lords of Ireland, and also many Englishmen are firmly persuaded that Don John [1] has already received the royal crown of the realm of

---

[1] The achievements and fame of the victor of Lepanto, Don John of Austria, half-brother to King Philip of Spain, and one of the foremost military leaders of the period, had been attracting the attention of the Vatican. Despite the difficulties that stood in the way of a Spanish rupture with Elizabeth, the Pope began to look to the young hero for a solution of the problem. He gradually came to entertain the notion that there was something to be said in favour of the proposal put forward by the Irish negotiators to the effect that all would be well if Don John could be crowned King of Ireland. His Holiness went a step further, and suggested to Spain that Don John should become King, not only of Ireland, but of England, which could be effected by ousting Elizabeth and marrying the imprisoned Queen of Scots. A proposal to that effect was

Ireland from the Supreme Pontiff, and they anticipate with the utmost delight the time when they shall welcome and embrace him as their King.

Cap. 21. Things necessary for the Taking of Ireland. It is necessary to have these two knights, that is, James Fitzmaurice and Thomas Stucley, as two captains who are brave men with their hands, zealous for the honour of God, known and beloved by the lords of the kingdom, and well versed, successful, and expert in warfare.

All the lords of the kingdom respect, love, and with reverential fear stand in awe of James, and this was evident in his last war with Lady Elizabeth, her presidents and captains, in which war, although the lords stood by the presidents and Viceroy in person, they sent away all their soldiers and men to help James.

It is necessary to have these two gentlemen to conciliate the others of the kingdom to come to terms of peace and concord and true obedience to his Catholic Majesty, and if necessary to make raids against the disobedient and the rebels, for they know well the routes and roads and the fortified places of that whole kingdom, and know well the intentions and inclinations of every one, together with their forces, potentialities and possibilities.

Given the Supreme Pontiff's commission and authority for the subjugation of that realm, I say that it might be accomplished with but little force. Howbeit his Catholic Majesty would be ill advised to send too small an army, lest the English should send a great army to oppose him. Don James [Fitz] Maurice told me that with his own men, and two thousand Spanish auxiliaries, he would have cleared all the heretic English out of the realm of Ireland. Sir Thomas Stucley, as I understand, said that with 4000 Spanish soldiers he would have subjugated all the realm. Ay, and I aver, that this is true alike of the one as of the other. But nevertheless I would not advise the despatch to that realm of fewer than 12,000 men, I mean 8000 soldiers and 4000 craftsmen, such as tillers of the soil, masons, carpenters, tailors, shoemakers, and other persons to make armour, and also citizens and merchants to settle in the cities and episcopal Sees, which, indeed, are most beautiful places and lack only inhabitants. Without such people, soldiers cannot keep going, nor live in the country, still less conquer the realm.

accordingly laid before King Philip early in January, 1574, which was supported by Dr. Sander, the ablest of the English refugees then in Spain. Letters from the Spanish Ambassador in London also assured the King that not only was the Queen of Scots willing to entertain the proposal, but that she could count on the assent of the English Catholics.

[Having requested that the Captain General of the army should be a duke or a great prince, and one zealous for the honour of God, he continues :] Above all he should have a care that women and girls be not dishonoured or corrupted by the soldiers, an offence most detestable in the sight of God and men, and also that which the people of the country most dread on the part of the Spaniards, as it is obtruded frequently on their view by the English when the talk turns on Spaniards or Italians. . . .

In speaking of sending 12,000 men into that realm I do not think I have said amiss, for as many Irish might be sent out of the realm to serve his Catholic Majesty in Flanders or elsewhere ; and they would gladly go, for they do but ask war and pay. Would to God that 12,000 of them might be taken out of the realm every year, that they with their barbarous habits might be totally eradicated and extirpated from the realm, for, indeed, it will be no easy matter to chasten them and keep them from their larcenies and other evil practices.

[Of Munster the writer says that it] is ruined by the operations of the English and Sir James [Fitz]Maurice during the last four or five years, and of the inhabitants some are dead and others have quitted the country, so that the land has not been tilled all that time. . . .

Since writing the foregoing I have learned that Gerald FitzGerald, Earl of Desmond, has escaped from prison, and betaken him to his country, where he keeps many soldiers ever in the field to prevent the English from entering his country, and constrains all the English that have been in his castles and fortresses in the service of the Lady Elizabeth to depart, and that he has done them no harm whatever. Richard de Burgh, Earl of Connacht, has done the like, and has a great army in the field ; and the two earls have joined their forces to make war upon the English. Princes O'Neill and O'Donnell have united in aid of the Earl of Desmond and the Earl of Connacht, so that now is the time to aid them, if his Majesty without prejudice to his honour in regard of the truce [1] would ever do anything in that country . . . and so I end, commending with all my heart myself and my son Maurice [2] and all the affairs of Ireland to your illustrious Lordship.

24 March, 1574, Lisbon [Letter in Italian].

[1] Commercial treaty with Elizabeth.

[2] The memorial was presented on behalf of James Fitzmaurice ; hence the allusion to his son Maurice.

This important description taken in conjunction with the previous account of Ireland by Father Wolf requires examination, especially in regard to the orthodoxy of the Irish Catholic bishops. Other letters of his must also be taken into account. In all he made five reports.

1. About 29 June, 1561, he sent to Cardinal Morone, Protector of Ireland, his first report containing an account of the Munster bishops. Unfortunately this document cannot be traced. It is referred to in his letter of 12 October, 1561, to the same.

2. On the same day (29 June) he wrote to the General of the Jesuits. He says nothing about the bishops, but gives a woeful account of the state of the clergy in general.

3. On 13 October, 1561, he wrote again to Cardinal Morone. The points that concern us now are that he states that Bishops Bodkin of Tuam and Burke of Clonfert " have given their vows [*voti*] to the Queen as I have already written of the others of Munster." He does not say how many others in Munster. The only ones of whom it could be said were Skiddy of Cork and Walsh [1] of Waterford. Wolf recommends three good and zealous priests for the vacant dioceses of ·Elphin, Achonry, and Raphoe in the persons of Andrew O'Crean, Eugene O'Hart, and Donald McGonigail. Later he recommended O'Herlihy for Ross. The four nominees were appointed to these Sees in 1561-62.

4. Father Wolf's Account of Ireland of 1573 (?) is based on a letter of 13 October, 1568, written evidently while in prison in Dublin Castle. In that letter he says that all the bishops except a few recognised the Queen as head of the Church, but only three opposed themselves courageously in defence of the faith. The three are Walsh of Meath, Creagh of Armagh, and Leverous of Kildare. [2] It is necessary to mention that Wolf had meanwhile recommended another good and zealous priest, Maurice MacBrien, for the diocese of

[1] Walsh, who had taken the Oath of Supremacy under Edward VI, was pardoned in the reign of Mary and was joined with Dowdall of Armagh and Walsh of Meath in depriving married bishops of their Sees. But Lynch says that Walsh of Waterford himself had taken a concubine instead of a wife.

[2] Redmond O'Gallagher's name was afterwards inserted as the fourth. Wolf might have included O'Herlihy whom he said was " steadfast and strong in the Catholic faith."

Emly, who was appointed, 24 January, 1567. Taking the five bishops recommended by Wolf himself, three of whom had assisted at the Council of Trent, it seems extraordinary that he should have had such a bad report to make of them within a few years. A few years afterwards some of them were actually exiled and on the Continent as negotiators in Rome and Spain for James Fitzmaurice seeking for help for faith and fatherland. How then are Fr. Wolf's words to be explained, for clearly they need explanation ?

It is necessary to understand what he means by the words : " acknowledge the Queen of England as Supreme Head of the Church." The bishops involved include some of the Marian Bishops and twelve others who were appointed by the Pope between the years 1560 and 1571. A clue to the solution of the problem is found in a treaty between Deputy Sydney and Calvagh O'Donnell, Chief of Tirconnaill, about the year 1566, in which O'Donnell agrees that " Her Majesty shall have the donation of all bishops and other ecclesiastical persons in Connalia " [1] (i.e. Tirconnaill). This treaty was witnessed by " Donald Magonnell, Bishop of Raphoe," who was appointed to the See by the Pope in 1562. To understand this situation certain distinctions must be borne in mind :—

(*a*) Oath of allegiance to the Queen as Head of the Church. Northern bishops, including Magonnell (McGonigail), took this oath in presence of Sydney and their chiefs. This meant that they recognised an heretical Queen as Head of a Church, but that is no more than Catholics to-day recognise in the English Sovereign. No doubt, in the sixteenth century it was a new departure, and, clearly, horrified Father Wolf.

(*b*) Holding Temporalities from an heretical Queen. This also was a new departure. Elizabeth, as Temporal Ruler, having unjustly-acquired Church lands in her hands, and the fact being recognised by the local chiefs, might bestow them on a Catholic bishop. This, likewise, in the circumstances, might be tolerated. In fact, 23 September, 1585, a composition was made between O'Hart, Catholic Bishop of Achonry, and Perrott as to Church lands. In all this there was recognition of a fact, not of a right.

[1] *C.P.C.R.*, *Eliz.*, i., pp 495-6.

(c) Induction of Bishops into their spiritual prelacies by the Queen. This need not imply more than that the Queen should recognise the Catholic bishops formally as bishops of their Sees, or at least as bishops over the Catholics in them. Here there is no exercise of any truly spiritual authority invested in the Queen. In the case of the Northern bishops Sydney recognised or approved those papally-appointed bishops as true bishops of their Sees, and thus he, as the Queen's representative, formally inducted them into their Sees. There was here no question of a veto as to their papal appointment ; it was a purely formal recognition. This likewise might be tolerated.

(d) Jurisdiction from the Pope. So far there has been not the slightest question about taking the Oath of Supremacy. It was never put up to the Northern Bishops who agreed to take the Oath of Allegiance to the Queen as the Head of her own Church, to take Temporalities from her hands, and to be formally approved by her as Catholic Bishops of their own Sees. A new feature is introduced into the subject on the occasion of Sydney's visit to Munster. The Munster Catholic bishops whom he met had also agreed to these three points, but they refused to take the Oath of Supremacy and to recognise the absolute authority of the Queen. They stuck, he says, at *salvo suo ordine*, namely, they insisted that their spiritual jurisdiction must necessarily come from the Pope. After a friendly theological discussion, and seeing he could not convert them, he parted with them in an equally friendly manner.

Wolf's wrath against the Irish bishops was then in reference to the three first points. No one knew better than he did that they took no Oath of Supremacy ; Bishop McGonigail and O'Donnell were great friends of his, and it was through an O'Donnell that he came to terms with Sydney. But not being a great theologian, and being rather impulsive, he was pleased to call those bishops, all except five, " hirelings." No doubt such an unprecedented situation was calculated to upset the equanimity of one who was burning to oppose might and main the recognition of an heretical Sovereign in anything that concerned Church affairs. Moreover, as the chiefs, by their selfish policy, prevented national combination, so the bishops, with the exception of five, pursuing a similar policy, made no combined national stand though the existence of Catholicism was at stake in the whole of Ireland.

Other reasons Father Wolf had for calling the bishops " hirelings and dumb dogs." It is clear that the bishops were not true pastors of their flocks. Discipline among clergy and people seemed to concern them little, as they themselves, in many cases, at all events, of which we have proof, did not show the good example. The neglect of preaching was universal and notorious. Dr. Sander said that " scarcely ever was there a sermon." [1] And James Fitzmaurice calls the bishops " blind pastors," and sees the " sheep in want of a pastor." The reason of this is not far to seek. Scarcely two dozen of the priests of Ireland at the time had any College education. There were no theological schools at home. Outside the friars who had some kind of theological training, there were few who had the necessary qualifications. No doubt, at the time, in Ireland, an ignorant priest was better than no priest,[2] and a supply was thus kept up, rough and ready though it was. It served its purpose, at all events, in keeping the Catholic Faith alive in Ireland. However this may be, the situation that presented itself to Father Wolf, who was in touch with the great continental schools, and who failed to induce the Irish bishops to erect schools in their dioceses, drew from him that severe castigation of those bishops from his prison cell in Dublin Castle in 1568.

5. The fifth report, dated 1574, is called Wolf's Description of Ireland, and appears to have been drawn up at the instance of James Fitzmaurice. Although the main account is the work of Father Wolf the document concludes in the name of Fitzmaurice.

Wolf, in his introduction to this report, states that although he, like his townsmen of Limerick, was brought up in due regard for the allegiance to Her Majesty, yet on account of the papal deposition of the Queen he was now free to speak out his mind freely. What is of importance in this 1574 report is that he has a different story to tell of the bishops.

---

[1] *Arch. Hib.*, vii. 248. *Ib. Ign.*, p. 21.

[2] Had Great Britain acted on this principle the leakage among Catholics, particularly in Wales, might not have been so notorious.

He says nothing about the northern bishops for the simple reason that they were carrying on in the way already indicated, lords and bishops being true to Rome. As to those of Connacht he admits that the majority was Catholic but that there were some schismatics who, however, he adds, would like to see the Church restored. Leinster was occupied by heretical bishops, some of whom he had reason to know were Catholics at heart but who were more concerned with keeping their Sees. But Wolf's summing up of the situation in Munster is quite interesting. All the Catholic bishops of Munster, he says, have been deprived of their Sees by Elizabeth, and some were exiled, such as Maurice MacBrien of Emly and Maurice MacGibbon of Cashel, and Thomas O'Herlihy of Ross was captive in England, " a true shepherd and strong in the Catholic faith." Hugh Lacy of Limerick was " now old and a fugitive among friends in the island."

As the 1574 report was rather a public political one for the information of Philip of Spain, Father Wolf omits his grievances against the Irish bishops for their recognition of an heretical Queen. On the other hand, the 1568 report was a personal one to Redmond O'Gallagher, Bishop of Killala, who was then in Lisbon and on his way to Rome, having been threatened with murder and driven from his See by his Catholic diocesans. No doubt it was intended to reach the hands of the Vatican authorities, and, amended in some minor details, and presented to Cardinal Morone, Protector of Ireland, it gave them the episcopal situation that had horrified himself.

CORRESPONDENCE BETWEEN THE HOLY SEE AND SPAIN RELATIVE TO IRELAND.

It is important to give here a synopsis of the correspondence carried on between the Holy See and Spain as to the advisability of immediate help to Ireland. On 22 April the Papal Secretary, Cardinal of Como, wrote to the Nuncio in Spain :—[1]

The Catholics of Ireland, by what we understand, are in great peril of losing the few bits of land that still belong to them ; you will therefore in his Holiness' name do your office with his Majesty,

[1] C.S.P., Rome, 1572-78, no. 306.

that some soldiers be sent them from Flanders by the Comendador Major that they may be able to defend and maintain themselves, and not fall into the hands of the heretics.

The Nuncio replied in May : [1] " in the matter of the aid for the Irish, he [Secretary Perez] says that his Majesty will consider all that can be done to that end." In a postscript (23 May) he says—

his Majesty told me it would not be long before there arrived here a Military man that had gone to Ireland to get information as to those matters, from whom much light will be had as to what is feasible, and that meanwhile thought will be given to the means to be adopted to help them, the whole question being whether it be well that his Majesty should now discover himself as the open enemy of the pretended Queen of England with little hope of success in the main matter, seeing that to declare open war against her would, perchance, but serve to warn her to prepare for the sequel,[2] and if he should go to war with her, he ought to do so in such a manner as to clear all scores.

On 17 July the Nuncio in France wrote to the Cardinal of Como :—[3]

So far as I can I shall not fail to aid the Irish Bishop of Meath [Walsh] to commend him to these prelates that they may help him to some benefice, which, you may conceive, they are not as a rule much inclined to do.

Having received no help in France, the Irish Bishop repaired to Spain where his necessitous condition induced the Cardinal of Como, 24 September, to write to the Nuncio in Spain :—[4]

His Holiness is apprised of what you write as to the necessities of the Bishop of Meath. Two years ago he received a letter from the said bishop, then in Flanders, and caused 100 crowns to be

---

[1] *C.S.P.*, *Rome*, 1572-78, no. 311.

[2] A news letter from Vienna, 3 August, 1574, states : " It is understood that the Queen of England, having armed many ships to oppose and harass the Catholic fleet that is to come from Biscay, now causes them to be disarmed " (*ib.*, no. 337). The Fleet of Spain was on its way to Flanders (23 July) for the recovery of Zealand (*ib.*, no. 329). It reached England on 17 August (*ib.*, no. 349). In a news letter of 24 August it is stated that the Queen had granted the passport for the Spanish fleet (*ib.*, no. 345).

[3] *Ib.*, no. 328.   [4] *Ib.*, no. 351.

given to him, and now he bids you give him other 100 crowns, from the *Collettoria* fund, for his maintenance until it is known what his Majesty will do for him. And if his Majesty shall provide him with a maintenance, then will be no need to do more ; but otherwise you will apprise us here ; for in that case the Pope will assign him an ordinary provision to meet his needs. Meanwhile you will exhort him to have patience, and to believe that his Holiness bears him good will.

In a letter of 10 October, 1574, to the Cardinal of Como, the Nuncio in Spain writes :—[1]

It seems that there is intelligence here from an Irish Catholic, resident in Portugal, that the Queen of England's Governor in Ireland had taken by stratagem one of the chief Catholic gentlemen who had risen in favour of the Queen of Scotland. And he writes that if succour, particularly munitions, be not sent, there is great danger of the Catholic party being completely crushed. So, by what I understand, they are discussing here how they may afford them aid by some secret method so as not at present to incense that lady, because the affairs of Flanders are not in such a condition as to allow hope of a greater enterprise against the said Queen.

In a letter of 20 October the Nuncio wrote to the Cardinal :—[2]

I have done my office afresh that some aid be given by some indirect way, as it cannot now be afforded openly, to those poor Irish Catholics, that they succumb not altogether. And some hope is afforded me that it will be given.

On 25 October the Nuncio wrote to the Cardinal :—[3]

There is no doubt that, as you write, these two princes, Spain and France, will, by reason of the mutual jealousy of their States, and for other reasons, hardly agree to make common cause in that enterprise (i.e. restoration of the Catholic religion in England).

In another letter, 14 November, the Nuncio wrote to the same :—[4]

I shall commend to his Majesty the Catholics of Ireland pursuant to the order that you give me and the contents of the memorial that you have sent me as to this matter.

---

[1] *C.S.P., Rome,* 1572-78, no. 355. [2] *Ib.*, no. 356.
[3] *Ib.*, no. 358. [4] *Ib.*, no. 363.

On the 27 November the Nuncio wrote to the Cardinal :—[1]

I spoke to the King of the affairs of Ireland : and he marvels at the advices furnished by the Bishop of Emly [MacBrien] which you have sent me with the letter of the 15 October, there being no advice of the sort here. I know not what hope I may entertain of help in this quarter, and that for many reasons. However, I am not debarred from the subject by his Majesty, who spoke to me thus : " You know well, Mgr., the course things have taken in those parts " ; by which he meant the untoward circumstances of Flanders and the Biscay fleet, which have precluded further progress.

The Nuncio in Spain wrote, 20 December, 1574, to the Cardinal of Como :—[2]

There has come hither from Ireland, Father David [Wolf] the Jesuit, who is of that country, to crave his Majesty's aid for James [Fitzmaurice FitzGerald] of the Earls of Desmond, a Catholic, and a valiant gentleman, who has taken arms against the heretics, and has sent one of his sons, a boy of twelve years, by way of hostage, who, however, remains in Portugal. This father [David] has told me of his business, and what has passed between him and the Catholic King, and as he got no speedy answer, he was about to depart hence for Rome. I exhorted him to wait, and have a little more patience, considering how busy his Majesty is ; nor has his Majesty been very slow to acquaint him with his decision, which is to send him back with some aid in money, that being the most secret mode of giving aid ; and the matter has passed through no hands but his Majesty's own and the Bishop of Cordova's whereby the money will be delivered to him with the utmost secrecy, which will afford some aid, and keep that gentleman true to his purpose. The son will not come here, as it is not a time to excite that lady's [Elizabeth's] suspicions. I fully believe that his Holiness is in great straits for money by reason of the great expenditure to which he is put in divers parts, but, if he could make some loving demonstration by ever so little aid to this gentleman, who with such zeal and ardour defends the cause of the Catholic religion and the Apostolic See, of which they profess themselves sons and likewise vassals, I consider that it would be of great service to the cause, and 2000 or 3000 crowns with those that the King will give would, I believe, suffice to keep things going until better times. I have kept my own counsel as

[1] *C.S.P., Rome*, 1572-78, no. 367.　　　[2] *Ib.*, no. 370.

to this matter, that it may be quite open to his Holiness to do as he please ; and if he should decide to give something, payment may be made here from the funds of the *Collettoria ;* and no time will be lost, for I believe Father David cannot depart so soon ; and should he do so, I have means to remit the money securely to him by way of Portugal ; and assuredly this alms in aid of the Catholic religion and these good Catholics will be a very fine thing.

In order to keep the foreign situation fresh in mind it will be useful to recapitulate what has been already stated.

Philip II was of the opinion that an expedition against England should be undertaken in common by the two Catholic powers, France and Spain. To assure this object the Pope endeavoured to establish an entente between the two rulers recommending marriage between the Duke of Anjou and a daughter of Philip. The project fell through as France demanded either Naples or Milan as a dowry for the King's daughter. Besides, Philip had no other idea in his mind in regard to the expedition than that of dethroning Elizabeth and making Mary Stuart Queen—at least so the Nuncio of Spain thought, 19 February, 1573.[1] He considered the Conquest of England impossible, as the English Catholics would lend no aid to a foreign conqueror. Spain was annoyed because France, in the event of Elizabeth's fall, wished the Duke of Anjou to marry Mary Stuart, and to make him King of England. Hence the jealousy that developed between the two Powers and the impossibility of an understanding. In April, 1572, an alliance was concluded between France and England.[2]

In 1573, to the disconcerting of many Catholics, a treaty was made between Spain and her greatest enemy, Elizabeth. To the remonstrances of the Nuncio, Philip replied that the treaty was merely a commercial one for two years. But still a commercial treaty meant the exclusion of any inimical attack on England. Gregory XIII and the Nuncio in Spain, however, did not lose sight of that nation. They suggested that Philip should utilise his friendly relations with the English Queen to try to convert her. Elizabeth knew so well how to keep every one in the dark in regard to her own

---

[1] Carini, 84 *seq.*   [2] Kretzschmar, 45.

religious persuasions that the attempt seemed not impossible, although the Nuncio was rather sceptical about it.[1]

Meanwhile the English fugitives in the Netherlands saw with dismay the increasing hesitancy of Spain. They now turned to the Pope to obtain a letter of recommendation for their countryman, the theologian Nicholas Sander. They sent the latter to Philip II with the papal brief and with several letters from English nobles as a kind of permanent representative. The remonstrances of Sander made some impression on the King of Spain, but the latter emphasised the risk of the expedition for which, in case of failure, the English Catholics would have to pay dearly. He pointed out likewise the many difficulties of the expedition, and especially the money difficulty, notwithstanding the assertions of the Nuncio. The latter, therefore, begged the Pope for the salvation of so many souls, to renew the subsidy granted by Pius V.[2] But, again, nothing was done.

Spanish King's Envoy to Ireland Reports on the State of the Country.

Fr. Wolf's report must have been laid before the King of Spain and must have made an impression on him, for he began at once to manifest a keener interest in Ireland. This is evident from the Nuncio's despatch (22 May, 1574) to the Cardinal Secretary in which it was stated that the King had sent a military expert to Ireland to make inquiries as to the conditions there. The Report, expected any day, would be bound to exercise a healthy influence on the King's mind. Meanwhile, the King was considering how best to help in the circumstances, and was of the opinion that open help would do more harm than good, and that it was better to strike unexpectedly and without warning.

The report,[3] drawn up by the King's envoy, Captain Diego Ortiz (24 June), tells how he had sailed from Spain, 26 April, had landed at Dungarvan, 3 May, and had visited

---

[1] Maffei, i. 85. Carini, 87.   [2] *Ib.*, 88.
[3] Royal Archives of Simancas. The original has marginal notes in the King's hand. See *Catholic Bulletin*, April, 1928, p. 418.

Waterford, Cork, and parts of the interior. His detailed description of these two cities and of their relations with the surrounding districts is decidedly interesting. Waterford, for instance, which was a walled town and fairly well supplied with artillery, was the richest town in Ireland, with the exception of Dublin. It had a good harbour capable of accommodating vessels of 400 tons, and did a brisk trade with Galicia, Andalusia, Biscay, and Portugal, to which it shipped fish, hides, salt-meat, wheat, and barley. There was constant traffic between the seaport towns and the surrounding country in articles of prime necessity, though it struck him as very strange that these did not include bread, which was little used by the people who lived mostly on meat. The land was very fertile and if properly cultivated would, he thought, produce all that is produced in Spain, except oranges and olives. The people took things easily, but indeed there was little encouragement for anyone to work, as raiding was not regarded as a great crime. The man who was most successful in looting his neighbour's property was held in high esteem. Outside the walled towns, which were governed with some regard to law and order, there was little of either to be met with. It was usual for each petty chief to live in a tower-shaped castle within which he maintained a number of bravos and idle men who lived on his neighbour's property.

The people, he found, were all Catholics ; but they were exposed to great disability in the exercise of their religion wherever the English had power. Thus, they were forbidden to have Mass in their old parish churches, and were constrained to assemble for that purpose in private houses. At Dungarvan, for instance, the Franciscans and Dominicans had to fly to the mountains or seek refuge in caves or cellars every time the English troops appeared on the scene ; but they returned the moment the way was clear, and went on with their work just as if nothing had happened in the interval. For this reason, particularly, they hated the English and longed for the coming of the Spaniards who would liberate them from their bondage and enable them to save their souls in peace. Everywhere he went he found the same desire to see the Spanish fleet sailing into one of the

Irish harbours ; and he, too, repeated the proverb that had been quoted by Father Wolf :

> He that England would win
> Let him with Ireland begin.

With these two remarkable reports the Nuncio, in the name of the Pope, impressed upon the King the necessity of the expedition if Ireland was to be saved.   In this he was supported by the Irish negotiators, Father Wolf, Archbishop MacGibbon, Bishop MacBrien of Emly, Bishop O'Gallagher of Killala, and Father Patrick O'Hely, then present in Spain. But although they dwelt on the absolute necessity of a speedy decision, yet precious time was being wasted by Philip's wavering.   The passing months wore out the patience of the Irish negotiators.

Father Wolf was so sick of the King's indecision that he made up his mind to repair to Rome, and was only prevented from doing so by the Nuncio towards the end of 1574.   This threat had some effect, for the King assigned a considerable subsidy for the Irish insurgents, which Father Wolf was to convey to Ireland.   The Nuncio, whilst recounting all this to Rome, was of opinion that if the Pope could spare a like sum for the same purpose it would be money well spent.

James Fitzmaurice, finding his position intolerable, and thinking, perhaps, that his presence on the Continent would be calculated to end the heart-breaking delay, quietly slipped out of Ireland in March, 1575.   He was accompanied by his wife, and the Seneschal of Imokilly, and a few weeks later was the guest of his old friend Captain de la Roche at St. Malo.

PART IV.

"WINE FROM THE ROYAL POPE."

FITZMAURICE SAILS FOR FRANCE.

DURING his four years (1569 to 1573) of unsuccessful struggle against the English, Fitzmaurice had learnt the necessity of a sufficient supply of arms and munitions. Experience had shown him that the real strength of the English had lain in the possession of lines of fortress-like castles that dotted the land and from which they were able to dominate the surrounding districts. The Irish had no cannon to batter them down, and, when perchance they had taken them, they had no desire to inhabit them, be a target for the enemy's galling fire, and be unable to return it. What the Irish chiefs, then, really wanted was a small but select body of officers and tried soldiers to train the native troops and undertake the capture or defence of the fortified castles that had hitherto been the great obstacle in the way of success.

A sufficient supply of money was likewise a necessity to pay the hired troops, such as the Scots, the Sheehys and the McSwineys. The men belonging to the ruling families who were bound to give military service only gave it for a month or six weeks, after which they usually returned to their homes unless there were prospects of regular pay. Moreover, it was hopeless, on account of jealousy, to expect any unity of action among the chiefs under any one recognised leader. There was always the fear that a leader would aggrandise himself at the expense of his neighbours. A Celtic O'Neill would not serve under the leadership of a Geraldine, or vice versa, though they might indirectly aid each other. To Fitzmaurice it seemed that the only way out of the difficulty was to call in a foreign sovereign or obtain from the Pope a commission for one of the native chiefs. To this end were directed all his best efforts and those of his agents from the day he set sail for the Continent.

The following account of the reasons for Fitzmaurice's going to France is worthy of being fully quoted :—

The confession of Thomas Bracke (1 June, 1575), one of James Fitzmaurice's men, and now a prisoner, concerning the departure of James and his company from the land of Ireland.[1]

He, being examined and deposed, saith, that if he were at liberty out of imprisonment, he should have departed with James, and that before his imprisonment, viz., in February last, James told him that inasmuch as the Earl of Desmond's force was by his means much weakened, and namely, for that Ballymartir, Castlemaigne, the White Knight['s], and the Knight of the Valley's lands are come into her Highness's hands, he intended to go to France or Spain, to the end that by intercession of the French King or King of Spain, or of the Queen's Majesty's ambassadors residing in those countries, restitution should be made of those lands to the Earl and the other ancient inheritors, which if he could not obtain, yea (said he) that the Earl may the rather have his own will of Her Majesty in other things by his (James's) being beyond the seas threatening disturbance to this land.

Item. This examinate saith that the seneschal of Imokelly had with him about an hundred marks sterling of the Earl's money collected in Imokelly and knoweth not whether the Earl gave his consent to his going, but he is sure that the seneschal would not go without the assent of Sir John upon whom he most depended. He assureth himself also that neither the White Knight's son nor the Knight of the Valley's son, nor the son of Morice FitzGaret of the Shian would go with James but with the Earl's assent, and namely, the White Knight's son, betwixt whom and James there was great enmity.

Item. He saith that, when James was ready to depart, Sir John repaired unto him, and had secret conference with him.

A collection of certain circumstances preceding the departure of James. In the beginning of February last Mr. Agarde and his assistants then keeping sessions in the County of Waterford, James with 200 and odd Gallowglasses and a dozen horsemen came to Imokelly, and in Clon (John FitzEdmund's house) Sir John and the seneschal [of Imokelly] met him, and were in secret

[1] *S.P.I.*, *Eliz.*, lii. 2, 5.

conference, after which it was bruited that Sir John and the seneschal should presently go to England.

Item. In the beginning of March, John Barnewall, one of the Earl of Kildare's gentlemen, came in the justice Dowdall's company to Cork, and the next morrow after his coming thither, departed towards the Earl [of Desmond] to Kerry, and within 10 days after it was secretly bruited that James was ready to go into France, whereupon the Earl came unto the County of Limerick, and sent Barnewall to James which had conference with him, and lay a night with him in the Castle of the Glann.

Item. The Earl was at Conelo a fortnight before James's departure and after the bruit raised of his going and he might have stopped the passage betwixt the Castle of the Glann and the water, or might have assaulted and taken the Castle in that time, for it is well known to many that the Earl made a grant to James of Cariggephoite, [Carricfoyle] the Glann and Tarrybirde [Tarbert] [1] until he should bestow a better living upon him, and, as James complaineth, and the Earl did not deny, promise was not kept for Carrigephoyle, because it was not subject to the Earl's force but was ready to be performed for the other castles as places not able to stand at defiance with him.

Item. It is bruited by many, and namely by David Harolde and other the Mayor of Limerick's friends that the Earl had conference with James after the bruit of his departure and before his going a-shipboard.

An objection refelling their opinions which believe that the Earl's unkindness, or his own unsafety caused James to determine his going.

Where James pretended that the Earl's unkindness in not bestowing Kerighurhie or other competent living upon him according to his former grant, or his own unsafety, or the doubt to be sued for the spoils that he made in his rebellion were the causes of his going away. The Earl's bond of ten thousand pounds made unto James, with his oath made in presence of many to pass security unto him of such and such lands, as the Justice Dowdall, Mr. Miagh, and John Barnewall would deem, being by him chosen as indifferent to deal in, that cause might have contented him. And also in the other, James was proferred Her Majesty's pardon, which he never took out ; and the Earl promised to put to silence as many as [be]longed to him ; and he was assured from some of his friends that an assured mean[s] should be provided to force him [James] from those suits.

[1] *C.S.P.I., Eliz.*, p. 19, no. 80.

Moreover, if those should be the causes of his going, those other gentlemen which went with him, and in especial the seneschal which stood in neither of those extremities, and the Knight of the Valley's son, a lad of 17 years old, would not have gone with him, neither would James bring his wife and children unless he feared that his attempts should breed them trouble in this land, or that he meant to pledge them for such promises as he should make to either of those princes that would give him aid.

NICHOLAS WALSHE.

Having arrived safely at St. Malo, Lady Fitzmaurice wrote to tell the news of herself and her husband. The first letter was "To my loving and most assured friend John O'Duyn in Kilvarry by Waterford in Ireland."

With my hearty commendations to you my trusty friend letting you to understand that my husband and I with the rest of our company came in good health to France, thanks be to God, advertising you that my husband was in the King's court at the writing hereof and that I did not receive his news at the departing of this letter, but you shall understand at his going to the court he was honourably received by the Governor of Britain [Brittany] and by the Bishop of Nantes, you shall further understand, I remain in Saint Malos upon my own charges, with a couple of gentlemen of my husband's cousins and my maidens, where I am well bestowed and honestly used. I desire you to have me commended to my cousin my Lord Power and to my cousin Richard, and to all my cousins and friends requiring them to be good to my poor servants in my absence, as Richard Cahill, James Ronan, and others that to me doth belong, you shall send this other letter to my mother, bidding her always to send all news to me with this bearer, and so I take my leave with you from St. Malos in France, the xxviii April, 1575. Your assured friend.

KATREN BURKE.

The enclosed letter was directed "To my loving mother Margaret Power."

Loving mother, after my hearty commendations premised, letting you to understand that we came in good health at Easter Monday to St. Malos in France where we were honestly and gently received by the Captain of the said town and other honest and gentlemen of the town, and within a sevennight after we have landed my husband went towards the court with half a dozen men honestly appointed, leaving me and my cousin Harry Rian in St. Malos, waiting for his news speeding, upon our own charges and at the writing hereof we had not his news, but only at his going up to court he met with the Governor of Brittain by whom he was honourably received. I desire you loving mother not to be offended with me for my coming, to you unknown, and to send me your blessing, with all news, with this bearer John Grud, beseeching you to be good to all my servants in my absence praying my brother in like case to be so : have me commended to my father your bedfellow and to all my friends and so I take leave with you from St. Malos the xxviii of April, 1575 : your loving daughter,

KATREN BURKE.

These letters did not reach their destination, as they were captured by the Mayor of Waterford who sent them to the Lord Deputy who enclosed them in a letter to Burghley, 15 May, 1575.[1]

Lady Fitzmaurice was the daughter of William Burke of Muskerry and a relative of the Burkes of Castleconnell who attacked her husband after the landing at Smerwick (of which later). It would seem that it was her uncle Theobald who was responsible for his death and who was in turn killed by Fitzmaurice. Lady Fitzmaurice seems to have had some suspicion that her mother would be displeased with her for leaving Ireland with her husband on his expedition to France. The Burkes also would seem to have been opposed to it. This may explain their action against James after his landing at Smerwick in 1579.

James had two sons, Maurice and Gerald, and two daughters, three of whom he brought to France. It has been said that James had put away a former wife, but this can scarcely be maintained. At all events there is considerable confusion about the whole affair and no proof that it was our James Fitzmaurice who was involved in a marriage with a certain Ellen Lee or Barrett or as others say Honora Ryan.

IRISH NEGOTIATOR IN ROME.

The Councils of the Franciscans were beginning to produce some result. Towards the end of June, 1575, an interview

[1] *C.S.P.I.*, *Eliz.*, li. 27, i., ii. See *Unpublished Geraldine Documents H.A.A.Ir.*, 1868-69, pp. 523-6.

took place at the palace of the Spanish Embassy in Rome between Fr. Patrick O'Hely, a Franciscan (a native of Dromohair : afterwards Bishop of Mayo ; executed at Kilmallock, 1579) and Don Juan de Zuniga, the Spanish Ambassador. After Fr. O'Hely had exhibited his credentials from King Philip, Zuniga tells what passed between them.[1] Fr. O'Hely said that a certain person (i.e. Fitzmaurice) was making preparations for an Irish insurrection against Elizabeth. All that was required was authorisation from the Pope and men, money, and munitions of war from Spain. The Irish Catholics would not only flock to the standard of a leader recognised by the Pope but were ready to accept a Spanish sovereign in the person of the King's half-brother, Don John of Austria. He (Fr. O'Hely) had laid the whole plan before the King of Spain who had expressed a desire to see it carried out.

Zuniga, without compromising himself, advised Fr. O'Hely to secure the Pope's approbation before proceeding further, and to omit Don John's name in his conversations with the Pope, as his Holiness was not in favour of him as a sovereign for either England or Ireland. The Pope, in fact, seemed to think that Spain had quite enough territory already.

It took the slow moving King of Spain two months to reply to Zuniga's letter. He informed him that the letter he had given to Fr. O'Hely was merely a letter of introduction and was not to be taken as an authority to negotiate matters of such public importance. It is quite certain that Fr. O'Hely did not look upon the letter in that light. The King expressed surprise that the Pope should show any opposition to a Spanish ruler for Ireland. Indeed the Pope's attitude was contrary to the terms of a memorandum laid before him by the Papal Nuncio in the name of the Pope in the month of March. In that document the Pope had expressly stated that the expedition against Elizabeth would not only secure the salvation of many souls but also confer temporal advantages on Spain if the King lent his aid. Moreover, the ruler who should be chosen for Ireland should be one who would be pleasing to the King.

[1] *Royal Archives, Simancas*, 24 June, 1575. See *Catholic Bulletin*, February, 1928, pp. 190-6.

The King then went on to inform Zuniga that he was willing to provide pay for 2000 men for six months, to provide the means of transport to their destination provided the expedition should sail in the Pope's name and on the Pope's responsibility. Zuniga was to communicate this offer to the Pope and to impress on him the necessity of secrecy, and to discuss with him the time of the departure of the expedition, the place where the force was to be raised, the intended landing-place, the commander, and the amount of money expected of the King.

On 17 October Zuniga informed the King that in his conversations with the Pope and the Cardinal Secretary, he gathered that they were of opinion that the expedition should consist of 5000 men, should set out from the papal port of Civita Vecchia, and should make for a point on the English or Irish coast to be determined by two or three persons keenly interested in the project who were summoned to Rome where they were expected in a few weeks. (Though their names are not mentioned in Zuniga's letter, it is known that one was Dr. Allen, another Sir Francis Englefield, and the third James Fitzmaurice, then at St. Malo.)

As regards Don John of Austria, or any other candidate selected by the King, Zuniga informed the King that as far as the Pope was concerned, the Prince was free to marry Mary Queen of Scots, the rightful heir to the English Crown, the moment the expedition had effected a successful landing. The commander should be one who had the confidence of the King, and the cost of the expedition should be borne by His Majesty who was to reap all the temporal advantages.

Having thus supplied the King with an outline of his conversations, Zuniga went on to indicate his own private view of the situation. This was to the effect that while the whole project was still too vague, and would cost more than the 100,000 crowns suggested by the Cardinal Secretary, yet it would be well worth the cost if it did no more than make Elizabeth confine her attentions to her own kingdom and keep her from helping the rebels against Spain in Flanders and elsewhere. Zuniga thought the commander should be a Spaniard, or, if that was not feasible, some distinguished Italian military man in sympathy with Spain.

Of the three personages expected in Rome to discuss the expedition, Englefield arrived at the appointed time from Flanders, Dr. Allen did not arrive until the following February, also from Flanders, but James Fitzmaurice, to the surprise of everybody, failed to put in an appearance. He was then at St. Malo in France, eagerly awaiting news of the efforts to secure papal authority to lead a national movement against Elizabeth.

FITZMAURICE IN FRANCE.

Fitzmaurice had an influential friend in St. Malo in the person of Captain de la Roche. As far back as 1571 he was in touch with this adventurous buccaneer who had authority from the French sovereign to see what could be done for the Irish leader. Indeed it was reported that de la Roche informed one of Fitzmaurice's agents that the King would furnish 5000 French troops if Fitzmaurice could undertake to support them with 20,000 Irishmen. Though nothing came of this promise, Fitzmaurice kept up intercourse with de la Roche, and was now about to visit him.

Fitzmaurice was presented by de la Roche to the Governor of Brittany, and a little later (April) to the young King Henry III and the Queen Regent of France, and afterwards (June) returned to St. Malo. His cordial reception at the French Court caused consternation among the English spies, and the English Ambassador entered a protest, but received the diplomatic reply that nothing serious was intended. In July, however, he warned the English Government that naval preparations on a large scale were being made at St. Malo, and that it was suspected that these were intended for Ireland. After a visit of de la Roche to the Queen Regent, it was reported that those interested did not conceal their intention of making things unpleasant for England at the earliest possible moment.

Naturally Fitzmaurice was closely watched, his letters were intercepted, and his movements carefully noted by English spies, who wrote (15 July) an account of his doings to London. They told how he was then residing at St. Malo with his wife and a household of twenty-eight persons, and that de la Roche was then at Paris trying to interest the King in the Irish movement. His object was to obtain a dozen ships to harass the English along the Irish coast, or even to effect a landing in Ireland, in return for which Fitzmaurice had agreed to accept Henry as King of Ireland. The dozen ships with 12,000 men were, they reported, now almost a certainty, and Fitzmaurice was actually being supported on a handsome allowance from the King.

Again the English Ambassador entered a protest at the French Court when he received the assurance that all that Fitzmaurice had asked for was the intervention of the Court [1] for his restoration to the good graces of the English Queen. Not satisfied with this reply he enlisted the services of Captain Thomas (Bath), who had already betrayed the Archbishop of Cashel, to ascertain the real attitude of the Queen Regent towards the Irish negotiators. Captain Thomas, pretending to be one of them, obtained an audience with her, but she was on her guard and directed him for information to de la Roche or the Duke of Guise. Defeated in his ruse, the Ambassador lodged a formal complaint against de la Roche, as he believed that at least five of the ships then at St. Malo were to be placed at Fitzmaurice's disposal. At the same time he was glad to notice that the Queen Regent appeared desirous of standing well with Elizabeth.

Towards the middle of August, 1575, the English Ambassador reported that Fitzmaurice was still at St. Malo " in great countenance and favour," and that five ships had been fitted up for him there. A fortnight later he learns that one of Fitzmaurice's agents had been at the French · Court and had had an interview with the King. A few days afterwards he mentions that one of the five ships had sailed for Ireland with three of Fitzmaurice's principal men, and that the other four had put out to sea in the direction of the Irish coast, doubtless to see what mischief they could do. Again the Ambassador protested but received the royal assurance that Fitzmaurice's only object in remaining at St. Malo was to wait until he had received news of his pardon from the Queen of England.

[1] See *Appendix VI, G.*

Towards the end of 1575 Fitzmaurice was back again in Paris, and about to return to St. Malo with some money and a handsome pension from the French Court.

On 20 July, 1575, the French King had written a letter to Elizabeth in behalf of Fitzmaurice in which he reminded her that on a previous occasion she interceded with him in behalf of his subjects (Huguenots) who, on account of their rising against him, took refuge in her Kingdom. And now one of her subjects Lord James Desmond has made known to the King his desire to return to her grace and pardon for the injury that he and his kinsmen have done against her and her authority in Ireland. The King accordingly begged Elizabeth to grant James her pardon and to send Letters Patent for the same to the Lord Deputy and the Earl of Desmond that they may restore to James and his kinsmen their goods and lands now in the hands of others, and may peacefully enjoy them, according to what will be further told to Her Majesty by the French Ambassador, de la Mothe Fenelon.[1]

Some months afterwards Captain Thomas was arrested for revealing the doings of Fitzmaurice and de la Roche. In a beautiful, pathetic, and pious letter written by James Fitzmaurice at St. Malo, 31 January, 1576, to the General of the Jesuits, having spoken of the many benefits derived by Ireland from the Society, especially from Father Wolf, he stated that the object of all his endeavours was the glory of God and the salvation of souls redeemed by the Blood of Christ. He desired, if possible, that Father Good be sent to him for the comfort of himself and his family. In this letter he referred to one of the order who was already delivered to death for his sake. He evidently meant Edmund Daniel.[2]

In August, 1576, Fitzmaurice was back again in Paris, had seen the King, and had returned to St. Malo with plenty of money. It is now time to transfer our attention to

---

[1] *S.P.I.*, *Eliz.*, lii. 66, v., P.R.O., London.
[2] Hogan. *Iber Ignat.*, pp. 21-3. Father Hogan thought that Daniel was a priest and intended as spiritual adviser for Fitzmaurice. He was not aware of the real date of Daniel's death.

Rome whither some of the Irish negotiators had repaired in the hope that the new Pope Gregory XIII and his Secretary, the Cardinal of Como, were more likely to lend a willing ear.

The Parties Engaged in the Expedition against Elizabeth.

To understand the reference to the leadership of Fitzmaurice it is necessary to get a clear idea of the various parties interested in the organisation of a Spanish expedition against Queen Elizabeth, and of the various aims that animated them.[1]

Firstly, there were the Irish negotiators in Spain and Rome, such as Maurice MacBrien (Bishop of Emly), Father O'Hely, and possibly Father Wolf. They aimed at ridding Ireland of Elizabeth and her Government. They wanted only a small amount of help from Spain in the way of money, arms and munitions, with a small force of experienced soldiers to train Irish troops and man Irish strongholds. In return for this help they were willing to accept and acknowledge a Spanish sovereign such as Don John of Austria. From the Pope they expected little more than sympathy, along with a document authorising their expedition and nominating a leader to whose banner all Ireland would flock as to the banner of the Church.

The English negotiators, such as Dr. Sander, Dr. Allen, Sir Francis Englefield, Dr. Lewis, and Dr. Clenoge naturally looked at the matter in the light of the interests of their own country. Their aim was to get rid of Elizabeth and her Government, place the Queen of Scots, whom they regarded as the rightful heir to the Crown, on the throne, and restore the old Catholic aristocracy to power. They were interested in an Irish expedition, and in favour of it, to this extent that they knew Elizabeth's difficulties in Ireland were England's opportunity. The relations between these two parties of negotiators were friendly enough, but the divergent motives were bound to lead to misunderstanding.

France and its people were interested in Mary, Queen of Scots, one time Queen of France, and in general not very

---

[1] *Catholic Bulletin*, Oct., 1928, pp. 1062-8.

friendly to England. But much as they should like to help the imprisoned Queen they were sufficiently occupied with their own factions and civil war.

Philip of Spain, whilst keenly interested in the welfare of the Catholic Church, had two cards to play. He was not unfriendly to Elizabeth, at least at this time, but he feared and hated France. In every move he made for the welfare of the Church he was confronted with the hostility of France. So he stood with folded arms whilst Elizabeth waxed powerful and the Catholic Church steadily declined under her rule. Had France and Spain listened to the voice of the Pope and continued to save Catholicism, the subsequent history of the world might have been written differently. It was a turning-point of history, but neither nation had the genius of vision. Each, actuated by jealousy of the other, looked on at the Catholic Church being torn asunder under the rule of Elizabeth.

STUCLEY IN ROME.

Stucley was in Rome during those negotiations and was evidently championing the English interest in the expedition to be sent against Elizabeth. On the subject of Stucley's offices in the matter it is interesting to hear what the Nuncio at Venice has to say in his letter to the Cardinal Secretary, 12 February, 1575.[1] He states that he has had a letter from Stucley from Rome, but believes that Stucley's day is past. In the time of Pius V " one could still think of force in connection with English affairs." It is otherwise now, and instead of affronting the Queen one should use " suavity, lenity, and negotiation with her personally, seeing that she is now growing old, and might perchance some day become weary of the life that she leads. Meanwhile, however, there is nothing that vexes her more than to hear this gentleman's name, not that she is in the least afraid of him, but because she dislikes him, and is incensed to think that he goes about sowing in the mind of powerful princes seed of evil against her, and that by this alone he has gotten some credit and favour with them."

[1] *C.S.P.*, *Rome*, 1572-78, no 377.

On the 19 February the Cardinal replied from Rome : " Here he [Stucley] meets with attentions and courtesies because of what he has suffered for the Catholic religion, not for any hope that may at present be entertained of any improvement to be made of affairs there " [England].[1]

He was thought so highly of in Rome at this time that a Brief was issued, 13 June, 1575,[2] entitled : " Grace and Indulgences attached by Pope Gregory XIII to the Crucifixes blest by him at the instance of Sir Thomas Estocley " [Stucley]. As this is substantially similar to a Brief issued at the request of Bishop Tanner, it will suffice to give the latter document (later). There is one paragraph in the Stucley Brief, not contained in the Tanner Brief, which is deserving of mention. It is as follows : " 3. For taking part in any warfare against the foes of our holy faith, seven years and seven quarantines of indulgence, and in case of death therein, for such as have at least confessed and communicated at the beginning of the said conflict, and are in a state of contrition for their sins, and invoke the most holy name of Jesus with their mouths or with their hearts, a plenary indulgence and remission of all their sins."

Settling Details of the Expedition.

During the second half of the year 1575 the two projects for the dethronement of Elizabeth and the restoration of the Catholic religion in Great Britain and Ireland occupied the attention of Pope Gregory XIII and King Philip of Spain. One was submitted by the Irish and the other by the English negotiators in Rome. The Irish project, as we have seen, consisted in an appeal for money, arms, munitions, and a few thousand experienced officers and tried soldiers to train Irish troops, and a papal commission for a leader, preferably James Fitzmaurice. In return for this the Irish undertook to hand over the Irish Crown to Don John of Austria, or to any other prince whom the King of Spain should select. The English project, similar to the Irish, and probably suggested by it, was put forward by influential British residents in Rome, principally two

---

[1] *C.S.P., Rome*, 1572-78, no. 379. [2] *Ib.*, no. 409.

Welsh ecclesiastics, Drs. Owen Lewis and Maurice Clenoge, who were warmly supported by Stucley.

Briefly the British project amounted to this : the Pope should furnish 1500 troops, with means of transport and supplies for six months ; the negotiators were to raise another 1500 in Italy or Sicily ; the ships carrying this force were to set sail from one of the papal ports in October, effect a landing at some suitable English harbour, rouse all Catholic England to arms, liberate Mary Queen of Scots from her prison in England, place her on the throne, and marry her to Don John of Austria. Thus the Catholic religion was to be restored, and the man marked out for the undertaking was Thomas Stucley.

The two projects had much in common, but there were certain differences in aim and scope which must be borne in mind for a proper understanding of the course of subsequent events. Although the Pope was anxious to place Mary Queen of Scots on the English throne, he was not so keen on Don John as her husband. He probably had an Italian prince for that honour, and considered that Spain had already enough territory. That question, however, could be decided later, but the urgent one was as to the commander of the expedition. Philip of Spain, moody and wavering, agreed with the last idea, although he had to move with caution on account of France's hostility to him and the Netherland revolt. But he would dearly love an opportunity of wiping off the old score against England. At present, however, as his hands were tied, he would not like to break with Elizabeth. Hence, although he agreed with the Irish and English projects, and agreed to provide the means of transport for the troops and their pay for six months, he stipulated that the expeditionary force of some 2000 men would be organised in the papal and non-Spanish provinces of Italy, that his name should not be mentioned in connection with it, and that the whole responsibility should rest on the Pope, in whose name and under whose flag the expedition should set out. There were some points, however, on which he would welcome further information from the Pope, namely, as to the leader, the amount of money, and the ultimate settlement of the English Crown.

In the course of conferences between the Spanish Ambassador, the Pope, and the Cardinal Secretary, it transpired that the Pope had no longer any objection to Don John, or any other selection of the King of Spain, as the husband of Mary Queen of Scots, the future Queen of England. The expedition would sail from the papal port of Civita Vecchia and the expenses should not be less than 100,000 crowns, which were to be paid down by Spain before His Holiness could undertake the preparations. The leader should be an Italian, but one agreeable to the King. In all this the Pope and the Spanish Ambassador were agreed that certain material advantages might accrue to Rome and Spain. Indeed, so optimistic was the Pope of the result that he suggested the desirability of preparing a concordat in which the ancient rights of the Holy See in the kingdoms of England and Ireland should be defined and recognised.

FITZMAURICE'S ABSENCE FROM ROMAN CONFERENCE.

The reason of the non-appearance of Fitzmaurice at the Roman conference is given by him in a letter,[1] 7 March, 1575, addressed to

His moste assured and moste estimde gosope and frende Father David Wolf at Rome.

In pace et tranquilitate, spes nostra Jesus et Maria.

Right Reverend Father and lovinge gosope My harti commendacions to youe. Premysed you shall understande I have sent Morys Whyth of Yoghul with our leters to Digo Falerio to receve such money as youe left yn Digo Felerio his handes, which I yought was two hundert and fifti. But Digo said it was but a hundred and seven ducates ; and for to recev the same sum he went by the Bishop of Emly his advice to Madryd with other leters as youe know. But he profited nothing, and have spent the same money in his journey, and brought me nothinge of it. Youe shall understande that the child [Fitzmaurice's son, then a hostage in Spain] is not very well where he is, for he that was wont to gyve his charges [expenses] gyves him nothinge. Therefore I desire youe, lovinge gosope, to write to youre frende Digo and byd him to send me the child. Why I send my newe leter

---

[1] Vatican Archives. This is the only English letter of his in Rome, and is partly in cipher. See *Catholic Bulletin*, Feb., 1928, pp. 193-4.

for him, if so be that youe will not bestow him accordinge to the tenour of youre former leter sent to me from Rome. And lovinge gosope I besyche youe to sende me the foundacyon of all youre mater in all haste. And as for any newes out of Ireland there is none but that Syr Henry Sydney is Lord Deputy, lying all quiet, havinge nott two hundred soyders in all the country; and they suffer no newes to come to me.

Therfor, moste dier and lovinge gosope, I besiche youe to rectyfy me in haste of youre proseydings, for it gryves me nott to hyre from youe, and I tought indeed that there was as moche money in Digo Falerio his handes; for I bade Morys Whyth to leav a hundred ducates in Digo his handes for the childe his apparel and charge.

And I besyche youe lovinge gosope to speake to the Pope and tell him that I am ready to performe his Holiness his will and pleasure, and if he doe furder the mater himself, that I will spend motch, body, life, and goodes to overcome his enemies. And this youe shall declare to the Pope; and I stay here in Saynt Malos, accordinge youre request in former leters; and I luke dayly for youre news, for it gryves me nott to hyre of youe; but I besyche youe, gentil gosope, send my in all haste the syr-cumstance and end of youre bysynes. It is my bed-fellow and all the children and young men send their commendacions to youe; and I besyche youre dispatch; and if all things fayl, youe shall obtain of his Holines a comysyon in Ireland, in hope that God should send us tyme, and this according to youre own desire, as to say, agaynst her [Elizabeth], when tyme doth requyre, and this I commende youre guydinge to the omnipotent God, from Saint Malos, the 7 of March 1576 [*recte* 1575] youre gosope and frende for ever.

My harti commendations to Patrizio O'Hely whom I love well.

JAMES FYTZ MORYS *of Desmond de Geraldinis.*

From this letter it is clear that Fitzmaurice had remained at St. Malo on the instructions of Fr. Wolf from whom he expected to hear further. But it is also clear that the Cardinal Secretary understood from the Nuncio in Spain that the latter had invited Fitzmaurice to go to Rome to discuss the expedition with Dr. Allen and Englefield, and the Cardinal Secretary was eagerly awaiting him. The Nuncio himself was surprised to learn that Fitzmaurice had not gone to Rome, and had heard, moreover, from Fr. Wolf that Fitzmaurice had decided to return to Ireland.

From all this it seems that there was something on foot to the detriment of Fitzmaurice. It is still clearer from the Nuncio's despatch (18 January, 1576),[1] in which he states that representations had been made to him to the effect that it would be well to hear the views of Thomas Stucley.

The Nuncio states : " I am surprised that [Fitz]Maurice should have changed his mind as to going to Rome, and determined to return to Ireland, as we are informed here by a letter from Father David [Wolf], who, by what I understand, has already arrived there, and will report to us. Dr. Sander here [at Madrid] has received from one that is with Stugli [Stucley] [at Rome] a letter urging that he too go to Rome." The Nuncio is of opinion that some one acquainted with the Irish business should be at Madrid, and then adds : " I know that some Irishmen, and perchance among them Father David, are instant that all the charge of the forces in Ireland be given to [Fitz]Maurice. On the other hand I am advised that this would not be to the advantage of the enterprise, as there are gentlemen there [Ireland] of greater capacity who would take it amiss. To satisfy all, and avoid offending any of these people, it would be best that there should be, as I have written, an Italian commander-in-chief, and that use should be made of the people of the country according to their several conditions." It is not clear from what quarter the opposition to Fitzmaurice's leadership came.

UNREST IN THE NETHERLANDS.

Just when mutual agreement had been arrived at between Rome and Spain on the subject of the proposed expedition against Elizabeth, a train of events was set in motion in the Spanish dominions of the Netherlands (Holland and Belgium). These events were bound to effect the destinies of the expedition, and even of the world at large. The people of the Netherlands, grown restive under Spanish rule, had continued to set on foot movements for the redress of grievances. At this stage the Spanish Governor-General died (5 March, 1576). With unaccustomed celerity, Philip

[1] *C.S.P., Rome*, 1572-78, no. 475.

appointed Don John, then at Naples, to the position, and insisted on the absolute need for haste.

The position afforded Don John great scope not only for adventure but for satisfying his ambition to wear the English Crown. He had at hand 10,000 veteran Spaniards, a like number of Italian auxiliaries, and a large number of German mercenaries, all ready for adventure, and all within a few hours' sail of England. Instead of going direct to the Netherlands, he took the bold step of sailing for Spain which he reached early in September. Although Philip agreed with Don John as to the necessity of an invasion of England in the interests of religion and of Don John, there was an important difference in the viewpoints of these men. Philip's watchword was " Flanders first "—pacify Flanders and then conquer England. Don John's was " England first " —prevent Elizabeth from supporting the rebels in Flanders, and then pacify that country.

When fifteen of the sixteen provinces of the Netherlands, Catholic and Protestant standing side by side in a national policy, demanded, on 3 November at Luxemburg, the withdrawal of the Spanish troops, Don John acquiesced. But his anxiety to secure their departure by sea aroused the suspicion that they were required for some sinister design. Accordingly, and evidently with the cordial support of Elizabeth, the provinces opposed this move. Philip, however, now fell in with Don John's viewpoint, and sent him elaborate instructions as to the disposal of the returning troops. They were to be used for the invasion of England, and to land preferably at the nearest port to Mary Queen of Scots' prison. Don John was not to lead the expedition, but to await a successful landing. The Pope's name was not to be mentioned, but if success attended its efforts, His Holiness was to be asked to supply the necessary benediction and briefs. The King concluded by expressing his wish to see Don John married to Mary, a marriage that he understood was desired by herself.

Although Don John had been commanded by Philip to keep the whole business a profound secret, even from the Pope, yet the enthusiastic Governor-General actually wrote to His Holiness for encouragement and practical support.

But before the letter was despatched the provincial delegates demanded a categorical answer to three questions one of which was " whether he was ready to withdraw the troops, and by land." Don John assented to all their demands except that of the withdrawal of the troops by land. Even on this, after a fortnight's delay, he was constrained to yield. On 17 February, 1577, according to the Perpetual Edict, signed at Brussels, the troops were to depart, " freely, frankly, and without delay, by land, never to return except in case of foreign war."

Although Don John's appointment to Flanders took place in March, it was not until August that the news reached Rome. The presence of the victor of Lepanto with 10,000 men at his command, and within striking distance of England, could not fail to open up possibilities for the projected invasion. The Pope, meanwhile, became most anxious to hasten the organisation of the 5000 troops in the Papal States at Philip's expense. But, in September, the latter declared that all must depend on the course of events in Flanders. All that the Nuncio could get Philip to do was to take an interest in the selection of a commander. The Pope, however, gradually came round to the view that, after all, the projected expedition from the Papal States was a matter of minor importance if only the Spanish troops in Flanders could be used for a descent on England. In this he was probably guided by Don John, who, in spite of Philip's prohibition, had written to the Pope about the business. The Pope gladly sent letters of authorisation to Don John, and a subsidy of 50,000 crowns, and early in February, 1577, sent a Nuncio, Bishop Sega, to Flanders to see the venture carried to success. But, as we have seen, Don John was forced on the 17th of that month to relinquish all hope of the expedition.[1]

The English Enterprise.

Although in Rome and Spain only one expedition seemed to be contemplated, namely, what was vaguely called " The English Enterprise," both the Pope and his Nuncio in Madrid

[1] *Catholic Bulletin*, Nov., 1928, pp. 1172-6.

seemed also to have in mind a separate expedition for Ireland with a leader of its own. This is indicated in the Nuncio's despatch (18 January, 1576). "Some of the Irish," he wrote, "are pressing to have the charge of the forces in Ireland given to Fitzmaurice." But he took care to add that there was opposition to Fitzmaurice as his nomination might create feelings of jealousy and distrust in other chiefs of equal or superior standing in Ireland. Indeed, he was himself of the opinion that an Italian as commander-in-chief for Ireland would be best, as the Irish chiefs as a body would be more ready to rush to the papal standard in the hands of a stranger than in those of one of their own countrymen. This opposition to Fitzmaurice on the part of some of the Irish chiefs actually took place some three years later when he landed at Smerwick Harbour.

As to the English expedition, two of its negotiators, Dr. Allen and Sir F. Englefield, appeared in Rome in February for the suggested conference. Although Dr. Sander, the ablest and most influential of the English Catholics, was summoned from Madrid, King Philip refused his assent as his presence in Rome would arouse Elizabeth's suspicion that something was being plotted against her.

Fitzmaurice's failure to appear at the Roman conference was as irritating as unaccountable to all concerned. His letter, however, explains the failure. Not only had he received no invitation, but he remained where he was, at St. Malo in France, in obedience to instructions that Fr. Wolf, one of his most trusted agents in Rome, had conveyed to him by letter. There was bungling or duplicity somewhere, but his non-appearance at such an important conference at a turning-point in his country's history was of supreme moment. This seems one of the most unsolvable problems in Irish history. Stucley, it would seem, wanted the glory and the gain of what he expected would be a grand invasion of Ireland. With two English representatives present, and no Irish negotiator, naturally England loomed large, and Ireland was scarcely mentioned in the deliberations of the conference.

Briefly the result arrived at was this: an expeditionary force of 5000 troops was to be raised in the Papal States and in the non-Spanish provinces of Italy, and when all was ready it was to set sail from the papal port of Civita Vecchia, flying the papal flag and under the command of Don John of Austria, or an Italian commander. To avoid causing suspicion and preparation among the English, it was to be given out that the expedition was being organised for service against the Turks or some similar enterprise. The King of Spain was to supply the expenses, calculated at about 100,000 crowns. So much did Philip throw himself into the project that he put the Nuncio into direct communication with his Council, and arranged for the shipment to Rome of half the sum demanded of him for expenses, promising the balance as soon as it could be raised.

Once more, however, Philip was moody and wavering, and the Nuncio, in April, 1576, had to complain of his dilatory tactics, but cherished some hope that he might be able to induce him to fix the departure of the fleet for the beginning of September. In his "Wait and See" policy Philip was remarkably like Elizabeth, except in this that it always succeeded in her case, whereas in his it spelt disaster. However, it soon appeared that Philip preferred to defer the expedition until the following February. In Rome the Pope was glad enough to bear with the delay, since the promised crowns were not forthcoming, without which he firmly decided not to act. The Nuncio was careful to remind the Cardinal Secretary (29 March), as he had already several times reminded him, that before embarking on the English expedition it would be necessary that the Pope should deprive Elizabeth of the realm of Ireland " because the deprivation made by Pope Pius V comprises only the realm of England." [1]

By November, however, the Irish negotiators had made their voices heard at Rome, when there was renewed activity on the part of the Pope to induce the King of Spain to act. Two briefs were proposed : 1. To the Catholic King, apprising him that some Irishmen, and chief among them Brother Patrick (O'Hely) of the Order of Observants of St. Francis, created by the Pope Bishop of Mayo, have several times intimated to His Holiness that there is now an excellent

[1] *C.S.P.*, *Rome*, 1572-78, no. 499.

opportunity of wresting the island from the hands of the English, provided they receive the necessary aid, and of offering to surrender it to His Catholic Majesty, or whomsoever he shall approve ; and that, as the Pope, by reason of the remoteness of the kingdom, is unable to lend such aid as he could wish to so good a work, the said bishop had resolved to betake him to His Majesty, to lay the whole scheme before him, and crave his aid. Wherefore His Holiness exhorts and beseeches His Majesty not to miss such an opportunity, if such it be as it is affirmed, seeing that it is a question of restoring the holy Catholic faith and religion, and augmenting the strength and reputation of His Majesty, etc.

2. To Don John of Austria, notifying him of the matter aforesaid, and exhorting him to use his influence with His Catholic Majesty to promote the desire and good intention of these Irishmen for the reclamation of that realm to the Catholic Church and devotion to His Majesty, or in such other terms as may seem best.

On 10 November the Pope wrote to the King of Spain in similar terms as above, calling the Queen of England " an impious Jezebel." [1]

End of Essex's Expedition ; Elizabeth's Duplicity.

Whilst all these events were taking place on the Continent, no open rebellion occurred in Ireland during the first half of the year 1575, though the usual burning and spoiling went on. Desmond was remaining quiet, but the Earl of Kildare had agreed with FitzWilliams to secure the Pale by taking command of the south and west borders with soldiers in the Queen's pay. Kildare was suspected of being in communication with the O'Tooles and the O'Byrnes, and of hatching a plot to obtain the Government as his ancestors had it.[2] The old hereditary enemy of the Geraldines, John Alen, was the first accuser. The task of arresting Kildare was entrusted to Essex who had doubts about the policy. " You must," he stated, " take heed that you transfer not the greatness of some to make it trouble in some other, so

[1] *C.S.P.*, *Rome*, nos. 558, 561.   [2] *S.P.I.*, *Eliz.*, xlix. 57.

were the second error worse than the first." Having been
first confined in Dublin Castle, Kildare was transferred by
Sir E. Fitton to London and placed in seclusion under the
charge of Lord Keeper Bacon.[1]

It was now Essex's turn on the wheel of fortune, and he
drew a blank in his Ulster expedition. His scheme for the
occupation of Ireland did not find favour with FitzWilliams
who was never too friendly to the Earl's amateurish plans.
FitzWilliams was not prepared to carry on the Government
unless with sufficient forces. The Earl resigned the Government of Ulster, and wrote to the Queen : " Being now
altogether private, I do desire your Majesty's good licence
so to live in a corner of Ulster which I hire for my money." [2]
Tirlogh Luineach profiting by this dissension thanked
FitzWilliams for not invading his country, professed loyalty
to the Queen, and desired nothing so much as peace and
friendly intercourse with the English Pale. Elizabeth's
heart was touched by Essex's failure in her service, and
consoled him by sending him a private letter [3] in which she
stated " we have great cause to think you a rare treasure
of our realm and a principal ornament of our nobility ; we
wish daily unto God we had many such ; and are sorry that
in anything you should be discouraged." Essex, in his delight
with the letter, sought a reconciliation with FitzWilliams,
and confessed that " reformation was never thoroughly intended until now, as I think." [4] He thought he was now
on the high road to success. Once more he started for the
North and agreed to discuss terms with Tirlogh at Drogheda.
There he received a letter (22 May) from the Queen which
swept away all the castles he had built on the sand.[5] She
told him plainly that she never intended his expedition other-

---

[1] *S.P.I.*, *Eliz.*, 15, 16. *Fiants*, no. 2582. The tidings of Kildare's arrest
reached Rome, and in a news letter of 21 June, it is stated :—

" The Earl of Kildare, a powerful Catholic Irish nobleman, has been brought
a prisoner to England with his two sons and a cousin the Baron of Meluin
[*sic* Delvin].

" The Earl of Vormonde [Ormonde], an Irishman, for many a year the
favourite of the Pretended [Queen], is deemed to be already a Catholic and
reconciled to the Church and a friend of the Earl of Desmond, a Catholic and
most potent lord." (*C.S.P.*, *Rome*, 1572-78, no. 411.) The news about Ormond
was, of course, quite inaccurate.

[2] *S.P.I.*, *Eliz.*, l. 32.   [3] *Ib.*, 57.   [4] *Ib.*, li. 9.   [5] *Ib.*, 38, 39.

wise than as a temporary measure when there was danger of general revolt. She had now made up her mind that the Ulster plantation was not a paying proposition, and must be abandoned. Whilst submitting loyally to the royal will, Essex reproached the Privy Council for allowing him to spend his substance and his health " in an action which, as it now appears, was never intended to be performed." [1] But before relinquishing, according to the Queen's wish, he constructed a miserable fort on the Blackwater, and came to terms with Tirlogh, the principal of which were that Tirlogh should confine himself in general to Tyrone, and give up his claim to superiority over his neighbours. [2] The obvious intention was to destroy the power of the O'Neills by taking from them their claims over the northern chiefs, and thus make English government easy by creating divisions among the Irish. But many of the English officials thought that this patch-work peace would not be of permanent value, it would " make much work for the tinker." Some better form of reformation should be devised. [3]

Just when Essex was settling the terms for the humiliation of Tirlogh, Gregory XIII, evidently inspired by the Irish agents in Rome, sent a Brief to the Irish chief encouraging him in his loyalty to the Church. On 26 April, 1575, he wrote to Shane Oge O'Neill, Earl of Tyrone, commending his proved faith and charity in those troublous times, and exhorting him to remain steadfast therein. Similar Briefs were to be sent to Lord Tirconnel, Macullian [MacWilliam Burke], Lord of Lower Connacht, and Gerald, Earl of Gesmond [*sic* Desmond]. [4]

Sydney's Grand Tour.

FitzWilliams, sick in body and mind, was anxious to be relieved of the hated Irish Deputyship. Waterhouse advised the reappointment of Sydney whose Secretary he had been, but Sydney was reluctant, and Elizabeth undecided, and more than a year and a half slipped by without any

---

[1] *S.P I., Eliz.*, lii. 3, 4.   [2] *Ib.*, 32, 33, 34.   [3] *Ib.*, lv. 5, 6.
[4] *C.S.P., Rome*, 1572-78, no. 398

appointment. " But whenever any alteration [in the deputy-ship] shall happen," said Waterhouse (14 June, 1574),[1] " let all offices be given to soldiers of experience and to none others. I would the Queen would also so bestow her bishoprics, for here is scarce any sign of religion, nor no room for justice till the sword hath made a way for the law."

Thus even in 1574, fourteen years after the promulgation of Supremacy and Uniformity, there was scarcely any sign of a " reformed " Church. Unless the " reform " was backed by force, there was little hope that persuasion and preaching would convert the natives to it. The remedy, therefore, was the Bible in one hand and the sword in the other, and preferably both in the hands of the " reformed " bishop. At all events, that was the considered opinion of Waterhouse before Sydney's re-appointment, and he evidently believed that Sydney was the one man to see the scheme operative.[2]

Another feature of the suggested reformation under Sydney was a new system of taxation. After the barbarous massacre of the inhabitants of Rathlin island, to the number of 600, for which John Morris had secret orders from Essex, the latter had nothing but praise for all concerned and Elizabeth vouchsafed her unqualified thanks. Sorley Boy, though he lost his children (most of his gentlemen lost theirs as well as their wives), did not lose heart, and when Sydney came to Carrickfergus he found him in possession of the coast from Larne to the Bann. Sydney abandoned Rathlin as a useless and expensive defence, although Essex had thought that 100 men there would be worth 300 in any other place in the North. Moreover, Sydney thought that the Glynnes might be handed over to Sorley. Such was the result of Essex's great piece of strategy and slaughter. Sydney did not think that the slaughter of Sir Brian MacFelim and his family had done much for the civilisation of Eastern

---

[1] *S.P.I., Eliz.*, xlvi. 64.

[2] On his arrival in Ireland, 14 September, 1575, Sydney landed as near the city of Dublin as he could safely do on account of a great pestilence. " The city beside the castle only was in a manner depopulated so that the grass grew in the city at the doors of the churches. The Archbishop had litanies said against the plague on Sundays, Wednesdays, and Fridays throughout his province and had a fast proclaimed." (Loftus, *Annals*.)

Ulster, or that the system of private conquest carried on by Smith and Essex was any great improvement upon native usages.[1]

Sydney found the northern portion of Armagh all waste and the cathedral in ruins. The southern portion had been granted by the Queen to the brothers Chatterton who were totally unable to manage the country, and were rapidly losing all. He did not visit Tyrone, Tirconnaill, Monaghan or Fermanagh on this occasion, but MacMahon came to Armagh, begging to be relieved of the tyranny of O'Neill on condition of paying rent to the Queen, and O'Donnell and Maguire wrote to the same effect. Tirlogh Luineach came to Armagh without hesitation or condition, but Sydney would grant his petition excepting the authority that he claimed over his neighbours. Sydney, however, would agree that he should be made Earl of Clan O'Neill for life, seeing that "his age, wounded and imperfect body, his ill diet, and continual surfeit, he cannot be of long life." Magennis also, whose country of Iveagh had much improved, might also be granted a title, that of Baron. The Lord Deputy's plan was to make all look to the Crown, not excepting the great O'Neill.[2]

Sydney now started on another journey. He found Louth greatly impoverished by the cessing for the soldiers who constantly passed north and south. The towns of Dundalk and Ardee were miserable enough, but Drogheda was somewhat better. The one bright spot in the general failure of the English plantation in Ulster was Newry, with its well-built town and well-cultivated lands. It was the settlement of Marshal Sir Nicholas Bagenall, and was strong enough to defend the north border of the Pale. Meath was "Cursedly scorched on the outsides" by O'Connors and O'Molloys. O'Reilly, on the contrary, used the Pale well, and he himself was "the justest Irishman, and his the best ruled Irish country, by an Irishman, that is in all Ireland." There was hope that Lord Delvin might by his courage and discretion save Westmeath from anarchy and unruly Irish

---

[1] *S.P.I.*, *Eliz.*, lv. 58, 15 June, 1576.

[2] Bagwell, ii. 304-5. Sydney to Privy Council, 15 Nov., 1575. *S.P.I.*, *Eliz.*, liii. 65, 67.

neighbours. The O'Ferrals had consented to have Longford made a shire and had taken estates of inheritance but had not yet paid their quit-rents. Cattle-raiding went on as merrily as ever in what is now the present Co. Wicklow, and Feagh MacHugh O'Byrne had risen to great notoriety. The country was tolerably quiet, but the Kavanaghs had not yet paid the Queen's rent. The absence of Agard, then in England, was dangerous to the peace of the Pale. In Leix and Offaly the English tenants were decaying day by day, and the old native inhabitants growing great and increasing in numbers. Though both countries did not contribute a twentieth of their cost, yet are " now not to be given over in any wise." Rory Oge O'More " occupieth what he listeth and wasteth what he will." [1]

Kilkenny, " the sink and receptacle " of stolen goods, was not found to have profited much by the continuance of coyne and livery, which was done by order. Ormond, though he had no love for Sydney, entertained him handsomely, and was appointed Lieutenant of Kilkenny and Tipperary. On the word of Ormond, O'More came and in the Cathedral of Kilkenny solemnly promised amendment in the presence of Sydney. Ormond then escorted Sydney to Waterford, where the citizens having received a great check from Sydney for their former disobedience to him, feasted him with shows and rejoicings by land and water.[2] Sydney went next to Curraghmore where he stayed with Lord Power, and found the country " comparable with the best ordered county in the English Pale," a proof of the

---

[1] " At this time Rury Oge, the son of Rury, son of Connell O'More, and Conor, Mason of Cormac, son of Brian O'Conor, opposed the English with their woodkerns ; and they were joined by all that were living of the race of Rossa Failghe, and of Conall Cearnach. Shortly afterwards these people formed troops of many hundreds. They burned and desolated large portions of Leinster, Meath, and Fingal." (*A.F.M.*, *ad an.*, 1576.) On 8 March, 1576, O'Carroll, chief of Ely O'Carroll, made his submission to Elizabeth. His district was now made parcel of the King's County. As in similar indentures he agreed in behalf of the other chiefs and people of his clan to surrender his lands, etc., and to have them back on certain conditions. He was to hold the country called Ely O'Carroll by two knight's fees in chief, and to be wholly discharged from bonaght and all other cesses and impositions.

[2] Sydney to Privy Council, 15 Dec., 1575. *S.P.I.*, *Eliz.*, liv. 17, 18. (Sydney *Papers*.)

benefit of "suppressing of coyne and livery." [1] Lord
Power's neighbour, Sir James Fitzgerald, who had succeeded
his brother Sir Maurice but without the title of Viscount
Decies, ruled a district four times as large which had " more
idle vagabonds than good cattle." [2] The smaller country
gentlemen, as well as the citizens who held mortgages, were
anxious to live quietly and pay their taxes. Desmond
himself came to Sydney at Dungarvan, and " very humbly
offered any service that he was able to do to her Majesty."
The town was half ruined through the late rebellion of James
Fitzmaurice. The people of Youghal pleaded that they
had suffered too much by the rebellion to bear the cost of
a viceregal reception, and Sydney passed by Castle Martyr
to Barry's Court, and thence to Cork. In the course of
this progress (January to April, 1576) Sydney remarks,[3]
the Bishops of Cashel (Miler Magrath) and Cork (Mathew
Sheyne) and " the elect of Roscarbery " (Cornelius O'Brennon)
" Came to do me honour." At Cork " we got good and
honest juries " and " with their help twenty-four malefactors
were honourably condemned and hanged."

At Kilmallock " the best and principallest gentlemen of
those parts submitted to my taxation for bearing of soldiers.
Thither came three or four bishops of the provinces of Cashel
and Tuam (which bishops albeit they were Papists) submitted
themselves unto the Queen's Majesty, and unto us, her
Deputy, acknowledging that they held all their temporal
patrimony of the Queen's Majesty, and desired humbly that
they might (by her Highness) be inducted into their ecclesiastical prelacy. Here was some hold between the bishops and me,
too long here to be recited, for they stood still upon *Salvo
suo ordine*, etc. and I of the Queen's absolute authority." [4]

[1] A commission was issued to William, (Protestant) Bishop of Limerick, and
others, to inquire by what services and of whom every tenant and freeholder in
Munster holds, and where doubtful, to determine the amounts of their rents
and services. Recites that though prohibited by the laws, conny, lyvery,
cuddihie, foye, kinduff, bony begg, sorhin, srahe, and other Irish exactions
were commonly levied on the Queen's poor subjects ; that the Lord Deputy
had issued a proclamation against them at Cork on the 31st January, 1576 ;
but that by the long use of these extortions between some lords and their tenants
the tenures were not certainly known. 23 April, 1576. (*Fiants*, no. 2771.)

[2] Bagwell, ii. 310-13.   [3] Brady, *State Papers*, x.

[4] Carew, *Cal.*, 1575-88, p. 352. Sydney's relation of all his services in Ireland,
1 March, 1583. (*Ib.*, pp. 334-59.)

The meaning of this recognition of Elizabeth on the part of the Catholic bishops has been already stated. That they objected to taking the Oath of Supremacy is clear from Sydney's words that in the discussion they insisted on recognising their Orders as coming from the Pope whilst Sydney wished to get them to recognise the absolute authority of the Queen as Head of the Church. The point to be noticed is that they refused, "stood still," and Sydney without causing any trouble went on his way. It is probable that the bishops referred to here were O'Molony of Killaloe, James Fitzmaurice of Ardfert, Lacy of Limerick, and possibly O'Dea of Kilmacduagh.

Munster was then in good "towardness" to be reformed, "but it never needed more a discreet and active government there continually resident, for these people are, for the most part, all Papists, and that of the malicioust degree." Sydney entered Thomond on 27 February, attended by the "Earl of Thomond and a cloud of O'Briens besides." "I there," he says, "subdued a rebellious race of the sirname of the Earl, the O'Breens [O'Briens]. Their captains were called the Bishop's sons and indeed the bastards they were [of] the Bishop of Killaloe,[1] which bishop was son to an O'Breen, captain of Thomond. Of these wicked generation, some I killed, some I hanged by order of the law, but all I subdued."

Sydney lodged the first night in the dissolved Priory of Coyne [Quinn], and on the next rather "encamped" than lodged in the ruined See of Kimlakohah (Kilmacduagh) where, "I and my company had bad fare and worse harbour."

At Galway Sydney was "continually attended" by the Earls of Clanricard and Thomond, the Archbishop of Tuam (Mullaly) and the Bishops of Clonfert and Kilmacduagh He found there "plenty of burning, rape, murder and sacrilege, besides such spoil of goods and cattle, as in number might be counted infinite and in quantity immeasurable."[2] He hanged a good many malefactors, who were guilty of

---

[1] Evidently Terence O'Brien, the Marian bishop. The sons, Mahon and Donough, are mentioned as rebels and outlaws in 1569 and 1570. (*C.S.P.I., Eliz.*, xxix. 70 ; xxx., 56, iii.)

[2] Sydney to Privy Council, 27 Feb., 1576. *S.P.I., Eliz.*, lv. 19.

the unpardonable crime of recovering what had been forcibly taken from them.

" The Earl of Clanricard caused his two most bad and rebellious sons, Ulick and John, to come to me with humble submission. I committed them, and in the chief church of the town had a sermon preached of them and of their wickedness by a countryman of their own, called Linch, sometimes a friar at Greenwich, but a reformed man, a good divine and preacher in the three tongues, Irish, English, and Latin. The young men publicly in the church I rebuked very sharply, and they as humbly submitted, and again to prison I committed them."

Sydney knew Ireland too well to be sanguine about the success of his grand tour. He hoped, however, that the Munster lords (except perhaps two) would consent to support 100 English foot and 50 English horse free of charge to the Queen. This would be very pleasing to Elizabeth from a monetary as well as disciplinary point of view. But a cloud was gathering on the horizon. James Fitzmaurice had fled to France, with the seneschal of Imokilly (son of the Knight of Glin) and Edmund Fitzgibbon (eldest surviving son of the late White Knight). How long this artificial peace would last largely depended on the amount of support which Fitzmaurice would receive abroad. But Sydney had carried out the instructions to settle all internal disorders and to quell all remains of commotion. One of the most important duties of the loyal Munster lords in whose territories lay the southern havens was to guard them well, to watch for all foreign vessels, and to examine all native merchants unloading there, so that neither news, money, men, nor munitions should gain an entrance. All this was zealously carried out to the great hurt of the foreign emissaries.

His Account of the State of the Church.

At the end of the account of his grand tour or " progress," as he called it, Sydney discoursed on the Reformation of Ireland, under three heads : [1] Firstly, the Church ; secondly, a standing army ; thirdly, three English lawyers for Chief

---

[1] Brady, *State Papers*, no. xi.

Justice, and an Attorney-General.   He thus treats of the Church :—

The first head is the church now so spoiled (as well by the ruins of the Temples, as the dissipation and embezzling of Patrimony, and most of all for want of sufficient ministers) as so deformed and overthrown a church there is not, I am sure in any region where Christ is professed, and preposterous it seemeth to me to begin reformation of the politic part and neglect the religious.

In a letter to the Queen, 28 April, 1576,[1] Sydney delivered himself more fully on

the lamentable estate of the most noble and principal limb thereof [realm of Ireland] : the Church, I mean, as foul, deformed and as cruelly crushed as any other part thereof by your only gracious and religious order to be cured, or at least amended.   I would not have believed had I not for a great part viewed the same throughout the whole Realm, and was advertised of the particular estate of the Church in the bishopric of Meath (being the best inhabited country of all this Realm) [2] by the honest, zealous, and learned bishop of the same, Mr. Hugh Bradye, a godly Minister for the Gospel and a good servant to your Highness, who went from church to church himself and found that there are within his diocese 224 parish churches, of which number 105 are impropriated to sundry possessions now of your Highness—and all leased out for years or in fee farm to several Fermors, and great gain reaped out of them, above the rent which your Majesty receiveth.   No Parson or Vicar resident upon any of them, and a very simple or sorry curate, for the most part, appointed to serve therein.   Among which number [105] of curates [presumably Catholic], only eighteen were found able to speak English—the rest Irish priests or rather Irish rogues, having very little Latin, less learning and civility.   All these live upon the bare alterages, as they term them (which God knoweth are very small) and were wont to live upon the gain of masses, dirges,[3] shrivings [4] and such like trumpery, godly abolished by your Majesty.   Not one house standing for any of them to dwell in.   In many places the very walls of the churches down, very few chancels covered

---

[1] *Loc. cit.*

[2] Where English law prevailed, where English interests were cultivated, and where nearly all the prominent men were of English stock.

[3] Requiem Office.   [4] Probably the Last Sacraments.

windows and doors ruined or spoiled.   There are 52 other parish
churches more in the same diocese [Meath]—who have vicars
endowed upon them [appointed by the bishop]—better served
and maintained than the other, yet but badly.   There are 52
parish churches more residue of the first number of 224—which
pertain to divers particular Lords.   And these, though in better
estate than the rest, commonly are yet far from well.   If this
be the estate of the churches in the best peopled diocese, and
best governed country of this your Realm (as in troth it is), easy
it is for your Majesty to conjecture in what case, the rest is, where
little or no Reformation, either of Religion or Manners, hath
yet been planted and continued among them.

Yea ; so profane and heathenish are some parts of this your
country become, as it hath been preached publicly before me
that the sacrament of Baptism is not used among them, and
truly I believe it.   If I should write unto your Majesty what
spoil hath been and is of the archbishoprics, whereof there are
four, and of the bishoprics, whereof there are above thirty, partly
by the prelates themselves, partly by the Potentates, their noisome
neighbours, I should make too long a libel of this my letter.   But
your Majesty may believe it, that upon the face of the earth,
where Christ is professed, there is not a church in so miserable
a case.   The misery of which consisteth in these three particulars :—

1. The ruin of the very temples themselves : 2. The want of
good Ministers to serve in them, when they shall be re-edified :
3. Competent livings for the Ministers, being well chosen.

For the first—Let it like your most gracious Majesty to write
earnestly to me—and to whom else it may best please you—to
examine in whom the fault is that the churches are so ruinous.
If it be found in the country of Fermors, to compel them speedily
to go about the amendment of them.   If the fault, for the churches
of your Highness' inheritance, be not in the Fermors, nor they
bound to repair them (and the most ruined of them are such as
are of your possession) it may like you to grant warrant that some
portion may yearly—of the revenues of every personage—be
bestowed on the church of the same.

For the second and third, which is that good ministers might
be found to occupy the places, and they made able to live in
them.   In choice of which ministers for the remote places where
the English tongue is not understood, it is most necessary that
such be chosen as can speak Irish.   For which, search would
be made, first and speedily, in your own Universities.   And
any found there, well affected in Religion and well conditioned
beside, they would be sent hither animated by your Majesty.

Yea, though it were somewhat to your Highness' charge, and on peril of my life, you shall find it returned with gain before three years be expired. If there be no such there, or not enough (for I wish ten or twelve, at the least) to be sent, who might be placed in offices of dignity in the Church in remote places of this Realm, then do I wish—but this most humbly, under your Highness' correction—that you would write unto the Regent of Scotland, where, as I learn, there are many of the reformed Church that are of this language, that he would prefer to your Highness so many as shall seem good to you to demand of honest, zealous and learned men, and that could speak this language. And though for a while your Majesty were at some charge, it were well bestowed, for in short time their own preferments would be able to suffice them, and in the meantime thousands would be gained to Christ, that now are lost, or left at the worst.

And for the ministry of the churches of the English Pale, of your own inheritance, be contented, most virtuous Queen, that some convenient portion for a Minister may be allowed to him out of the Fermors' rents. It will not be much loss to you in your revenue, but gain otherwise inestimable. And yet the decay of your rent (will be) but for a while, for the years once expired of the leases already granted, there is no doubt but that to be granted to the Church will be recovered with increase.

I wish and most humbly beseech your Majesty that there may be three or four grave, learned and venerable personages of the Clergy there, be sent hither, who in short space, being here, would sensibly perceive the enormities of this overthrown Church and easily prescribe orders for the repair and upholding of the same, which I hope would confirm, and I find no difficulty but that your officer here might execute the same. Cause the bishops of that your Realm [England] to undertake this Apostleship, and that upon their own charges. They be rich enough, and if either they be thankful to your Majesty for your immense bounty done to them, or zealous to increase the Christian flock, they will not refuse this honourable and religious travail. I will undertake their guiding and guarding honourably and safely from place to place. The great desire that I have to have such from thence is for that I hope to find them not only grave in judgment but void of affection.

I most humbly beseech your Majesty accept these my rude letters as figures of a zealous mind for reformation of this your church and country, wherein methinketh I work waywardly when the latter is preferred before the former. . . .

Lord Burghley and the Privy Council in England, in their reply (10 July, 1576) to Sydney's letter on the State of the Irish Church, state that it is more meet that he should first consult the Irish Council upon these matters and give his opinion under proper headings, and also send over to England some persons well instructed and acquainted with the government of Ireland, such as Sir Luke Dillon and Mr. Agard— representatives of the two nations.[1]

Sydney had, therefore, to content himself for the present with pointing out that the misery of the situation consisted in the way in which the parish churches had been allowed to fall into ruin ; the scarcity of a fit and worthy Protestant clergy ; and the absence of a suitable provision for those who might offer their services, or be called over from England or Scotland to help on the work.

In similar terms Essex laments the state of the Church :—

" When he had come to Dublin he considered how ruinous the state was, yet nothing in comparison of the ecclesiastical state, and that it was too far out of order by the wars, the temples ruined, and the parish churches almost without curates or pastors for to read service or to preach the Gospel to the people ; " that several were born and then yet living who were never christened, the patrimony of the Church was wasted and the lands embezzled.[2]

Connacht again Disturbed.

Sydney scarcely believed that his mere visit to Connacht would keep the sons of Clanricard in dutiful obedience. Their father's word weighed little with them, and the presence of the few English officers left by Fitton was not calculated to overawe them. Moreover, the delay in appointing a President for the province gave them fresh courage in their exasperating habits of taking it into their own hands. The loyal town of Athenry, with its few houses lately restored and its stone, with royal arms built into the town wall, was a particular object of their wrath. A complaint was immediately forwarded by Gregory Botken (probably a

---

[1] Brady, *State Papers*, no. xiii.   [2] Loftus, *Annals*, 1576.

relative of the former Archbishop of Tuam) to the Council on behalf of the townsmen that a black rent had been levied on them by the Earl and his sons, and that their goods had been seized. The usual remedy was adopted in the nature of a commission (23 May, 1575), in this case consisting, among others, of Adam, Archbishop of Dublin, William Lealy, Archbishop of Tuam, and Roland, Bishop of Clonfert, to inquire into the statements, and cause justice to be done.[1] To add to the discontent of Ulick and John, a grant had been made to Oliver Burke to be chief of his race and seneschal of his nation (10 May).[2]

When Sydney was about to set out for Waterford to instal Sir William Drury [3] as President of Munster, he heard that Clanricard's sons—the MacIarlas as they were called —had burnt Athenry and held the open country with 2000 Scots. Sydney received the news on Tuesday, and by Friday was at Athlone. Meanwhile the young Burkes had fled to the mountains, and Clanricard came to the parish church of Athlone where on his knees he implored Sydney's pardon for himself and them. Sydney, receiving him sternly, made no promises, but expressed the hope that he would soon have " the bastard brats " dead or alive in his hands. In his letter to the Privy Council, 9 July, 1576,[4] he declared his anxiety that the Queen should now seize Clanricard's lands [5]

---

[1] *Fiants*, no. 2575.   [2] *Ib.*, nos. 2764, 2791.

[3] Drury was a native of Suffolk, who had served England well by sea and land at home and abroad. He had been Governor of Berwick and had superintended the siege of Edinburgh Castle.

[4] Brady, *State Papers*, no. xii.

[5] Some of Clanricard's lands were taken from him two years later as appears by the following grants :—

" Lease under the queen's letter, 8 July, 1578, to the mayor, bailiffs, and commonalty of Galway of the monasteries of S. Francis, S. Augustin, and S. Dominic, by Galway, and their possessions." (*Fiants*, no. 3465.)

" Lease under the queen's letter, 8 July, 1578, to the warden and vicars of her majesty's college of Galway, of the site of the priory of Anaghedowne *alias* Anaghcoyne, Co. Galway, land in Anaghedowne, Lisdugh in O'Flaheries [O'Flaherty] country, Knockan in same, Shankill, Muckkerys, and Owre, ditto, a ruinous chapel and land in the island of Aryne (Arran), chief rent out of Laspydell, all in said Co., the rectory of Ballencourt in Clanricard with a moiety of the tithes and alterages extending to Ballencourt, Ballenecloye Garrane, Ballenemanaghe and Cregane, the other moiety belongeth to bishop of Tome [Tuam] and the vicar that serveth the cure, the rectories of Kilcomen in O'Flaheries country, Karygne, and Lisduh, all in said Co. (the tithes and alterages due to

and extirpate him and his from Connacht. Unless the
Queen consents to decided steps, Sydney, for his part, will
only " trundle Sisyphus' stone," and she will " lose honour
and treasure." Whilst professing himself glad to gain an
Earl and his castles, he admitted the power of the sons to
annoy, and pressed for a President.

Having secured Galway and Athlone, Sydney went to
Limerick where he settled Drury in his presidency. Though
the country was free from any great disturbance, Drury
had to show his martial spirit by hanging forty-two persons
at the Cork assizes, and pressing one to death. A MacSwiney
galloglass who displayed a banner whilst driving cattle
from under the walls of Cork was treated to the hanging
rope for his stupid error. In derision the same banner was
borne before the unfortunate culprit to the place of execution.
Drury was obsessed with the idea of making an example
of local ringleaders of the people, and had another forty or
so hanged at the Limerick assizes. " The head of the salmon
is worth a many small fishes." [1] He boasted that in all
he " put 80 idle persons to execution."

A few months later (3 June, 1577), in a commission for
military affairs in Connacht the Archbishops of Dublin,
Armagh, and Tuam are named along with the Bishop of
Meath, and the name of Roland, Bishop of Clonfert, is substituted for that of the Earl of Essex.[2]

Death had cut short Essex's career. Having received
a grant of the barony of Ferney in Monaghan, the peninsula
called Island Magee in Antrim, and of the office of Earl
Marshal in Ireland for life, he returned to Dublin, July 23,
1576, but was carried off by dysentery within three weeks.

NEW PLAN OF REFORMATION.

The Government of Ireland from 1 April, 1573, to
30 September, 1575, cost the Queen more than £130,000 in

---

the vicars or curates excepted). To hold for 50 years. Rent £6 11s. 4d. In
consideration of their continuing together and maintaining a Godly learned
preacher amongst them from time to time at their own charges." (*Fiants*,
no. 3466.)

[1] Drury to Walsingham, 24 Nov., 1576. *S.P.I.*, *Eliz.*, lvi. 51.
[2] *Fiants*, no. 3048.

ready money sent from England, besides the Irish revenue and debts incurred but not discharged. It was a principal part of Sydney's instructions to devise some means of checking this outflow. In some notes (February, 1575) in the *State Papers*,[1] Burghley sets out his scheme :—

> The best is to seek the reformation of Ireland as well by force as by order of justice, that the English may obey laws and the Irishry be kept from rebellion, and so by success of time the Irish to be brought to be governed either by the law of England, or by some constitutions to be compounded partly of their own customs and Brehon laws that are agreeable to reason and partly by the English laws. . . . That means be used with the bishops, noblemen, and freeholders, to contribute in victuals a convenient portion both for the soldiers and for the justices, whereby they may the better live of their fees and wages. That every nobleman, and other captain of the counties, which hath of late years used to take coyne and livery for maintenance of men of war, may be treated withal to reduce his number to a certainty and his cess also of victuals ; so as the people chargeable herewith may know what to yield, and the rest to retain to their own profit. . . .
>
> This manner of cess for victuals to wage men of war to continue, until the power of the Irishry may be diminished, and they brought to live in a more peaceable manner.
>
> That as many of these captains of countries as may be induced, will take their countries of her Majesty by her grant to them . . . and to pay to her Majesty some yearly rent in victual for a knowledge . . . their heirs be brought up in English sort. . . . For such as will not take their countries by grant of Queen's Majesty, there should be sought means to procure and entice some others of the same countries, being of some sept of strength, to take the same countries by grant.

The tranquillity induced by the appointments of Drury to Munster and Malby to Connacht was but short-lived, as the new system of taxation suggested by Burghley and adopted by Sydney became the occasion of new discontent.[2] For many years it had been customary to impose a cess or taxation upon the English districts, of a certain proportion of the provisions, horse meat and man's meat, required for the royal garrisons, and for the maintenance of the governor's household.

---

[1] Brady, *State Papers*, no. viii.   [2] Leland, ii. 261 *seq.*

The principal inhabitants of each district used to attend the deputy and council to settle the contribution and the rates to be paid. Sydney now conceived the plan of converting this occasional subsidy into a regular and permanent revenue, by substituting a composition in place of the assessment, and by exacting it from all the subjects. He communicated it to the English Court, and was encouraged to pursue it.

He first began by a proclamation to dissolve those liberties that had ever claimed an exemption from the ancient charge of purveyance, and then proceeded to the general imposition of the new tax, by the mere authority of Council, and by virtue of the Queen's prerogative. On all sides there was violent discontent with this bold act. The numbers and position of these opponents would secure them a respectful hearing. Sydney was aware of this and remained indifferent. But other parts of the realm joined in the opposition to the edict. This encouraged the inhabitants of the Pale to assemble and to entrust their cause to three agents who were to lay their complaints before the Queen and Council. The letters they bore were signed by Lords Baltinglass, Delvin, Howth, Trimbleston, Bellew, Nangle, by members of the Plunket and Nungent families, and other distinguished inhabitants of the counties of Meath and Dublin, in the names of all the subjects of the English Pale. The matter was referred to the Council, and Lords Kildare, Ormond, Gormanstown, and Dunsany, attendants at the Court, supported it, confining themselves to the heavy burden of the imposition and cautiously avoiding the question of the Queen's prerogative. Though the Queen pretended to listen with sympathy to the grievances, she was more readily led by her Ministers to maintain her prerogative. The unfortunate agents were confined to the Fleet, and the signatories were threatened with imprisonment if they continued to impugn the royal prerogative. This did not deter the Lords of the Pale from pressing the legality of their plea, but their reward was close confinement in Dublin Castle, and their agents were sent to the Tower. Submission to the royal prerogative ultimately brought relief to some of the offenders, but a composition was necessary to move the more obstinate.

A period of seven years was fixed for the provisions.[1] As in all such cases the odium of the dispute fell upon the governor, who pleaded to be recalled.

By the composition the counties of Dublin, Meath, Westmeath, Louth, Kildare, Carlow, Wexford, and Kilkenny acknowledged themselves bound to victual as many of the 1000 soldiers and officers as the Lord Deputy should appoint, and to pay 1d. a day for the soldiers present or not, deducting that sum in the case of those men whom they were required to victual fully. They were to furnish 9000 pecks of oats to the horsemen at 10d. sterling, and to sell fresh provisions to the Lord Deputy at reasonable prices for ready money. The Queen consented to repair the old-stores thoroughly, but not to build new ones, and no other charge was to be made against her. To this arrangement the cess-payers submitted with a tolerable grace, but officials complained that the Queen had made a very bad bargain.[2]

EDMUND TANNER ANXIOUS TO RETURN TO IRELAND.

Edmund Tanner, a native of the diocese of Dublin, and afterwards Bishop of Cork, wrote in his *Book of Novices:* " Edmund Tanner, Irishman, 39 years of age, entered the Society [of Jesus], 14 June, 1565." [3] For many years, said Brodin, he made singular progress in virtue in the Society, yet constrained by ill health, and with the goodwill of the Fathers, he left the Society.[4] Having left the Jesuit house in Rome, he wrote from that city a letter, 26 October, 1571, to John, Cardinal Moroni, Protector of Ireland, in which he tells him of his story and his desire.

An exile for religion's sake, he says,[5] for more than twelve years from his native country Ireland, he has lived, the sport of fortune, among Spaniards, Italians, and Germans, during which time Ireland has been sorely afflicted by the tyranny of the heretics, and other calamities. Now, if he might be of any service to his country, he would fain return thither, but submits himself to the direction of the Protector.

---

[1] Privy Council, 31 March, 1579. *S.P.I., Eliz.*, lxvi. 16, 17, 18.
[2] Bagwell, ii. 333. [3] Hogan, *Iber. Ignat.*, p. 16.
[4] *Ib.*, p. 25. [5] *C.S.P., Rome*, 1558-71, no. 845.

He is assured by grave men that during all this time not a hundred Irishmen in all Ireland have been infected with heresy, though not a few, for fear of penalties and confiscation of goods, attended the profane rites of the heretics, and the demoralisation of the people is such that a pious Catholic is hardly to be found : and no wonder since the clergy are the most depraved of all. Moreover, there is so little instruction to be had in the Christian faith that few can so much as repeat the Lord's Prayer, the articles of the faith, or the commandments, and still fewer understand them. Sermons are so uncommon that there are many that have never so much as heard one ; the sacraments are so rarely administered, so much more rarely understood, that the ignorant people know not whether they were appointed by God or by men. In fine, so gross is the ignorance of the people that there are many who, passing all their lives in the grossest sin, have grown so accustomed thereto that they dare to say that it is just as lawful for them to live by theft or rapine as for him that worthily serves the altar to live by the altar. And nevertheless, so well inclined are they, or rather prompted by the Holy Spirit, to a good life, that it needs but the admonition or reproof of a good man and forthwith they are dissolved in tears, lamenting that they knew not that such things were sins, or contrary to the commandments of God.

Touched by a sense of their woeful plight, Tanner says, he has come from Louvain to Rome to offer his services, such as they are, in that deserted field. As to his qualifications, he refers the Cardinal Protector to the Bishop of St. Asaph and the Bishop of Emily, both of whom are in Rome, and the " London " Prior of the Knights of Malta who will soon be there ; and for fuller information to Father Natalis, Vicar of the Institute of the Society of Jesus, and Father Everard, of the same Society, Alan Cope, Cardinal Hosius' theologian, and the Warden of the English hospital at Rome, and other priests of the said hospital.

That the state of religion among Catholics was as bad as Tanner's informants told him we have sufficient evidence in corroboration. James Fitzmaurice had likewise written to Miler Magrath about the necessity of preachers to keep religion and morals alive among them. No doubt the horrible state of war and unrest which prevailed in Munster, to which province Tanner probably referred, had deprived the people of any systematic ministration or education. But that the clergy that still remained were " the most depraved of all " is not what one would have expected, but which we are inclined to believe is in the main true. Fleeing from place to place, insecure not only as to abode but as to the means of sustenance through the misery and poverty created by the rebellions and wars, it is only to be expected that many of them may have become lax in their religious life. It is difficult, however, to realise that the Catholic fathers and mothers were so forgetful of their duties to their young as to neglect to instruct them in the Lord's Prayer, the Creed, and the Commandments. In general, it may be said that exaggeration was not uncommon at the time among all classes and creeds. The picture painted by Tanner might influence the Holy Father and, at the time, it could do no harm to anyone. Yet, in the main, one must accept Tanner's statement.

Tanner's letter did not produce the result he expected, to return to his own country, for, 5 January, 1573,[1] that is, more than a year after his previous letter, he again wrote to Cardinal Moroni from Milan stating that though provided by Cardinal (St. Charles) Borromeo with a Canonry at Milan, he yearned to return to Ireland to minister to the souls that there " sit in darkness and the shadow of death," and encouraged by Moroni's previous kindness, he craved his good offices to that end. Doubtless, he was a sincere lover of Ireland and most anxious to minister to the people, whether as priest or perhaps bishop, undeterred by poverty or persecution.

TANNER, BISHOP OF CORK, LANDS IN IRELAND.

The next reference to Tanner is in a Brief of 5 November, 1574, nearly two years after his letter to Cardinal Moroni, during most of which time he, presumably, remained as Canon at Milan enjoying the friendship of the saintly Charles

[1] C.S.P., Rome, 1572-78, no. 139.

Borromeo. The Brief [1] describes him as " Master in Theology," priest, and in the fiftieth year of his age, and as having " made profession of the Catholic faith in accordance with articles recently drawn up by the Apostolic See." It then describes him as having the usual virtues required in a bishop. The Brief continues with an address to the clergy and faithful to accept him as their pastor and father and to obey his monitions and commands.

It continues with an important clause : " We desire all occasion and reason of wandering outside the cities and dioceses of Cork and Cloyne be taken from you and that you do not exercise the pontifical office [outside these dioceses] even with the permission of the Ordinaries of the dioceses, as in those cases we decree such functions to be null and void." This latter clause was subsequently modified.

Tanner, although appointed Bishop of Cork and Cloyne, 5 November, 1574, was not consecrated until 6 February, 1575. On the day of his consecration the following Brief [2] was issued to him :—

Indulgences granted unto all those that bearing about them one of grains [beads] blessed by our Holy Father Gregory the Third,[3] at the humble request of the Reverend Father E. Th., Bishop of Cork and Cloyne in Ireland, the day of his consecration which was 6 February, 1574 [i.e. 1575]. At St. Peter's Church in Rome.

First, whoso hath one of the said grains about them being contrite and confessed, intending to receive the Blessed Sacrament as soon as they may, and do say the Corona or Rossaire or read the Passion of Christ, or the 7 Psalms or Litany, praying for the Pope's Holiness, for the preservation of the Catholic Church, for the conversion of the kingdom of Ireland, England, and Scotland, and of all heretics, both obtain plenary Indulgence.

Secondly, he that is contrite and confessed and receiveth the Blessed Sacrament at the Nativity of Our Lord, at Easter, or on Ascension Day, at Whit Sunday, Corpus Christi Day, or all Saints, or at the Annunciation or Visitation or Assumption, Nativity, Conception, or Purification of Our Blessed Lady, or

---

[1] *Ex Secr. Brevium Romae, I.E.R., I.,* i. 314-18. *Arch. Hib.,* v. 172.

[2] *S.P.I., Eliz.,* xlix. 55, P.R.O., London. This document was evidently confiscated on his landing in Ireland ; hence the copy among the *State Papers.*

[3] Mistake for thirteenth.

in the feast of St. Patrick or St. Bryd [Brigid], or in the feast of the Patron of his Church, hath plenary Indulgences.

Thirdly, is granted to all those that be contrite, as above, going about to make peace whereas is discord, or to convert any heretic by counsel or virtuous example, or doeth the works of mercy, or do withdraw himself from the communion of heretics or from their preaching, also indulgences of Nostre Dame de Loretto, St. Marie Maior, and of the Holy Church of St. John de Lateran in Rome.

Fourthly, if the bearer of this bead or grain do fast in the vigils of the feasts Our Blessed Lady, as the Annunciation, Visitation, Assumption, Nativity, Conception, or Purification, being content with one refection, then have 500 years of pardon ; if thou hast bread and water, 1000 years of indulgence, being confessed with contrition, receiving or portending [intending] to receive the Blessed Sacrament.

Fifthly, whoso exhorteth any person to leave their sinful life, or desisting any heinous offence as heresy, schism, blasphemy, or swearing, shall obtain 1000 years of indulgence.

Sixthly, in saying 7 Pater Nosters and 7 Aves, or the Corona or Rosary, the 7 Psalms or Litany before any altar or image of Christ or of Our Blessed Lady or the Crucifix, for the conversion of England, Ireland, and Scotland, shall have the Indulgences of the 7 churches in Rome which are St. Petre, St. Paule, St. Sebastian, St. John de Lateran, the Holy Cross, St. Laurence, and St. Marie Magdalene.

On 10 April, 1575, special faculties were granted to him, and, notwithstanding the clause in the above Brief of his appointment, he was empowered to exercise them not only in his own united dioceses of Cork and Cloyne but also " throughout the whole province of Dublin, of which he was a native (*universae provinciae Dublinensis ex qua exoriundus*), as well as throughout the whole province of Munster, so long as the various Archbishops and Bishops were obliged by the fury of the persecution to be absent from their respective Sees." [1]

On 12 May Gregory XIII gave him a letter,[2] as he was on his way to Ireland, recommending him heartily to all Bishops and other Prelates who might be able to render him assistance.

---

[1] *Ex Secr. Brevium Romae.*
[2] *C.S.P.*, *Rome*, 1572-78, no. 402.   Theiner, *Annals*, ii. 133.

Tanner made his way to Madrid, where evidently he made some delay or was delayed on his voyage from Rome to Spain. At all events he was in Portugal a sick man, 23 November, on which date the Nuncio wrote to the Cardinal Secretary of State :—[1]

The Irish Bishop of Cork was earnestly commended to me by the Nuncio of Madrid. I have done him every service in my power that a sick man requires : *inter alia*, I have procured him safe passage for England on one of the Venetian ships, whence he will readily make his way to Ireland ; he has departed with a good wind and a good purpose to do his duty in his church to the honour of God and the weal of those souls, who are in the utmost need thereof. I cannot but bear good testimony to his virtue and zeal for the service of God. All this, I believe, will be gratifying to the Pope.

For this act of kindness the Nuncio in Portugal received the thanks of the new Cardinal Protector of Ireland, Francis Alciati, 3 January, 1576 : [2] " You have done very well in being courteous to the Bishop of Cork, and have afforded his Holiness much gratification."

Between November, 1575, and June, 1576, we have no information about Tanner. What precise difficulties he encountered on his landing in England we do not know, but he succeeded in taking another ship to Galway where he landed, 21 June, and evidently remained a few months. " Yesterday " (17 October), says the Commissary in Portugal, to his master, the Cardinal of Como, " I received letters from Edmund, Bishop of Cork, to the effect that after infinite perils he arrived at the port of Galway in Ireland on Corpus Christi day, and that the country is full of heretics and robbers. Nevertheless, he evinces great courage." [3]

He probably took another ship to some of the Munster ports, but was taken prisoner with his chaplain at Clonmel. In a letter of 11 October, 1577, written at Ross, he tells the General of the Jesuits that in the midst of persecutions from heretics he was taken prisoner, but by the grace of God and the help of a nobleman, he escaped, eluding twelve warders. Every day they diligently seek his death. " In

---

[1] *C.S.P.*, *Rome*, 1572-78, no. 451.   [2] *Ib.*, no. 470.   [3] *Ib.*, no. 534.

those straits," he adds, " aided by the grace of God, we have reconciled many of the nobles of the kingdom, many of the citizens of various cities and nobles we have received back from the cesspool of Schism into the bosom of the Church, and receive them from day to day, and many more we should receive if the present persecution, and privation of goods, life, and liberty did not prevent us. By that means a very great number, otherwise well disposed, are kept back from us ; but I hope in Christ that ultimately the cord shall be cut and that we shall be freed. The Rev. Father Charles and Master Robert Rochford spread everywhere the good odour of their Society of Jesus, conduct a school in the town of Youghal in the diocese of Cork in Munster. Its pupils and people are every day instructed in the Christian doctrine, and in the frequentation of the Sacraments and good morals, as far as time will permit, not indeed without molestation ; yet the Lord gives them perseverance, and their hearers abundant fruit." [1]

Other particulars of his activities are mentioned in a letter, of 24 November,[2] from the Commissary in Portugal, to the Cardinal Secretary of State :—

I have received another letter, to wit, of the 25th of September, from the Bishop of Cork in Ireland, who likewise writes the enclosed to Cardinal Alciati ; and apprises me that he has not been able to avoid the nets of the heretics ; they were not, however, treating him harshly, but had committed him to the custody of the heretic Bishop of Waterford pending the Queen of England's answer to their request to know what was to be done with him ; and the bishop says that, propagating the Gospel even in prison, he has converted the said bishop, his keeper, and induced him to abjure all heresies with many a tear and token of penitence.

The tears and tokens did not last long.[3]

---

[1] Hogan, *Iber. Ignat.*, p. 23. [2] *C.S.P., Rome*, 1572-78, no. 562.
[3] On 20 November, 1629, Thomas Strange, Guardian of the Order of St. Francis, Dublin, wrote to Luke Wadding, Guardian of St. Isidore's, Rome : " Be it known that Father Patrick, Lord Bishop of Waterford, showed me in private an authentic copy of his Bull, in which I observed a clause to which I drew his lordship's attention, and which I refer to Your Paternity for amendment, if need be : it is that where mention is made of the time during which the said See has been vacant there occur the words *per obitum cujusdam Walshe bonae memoriae, etc.* I suppose that neither Your Paternity nor his lordship were acquainted with the facts touching this Walshe at the time when the Bull

Tanner, as Papal Commissary, travelled almost the whole of Ireland, administering the Sacraments, " but secretly on account of persecution. In spite of ill-health he persevered until at last, worn out, he died 4 June, 1579, in the diocese of Ossory." He was the author of *Dissertations on the Summa of St. Thomas*.[1]

A few references to another Irish bishop about this time are worthy of notice here. William Walsh, Bishop of Meath, who had been imprisoned and who escaped to Spain, received several grants of money from Francis Alciati, Cardinal Protector of Ireland at Rome. Authority was issued, 20 February, 1576, by the Cardinal to the Nuncio in Spain to pay to Walsh, or his proctor, if he have left for Brittany, a further sum of 100 crowns of gold from the Collettoria. In a letter (of 1576, undated) of thanks to the Cardinal for his bounty, Walsh, referring to the presence of Fitzmaurice and Stucley in Rome, craves the Cardinal's zealous support for their scheme for

was obtained, and therefore I have determined to apprise Your Paternity that this Walshe was Patrick Walshe a Catholic bishop by election and consecration, a man of learning and of great repute throughout the kingdom for his gifts of teaching and preaching, insomuch that in Parliament all the bishops of Ireland spoke *ad nutum ejus*, and stood firm while he stood firm, and when he fell, all fell with him, save only the Bishop of Kildare. Not content with taking the Oath of Supremacy, he married, they say, and had sons—to wit, Nicholas Walshe, who was pseudobishop of Ossory, and was murdered by a kearn—and Abel Walshe, and the wife of one Magheraghty, Anna Walshe, so that Your Paternity may see that this clause in the Bull stands in need of correction, for that Walshe died a confirmed heretic." (*Report on Franciscan MSS. Hist. MSS. Commission*, p. 15.) See p. 23, note.

The reference to the " bishops of Ireland " is, as we have seen, rather inaccurate. He may have influenced some. As to his marriage, a few dates will help to elucidate the subject. He was born probably about 1508, as he took his M.A. degree in Oxford in 1534. He was consecrated Bishop of Waterford in 1551 by virtue of a mandate from Edward VI, but according to the Roman Ordinal. Evidently he was not married during his reign as he would have been deprived of his See during the reign of Mary. He was continued in office, but went over to the " Reform " in 1560. His marriage, therefore, must have taken place about that date. His son, Nicholas, succeeded to the See of Ossory in 1577. We have seen no reference to any question of illegitimacy or defect of age. If we take him to have been at least thirty years of age at that time he must have been born about 1547, that is four years before his father was appointed Bishop of Waterford. It seems, therefore, that Patrick Walshe took unto himself a concubine early in his career, either during Henry VIII's reign or early in Edward's, and that his children were recognised as legitimate. It is interesting to note that Nicholas, his son, was called by one of Elizabeth's officials, " the scare-crow bishop of Ossory."

[1] Hogan, *Iber. Ignat.*, p. 25.

35 *

the expulsion of the heretics and schismatics from Ireland, and the restoration of the Catholic faith and religion in the country. He solicits also the Cardinal's interest to procure for him means of subsistence in " Lesser Britain " (Brittany), as he can no longer endure the intense heats of Spain, and the proximity of Lesser Britain to Ireland would enable him to exhort his flock by letters, if not otherwise. Moreover, it is extremely irksome to him, a foreigner and an aged man, to be compelled to extort the stipend allowed him by the Catholic King month by month from the hands of laymen.[1] Walsh died in a house of the Cistercian Order in Alcalá about the year 1579.

State of Religion in Waterford ; " Masses Infinite."

One of the most damaging accounts [2] of the failure of the " reform " in Munster is that given by Sir William Drury, Lord President of Munster, in a letter to Walsingham, the Queen's Principal Secretary of State, written at Dungarvan, 14 April, 1577. Having stated that James Fitzmaurice (Geraldine) is at Rome and is expected to be in Waterford in harvest time, he continues :—

He [Fitzmaurice] is sure of the favour and goodwill of the whole Peers of the Realm whom we call Earls of Ireland . . . the students of Ireland that are in Louvain, and come from thence. They are the merest traitors and breeders of treachery that liveth, by whose means I doubt not James [Fitzmaurice] hath much favour in Rome . . . whereof there are in these parts, about Waterford and Clonmel, four principal prelates.

The first is called John White, who is worshipped like a God, between Kilkenny and Waterford and Clonmel. He suborneth all the dwellers of those parts to detest the true religion, established by her Majesty. He is a chief preacher to the contrary, an arrogant enemy to the gospel, and one that denieth all duties to her Majesty. If he were not, and his auricular teaching were not, one nobleman, to the comfort of a great number, should be converted from this Popery. He said, over in Bristol, that he would be our inquisitor in England to burn a thousand in England for religion.

---

[1] *C.S.P.*, *Rome*, 1572-78, nos. 490, 566.
[2] Brady, *State Papers*, no. xv. *S.P.I.*, *Eliz.*, lviii. 2.

He wrote several letters unto my brother, most contemptuous, menacing him for the religion by his writings : then I suspect he wrote part of those letters unto James out of Ireland.

The second is James Archer, of Kilkenny, a detestable enemy to the Word of God. He did swear against her Majesty's jurisdiction in Louvain, and to read not in no English book [of Common Prayer]. He arrived the last March and came then out of Louvain.

The third is Doctor Quemerford, of Waterford, also of late come out of Louvain. He and all the rest taught all the way between Rye and Bristol against the religion, and caused a number to despair.

The fourth is Chaunter Walsh of Waterford, one that hath procured dispensation of the Pope to use the English service, to receive benefits of the same, and to abjure himself without hurting his conscience.[1] He came over last March. He preached praying to Saints and going on pilgrimages. Belike they are come as Reformators of Living before the coming of that wicked limb James.

There are a great number of students of this city [Waterford] in Louvain, at the charge of their friends and fathers. They will never come hither before a change [in the government of Ireland], which God grant them not.

By whom and by the others aforesaid the proud and undutiful inhabiters of this town are so cankered in Popery, undutiful to her Majesty, slandering the gospel publicly as well this side the sea as beyond in England, that they fear not God nor man, and hath their altars, painted images and candlesticks, in derision of the Gospel, every day in their Synagogues, so detestable that they may be called the unruly neuters rather than subjects.

Masses infinite they have in their several churches every morning, without any fear. I have spied them, for I chanced to arrive last Sunday at 5 in the clock in the morning, and saw them resort out of the churches by heaps. This is shameful in a reformed city, but I judge them rather enemies than subjects. Let it not deceive you, although they should make their vaunt to be as true to her Majesty without conscience as others with conscience.

So that in spite of the terrorism of Drury the Catholics in Waterford openly assisted at Mass and carried on just as of yore, whilst they professed loyalty to Elizabeth as the Head of the State.

---

[1] This, of course, is a slander.

Brady Reports Progress of Papistry.

Bishop Brady of Meath tells a similar story of his own diocese to the Lord Deputy :—[1]

My singular good Lord, according to my duty and promise I have been a diligent searcher of the state of things here since my coming home. I find great boldness generally, as well by word as action, against the received religion, Masses be rife, little less than openly said, friars show themselves openly, two of them being here at the Navan of late were apprehended by some of my men, but quickly rescued, and my men put in hazard of their lives ; this was done by no worse than by the Portrief of the town and some other of his brethren, which act they durst not for their lives have committed (as I thought), within this quarter of a year, such courage is now gotten as these disorders be generally committed, by which I gather that there is some greater mischief purposed, which I trust will fall upon the necks of the devisers, a great number of this treacherous clergy goeth towards Armagh ; the bruit of that meeting is openly spoken of here. I have made choice of three several persons, the fittest I could find, the one of them not knowing the others' errand, severally sworn to me, faithfully to execute that I gave in charge, some of them be such as have both acquaintance and credit with the best of that pestiferous congregation. I have given myself reward, and have promised from your Lordship both reward and credit if their diligence and faithful dealing shall deserve it. I have a meeting tomorrow with O'Reilly's sons, John and Philip, partly by their own procurement, whereof I was very glad, for I trust by their means I shall be able to inform your Lordship more perfectly of these northern causes. O'Reilly himself is upon recovery and requireth a meeting upon the borders with the Chief Baron and me, betwixt this and the holidays which were very requisite so as the Chief Baron might be present. What I shall further learn according to my duty I will advertise your Lordship praying the Almighty God to bless and prosper yourself and your enterprises, I humbly take my leave.

From Ardbraken this 12th of May 1577.

(Endorsed) 13 May 1577.

My Lord Bishop of Methe, touching the disorder of the portriff of the Navan, and to what courage they are grown to of late in matter of Papistry and lewd superstition.

[1] *S.P.I., Eliz.*, lviii. 16, P.R.O., London.

What the meaning of the concourse of priests towards
Armagh was we do not know ; probably it was some kind of
a synod of the province. The impunity with which they
went about shows how Catholics had begun to bestir themselves again, especially as there was no disturbance at the
time in the North. The boldness of the Catholics in Munster
confirms the suspicion that the country was aware of Fitzmaurice's intended visit to Rome and doubtless expected
great results from it. Even in Dublin and its vicinity there
seemed to be an air of expectancy.

When Catholics began to grow too bold in the mani-
festation of their religion, Elizabeth and her Council usually
resorted to that panacea for all religious ills, namely, an
ecclesiastical commission. Accordingly, in May 1577, one
was issued [1] " to William Gerard, lord chancellor, Ormond,
Thomas, archbishop of Armagh, Adam, archbishop of Dublin,
Gerald, earl of Kildare, Hugh, bishop of Meath, Robert,
bishop of Kildare, Nicholas Walsh, chancellor of S. Patrick's,
John Kerny, treasurer, John Ball, archdeacon of Glendalagh,
David Clare, dean of Waterford, among others, to be commissioners for ecclesiastical causes throughout the realm, to
inquire by all means, of offences against the acts of supremacy
and uniformity, and all heretical opinions, seditious books,
conspiracies, and scandalous words against the queen, to
search out and correct all persons who obstinately absent
themselves from divine service as by law appointed ; to
determine all disturbances in church against the service, to
correct all heresies, schisms, and offences spiritual and ecclesiastical which by ecclesiastical power may be corrected
by censures, ecclesiastical deprivation or otherwise ; to search
out all masterless men, quarrellers, vagrants and suspect
persons, and all assaults and frays, to hear complaints of
any who for religion or the contracting of lawful matrimony
have been deprived of lands or offices spiritual or temporal,
and to restore such, removing the usurpers, to hear and
determine adulteries, fornications, and other ecclesiastical
crimes,[2] with power to summon witnesses and to punish by
fine and imprisonment. The lord chancellor to appoint a

[1] *Fiants*, no. 3047.
[2] I.e. crimes that came within the jurisdiction of the ecclesiastical court.

registrar and a receiver of fines. The commissioners may also administer the Oath of Supremacy to ecclesiastical persons and all temporal officers having the queen's wages."

A similar commission was issued to Sir W. Drury, Lord President of Munster, Meiler Magrath, Archbishop of Cashel, Matthew Sheyne, Bishop of Cork, William Casey, Bishop of Limerick, Walter Travers, preacher, and others, including the mayors of Cork, Waterford, Limerick, and Youghal, to be commissioners of ecclesiastical causes in the province of Munster.[1]

Unrest in the Country.

The controversy between the gentry of the Pale and the Government had a disturbing effect on the rest of the inhabitants. At the assizes it was impossible to have indictments properly drawn up or prisoners duly arraigned. The juries refused to pass verdicts against their own people. Lord Chancellor Gerrard's picture (8 February, 1577) is decidedly dismal, and suggests that English judges should be sent to secure verdicts and provide the hangman with occupation, or send some of the causes to the Star Chamber. The Pale must be gradually stretched by bringing the Irish counties under law by degrees. The Lord Deputy should endeavour to keep the Irish from actual rebellion, and to persuade them to make some contribution to the revenue. In this way, as the Queen will not go to the cost of military operations on a large scale, the revenue of England will be saved, and in fact a contribution will be made to it from Ireland. If the Deputy can keep Ireland with a small garrison, it is well, but, he adds, " if, in ten years past, the Governors had been enabled to subject the whole Irishry to the sword—which manner of government, if ever Ireland shall be thoroughly reformed, must be practised—Ireland had been in other terms of wealth and obedience than it is this day." [2]

The peasants of the Pale were all Irish and had been hitherto induced to remain on good terms with the English. Even in the County Dublin those of the English race delighted

[1] *Fiants*, no. 3156.
[2] Brady, *State Papers*, no. xiv. *S.P.I.*, *Eliz.*, lvii. 16 ; lviii. 10, 11, 12. Carew, *Cal.*, 1576, p. 476.

in talking Irish, and habits and feelings followed the language. The Irish population was growing so rapidly that the process of " civilizing " them was becoming more difficult. Some might be civilised, but the rest should be extirpated, and English farmers with good leases and moderate rents substi- tuted for them.[1] From this nucleus the Celtic wilderness might be gradually reclaimed. The Dublin mountains har- boured raiders and cattle-stealers who came within four miles of the city. Gerrard thought that Dublin county might be made quiet if compositions for crimes were sternly abolished and if successive Lord Deputies would " work hanging instead of agreeing to recompense felonious offices."

All this was very fine talk, but it showed that in spite of the energetic Sydney and his two martial lieutenants, Malby and Drury, there was a feeling of uneasiness as to what was going to happen next. The intrigues of James Fitzmaurice were known to all, and in Munster complaints about excessive cess were frequent. Rents were as uncertain as the titles to the lands, and landlords and tenants distrusted one another. Yet, Drury boasted that the unusual quietness was owing entirely to the just severity with which he ruled, having, as he oddly expresses it, executed " divers malefactors of good account." [2]

[1] On 2 May, 1578, Swords was granted a charter of incorporation with bailiff and burgesses (*Fiants*, no. 3276), and, on 16 June, was issued a " com- mission to Adam, Archbishop of Dublin, John Challoner, principal secretary, and Edward Fitzsymondes, to measure and appoint from the town of Swords two miles every way and to indicate it by certain bounds for the liberties of the town." By patent, 2 May, 1578, the Queen had " incorporated Thomas Molyneux, his wife, children, and family, and so many strangers as he could induce within five years to inhabit in Swords, Co. Dublin, by the name of two bailiffs burgesses, and inhabitants of the town and liberties of Swords." (*Fiants*, no. 3325.)

Eight years previously, namely, after the Parliament of 1569, Sydney had colonised Swords with refugees from the Netherlands. In his account of his services in Ireland he says : " I caused to plant and inhabit there above 40 families of the reformed churches of the Low countries flying thence for religion's sake, in one ruinous town called Surds [Swords], and truly, Sir, it would have done any man good to have seen how diligently they wrought, how they re- edified the quite spoiled old castle of the same town, and repaired almost all the same ; and godly and cleanly they, their wives, and children lived. They made diaper, and ticks for beds, and other good stuff for man's use, and excellent good leather of deer skins, goat and sheep fells, as is made in Southwark." (Carew, *Cal.*, 1575-88, p. 350.)

[2] *S.P.I.*, *Eliz.*, lvii. 27, 42.

Desmond complained loudly that the soldiers ill-treated his tenants, and exacted cess, both in kind and money ; that he and his were much the poorer, and that the Queen was never a penny the richer. It was recognised by all that ill-paid soldiers could not be kept in proper order. The Queen refused a loan of £500 for the Munster service, but Drury warned her that she would be put to greater expense by her refusal. He begged for a galley to cruise on the coast, but this appeal met with no response. Sir John Desmond, suspected of complicity with Clanricard's sons, was arrested, whereupon the Earl of Desmond retired to Kerry, flouted Drury's entreaties and collected a force of 1000 on the plea that his life was in danger.[1] Drury had at this time but 100 available troopers.

It is quite probable that there were intrigues at the time between the Desmonds and Clanricard's sons, who by keeping the Government on the move hoped to prevent the adminis trative reform that was already looming on the horizon. No doubt the Burkes were not disposed to allow the " reform " Acts operate in the country under their sway. In order to cut off communications between them and the Desmonds, Drury granted all the privileges that Thomond, a vain and wavering individual, asked for. On the head of another O'Brien Murrough, who had been joined with Fitzmaurice in the late rebellion, £300 was placed, and more if necessary.[2]

Meanwhile, Malby took up the military command of Connacht, and having imprisoned Clanricard, gave his sons eight days to make up their mind if they would surrender or not. Loyal professions to gain time and a few skirmishes in which a few soldiers were killed and two officers captured showed Malby how matters stood. He lost no time in enter- ing the mountains, attacking first John Burke's district and then Ulick's. " I spared," says Malby, " neither old nor young." He put all at the mercy of the soldiers who had lost their lieutenant, and who slew twenty-two, " all tall men." Everything that would burn was burned, and every person met with was killed. With a great show of consideration he granted a pardon for five weeks that the crops might be sown,

---

[1] *S.P.I., Eliz.*, lvii. 43.

[2] *Ib.*, lviii. 60-2. The *Four Masters* call Murrough O'Brien " the most renowned of the heirs of Carrigogunnel and Aherlow."

but where the men were to come from or the seed obtained he did not pause to think. After this terrifying lesson Connacht was quiet, and Malby and Drury conferred as to how the two provinces " being ragged countries as we found them " might be brought to order. It was evident that the Burkes would break out again wherever they had the power, notwithstanding the good opinion the Presidents had reported of them that " they be a people that do now seek much unto the administration of justice."

For a year or more Rory Oge O'More, after his profession of loyalty before Sydney in the cathedral of Kilkenny, kept very quiet. But the restlessness all round—the Burkes in Connacht, the cess dispute in the Pale, the Desmond call to arms, and the rumours of the Spanish invasion—contributed to rouse his ardour. Joined by his old ally Connor MacCormac, Rory, on the night of 3 March, 1577, at the head of a band of 100 men, entered the town of Naas which they burned. Not a townsman, however, was killed.

So frightened were the Council in Dublin at the turn events had taken that a commission was issued, 30 September, 1577,[1] to Adam, Archbishop of Dublin, Sir William Sarsfield, Edward Barnewell of the Dromynagh (Drimnagh, Co. Dublin), and William Fitzwilliams of Jobstown, Co. Dublin, to take muster and array of the inhabitants of the barony of Newcastle, Co. Dublin, between 16 and 60 years of age, and fit for guard and defence to view the aptness of body and courage, and the armour and weapons of each, and to take notice of the amount of their lands and goods, and what horses, armour, and weapons they are bound by law to be furnished with, and to oblige them to be so furnished, to return a book of the muster to the lord deputy, to appoint men to keep English watch and daily ward at every village, bridge, and ford, where they think it necessary, to make arrangement for the following of hue and cry after enemies, rebels, and robbers ; Sir William Sarsfield to have command of the men of the barony when raised.

[1] *Fiants,* no. 3118.

Massacre of Mullaghmast.

At the year 1577—the *Four Masters* describe :—

A horrible and abominable act of treachery was committed by the English of Leinster and Meath upon that part of the people of Offaly and Leix that remained in confederacy with them, and under their protection. It was effected thus : they were all summoned to show themselves, with the greatest number they could be able to bring with them, at the great Rath of Mullagh-Maistean [1] and on their arrival at that place they were surrounded on every side by four lines of soldiers and cavalry, who proceeded to shoot and slaughter them without mercy, so that not a single individual escaped, by fight or force.

The *Four Masters* are not the only Irish chroniclers who relate what has been characterised as " one of the ugliest [deeds] ever committed in Erin." [2] Although they differ as to certain details and the date, they agree in the main. The memory of the treachery, however, has been handed down from father to son in the district and has been committed to writing with a number of details not recorded in the cut-and-dry pages of the chroniclers.

It will be well first to refer briefly to some incidents that occurred in Leix and Offaly some years before the massacre. During the reign of Queen Mary, the territories of Leix and Offaly were brought to a state of submission. Leix was, after her, called the Queen's County, with Maryborough as its capital, whilst Offaly became the King's County, with its capital, Philipstown, after Philip of Spain. The best parts of these two counties were gradually planted with those military officers who had taken part in their reduction, such

---

[1] The high ground lying to the west of the town of Ballitore, in the south of Kildare, is called Mullaghmast (Mullach Maisten or Maistin's Hill). It was situated in the ancient territory of the O'Tooles, called O'Murethy, which comprised the southern portion of the present Co. Kildare. From a very early date it was a place of great importance. On the summit is a large circular Rath inside of which is to this day a deep hollow by the name of " the Blood Hole," and here it was, the peasants say that the chiefs were executed one after the other to the number of one short of four hundred. At this Rath was held Daniel O'Connell's Monster Repeal Meeting, Sunday, 1 October, 1843.

[2] See *Annals of Lough Ce*, and Dowling's *Annals*, compiled by men living at the time. Dowling, Protestant Chancellor of the Diocese of Leighlin, lived on the borders of Leix at the time. See also O'Sullivan Beare, *Catholic History of Ireland*, published about forty years after the event.

as the Cosbys, Bowens, Hartpoles, Hovendens, Parsons, Molesworths, Armstrongs, etc. Needless to say, they had not a quiet time of it from the natives. The O'Mores and the O'Connors were ever endeavouring to recapture the lands taken from them, and in particular, Rory Oge O'More was the strong leader who made things lively for the English planters. At the time of the massacre, Captain Francis Cosby, described as of Kildare, and then of Monasterevin, was in command of the English troops stationed in the Rath. Twenty years previously he had been appointed General of the Kerne (native light foot-soldiers) retained in the pay of the Government. Under him was an officer named John Bowen, one of the Ballyadams (Queen's Co.) family. He was known as Shawn-a-feeka (John of the Pike) by the Irish, on account, it is said, of his being usually armed with that weapon.[1]

The story of the massacre as told by the natives is as follows : " The principal men of the O'Mores and their allied ruling families, under Morris (Murty) O'More, chief of Margy, were invited by Francis Cosby and Robert Hartpole, who at that time were responsible for law and order in Carlow and Leix, to meet them in a friendly conference at the Rath of Mullaghmast, to devise means to preserve peace and good-will. Relying on the good faith of these two officials, a large number of the principal men of Leix, including Murty O'More, made their way to the appointed place, entered the old Rath unsuspectingly, and without a word of warning were surrounded by soldiers who were in readiness and who slaughtered them almost to a man. The only man who escaped was Henry Lalor, who, noticing that none of those who had entered before him was to be seen, had his suspicions aroused, advanced with sword in hand, saw the bodies of the slain, fought his way back, and warned those still outside, with whom he managed to escape across the Barrow." The chief English planters were all implicated in the deed, whilst the slaughtered included not only the O'Mores, but the other seven septs of Leix, the O'Kellys, O'Lalors, Devoys, MacEvoys, Dorans, and Dowlings. The traditional account handed down in the locality was committed to writing by one Cullen who had

---

[1] *Kild. Arch. Journ.*, i. 382 *seq.*

often heard it from the lips of two old men named Dowling and Dwyer, both of whom remembered the massacre as having taken place in their young days and in their own district.

The curious thing about this wholesale massacre is that the name Mullaghmast is not even mentioned in the official correspondence of the time between Dublin and London. There are, however, a couple of allusions which may be taken as referring to it in rather discreet fashion. One is found in the order to FitzWilliams in 1582 to investigate the serious complaints that had been made against the Queen's captains and soldiers. It was alleged that they " have dealt very treacherously and barbarously with some of them [the Irish] by inviting them to banquets and parleys and afterwards slaying them in most cruel manner when they had them in their hands." The other allusion is found in an indictment drawn up by Captain Thomas Lee, who had been in the Queen's service for many years in the vicinity of Mullaghmast, against the conduct of the English officials in Ireland. In this document of the year 1594, presented to Elizabeth, he states : " They have drawn unto them by protection three or four hundred of those country people, under colour to do your Majesty service, and brought them to a place of meeting, where your garrison soldiers were appointed to be, who have there most dishonourably put them all to the sword ; and this hath been by the consent and practise of the Lord Deputy for the time being." [1] The real date of the massacre appears to be rather the year 1572. In June, 1572, Fitz-Williams, in order to pacify the country had commissions issued to have lists drawn up of the men in each of the ruling families severally within his reach expected to furnish a certain quota for military service. One of these commissions was issued for the Co. Wexford, and the contingents from each county severally were to muster and take their places in the ranks assigned to them on a certain day and in a certain place. About the same time Rory O'More had been giving such trouble that Ormond and Kildare (at this time a loyal subject) had been sent against him, early in August, but with such poor results that it was considered advisable " to reclaim him

---

[1] *Kild. Arch. Journ.*, i. 372-90.

by peaceable treaties to become a peaceable and dutiful subject." After much reluctance and delay, Rory was induced,
under safe-conduct, to visit Kildare at the castle of Kilkaa.
In a letter, 23 August, the Earl was able to report that he
had succeeded in inducing Rory to submit and that he had
every hope of like success with Fiagh MacHugh O'Byrne
and the Kavanaghs.

It was precisely at this time that something of great
gravity must have occurred to break off the negotiations, for
Fiagh and the Kavanaghs at once made a desperate and
destructive raid on Wexford. It was this raid that the *Four
Masters* give under the year 1579, but in reality it was 1572.
They state that Fiagh MacHugh was invited " to a treacherous
conference ; but Fiagh, having received intelligence that
the seneschal had appointed this conference for a treacherous
purpose, lay another snare for the seneschal and slew one
hundred of the youths and chieftains of the Co. Wexford on
that occasion, besides several of the common sort of people."
This incident is narrated in a letter written late in August
or early in September to the Lord Deputy by Sir Nicholas
Devereux of Belmagir in the Barony of Forth, in which he
states that the incident occurred on 26 August.[1] This act
of Fiagh was evidently a reprisal for the treachery against
the O'Mores.

Mullaghmast, the most prominent landmark in the district, runs down like a neck towards Carlow between the
counties of Wicklow and Wexford on one side, and that of
Leix on the other, thus forming the most central meeting-
place that could be selected for a gathering of the O'Byrnes,
O'Mores, and Kavanaghs. The chiefs and men who showed
willingness to submit were actually coming to the appointed
place for the taking of the musters of the quota of men for
military service to preserve the Queen's peace. The O'Mores,
living nearer to Mullaghmast, were the first to arrive, with
the disastrous results described already. The O'Byrnes and
Kavanaghs, having a longer journey to make, arrived later,
and, being warned of the danger, sped in all haste to Wexford
where they engaged in the reprisal also mentioned above.
This seems to be what actually occurred in connection with

---

[1] *S.P.I., Eliz.,* xxxvii. 59, vii.   *Ib.,* 41.

this memorable massacre mentioned in legend, song, and story.[1]

Fitzmaurice in Rome ; Papal Brief.

The eyes of Ireland were now centred on James Fitzmaurice who had gone to Rome from France. During 1576 little attention had been given by the Pope to the Irish side of the expedition against Elizabeth, and Ireland was rarely mentioned in the diplomatic correspondence. In November of that year a change came about when Bishop O'Hely succeeded in getting the Pope to write to the King of Spain to lend aid for the recapture of Ireland from Elizabeth. The appointment of Don John to Flanders awakened fresh hopes in the heart of Fitzmaurice who repaired to Rome to ask for papal authority to rally his fellow-countrymen round the papal standard in a united effort for freedom. This doubtless appealed to the Pope as a useful auxiliary to the great expedition from Flanders to England.

Fitzmaurice remained some weeks in Rome, early in the year 1577, until he obtained the papal authorisation he had been long seeking. The Brief was as follows :—

Gregory XIII to the Hierarchy, Princes, Earls, Barons, Clergy, Chiefs and People of the Kingdom of Ireland.

Of all the regions of the Christian world, separated from us by many lands, the Apostolic See has always cherished a special love and singular affection for the Irish nation because of its constant fervent devotion and unshaken attachment to the Catholic religion and the See of Rome.

Deeply moved, therefore, by the sufferings and afflictions of that Kingdom, we are anxious to do all in our power to secure the peace and liberty of its people and the salvation of their souls.

A prominent nobleman, James Fitzmaurice, chief of Kerry-currihy, and, as he states, governor-general of Desmond in the Earl's absence, has come to Rome to cast himself at our feet and to pour into our ears the sad tale of the many and sore tribulations which the good have to suffer for the true religion and their love of the faith at the hands of Elizabeth, the enemy of God and

[1] *Catholic Bulletin*, June, 1927, pp. 643-9. Whether the date be 1572 or 1577 does not alter the facts of Mullaghmast. If its date be 1577, then a similar treachery may have been the occasion of Fiagh's reprisal in 1572.

man, who brazenly and impiously wields the sceptre over England and Ireland.

Now, the said James, impelled by zeal for the glory of God's house, by the desire of seeing our holy religion restored in his country, by love of his native land, and by his own innate virtue and magnanimity of soul, is determined with God's help to shake that hard and intolerable yoke from off your necks, and hopes to find many to co-operate with him in carrying out his intention and design.

We therefore, through the bowels of divine mercy, counsel each and all of you to the best of your ability to seize on the opportunity now offered and strenuously to support the holy and brave efforts of this undaunted leader against that woman who, already fulminated against and abased by anathema, has been cut off thereby from the Church and will surely be overtaken by evil according to her deserts.

That you may be enabled to do this all the more readily, we hereby grant to each one who, confessing his sins or intending to confess them with contrite heart, shall join Fitzmaurice's army for the defence and preservation of the Catholic faith, or shall aid them by counsel, countenance, contribution, arms, or in any other way whatsoever, a plenary indulgence and remission of all sins, similar to that granted by the Apostolic See to those going to war against the Turks for the recovery of the Holy Land.

In order that this document may reach those for whom it is intended as quickly and as readily as possible, it is our will that all printed or written copies which shall have been duly issued by a notary public and attested by the seal of competent ecclesiastical authority shall be everywhere accepted with the same respect as would be accorded to the original.

Given at St. Peter's Rome, under the Fisherman's Ring, the twenty-fifth day of February, 1577.[1]

On 25 February the Cardinal of Como gave Fitzmaurice a letter to bring to the Collector of Portugal where the Irish chief intended to visit his little son at the Jesuit College in Lisbon, before departing for Ireland. The Cardinal continues : " While he has been here he has been received with favour, and gladly seen by the Pope as being a very honourable gentleman and most devoted to the Catholic religion. And now His Holiness has commissioned me to commend him to

[1] *Catholic Bulletin*, Nov., 1928, pp. 1178-9.

36

you, that he may not lack your favour whereinsoever you shall find yourself able to gratify him ; and in particular in aiding him to find a ship and other conveniences for safe passage to his home, which, as you will learn from him, is what he particularly desires." [1]

Fitzmaurice's route lay by Genoa where he expected to take ship for Spain.   He was there in March, and on 15th, the Collector Apostolic reported to the Papal Secretary that " James is well ; it irks him much to be so delayed in travelling but it must needs be so if risk is to be avoided." [2]   Here during those days was Stucley also.   He had been the bearer of the papal Brief to Don John who (17 February) recommended Stucley's return to Rome, entreating the Pope " ever to make special account of Thomas Stucley, for I warrant you his good qualities merit it, and will daily merit it more and more." [3]   On the same day Don John wrote to the King of Spain begging him to supply Stucley with the means of getting out of debt as he was in extreme need since he quitted that Court.[4]

As nothing was to be hoped for in the matter of the expedition by Flanders, Don John evidently suggested through Stucley to the Pope the sending of one from Italy.   But such, said His Holiness, was out of the question on account of its difficulties, and on account of the suspicion that would be aroused in England which had its spies everywhere.   The Pope, however, is not losing heart, and will abate none of his zeal.   The Papal Secretary, in this letter, 2 April, to Don John,[5] then speaks of Fitzmaurice :—

I wrote your Highness that James Geraldine, one of the chief men of the realm of Ireland, had been here, and that his Holiness had sent him to Portugal with a handsome largesse, there to embark privily, and betake him to Ireland, where he is eagerly expected by many friends, who are already in arms against the Queen of England.   This will be a rising of moment, and one that will harass that wicked woman not a little, so that, were but as much trouble given her in England, her affairs would readily be thrown into confusion, and the Catholics of those kingdoms, who are numberless, would be encouraged to take up arms in earnest.

[1] *C.S.P.*, *Rome*, 1572-78, no. 575.   [2] *Ib.*, no. 582.   [3] *Ib.*, no. 570.
[4] *Ib.*, no. 571.   [5] *Ib* , no. 588.

If the contemplated enterprise be speedily accomplished there will be no need to think of another, for that will be remedy enough and to spare; but though your Highness would discover difficulty in the said enterprise, you would see the need of it at least thinking of supporting an Orange on the flanks of that wicked woman [Elizabeth], to harass her and wear her out, as [the Prince of] Orange has worn us out; and such an Orange would be Stucley, who with a few ships and a few troops would be able in this case to do great things; and as we have promised Geraldine that, if he begin harassing the Queen, we will send him for sure some aid in the course of a few months, Stucley's going would be an excellent form for the aid to take. . . . What I have said as to sending Stucley has reference only to the event of lawful impediments precluding the general enterprise, but if that is feasible, this other enterprise should not be attempted, because we should thereby give the Queen occasion to arm, which would increase the difficulty of the general enterprise.

FITZMAURICE IN SPAIN; THE KING'S IRRITATING HESITATION.

A few weeks before the news reached Rome of Don John's surrender to the demands of the provinces of Flanders, and whilst the Pope still hoped for the descent of the Spanish forces on the English coast, Fitzmaurice set out from the Eternal City for his native country armed with the papal Brief. He was comforted also by the papal promise that, if he rallied the country round the Catholic Standard in the name of the Pope, he might expect further help from Rome or Spain or both. He carried with him papal letters to the Nuncio in Portugal, directing him to assist the Irish chief in securing a ship and accessories for his journey to Ireland.

A month later the Pope, writing to Don John on the new situation that had arisen in Flanders, mentioned Fitzmaurice's departure with a handsome sum from the papal purse, and how advantageous to Don John's rule in Flanders would be the harassing of Elizabeth 'in Ireland. Six weeks later the Nuncio was informed by the Cardinal Secretary of State that the Pope was most anxious to hear what was being done for the Irish chief, " for," he added, " it would be a great crime to desert James Fitzmaurice, who has gone ahead." [1] Again, towards the end of July the Cardinal Secretary directed the Nuncio in Spain to urge the King to find some other way " for aiding Fitzmaurice in accordance with the promise given to him ; for it would be shameful, indeed, if he was abandoned by us." [2] Fitzmaurice had been experiencing difficulty in securing shipping accommodation in Lisbon.

Fitzmaurice had made his journey by sea from Genoa where, strange to say, whilst he was waiting a suitable ship, Stucley spent a few days on his way to Rome bearing despatches from Don John. It does not appear, however, that the two leaders met. Fitzmaurice was accompanied on his journey by his most trusted agents Bishop Patrick O'Hely of Mayo, and Father Wolf. [3] He took up his abode at Villaverde, a quiet place some three miles from Madrid, at the suggestion of King Philip, in order not to arouse the suspicions of the English spies. [4] Near at hand in Spain or Portugal were other Irish supporters of his, such as Maurice MacGibbon, Archbishop of Cashel, Maurice MacBrien, Bishop of Emly, Donat O'Gallagher, Bishop of Killala, Cornelius Ryan, Bishop of Killaloe, with whom was Dr. Sander, the representative of the English Catholics at the Court of Spain, who warmly espoused the Irish movement, and afterwards accompanied Fitzmaurice on his adventurous expedition.

Writing to Rome on 31 May, the Nuncio in Madrid was unable to report much progress with the King in favour of the Fitzmaurice expedition owing to the disturbed state of Flanders. However, the business was in good hands, namely those of the King's most trusted minister, Antonio Perez, with whom the Chief Inquisitor was joined, who promised to keep up pressure on the King. Bishop O'Hely and Dr. Sander, who were in Madrid, were also doing their best to interest the King in the project. Even Don John was bringing his influence to bear on Madrid, so that the signs were hopeful enough, provided there was no fresh trouble in Flanders. [5]

---

[1] *C.S.P., Rome,* 1572-78, no. 605.   [2] *Ib.,* no. 637.
[3] He seems to have severed his connection with the Jesuit Order about this time.
[4] *C.S.P., Rome,* 1572-78, no. 613.   [5] *Ib.,* no. 606.

The Pope, however, was getting tired of the King's hesitation, and a strongly-worded letter was despatched to the Nuncio, 2 July, complaining of Philip's irresolution " of which God grant he may not have to repent one day, and perhaps sooner than he expects." On account of his irresolution matters were going from bad to worse in Flanders, so it would be well if he " put off the mask in his dealings with that she-devil [Elizabeth] and give her bread for flour " [i.e. tit for tat]. As His Holiness was giving to the enterprise his name and authority, and anything else that the King might deem meet and proper, Philip was to be induced to give a decision, particularly because " poor Fitzmaurice will be awaiting the promised help, and to disappoint him would be a great sin against God and a stain on our own honour." [1]

Letters to a similar effect were sent, 24 July, to leave no stone unturned. Mgr. Sega, who had been sent as Nuncio to Flanders for the special purpose of promoting the enterprise against England, was now transferred to Madrid in the hope that by his influence, knowledge, and experience, he might be able to bring the King to a decision. " Go then, in good cheer," the Pope wrote to Mgr. Sega, " and as soon as you are in Madrid deliver a powerful attack in support of the good cause ; for if action is to be taken at all there must be no further delay." Sega had informed the Pope (23 July) that matters were going from bad to worse in Flanders owing to Elizabeth's evil influence there, and that Don John was endeavouring to recall the departed Spanish soldiers in order to be ready to attack England as soon as Philip could be induced to make up his mind. [2]

Fresh instructions were now sent by the Pope to Sega to the effect that if the King intended to take no action, the Nuncio was to try to secure at least some help for Fitzmaurice, even if it was no more than a single ship, with plenty of firearms and other weapons. This, said the Pope, " would give us breathing time to wait for the English enterprise to mature and would prevent the Queen from harassing others." [3]

---

[1] *C.S.P., Rome*, 1572-78, no. 619.   [2] *Ib.*, no. 635.   [3] *Ib.*, no. 637.

Fitzmaurice Sets Out for Ireland; Robbed of his Ship and Munitions.

Accompanied by Bishop O'Hely of Mayo and some eighty soldiers whom he had been able to get together in Spain or Portugal, James Fitzmaurice sailed out of the harbour of Lisbon on 19 November, 1577. The ship that he had hired of Captain Stonbec of Le Croisic, Brittany, carried 200 calivers with twenty-two pieces of ordnance, a quantity of gunpowder, and other munitions of war.

On receipt of a letter from the Nuncio in Spain, the Papal Secretary wrote to him (18 January, 1578) lamenting the King's base treatment of Fitzmaurice, who, he says, to use the Irish Chief's own words, has departed from Lisbon " *sine armis, sine classe, et sine hominibus* . . . a thing which verily might dishearten any giant." He begs the Nuncio to plead with Philip " not to be false to himself in an emergency of such importance, and if His Majesty should be loth to send soldiers for fear of discovery, he can succour Geraldine in arms defensive and offensive, in powder, balls, and other sorts of munitions, and in money, for supplies of this sort can be sent very secretly by way of Portugal. In fine, everything depends on the succour being to hand while Stucley is in those parts, so that the twain may make the better progress together.[1]

Before leaving, Fitzmaurice wrote a last heartbroken appeal to the papal representative in Portugal :—

I came to Lisbon to set sail for Ireland, and I would have been there long ago were it not that the Spanish Nuncio, in his anxiety to procure me a subsidy from the King of Spain, induced me to tarry. In a recent letter he now gives me to understand that there is nothing for me.

Unarmed, therefore, without a fleet and without men, in the name of our Lord Jesus Christ, and relying on the authority of the Apostolic See, I am setting out without any further delay for Ireland, trusting much to your prayers, through which, I have no doubt, the most merciful Lord will be propitious to me and will give me victory over the foes of Holy Mother Church.

To conclude : I have looked for aid and having failed to find it, my friends, who have all been eagerly expecting me, will be luke-

[1] *C.S.P.*, *Rome*, 1572-78, no. 731.

warm and dispirited, while my foes will be all the more ready to
face me, when they see me coming back unarmed and unaided.
I therefore beseech your Excellency, in whom I trust, to speed the
promised aid after me into Ireland, and to press for the despatch
of help in accordance with the promise made by the King of
Spain to the Bishop of Mayo.

Farewell !

Lisbon, November 5, 1577.[1]

Bishop O'Hely wrote in a similar strain to the Nuncio
at Madrid, mentioning, with unconscious irony, that, at the
intercession of the Spanish Ambassador, the King of Portugal
had allowed them to hire at their own expense a ship they
were about to set out in, in the name of the Lord and of
the Apostolic See. "Our leader, like another Maccabæus,
cannot but achieve a victory commensurate with his zeal
and fervour."

Fortune for a while seemed to smile on them. They
were not long at sea when they fell in with a large English
ship which they attacked and captured. They handed the
soldiers over to the Spanish Inquisition, and took the ship,
which was a good one, along with them. Soon, however,
high winds and raging seas forced them to seek shelter in
the harbour of Bayona on the Gulf of Vico in Galicia.
Having repaired the damages to their vessel, and having
again set out they were again compelled to seek shelter in
a harbour of Monuiero near Corunna where they spent twenty
days. Misfortune had indeed frowned on them, but worse
was to follow. While engaged in provisioning their ship,
some of the hired soldiers deserted, and their Captain, whom
they had secured somewhat against his will, showed reluctance
to go ahead. Legal proceedings had to be taken against him
to compel him to carry out his contract, and a decree was
obtained against him, but still he flatly refused to obey.
Both Captain and crew were now committed to prison. On
the night of 5 January, they broke out of prison, boarded
their ship and stole out of the harbour in the early morning.
When Fitzmaurice returned from Church where he had
been attending Mass for the Feast of the Epiphany, he found

[1] *C.S.P., Rome*, 1572-78, no. 686.

his ship gone, and with it all his artillery, guns, munitions, and even his personal effects, as well as those of Bishop O'Hely.[1]

BISHOP OF MAYO APPEALS TO ROME IN FITZMAURICE'S BEHALF.

These adventures were graphically set forth in a Latin letter written by Hely, Bishop of Mayo, nearly three months later, to the Cardinal Secretary of State. He then continued:—

We have followed him [Shipowner or Captain] into France and are trying to recover our property. Fitzmaurice has gone to St. Malo for this purpose, while I am here in Paris seeking a royal mandate for the restoration of what was taken from us. But in the meanwhile those who made off with our belongings have warned the Queen of England to look out and keep us from landing in Ireland ; and as for the royal mandate, I have not yet succeeded in procuring it.

All these misfortunes have befallen us for the very simple reason that when Fitzmaurice reached Portugal he had not the means to purchase as much as a single ship ; there was no Spanish or Italian ship for hire, and in his eagerness to carry out the order of His Holiness, he almost flung himself into danger by entrusting himself and his all to French sailors in whom no trust was to be placed. Had I been his spokesman the second time I visited Rome, as I had been on a former occasion, and if my advice had any weight,[2] His Holiness would never have given him the Church's Standard without soldiers, nor his Commission with nothing to back it up, and I would thus have saved the authority of the Church from being exposed to the contempt and derision of the enemy ; nor would Fitzmaurice ever have set out from the Roman Curia under conditions like these, had he not had reason to hope that he would receive assistance from the Papal Collector in Portugal, to whom he had letters to that effect from your Eminence.

However this may be, the venture is now on the way, and there is no turning back without dishonour. Neither the influence of the Church, nor the dignity of the Holy See, nor the safety of our Nation, nor the salvation of souls, which should be dearer to us than life itself or any earthly consideration, nor even common charity or any temporal interest or design, will now allow us to

---

[1] *Catholic Bulletin*, Jan., 1929, pp. 48-56.
[2] This seems to confirm the deal between Stucley and Fr. Wolf.

withdraw from what we have set out to perform—we must go
ahead courageously, and Fitzmaurice must on many counts be
given the help he needs to cross over into Ireland. He is now in
Brittany. He expects no help from the King of France, from
whom it is idle to seek or expect anything ; but he does expect
His Holiness to hold out a helping hand ; and if this is not stretched
out promptly it is greatly to be feared that the prestige of the
Holy See will suffer sorely in the eyes of the enemy—and assuredly
it will not redound to the credit of that See to have entered on an
enterprise which it is unable to carry through. Not only this ; but
it is not a little to be feared that the Irish magnates and chiefs,
who are friendly to Fitzmaurice not to speak of all the Catholics
of England and Ireland, will be slaughtered ere long if he fails to
reach Ireland ; and in this event, which may God forbid, the door
through which aid could be brought into the other two kingdoms
will be closed up, and the Queen, who has already heard rumours of
the doings of Fitzmaurice and Stucley, will act with greater violence
than ever before against the Catholics of her dominions. On the
other hand, however, a favourable opportunity now offers itself
for going ahead with the work which has been undertaken ; for
the Scots, who speak the same language as ours, and are bound to
us by ties of friendship and treaty, are up in arms and on the
move ; while three of the chief Irish magnates, O'Neill, O'Donnell,
and O'Rourke, have, we understand risen out in revolt and will
strongly support Fitzmaurice if only he reaches Ireland in time.
Great, then, is the danger of delay.

His Holiness, in my opinion, can help Fitzmaurice in two ways.
First of all he can help by issuing an Apostolic Brief to all sovereigns,
princes, and magnates of the Christian world, no matter what their
nation, offering remission of their sins together with a plenary indulgence to all and every one who will hold out a helping hand to
Fitzmaurice and promote the good of religion against the Queen
of England ; and at the same time under pain of *ipso facto* excommunication strictly forbidding anyone to impede Fitzmaurice
in the execution of his commission, or to help the enemy by word
or work openly or secretly. The second way in which help can
be given is that of transmitting to Fitzmaurice through the Nuncio
in France a sum of money sufficient to purchase at least one well-
equipped and well-armed ship, where the public weal of kingdoms
and the cause of religion and piety are concerned, not only the
spiritual but the temporal treasures of the Church should be thrown
open and expended.

Should His Holiness not see his way to take this step, it is
greatly to be feared that the undertaking we have entered on will

meet with little or no success, and is a mere waste of time and effort. Without Fitzmaurice's presence in Ireland, Stucley can accomplish nothing, even if he had a thousand soldiers for every hundred he really has at his command.

If he had but one ship, Fitzmaurice and we of his company will neither hesitate nor fear to set out once more in God's name and in obedience to the Apostolic See on the voyage towards our native land, no matter how many English ships may infest the seas between France and Ireland. The work to which we have set our hand is of the last importance ; it is one that permits of no delays, and the moment this reaches your Eminence you will, we feel confident, approach His Holiness and see that a decision is come to with all speed and that a reply reaches us at the earliest possible moment in order that we may be in a position to know what is before us.

Your Eminence may perhaps think that the language I am using is too plain, or that I entertain doubts or faint hopes of help coming from His Holiness ; but please also remember that with the help of God's grace I shall be much more free and ready to give up life and blood and all I have, should need there be, for the safety and exaltation of the Apostolic See, for the propagation of the Catholic faith, and the spread of the Christian religion, and that I have every confidence in the bountiful liberality of His Holiness, which in my experience I have found to be great and prompt. Necessity urges me, the importance of the issue impels me, common charity forces me, zeal for religion and the common weal inspires me,—in a word, I am stirred by care for the salvation and safety of my brethren, and by the unique opportunity that now offers itself for effecting a great achievement, so that in this holy and most pressing cause I have to write in language much stronger than I should think of using in normal circumstances thus exposing myself to the risk of being interpreted as doubting the likelihood of receiving help from His Holiness, or even as mistrusting his prompt liberality. I am writing to the illustrious Cardinal Protector in a similar strain in order that both of you, like the pillars of the Church which you are, may support that Church which in our part of the world is weighed down by a bitter burthen and has to groan under the intolerable yoke of slavery.

Paris, March 31, 1578.

> Your Eminence's ever grateful
>
> PATRICK, *Bishop of Mayo.*

To His Eminence, The Cardinal of Como, Rome.

To this letter there was added the following postscript :—

I lost with that ship the bulls of my appointment to the diocese of Mayo, and there is no one I can send to Rome to have them replaced, while the Irishmen who were in Rome and could have acted for me are, I believe, no longer there, but have left with Stucley. But should there be anyone available I shall be eternally grateful if he will procure and transmit them to me, even though I may add that they are likely to be of little use to me, just as similar bulls will be of little use to the other Bishops of Ireland, unless Fitzmaurice receives real, and prompt help.[1]

Whilst at Paris, Bishop O'Hely obtained the royal mandate, 7 April, which was addressed by the King of France to the Seneschal of Nantes, who was instructed to compel the ship-master, Thomas Strubec of Le Croisic, " to make restitution of the property belonging to the deponents [Fitzmaurice and Bishop O'Hely] and to pay their expenses with damages and interest." This document fills in some gaps in the Bishop's narrative. It states that Fitzmaurice and the Bishop had hired the services of Strubec " to take them and their people in a vessel of his from Lisbon to Ireland, and that the said Strubec having sailed, kept them eighteen days at sea in company with other vessels from Le Croisic." It then relates the details already given by Bishop O'Hely. It ends thus : " Our will, therefore, is that you proceed against the said Strubec, master-mariner and his sailors."

Fitzmaurice Betrayed by a Franciscan Friar.

Bishop O'Hely, as a result of these vicissitudes, was obliged to seek hospitality in some of the houses of his Order in Paris.[2] Even here was to be found a traitor who is now discovered to be no other than Denis Molan, a Franciscan friar. Through information from him the English Ambassador was able to report to London, 8 June, that " James Fitzmaurice arrived in this town on the 4th, and being in-

---

[1] *C.S.P.*, Rome, 1572-78, no. 776. *Catholic Bulletin*, Jan., 1929, pp. 49 *seq.*

[2] He repaid his benefactors by assisting in training novices whom he impressed profoundly by his deep humility, his vast erudition, his wonderful memory, his brilliant genius, and his enthusiasm for the great Duns Scotus. (Fr. Thomas Bourchier or Bowser, *Franciscan Martyrs*. He was an English Franciscan and a guest in the same religious house with the Bishop.)

formed by a friar of the shape and fashion of one of his servants
I caused him to be followed so long that I have now found
his master's lodgings and hope to be able to render you some
account of his behaviour here." A few days later the
Ambassador was able to supplement his information by a
document entitled " Considerations on the State of Ireland "
which runs as follows :—

Considering what is the vein and fountain whence comes all
our unquietness, especially in Ireland, I remarked three things
causing our rude unquiet people there to rise against their godly
quiet Prince [Elizabeth]. The first and principalest is the *long
suffering* of monks and friars, and especially of their fair mighty
houses, whereby they are not only maintained themselves, but also
those who with their counsel remain in perpetual rebellion. The
remedy is no better than to pluck down such houses. When the
fox has no hole he must run away, and the bird having no nest
cannot breed.

The second is the *large* imprisonment of Richard Craigh called
the Primate of Ireland, now bearing the name of a prisoner in the
Tower of London, whose letters come almost daily to France, Italy,
and Spain, alluring all evil-disposed persons against our good and
merciful Prince. This fellow ought to be regarded according to
his service.

The third and not the least is, doubtless James Fitzmaurice,
having the name of the greatest rebel, Shane O'Neill only excepted,
in all Ireland, running from one Papist Prince to another with the
Pope's commendations and his proud letters to his foolish friends
in Ireland, comforting them to resist their Prince ; and this
Episcopus Maionen [Bishop of Mayo] preaching in Spain and
craving in every other where for him. God will, I doubt not,
plague these two fellows, and if a man could reward them according to their deeds he should do a right good service to God. It
were better that these two did perish than all the people. I write
what my conscience doth bid me :

In Witness whereof I subscribe my name, the 7th day of June,
1578.

(Signed) DENIS MOLAN.[1]

---

[1] *C.S.P.F.*, 1578, no. 7. The Editor of the Calendar who remarks that
the document contains what looks very like a proposal to assassinate Fitzmaurice
was unable to identify the writer and could only hazard the guess that his name
" suggests that he, too, was an Irishman abroad."

With the help of a document in the Vatican Archives it is now possible to lift the veil that shrouded this Irish traitor. Owing to the circumstances of the period, many unworthy men found their way into the houses of Religious Orders in Ireland, and just as easily found excuses for making their way to foreign lands. Trading on the persecutions that raged at home, they laid themselves out to captivate the good graces of the mighty and to win high positions for themselves. In doing so intrigue and jealousy played an ignoble part, and these men did not hesitate to decry and defame their fellow-contemporaries who were likely to be competitors or to stand in the way of their own honour and glory. Fortunately, they were few but their work was considerable and harmful. To this class belongs the writer of the " Considerations," Denis Molan.

Molan was a Franciscan friar [1] then resident in Paris, very probably in the same house as Bishop O'Hely. The Bishop, who suspected him of playing a double game, warned the Papal Nuncio in Paris, who in turn warned the Holy See, that the friar, who was about to visit Rome in August, was on friendly terms with Queen Elizabeth. The Friar pretended to be against her, " probably in order to work mischief with greater ease " ; but in reality he should be regarded as " an apostate and a heretic."

A couple of weeks later Fitzmaurice was back in Brittany, and Paulet sent one of his spies to watch and report his movements. While there were no signs of immediate danger there was always the possibility that Fitzmaurice might set out with a ship or two for Ireland ; " the subtle malice of this time gives us just cause to fear rather too much than too little." One of Paulet's spies returned on 7 July, and reported that having visited every haven from St. Malo to Vannes, some twenty leagues from Nantes, he had not seen

---

[1] In a MS. account of the sufferings of the Irish Franciscans, written in the early seventeenth century, there is an entry to the effect that " Father Roger Mac-Comghuil, Eugene Mac-an-Taoir, Donat Molan, Charles O'Hamvill, and Patrick Thadaei of the Convent of Carrickfergus, were captured by the Protestant magistrate of the place, and suffered various afflictions at his hands, but were eventually liberated on handing over some chalices to him, in the year 1560." It seems just probable that the Donat Molan here mentioned is the Denis Molan of the " Considerations."

as much as a single ship or barque prepared for war, and that even la Roche, who had put out to sea with a ship and pinnace, had been forced by foul weather to return to harbour. He found James Fitzmaurice at Dinant, " where counting himself and his wife he has eighteen persons in his house, which argues that he finds liberal friendship in this country ; and there is no appearance that he is preparing for any new voyage." As a matter of fact Fitzmaurice was so short of funds at this time that he had to pawn some plate that he had brought with him from Ireland. This, however, he was enabled to redeem a couple of weeks later on receipt of a subsidy of 1000 crowns sent by the Pope.[1]

At this time Fitzmaurice seems to have been anxious that Jesuits should be sent into Scotland and Ireland, and that Father Wolf should accompany him to Ireland. Accordingly, he wrote from Paris to Everard Mercurian, General of the Jesuits at Rome, 6 June, 1578, and to know if his friendship for Father Wolf was in any way displeasing to the General. The latter replied, 28 June, that he was sorry that two or three letters of Fitzmaurice's were lost and that he considered that the present was not a fitting time to send his men into Scotland or Ireland, but that he will embrace a fitting opportunity. As to Father Wolf, he will be glad of any employment for old David Wolf.[2] From this it is clear that Father Wolf had left the Jesuit Order before this time.

Rome Anxious About Fitzmaurice's Departure.

During the first three months of 1578 it was assumed in Rome that Fitzmaurice had reached Ireland ; and letters continued to be dispatched to the Nuncio in Spain urging him to bring increased pressure to bear on the King with a view to procuring the promised reinforcements in men and arms for the Irish Chief.

The King would not listen to the entreaties of the Bishop of Killaloe and refused him an audience.[3] The first news of

---

[1] *Catholic Bulletin*, Jan., 1929, pp. 53-6.
[2] *S.P.I.*, *Eliz.*, lxi. 11. Hogan, *Iber. Ignat.*, p. 24.
[3] *C.S.P.*, *Rome*, 1572-78, no. 749.

Fitzmaurice's misadventure is contained in a letter from the Nuncio, 22 March.[1] This was followed by other letters from the Nuncio and the Bishop of Killaloe, to the effect that not only had Fitzmaurice succeeded in recovering the property carried off by Strubec, but that four or six ships with 2000 soldiers had been placed at his disposal by his friend de la Roche of St. Malo, and that he would probably set sail any day for Ireland.

The Pope, however, was growing weary of the whole affair, and was not in a mood to listen to the request for additional funds set forth in Bishop O'Hely's letter, especially as the King of Spain had shown such supreme indifference to the success of the venture. All this was pointed out in a letter of 2 May by the Cardinal Secretary [2] who went so far as to express some doubt as to whether it was not possible that Fitzmaurice had not magnified his loss. He even hinted in rather an undignified manner that perhaps Fitzmaurice turned his loss into an excuse for dawdling at St. Malo with his wife and children rather than face the dangers of a campaign in Ireland.

Subsequent information, however, reassured the Pope of Fitzmaurice's sincerity. The news that de la Roche was coming to the Irish chief's aid induced a more generous frame of mind in His Holiness, who sent a thousand crowns to Fitzmaurice along with a letter, 2 June, in answer to Bishop O'Hely's request of 31 March.[3] The Pope was not altogether satisfied with Fitzmaurice's management of the ship in which he had set out and hoped that the report of de la Roche's aid was true. Should this be really the case, and should Fitzmaurice make a brilliant beginning, he could count on the support of His Holiness. Unfortunately the report as to the aid from de la Roche was untrue. It was Bishop O'Hely's painful task to inform the Cardinal Secretary, 22 June, that Fitzmaurice had not even been able to charter a vessel of any kind to carry him into Ireland, and was still in Brittany awaiting orders from His Holiness.[4]

---

[1] *C.S.P.*, *Rome*, 1572-78, no. 770.   [2] *Ib.*, no. 813.
[3] *Ib.*, nos. 851, 852.   [4] *Ib.*, no. 868.

PAPAL EXPEDITION ; STUCLEY IN COMMAND.

A few days after Fitzmaurice had set out from Rome on his journey to Ireland in 1577, the news reached the Pope that the project of sending an expeditionary force from Flanders against Elizabeth was impracticable. His Holiness, therefore, fell back on the plan agreed in 1576 between Rome and Spain. But as the King of Spain had his hands full in Flanders, and as there was no hope of his co-operation with the 100,000 crowns expected by the Pope, the latter concluded that if anything was to be done for Ireland or England, it must be done by himself. It should take the shape of a small expeditionary force, of a certain number of soldiers in a vessel that would also carry what the Irish chief required more than anything else, a considerable supply of arms and munitions of war with which to equip his fellow-countrymen for the struggle that lay ahead.

The important question of the commander was without hesitation settled by Dr. Lewis, Archdeacon of Cambray, and the Pope's chief adviser on English matters. The person selected was Thomas Stucley, the adventurer in many lands, who was at that time in Rome and attached to the papal household in the capacity of what would now be known as privy chamberlain. Not only was he regarded with some reason as a man of great experience in military affairs on land and sea, but, more important still, he was well known in Spain, to the King himself. He had just returned from Flanders whither he had accompanied Don John, and had letters of recommendation from him to the Pope as a man who could render great service to the cause of religion in England and Ireland.

In a letter to Don John, 2 April, 1577,[1] the Cardinal Secretary pointed out that as things stood now His Holiness was inclined to think that he could best help Fitzmaurice by supplying Stucley with ships and troops to come to his assistance. The Cardinal stressed the advantages accruing to Spain from the expedition and the Pope's expectation that the King would help with the force of some 6000 men already agreed upon. To spur on the King the Pope had

[1] *C.S.P.*, *Rome*, 1572-78, no. 588.

sent as Nuncio to Spain the influential Mgr. Sega. Although the Nuncio did his best, yet, in September, 1577, he had to report that whilst His Majesty was keenly interested in the invasion of England, he did not approve of making any move in regard to the Stucley expedition.[1]

The Cardinal Secretary pointed out to the Nuncio the injury done to the cause by this delay and indecision. Stucley was becoming restless, and it was now impossible to restrain him any longer. The Pope was now determined to go on with the expedition no matter what the King thought (15 Oct.).[2] Between Stucley and Fitzmaurice, he added, the Queen of England would have too much to do at home to allow her to send further help to Flanders. " His Holiness has definitely decided to provide Stucley with a good ship as well as men, arms, munitions, victuals, and sufficient money for some months, and to let him join Fitzmaurice, so that these two, acting in concert, may do all the harm they can to that wicked woman. The expedition will start in a few days, and Stucley is now at Naples engaged in finding a suitable ship." (27 October.) The Cardinal Secretary expressed the hope that even now the King of Spain would try to do for Fitzmaurice something like what His Holiness was doing for Stucley.[3]

Preparations and Voyage.

It was not until 3 January, 1578, that the Cardinal Secretary was able to report to Spain that everything was now in readiness. " A ship of the largest size had been chartered, and 600 picked soldiers are being put on board with plentiful supplies of all things needed for six months—victuals in good abundance, money to meet all expenses, and arquebuses, pikes, and other arms for 3000 men—all of which will cost His Holiness thousands and thousands of crowns." Just as before, he added : " I trust that by God's grace the King of Spain has furnished Fitzmaurice with like aid ; and should he not have done so, it would assuredly be well that he should

---

[1] *C.S.P.*, *Rome*, 1572-78, no. 659. [2] *Ib.*, no. 668.
[3] *Ib.*, no. 678. *Catholic Bulletin*, March, 1929, p. 254 *seq.*

do so as soon as possible.[1] We have seen how Philip treated Fitzmaurice. The Stucley ship was called the *St. John*, and the troops were raised in the Papal States by Paolo Giordano Orsini, Duke of Bracciano, who was a warm admirer of Stucley, and easily found volunteers among his own vassals.

On the 18 February the ship reached the papal port of Civitá Vecchia where it was visited by Stucley who considered her " very good, but ill-furnished with artillery," for which reason he asked the Pope to let him have four of the pieces that were lying idle in the fortress of the port.[2] These were duly handed over to him, together with two culverins and their gear and a number of cannon balls, as well as two smaller culverins known as *mogliana*.[3]

On 22 January Captain Bastiano wrote to the Cardinal Secretary[4] that he went to Rocca Nuova with Stucley " and thence have taken four small pieces of the sort that could best be spared ; to wit, first an old and small mogliana without arms thereon, and an old pitriera[5] with the arms of Malta thereon, which Sir Thomas besought them to be pleased to allow me because it has the Cross upon it, and an old square *morana* [*moyen*] with the arms of Pope Paul III thereon ; and also a Turkish saker ;[6] which said pieces are all mounted on iron wheels for horse traction ; there have also been taken 300 balls with the implements for charging, and other gear of the said pieces."

Bastiano, who was to accompany the expedition as paymaster and treasurer, was less pleased with what he saw. He sent a despatch to Rome[7] pointing out that many things were still lacking, and that in fact, the accommodation was insufficient for such a large number of men. They would be packed like " pinkins and pipes,"[8] and, moreover, the funds would be inadequate. Eventually, all things were considered

---

[1] *C.S.P., Rome*, 1572-78, no. 713.   [2] *Ib.*, nos. 732, 733, 734.

[3] A *Mogliana* (*Fr.* moyene) was a piece of ordnance of about 8 ft. long, of a demi-culverin bore.

[4] *C.S.P., Rome*, 1572-78, no. 738.

[5] I.e. *petriero*, a piece discharging a stone missile.

[6] An old form of cannon, of 5 to 12 pounds calibre.

[7] *C.S.P., Rome*, 1572-78, no. 739.

[8] Equivalent to " herrings in a barrel."

in good order, and preparations were made to hoist sail
23 January.[1]

So keen was the Pope on the expedition that he decided
to visit the ship and her company before their departure :—

> On Monday morning the Pope departed for Civitá Vecchia, and,
> after riding some miles, got into a carriage lined with crimson velvet
> in which were Cardinals Austria, Sermaneta, and Farnese. After a
> splendid reception by Farnese at Palo, His Holiness departed for
> Civitá Vecchia to confer his blessing on the soldiers that are going
> on the galleon of the English Duke ; [2] but having learned that an
> uproar and mutiny had broken out among them, as they insisted
> on having two instalments of their pay before embarking, the
> Pope decided to hold aloof and not expose his person to disrespect.[3]

He therefore did no more than give such orders as were
necessary to pacify the soldiers, and returned to Rome
without seeing them.

An incident now occurred which put a rather unpleasant
complexion on the expedition. In a letter to Stucley
(17 January),[4] just a few days before his departure, the Cardinal
Secretary informed him that in reference to the matters to
which Dr. Lewis had drawn his attention, he could give no
answer until he had first spoken with Donat O'Gallagher,
Bishop of Killala, but that he hoped to satisfy Stucley in
this respect also. The question referred to concerned the

---

[1] *C.S.P.*, *Rome*, 1572-78, no. 741.

[2] Thus was Stucley styled. According to his own story two brothers
(names not mentioned, but indications point to the Clan Magennis) had quarrelled
about the succession to the family estates, and as they could not agree as to
which was to have them, they decided to sell them to Stucley, who was then in
Ireland as intermediary with Shane O'Neill. Owing to the hostility of Elizabeth,
he had not been able to enter into possession. Now that he was about to sail
on an important mission, the Pope, taking his statement to be true, confirmed
him in his right to these estates, and raised him to the rank of Marquis of
Leinster [*sic*] ; and in all subsequent documents he is addressed and referred
to as the Marquis of Leinster, or simply as the *Marchese*. In an interesting
passport that he subsequently issued to some English sailors whom he fell in
with on the way, he signed himself " Thomas Stewkeley, Knight, Baron of
Ross and Idrone, Viscount of Murrows and Kinshelah, Earl of Wexford and
Carlow, Marquis of Leinster, General of our most holy Father Gregory XIII."
Leaving aside his claims to the titles of Marquis and General, his claim to the
other titles was based on his office of constableship of Wexford and Leighlin
which Sydney had obtained for him and of which he was deprived by Elizabeth.

[3] *C.S.P.*, *Rome*, 1572-78, no. 742.   [4] *Ib.*, no. 730.

Irishmen then present in Rome, chiefly ecclesiastics living on the bounty of the Pope. They were the Bishop of Killala, Fathers Cornelius Neachton, Cornelius O'Boyle, Laurence O'More, Patrick Synnott, Dr. Nicholas Comerford, and three students, Nicholas Fegan, Richard Galway, and Nicholas Sedgrave.[1]

" Stucley [2] suggested to the Pope, probably in order to display greater zeal and sincerity, that it would be well to make use of these and carry them with him into Ireland, so as to render the expected rising in that country easier and more imposing. The hint was not thrown away. But as the Irishmen displayed great reluctance to accept the invitation and had little hope of anything good resulting from the venture, he had them seized in their hotels at night, and brought straightway by car to Civitá Vecchia where they were closely confined in a hospice, with the windows and doors secured, and without permission even to write until the arrival of Stucley, who, much against their will, had them carried on board his ship."

Not only were the Irishmen distrustful of Stucley and hostile to him, but they were determined to have nothing to do with the expedition under his command. Fitzmaurice, the chosen leader of the Irish chiefs, was in their opinion the man who should have been chosen, and who alone might be able to rally the country round his standard. The selection of an Englishman at such a crisis seemed to them to bespeak disaster. The counsel of the poor uninfluential Irishmen was unheeded, and the Pope, attaching more weight to the advice of Dr. Lewis, the representative of the powerful English Kingdom at the Vatican, entrusted the great venture to Stucley. Had Fitzmaurice been placed in command, the whole history of these islands, and indeed of the English-speaking world, might easily have assumed a different hue. It was one of the biggest " If's " in the history of Ireland, the existence not only of English power but of the Protestant

---

[1] " On 2 February, 1573, Nicholas Sedgrave, 35 years of age, born in Dublin of James Sedgrave, merchant, and Margaret Bath, both dead, entered the [Jesuit] novitiate of St. Andrew's. He spent three years and eight months in the German College " (Rome). (*Iber. Ignat.*, p. 19.)

[2] Maffei, *Annals of Gregory XIII. Cath. Bulletin*, March, 1929, p. 259.

religion in this country depending on the selection of one man.

Stucley's ship, the good *St. John,* sailed out of the port of Ercole on the 3 February, with 600 men, arms, and ammunition, and with " a most favouring breeze." It carried also some men given by Prince Orsini who were the first to cause trouble to the Marquis. Having landed at the Port of Palamos, and giving them leave to go on shore, five of them deserted. Something in the nature of a mutiny had occurred during the voyage which was raised by Lorenzo Cerchi who fraternised with an Englishman, named Thomas Meyners or Miners who was regarded as a spy. Bastiano San Joseppi informed the Cardinal of Como that had she been a good ship she would have reached her destination by now, namely 14 February. Stucley, on the same day, also wrote from Palamos, to the Cardinal that he will have to put in probably at Lisbon to " refit the ship with timbers, ropes, and gear, and sails, and have her well caulked, as otherwise she runs a risk of going all to pieces in the sea." For some reason or other he refers the Cardinal to Owen Lewis, Archdeacon of Cambrai, who will give all particulars.

How the ship and the crew fared between Palamos and Lisbon is told by Captain Bastiano in a letter of 23 April from Lisbon to the Cardinal Secretary.[1] Having accorded the soldiers some recreation, and with great difficulty and at much cost having got a supply of water, they left the port of Palamos on 17 February, and arrived on the 27th at Salou, hard by Tarragona. Having got some necessaries there for the sick, they departed on 5 March and arrived at Alicante on the 11th, " where they were at much expense in recreating the troops, who were in much need thereof in divers respects which I forbear to specify." They departed on the 19th, and arrived at Cadiz on 5 April, where, having got some wine and water they took aboard a pilot to guide them to Lisbon. They set out again on the 7th, but caught by a gale, they had to return towards Cadiz and Porto Sancta Maria, where they put in on the 8th. Again they procured wine and water with much trouble and at great cost. In

[1] *C.S.P., Rome,* 1572-78, no. 800.

fact " in all the ports on the Spanish seaboard water was sold very dear, and was very hard indeed to come by." They got away again on the 12th, and on the 17th were about fifteen miles from Lisbon when they received the Collector's letter forbidding them to come any nearer.

Spain Refuses Fleet to Fitzmaurice.

While all this was taking place, much was being done at Madrid, by the Nuncio and Cornelius Ryan, Bishop of Killaloe, to induce the King to provide some practical assistance for Fitzmaurice. But as usual the King hesitated, and even refused the request of the Nuncio to grant an audience to the Bishop of Killaloe. The Pope made known to the Nuncio how distracted he was at the King's treatment of Fitzmaurice, and how disgusted he was when he learned that the Irish chief, after months of weary waiting, had to leave Lisbon without fleet, men or arms (19 November, 1577). So far Fitzmaurice had to be satisfied on his difficult and dangerous mission with a sum of money, almost grudgingly granted, and with doubtful promises.

Eventually, by dint of continual pressure, the Nuncio succeeded in extracting the not inconsiderable sum of 20,000 crowns out of the royal treasury, half of which was to go to Stucley and the other half to Fitzmaurice. Somewhat elated by his success, the Nuncio addressed letters to the Irish bishops exhorting them to do their part in promoting the success of the expedition, and sent instructions to the papal representatives at Lisbon to interest himself in Stucley whose arrival was expected any day. At the same time Dr. Sander drew up a powerful manifesto that was to be published in Ireland on the landing of the troops (of which later). It was at this time that the Nuncio informed the Pope of the misfortunes that had overtaken Fitzmaurice at the hands of the Breton sailors. Such was the position in March, 1578. So keen was the Nuncio on the success of the undertaking that he wrote to the Pope (25 March) volunteering to accompany the Stucley expedition in person. He made the offer all the more readily because of the fact that the King had refused permission to Dr. Sander to accompany it on the ground that on account of the latter's well-known connection with the Spanish Court, his presence in the expedition would be tantamount to a declaration of war with England. " There is no more acceptable sacrifice I can offer to God for my sins," wrote the Nuncio, " and no better way in which I can repay the obligations I am under to His Holiness and the Apostolic See, than by dedicating my zeal to their service in the manner I propose." [1]

A couple of weeks later he wrote : " I am here in the thick of affairs, and I plainly see that if we continue to wait for the King to make a move we shall lose our pains, because the people here are so obsessed by hesitation in making up their minds that plans are abandoned until it is too late." [2]

PAPAL EXPEDITION ARRIVES AT LISBON ; STUCLEY'S TREACHERY.

Early in April, 1577, the news reached Lisbon that a papal expedition of 600 picked men under Stucley had set sail from Italy with orders to assail the enemies of the Church in the British Isles. To the young and enthusiastic Don Sebastian, King of Portugal, the coming of such a force to Lisbon on its way appeared as a great God-send for his own personal purpose. He was at the time raising an imposing army for the purpose of crushing the Moors in Africa, under Muley Moloch, King of Fez, Morocco, and Taradant. In addition to his own 900 men, he had managed to secure 300 hired soldiers from Germany, and 2000 from his uncle, the King of Spain. If he could secure the 600 veterans of the papal expedition it would be a decided acquisition. He had little difficulty in persuading himself that the Moors were to be counted, equally with the English, amongst the Church's enemies. Besides, if Stucley and his men accompanied him to Africa, on their return, after a few months, it would be easy to increase their force to a couple of thousand men, and send them on their way to Ireland.

This design reached the ears of Mgr. Fontana, papal representative at Lisbon, who had had definite instructions

---

[1] *C.S.P.*, *Rome*, 1572-78, no. 774.
[2] *Catholic Bulletin*, March, 1929, pp. 259-61.

from Rome to expedite the sailing of the Stucley expedition to Ireland. At once he sought and received an interview with the King to whom he explained the urgency of this expedition. Seeing, however, that the King was " bent on arranging for the papal ship to go with him for two or three months to Africa," he despatched couriers to warn Stucley, who had at this time arrived at Cadiz, to avoid Portuguese waters and to make for some harbour on the Spanish coast, in case he should find it necessary to touch land. Great was his surprise, therefore, when on the morning of 18 April he learned that Stucley's ship had been sighted making for the port of Lisbon. Displeased with Stucley's disobedience, he sent out a boat to intercept his ship, with an intimation that he was to anchor outside the harbour and await a visit from him early next morning. At dawn, next day, he sailed out towards the place where he expected to find the ship, but to his great surprise he saw that Stucley was actually sailing towards the port. On receiving a peremptory order from the papal representative, Stucley cast anchor outside the harbour, where the two men entered into an animated conversation.

Mgr. Fontana gathered from Stucley that he was inclined to consider the King's suggestion, and, by way of excuse, was stressing the ship's unfitness for the long and stormy journey, and the necessity of repairs which would take a couple of months. To Fontana's reminder that he was bound in conscience to go ahead on his mission, Stucley easily replied that it was idle to talk of going ahead until he had procured a seaworthy vessel. He must first see the King and find out if he could help him in the matter.[1]

According to Stucley's account [2] of the royal interview, reluctantly arranged by Fontana, he was pressed by the King to join the African expedition and promised additional forces on his return ; he resisted with all his might, and begged for leave to land his troops, a place for his stores, and a seaworthy ship for his voyage to Ireland. In a letter of 23 April to the Pope he states that he will not " fail to take care of your soldiers in accordance with your command, for it will

[1] *C.S.P.*, *Rome*, 1572-78, nos. 796, 797, 798, 800.
[2] *Ib.*, nos. 802, 805.

not be long before they are engaged in those operations which your Holiness desires, and that of a surety." On the same day he wrote to the Nuncio in Spain telling of his arrival, " to me a miracle," considering how the sails were all in pieces, all the timbers broken and rotten " so that, when it rains, the poor soldiers get all there is of it." The ship is so damaged as to be quite unseaworthy, and if the soldiers had not been allowed to land at Lisbon but had been confined to the ship " some pest and disease would befall them, incapacitating them all, and likewise the vessel " ; that it was with great reluctance that the King of Portugal suffered them to land.

He tells how the King had tried to force him to go with the soldiers " on this enterprise of Barbary," but he answered " that he would on no account do so, but would certainly continue his voyage." But the King refused to yield, and now he is unable to contend any longer with him. He therefore asks the Nuncio to induce His Majesty to allow him depart on a good ship and that, his men being in excellent condition, he will embark at an hour's notice. He adds that he will not give up the voyage. " I had rather die a thousand deaths, were it possible."

In the game now being played, Alcazzova, the King's official, took a hand and informed Fontana and Stucley that as the ship was unfit and the prospects of the voyage very remote, the King was of opinion that the papal troops could not be better employed in the interval than in accompanying the Portuguese army against the enemies of the Church in Africa.

Fontana at once pointed out that the only thing needed for the voyage was a suitable ship, for the chartering of which in Lisbon they were simply asking the King's leave, and for which they themselves were ready to pay. Through Alcazzova the King bluntly replied that he was prepared to give the desired facilities only on the condition that the papal troops first accompanied him to Africa. At an interview with the King on the 23rd, Stucley accepted the ultimatum that he should lead the expedition to Africa, and proceed later to Ireland. Fontana was informed of this next day, and neither by prayer nor appeal could he move the King or Stucley from their decision. All he could do was to secure possession of the arms and munitions of the papal expedition which he placed in the custody of Captain San Joseppi.

Now that people had an opportunity of voicing their opinions about Stucley many things were revealed to his discredit from the first day he went on board the *St. John* at Civitá Vecchia. He was hated by the Irish, not loved by the English, and detested by the papal troops.[1] The Bishops of Killaloe and Killala were dissatisfied with him and were inclined to think that the whole enterprise had been ruined from the beginning by being entrusted to his leadership.

Gamberini, who had been sent to Lisbon by the Madrid Nuncio to investigate the state of affairs on the spot, reported [2] that he found great instability in Stucley, great distrust between him and his troops, and great dissension in the ranks of the latter. " Stucley," he noted, " was abandoned by all the Irish who had accompanied him from Rome, on the plea that they had sailed under compulsion, and that they ought not to have been forced, even by the Pope, to set out on a voyage of the kind against their wish. Indeed, the whole business was a sea of confusion." Finally, Fontana noted that the two bishops and the Irish priests in Lisbon had been very severe in their criticisms of Stucley [3] whom they bluntly accused of having deceived the Pope and betrayed them. So keen was their resentment that most of them flatly refused to accept an allowance which he offered them for their support during their enforced stay in Lisbon.

Eventually, 26 June, Stucley sailed out of Lisbon and out of Irish life. It is unnecessary to follow him on his journey to his end on the desert sands of Africa where he received the fatal bullet on 4 August. Only about fifteen of his 600 men escaped the general slaughter wrought on the army by the Moorish King. Such was the disastrous climax to the ill-starred decision to put the expedition in the hands of such an adventurer. For, taking everything into account, perhaps this is the best term with which to describe Stucley.[4]

[1] *C.S.P., Rome*, 1572-78, no. 880. [2] *Ib.*, nos. 834, 836. [3] *Ib.*, 843.
[4] *Catholic Bulletin*, April, 1929, pp. 341-50. A few references to Stucley's belongings will be of interest. One of his pages who survived the slaughter in Africa got away with all the writings of most importance. These came into

DR. SANDER JOINS FITZMAURICE.

When James Fitzmaurice reached Madrid on his way from Rome to Ireland, in May, 1577, he came into close contact with Dr. Nicholas Sander, the most influential and energetic of the English Catholic refugees on the Continent, and the most enthusiastic preacher of a Catholic crusade against Elizabeth. Born in Surrey in 1530, he became a fellow of New College, Oxford, and graduated B.C.L. in 1551. Early under Elizabeth (1559) he escaped to Louvain with ten priests, went to Rome in 1562, and was ordained priest.

Since 1573 he had been endeavouring to induce Philip to take decisive action against Elizabeth, and pointed out that no move could be made by the English Catholics until an expeditionary force had first landed in England. Gradually he came to see that there was no hope to be placed in the King of Spain, and that all rested on the Pope. Through contact with Fitzmaurice, he learned of the possibilities in an Irish invasion, and made up his mind that if anything was to be done a start should be made in that country. Henceforth, all his energies and all his hopes were to be linked with those of the Irish chief. Hearing that the Pope had fitted out the Stucley expedition he rejoiced at the prospect of success, if it was followed by another against England. His hopes having been dashed to the ground by the turn taken by Stucley, he set himself to the task of repairing the disaster.

In Madrid at this time he found one of the most influential diplomatists of his age in Mgr. Sega who had been specially sent as Nuncio to Philip for the purpose of spurring on the slow-moving King to decisive action against Elizabeth (July, 1577). He soon saw that as long as the situation in France and Flanders was critical there was little use in expecting Philip to take such action. He therefore confined his activities to a request for help for Fitzmaurice and Stucley

---

Sander's possession, except three—the Papal Brief raising Stucley to the Marquisate which was taken possession of by the Nuncio of Spain, and two Briefs to O'Neill and O'Donnell which remained at Lisbon. The Mass vestments, Chalice and Missal, which were a gift of the Pope to Stucley, fell into the hands of the Collector Apostolic at Lisbon. He wrote to the Papal Secretary that they might be granted " To the Madonna of Loreto here, the shrine being subject to the Italian nation." (*C.S.P.*, *Rome*, 1572-78, nos., 989, 997.)

who had sailed from Italy. Stucley's expedition having proved a fiasco, Sega decided to recall Fitzmaurice from France to Madrid, where in consultation with Dr. Sander and the Irish bishops, he set about to gather the threads that had been so rudely scattered by the unfortunate Stucley. The most that could be hoped for was some little help for Fitzmaurice. As the Pope had already spent the large sum of 50,000 crowns on the Irish venture, the Cardinal Secretary of State directed Sega to suggest to Philip to provide a like sum for Fitzmaurice, as the Irish chief, by keeping Elizabeth employed at home, would prevent her from sending supplies to the King's enemies in Flanders. Meanwhile, the Pope was of the opinion that the 20,000 crowns that had been set aside by the King for the projected expedition under Stucley and Fitzmaurice could now be placed at the disposal of the latter. With this sum it was considered that the Irish chief could enlist in Spain, Portugal, and France, a force of about a thousand hired soldiers who could be transported into Ireland in a couple of hired ships with the arms and ammunition that had been saved out of the Stucley wreck. This was all that could be expected at the moment ; but it was important to expedite the departure of Fitzmaurice to Ireland with whatever forces could be gathered together, for if there was any further delay " his fellow-countrymen, who are expecting him in Ireland, will lose heart, if indeed they are not utterly crushed before he arrives." [1] The Nuncio was accordingly empowered to take charge of all the negotiations, plans, and arrangements required to enable the Irish chief to proceed on his journey. The papal representative in Lisbon was likewise ordered to receive the Nuncio's instructions as to the making good of the losses caused by the late King of Portugal's deflection of the Stucley expedition from its original destination.

MADRID CONFERENCE.

When the Cardinal Secretary wrote to Fitzmaurice, 26 August, to shift his quarters to Lisbon under pretext of seeing his son, the news of the Stucley debacle had not yet

---

[1] *C.S P., Rome*, 1572-78, no. 962.

reached him.[1] On the same day Mgr. Sega wrote to the Secretary that Geraldine had arrived at a villa a league and a half from Madrid, but had been forbidden by him to come to Madrid. Their conferences should be held in a house of the Discalced Friars outside the city. He encloses the following document drawn up by Dr. Sander :—[2]

A. Besides James [Fitzmaurice] a Nuncio Apostolic should accompany the army with the most ample powers in order : (1) that the cause of the faith, which once hurt will not easily be made whole again save by the authority of a most prudent protector, may ever be unimpaired ; (2) that ecclesiastics, who from all parts will flock to the holy war, may not lack their chief from whom they may receive authority to grant absolution to others ; (3) moreover, that secular princes, Irish, English or Scottish, who might be loth to submit to James may without envy and rivalry submit at least to a Nuncio Apostolic ; (4) finally, that should perchance a Legate Apostolic be afterwards sent to them, none may deem the advent of the Legate to be an innovation, the place of the legate having previously been supplied by the Nuncio. It is indeed a matter of much importance with what authority the conduct of affairs in the first instance rests.

B. The Nuncio should be an Italian, lest offence should be taken by the English, that an Irishman, or by the Irish, that an Englishman, should be preferred to them ; and the same reasoning holds equally good as to the Scots.

C. And if two of the fathers of the Society of Jesus, one to succeed the other, be appointed to this office, their venerable sanctity and grave wisdom will be extremely helpful to the cause in every respect.

D. With this Nuncio Apostolic there should be associated English, Irish, and Scottish priests, two at least from each of these nations, as well that they may make known to the Nuncio the plight of persons and things, as that they may conciliate the minds of the people by orations ; and that, if need be, there may never lack persons to be sent hither and thither with mandates. For it is scarcely possible but that upon the outbreak of war in any one of these islands, it must soon be begun in another also, especially if the business be managed with prudence and address.

E. Nor indeed is there lack of such priests either *in Urbe* [Rome], or in other cities of Italy.

F. It would be much to the purpose if His Holiness were to

---

[1] *C.S.P.*, *Rome*, 1572-78, no. 939.   [2] *Ib.*, no. 943.

give his Nuncio faculty of a bull of composition, so that it might be lawful for him to compound and dispense touching ill-gotten ecclesiastical goods, and disputable debts, with those that join the army, being penitent, and having confessed, *pro modo facultatum cujusque*.   For thus the war would be fed, and more by far would join therein.

G. A procedure should be adopted whereby the Kingdom of Portugal may make amends, as well to His Holiness as to the Catholics, Irish, and English, both for thwarting us and for depriving us of six hundred soldiers ; for that which the King did must also be deemed to have been done by all the realm.   Therefore, James [Fitzmaurice] having by His Holiness's letter been appointed Commander-in-Chief of the Catholics in Ireland, is competent to appoint some one his agent to claim compensation for this loss ; and should he fail to obtain all that is due, yet he can hardly fail to obtain ships and seamen, and at least some soldiers, or at any rate soldiers' stipends, especially if His Holiness plainly write that he cannot exonerate the Portuguese of this loss ; both because it has ceased to be *res integra* and some right has already been acquired by a third party, and also because it was God's business, and to God one must discharge one's obligations as it were *ex voto ad unguem*.

H. Besides three of the Irish Clergy, who are at Madrid, there is said to be resident in a town of Portugal which they call Portus [Oporto] Dr. [Nicholas] Quemerford who, I am informed, is of great authority among the Irish by reason alike of doctrine and of probity.   It would be well that he were admonished not to depart thence, as it was said he thought of doing.

I. As James [Fitzmaurice] says that he not only had very many friends in Ireland, but also of late has received by letters, from—among others—the Earl of Desmond himself an invitation to return as soon as possible, armed or unarmed, we have reason to entertain the greatest hope of doing the business splendidly ; nor should we allow the avoidance of a trifling pecuniary loss to deprive us of the greatest of gains.

L. Therefore, though the Nuncio say that he is loth that a greater sum of money should be hazarded before he learn that James has landed in Ireland ; nevertheless, since a war of this sort demands the utmost despatch, both lest the Irish should grow weary by prolonged exertion and lest larger reinforcements should be sent privily from England to Ireland, it is expedient that on landing James take charge of all the war ; and as he will be much more at ease in so doing if he have no lack of means to pay the soldiers, it is at least desirable that His Holiness should, from the money which he has in Spain, lend James some thousands meanwhile and afterwards recover them by the Nuncio. And certainly there will be much more difficulty in transmitting money subsequently, since there will neither be the same leader, nor so many soldiers to preserve it from the pirates.

M. It is of the utmost importance that his Holiness write to the Earl of Desmond, exhorting him to defend the cause of the faith ; for he is more potent than the rest and more intimate with James.

FITZMAURICE'S REQUISITES FOR HIS EXPEDITION.

On Friday, 28 August, 1578, Mgr. Sega, Dr. Sander, and Fitzmaurice met in conference at a Franciscan monastery outside the city for the purpose of examining the situation created by the defection of Stucley. It was indeed gloomy, as all that Fitzmaurice could show for his four-and-a-half years of weary waiting was a Papal Brief appointing him Captain-General of the Catholic forces in Ireland, a small store of arms and ammunition, a few score volunteers and hired soldiers, and a single ship, but without money. He had had letters from O'Donnell of Ulster and the Earl of Desmond who were anxiously awaiting his arrival. Indeed, it was said, all the magnates of Ireland were similarly minded.

Dr. Sander, however, was somewhat optimistic, and doubtless introduced for discussion the above document which he had drawn up. Something must be done at once " if the Irish are to be kept from growing weary of the prolonged struggle." Above all sufficient money must be forthcoming to maintain a standing army in the field, and for this purpose the Holy See might advance a certain sum, at least by way of loan. The Earl of Desmond should also be written to to defend the faith as he was more influential than the other chiefs, and more intimate with Fitzmaurice.

The following memorial [1] was handed in at the conference by Fitzmaurice (27 November) :—

James Fitzmaurice will cross over into Ireland with a firm determination to do all in his power to divert the forces of the Queen of England from causing loss in Flanders, and with the help of his

---

[1] *Catholic Bulletin,* June, 1929, p. 552. *C.S.P., Rome,* 1572-78, no. 1020.

friends and relatives, to rouse the whole country in support of the Catholic religion, of His Holiness, and of your Majesty. In this service he will be faithful to the day of his death : and even in death he will hand the same duty on to his [two] sons, whom in the meanwhile he will leave with his wife in Spain as hostages for his good faith. Not only this, but on the credit which he enjoys with his kinsmen and friends he relies for the successful issue of the venture. This he can do all the more readily because he can undertake to have 5000 foot-soldiers under arms with him within eight days after his landing, if only conditions in Ireland continue to be as reported some months before. There are already available for transport two bronze pieces of artillery, ten smaller iron pieces, fifty arquebuses, two hundred pikes, and twenty-four corslets. . . .

But to facilitate the enterprise, and to encourage the insurrection of his friends and kinsmen, he begs to be supplied with the following :—[1]

Fitzmorishe's instructions and advices of the number of soldiers, proportion of munitions, armour, and other necessaries to be provided by the Pope and King of Spain for the maintenance of this rebellion :

1. One ship of 400 tons.
2. Another ship of 50 tons.
3. A third ship of 20 tons.
4. 3 Small ships for entering rivers.
5. 600 soldiers.
6. Arms for same.
7. Wages for same for six months.
8. At least 10 skilful leaders from Italy or Spain.
9. 6 large engines of War.
10. Arms for at least 3000 soldiers.
11. At least 15 small Engines of War.
12. 10 barrels (*dolia*) of Cannon powder.
13. Balls and lead.
14. License to capture English ships.
15. License to sell the spoils in Spain.
16. 4 horses.[2]
17. That any of the Geraldine [Fitzmaurice's] possessions retaken in the war by Geraldine [i.e. James Fitzmaurice] may remain in that family.

---

[1] *S.P.I., Eliz.*, lxiv. 7, P.R.O., London.
[2] To enable him to convey to his friends and kinsmen the news of his landing.

18. That if any harbour belonging to the Geraldines or their confederates be delivered to the Captain in the name of His Holiness or of His Catholic Majesty, and afterwards other harbours and other places are delivered to the same captain, then its possession be given to Geraldine or the confederates.

19. That a legate or Apostolic Nuncio be sent with 20 learned priests.

20. That, if Geraldine should happily triumph then, at latest within six months, reinforcements of 6000 men be sent to him.

21. If His Catholic Majesty would be pleased to subscribe to this one article—i.e. that if the Princes of Ireland drive the English heretics out of the island, he will afterwards defend them against Elizabeth—then the whole business is transacted.

22. If Geraldine succeeds, then His Holiness and his Catholic Majesty should confer the title and possessions on himself and his children.

It is to be understood that all these petitions are made for the honour of God, and the good of His Holiness, and of his Catholic Majesty.

Jesus and Mary our Hope
James Geraldine Desmond.

It seems that God is united to aid this purpose of Geraldine, because [Sir] Henry Sidney, Viceroy of Ireland, is persecuted by the Earl of Ormonde, who is urged in England for his discharge from office; and he [Sydney] having a thorough understanding with [Turlough Luineach] O'Neill makes excuse with the Queen alleging obstacles to his return [to England], while the said O'Neill has written to the Queen to the express effect that, if she remove him, he will not suffer another Viceroy to go there. This Henry is friendly to Catholics, and it is for that reason that it is sought to compass his removal; and as he is apprehensive on his own account, it would be likely enough that at their instigation he should rise with the Province against the Queen, if he be assured of support.

The rising of the Scots gathers strength, and their movement will impart energy to this, and vice versa; and aid may be given in two ways, first, by money to be carried by Geraldine for disbursement to the King of Scotland himself; which money should be sent to him by one of the very same ships that will carry him to Ireland, the said ship sailing round the northern part of the island so as to pass safely to Scotland ; and secondly, by means of the expedition of Baron Dacre who, despatched in hot haste by Don John with a few men by way of Sweden to Scotland, may thence reach England to raise his people, who are near neighbours of the Scots, against the Queen, and assure the passage by that part of Ireland into England, if matters should take such a course as that Geraldine might go there.

But it is necessary that a decision be speedily reached as to what may be done :

(Italian copy. Found in conjunction with a letter of 29th Dec., 1578. Apparently the writer had not heard of the death, 2 Oct., 1578, of Don John of Austria.)

It was not until the middle of October that the Nuncio received the reply from Rome of 2 October, to the effect that " this clumsy dance of Geraldine and Stucley has by this time cost the Pope more than 50,000 crowns . . . for the present it will suffice to mobilise the 20,000 crowns that are at Lisbon, which will enable Geraldine to enlist a thousand picked soldiers picked up wherever he can find them, and with two ships to sail forthwith to Ireland ; and the Pope is content to supply him with whatever Captain Sebastiano San Joseppi has at his disposal, to wit, the arms and what few victuals remain [of the Stucley expedition]. . . . It seems that it is impossible to send any more troops or moneys from here." [1]

As the Pope suggested to act in concert with the King, the Nuncio discussed the situation with him with Fitzmaurice's petition for the 600 troops and other aids. Antonio Perez, the Spanish Secretary of State, was appointed by the King to confer with the Nuncio on the whole subject, but nothing came of it. The usual " sluggishness of the ministers " caused Fitzmaurice to lose his patience. The two Irish bishops, the Irish priests, and the soldiers that escaped from Africa were all anxious to start at once for Ireland. This was the report of the Nuncio, 18 October, who stated that " I discern here little hope of the King applying his mind to the matter in such good earnest as it requires." [2]

At last, 22 November, the Nuncio was able to report to

---

[1] *C.S.P., Rome,* 1572-78, no. 962.   [2] *Ib.,* no. 968.

Rome that the King had agreed that the Irish chief was to
go ahead, and that he was to have whatever remained of the
20,000 crowns, together with such sums as could be raised
for the purpose, and that Dr. Sander might accompany the
expedition. " I am now occupied," he says, " in hastening
the preparations for their speedy departure. Fitzmaurice's
boys are to remain under my care at Alcala : but he is to take
his wife with him, in the hope that her presence will move
her relatives to action when they see her." [1]

Fitzmaurice in " Great Straits."

In order to assist Fitzmaurice in his pecuniary embarrass-
ments the Nuncio in Spain had recourse to an ingenious
device. Lady Jane Dormer, Duchess of Feria, one of the
leaders of the English Catholic refugees at the Court of Spain,
had in her possession " two images of Our Lady with the
Saviour in arms, of St. Paul's Church at London in England ;
the one being of gold, and enamelled weighing sixteen and
a half marks or thereabouts, and the other of mere silver,
weighing about twelve marks." These were probably saved
at the time of the desecrating of the Catholic churches by
the iconoclasts and taken care of by the Duchess who managed
to carry them with her into Spain. The Nuncio requested
the Duchess to let him have the statues on loan in order
to raise money on them for Fitzmaurice. This she readily
agreed to, and the Nuncio sent them to the Collector Apostolic
at Lisbon as securities for a loan of " 600 ducats, the ducat
being reckoned at 375 maravedis ; that is to say, 6617 reals
and 22 maravedis." This money was to be paid into the
hands of Fitzmaurice, but Sander thought well of petitioning
the Pope, 27 November, for his approval. Before, however,
word could come from Rome the deal was made as there was
no time to be lost. But the Nuncio sent word, 15 December,
to the Cardinal Secretary that he had—[2]

caused the Collector to lend them 600 crowns upon certain images
that are worth much more. . . . Besides which I purchased a suit
of armour, and gave it to Geraldine; and to Sander I gave a

---

[1] *C.S.P., Rome,* 1572-78, no. 993.   [2] *Ib.,* nos. 997, 1005, 1012, 1013.

complete set of the ornaments of the Mass. And as I am sending with them four discalced friars of the Order of St. Francis, I have purchased for them a young mule, crucifixes, and some other trifles which they must needs have, that they may go more cheerfully, all which expenditure I mean to bear on my own account as first fruits of the church which it has pleased His Holiness to give me, as I deem it applied to very good purpose. Besides which, as there has returned hither from Lisbon one Thomas Miniers [Miners] after a long incarceration, without cause, as he proves, by Stucley, I have resolved to send him back again; and I shall give him money for the journey and letters of recommendation to Geraldine and Sander, who have departed, the one for Biscay to fetch his wife, and the other for Lisbon; thence the commissary already writes me that he had virtually arranged for the ship in which he was to depart. They will assemble in a port of Galicia, and thence will set sail for Ireland in God's name. . . . There is here a son of Geraldine, twelve years of age, and in Lisbon there is another 13 years of age, who will come here. They will both be under my protection until some other decision is taken; and I have 400 crowns to expend in relief of their needs. Geraldine would be pleased if it should be agreeable to His Holiness that I should send them to Rome to be brought up in one of the Colleges there.

The Cardinal wrote to the Nuncio in Spain on 29 December that His Holiness was pleased to grant to all the Irish bishops who have joined the army faculty to preach, and absolve in all cases, even the most reserved, as requested by Sander, and that he " approved the alienation of those two images of which you write, seeing that the money thereby raised is to subserve a work so just and holy." [1]

An Irish priest, John White, starting for Ireland, was also granted by a Brief of Gregory XIII, 4 November, faculty to absolve all penitents, applying to him in the realm of Ireland, of all sins, including those reserved to the Holy See and comprised in the Bull *Coenae Domini*, and likewise heresy and schism; with ample powers of granting dispensations in other matters.[2]

Provisions also were being made for the education of some Irish students. The Nuncio in France wrote to the Cardinal on 1 September, 1578 : " I am besought by one of the Jesuit Fathers, an Irishman, to notify the Pope that some

---

[1] *C.S.P., Rome*, 1572-78, no. 1019.   [2] *Ib.*, no. 985.

of his fellow-countrymen, and in particular some of those who, by means of His Holiness, have on former occasions been in receipt of aid in the Universities of Louvain and Douai, have come hither, being dispersed by the tumults of Flanders ; among whom are some priests ; and so poor are they that they are unable either to pursue their studies or to maintain themselves." They desire His Holiness to maintain a little establishment of twelve of these priests in Rome or where else he please.[1]

On the 10th December the Nuncio in Spain wrote to the Cardinal recommending the bearer, a young Irishman named Nicholas Hickey, commended to him by Geraldine that he may continue his studies for the priesthood at Rome, " sharing with the rest of his compatriots in the benignity of the Pope." [2]

BISHOP OF EMLY'S PERSONAL PROPERTY LANDED AT WATERFORD.

Maurice MacBrien, Bishop of Emly, had been in Rome in April, 1573, and brought a letter from the Pope, of 7 April, to the Nuncio at Madrid, who assured the Cardinal Secretary, 17 June, that he would not fail to afford him all the help he could with the King, in conformity with His Holiness's instructions.[3] The Cardinal had stated in his letter that MacBrien had been expelled from his See by the heretics, and had repaired to Rome where he was graciously received by the Pope.[4] From June, 1573, to 27 November, 1574, MacBrien seems to have remained in Spain or thereabouts. By a letter of the latter date the Nuncio in Spain informed the Cardinal Secretary of a conversation he had with the King about some requests of MacBrien to His Majesty, where-upon the King said he had advices from Rome on the subject.[5] The matter evidently referred to a subsidy from the King to the Irish chiefs. Nothing more is heard of the Bishop until his packet of belongings was held up at the Quay of Waterford by one of Drury's men, 25 March, 1578. The

---

[1] *C.S.P., Rome,* 1572-78, no. 947.
[2] *Ib.,* no. 1009. See *Hist. MSS., Merchant's Quay,* p. 86, for the Hickey family.
[3] *C.S.P., Rome,* 1572-78, no. 205.
[4] *Ib.,* no. 174.   [5] *Ib.,* no. 367.

Bishop had landed at Liverpool and intended to take ship for Galway.

One of the most interesting lists of a Catholic Bishop's personal property is described in the document drawn up by Drury's man who examined the ship and found—

certain papistical garments and other like ceremonies belonging to one Morr McBrien, a pretended bishop of Emlye,[1] in this province [*blank*] which stuff and nigling boxes, with other like varieties [. . .] were by the said Bishop's man brought aboard [. . .] at their departure from Calais. The trumpery I have [. . .] seen. There is besides the parcels contained in the inventory certain bones of men which by writing under seal [. . .] are alleged to be the bones of saints. Other writings of authority were brought over among the said Bishop's things and because your honour shall the better be acquainted with the devices now brought hither as instruments of sedition, I send you honour of every part of those writings [2] a piece to peruse [. . .] for as I take these persons and their furniture to be the forerunner of some great mischief, either by foreign invasion or civil rebellion. So, so far as I learn, they are set on thereto by James Fitzmaurice.

[He has sent to Galway to Sir Nicholas Malby to cause the Bishop to be apprehended.]

A note of such things as are brought into this realm of Ireland, landed at Waterford in two budgets [packets] belonging to the pretended Bishop of Emly, of late come from Spain, and as is said arrived at Galway, 28 March 1578.

Item. 3 Vestments with an Altar Cloth.
,, A silver cup gilt within and without.
,, 12 coletts of blue and white taffeta.
,, 3 coletts of black taffeta.
,, 2 ounces of gold wire.
,, A coat, and a gown and his rocket.
,, A girdle of black silk.
,, A gold ring.
,, 2 ounces of black silk.
,, 1 ounce of black passamano.
    an Inkhorn wherein is balsam.
,, 7 pair of beads.

---

[1] Maurice MacBrien was appointed by the Pope to this See, 22 Jan., 1567. In the Protestant arrangement the See was united to Cashel by Elizabeth in 1568.

[2] These extracts are not attached to the document in the P.R.O., London.

Item. 4 primers of Latin.
  ,,   3 Combs.
       a tooth-pick of Ivory bone.
       a white doublet, a red cap, and a primer of Latin.
  ,,   2 felts of taffeta.
       a silver cross.
  ,,   6 Corposstes.
       A box wherein is relics which is in a bag with the Cross.
[Underneath is written in another hand] :

After the letter was sealed, in farther searching, Bulls from
Rome, bones and relics were found, with a testimonial under a
great seal avouching the virtue of them which caused me to break
off the letter being sealed.

W. Drury.[1]

Fitzmaurice Anxiously Awaited in Ireland.

For the past year the burden of the many letters received
from Ireland was that Fitzmaurice " was eagerly expected
by many friends now in arms against the Queen of England,"
and that " a rising of importance is likely to follow his advent
to the country." Fitzmaurice had put this aspect of the
case before Rome and Spain in his appeals for help. When
he was driven by the gales into Baiona in Galicia, he wrote
to Dr. Sander, 3 December, 1577, " that he had letters from
two potent princes of Ireland, O'Donnell of Ulster, and the
Earl of Desmond, by whom he is very affectionately invited." [2]
Four months after that, his friend and colleague, Bishop
O'Hely of Mayo, wrote to Rome that O'Neill, O'Donnell, and
O'Rourke were out in insurrection, and would strongly
support Fitzmaurice if he but returned quickly, but, he continued, " there is not a little reason to apprehend that, unless
he get to Ireland as soon as possible, all the magnates and
nobles of that country, and his friends, and indeed all the
Catholics of England and Ireland may shortly be slain. . . .
For the Queen of England, having heard some rumours
about James and Stucley, is much more ruthless against the
Catholics than she has ever hitherto been, and patrols and

[1] *S.P.I.*, *Eliz.*, lx. 27, P.R.O., London.
[2] *C.S.P.*, *Rome*, 1572-78, no. 714.

searches the ocean and most of the ports of Ireland with her ships. Moreover, it is no ordinary opportunity that now presents itself of doing the business once and for all; for the Scots, who speak the same language as the Irish, and are united with them by a league of friendship, are all in arms and bestirring themselves might and main." [1] In July, 1578, the Irish chiefs then in arms are given as O'Neill and O'Donnell in the North, de Burgo in Connacht, and Rory O'More in Leinster.

In October, 1578, the Collector Apostolic in Lisbon received a letter from the Bishop of Killaloe [2] stating :—

Five days ago there arrived here ships from the city of Waterford in Ireland. . . . In one of those ships there came . . . an intimate friend of mine who explained all things to me exactly. For he, shortly before his arrival, was conversing with the Earl of Desmond and his brother, Lord John Desmond ; who asked him to meet Lord James [Fitzmaurice] wherever he might be, and persuade him not to postpone going to Ireland, because in all Munster there are no Englishmen, and likewise the people are ready to harbour and aid him ; and since the Viceroy of Ireland [Sydney] was about to go to England, there was now more possibility than hitherto of something being accomplished before more Englishmen should be sent to Ireland, seeing that he might make a stand at the outset before they should capture munitions and some cities ; which being taken, though all England should attack Ireland, it would be in vain. Lastly two sons of the Earl of Clanricarde, who formerly aided Lord James [Fitzmaurice] in war, have just of late risen against the English, and are able to lend no little aid and support to the affair. Also the sons of the late Lord John Ynell [Shane O'Neill] will march with 600 Scottish soldiers to join Lord James as soon as they are apprised of his advent ; besides which all the more eminent nobles of all the realm await him, and most eagerly desire his advent ; nor is there any watch or aught else to hinder it.

Among the common people of our country the general bruit is that Lord James [Fitzmaurice] has gone to Flanders, thence by way of Scotland to come to Ireland. Such is the news that I have been able to learn ; and if His Most Reverend Lordship has learned aught either at Rome or at Madrid touching our business, may he deign to inform me thereof.

---

[1] *C.S.P.*, *Rome*, 1572-78, no. 776.   [2] *Ib.*, no. 976.

The friend or messenger referred to by the Bishop of Killaloe was probably the Franciscan Father Sean O'Farrell of Askeaton. This appears from evidence given by another Franciscan, James O'Hea, who, falling into the hands of the English at a later date, was examined on 17 August, 1580, as to his relations with Fitzmaurice in Spain at this very time. Father O'Hea stated that Father O'Farrell had brought messages from the Earl of Desmond to Fitzmaurice at Madrid, and then came to Bilbao where he (O'Hea) met him. O'Hea asked O'Farrell, " What news from Ireland, and he said both good and bad. And he asked him how the Earl of Desmond did. He answered that he was well if he had James Fitzmaurice home and that the Earl had sent him to see and visit him, and willed if James had found any favour or succour there that he should bring them over into Ireland ; and if he found no favour, that then he should come himself." He added that " the Earl could not live without Fitzmaurice."

The Franciscans were very busy at this time as intermediaries, and many of them suffered the extreme penalty for " seditious practices." The Father O'Farrell mentioned above, is probably a certain Father Geoffrey or Godfrey O'Farrell, who is mentioned as having suffered death at Askeaton about a year later. Another Franciscan who suffered death for " seditious practices " is mentioned in a report from Waterford, 24 March, 1578, by Drury, President in Munster, to the Privy Council :—[1]

There have been, to my judgment, since my first entry into office, about four hundred executed by Justice and Martial Law within this province, among the which some have been so notorious and so well allied, and one so dear to James Fitzmaurice, as when he heard of his death, he wept, for whom and for others as also for one Cormac Doune, of late hanged on chains for a murder, I could have had large sums to have consented to their pardoning, if I could have regarded mine own commodity than the profits of the commonwealth.

Among the which a Friar was of late apprehended arraigned and hanged in his habit at Limerick for having about him certain letters with blanks and the seals of several Abbeys and Friaries in this province, with letters of commendation to the Provincial of

[1] Brady, *State Papers*, no. xvi.

Portugal, importing seditious practices to be intended and he as a trusty messenger sent to negotiate.

He was apprehended, being ready to depart to the sea into Portugal from the river of Limerick for whose life also a good sum would have been given.

A judge also of Rory Oge's, termed a Brehon, who was much esteemed among the common people, and taught and practised only such laws as are repugnant to her Majesty's laws, was likewise hanged at Limerick.

On Drury's way to Waterford from Limerick, he held sessions at Cashel and Clonmel, where ten were executed for treason and felony and one was pressed to death.

The Franciscan referred to by Drury was probably Father Thady O'Daly, a native of Askeaton and a member of the community of Roscrea.

Only one of the letters sent about this time to Fitzmaurice has survived. It fell into the hands of the English authorities by whom it was sent to London. It is written in Irish and purported to have been written by one William of Danubi,[1] who refers to the Earl of Desmond as his lord or patron. He speaks in the name of the Earl and urges Fitzmaurice to hasten to Ireland with such help as he could gather together. " I beseech you in the name of God and in my master's name to bring relief soon," to co-operate with those who are in the field, de Burgh of Connacht, Rory O'More in Leinster, and others elsewhere. " The flame of war," he says, " has grown up in many of the men of Erin against the Saxons, if they but get help. . . . Be assured of it that we cannot tell how much we are in want of you ; and though we should like that a host of men should come along with you, we would be exceedingly glad that you yourself should come to our aid . . . for we think that the greatest part of the men of Erin are ready to rise with ourselves, and we would be much the better of you. Do not wait for the harvest, for there is danger that the whole affair be set aside by that time. . . . I do not write this of my own accord, but at the request of my master." He adds that it is dangerous to write at all, for other letters of the same nature have fallen into the hands of the English, one of which was from the Seneschal of Imokilly,

---

[1] *Kilk. Arch. Journ.*, 1858-59, pp. 360-1. Irish and English versions.

who had written to Fitzmaurice that " the wheat of the friars has grown well, and the wheat of the country has failed." This phrase was evidently pre-arranged and doubtless conveyed much meaning.

All kinds of alarming letters were being received in London conveying often exaggerated news. It was reported, in April, 1579, that " certain Irishmen are preparing in Biscay, and that 1500 Scots Highlanders have gone over to Ireland." [1] It was apparent, however, to all that rebellion was in the air, and Drury complained that the rebellious tendency had been accentuated by the Queen's parsimony. He had been, he said, left " wholly destitute of money, victuals, and munitions " for the defence of the country against foreign invasion and native insubordination. The situation in Ulster, too, was not without its dangers. One of Tirlogh Luineach's daughters had been given in marriage to young Hugh O'Neill, and another to Sorley Boy, thus consolidating on the one hand the power of the O'Neill family, and on the other enlisting the support of the well-armed auxiliaries from the Highlands of Scotland when he considered the time meet for a conflict with the English. But the situation in Munster was not so rosy from the Irish point of view. The power of the chiefs had been gradually undermined by Drury's presidency, and the Earl of Desmond had been driven from concession to concession. He had been able to stave off complete ruin by armed protests and by the abject submissions he had made under the dominating influence of the Countess whose main concern was the safeguarding of the family estates for her son, who, however, was never to enjoy them but to spend all his life in the Tower of London. [2]

EXPEDITIONARY FORCE FOR IRELAND.

The plan of the expedition having been arranged by Mgr. Sega, Dr. Sander, and Fitzmaurice at Madrid, the next thing was to raise the small force and to charter a ship to carry the Irish chief and his men. This could not be done in Spain, as the King would not break with Elizabeth by

[1] *S.P.I., Eliz.*, lxvi. 50, 51, 52.
[2] *Catholic Bulletin*, July, 1929, pp. 626-33.

allowing troops and ships to be raised in his country. It was agreed by the three confederates that Lisbon was a suitable place, chiefly because greater secrecy could be observed there. Captain San Joseppi, the Papal Commissary in Lisbon, was accordingly instructed to recruit a couple of hundred Spanish and Italian troops in the neighbourhood, and to charter a suitable ship to convey them into Ireland. Letters were also sent to the Papal Nuncio in Portugal, Mgr. Frumento, to render every assistance, and to the King of Portugal for his good-will and support. Dr. Sander and Fitzmaurice's agent, Captain Fleming, were despatched to Lisbon to supervise the preparations, and to bring influence to bear on the King and his ministers. Fitzmaurice was directed to return to France, get his ship and supplies, and as many men as possible ready in the harbour of Ferrol in Northern Spain. Dr. Sander and the Lisbon expedition would pick them up there as soon as they were able to sail, which they expected would be early in the new year (1579).

Although the King of Portugal showed his sympathy in a practical way by a handsome contribution towards the expenses of the expedition, he insisted that the preparations should be managed in such a way as not to arouse the suspicions of Elizabeth. It was thus necessary that a Catalan rather than a Portuguese ship should be chartered, and that it should be given out that it was intended to carry back to Italy the arms and munitions that remained in the hands of San Joseppi, and that the troops were required to act as a convoy to Civitá Vecchia.

Notwithstanding all the delays, due to the secret method of working the arrangements, the Nuncio was able to report, 15 February, 1579, that "they have now shipping, munitions, arms, money, and about 200 soldiers," Spanish and Italian. Everything looked promising for the success of the expedition when an incident occurred which terminated it miserably. Delay and disaster seemed to be for ever dogging the footsteps of Fitzmaurice. The soldiers were actually under orders to embark "when one of them was arrested on some charge or other, and tried to save himself from the arm of the law by proclaiming that he was the Pope's soldier, thus making the affair public property, whereupon the King of Portugal, who did not wish to have it known that he had any hand in the transaction, ordered Sander to depart out of the kingdom, sequestrated the ship, and disbanded the soldiers, so that everything was upset, and despite every effort that was made it was found impossible to recover the ship until several months had passed." [1]

Meanwhile Fitzmaurice had made his own preparations, and had gathered his own company, including his wife, the Bishop of Killala, Father Matthew de Oviedo (afterwards Archbishop of Dublin), with some Franciscans, and a number of soldiers amounting in all to some seventy souls. All were ready to embark on the ship that lay safe in the harbour of Ferrol. But their optimism was rudely shaken when Dr. Sander arrived in haste from Lisbon to tell them the sad news of the Lisbon contingent. Four weary months passed by in the hope that something might be done to release the ship and its company which was still held up in the harbour of Lisbon by order of the King. Tired of waiting, they arrived at a decision that was to prove one of the most fateful in the whole course of Irish history. [2]

Bishops of Killaloe and Killala at Lisbon ; Ship and Soldiers for Ireland.

The official spies and watchers on the south coast had their ears open for every piece of stray news brought by the merchants plying between the Irish ports and Spain and France. The following is one of the fullest declarations made :—

At Limerick. The declaration of James Fagan of the City of Waterford, merchant, made before Sir Edward Fitton, Knight, Vice-Treasurer and Treasurer at Wars for Her Majesty in the realm of Ireland, and Sir Lucas Dillon, Knight, Chief Baron of Her Majesty's Court of Exechequer in the said realm, the 23rd day of March 1578 [i.e. 1579], by the appointment of the right honourable the Lord Justice, and being present likewise James Golde, Her Majesty's Attorney in the province of Munster.

---

[1] Mgr. Sega's *Relazione Compendiosa* (*Vat. Arch.*) ; a detailed account of the Desmond wars, 1579-83.

[2] *Catholic Bulletin*, June, 1929, pp. 555-6.

He saith that the 15 day of February last past he was at Lisbon in Portugal and there saw two Romish bishops, the one naming himself Bishop of Killaloe beside Limerick, and the other of Killala in Connacht, who late were come from Rome, both of this country birth, and the one called Conoghor O'Mulryan [1] and the other Donoghe Oge O'Gallagher. [2]

And that they had in their company attending upon them three hundred lusty soldiers of Italians and others, and one goodly ship of 300 tons very well appointed, which bishops and their company were, at the departure of the said James Fagan, ready to go to the sea to meet James Fitzmaurice in Galicia or in Biscay. Being demanded what company James Fitzmaurice was, he answered he saw him not but that they reported that he had 6 or 7 shallupes which he provided in Biscay, and there did furnish and man them. Being questioned with—what was the pretence of their voyage—he said it was given abroad there openly, and one of their own men told the said Fagan, and himself thought it most likely, that it was to land in Ireland, either in Connacht or Ulster, and did retain one William Roche, sometime having charge of Ordnance at Castlemayne, in Sir John Perrott's time, as a man of best skill to pilot ships upon the west coast of Ireland ; and another James Den of Galway, a pilot upon the said coast, for that purpose.

Further being asked who bore the charge of that company, he answered that the Pope did bear all and that the Collector of his finances in Lisbon did pay the entertainment of the soldiers and all other things that the bishops wanted.

Being questioned with—what gentlemen or others came with them—he said " he heard of none but one Dr. Sander, who was by letters from the Pope commended to attend upon James Fitzmaurice (as was reported) and saith that accordingly Doctor Sander departed out of Lisbon aforesaid two days before he left Lisbon, toward the said James. But what message he had or whether he were to return or not he cannot affirm.

Being asked whether the bishops had the ship, he answered that the ship was Stucley's, and that she went in the late Portugal voyage into Barbary, and upon her return, the Pope sent direction that she with all her furniture should be delivered to the said bishops to attend upon James Fitzmaurice.

Being demanded at what time he left Lisbon saith that he departed thence the 20th of the last month, and that the said

---

[1] Cornelius Ryan who was appointed by the Pope, 22 Aug., 1576, to Killaloe in the place of Malachy O'Molony who was translated to Kilmacduagh.

[2] He succeeded to Killala in 1570. He had been to Rome on other occasions.

bishops were to go thence within 6 or 7 days after. Affirming further that there is no doubt (unless God let them) but that they will land here in Ireland very shortly, for the men be willingly, they want no treasure, they lack no furniture, and they have skilful leaders.

Item. Leonard Sutton of Wexford, merchant who passed in the same ship from Lisbon to Galway with the above mentioned James Fagan, affirmeth the declaration of the said Fagan on all points.[1]

The ease with which sailors and merchants picked up information in foreign ports is quite remarkable, the very sailors of Fitzmaurice's crew furnishing it themselves readily. The only item practically in which they were astray was in regard to the Irish port for which they were bound. This was probably kept a secret.

The Ill-starred Expedition Sets Sail.

The King of Portugal, who was sadly in need of friends, and who did not wish to make an enemy of Elizabeth, not only forbade the expedition to leave his shores but disbanded the papal soldiers and ordered San Joseppi and Dr. Sander to quit the kingdom within ten days. Although Sander repaired in haste to Fitzmaurice to tell him the sad news, San Joseppi insisted on remaining in Lisbon as he was a papal official. He had had orders from the Pope to keep the arms and munitions in his custody, and he would not leave until he could take them back to Italy. Having applied to the Madrid Nuncio for directions in his difficulty, he was ordered by him to remove the arms from the ship and to deposit them safely at Lisbon, pending the arrival of the new Nuncio Lisbon, who was expected shortly. Reluctantly San Jose__ __emoved them to Portuguese territory, consoled by the idea __ __ perhaps the new Nuncio would be able to induce the King to release the ship and arms for Fitzmaurice's use.

The months were passing and still nothing would move the King to consent. Meanwhile, Fitzmaurice wrote, 28 April, from Corunna in Galicia, that he was determined to set out for Ireland in the near future, help or no help, " in the hope

---

[1] *S.P.I.*, *Eliz.*, lxvi. 14, i., P.R.O., London.

that after all his trials God will assist him in the end." With this determination, he was able to state, Sander thoroughly agreed. After a delay of four months, the King yielded to the pressure of Rome and Madrid, and consented to the departure of the ship. On 22 June San Joseppi announced to Rome that they were sailing that very day and hoped to be with Fitzmaurice in a few weeks.

Misfortunes were gathering more thickly around this expedition. Having sailed out of the port of Lisbon with favourable winds and well equipped for its long journey, the ship was compelled by adverse weather to put into the harbour of Noya, on the north-west coast of Spain, where it had to suffer the fate of all foreign shipping. It was held up until word should come from Madrid that it should not be included in the general orders for shipping. But before the word arrived, the ship in the apparently safe waters of the port was struck by a violent storm which dismantled her of masts, sails, etc., thus rendering her unfit for proceeding on her journey until the necessary repairs were made. As funds were low, the delay was all the greater.

Meanwhile Fitzmaurice, who had taken up residence in the neighbourhood of Bilbao with his wife and family, was busy enlisting soldiers and chartering ships. On the strength of letters from the Spanish King to the Governor, Don Juan Alonzo, the latter offered to let him have 300 men, but, as these were raw and unarmed, Fitzmaurice contented himself with some fifty veterans whom he had collected. As to his ship, he was fortunate in securing the *St. Francis* of Portogalete, with all its equipment, stores, artillery, and ammunition, the contract for which was witnessed by his chaplain, Father Laurence Moore. This took place about the middle of February, 1579.

A few weeks later Dr. Sander arrived at Ribadeo, whither Fitzmaurice had gone, with the unpleasant news of the disbanding of the troops by the King of Portugal. Neither of them had yet learned of the still further disaster of the dismantling of the ship by the storm. Eager to be on his way Fitzmaurice cried out : " I care for no soldiers at all ; you and I are enough ; therefore, let us go, for I know the minds of the noblemen of Ireland." On reflection, however, they agreed that they must first ascertain the views of the Nuncio at Madrid, which they awaited at Corunna and which was favourable to their proposal.

In the midst of their preparations they found time to write to the Lisbon Nuncio, 31 May, whom they thanked for his efforts in their behalf. At the same time they expressed their indignation very forcibly against the King of Portugal :—

As our only object [they say] is to secure the administration of Christ's Sacraments to a Catholic people in a Catholic rite, and as to have a care of these things is religion pure and undefiled, let those who hinder this holy work ask themselves to what religion they will be considered to belong by Him Who judges not by word but by work. . . . If we have the arms without further delay, the salvation of Ireland and England, not to say of Scotland, Flanders and France, will be ascribed to your efforts ; for it is from England that the great evil of schism is propagated into all the neighbouring countries. But if you see no hope of success for your efforts, care should be taken lest by pretending to hand over the arms soon, and by failing later on to do so, those responsible should hinder us still further from rendering to the Catholics such small help as we can bring them without the arms in question. Let them therefore give up the property which belongs to others and which they are detaining against the will of the owners, or let them feel that whatever they may urge they are refusing them to us, to His Holiness, to Christ Himself. Let them remember the damage they have been causing by making so many persons incur so many months' expense in a foreign country ; and let them bear in mind that there is a just Judge Who will requite them for their work. Good cause we have to be angry, for we have been subjected to great inconvenience and injury ; but the greater these are the more glorious will be your achievement if you but succeed in bringing them to an end.[1]

To Fitzmaurice only one thing mattered now, namely, his own return, with or without foreign help, as he was eagerly awaited by the Irish chiefs, and in the capacity of, what was of the greatest importance, Captain-General of the Catholic forces in Ireland duly appointed by the Pope. After mature consideration, Sander and he decided to set out for Ireland with the shipping, soldiers, and arms they

[1] *Catholic Bulletin*, July, 1929, pp. 626-33.

had at Ferrol. In coming to this decision they were influenced to a great extent by the repeated assurances of Rome and Madrid that, if they were successful in inducing the country to rebel, they might rely on substantial help from Pope and King. Whether this was seriously meant or not it is not easy to say, but the weakness of such an expedition must have been apparent to Madrid and Rome. The Pope, while over and over again bewailing his inability to contribute more funds, relied on the magic of his name and authority to rally the chiefs around Fitzmaurice. In this he was mistaken, as he took no account of the petty differences that were for ever hurling them at one another's heads. They believed that they could look after religion in their own way in their own territories, but to unite for that purpose under any one of them was the supreme difficulty. This will become abundantly apparent in the sequel to this disastrous expedition.

Having left Cornelius Ryan, Bishop of Killaloe, in Spain, to look after the ship and arms detained in Lisbon which they hoped would soon follow them to Ireland, Sander and Fitzmaurice, with their little band, set sail from Ferrol, 17 June, for the Dunanoir of Smerwick at the entrance to Dingle Bay.

EXPEDITION ARRIVES AT DINGLE.

Never did such a tiny force set out to face such a mighty foe as that which sailed out of Ferrol, 17 June, 1579. In all it did not exceed some seventy souls which included Fitzmaurice, Sander, O'Gallagher, the Bishop of Killala, four Irish priests, four Franciscans, including Father de Oviedo, and fifty Spanish and Italian soldiers. "Their strength," says Mgr. Sega,[1] "lay in Fitzmaurice's name, which was itself a firebrand, in their being representatives of the Pope, and in the precious banner blessed by His Holiness's hands, on which was emblazoned a Christ upon the Cross." Besides the ship that he had already bought, Fitzmaurice chartered three boats that were about to leave the Asturias for the fishing off the Irish coast. Such was

---

[1] *Relazione Compendiosa (Vat. Arch.).*

the fleet, and such the army that after years of waiting and
begging from Kings and Pope the Irish chief was with the
greatest difficulty able to muster.

During their few weeks at sea, they captured a French
ship which they immediately released as it belonged to
Catholic sympathisers, an Irish ship which they released for
a like reason, and an English one carrying a valuable cargo
of iron which they handed over to the owners of the Spanish
fishing boats by way of payment for their services. The
only other incident of their voyage was an attack by an
English corsair that, after a fierce fight, they completely
routed.

Reaching Dursey Sound on the 14 July, they fell in with
a fishing smack, and taking the men on board, they sent one
of them with a message to Sir Owen O'Sullivan to say that
the strangers would like to have conversation with him.
The result of the message was a despatch from O'Sullivan
to the Mayor of Cork to the effect that strangers were off the
coast and that he suspected them to be none other than
Fitzmaurice's men. Having received no favourable reply,
the boats put out to sea again, sailed past Dursey Head and
the Skelligs, and late in the evening of the 17th sailed into
Dingle Harbour. The Harbour Master sent word next morning to the Earl of Desmond that six Spanish ships were in
the Bay and that he suspected they belonged to Fitzmaurice.
Spanish ships and Fitzmaurice were at the time uppermost
in everybody's mind. When the Constable of Castlemaine
heard that the strangers had landed at Dingle and taken
some of the townsmen prisoners, he at once sent word to
the authorities.

In a letter, 22 July, James Golde informed the Mayor of
Limerick " in post haste for life " that " the traitor [Fitz-
maurice] upon Saturday last [18th] came out of his ships in
this manner : Two friars in their habits were his ancient
[standard] bearers, and they went before with two ancients
[standards]. A Bishop with a crozier staff and his mitre
was next the friars. After these came the traitor himself
and had in his company about a hundred, and went to speak
for flesh. Eight kine only they found, and so returned to
his ships. The number of his company are six vessels ;

39 *

two of them about three score tons apiece ; the rest are small barques. The number of his men are unknown. Every night he makes beacons or fires upon the highest hills, and gives abroad that he looks for more ships to follow. He has taken a little fort called Downyn [Duinin, i.e. Dun-an-oir] in Smerwick haven, whither he is removed from Dingle, a high rock upon the top whereof [he has raised] a wall for defence. Look well to yourselves and have spies continually abroad. To-morrow, God willing, we will beat him out of his fort or else he shall beat us. As far as I gather he looks for help in Connacht. As soon as you read this letter send it away in a letter enclosed to the Lord Justice at all post haste." [1]

As many inaccurate and coloured versions of what followed the landing of Fitzmaurice have been handed down by partisans of both sides,[2] it is important to get at the narratives of those who were on the spot and who knew what they were talking about. The story, as woven from the accounts of those who had a hand in the business, may be briefly stated.

The expedition, arranged in processional order, landed at Dingle pier, shortly before noon on Saturday, 18 July, to the chant of the Litany of the Saints. Leading the procession were two Franciscans, bearing banners, one of which was the Papal Standard emblazoned with the emblem of the Holy Cross. A Bishop in mitre and crozier followed. Then came Fitzmaurice, Dr. Sander, priests and friars, the members of Fitzmaurice's family, fifty or sixty soldiers, the crews of the six vessels, and perhaps a number of prisoners captured on the voyage from Spain. The priests who were four in number, were probably Fathers Laurence Moore, Cornelius Neachtan, Cornelius O'Boyle, and Patrick Synnott. The friars also were four, and were probably Fathers James O'Hea, Sean O'Farrell, and Patrick O'Rourke, with Father Matthew de Oviedo at their head.[3]

As provisions for the party were of supreme importance

---

[1] *S.P.I., Eliz.*, lxvii. 41, P.R.O., London. *Catholic Bulletin*, August, 1929, pp. 720-2.

[2] The accounts given by O'Sullivan Beare, O'Daly, and Russell must be regarded as having as little value as those given by Hooker, Camden, and Bishop Carlton.

[3] *Catholic Bulletin*, September, 1929, pp. 827-8.

they seized some cattle, took as prisoners some of the loyal townsmen who opposed them, and burned their houses. Taking to their boats again, they put out to sea, sailing by the Blaskets, and entered the little harbour of Smerwick. Here was a small promontory jutting out into the bay, and connected with the mainland by a narrow neck of land. This was Dun-an-oir, or The Golden Fort, destined to become one of the saddest landmarks in the annals of Ireland, whilst in the district around lay the stone monuments of a glorious Celtic past, Gallerus' Oratory, beehive cells, and Kilmakeldar. Having erected a stone wall across the neck of land, with trench and mound, they mounted on it their cannons, conveyed to the fort from the ships their stores of wine, oil, beer, sea-biscuits, and meat, and waited eagerly for good tidings from the neighbouring chiefs.

FITZMAURICE'S CALL TO ARMS.

Whilst bonfires blazed on Brandon Head and Connor Hill, and were repeated on the other hill-tops around Dingle, giving the alarm along the coast to Tralee and inland to Castlemaine, telling of strange happenings, perhaps long expected and understood by the people of the surrounding country, messengers were sped in all directions with proclamations and letters to chiefs and people calling upon them to take up arms and join the Papal General in the great and new struggle for faith and country. One of these was the following appeal :—

TO THE RIGHT HONOURABLE PRELATES, PRINCES, LORDS, ESTATES, CITIZENS, AND PEOPLE OF IRELAND : [1]

Our Holy Father Pope Gregory XIII, Christ's Vicar in earth, perceiving what dishonour to God and His Saints, what destruction to Christian souls in Ireland and England, what sedition, tumult, spoil and murder, hath fallen to Scotland, France and Flanders by the procurement of Elizabeth, the pretended Queen of England— perceiving also that neither the warning of other Catholic princes and good Christians, nor the sentence of Pope Pius V, his predecessor, nor the long sufferance of God, could cause her to forsake her schism, heresy, and wicked attempts—as he now purposes,

[1] *Kilk. Arch. Journ.*, 1858-59, pp. 364-8.

not without the consent of other Catholic powers, to deprive her actually of the unjust possession of these kingdoms, which she uses for the chief instruments of her impiety ; so he first of all attempts her said actual deprivation by the means of our dear country, wherein he does us more honour and favour than can easily be expressed in words. For whereas he understands that other great princes wait for a due time and good occasion to revenge the manifold injuries which they have received by the said Elizabeth, he, like a good father, knowing that commonly the commons do bear the pain which is due for the prince's fault, has taken the correction of these disorders into his own hands, thereby desiring to save and excuse us from all foreign invasions, which otherwise ought and shortly would have been made into our lands, possessions and houses, to our great damage and perhaps utter destruction. . . . If we then dispossess her first, shall not the country of Ireland obtain the greatest glory that ever it had since it was an Ireland ? Shall not also this our glory be accompanied with God's honour, with liberty of conscience, with doing good to our neighbours, and with enjoying our own goods, which hitherto have been at the unjust commandment of heretics ?

Now, in that His Holiness sends no greater foreign power with us to do this act, it declares, first, that he would not have the country oppressed with strangers ; it declares, secondly, that he has great trust and confidence in our faith towards God and in our obedience towards himself ; it also declares that he himself considers the proper power of our country sufficient for this exploit ; and no wonder ; for if we ourselves list not to hinder one another, but do agree and join together (as he trusts we will, and indeed we ought to do), it is certain that there is no power in this realm able to withstand our forces. . . .

What an extreme folly it is to fear the power of man more than the power of God ? If any man die for the defence of Elizabeth, can she save him before the throne of God ? Shall not he rather be contemned there for maintaining a heretic against the command of Christ's Vicar ? For if Christ left St. Peter as the chief pastor and governor of His flock, seeing the Pope of Rome is St. Peter's lawful successor, are we not bound, that are the flock of Christ, to assist our chief pastor when he commands one that by baptism is a member of the same flock to cease from the evil government which she has so long usurped, to the utter undoing of a great part of Christendom ? If then our war be of God, and therefore God be with us, who is able to stand against us ?

This being so, I, although unworthy of that preferment, yet

being put in trust by His Holiness, do expect all my noble and valiant countrymen to arm themselves with a strong faith, and not to fear any power that is against God, but rather to win with Christ's banner, under which both I and they may warfare together.

And that this our desire may be the better brought to pass, may it please my good lords, the princes, leaders and rulers of this our dear country, *to meet together with me in some convenient place*, where order may be taken in common for the common good and weal of this noble Ireland ; for although I alone was present with His Holiness (and your honours not only absent, but also within the dangers of the said Elizabeth's power) I only was named general captain in His Holiness's war, yet it both was and is my meaning to be advertised and counselled of your honours and lordships, whom I take in great part for my betters, but every one of you for my well-willers and friends. . . . I wish, moreover, the case stood so that your lordships might name the place of our assembly, whereunto myself would gladly resort ; but for so much as that cannot be done by your common consents, but after long conference, and much sending to and fro, and the matter we take in hands requires no long delay, but speedy execution, therefore I crave pardon if I be so bold as to request your honours to *come with all speed possible*, or to send your lawful attorneys, *to the place where I am*, to the end that we there make a perpetual peace, league and friendship, first to the utter destroying of all schism and heresy, and next to the establishing of true love and amity amongst ourselves, whereof the perpetual weal of our dear country is like to ensue.

And here, considering the wariness, or rather the wiliness, of some men, who, for their own worldly security, will see what others do before they themselves move out of their place ; and others pretending the better to prepare themselves for their self-coming, will also use delays only to see what event the time is like to have ; and knowing that in the meantime the common enemy of God and of us all will not cease to do his best against me, and thereby great damage may come to me and my company before my friends resort to me ; for this cause I must needs most earnestly request those that in deed have zeal for God's honour and their own country, not to use such delays, but with all speed to show good example to others, being assured that, besides the favour of God Almighty, His Holiness and such other potentates as in this behalf join with His Holiness, will reward any man with honour, goods and inheritance according to the readiness which he shall show in furthering this holy cause. . . .

Special letters were addressed by Fitzmaurice to the Earls of Desmond [1] and Kildare. The first of these is worth giving in full :—

Right honourable and my singular good Lord.—After due and hearty commendation in most humble manner premised : Forasmuch as James Fitzmaurice, being authorised thereunto by His Holiness, warfareth under Christ's ensign for the restoring of the Catholic faith in Ireland, God forbid the day should ever come wherein it might be said that the Earl of Desmond had forsaken the poor kinsman his faithful servant, the lieutenant of his spiritual father, the banner of his merciful Saviour, the defence of his ancient faith, the deliverance of his dear country, and the safeguard of his noble house and posterity.

For as the proper reward of them that build up God's house and temple is to have their own houses and families built up and maintained by God, insomuch that King David had no sooner the intent to build a temple unto God, but immediately God promised that He Himself would build up and preserve King David's royal throne—even so, all they that pull down God's temple or otherwise favour and help the pullers-down thereof are sure to have their own houses and families shortly after pulled down and overthrown. Hereof it came to pass that when the Kings of Samaria had once forsaken the house and temple of God in Jerusalem their own days were so shortened and their own houses so speedily overthrown that within two hundred and forty years there reigned nineteen kings, and their blood royal was nine times rooted up and changed from one family and surname to another ; and in the end the royal state with all the nobility and people was vanquished, banished and extinguished.

But what need we speak of foreign examples ? Whereas King Henry the Eighth left behind one son and two daughters, how came it to pass that none of them at all could have lawful issue of their own bodies, but because even as King Henry had overthrown many houses in England which bore the name of God, and as it were represented God's majesty and mercy towards us, even so God hath determined to root up all them by whom King Henry's name and blood might have been maintained and preserved in this world—insomuch that although Queen Mary was a builder-up of God's house for her own part, yet for the revenge of her father's fall (whose person she by nature represented) she left no heir of her own body behind her.

[1] *S.P.I., Eliz.*, lxvii. 32, P.R.O., London.

If, therefore, you are resolved, my dear cousin, to make an end of our noble house and blood in your days (which God forbid), then dissemble with God's honour a little, bear with them that pull down God's house and destroy His monasteries, forsake the banner of Christ, and profess yourself to be the soldier of Antichrist.

But if as well the punishment to come, as the present infamy of such an act, ought worthily to make your honourable heart to abhor all such counsel or advice, then without any further delay resolve to be the first that shall stand for God's honour, for the health of our country, and for the restoring of the Catholic faith again. For as he that defends God's honour shall be defended and honoured of God, so he that does it first and chiefly shall have the first and chief reward for his service. For this cause I came to this part of the Island rather than to any other ; for this cause I send the messenger so speedily to your honour.

As for my part, I am, God be praised, long since resolved to die for God's honour and faith ; but God forbid that any of the Geraldines should stand in the field against the Cross of Christ, which is the ensign of our salvation. As we live now because our ancestors were builders-up of God's house, so let not our lack of courage in restoring God's house hinder the seed that hereafter may spring out of our children—and indeed how can their seed flourish that will defend Elizabeth, a woman that is hated of all Christian princes for the great injuries which she has done them, hated of her own subjects, as well for the compelling them to for-swear their Christian faith touching the supremacy of Christ's Vicar on earth, as also for not publishing the heir-apparent to the crown—a woman that leaves no issue of her own body either to reward them that should fight for her or to revenge them that shall fight against her—nay, rather a woman that is surely hated of her successor, whosoever he be ; and therefore they that seek to please her cannot be but unpleasant to the next heir of the crown, whose right she so tyrannously forbids to be published. But hereof I have written in my *common letters* directed to all the nobility of this realm, the copy whereof, as also of my *proclamation*, your honour shall receive either by this bearer, or shortly after.

For these letters which you now receive, as they are proper to yourself, so they come from such an affection and love towards your own honour and your house hereafter, that I cannot tell what worldly thing could grieve me more than to hear not only that your honour should not assist the Christian banner, but also that any other nobleman should prevent you in this glorious attempt.

All that I write to your honour I understand to be spoken also to my good Lady your bedfellow, and to my good Uncle your brother, to all whom I commend myself, as also my bedfellow most heartily does the like ; no less desiring to hear of your valiant courage and virtuous resolution in this behalf, than offering to serve your honour as well with my person as with all that I ever have besides, here and wherever your honour shall command me, trusting in Almighty God that as His Holiness has made me General Captain of this holy war, so your honour, being head of my house, will also be the chief protector and patron of this no less your than my quarrel.

Beseeching God to give us His grace and true wisdom to know what honour is now offered us and our posterity for ever, and not to come less this good occasion which being once refused is hardly again recovered. But God, I trust, will be more merciful to you and me, to whose gracious direction I commit your honour, with my humble recommendations to yourselves and to all my good cousins your children, and to my dear Uncle your brother, longing to see us all one, first as in faith so in field, and afterwards in glory and life eternal.

Special letters were also sent to the leaders of the gallo-glasses and mercenary clans, whose swords were to be had for a consideration. A sample survives in that sent to Austin McDonnell in Irish.

James Fitzmaurice to Austin Kittagh McDonnell, 18 July, 1579 :—

Life and health with thee, O writing, to Austin Kittagh McDonnell from his friend and companion, James, Son of Maurice, Son of the Earl. And be it known to him that I have come safe to Erin with power, after all I have travelled and traversed of foreign countries ; and for this reason I implore of him to come to me with as many bonaghtmen as he can bring with him ; and, moreover, be it certain unto him that he never came to any war coming into which he should have greater courage than this war, for many reasons : first, inasmuch as we are fighting for our faith and for the Church of God ; and next that we are defending our country and extirpating heretics and barbarians and unjust and lawless men ; and besides (let him remember) that he was never employed by any lord who will pay himself and his people their wages and their bounty better than I shall, inasmuch as I was never at any time more competent to pay it than now, thanks be to the great God of mercy for it, and to the people who have given me that power under God, and who will not suffer me to want henceforth. And this is enough ; but let him not neglect coming, that he may get some compensation for all the toil and labour that he suffered in my cause before now ; let him request his brethren and the gentry of his territory to respond to the time, and to rise with one accord for the sake of the faith of Christ, and to defend their country, and, moreover, that all their bonaghtmen will get their pay readily ; and that we shall all get a place in the kingdom of heaven if we fight for His sake.[1]

The proclamation referred to above was in the Latin tongue, and ran as follows :—

PROCLAMATION OF THE NOBLE KNIGHT JAMES FITZMAURICE ON THE JUSTICE OF THE WAR WHICH HE IS WAGING IN IRELAND FOR THE FAITH.

Three conditions are required for a war to be a just war, namely, a good cause, lawful authority, and fair fighting. That these three conditions are fully verified in the present case, is easily made plain to all.

First, the cause for which we are waging this war is the glory of God, to whom we are striving to restore the outward rite of sacrifice and the visible honour of our holy altars, which heretics have impiously overturned ; it is the glory of Christ, to whose Sacraments the heretics blasphemously deny the power of conferring grace, thus attributing to Christ's Gospel that weakness on account of which the old law was condemned ; it is the glory of the Catholic Church which in the teeth of Sacred Scripture the heretics lyingly assert to have become obscured and consigned to oblivion in recent centuries ; whereas our salvation chiefly depends on the name of God, Who sanctifies us by Christ's Sacraments, and on the preservation of the unity of His Church.

Secondly, our authority for this war is based on the natural and the evangelical law. The natural law justifies us in defending ourselves against the manifest tyranny of those heretics who in defiance of the law of nature are forcing us under pain of death to forsake our old faith in the primacy of the Roman Pontiff, and are constraining us to accept and profess a new religion which we do not want, thus imposing on us a yoke the like of which has never been imposed by Christians on Jews or Turks, nor thus far by heretics on us. Again, Christ in His Gospel gave to St. Peter the keys of the Kingdom of Heaven, that is, the supreme administration of His Church. Now, the lawful successor of the Prince of the

[1] *Kilk. Arch. Journ.*, 1858-59, pp. 362-3.

Apostles in the See of Rome, Pope Gregory XIII, has appointed us Captain General in this war, as his letters patent show ; and he has done this all the more readily because his predecessor, Pius V, had deprived Elizabeth, that patroness of heresy, of all royal power and dominion, as is witnessed by his decree, a copy of which we hold. Thus, then, we are not at war against the legitimate and honourable crown of England, but against that she-tyrant who, by refusing to hear Christ in the person of His Vicar, and even by daring to subject the Church of Christ to the ruling of a woman in matters of faith, on which she has no right to pronounce, has deservedly forfeited her royal authority.

Finally, as regards the right conduct of this war, we intend neither to invade the rights of our fellow-countrymen, nor to pursue private enmities, which are far from our thoughts, nor to acquire political power. Let God's honour be but restored to Him, and we at once propose to lay down the sword and yield obedience to whoever shall be lawfully placed over us.

God forbid that there should be found any to continue to favour heresy and thus rob God of the honour due to Him ; but should there be any such, it is they, not we, that deprive Ireland of true peace ; it is they, not we, that make war on their country ; and to them we can truly say with our Saviour : " I came not to bring peace on earth, but the sword." As for those who are ready to repent of the past, we war not against them, nor shall we ever think of doing so.

If, then, the war we are waging for the sake of peace with God is most just, those who oppose us in our struggle are purchasing their own damnation and will have for their enemies not only all the saints whose relics and images are being trampled underfoot by the heretics, but also God Himself, whose glory they are lessening.

This much ought to suffice for the present ; but if anyone requires further information on this head he has only to read the more ample exposition which is appended to this Edict.[1]

Another letter in Irish was sent by Fitzmaurice, 31 July, to Randal MacDonnell : " The custom of the letter [i.e. salutation], O billet, from James, son of Maurice, son of the Earl, to his friend and companion, Randal, son of Colla Maeldubh ; [2]

---

[1] *Kilk. Arch. Journ.*, 1858-59, pp. 368-9 (Latin Copy). *Catholic Bulletin*, August, 1929, pp. 364-8. The ' exposition ' was evidently that of Sander.

[2] Evidently another of the sept of MacDonnells, and a galloglass leader in Munster.

and tell him that I told him to collect as many bonachtmen as he can, and to come to me, and that he will get his pay according to his own will, for I was more thankful to God for having great power and influence than now. Advise every one of your friends (who likes fighting for his religion and his country, better than for gold and silver), or who wishes to obtain them all [i.e to fight for his religion and country, and also for gold and silver] (as their wages) to come to me, and that he will find each of these things." [1]

Preparations Against Fitzmaurice.

Not many days elapsed before the party in the fort began to get into touch with the Munster chiefs and mercenary bands. In the first few days they easily repulsed an attack by some of the local loyalists who, thinking the fort of little consequence, attempted to carry out the threat of James Golde (to the Mayor of Limerick). Five days after their arrival, Fitzmaurice and his men rejoiced to see two galleys of the O'Flahertys and O'Mallys of Clew Bay coming on the waters of Dingle Bay and entering the harbour. Agreement was come to with these to enter the service of the Papal General. Other arrangements were made with the mercenary bands of the Sheehys, MacSwineys, and O'Connors. In a few days contact was established with the Munster Geraldines, the leaders of which were of opinion that before any general revolt could be expected the promised ship and arms should come from Spain.

For the purpose, therefore, of informing Spain and Rome that a beginning had been made, and of convincing them of the necessity of further supplies of men, money, and arms which had been promised to them, they sent Father de Oviedo to the Nuncio in Spain. Sailing out of Smerwick harbour on 26 July in one of the Spanish ships, he was in touch with the Nuncio at Madrid within a month. In a letter, 26 August, the Nuncio informed the authorities in Rome of all he had learned from the Franciscan Father ; that Fitzmaurice was satisfied that the majority of the

[1] *Kilk. Arch. Journ.*, 1858-59, p. 364.

nobility would break out into rebellion when they could believe that the King of Spain had his heart in the project; and that for the present they would be satisfied with a sum of 10,000 crowns along with 300 soldiers and the arms that they had gathered together at Lisbon. If these supplies arrived before the end of September, they had great hopes of ultimate success.

Whilst all these preparations were being made at Smerwick and Madrid, the Council in Dublin were hastily summoned to consider the ominous news from the South. A meeting was held on the evening of 22 July, under Lord Justice Drury, at which were present Loftus, Archbishop of Dublin; Gerald, Earl of Kildare; Lord Chancellor Gerrard; Sir N. Malby, Governor of Connacht; and Chief Secretary Edward Waterhouse. The news they came to consider was contained in a letter from the Earl of Desmond,[1] at his castle of Cullen,[2] on the borders of Tipperary and Limerick.

The Earl informed Drury that he received, at 8 o'clock on the evening of the 19th, a despatch dated the 18th from the harbour authorities of Dingle, stating that the previous evening six Spanish ships, great and small, had appeared in the Bay and that it was understood they belonged to Fitzmaurice; that he deemed it right to lose no time in informing the Council so that steps might be taken at once to stay the traitorous attempt; that he was awaiting instructions, and that he was ready to risk his life and the lives of his men in Her Majesty's defence. Meanwhile, he was writing to the Mayors of Cork and Limerick, and others in authority in Munster to be ready to defend themselves and to assist in the expulsion of the traitor. In another letter he told how the town of Dingle had been burned and his tenants spoiled by Fitzmaurice's men, and that, acting on the advice of Meiler Magrath, Protestant Archbishop of Cashel, and William Apsley, who were now accompanying him to Kerry, he hoped to drive out the traitor and his men and " with the mighty hand of God to make an end of this service." He had written, he said, to all the chiefs and nobles of Munster to muster their forces and meet him in

---

[1] *S.P.I., Eliz.*, lxvii. 40, i.   [2] Quite close to Limerick Junction.

Kerry. Above all he implored the Lord Justice to come South without delay and to be prepared for the worst.[1]

The news sent by Desmond threw the Council into a veritable panic, and with other reports from North and South the situation was decidedly grave and the outlook discouraging.[2] By a loyal Irishman of Waterford, named Edward White,[3] it was urged that " the state of this realm was never in greater danger than it is at this instant." The trouble, he said, was not from the native Irish but from the noblemen of English blood, like the Desmonds, who loudly profess loyalty and yet go on dissembling, playing a game in order to overthrow Her Majesty's authority and take the rule into their own hands. These noblemen would never have broken out unless they had " hope of assistance and aid of other nobles' houses." " If this present action," he urged, " be not well provided for in time, I am afraid you shall see the fire in every corner of the realm all our time ; for the practices and devices of the enemy are great and have their favourers in every place, some for the cause of religion, some to shake off the government, and such other devices. I speak of knowledge, not by guess."

The situation in Ulster also gave Gerrard and Loftus, who were entrusted with affairs in Dublin during the absence of Drury, " great cause of suspicion of a general combination " throughout the whole of Ireland.[4] The O'Neills were probably, they said, in league with Fitzmaurice, and had 2000 foot and 500 horse some six miles south of Armagh.[5] In Dublin but a few soldiers had been left behind to deal with the O'Neills, all the rest having been sent after the Lord Justice into Munster. To make matters worse there was not a penny in the Treasury, and the stores had been emptied of " all the munitions, powder, and shot," which had also been sent into Munster. All might be well, they added, if the Earl of Desmond would only act up to his loyal professions.[6]

As the days and weeks went by, the letters from the officials revealed only still more the gravity of the situation. Secretary Waterhouse [7] wrote : " This rebellion is the most perilous that was begun in Ireland, so is foreign help in

[1] *S.P.I., Eliz.*, lxvii. 43, i.   [2] *Ib.*, 40, ii.-viii.   [3] *Ib.*, lxviii. 22.
[4] *Ib.*, 46 ; lxviii. 7.   [5] *Ib.*, 7, i.   [6] *Ib.*, lxvii. 49.   [7] *Ib.*, 45.

multitudes, as the rebels give forth, looked for to arrive presently here . . . since nothing is to be looked for here but a general rebellion, aid must be sent [from England] in due time. If the Queen's force and some shipping come before the strangers or before Ulster stir, all will be well and with honour and safety to this state—if otherwise the case will be hard." Friars were practising with O'Rourke, O'Donnell, Tirlogh Luineach, and the Scots. John Burke was to be carefully watched.

The Lord Justice showed himself also quite despondent of the situation.[1] " Some of his [Fitzmaurice's] confederates have burst out into open rebellion," he wrote, " and many others have gathered great forces and with them do commit all the outrages they can. . . . The rebellion of James Fitzmaurice, who has practised with many foreign princes, is not like other ordinary stirs that have fallen out upon small occasions within this realm, for we see great evident appearance of general combination." Still more he lamented the fact that he had not more than 200 horse and 400 foot, while some of the latter had to be left here and there to garrison forts and castles to guard their lines of communication. Consequently he entreated the Council in England by furnishing him with sufficient means " by speedy aid of men, money, and munition to prevent the dishonour and inconvenience that may ensue both to Her Majesty and to the whole realm of England." The Lord Justice's brother, Drew Drury, also wrote [2] in gloomy fashion of " the desperate estate of this most miserable country." The only consolation, he added, that he could offer was that his brother had begun " by giving religion and the gospel his free course." This consideration indeed was calculated to relieve the gloom, as Drury, the Lord Justice, was an experienced soldier and knew Munster intimately where he had been President for two and a half years, and which he ruled with vigorous determination, having recourse on many occasions to hanging and torture.

Though he boasted but a year ago that he had hanged about four hundred malefactors, yet he thought it necessary

---

[1] *S.P.I., Eliz.*, lxvii. 40.   [2] *Ib.*, lxviii. 19.

to apologise for the moderation of his methods by stating : " I chose rather with the snail slenderly to creep than with the horse to run." He was suspected of being not unfriendly to Catholics, and was on rather good terms with the Earl of Desmond, although he had driven him from one submission to another. He therefore was glad of the Earl's new evidence of loyalty in acquainting him of the recent danger to Her Majesty's peace, and wrote to him to thank him for it, promising at the same time to send him forces sufficient for his relief.[1]

Drury now got busy to raise the necessary forces and to call upon the chiefs and municipal authorities to give Desmond their best assistance and to defend the cities and towns. In this strain he wrote to Clancarty, Barrymore, Roche, and Fitzmaurice of Kerry, on whose loyalty he felt he could rely.[2] In a despatch, 24 July,[3] he authorised Humphrey Gilbert to press into the service of the crown all ships, vessels, barques, all men and mariners, as well as all supplies, and to pursue Fitzmaurice and plague him and his accomplices " by all ways and means in war usual." Prisoners were to be well guarded and sent to him, Drury, so that he could examine them on the extent of the conspiracy, and spies were to be procured who would furnish him with the names of the chief personages " arrayed in this rebellious company." A week later, fearing that he had not given sufficient authority for the capture of Fitzmaurice in the event of his taking to sea, he wrote from Kilkenny, 29 July, authorising Gilbert to " follow him into any place or harbour, and there to apprehend him and stay himself, his ships and company, and to detain them until further order."

Gilbert was to be assisted in his commission and advised by Justice Walsh, Justice Miagh, Henry Davells, Sheriff of Cork, and Arthur Carter, Provost-Marshall of the forces of Munster. Warham St. Leger, with the Mayor, was to take charge of Cork ; Malby, with the forces of Connacht, was to join Drury ; Bagenall was to look after the O'Neills, and Loftus and Gerrard were to look after the Pale. Having made all these arrangements, Drury, accompanied by the Earl of

---

[1] *S.P.I., Eliz.,* lxvii. 40, ix.   [2] *Ib.,* 40, x., xi.   [3] *Ib.,* 66.

Kildare and Secretary Waterhouse, started for Kilkenny, 28 July, and having made a short stay there, proceeded to Limerick where he arrived 3 August, and remained for a couple of weeks preparing his great attack on Fitzmaurice.

Desmond Plays a Game.

The attitude of the Earl of Desmond in sending immediate news of the landing of James Fitzmaurice, his cousin, may appear an enigma. It is important, therefore, to understand the situation in which he was placed at this time. It is true that he had sent pleading letters to James to return quickly lest the opportunity for successful rebellion should pass. These were precarious days when the military expert, Drury, was driving him from post to post. Whilst he was writing to James, he was at the same time, in 1578, trying to keep in Drury's good graces. So satisfied was the Lord Justice with Desmond's loyalty, that he wrote on several occasions to London that the Earl was "excellent," "more and more obedient," and "in good tune," whilst the Countess, blamed by some for spurring on the Earl and yet at the same time regardful of the future, was praised for her anxiety that all should be done "in the English way."

Desmond, like Clanricard, O'Neill, and O'Donnell, was playing a game. It was a matter of preserving an inheritance of some four hundred years' standing and of handing it on to his heirs. When he succeeded to his title in 1558 as sixteenth Earl he was almost an independent ruler over some half a million acres. But during the intervening twenty years he had suffered many reverses from the energetic Sydney and from his neighbouring chiefs. When the opportunity offered he could refuse allegiance to Elizabeth just as readily as he could render it. Worn out by seven years of close restraint either in the Tower or in the city of London, he did not shirk the galling oath to follow English law, customs, civilisation, and religion. But back in his native glens, with his fighting men, a thousand strong, he returned to his Irish customs in dress and law, and practised and defended the Old Religion.

Between 1573 and 1576 he continued to preserve his principality practically intact, but the coming of the iron-

handed Drury into Munster as president put a different complexion on his tenure.   With sheriffs, justices, etc., planted in
his territory for the execution of English law, with some of
his castles, especially Castlemaine, taken from him, which
latter was all important for the control of Spanish intercourse
with the Kerry coast, it is scarcely to be wondered at that
again he bowed to the inevitable.   He might disband his
fighting men, suffer the ancient privileges of his liberties to be
torn from him, but it was all in the game.   Some day he would
hope to regain them all.

Faced with the present situation of Fitzmaurice's expedition about whose strength he knew little, and with the heavy
hand of Drury and his English forces over him, Desmond's
position was indeed bewildering.   Spies were abroad watching
his every movement and only waiting for an opportunity to
report any misdemeanour of his to Drury whose plan of con-
fiscating the Desmond territories was not yet abandoned.   He
had no information as to what aid was expected from Rome or
Spain, and he had grave reason to doubt the assistance that
would be offered by the other chiefs especially those of Munster.
His pretence of loyalty by sending reports to the Council in
Dublin and others gave him the required opportunity of
making himself acquainted with the strength of the forces at
Smerwick Harbour without exciting the suspicions of Drury's
agents.[1]   At the same time his calling on the Munster chiefs
to meet him in Kerry with their forces just fell in with Fitzmaurice's plan of a conference with them at Smerwick.
That was the best that he could do at the moment, as he had
been taken unawares, and he could not come out into the
open for want of resources and because he saw too well that
Fitzmaurice's forces were quite inadequate against the English.
He had to save his face and pretend that he meant the expulsion of the traitor, and whilst playing the waiting game he
would quietly lend as much help as possible to James.

Leaving Cullen, 20 July, with about 300 horse, Desmond
reached Smerwick in three days and encamped just outside
the narrow passage that led to the fortified rock.   He pretended in his report that the traitor within the fort would

[1] That this was Desmond's plan is clear from Dr. Sander's reports to Rome
and Spain, and from those of the English officials to London.

40 *

be starved out before many days, and that he was skirmishing with him. But on the 29th, a Captain Courtenay appeared in the harbour, and having put Fitzmaurice's three remaining ships out of action, thus cut off his communication by sea. James was thus caught in a trap, but the strange thing is that Desmond simply sat down and did nothing, although it was found afterwards that he could easily have taken the fort. Desmond knew this quite well, but it did not suit his game. Fitzmaurice, too, knew the Earl's intentions and that the skirmishing was merely play-acting, for, at nightfall, " the chief men amongst them came to us, congratulated us on our arrival, told us that they held our lives to be dearer to them than their own blood, and placed themselves and their all at our service : owing, however, to the scarcity of powder, guns, money and arms, they could not venture openly to proclaim their adhesion just then. . . . But it is certain, that their hearts are with us and that they are ready to obey the Holy See if only we receive reinforcements in good time." [1] The sending of Father de Oviedo to Spain on the 26th was to hurry them and in particular the Lisbon ship with its store of arms and ammunition.

Meanwhile Drury had ordered Captain Gilbert to pursue and plague Fitzmaurice and to set spies on him, and to be advised by Justice Walsh, Justice Miagh, Provost-Marshal Carter, and Henry Davells, Sheriff of Cork. Davells repaired to Kinsale and persuaded Courtenay, a privateer, to sail round to Smerwick and see what harm he could do to Fitzmaurice's ships. He is next seen with Commissioners Miagh and Carter near Smerwick towards the end of July. Davells and Carter appear to have visited Desmond in the hope of inducing him to attack the fort, but the Earl pleaded that it was useless to expect his galloglasses to face trained soldiers. Seeing that their efforts were unavailing they withdrew with their retinue to Tralee to settle on the best means of dislodging Fitzmaurice.

[1] Fitzmaurice to the Nuncio at Madrid, 26 July, 1579. This is corroborated by Sander who wrote on the same day, and by Father Matthew de Oviedo, who sailed that day with the despatches to the Madrid Nuncio. Desmond also tells a similar story in his letter of 17 January, 1580, to the King of Spain and the Nuncio, and gives the reasons why he had not come out into the open at the beginning.

Desmond saw the danger to himself and James if these commissioners were allowed to get into touch with Drury and the Council. It would mean that he would have to decide which side to take, whereas by putting them out of the way, he could still play for time. Accordingly, with or without his consent, his two brothers, Sir John and Sir James, with the O'Connors and others, attacked the town of Tralee during the night of the 1st August, and put Davells and Carter with their retinue to the sword. The result of putting the two commissioners to death was, as Sander laconically expressed it, that they were "enabled to move out freely into the open." It was war, and the attackers looked at it from that point of view, although Drury called the war "apparent and dangerous rebellion," and the deed "shameful murder." Of course, Desmond, who was still waiting to see what was going to turn up next, characterised the deed as "that detestable act." [1]

DEATH OF JAMES FITZMAURICE.

The truth about the events that were crowded into the last days of James Fitzmaurice's life is to be found only in the eye-witnesses' reports that Mgr. Sega made the basis of his *Relazione Compendiosa*,[2] and one cannot take as reliable either the reports of the Castle officials or the versions filled in afterwards by Russell, O'Daly, and O'Sullivan Beare on the one side and by the Camden school on the other.

Such was the panic created in the ranks of the Castle officials that very little attention was given to Fitzmaurice's landing. They were chiefly occupied in considering reports from North and West, which gave them reason to fear a general confederation of all the Irish chiefs under the papal banner. Waterhouse (Limerick, 3 August)[3] had no hesitation in declaring that the insurrection was "the most

[1] This act was used extensively for propaganda purposes and later for justifying confiscation by historians such as Hooker, Camden, Russell, and Carlton.

[2] *Catholic Bulletin*, November, 1929, pp. 1029-36. *Arch. Hib.*, vii., pp. 187-95.

[3] *C.S.P.I., Eliz.*, lxviii. 2.

perilous that was ever begun in Ireland." Malby, writing from Connacht, was no less pessimistic, and, knowing the Burkes, reported that " the practices and devices of the enemy are great and have their favourers in every place, some for a cause of religion and some to shake off the governor, and such other devices." [1]   Reports from the North showed that Fitzmaurice's messengers had already reached there and that matters were threatening. Even Desmond was reported as merely keeping Drury " in tune " and as one who " will not be a subject," for, says the report, he had drawn no rebel blood when he could easily have done so.

All these adherents of Fitzmaurice were simply playing for time. They saw clearly that the forces that he had brought with him were useless as an attacking party, but they looked anxiously for the promised aid from Spain. They were all ready to move the moment the trained soldiers, money, and munitions were forthcoming. But Fitzmaurice, poor and unprovided, could not convince them that the time had yet come for a general insurrection. He had sent Father de Oviedo, 28 July, to Madrid to hasten the small assistance for which he asked and with which he hoped to hold out if it arrived before the end of September. Meanwhile, he was inducing as many as he could to join him openly.

The events that immediately followed the landing are told in a statement drawn up by the Earl of Desmond two months later.[2] After the sacking of Tralee by Desmond's brothers, the Earl, having had a talk with Justice Miagh, thought it better to retire from Smerwick, and ensure the safety of his wife and son at Askeaton. He then, 4 August, set out for Limerick, saw Miagh again and started in pursuit of Fitzmaurice. The Earl, of course, had to save his own face as the English forces were gathering under Malby at Limerick. But even his pursuit of Fitzmaurice did not convince Waterhouse that he was in earnest, as James had been able not only to fortify the fort at Smerwick, leave it in command of the Spanish soldiers, but sally out with his wife, daughters, Dr. Sander and others, and move inland.

---

[1] *C.S.P.I., Eliz.*, lxviii. 33.   [2] *Ib.*, lxix. 51.

As the Earl's brothers, after the sacking of Tralee, had been able to bring over to their side most of the Earl's armed followers, so Fitzmaurice was free to proceed inland to enlist all those whom he met in his way.

Although the Earl pursued him he was not given the credit of hunting him out of the woods. Waterhouse, 22 August,[1] stated that it was Malby who was responsible for driving him across the mountains to Castleisland, Co Kerry, thence to the Great Wood, and then to Castletown, Co. Limerick. James was forced to disperse his followers, who sought shelter where they could best find it, whilst he himself, 17 August, set out for the country of Mulryan, east of Limerick.

The tragedy, or whatever else one is pleased to call it, which ensued is not as described in the wild tales told by O'Sullivan Beare and by the Geraldine chroniclers, Russell and O'Daly, on the one side, and by Camden and his school on the other, but as was told by Captain Bertoni and by the courier sent by Dr. Sander to the Nuncio in Madrid who were eye-witnesses of the encounter.

Having agreed on a plan of campaign with John and James of Desmond, Fitzmaurice and his confederates set out in different directions to raise forces, and according to Mgr. Sega, " on the 18 of August,[2] Fitzmaurice, accompanied by Captain

---

[1] *C.S.P.I., Eliz.*, lxviii. 48.

[2] On one of these eventful days, 15-18 August, Bishop O'Hely of Mayo and a certain scholar were hanged by Drury at Kilmallock. Bishop O'Hely was undoubtedly the bishop who appeared with crozier and mitre in the procession that landed with Fitzmaurice at Dingle. This conclusion is supported by a letter, 14 November, of the Papal Nuncio in Portugal (*A. Hib.*, vii. 220), who states that, a few weeks before, he had received news of Fitzmaurice's death and that " the bishop who was with him was captured and, having been tempted to abandon the Catholic side, was hanged." The Earl of Desmond's letter, 10 October, also confirms the conclusion : " First, before the Traitor arrived there landed at Smerwick haven three Irish scholars in mariners' attire, which upon suspicion I caused to be examined and sent to the gaol of Limerick, who, in fine, were known to be gentlemen, and one of them a bishop, who were sent by the Traitor to practise with the North to join with him, for which they were by my Lord Justice executed." What happened to Bishop O'Hely after his landing is told by his biographer, the Franciscan Father Bourchier or Boverius, in his work published in Paris, 1582. O'Hely, accompanied by Conor O'Rourke, one of the " scholars " and son to O'Rourke, chief of Brefni, set out to visit the Earl of Desmond at his residence at Askeaton. In the absence of the Earl, the Countess received the visitors cordially, but contrived within three

Alexander Bertoni, six horse, twenty-four foot, and two gunners, was on his way to meet a certain Catholic chief named David Barry [?] when he was confronted by a force composed of eight horse, a hundred and twenty foot, and four gunners, under the leadership of three of the Burkes [of Castleconnell] who had sided with the Queen. In the encounter that ensued Fitzmaurice with his own hand killed eighteen of his opponents, including three horse, and put the rest to flight. But just when victory had crowned his efforts, and when he was about to abandon the pursuit of the fugitives, a bullet passed through his body. He had time to make his confession and then he died a most holy death. Not a single man of his was slain." Amongst those killed on the other side was their leader Theobald Burke, eldest son to Sir William Burke of Castleconnell.

days to send word to the authorities at Limerick. Unconscious of his betrayal the bishop next day left for Limerick where he hoped to learn the whereabouts of the Catholic forces among whom his work was to lie. In or on the way to Limerick he was taken prisoner by the Mayor (or attorney) who was on the look-out for him, and had him transferred to Kilmallock, a strong garrison town where there was little fear of rescue. Here he was tried by court-martial under President Drury, who promised him life and the peaceful possession of his See with honours and emoluments if only he would renounce his faith and confess the real purpose for which he had come. As for the faith, the bishop replied that no earthly consideration would induce him to renounce it ; whilst as regards the second, he replied that he had come as a bishop to promote the cause of religion and the salvation of souls. Drury then pressed him to state what plans had been made by the Pope and the King of Spain for the invasion of Ireland. To this demand the Bishop turned a deaf ear and could not be made to speak even during the cruel torture to which he was at once subjected by means of sharp spikes driven with a hammer through his fingers severing them from his hand. Seeing that nothing could be extracted from his victims, Drury ordered them to be led out to execution ; and on a mound just outside the town walls at the rear of the present church, Bishop O'Hely and Conor O'Rourke were hanged by the neck till they were dead. (Boverius or Bourchier, *Franciscan Annals ; Catholic Bulletin*, December, 1929, pp. 1116-24.) It may be remarked here that Desmond's statement, in his letter, of 10 October, of his capture of Bishop O'Hely is a mere boast ; he was posing as a loyalist and expected consideration for his supposed deeds. As to Father Bourchier, whilst narrating with pride the noble death of Bishop O'Hely, a member of his Order, passes over, through political prejudice, the deeds of the Bishop on the Continent in favour of Fitzmaurice. Bourchier was one of a group of English Catholics who thought that Elizabeth could be induced by persuasion to grant toleration of their religion, and were opposed to the use of arms against her. His attitude is apparent in a letter of the English Ambassador at Paris, 23 June, 1578, and in the *Autobiography* of Father Parsons, 1546-84. (*Catholic Record Society, Miscellanea*, ii. 34, 206.)

Around this simple story O'Sullivan Beare, Russell, and O'Daly have woven fanciful legends that tell how Fitzmaurice, having been wounded " gave in with great violence amongst his enemies, where, meeting with Theobald Bourke, with one blow he clave his head, and perceiving the said Theobald's brother William Bourke, not far from him, he ran at him, and with the second stroke slew him," etc.

The encounter between Fitzmaurice and the Burkes has been usually represented by those historians as a chance affair, but such a version cannot be admitted. It was the deliberate engineering of Drury who had united his forces at Limerick with those of Malby who had come from Connacht. North-east of Limerick was the country of the Munster Burkes. Theobald and William Burke were nephews of the Earl of Desmond, and their sister was married to James Fitzmaurice. Theobald had already put his signature to the Desmond Combination, but afterwards he took the side of the Queen. It is clear that he was persuaded by promise of reward to attack Fitzmaurice who was on his way northward to join the Clanricard Burkes in Connacht, his passage being through the country of the Munster Burkes before coming to O'Brien's Bridge across the Shannon above Limerick. Perhaps much persuasion was not needed, as it would seem that there was already enmity between Theobald's people and Fitzmaurice. When Lady Fitzmaurice arrived in Brittany with her husband and family, she wrote a letter to her mother entreating her in very significant terms not to be displeased with her for having hastily left the country with her husband, and begged her to write to that effect. It would seem that the Burkes did not approve of Lady Fitzmaurice's action, as they had broken away from the Confederation, and thus when given the chance of revenge and reward they took it.

That they were enlisted on the side of Drury for the deed is quite clear, for, four days after the encounter, Malby wrote from Cork to London (22 August) [1] that of all the Munster chiefs only two had really resisted the rebels, namely, Sir Cormac MacTeig MacCarthy of Muskerry and " Theobald Burke's sept lately slain." Waterhouse also, writing on the same day, [2] gives the credit of the defeat of the rebel

---

[1] *C.S.P.I., Eliz.,* lxviii. 46.   [2] *Ib.,* 48.

not to the Earl of Desmond but to Drury "who sent the force under Sir Nicholas Malbie that bolted him [Fitzmaurice] out of the wood, and gave the cause to Tibet Burke, both by reward and persuasion, to give that last attempt [attack] that indeed he did." To confirm all this, Burke's widow put in a claim for a reward for Fitzmaurice's head. No reward had been offered in the general proclamation against the rebel chief, but the widow Burke evidently considered herself entitled to it on the strength of the agreement between her husband and Drury. Moreover, the Queen in recognition of the noble deed done wrote to the widow a letter of thanks and conferred the title of Baron of Castleconnell on her husband's father. It is said that so overwhelmed with joy was the old man that he died suddenly when he heard the good news that he was to be the first lord of Castleconnell.

As to the report of Mgr. Sega, based on the information of Captain Bertoni and the courier of Dr. Sanders, there is one point that must have already appeared inconsistent to the reader. Who was the Catholic chief to whom Fitzmaurice was repairing when he was met by the Burkes? These authorities, reliable and first-hand, mention the chief as David Barry, who was son and heir to Viscount Barry of Buttevant. That is clearly an error of judgment; the real person being John Burke of Connacht. The journey from Smerwick to Castlemaine was accomplished by Fitzmaurice easily enough, but between Castlemaine and Castleisland he met with opposition and was driven out of the woods and across the Slieve Mish mountains to Castleisland in a north-easterly direction. From this he was driven to Castletown near Kilmallock, still in a north-easterly direction, into the Co. Limerick. If he wished to go to Buttevant to meet David Barry, who was already a supporter of his, he should then go directly southward, whereas when he met with the Burkes in their own country he must have gone in a north-easterly direction. Drury's forces had set out from Limerick and had gone towards Castlemaine and had intercepted Fitzmaurice who bent his way northward to O'Brien's Bridge to cross the Shannon in order to join with John Burke of Connacht. The latter had been brought by Malby to Limerick and kept there quietly for some time, but he had escaped his meshes (12 August), of which Fitzmaurice was evidently aware, and the two chiefs were bent on a meeting for the purpose of discussing the plan of campaign. The direction of Fitzmaurice's flight is confirmed by the Earl of Desmond in a letter in which he states that James went from Balingarry, Co. Limerick, into the country of Owney Mulryan. This country lies east of Limerick. It is said that he fell at a place called *Bealantha-an-Bhorin*, which has been identified by some as Barrington's Bridge at Limerick, and by others as Boher between Limerick Junction and Cappamore.

Russell tells what happened to the body of Fitzmaurice : " Now as soon as James Fitzmaurice was dead, his cousin, Maurice Fitz John, caused his head to be cut off from his body ; and, having no leisure to bury the body, left it wrapt in a caddowe under an old oak, where being soon after found by a huntsman, the body without head was brought to Kilmallock, and there hanged on a gibbet, and shot by the English soldiers, that were glad to see him dead whom they so much feared living, as they durst not look him in the face. You have heard the end of the chiefest actor in this remarkable tragedy."

According to Russell, " This James Fitzmaurice was (rightly for to describe him) a brave and gallant gentleman, witty, learned, impassionate, circumspect, active, generous, devout, subtle, and quick of apprehension, eloquent, of a high and adventurous politic, and dissembling mind ; too forward and apt to travail, to take great pains, and to endure thirst, cold, and hunger ; not much given to the pleasure of Bacchus or Venus, as Dr. Meacy at large writes of him." Having lamented the untimely death of " so brave a leader, whose equal they were sure never again to meet out of his own race," he continues : " Well, there was no remedy—God's will must be done, punishing the sins of the father in the death of the son. Fitzmaurice made a godly end of his life (only that he bore arms against his sovereign princess, the Queen of England), and within an hour after receiving his wound gave up the ghost, to the lamentable grief of all those of his faction. The death of James Fitzmaurice was the beginning of the decay of this honourable house of Desmond, out of which never issued so brave a man in all perfection, both for qualities of mind and body ; besides the league between him and others for defence of religion. . . . This Fitzmaurice was well worthy to serve any prince in Christendom, both for his manhood, policy, and good direction ; he was a noble and valiant gentleman—grave, affable, wise, learned, and religious ; a man of far·reaching wit, of a voluble, sweet tongue, and have a comely behaviour ; and if his means had been able to second the plot he laid, out of all question he would have performed much in that last action. But all his haughty designs died with his life, and the downfall of his house presently ensued. The English through his death took heart and courage ; and the Irish were daunted, having lost their leader, being never like to find such another. Let no man be offended, if I give him his due praise ; for I hold it lawful to commend worth even in enemy, for what I have delivered of him I speak without passion or partiality."

Such is the verdict of one who blamed Fitzmaurice for the downfall of the house of Desmond. It is a verdict that will doubtless commend itself to all who followed his career in these pages, for it can scarcely be denied that he was a man of great parts, of genius, energy, and marvellous perseverance, which made him a born leader and one of the bravest and greatest Irishmen of his own or of any other age. His indomitable will amid dangers and disappointments that would have broken the heart of a weaker man rallied for the first time in hundreds of years of Irish history practically every Irish chief in a formidable organisation that required only the necessary arms from abroad to put an end to English rule in Ireland and to restore freedom to Irish homes and altars. That likewise was the opinion of President Perrott. That Fitzmaurice had consolidated his colleagues is evident in the stern struggle that they made within a few weeks after the shock of his untimely end had passed away. The subsequent defeat and the shameless massacre of Smerwick are too well known to be dealt with here. They form rather the opening of a new chapter in Ireland's history, an era of blood and martyrdom, which cannot yet be told in all its horrible details.

APPENDICES.

I.

CATHOLIC CHURCH IN IRELAND IN 1580.

(Document [1] put together probably by Dermot O'Hurley afterwards Archbishop of Cashel, 1581, who laid down his life for the Faith two years later.)

THE author having pointed out the ancient love of Ireland for the Holy See, goes on to show how vast numbers " did not bend the knee before Baal, and that they are still whole-hearted in their obedience " to that See.

All Ireland is divided into three parts.

The first is called Ulster in the North. It continues to this day to keep itself intact from all heresy and error, and wages continuous war with its English neighbours and with their Queen with that intent. There are many Franciscan Houses here and both prelates and people publicly profess their faith and obedience to the Roman Pontiff.

The second part is Munster and Connacht, which is under the rule of the English, and so it is not possible to worship in public. Yet, practically all are still Catholics, and there are many diligent workers, of whom we shall speak later, producing much fruit in the Lord's vineyard.

The third part is Leinster, which is even still more oppressed by English tyranny, against which it is impossible to move on

---

[1] *Vatican Archives (Archiv. Hib.,* v. 157-67).

account of inferior forces, and which is constrained to admit their sacrilegious rites ; but even those it is found for the greater part still hold the faith of the Roman Church, and what is more praiseworthy, many of them maintain their own priests from whom they receive the Sacraments ; and with what constancy and courage in dire straits and in undergoing tortures for the faith many of them have often shown their spirit. For the Bishop of Meath has suffered imprisonment for sixteen years. The Bishop of Kildare, deprived of all his goods and expelled, after continual labours and inconveniences laid down his life in exile. Moreover, the Bishop of Armagh, who for many years in the cause of Christ was detained in prison in England, a pious and truly saintly man, in the opinion of all, has been continually submitted to many hardships and torments. A few years ago Rev. Edmund John [= Daniel] of the Society of Jesus, was, because of his profession of faith, first hanged and then quartered. There are many others whose names it would take too long to mention, who, deprived of all their goods, exiled, tormented, prefer to lead a miserable and indigent life rather than be unfaithful to their office and religion, and it would require a huge book to set forth all this and the many wonderful fruits produced by such constancy in virtue.

If it is asked whether there are any good and suitable workers who might be sent to the province at once ; these are not, through God's mercy, wanting. So, the first list will show those who are in Ireland scattered about doing great work in convincing heretics, encouraging Catholics and confirming them ; then there are those outside Ireland in various places, all well educated, and with many degrees for carrying on the work, who are prepared at the will of the Sovereign Pontiff to devote their lives to the Catholic faith. In both lists I give only those whose names I recall ; there are very many others whom I once knew but their names escape my memory, and there are many whom I never knew, but whose names I could easily obtain.—(*Archiv. Hib.*, v. 157-60.)

Eminent workers in Ireland :—

Most Rev. Edmund, Bishop of Cork, driven from his See.
The learned Bishop of Ross, who was at the Council of Trent, now exiled.
Bishop of Achonry, Order of Preachers.
Bishop Malachy of Kilmacduagh, also driven from his See
Thomas Cooney, Archdeacon of Waterford, a very pious man.
James Gould, Archdeacon of Limerick.
Thomas Barnoel [Barnewall], treasurer of St. Patrick's, Dublin.

Edmund Arthur, archpriest of Limerick.

Thomas Moran, dean of Cork.

(All deprived of their benefices, and well learned, to whom the
Pontiff might commit any office).[1]

Richard Valtius [Walsh], deacon, who taught youth in Waterford
in religion and letters.

Father Charles Leus [Lea] and Father Robert Risford (Rochford), both of the Society of Jesus, who in various places teach
letters under the care and command of the Bishop of Cork.

Friar William O'Keane, Dominican, celebrated preacher.

Friar Thady Fergallus [Farrell], Dominican, schoolmaster.

Friar Matthew Machuar [MacCourt], Dominican, in the same
offices.

Friar Eugene, Franciscan, an eminent man, who like an apostle
goes about to castles, towns, and villages, producing much fruit.

There are also very many Franciscans, who preach with much
fruit in their monasteries, numbering more than 20.

Those outside Ireland :—

Rev. John Vittius [White], Paris, about 36 years of age.

Rev. Nicholas Comerford, about the same age, Oporto.

David Delahyde, about 40 years, learned theologian, Rouen.

Leonard Fitsimon, Douay, professes Theology, learned in many
sciences.

(All four are very eminent in letters.)

Thomas Strong, Paris, 32 years.

Walter Bath, Alcalá, 33 years.

Dermot Creagh [Craticus], Rome, 30.

Nicholas Fagan, Portugal, 35.

Nicholas Siretus [Skerret], German College, Rome, 26.

Nicholas Segrave, Spain, 30 years.

Cornelius Obovilius [O'Boyle], Spain, 35.

Patrick Sinnot, Spain, 35.

John Hay, Paris, 30.

Friar Thady Solan [O'Sullivan], Franciscan, Bononia, 35.

Friar John Casey, Franciscan, Paris, 30.

Friar Patrick Kotz, Spain, 28.

David Dulius [Dooly ?], Louvain, 33.

(All theologians, and experienced workers.)

[1] Another copy has an additional entry here : Nicholas Eustace, whom
the Bishop of Cork calls a ceaseless worker in Ireland ; he is a noble and is
acquainted with the chief personages of the whole nobility.

Suitable as Confessors but not as learned as those mentioned above :—

Patrick Frentius [French], Louvain, 32.
Laurence More, Spain, 36.
Cornelius O'Neachtan, Spain, 35.

Youths of great promise, Masters in Arts, and Theology Students :—

Peter Lombard,[1] who was first in his Philosophy course, and studied four years Theology, 25 years.
Michael Walter, Academy of Evora, Spain.

Patrick Seadgrave, Douay.
Edward Bornell, Douay.
Walter Curchius [de Courcy], Douay.
William Comerford, Louvain.
Mark Lea, Rheims.

Richard Lea, Louvain.
James Arthur, Louvain.
Edward Aylner, Douay.
Richard Field, Douay.
Thady Olan, Paris.

Philosophy Students :—

George Aylner, Douay.
Henry Sedgrave, Paris.
Matthew of Armagh, Paris.

James Walter, Paris.
Patrick Plunket, Louvain.

There are also many others studying in Spain, Portugal, France, whose names I cannot now recall. But information can easily be got if His Holiness wishes.

Irishmen in the Society of Jesus :—

Father Richard [Fleming], professor of Theology in France, about 40 years.
Father Charles Lea, now teaching the people and the youth in Ireland.
Robert Rochford, also teaching youth in Ireland.
David Stackpole, Paris, teaching Philosophy, and learned in Theology, about 28 years.
Maurice Haley, Pavia, student of Theology, about 30.
Thomas Field, Portugal, about 26.

List of those now in Ireland, faithful workers, or who can easily be sent there :—

Rev. White, knows English and Irish, the former better.
Rev. Nicholas Comerford, knows both, English better.
Rev. Thomas Cooney, Waterford, likewise.

[1] Afterwards Archbishop of Armagh.

From Munster :—

Rev. Richard Walsh, also, English better.
Rev. Edmund Arthur, speaks Irish better.
Rev. Dermot Creagh, also Irish better.
Rev. Richard Maurice, likewise.

From Connacht :—

Friar Thady Fergall, Dominican, Irish only.
Friar Matthew Machuard, Dominican, likewise.

From Ulster :—

Rev. Walter Bath, Irish better.
Rev. Cornelius Obovilius [O'Boyle], Irish better.

From Leinster :—

Rev. Nicholas Eustace, English better.
Friar Eugene Odouhius [O'Duffy], Provincial of Franciscans in Ireland ; no English ; but goes about all Ireland preaching and teaching like an apostle.

In this last province those who know English will be very useful and suitable, as this part of Ireland is more and for a longer time subject to the English.

Bishoprics :—

Those marked (*) are either vacant or are held by heretics ; administrators or vicars might be sent to those set out in the list so that the temporalities may not be confiscated altogether or at least their divisions, but greater diligence and foresight should be used as to the spiritualities and the cure of souls, presupposing their sufficiency.

Those marked ‖ are indeed Catholic bishops and canonically instituted, but afterwards they became schismatics, taking the royal oath.

Munster : Archbishopric of Cashel,* with its suffragans .	Lismore and Waterford.‖ Cork and Cloyne. Limerick.*	Ross. Ardfert.* Emly. Killaloe.
Connacht : Archbishopric of Tuam,* with its suffragans .	Anaghdune.* Mayo. Achonry.	Clonfert.‖ Kilmacduagh. Kilfenora.*

Ulster : Archbishop-ric of Armagh and Primacy with its suffragans . .	Meath.* Raphoe. Derry. Down and Connor.*	Kilmore. Ardagh. Brenny [Kilmore]. Clonmacnoise.*

Two or three others whose names we know not.

Leinster : Archbishopric of Dub-lin, with its suffragans * .	Kildare.* Leighlin.* Ossory.* Ferns.*

Two others whose names we know not.

Archbishopric of Cashel occupied by Meiler, formerly bishop of the united churches of Down and Connor, vacant by the death of Maurice Gibbons, who went out to Spain, and died last year.

Limerick by the death of Hugh Lacey in his diocese. Vacant.

Ardfert by the death of James N. [Fitzmaurice] a few years since.

Tuam by the death of Christopher Bodkin,[1] if he were the true Archbishop, as he had 4 [Sees] and litigated for Mayo, of what diocese he was the legitimate bishop we know not. The Archbishop of Tuam was generally excepted.

Anaghdune by the death of William Mor [Morius].

Kilfenora by the death of the bishop whose name we know not.

Meath by the death of William Walsh who died some years ago at Alcalá, suffragan to Archbishop of Toledo.

Down and Connor by deposition of Meiler [2] the apostate, and a married man, by the Holy See last year.

Clonmacnoise by death of Peter Wall, Order of Preachers.

Archbishopric of Dublin by death of the bishop in the time of King Henry, whose name is forgotten as it was so long ago. The whole city, however, perseveres in the Catholic religion, although it is occupied by an heretical bishop. This diocese is the richest in all Ireland.

Kildare by death of William or certainly James [? Thomas] Lauricius [Leverous].

Leighlin, for many years occupied by heretics, after the death of the true bishop.

Kilkenny or Ossory, similarly, after the death of the true bishop.

Ferns likewise by death of the true bishop. Now occupied by

---

[1] His successor was appointed in October, 1580.

[2] March 14, 1580. His successor was appointed 23 March.

some one who although Catholic in spirit, yet as he was instituted by the Queen he administers as a heretic.

Of the above dioceses there are two in which freely and without danger bishops or vicars may reside. One is Ardfert, which is situated in the Desmond country, called Kerry, in which the Earl of Desmond has full liberty, and has the right of king ; the other is Down and Connor, which is under the command of the O'Neills, who wage war continually against the Queen, and are most Catholic princes. In Connacht if indeed not all the possessions of Anagh-dune and Kilfenora can be enjoyed on account of the tyranny of the English, a good portion of them can, through the two sons of the Earls of Connacht, who with the whole nobility, which is a good number, constantly wage war in that part of Ireland against the Queen. So that those who are sent can freely preach.

If the above bishoprics and others perhaps vacant in Ireland be bestowed on those named in the list, at least administrators or vicars, the following good results will follow :—

1. The Holy See will keep possession of its jurisdiction.

2. The people will have lawful pastors of whom they are now in need.

3. They will be edified and refreshed in a wonderful manner by paternal care and beneficence of the Supreme Pontiff for them and will be encouraged to persevere.

4. Doctrine and ecclesiastical discipline will be preserved by private sermons and by the administration of the Sacraments.

5. The labourers [clergy] themselves seeing that their merits are recognised by the Supreme Pontiff will more diligently and faith-fully give themselves to the work of God, although they may think nothing of such honour and dignity.

6. Even as to the temporalities some good may follow. For although in a great measure they are in the hands of the heretics, yet where the princes, as has been said, wage war with the Queen, as in Connacht, Desmond, and Ulster, they could not only easily pos-sess those not yet confiscated, but also recover those already taken. But in other parts it may not be so difficult to recover in whole or in part those possessions which Catholics have bought from the heretics and schismatics. Finally, the memory and the location of these possessions will be preserved. If one ask how they can live in such heretical tyranny, we reply first by the protection of the Catholic nobles with whom it is lawful for them to reside, and secondly by the help of the people who are almost all Catholic. Above all by the grace and providence of God whose cause is here in question and who it is to be hoped will not fail them in the hour of need.

II.

BISHOPS OF IRELAND, 1558-80.

PAPAL APPOINTMENTS.[1]

Diocese.	Bishop.	Date of Appointment.	Succession to
1. Ross	Maurice O'Hea	1559, 7 April	Maurice O'Fihil (*d.*)
2. Kilmore	Hugh O'Sheridan [2]	1560, 7 Jan.	John MacBrady (*d.*)[3]
3. Armagh	Donat Taig	1560, 7 Jan.	George Dowdall (*d.*)
4. Clogher	Cornelius Macardel	1560, 29 May	Raymund MacMahon (*d.*)
5. Ross	Thomas Herlihy	1561, 17 Dec.	Maurice O'Hea (*d.*)
6. Elphin	Andrew O'Crean, O.S.D.[4]	1562, 28 Jan.	Bernard O'Higgins, O.S.A. (*res.*) [5]
7. Achonry	Eugene O'Harte, O.S.D.	1562, 28 Jan.	Cormac O'Coyn (*d.*)
8. Raphoe	Donald MacCongail	1562, 28 Jan.	Art O'Gallagher (*d.*)
9. Armagh	Richard (Creagh)	1564, 22 March	Donat Taig (*d.*)
10. Down and Connor [6]	Miler Magrath, O.S.F.[7]	1565, 12 Oct.	Eugene Mageniss (*d.*)
11. Emly [8]	Maurice M'Brien	1567, 23 Jan.	Redmund de Burgh (*d.*)
12. Cashel [9]	Maurice M'Gibbon, C.O.[10]	1567, 4 June	(*Vacant over* 16 *years*)
13. Cork and Cloyne	Nicholas Lailes [11]	1568, 27 Feb.	John O'Heyne (*d.*) [12]
14. Derry	Redmund (O'Gallagher) bp. of Killala	1569, 22 June	Eugene O'Doherty (*d.*)
15. Killala	Donat O'Gallagher, O.S.D.	1570, 2 Sept.	Redmund O'Gallagher (*tr.*)
16. Killaloe	Malachy O'Molony	1571, 10 Jan.	Terence O'Brien (*d.*)

[1] *Vatican Archives.* See *Arch. Hib.*, v. 168-75.

[2] Canon of Raphoe.

[3] Ware and Harris are confusing about John and Richard Brady. (*Bishops*, 230.)

[4] Order of St. Dominic.

[5] Order of St. Augustine. Ware gives him as a Dominican (p. 633).

[6] Vacant 3 years.

[7] Order of St. Francis.

[8] Vacant more than 4 years.

[9] Vacant more than 16 years. No account, therefore, is taken of Roland Baron. It is probable that he was never consecrated, although Ware gives : " consecrated in December, 1553. (*Bishops*, 483.)

[10] Cistercian Order.

[11] *Alias* Landes (?).

[12] Probably John FitzEdmund (died *circa* 1536). No account is taken of Dominick Tirrey (1536), or of Roger Skiddy (1557-66). Skiddy was probably never consecrated. O'Heyne is called the " last Catholic Bishop."

PAPAL APPOINTMENTS—*Continued.*

Diocese.	Bishop.	Date of Appointment.	Succession to
17. Mayo [13]	Dermot O'Clery, O.S.F.	1574, 12 Feb.	Eugene MacBrehon (*d.*)
18. Cork and Cloyne	Edmund Tanner	1574, 5 Nov.	Nicholas Lailes (*d.*)
19. Ardagh	Richard MacBrady, O.S.F.	1576, 23 Jan.	Patrick M'Mahon (*d.*)
20. Dromore	Patrick Macival	1576, 23 Jan.	Arthur Mageniss (*d.*)
21. Mayo	Patrick O'Hely, O.S.F.	1576, 4 July	Dermot O'Clery (*d.*)
22. Kilmacduagh	Malachy O'Molony (*tr.*)	1576, 22 Aug.	Cornelius O'Dea (*d.*) [14]
23. Killaloe	Cornelius Ryan, O.S.F.	1576, 22 Aug.	Malachy O'Molony (*tr.*)
24. Kilmore	Richard M'Brady (bp. of Ardagh) (*tr.*)	1580, 14 March	Hugh Sheridan (*d.*)
25. Down and Connor	Donat O'Gallaghair of Killala (*tr.*)	1580, 24 March	Miler Magrath (*dep.*)
26. Killala	John O'Casey, O.S.F.	1580, 11 July	Donat O'Gallaghair (*tr.*)
27. Cork and Cloyne	Dermot Magrath [15]	1580, 12 Oct.	Edmund Tanner (*d.*)
28. Tuam and Anaghdune	Nicholas Skerett	1580, 17 Oct.	Christopher Bodkin (*d.*) [16]

[13] Called " Magionen." Eugene is called " the last legitimate possessor."
[14] Takes no account of Christopher Bodkin who was appointed by Henry VIII to Tuam and who held Kilmacduagh also.
[15] " Irish priest of the diocese of Lismore."
[16] Called " the last bishop."

Thus in 22 years the Pope made 28 appointments to dioceses in Ireland ; in the first 33 years of Elizabeth's reign there were 43 appointments. The average yearly appointment then was at least equal to the average present appointment. Episcopal succession therefore was continued in places where it was possible for an Irish bishop to officiate, and indeed in places like Cork where there was a chance that the Catholic bishop could exercise his office. Within the Pale, of course, it would have been hopeless to expect that a Catholic bishop could even reside.

ROYAL APPOINTMENTS.[1]

Diocese.	Bishop.	Date.	Remarks.
1. Kildare	Alexander Craik	1560, 21 Aug.	*d.* 1564
2. Armagh	Adam Loftus	1563 (conscr.)	*tr.* 1567
3. Meath	Hugh Brady	1563, 21 Oct.	*d.* 1583
4. Kildare	Robert Daly	1564, 2 May	*d.* 1582
5. Ossory	Christopher Gafney	1565, 4 Dec.	*d.* 1576
6. Ferns	John Devereux	1566, 19 Oct.	*succ.* A. Devereux
7. Leighlin	Daniel Cavanagh	1567, April?	*succ.* Th. O'Fihil
8. Dublin	Adam Loftus	1567, 24 Aug.	*succ.* Curwen
9. Cashel	James M'Caghwell	1567, 2 Oct.	*d.* 1570
10. Armagh	Thomas Lancaster	1568, 12 March	*succ.* A. Loftus
11. Down and Connor	John Merriman	1569, 19 Jan.	*d.* 1572.
12. Cork and Cloyne	Richard Dixon	1570, 6 June	*succ.* Skiddy (*resig.*)
13. Killaloe	Maurice O'Brien	1570, 15 May	*resig.* 1612
14. Clogher	Miler Magrath	1570, 18 Sept.	*resig.*
15. Cashel	Miler Magrath	1571, 3 Feb.	*succ.* M'Caghwell
16. Limerick	William Casey	1571	*restored*
17. Cork and Cloyne	Matthew Sheyn	1572, 29 May	*succ.* Dixon (*depr.*)
18. Tuam	William Laly	1573, April	*succ.* Bodkin
19. Kilmacduagh	Stephen Kirvan	1573, 13 April	*tr.* 1582
20. Down and Connor	Hugh Allen	1573, 21 Nov.	*succ.* Merriman
21. Ossory	Nicholas Walsh	1577, 23 Jan.	*d.* 1585
22. Waterford and Lismore	Marmaduke Middleton	1579, 31 May	*succ.* P. Walsh

[1] See *Ware's Bishops.* Cotton, *Fasti.* Brady, *Episcopal Succession; Alleged Conversion of Irish Bishops* (5th ed.).

Kilmore—no royal appointment between 1558-1603, except John Garvey 1585-89 ; namely 42 years.

Ardagh—no *ditto* until 1583 ; namely 25 years.

Dromore—no *ditto* until 1606 ; namely 48 years.

Raphoe—no *ditto* until 1605 ; namely 47 years. Montgomery had patent for Raphoe, Clogher, and Derry in 1595 ; not consecrated until 1605.

Derry—no *ditto* until 1605 ; namely 47 years.

Emly united to Cashel by Elizabeth, 1567.

Clonmacnoise united to Meath.

Ross—no *ditto* until 1583 ; namely 25 years.

Kilfenoragh—no *ditto* until 1606 ; namely 48 years. One Daniel appointed 1585 ; no record of consecration.

Killala—no *ditto* until 1591 ; namely 33 years.

Achonry—no *ditto* until 1608 ; namely 50 years. Miler Magrath received the charge of it.

Kilmacduagh held by Bodkin (*d.* 1572). Roland Lynch received it 1587.

See discussion on the continuity question: Rev. J. H. Lawlor, *The Reformation and the Irish Episcopate*, and a reply by Rev. T. Gogarty, *Are Our Bishops Intruders ?* (*I.E.R.*, Feb. and March, 1914.)

It is abundantly clear from the foregoing and from the whole narrative of these twenty-two years of Elizabeth's reign that the Established Church in Ireland was simply the church of the Pale, and in its growth followed the march of the Pale. Where English force was of no permanent value there was no entrance for a " Reform " bishop. That was clearly exemplified in Armagh and some of the northern dioceses. In Connacht, Fitton admitted in 1574 the occupation of the Sees by Catholic bishops whom he correctly names. The Established Church could not then be called the Church of the people, and, therefore, not the Church of Ireland. That is the situation at this period. As time advanced, the policy, spoken of in 1577, of bringing the Irish counties under law by degrees and stretching the Pale gradually further, was carried out. But the process was slow. It took many years to introduce English law and order, and to establish courts of justice in the corporate towns, and it took many more years before the assize circuits were aught but travelling courts-martial. The reign of Elizabeth had ceased before her sovereignty had been practically exercised in some of the remoter parts of Ireland.

Brady says : " In fact the establishment, which Elizabeth founded was an establishment and no more. It could not in her day be called a Church except by a kind of fiction. If it possessed a staff of dignitaries as well as bishops, it was entirely wanting in the essential and principal part of a Church, namely, people to be ministered to. It has been correctly likened unto a body of shepherds without a flock. It is impossible, upon any recognised principles of Christian ethics, to associate the idea of true religion with such an establishment, even though its ritual may be regarded as excellent and its doctrine as pure. The Church of Christ, be it ever so pure in creed, ceases to be a Christian Church when it begins to teach the Gospel by fines and imprisonment and deprivations. The Establishment in Ireland commenced its career by violating the simplest rules of Christianity when it prescribed penalties for its support. Morality was outraged when the Establishment became the recipient of the confiscated Church property of the Irish nation. . . . History is falsified when it is said that the Irish Church thus reformed itself. Against such falsehoods and sophistries the very stones of the temples and churches which Sydney saw ruined in his day cry out in the present generation. A voice from the ancient graveyards with their broken chancels, mutilated crosses, and shattered towers is lifted up in protestation against such an untruth." [1]

---

[1] *English State Church in Ireland*, pp. 79-80. Maziere Brady was at this time a Protestant clergyman.

In concluding this subject of the Irish bishops, it is important to insist once more on certain well-marked dividing lines.

A. *Catholic Bishops.*

(1) Taking the Oath of Allegiance to the Queen.
(2) Holding Temporalities from the Queen.
(3) Being inducted into the Spiritual Prelacy by the Queen.

These bishops could be tolerated. Under these three heads would come nearly all the cases except those of the seven bishops who accepted the Supremacy.

B. *Catholic Bishops.*

(1) Taking the Oath of Supremacy or apostatising openly.
(2) *Acting on* ecclesiastical commissions against " heretics," etc.
  (a mere mention of their names in those commissions proves nothing; there is no proof that any of the Catholic bishops *acted* on them).
(3) Ordaining priests for Protestants (e.g. O'Molony of Killaloe, who thus yielded for a time, see Appendix IV).

Bishops who acted thus could not be considered Catholics.

III.

ELIZABETH'S APPOINTMENTS TO BENEFICES, ETC.[1]

Province of Armagh :—

1560, 14 July. John Garvey to the archdeaconry of Meath, with rectory of S. Columba of Kells, vacant by deprivation of Robert Luttrell (*no. 262*).

1565, 29 January. William Kegane, clerk, to the vicarage of S. Katherine the Virgin, of Killdemoke, County Louth, vacant by death of John M'Ekihe (*no. 699*).

1571, 30 June. Henry Fulks, clerk, to the vicarage of Kilpatricke, diocese of Meath, vacant by death of John Maryman, clerk (*no. 1820*).

1578, 11 September. Sir Thomas Cornwalshe was vicar of Stamullen, and Walter Caddell, chaplain (*no. 3475*).

1578. James Butler, clerk, was vicar of S. John Baptist of Clonnalve, diocese of Meath.

---

[1] *Fiants of Elizabeth.*

Province of Dublin :—

1562, 30 April. Pardon to Stephen Hay, vicar of St. Patrick's in Wexford, and Robert Chever, chaplain, and alienation to them of lands and house of the Friars Minors, Wexford (*no. 417*).

1565, 1 February. Robert Cusake, chaplain, to the vicarage of Cloncurry, diocese of Kildare, vacant by death of William Veldon (*no. 702*).

1565, 24 March. Laurence Bryan, clerk, to the vicarage of S. Molunan, of Clonecurr, diocese of Kildare (*no. 706*).

1565, 8 April. Grant to John Garvey, archdeacon of Meath, and prebendary of Tipperkevin (diocese of Dublin), enabling him to hold the deanery of the Holy Trinity, Dublin, with those benefices (*no. 712*).

1565, 16 July. Grant to John Maguyre, clerk, rector of S. James of Uske, and vicar of S. Edan of Kynneghe, diocese of Dublin, enabling him to hold a third benefice, and licence to be absent in England for five years for the purpose of study (*no. 740*).

1565, 20 August. William Dalye, clerk, to the vicarage of Geshill, diocese of Kildare, vacant by resignation of Patrick Helye (*no. 748*).

1565, 28 September. Patrick Helye (as above) to vicarage of Oughterard, diocese of Kildare, vacant by deprivation of Edmund Walshe (*no. 757*).

1565, 25 October. William Kegho, clerk, vicar of Kilcolme, diocese of Ossory ; leave to hold two benefices with present one (*no. 767*).

Same to prebend of Kilmannaghe, vacant by death of James Joice, clerk (*no. 768*).

1565, 25 October. Edmund Sentleger, clerk, to vicarage of Tullighanebroge, Co. Kilkenny, vacant by death of James Joise (*no. 769*).

1565, 7 November. Bartholomew Mason, clerk, to Treasureship of Holy Trinity, Dublin, vacant by resignation of Thomas Mason, clerk (*no. 771*).

1566, 10 January. Licence to Thomas Mason, Treasurer, to be absent in England for four years for study (*no. 794*).

Licence to George Hopton, rector of Kylcolmbane, diocese of Leighlin, to be absent in England for five years for study (*no. 801*).

1567, 30 June. Licence to Geoffry Crosse, prebendary, of a moiety of Donamore Amayle (Ui Mail, diocese of Dublin), to be absent in England for six years (*no. 1091*).

1569, 20 February. Licence to John Bryan, vicar of Eyrke, diocese of Ossory, son of Lewis Bryan, of Dammaghe, to be absent from Ireland for three years for study (*no. 1271*).

1574, 25 July. Richard Thompson, clerk, precentor of Christ Church, Dublin, to be absent in England for three years to study at either of the universities there (*no. 2438*).

1577. Licence to Donald Dowlinge, clerk, vicar of Calfeston, Co. Kildare, diocese of Dublin, to obtain and hold two additional benefices (*no. 3159*).

1578, 16 July. Commission to John Garvey, dean of Christ Church, Dublin, etc., Henry Ussher, Treasurer of same, John Magwyr, prebendary of Donlowan (Dunlavin), and Richard Johnson, prebendary of Mynoth (Maynooth), to hear an appeal by James Weslye, vicar of Maniam, diocese of Kildare, from an institution to that vicarage of Nicholas Duchman, a foreigner, by the sentence of Geo. Ackworth and Rob. Garvey (*no. 3367*).

1578, 1 August. Cornelius Coinge, clerk, rector of Dromkaye (Wicklow), diocese of Dublin (*no. 3394*).

1578. William Clerie, clerk, to rectory of Killmaboy, diocese of Ossory, vacant by death of John M'Hugh Smith (*no. 3485*).

1578, 14 November. Appeal of Sir Owen Rogers, clerk, against Henry Luttrell, concerning vicarage of Donebate (*no. 3510*).

1578. Appeal of Nicholas Whittey, clerk, perpetual vicar of Carne, diocese of Fernis, against Thomas Codd in reference to institution to vicarage (*no. 3511*).

1578, 26 June. Richard Deverox, archdeacon of Ferns (*no. 3558*).

1577, 13 September. Richard Quyne and Barnaby Byrne dispute as to clerk of church of St. Patrick's, Wicklow (*no. 3105*).

1578. Henry Ussher, Treasurer of Christ Church.

Thomas Jones, Chancellor of St. Patrick's.

William Berge, vicar of Rosse.

William Fitzgerald, vicar of Kyllussye, diocese of Kildare.

Province of Cashel :—

1564, 26 November. Richard Beard, clerk, to archdeaconry of Cashel, vacant by death of Master John Rian (*no. 686*).

1564, 28 November. John Archdeacon, chaplain to Treasurership of Cashel, and the churches of Leighemockomocke and Galvolie, vacant by resignation of Nicholas Archdeacon *alias* M'Cody, chaplain (*no. 687*).

William Roghan, chaplain, to Chancellorship of Cashel, vacant by resignation of John Archdeacon (*no. 688*).

1565, 19 March. Edmund Fleming, Treasurer of Waterford Cathedral and vicar of Dungarvan ; licence to hold one or two other benefices (*no. 417*).

1565, 26 March. Richard Beard, Archdeacon of Cashel, to hold also vicarage of SS. Quan and Brogan, of Mothell, Co. and diocese of Waterford, vacant by death of Florence Mahini (*no. 707*).

1569, 12 November. Christopher Sheale, clerk, to vicarage of Carekenlis, diocese of Emly (*no. 1443*).

1571, 23 March. Sollo M'Kegan, clerk, to rectory and vicarage of Ardpatricke, Co. and diocese of Limerick (*no. 1791*).

Master Golde, Chantor of Cork (*no. 3519*).

1578, 22 May. David Clere, Dean, John Wise, Chancellor, and Edmund Fleming, Treasurer of Christ Church, Waterford. Donogho M'Craghe, Archdeacon of Lismore. Nicholas Poer, vicar of Kilmedan, Waterford (*no. 3531*).

Nicholas Whittey, prebendary of Cloyne.

Province of Tuam :—

1561, 26 January. Protection for William Lealy, *alias* O'Mullaly, clerk, and confirmation, under the Queen's instructions in the deanery of Tuam, of the rectories of Bolomy, Aghasgarraghe, Killosaylaryn, and the prebend of Lekaghe, in the diocese of Anaghdune, Tuam, and Elphin, which he had obtained by provision from the Court of Rome (*no. 287*). (Elizabeth afterwards appointed Lealy, Archbishop of Tuam.)

1566, 13 October. Lease to Florence Lylly, chaplain, of the site of the monastery of S. Augustin of Anaghdwyn in Connacht, the lands of Lydsdough, Little Grange, and Shankyll, Towerre, and land in the island of Arran, and the rectories of Ballnecort and Cargyne, the tithes and altarages due to the vicars excepted (*no. 1061*).

1571, 23 March. Edmund Rowe O'Kelly, clerk, to rectory of S. Kelly of Beeghe, Co. Galway, diocese of Kilmacduagh (*no. 1792*).

IV.

ELIZABETH'S COURT OF FACULTIES.

An order was issued by the Lords of the Council in England, 20 June, 1576,[1] that dispensations were to be utterly abolished, except : (1) faculties to hold two or more benefices ; (2) dispensations for young men and children under age to hold benefices, the tax to be greater for those under 14 years ; (3) *perinde valere*, i.e. making grants good which by law were void ; (4) to take orders

[1] *S.P.I.*, *Eliz.*, lv. 63, P.R.O., London.

in another diocese or all Orders at one time; (5) from banns in marriage.

In 1577 a commission of faculties was granted to George Ackworth, Doctor of Civil Law, and Robert Garvey to grant all manner of licences, dispensations, compositions, as by 28th Henry VIII.[1] This commission did not please Archbishop Loftus, who objected to Ackworth as one who was said to have been put away from his living in England for disordinate life, and to Garvey who was neither in orders nor a doctor of laws. Besides, the question of the division of the fees for the dispensations was an important one for Loftus as archbishop who should have a very considerable share of them, about a fifth of the whole, the four-fifths being divided between the Queen, the Lord Chancellor, and the officials of the court.

Loftus gained a point, as a commission was drawn up, December, 1578, to be granted to himself and Garvey,[2] but Garvey refused to be a commissioner with any bishop. A bitter quarrel arose between Garvey and Loftus as to the unlawful exercise of the faculties made by Ackworth and Garvey (still carrying on the commission), which was not ended until 25 February, 1579, when an order was issued to restrain the two commissioners from the exercise of the office of faculties.[3] Loftus had thus triumphed.

The accusations of Loftus and the replies of Garvey furnish some unexpected information.

It was objected that the commissioners should have no control over the ecclesiastical state, archbishops, bishops, and clergy, as between 1575 and 1577 dispensations were issued by them to some candidates who " received their orders of traitors, runagates, which came from Rome, pretending themselves to be bishops by the Pope's authority." The Catholic Bishop of Killaloe, Malachy O'Molony, is mentioned as one of those bishops who conferred orders, and Robert Gafney, Chantor of Kilkenny, received a dispensation from the commissioners confirming his orders which he had received from that bishop.[4] We are not told why and how

---

[1] *S.P.I., Eliz.*, lxvi. 35. " Fees paid to the Clerk of the Chancery Faculties to the Queen's only use, since Easter term, 1577, to Michaelmas term, 1578, amount to £88 14s. od. *ster*. Fees of the great seal paid to the Clerk of the Hanaper, to the Queen's only use for 117 presentations come to Her Majesty by devolution from the 4th July, 1577, to 26th June, 1578, amount to £117 *Irish*, making £84 15s. od. *ster*" (*c. £1000 1914 value*). (*Ib.*, lxiii. 43.)

[2] *Ib.*, lxiii. 56.   [3] *Ib.*, lxv. 48.

[4] *Ib.*, lxv. 28. Brady, *S.P.*, xix., xx. O'Molony's firmness in the faith at this time is very doubtful. For a while he evidently fell away in order to get the Queen's favour. (*Cf.* Maz. Brady, *Ep. Succ.*, ii. 159.)

O'Molony was induced to confer orders on a Protestant candidate, but the point to be noticed is that Protestants were presenting themselves to Catholic bishops for the reception of orders. In this case Chantor Gafney had received licence from his bishop, Christopher Gafney of Ossory, to receive the orders from O'Molony as Bishop Gafney " never gave orders himself." [1]

Garvey in his reply states, among other things, that his authority over bishops is necessary in order to prevent Protestant laymen from intruding themselves into Sees, such as Cornelius O'Brennan into Ross and Tirrelagh O'Brien into Kilfenoragh, and to drive out Catholic bishops such as Tanner of Cork and O'Molony of Killaloe. Garvey also held that Simony on the part of some of the " reform " bishops made the jurisdiction of lay commissioners over the bishops advisable as for instance in the cases of Gafney, Bishop of Ossory, and Matthew Sheyne, Bishop of Cork, who sold livings in their collation. Sheyne, in answer to the charge " that he sold the livings of his diocese to horsemen and kerne, answered both privately to them and openly in a sermon, made in the church of Cork before Sir Wm. Drury, Knight, Lord President of Munster, and the said commissioners and the whole audience then present, that except he sold the livings of his collation he were not able to live, his bishopric was so poor." Bishop Gafney had sold the archdeaconry of Ossory to one Keho. Garvey was able to mention other cases in which the bishops admitted to livings " boys, kearne, laymen and other incapable persons." Some of these were deprived by the commissioners, as for instance " George Cusack, a lay serving man, usurper " of Kenstown, in Meath ; and " Lucas Plunkett, prentice to a vintner in Dublin," who had Killavy, a parish of which the Baron of Slane was patron ; and " Robert Nugent, a horseman of the Baron of Delvin's retinue," who held Galtrim and " John Barnewall, a young boy of Dublin who had Kilmessan," and " Thomas son of Edmund Power, a boy of ten years of age " who held Mothel vicarage.

Garvey likewise retorted [2] that there was " no disposition in the ordinaries themselves to reform and amend " abuses, and that the commission of himself and Ackworth was necessary in view of the fact that " one Robert [David] Wolfe had a commission from the Pope to grant licences and dispensations in Ireland, and did

---

[1] Bishop Gafney was evidently a time-server, unwilling to perpetuate the Protestant Church, and perhaps doubting the validity of the Edwardine Ordinal. It might be argued from this that other Elizabethan bishops would be equally unwilling to consecrate Protestant bishops.

[2] *S.P.I., Eliz.*, lxv. 9. Brady, *S.P.*, xxi.

execute the same in the west part of the realm, dangerously seducing the subjects and making them believe that their licences and dispensations were to be obtained of him. A like commission [1] was exercised by one Redmund Gallacher supposed Bishop of Rapotensis in the north part of the said land."

Not only did Loftus succeed in having the commission of faculties to Ackworth and Garvey abolished, but during his ten weeks in England he drew up a petition [2] to have enforced the statutes for erection of schools, repairing churches, placing curates on impropriated benefices, and for " compelling noblemen and gentlemen to go to [Protestant] church." These requests of Loftus resulted in the issue of a memorandum, 22 February, [3] called a " Note to Lord Justice of Ireland for some order to be taken in matters touching the Pastoral care of that Realm." It states that the Statute lately enacted for the erection of schools is to be put in execution at once, with special reference to the " use and increase of the English tongue " ; severe penalties to be enforced against those who oppose the teaching of this language. " The farmers of impropriate benefices where there are no Vicarages would be dealt withal to find sufficient and able curates which hitherto for their private gains sake they have refused to do, not contented to yield any reasonable stipend for that purpose." The Statute is especially to be used in " compelling noblemen, gentlemen and people of all sorts to come to the church in times of services and common prayers," being a course " so needful and convenient for the establishment and maintenance of good government."

V.

ELIZABETHAN CHURCH IN IRELAND IN 1580.

The following letters will be sufficient to show the condition of the Established Church in Ireland at the end of the first twenty-two years of Elizabeth's reign :—

On 7 December, 1579, Sir William Pelham, Lord Justice, wrote to Walsingham [4] that he desired to put him

---

[1] This commission was probably the result of the provincial synod held in the province of Armagh about 1569 for the purpose of promulgating the decrees of the Council of Trent.

[2] *S.P.I.*, *Eliz.*, lxv. 42. Brady, *State Papers*, no. xxii.

[3] *S.P.I.*, *Eliz.*, lxv. 43. [4] Brady, *State Papers*, no. xxiii.

in mind of the miserable state of the clergy of this land, among which I cannot but marvel to see so few able ministers, or so little order taken for their maintenance. I have heard it constantly affirmed by the bishop of Meath [Brady] in whose diocese this town [Trim] standeth, that some one of her Majesty's farmers of parsonages impropriate near to this place, hath sixteen benefices in his hands, and amongst those not one vicar or minister maintained that can read English or understand Latin, or give any good instruction to his parishioners.

He states that among those few that deserve good opinion,

the Bishop of Waterford [Marmaduke Midleton] is one that hath been lately placed by Her Majesty and hath since received many injuries, partly through the contemptuous and obstinate behaviour of the Mayor [Sir Patrick Walsh] and his brethren of that City, and partly by the clergy of that Church, namely the Dean, one Clere [David Cleere] who hath been heretofore commended to England to be bishop of Ferns, but as his behaviour deserveth rather to be deprived of the dignity which he now enjoyeth, so a time may serve for the reforming of the townsmen there who are the most arrogant Papists that live within this state. In the meantime, since Mr. [James] Proctor of Salisbury, who, as I have heard was elected to Ferns, doth not mean to accept it, I could wish the Bishop of Waterford [Middleton] were appointed thither.

Marmaduke Middleton, Protestant Bishop of Waterford and Lismore, in a letter of the 29 June, 1580, to Walsingham,[1] describes the state of his diocese :—

Such is the miserable state of this wretched City [Waterford] that all things are done contrary to the sacred word and blessed will of the Lord, and also Her Majesty's most godly proceedings in causes spiritual. The Gospel of God is utterly abhorred—the church, in time of divine service, of all lands eschewed (*nisi a paucis et id forma tantum*) [i.e. unless by a few and that for appearance only]. The sacraments contemned and refused—Massing in every corner—No burial of the dead according to the Book of Common Prayer, but buried in their houses with dirges and after cast into the ground like dogs—Romerunners and Friars maintained amongst them— Public wearing of beads and praying upon the same—worshipping of images and setting them openly in their street doors, with ornaments and deckings. Ringing of bells and praying for the dead, and dressing their graves divers times in the year with flower pots and wax candles—No Marriage agreeing with God's law and Her Majesty's proceedings, for either they marry in houses with Masses, or else

[1] Brady, *State Papers*, no. xxv.

before two or three laymen without any minister taking of hands, and so they live as man and wife. No punishment for this or any other sin. The windows and walls of the churches full of images— They will not deface them, and I dare not for fear of a tumult— None of the women do come either to service or sermons—And to conclude, virtue is rejected and all vice embraced. This Right Honourable, is the lamentable condition of this proud and haughty city of Waterford—God convert their hearts.

The greatest support of this is he, which was the last year, Mayor, whose name is Sir Patrick Walsh, a countrified christian, and a great enemy of God's truth. And [he] is coming over to obtain something of Her Majesty to maintain his Knighthood withal. As hypocrites and crafty enemies of the Gospel are to be eschewed and taken heed of, so are they not to be preferred lest their force might be strengthened the better to work their malice ; wherein I dare be bold to say, no man exceedeth the said Sir Patrick with whom, the living God knoweth—the whole city are partakers, for there is no obedience in any of them concerning any of Her Majesty's proceedings, but in those points, wherein if they should fail, it may touch their lives, goods and lands. That obedience deserveth no thanks, much less any reward.

[He speaks of the " stiffnecked, stubborn, papistical and incorrigible people of the City of Waterford."]

There is no difference betwixt the Clergy and the laity here, for they have joined together to prevent Her Majesty's most Godly proceedings—both by defacing of the See, which is not annually, at this instant, worth thirty pounds a year, and all the spiritual living in temporal men's hands so sure linked that they cannot be redeemed. And the most of the incumbents [are] little better than Wood Kerne, so that neither the bishoprick is able to maintain a bishop, neither the spiritual livings fit for any honest men. This is pitiful and lamentable hearing.

[Middleton then says :] The Lord Justice Pelham wanted lately to prefer me to the bishoprick of Ferns, as quieter than this, and because I was in danger here from the papists. He mentioned also, in a letter to you about it, one David Clere, Dean of Waterford, as a suitor for the same bishoprick, and his unworthiness, both for his wicked life, want of knowledge, weakness of religion. . . . I know the man, his life, doctrine and conversation (because he is dean in my Church) better than some others. In religion he is but a hypocrite [i.e. a Catholic] and by nature malicious. Neither a preacher, neither hath he sufficiency thereto—An arguer, with that little knowledge he hath, against the truth. This man I hold an unfit bishop, yet so well friended, as none better in this world than the wicked, as both his preferment shall be sought, and who shall withstand him shall hazard a displeasure. God knoweth we have too many such bishops in Ireland. [i.e. Catholic at heart, e.g. Devereux of Ferns.]

Sir Nicholas Malby, writing from Dublin, 7 September, 1580, to Walsingham,[1] states that the rebellion is now general throughout the realm. Tirlogh Lynagh (O'Neill) threatens Dundalk with 6000 men. O'Rourke is in arms again in Roscommon, and Malby must hasten back to Athlone. He then continues :—

I perceive, by your Lordship's last letters, that the Irish complaints have good hearing there. I am sorry for it, and hard is it for us that serve when rebels, tales and the surmises of such as be friends to rebels, shall work us disadvantage and misliking, for so often adventuring of our lives, which we do only in respect of our duty to her Majesty. No man can hold it for a pastime, neither will any man of discretion desire to govern by fighting if it may be done by honest policy. But my hap is worse of any man's in that I hear it is said I use the sword over severely. I am sorry I have spared it so much, and if it be not used more sharply than hitherto it has been, Her Majesty is like to lose both sword and realm. It is now a quarrel of religion and the expectation of foreign aid doth much further it.

VI.

Original Latin Letters.

A. *Shane O'Neill to Elizabeth, 11 September, 1563 (P.R.O., London, ix 7).*

Item Humillime petit clementissimam Maiestatem Regiam restituere ecclesiam Armachanam ad pristinum statum tam ut ibi preces effundentur pro ejus felici statu et prospero successu quam ut ibi divinus cultus exercebitur et mortui sepelientur, et instanter petit ut magna campana dicte ecclesie conservetur sine fraccione, ut dedit in mandatis Dominus Locum Tenens, et omnia alia ornamenta et bona dicte ecclesie ubicumque inveniri poterint restituantur et sic fiat quod durante hoc evo incessanter in dicta ecclesia pro ejus Maiestate ad Deum preces fundentur, et plurimum ad hoc debet monere ejus solitam clementiam quoniam nulla est ecclesia alicujus precii vel decoris in boriali parti Hybernie nisi illa sola.

B. *Shane's Bond with Elizabeth, Benburb 16 November, 1563 (P.R.O., London, ix. 59).*

Amovebit presidium ex ecclesia Ardmachana et cum tradi voluit ad pristinum statum hoc est ad divinum cultum, mortuorum

---

[1] Brady, *State Papers*, no. xxvi.

sepulturam et ut ab antiquo est metropolitana et cathedralis ecclesia et primitialis totius Hybernie ita in futurum perpetuis temporibus duranturis permanebit, ea tamen conditione quod ego in eodem statu permittam et sinam continuare.   Ego autem Clementiae ejus Majestatis quantum possum . . . referro gratias pro hac benevolentia mihi ostensa.   Et pollicior per meam fidem et juramentum majorumque subditorum coram omnipotenti Deo et dicto Magistro Thoma Cusake quod non solum non impediam cultum divinum fieri in dicta ecclesia verum viis et modis quibus potero dabo operam ut augebitur decor et venustas dicte ecclesie ad preces effundendas ad Deum magnum optimum.

C. *Shane to Elizabeth,* 18 *November,* 1563 (*P.R.O., London,* ix. 62).

Quod celsitudini vestri placeat ex plurima gratia et bonitate vestra ut templum Armaghense Decano et clero restituatur ut ibi mortui sepelliantur et sacre orationes exerciantur quum in tota patria ista non extet aliud templum ad ejus usus accomodatum preter Armaghanense, hac videlicet conditione ut ego sim bonus et fidelis subditus post hac futurus et patiar illud templum permanere in eo usu ad cultum divinum juxta directionem vestre Maiestatis innotescat Amplitudini vestre quo premissa omnia integre et inviolate prestentur et observentur.   Ego et omnes prestantes viri de patria mea sub multis penis tenemur et firmiter obligamur Maiestati Vestre praestito etiam juramento nostro non solum nos futuros fideles subditos et prestituros quidquid promisimus sed etiam passuros ut templum illud in dies ornatius crescat, nihil enim nobis jucundius et gratius esse potest sanctissima ista vestra restitutione, quoniam omnes parentes et generosi viri Tyroni sepulti recondiuntur.

D. *Shane to the Cardinal of Lorraine,* 25 *April,* 1566 (*P.R.O., London,* xvii. 35).

Reverendissimo Cardinali Ludivico Nos Dominus ONeill princeps hybernicorum Ultoniae et defensor fidei in partibus Hiberniae Salutem dicimus.

Notum Vobis facimus per presentes quod missimus nostras litteras ad Christianissumum principem regem Franciae petentes ab ejus Maiestate mittere nobis in nostros favores quinque vel sex millia Francorum bene armatorum ad repellendum Anglos de Hybernia qui sunt heretici et sissimatici et inimici Dei omnipotentis et Romane Ecclesie nec non francorum et hybernicorum.

Cum autem in partibus Hybernie fidem Catholicam defendimus ad posse nostrum et regulas Romanorum Pontifficum imitemur rogamus vobis omni reverentia et humilitate qua decet suadere Christianissimo regi Francorum (cum nunc tempus est et omnes Hybernici sunt in nostro consilio) mittere nobis dictum numerum Francorum ad repellendum dictos hereticos de Hybernia et ad coniungendum Hyberniam Coronae Franciae et sic quam optime valete.

Ex Dungenaind xxv Aprilis 1566.

Misi ONeill.

[Watermark of paper : Hand of Ulster.]

E. *Miler Magrath to Privy Council*, 11 *April*, 1570 (*P.R.O., London*, xxx. 41).

Vereor post tantam expectationem et diutiunam captivitatem a conspectu vestri illustrissimi Consilii discedere absque meorum negotiorum certitudine, ideoque supplico vestris illustrissimis duobus ut me certiorem facere dignentur quid mihi Regia Maiestas et vestrae celsitudines dare constituerint, videlicet, utrum illam dignitatem quam olim obtinui, aut alteram aut nullam omnino dare constituerint. Quod si in ea jam obtenta, ob concessionem Domini Deputati, alteri (ut fertur) iamfactam aliqua difficultas esse videatur, quominus iterum mihi a Regia Maiestate concedi possit, in hoc facilis esset responsio. Dominus Deputatus non difficilius (vel ut rectius dicam) eadem facultate potest illum quem in meo loco constituit ad alteram dignitatem transferre, qua et meipsum et presertim quum (ut intelligo) nullas Regiae Maiestatis patentes vel concessorias accepit litteras. Causa non est, ob quam Regia Maiestas et Vestrae Celsitudines illam dignitatem potius mihi quam alteram concedere deberent, quum in illa diocesi existens, multo melius et efficacius suae Regiae Maiestatis inservire possum, quam in aliqua alia parte Hiberniae ; nec ipse qui Deputato constitutus est tale servitium exhibere potest, quod ipse possum, ut prefatus Deputatus et illi qui utrumque norint, judicare possunt. Sed si res ita se habeat, ut Regia Maiestas factum Domini Deputati nullo modo revocare velit ego eandem Maiestatem suppliciter oro, quatenus id ad quod me idoneum existimavit, mihi concedat, in loco tuto et ubi suum regimen custoditur, quum de cetero inter rebelles et inciviles illos Hibernicos inter quos natus fui, vitam conducere nolo. Ut autem Regia Maiestas specialis mihi in illa Anglia Hiberniae parte providere possit, Corkaiensis Clunensis episcopatus

42 *

vacatione per diutina tempora eidem Maiestati et Vestris Celsi-
tudinibus ostendo, quem ego lubens accipiam, nisi priorem potero
recuperare, quod tamen mihi multo gratius foret, quia ibi multo
melius et commodius Regiae Maiestati inservire possem quam in
altero. Nam in eo et in vicinis locis multos habeo amicos et
consanguineos ex quibus quidam non nunquam rebelles existunt
quos ego meo consilio meisque persuasionibus ad pacem et ad
subiectionem Regiae Maiestati praestandam revocare sperarem, et
insuper in eadem diocesi doctrinam veritatis (quantum in me
esset) in publicum dicere, nullus me monachorum vel aliorum
Papistarum impedire posset, et nonnulla alia hic ostendere possem,
que modo brevitatis causa omitto. Preterea rogo Regiam Maiestatem ut minora illa beneficia, videlicet, prioratus, rectoriasque
simplices et capellas quas etiam pro me ac meo fratre ab episcopo
Romano impetravi, mihi denuo concedere dignetur, et suas litteras
ad Dominum Maguire, in cujus patria sita sunt, dirigat, jubendos
ut ipse mihi eadem beneficia integre et cum effectu persolvi faciat.
Nomina vero dictorum beneficiorum satis clare in litteris quas
Dominus Secretarius prae suis manibus habet, reperiri possunt,
et illas cuperem remitti ad Dominum Deputatum ut illas inspiciens
expeditius mihi ea conferre possit. Ea vero omnia a Papistis et
rebellibus sue Maiestatis obtinentur, tamen amicorum et consan-
guineorum favore et auxilio aliquid fructus inde colligi a me possit,
dummodo Regiam concessionem ostenderem et prae manibus
haberem.

Postremo rogo Vestras Celsitudines ut me diutius hic expectare
non cogatis, ne iterum in febres incidens, Regiae Maiestati et vobis
amplius sim molestus, etc. Deus eternus Pater, qui est casti
consilii amator, vestrum consilium regat dirigatque in suam gloriam
et publicam utilitatem. Amen.

Post scripta.

Oro vestras Celsitudines ut considerent me in hoc inclyto Regno
omnibus humanis praesidiis destitutum esse, ita ut neminem habero
a quo pecuniam vel dono, mutuo habere possim, vel sperem, nisi a
Regia Maiestate et a vestra beneficia. Proinde vos obnixe rogo ut
aliqua ratione pecuniam mihi pro itinere necessariam a Regia
Maiestate impetretis.

Vestre Celsitudinis Humillimus Servitus

Milerus Magrath Hibernus

11 Aprilis 1570   Inclytis Conciliariis Regni Angliae.

(Endorsed : Memoriale pro Milero Magrath Hibernico aliquando
nuncupato episcopo.)

F. *Wm. Mullaly and Roland Burgh to Sir E. Fitton*, 5 *March,*
1574 (*P.R.O., London*, xlv. 15. 1).

Illustri viro Domino Edouardo hujus regni Hiberniae Thesaurario
salutem Sanctique Spiritus consolationem. Litteras vestras cum
omni benevolentia accepimus, quibus citati fuimus ad Athluin ad
sextam diem instantis mensis Martii : sed cum nuper adeo periculum est quod vix potest quis de uno loco ad alium transire sine
corporis sui periculo, quia undique Scoti concurrunt in Clanricarde
et ibique morantur, et praecise in nostris locis, cum sentiunt nos
partem vestram fovere : nec contentantur praesentibus Scotis,
quia alii Scoti numero septies centum in proximo venturi sunt cum
Johanne filio Comitis, ut comuniter a pluribus invenimus, ac etiam
inter Succam et Shynenam, ubi via communis erat, tantae angustiae
et discrimina sunt, quia ad presens resurgunt quidam de Kylkellay,
qui insidiantur illic omnibus itinerantibus, ac ut accepimus, Duces
Scotorum sunt ad partes illas, nec alias possumus ire ad locum
destinatum, viz., Athluyn quam ire ad Clonfert, nec dehinc transire
sine salvo conductu possumus. Ideoque nos vestramque Domina-
tionem enixe in Domino rogamus, cum alias sub Deo locum refugii
non quaerimus, ut de gratia Edmundum Offalluyn aliosque fideles
cum tuto navigio ad portum de Clonfert ad diem Martis proxime
futurum transmittere non postponatis ac (Deo Duce) nisi aliud
obtaverit in eodem loco apud Clonfert erimus, licet non sine periculo
omnium rerum, quae post nos relinquimus, ut nobis antea accidit,
prout nostis. Non alia hac vice, quam quod Deus Optimus vos
conservet, et ad altiora ascendet, et sic feliciter valete.

Ex Kilconayll. Quinto Martii.
Willmus Tuamensis.
Rolandus Clonfertensis.

Vos in Domino exhortamur, ut mox literis nostris lectis cum
latore praesentium nobis scribi faciatis utrum citius aut tardius,
prout res exigit ad locum assignatum de Clonfert respondebimus,
et alia quae fuerint nobis necessaria pro tutela itinerum, cum cor-
poribus nostris summum periculum est, prout latius dicemus cum
simul erimus. Ex Kilconayl. 5 Martii 1574.

Subscribed as afore.

G. *King of France to Queen Elizabeth, July*, 1575 (*P.R.O.,
London*, lii. 66).

Reginae Angliae.

Altissima Principum amicorum communia sunt officia ut
mutuo reconsiliacione illorum ex suis subditis procurent qui parum

considerantur ab officio obedientiae principibus suis ac supremis debito dicesserunt. Quemadmodum antea tibi placuit a nobis postulare et intercedere pro nostris subjectis, qui propter tumultus et armorum dilationem contra nos, in tuos [sic] regnum et patriam refugerunt : pro qua re cum Dominus Jacobus Desmonde unus tuorum Hirlandiae subditorum, nobis narrare et ediscere fecerit illi desiderio esse in tuam redeundi gratiam veniamque impetrandi noxiae quam ille et sui consortes in te committere et perpetrare potuerunt arma in Hirlandiam defferendo contra te ac tuam aucthoritatem quodque nos libenter supplicaret hac de re pro ipso erga te intercedere velle auxilium nostrum et intercessionem illi non denegantes hanc tibi scribere litteram optime voluimus pro illius commendatione quo te precaremur ignoscere et veniam dare velle (pro tua bonitate assuetaque clementia) dicto Domino Desmond necnon suis consortibus, offensamque ab illis in te allatam oblivisci, quamquidem (ut accepimus) moleste ferunt, eamque fecisse paenitet. Illis concedendo et ad huiusmodi effectum conficere faciendo tuas veniae generalis litteras patentes, in bonam et amplam formam et modum, dignerisque expresse injungere generali tuo locum tenenti in Hirlandia, ac etiam domino Comiti Desmond cognato dicto James, ut ipsi James suisque consortibus sua bona, terrasque tam ab allis quam iliis quibusvis detentas et occupatas reddant illisque pacificae frui relinquent, juxta id quod amplius nostra ex parte tibi dicetur a Domino de la Mothe Fenelon, Consiliario ac Legato illic residente cui quidem scribimus. Super quo te precamur illi auditum praestare tantamque quam nobismet ipsis fidem adhibere Deum rogando, etc.

INDEX.

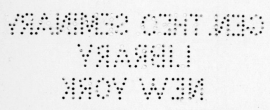

PRINTED IN GREAT BRITAIN BY THE UNIVERSITY PRESS, ABERDEEN